Foundations of Mind

Foundations of Mind

Philosophical Essays, Volume 2

TYLER BURGE

CLARENDON PRESS · OXFORD

OXFORD
UNIVERSITY PRESS

Great Clarendon Street, Oxford OX2 6DP

Oxford University Press is a department of the University of Oxford.
It furthers the University's objective of excellence in research, scholarship,
and education by publishing worldwide in

Oxford New York

Auckland Cape Town Dar es Salaam Hong Kong Karachi
Kuala Lumpur Madrid Melbourne Mexico City Nairobi
New Delhi Shanghai Taipei Toronto

With offices in

Argentina Austria Brazil Chile Czech Republic France Greece
Guatemala Hungary Italy Japan Poland Portugal Singapore
South Korea Switzerland Thailand Turkey Ukraine Vietnam

Oxford is a registered trade mark of Oxford University Press
in the UK and in certain other countries

Published in the United States
by Oxford University Press Inc., New York

British Library Cataloguing in Publication Data

Data available

Library of Congress Cataloging in Publication Data

Burge, Tyler.
    Foundations of mind / Tyler Burge.
      p. cm.—(Philosophical essays ; v. 2)
    Includes bibliographical references and indexes.
    ISBN-13: 978–0–19–921623–9 (alk. paper)
    ISBN-10: 0–19–921623–1 (alk. paper)
    ISBN-13: 978–0–19–921624–6 (alk. paper)
    ISBN-10: 0–19–921624–X (alk. paper)
  1. Philosophy of mind. I. Title.
    BD418.3.B77 2007
    128′.2—dc22   2006103408

Typeset by Laserwords Private Limited, Chennai, India
Printed in Great Britain
on acid-free paper by
Biddles Ltd, King's Lynn, Norfolk

ISBN 978–0–19–921624–6
ISBN 978–0–19–921623–9 (Pb)

10 9 8 7 6 5 4 3 2 1

Dedicated in Loving Memory
to my Father
DANIEL BURGE

Contents

Preface

This volume of essays centers on basic aspects of mind. I discuss the main themes of the volume in the Introduction. Here I want to make a few more personal remarks. Some pertain to general attitudes toward the substance of the early essays in the volume. Some pertain to memories, feelings, and debts regarding the circumstances of their birth.

The birth dates of the essays span a period of more than three decades. In this Preface, I will confine myself to the earlier essays in the volume. The early essays established a direction for the rest, with the exception of the two papers on consciousness. The volume includes the essays ("Belief *De Re*" and "Individualism and the Mental") in which I learned to sing—communicate with a distinctive philosophical voice. It also includes the papers (those two, together with "Other Bodies", "Intellectual Norms and Foundations of Mind", and my early work on perception) that set the direction for what I think of as my primary philosophical work. In returning to these essays for this occasion, I experience a combination of familiarity and distance. I suppose that these feelings are common emotional embellishments of long-term memory. The feelings have particular substantive content as well as typical emotional coloring, however.

The early papers in this volume were written during heady philosophical times. With regard to the work by Donnellan, Kripke, and Putnam on linguistic reference, there was a sense abroad in the philosophical community, which I shared, that something of long-term philosophical importance was occurring. This sense remains palpable and familiar. It has been confirmed with the passage of time.

On the other hand, aspects of these developments now seem philosophically blinkered. The methodology of the time was to separate linguistic matters as sharply as possible from issues in the philosophy of mind and epistemology. There are scientific advantages in this procedure. It constitutes an idealization of the sort that often serves science and understanding well. A phenomenon is simplified, the better to study some of its basic features in as pure a form as possible. This methodology has, I think, yielded dividends, particularly in philosophy's contribution as midwife to the birth and development of semantics in empirical linguistics.

The methodology was, however, philosophically limiting. The roots of reference lie in mental capacities—in particular, in perception and in various

x   *Preface*

mechanisms, especially memory and belief formation, that preserve perceptual reference. A serious philosophical limitation of the initial work on linguistic reference is that it was not coupled with comparably sophisticated reflection on mind. Perception, which clearly grounds the sorts of reference that drove the work on language, received little serious philosophical attention at all. Some of these limitations still weaken parts of philosophy of language, in my opinion, although, as noted, some parts of idealized, relatively "pure" approaches to philosophy of language have made steady, valuable contributions to knowledge through association with linguistics.

A similar mix of identification and distance marks my attitude toward my philosophical contributions from the period immediately following the breakthroughs on linguistic reference. Not surprisingly, the element of identification dominates. Seen at this distance, I think that my main contributions were, broadly, threefold. First, I developed philosophical issues about representation, including reference, in the domain in which I think they more fundamentally arise—the domain of mind. Second, I explained and systematically explored ways in which the *natures* of mental states constitutively depend on relations to an environment beyond the individual. Third, I extended (past the paradigms of demonstrative reference, proper names, and natural kind terms that had dominated the thinking about language) the types of representational phenomena that constitutively depend on relations to a broader environment. The sense that I was on to new, foundational directions in philosophy was vivid at the time of writing "Individualism and the Mental". This sense remains vivid.

On the other hand, there are passages in these early papers that show that I had not always adequately separated phenomena that are relevant to understanding language use from phenomena that are relevant to understanding mind. Some aspects of language serve communication rather than expression of thought. Some are relevant mainly to practical exigencies, and give only the most indirect clues to mental or even linguistic structures. I was aware of these general points, and made use of them. But I did not apply them as well as I might have. My improved understanding of these matters is marked in the postscripts.

I was on sabbatical in Graz, Austria, during the Fall of 1977 and in London during the Winter and Spring of 1978. This was the period in which I conceived the ideas of "Other Bodies" and wrote "Individualism and the Mental". The time in London was particularly stimulating. During the mornings, I worked. Afternoons, my wife Dorli and I got to know London. In the evenings, we attended concerts or the theater. Although I put fewer hours into philosophy than I sometimes do, I believe that I worked more efficiently than at any other time in my life. Inspiration from Rembrandt, Velasquez, Shakespeare, Mozart, Schubert, Wren, and Newton seemed to buoy my thinking. The joy of discovery was very intense during that period. Those two papers—and another on semantical paradox—developed toward birth in parallel with the pregnancy that led to our first son, Johannes.

After returning to California, I discussed final drafts of "Individualism and the Mental" in two long late-night sessions with Rogers Albritton. Albritton convinced me to make the arthritis example, which had been a secondary case, the lead example—suppressing an example about sofas to secondary status. (A variant of that sofa example eventually took center stage in "Intellectual Norms and Foundations of Mind".) I remain grateful to Albritton, now deceased, for his searching criticism, for his perspective on the issues, for his charm in discussion, and especially for his encouragement.

Many others helped in the gestation of the papers collected in this volume. I despair at recording my gratitude to most of these people individually, since most of the encounters are lost to memory. Regrettably, in most cases, I have to express my indebtedness in generalized form. Some specific acknowledgments occur in the notes of the individual papers. I will mention just a few individuals. During a semester-long visit to MIT in 1982, Ned Block went to the trouble of trying to get my views exactly right. He cemented a long-term personal and intellectual friendship. He remains a valuable interlocutor, as the notes in some of the newly published material here will attest. During the same visit, I had several formative discussions with Jerry Fodor and Noam Chomsky. Fodor, along with courses that I took at MIT on the psychology of vision, sparked my long-term interest in empirical psychology. The talks with Chomsky established a personal *rapport* that survived and even fructified our philosophical differences.

Among students during the formative years, I am particularly grateful to Joseph Owens, Bernard Kobes, and Martin Hahn. Each wrote dissertations on aspects of anti-individualism. I have continued to learn from them long after they graduated.

My debts to my family remain primary. My wife Dorli gave love, support, inspiration, and encouragement despite my frequent absences of mind. Involvement with the lives of my sons, Johannes and Daniel, especially in sport and music, provided outlets into other types of reality. Their support was often implicit but nonetheless fundamental. Both have grown, in different ways, into intellectual partners. Sadly, my parents are no longer around to receive thanks. I thank them anyway. My mother, Mary, tried bravely and touchingly to read some of my early work, and maintained confidence and support that transcended understanding. This volume is dedicated to the memory of my father, Dan. His intense involvement with music helped develop one of the loves of my life. He also provided for me the single most influential example of intellectual breadth and curiosity. And he too believed in me without being able to assess what I was doing.

Acknowledgments

'On Knowledge and Convention', *The Philosophical Review* 84 (1975), pp. 249–355

'Kaplan, Quine, and Suspended Belief', *Philosophical Studies* 31 (1977), pp. 197–203

'Belief *De Re*', *The Journal of Philosophy* 74 (1977), pp. 338–362

'Other Bodies', in *Thought and Object*, ed. A. Woodfield ed. (London: Oxford University Press, 1982)

'Individualism and the Mental', *Midwest Studies in Philosophy* 4 (1979), pp. 73–121

'Two Thought Experiments Reviewed', *Notre Dame Journal of Formal Logic* 23 (1982), pp. 284–293

'Cartesian Error and the Objectivity of Perception', in *Subject, Thought, and Context*, ed. P. Pettit and J. McDowell (Oxford: Clarendon Press, 1986)

'Authoritative Self-Knowledge and Perceptual Individualism', in *Contents of Thought*, ed. R. H. Grimm and D. D. Merrill (Tucson: University of Arizona Press, 1988)

'Individualism and Psychology', *The Philosophical Review* 95 (1986), pp. 3–45

'Intellectual Norms and Foundations of Mind', *The Journal of Philosophy* 83 (1986), pp. 697–720

'Wherein is Language Social?', in *Reflections on Chomsky*, A. George ed. (Oxford: Blackwell, 1989)

'Concepts, Definitions, and Meaning', *Metaphilosophy* 24 (1993), pp. 309–325

'Social Anti-Individualism, Objective Reference', *Philosophy and Phenomenological Research* 97 (2003), pp. 682–690

'Individuation and Causation in Psychology', *Pacific Philosophical Quarterly* 70 (1989), pp. 303–322

'Intentional Properties and Causation', in *Philosophy of Psychology*, ed. C. Mac-Donald and G. MacDonald (Oxford: Blackwell, 1995)

'Mind–Body Causation and Explanatory Practice', in *Mental Causation*, ed. J. Heil and A. Mele (Oxford: Clarendon Press, 1993)

'Zwei Arten von Bewusstsein' in *Bewußtsein*, ed. T. Metzinger (Paderborn: Ferdinand Schöningh, 1995)

'Two Kinds of Consciousness', in *The Nature of Consciousness*, ed. N. Block, O. Flanagan, and G. Güzeldere (Cambridge, Mass.: MIT Press, 1997)

'Descartes on Anti-Individualism', a large part published as a portion of 'Descartes, Bare Concepts, and Anti-Individualism: Reply to Normore', in

Reflections and Replies: Essays on the Philosophy of Tyler Burge, ed. M. Hahn and B. Ramberg (Cambridge, Mass.: MIT Press, 2003)

'Philosophy of Mind: 1950–2000', a large part published as a portion of 'Philosophy of Language and Mind: 1950–1990', *The Philosophical Review* 101 (1992), pp. 3–51; the present paper in *Edinburgh Companion to the Twentieth Century Philosophies*, ed. C. Boundas (Edinburgh: Edinburgh University Press, forthcoming)

The author and publisher would like to thank the publishers for permission to reproduce these papers in this volume.

Introduction

The essays in this volume center on philosophical issues about mind, and about language insofar as it is an indication of mind. The volume includes most of the essays in which I defend anti-individualism. It also includes discussion of other aspects of mind—mind–body causation, the mind–body problem, and consciousness. In this introduction I sketch some background. I also comment on the individual essays and how they relate to one another.

Before I explain what anti-individualism is, I want to explicate some terminology briefly. Anti-individualism is a view about the *natures* of representational mental states and events. 'Nature' is a relaxed, semi-technical term. The traditional term is 'essence'. I do not have anything against essences. To begin uncontentiously, however, I take as little stand as possible on traditional metaphysical issues about essences. Something's nature remains with it as other properties or relations come and go. Insofar as there are more or less basic ways of categorizing things, natures are more basic ways. In the background, I hold a stronger view: Something's nature constitutes what it is, without which it could not be. I do not assume that there is always a sharp answer to the question what the nature of a thing is. Usually, however, at an initial level of inquiry, the nature of something is unsurprising. The nature of the tree is being a tree—it is not being thirty feet tall, or being an ornament in the garden, or being covered with green leaves. Less obviously, the nature of the tree might be: being a certain type of realization of a certain genetic profile.

I will be discussing what *constitutively* determines the natures of mental states. What constitutively determines a nature is not always just the nature itself. What constitutively determine a nature are conditions that are necessary (or sufficient, or necessary and sufficient) for something to have the nature it has and that help explain the nature. Having a certain DNA profile and having certain further properties may be the nature of a tree. Certain topological properties of space may help constitutively determine the nature. Being a shovel might be the nature of a given instrument. The nature may be partly constitutively determined by someone's intentionally making a tool out of certain material, or using it with a certain purpose. The line between nature and constitutive determining conditions is not always clear or important. Sometimes it is, however. The distinction sometimes corresponds to different types of explanations. I will refine this point later.

Anti-individualism is a view about the natures of *representational mental states and events*. Examples of representational mental states or events are thoughts, beliefs, intentions, desires, perceptions, hallucinations, misperceptions, imaginings. An aspect of their function is to be about something—to present a subject matter as being a certain way. Such states can represent veridically or non-veridically.

Representational states and events have *representational content*. Representational content is a structured abstraction that can be evaluated for truth or falsity, or for perceptual correctness or incorrectness. A propositional attitude, like a belief that not all that glisters is gold, has a propositional representational content. The representational content is that not all that glisters is gold. A perceptual state, like a perception of a particular body as being a body and as glittering, has another sort of representational content. What sort is a matter that would require more detailed specification than I want to go into here. But roughly, if someone perceives a particular body as a glittering body, the perception's content makes singular reference to the body and involves a perceptual grouping or perceptual attributive that presents it as a body and as glittering. The belief's content is true or false, depending on whether or not all that glitters (glisters) *is* gold. The perception's content is accurate or inaccurate, depending on whether the perception singles out a body that glitters.

Representational content is not only evaluable for veridicality. It helps type-identify the mental state with that content. Or, to put it another way, it is part of the psychological kind that the associated mental state is an instance of. Thus the above cited belief is a not-all-that-glisters-is-gold belief. Psychological kinds typed partly by representational content are cited in psychological explanations. The representational content has a structure that corresponds to different aspects of the mental ability or mental state that it type-identifies. Thus the representational content of the belief cited above is made up of *concepts*, certain types of sub-propositional contents—for example, the relevant gold concept. There are other kinds of components of full representational contents besides concepts—*applications* and *perceptual attributives*.[1] These components, in turn, type-identify aspects of representational states that have the representational contents, or are of the representational kinds.

The foregoing should give some handle on some of the terminology that I will be using. I now want to explain the key view that dominates this volume—anti-individualism.

---

[1] Applications will be discussed later in some detail, especially in 'Belief *De Re*' (Ch. 3) and its Postscript. Perceptual attributives will not come in for much discussion in this volume. They are the perceptual analogs of predicative concepts. Thus, in a perception of something as a *body*, the perceptual grouping *body* (or some specific version of this grouping) is a perceptual attributive.

Individualism is the view that all of an individual's representational mental kinds are constitutively independent of any relation to a wider reality. *Anti-individualism* maintains that many representational mental states and events are constitutively what they are partly by virtue of relations between the individual in those states and a wider reality. More specifically, anti-individualism holds that the natures of many such states and events constitutively depend for being the natures that they are on non-representational relations between the individual and a wider environment or world. Such relations are constitutively necessary for the states and events to be the specific kinds of states or events that they are.

The intuitive idea of anti-individualism is that representational states cannot occur in a vacuum. One cannot have conceptual or perceptual abilities to represent matters beyond the mind unless they are associated with supplementary or collateral connections between the individual's psychology and some aspects of the subject matter. The specific representational content that these abilities have—the specific kinds of representational abilities that they are—is partly determined by specific aspects of the subject matter that those abilities relate to. Most commonly, the subject matter is the physical environment. Representational abilities are possible only by being supplemented by systematic non-representational relations between the individual and a subject matter. Most commonly, the non-representational relation is causation.

To illustrate the point in the crudest way: an ability to believe something about aluminum *as aluminum* requires some collateral causal connections between aluminum and the individual's cognitive system. A collateral causal connection might be light's bouncing off the aluminum and impacting the visual system of the individual, ultimately engendering perceptions of aluminum. An ability to perceive a rigid body as red and spherical depends on similar causal connections to relevant shapes and rigid bodies, and to red surfaces or red light.

The point is not merely developmental. It is not just that individuals acquire their beliefs by being in causal contact with relevant features of the environment, perhaps through the teaching of others. The point is constitutive. It is that, in many cases, a belief or perception is the kind of psychological state it is through being embedded in a network of collateral non-representational relations to aspects of the wider environment.

The illustrations just given are exaggerations for effect. They are not quite correct as stated. The relevant collateral relations do not have to be as simple as the examples suggest. They can be quite complex and indirect. For one thing, they need not occur in the individual's own life. The relations to the environment can route through other people, or through the evolution of an individual's perceptual system.

Moreover, the relevant constitutive relations need not be relations to the thing represented. One can think about aluminum as aluminum even though one's cognitive system never interacts with aluminum. For example, a Martian scientist could theorize about the structure of aluminum and imagine its macro-properties.

That would be enough to have a concept of aluminum—to be able to think about something *as aluminum*—even though there is no aluminum in the scientist's environment. Light from aluminum never entered the scientist's visual system. The scientist's perceptual systems never evolved from perceptual interaction with aluminum. The scientist never had any other indirect causal transactions with aluminum. It never caused anything that the scientist did perceive. And the scientist never communicated with anyone who had such causal relations to aluminum in perception. The scientist's capacity to think about aluminum depends, however, on this capacity's being linked to other cognitive capacities that are causally affected by matters that the scientist thinks about. For example, to theorize about the structure of aluminum, the scientist might have thought about hydrogen and about chemical bonding. These aspects of reality do bear (complex, indirect) causal relations to the scientist's psychological systems.

One can also have concepts that apply to nothing. Such capacities are not causally related to anything that they apply to. For example, in a conjecture that phlogiston is contained in combustible bodies, or a thought that Vulcan's orbit is close to Neptune's, or a belief that Santa Claus lives at the north pole, the representational contents phlogiston, Vulcan, and Santa Claus do not apply to anything in reality. It is possible to think these thoughts only because these representational contents are connected in the individual's psychology to other mental states that do have relevant constitutive connections to subject matters that they apply to.

There are many ways in which a thought content can be about a property, kind, relation, or object as such, even though the individual does not bear causal relations to it. Representational states may be products of inference, perceptual or conceptual composition, or various forms of unconscious amalgamation or association. In all these ways, thoughts need not bear a causal relation to what they represent. A representational ability must, however, be grounded in some systematic, non-representational relations to some subject matter.

So the general idea is that what kinds of representational mental states one can be in are limited by what relations one bears to one's environment. Minds bear constitutive relations to matters beyond them. This basic idea is spelled out in more detail in the essays.

A corollary of the basic idea is that representational mental kinds are individuated in an explanatory context that is wider than that of the individual's mind or body. For example, a belief that aluminum makes foil is a specific kind of belief. Its being the kind that it is, is fixed by a representational content suggested by the words 'that aluminum makes foil'. The belief is an aluminum-makes-foil kind of belief. Explanations of an individual's activity that make reference to this kind of belief connect it not only to other mental states and to bodily movements by the believer, but also to perceptual, practical, or communicative relations to a wider environment. In actual fact the environment includes relations between believers and aluminum itself. But even if aluminum did not occur in the environment in which the belief was constitutively formed, explanations that appeal to the belief connect it to a background that includes an environment wider than that of the individual's mind or body.

The ramifications of these points are considerable. They touch the natures of representation, thought, perception, action, communication, apriori knowledge, self-knowledge, empirical knowledge, psychological explanation, and personal identity; the relations between persons and animals; the mind–body problem; and the problem of scepticism. Some of these ramifications are suggested in these essays. Others will be developed in subsequent volumes of essays, or in subsequent work.

The origins of anti-individualism lie in Greek philosophy. Aristotle took the form of perceptual and other psychological states to be systematically and non-accidentally related to the forms of physical entities which they represent. Aristotle's notion of form here is closely related to our notion of kind. Mental forms or kinds are what they are through systematic relation to physical forms or kinds that they represent and on which they are causally dependent.[2]

This Aristotelian view dominated the Middle Ages. I once believed that Descartes rejected anti-individualism. I no longer believe this to be true. 'Descartes on Anti-Individualism' (Chapter 19) explains my current view. I think that Descartes carried on and deepened the Aristotelian tradition in this respect. The empiricists constitute complex cases, as do Leibniz and Kant. Hegel and Frege are, I believe, clearly anti-individualists.[3] These issues are ripe for treatment by historians of philosophy. Anti-individualism is a prominent, even dominant, view in the history of philosophy.

During the twentieth century a number of philosophical currents conspired to encourage individualism. One such current was a focus on qualitative aspects of the mind in theories of perception in the first half of the century. Both sense-data views, in the British tradition growing out of the work of Russell and Moore, and phenomenological views, in the Continental tradition growing out of the work of Husserl, encouraged the idea that one can construct mental reality (and sometimes physical reality as well) from introspectable, qualitative, intrinsic aspects of consciousness. Indeed, any position that gives the first-person point of view uncritical hegemony in philosophical reasoning will be tempted to forget some of the necessary constraints on representation or intentionality.

Behaviorist and neo-behaviorist movements encouraged individualism in a different way. Thinking that one can reduce attribution of mental states to

[2] Aristotle, *De anima* II, 5–12; III, 4–5; *On Generation and Corruption* I, 7. Plato took the mind to be capable of representing reality only by being in relation to abstract, objective forms that are certainly individual-independent. I believe it plausible that Plato as well as Aristotle was an anti-individualist, but I regard this case as more complex than I can confidently advocate.

[3] These assessments constitute more caution about the empiricists than is present in the historical remarks at the beginning of 'Cartesian Error and the Objectivity of Perception' (Ch. 7). Kant's 'Refutation of Idealism' has definite anti-individualist elements, but his idealism greatly complicates the historical issue that I am sketching. For remarks on Hegel, see the beginning of 'Individualism and the Mental' (Ch. 5). For remarks on Frege, see my *Truth, Thought, Reason: Essays on Frege* (Oxford: Clarendon Press, 2005), Introduction, pp. 54–63.

attribution of dispositions to bodily responses, or to networks of causal relations that mediate surface stimulation and bodily movement, proponents of these movements thought that mental states can be individuated and accounted for entirely in terms of dispositions or functions of the individual's body.

Early materialist movements in philosophy also provided impetus to individualism. Several prominent philosophers thought that mental kinds are reducible to physical kinds. Insofar as the relevant physical kinds seemed to be neural, there seemed to be no role for relations to a wider reality, in determining conditions for being particular kinds of mental states.

Most of these movements were waning by the time I developed arguments for anti-individualism. But all of them left residual inclinations that tempted philosophers to neglect the anti-individualist tradition. So when it re-emerged, anti-individualism had a feel of being a new view.

There were, to be sure, immediately antecedent currents in philosophy. One was Wittgenstein's emphasis on social practice and social use. I have no question that Wittgenstein was an anti-individualist. However, the tradition flowing from Wittgenstein's work harbored a broad suspicion of psychological explanation. It flirted with a social behaviorism about representational states that leaves the environmental and social emphases of the tradition only tenuously related to mind—because it leaves mind tenuously related to anything.[4]

The more important immediate antecedent was the major change in the theory of linguistic reference brought about in work by Donnellan, Kripke, and Putnam. This work showed that the reference of various linguistic terms, especially names and natural kind terms, depends on causal and other not purely representational relations to the environment, sometimes through the mediation of other language-users. Apart from these relations, even descriptive abilities of the individual were shown to be incapable of accounting for definite reference carried out in the individual's language.[5]

Although my work was strongly influenced by these antecedents, it took a new direction. Anti-individualism concerns not just language but mind, not just reference but mode of representation, and not just a few types of representation but nearly all types.

Let me turn from the broader history to some narrower, autobiographical remarks. In my work, three lines seem to me to have been the main antecedents

---

[4] Saul Kripke's exposition, in *Wittgenstein on Rules and Private Language* (Cambridge, Mass.: Harvard University Press, 1982), evinces the ambivalent bearing of Wittgenstein's views on the individuation of psychological states. The solution is a sceptical solution to a sceptical problem. Some of the scepticism is, in effect, about the full reality of representational mental states. Such a view is at least suggested in Wittgenstein's work, and is explicit in the work of many of his followers.

[5] Saul Kripke, *Naming and Necessity* (Cambridge, Mass.: Harvard University Press, 1972); Keith Donnellan, 'Reference and Definite Descriptions', *The Philosophical Review*, 75 (1966), 281–304; *idem*, 'Proper Names and Identifying Descriptions', *Synthese*, 21 (1970), 335–358; Hilary Putnam, 'Is Semantics Possible?' (1970) and 'Explanation and Reference' (1973), in *Philosophical Papers*, ii (Cambridge: Cambridge University Press, 1975).

of anti-individualism. One line is my early work on linguistic reference.[6] Here I was certainly influenced by the revolution in the theory of reference mentioned above. My focus was somewhat different, in that I was mainly concerned with the logical form of the relevant linguistic devices.[7] This concern was an early instance of my interest in mode of reference and mode of presentation. The way the reference is carried out, within a representational system—in this case, within a language—was as important to me as the causal and contextual factors that make successful reference possible.

The second line is represented by 'On Knowledge and Convention' (Chapter 1 in this volume). This article criticizes David Lewis's theory of convention.[8] What seems to me interesting about the article now is not the particular critical point. It is the article's caution against hyper-intellectualized accounts of meaning and representational practice. Language functions quite well even if individual speakers misunderstand basic facts about its functioning. A language can be conventional even though its users do not know that it is conventional. They may disbelieve that it is conventional. These facts leave room for the determination of the nature of the practice by facts about it that are beyond the ken of the practitioners.

This point is broadly parallel to a point driven home by the theory of linguistic reference: Reference can be definite even though the language-users who carry out the reference may not know enough to be able to describe the referent or fix it in a knowledgeable way. The point about convention, made in 'On Knowledge and Convention', bears not only on linguistic reference, but also on cognitive implications of acts of reference, and on the nature of the language itself.

The third line is represented by 'Kaplan, Quine, and Suspended Belief' and 'Belief *De Re*' (Chapters 2 and 3). The former article makes some technical points about an issue in the logical form of belief attributions. The interest of the article to me now is its insistence on the priority of *de re* belief over *de dicto* belief—a point that is elaborated in the latter article. 'Belief *De Re*' is the closest antecedent in my work to the articles on anti-individualism.[9] This article begins my shift in focus from pure philosophy of language to issues regarding thought and mind.

---

[6] Burge, 'Reference and Proper Names', *The Journal of Philosophy*, 70 (1973), 425–439; and *idem*, 'Demonstrative Constructions, Reference, and Truth', *The Journal of Philosophy*, 71 (1974), pp. 205–223. These articles are not reprinted here. I hope to have them collected later in a further volume.

[7] This angle on reference was influenced by the work of Donald Davidson. A focus on logical form of demonstrative devices is also present in David Kaplan, 'Dthat', in P. Cole (ed.), *Syntax and Semantics*, ix (New York: Academic Press, 1978).

[8] David Lewis, *Convention: A Philosophical Study* (Cambridge, Mass.: Harvard University Press, 1969).

[9] For further discussion of this article, see my Postscript to it in this volume. Cf. also my 'Davidson and Forms of Anti-Individualism: Reply to Hahn', in Martin Hahn and Bjorn Ramberg (eds.) *Reflections and Replies: Essays on the Philosophy of Tyler Burge* (Cambridge, Mass.: MIT Press, 2003), 347–350.

I make two primary claims in 'Belief *De Re*' that are relevant to anti-individualism. First, I argue that there is an irreducible occurrence-based, non-conceptual element in thought.[10] Such thoughts are not to be understood purely in terms of representational contents that mark abilities that can be individuated independently of specific contextual psychological occurrences. Second, I argue that having any thought at all requires having thoughts whose representational contents include such occurrence-based, non-conceptual elements—specifically *de re* thoughts whose contents contain such elements. The idea is that for a being to have representational capacities, it must be able to apply or connect those capacities to particulars in a subject matter. To have definite thoughts, it must have some thoughts that are actually applied in a way that depends on occurrence-based representational elements that are supported by non-representational relations (for example, causal relations) to a subject matter. That is a constitutive condition on the capacities' and thoughts' being representational.[11]

These points are closely connected to key elements of anti-individualism. For anti-individualism maintains that the *specific* natures of many representational states and events (including capacities type-identified by perceptions and concepts) are constitutively derivative from specific aspects of the environment to which those states and events are related in non-representational ways. 'Belief *De Re*' does not make this claim. It does postulate occurrence-based representational contents (applications) that depend for their identities in subtle, partial ways on relations to the environment.[12] It says nothing about individuation of ability-general, non-occurrence-based psychological abilities, particularly those marked by concepts or perceptual attributives.

The claim of 'Belief *De Re*' is more general. It bears on conditions for representation itself. It indicates that *de re* representation is necessary for having any representation at all. It indicates that a particular type of non-conceptual representational capacity is necessarily the vehicle that capitalizes on supplementary non-representational relations to make other representational contents and capacities possible—by connecting them to a subject matter.

---

[10] A similar point applies to perception, as I indicate in 'Five Theses on *De Re* States and Attitudes', forthcoming in a volume edited by Paolo Leonardi, honoring David Kaplan (Oxford University Press). In some respects, this article belongs in the present volume. It contains, in its last section, a conception of the *de re/de dicto* distinction that improves on that in 'Belief *De Re*'. It confronts somewhat more fully issues about *de re* attitudes in mathematics. It also develops, much more deeply than 'Belief *De Re*' does, an account of the essential elements in *de re* attitudes. On the other hand, much of the work in 'Five Theses' centers on issues about representation in perception, and on epistemic issues. In this respect, the article is better grouped with discussions of epistemology or perception. I have gone with this latter consideration.

[11] In subsequent work, I recognized the need to liberalize this claim somewhat. The being can rely on applications in a progenitor. It need not carry out the applications autonomously. Here I allow for innate capacities that are dependent for their meaning on applications of ancestors. Cf. 'Davidson and Forms of Anti-Individualism: Reply to Hahn'.

[12] I discuss this matter in some detail both in 'Five Theses on *De Re* States and Attitudes' and in 'Disjunctivism and Perceptual Psychology', forthcoming in *Philosophical Topics*.

In a Postscript to 'Belief *De Re*', I discuss four elements of the article. One is the inadequate sorting out of linguistic considerations from considerations bearing directly on mind. A second is the relation between my two epistemic accounts of the *de re*/*de dicto* distinction. I explain that the accounts are not equivalent. I discuss how the difference bears on possible *de re* thought regarding mathematical objects and objects of understanding. A third element is the notion of an occurrent application of incompletely conceptualized representational contents. I explain why I take such application to be an element in the representational contents of *de re* mental states. I believe that this notion is fundamental to understanding mind in general, and *de re* thought and perception in particular. A fourth feature is the argument that for an individual to have any propositional attitudes at all, the individual must have *de re* states or attitudes. This argument provides the immediate background in my work for development of anti-individualism.

The arguments for anti-individualism in these essays are laid out in four stages, dealing with four different aspects of anti-individualism. Each stage is associated with a different type of thought experiment. The third stage, centering on perception, couples its thought experiment with independent scientific considerations. Most of the articles in this volume either articulate the arguments in these four stages or refine them.

The article that provides the best entry into the series, although not the first one written, is 'Other Bodies' (Chapter 4). The thought experiment in this article is the simplest and the one most closely related to earlier work on linguistic reference. The relevant earlier work is that of Kripke and Putnam on reference by natural kind terms in language. The thought experiment in 'Other Bodies' uses Putnam's twin-earth methodology and centers on thoughts that use natural kind concepts.

Putnam considers an individual using language to represent instances of natural kinds. He then imagines a physically similar *doppelganger* in a mostly 'twin' environment, except that certain natural kinds in it are different. I use Putnam's illustrative device. The point of my thought experiment is to elicit a recognition that the representational natures of mental states vary with the differences in the individuals' relations to their environments, even though psychologically relevant physical aspects of the individual, considered in isolation from relations to the environment, are more or less constant. My thought experiment, and the basic conclusions that I draw from it, are importantly different from Putnam's superficially similar use of the twin-earth methodology. Bringing out these differences is the main point of the article. The differences signal how anti-individualism differs from the view that Putnam sought to establish.

Two main innovations mark 'Other Bodies'. (The innovations were present in the earlier 'Individualism and the Mental'.) One is a shift of focus from

---

[13] Hilary Putnam, 'The Meaning of "Meaning" ', in his *Philosophical Papers*, ii.

language to mind. The other is a shift of focus from reference, in language or in thought, to representational content. Putnam and Kripke discussed the reference of natural kind terms. Their focus was very strongly on language, with, I think, little direct insight into mind.[14] In 'Other Bodies' and 'Individualism and the Mental' I argue that not just the referents of natural kind terms but the specific natures of mental states about natural kinds, as marked by their representational (conceptual) contents, depend constitutively on causal relations to specific aspects of the environment.[15] These relations may not be specifiable by the individual thinker.

A key aim of 'Other Bodies' is to show that natural kind concepts are not indexical. They do not shift reference from context to context. The concept <u>aluminum</u> is true of the same stuff, aluminum, no matter in what context it is used in thought. I made this point against Putnam's view. The mistake underlies the key difference between his view of linguistic reference and meaning and my view of mind.[16]

---

[14] There is an astonishing lack of reflection on perception among many of the main philosophers of language in this group, even though perception clearly lies at the base of the relations that establish linguistic reference, in most of the cases that they discuss. The methodology of the time was to consider language more or less independently of any developed account of mind. Donnellan does give an account of referential use of language in terms of having an object 'in mind' and in terms of intended reference. But there is no elaboration of either of these notions. Putnam offers more on mind in "The Meaning of 'Meaning'". Putnam's account of non-factive thought in that article is basically individualist. Some of his account of mind contains fundamental errors that stem from thinking of some aspects of mental states too much in terms of linguistic reference. I discuss the specifics of Putnam's views in more detail below in this Introduction (cf. note 16), in 'Other Bodies', and in the Postscript to 'Individualism and the Mental'. All three philosophers failed in their work on language, I think, to see that the linguistic facts that they uncovered are derivative from more pervasive and deeper facts about the representational nature of mind. Despite these critical remarks, I think that the work of all three philosophers was ground-breaking and brilliant. I depended on their insights about language in my development of anti-individualism about mind.

[15] Throughout this Introduction I use 'referent' in a very broad sense. I mean it to apply to what singular terms denote, refer to, or apply to. I also mean it to apply to the semantical values of predicative and functional expressions—what they denote, indicate, or attribute. I sometimes also write of the referents of components of thought. Again, the relevant components can be singular, predicative, or functional.

[16] Cf. Putnam's "The Meaning of 'Meaning'". Putnam concedes the point in Andrew Pessin and Sanford Goldberg (eds.), *The Twin Earth Chronicles*, (London: M. E. Sharpe, 1996), p. xxi. I do not want to discuss Putnam's 1975 account of meaning in any detail here, but I will make a few remarks. I think that there are various legitimate conceptions of linguistic meaning, including meaning of natural kind terms. I regard Putnam's tendency simply to count the reference of a natural kind term as its meaning, on one conception of the meaning, as not particularly illuminating for any conception, much less as an account of representational mental states.

I think that his conception of a stereotype does illuminate one aspect of meaning. His use of the notion of stereotype is, however, a part of his mistake in regarding natural kind terms as indexical. The stereotype is supposed to be the constant element whose referent shifts with context. None of these ideas illumines the *way* an individual thinks of a referent. Individuals think of water as water. The referent itself does not illuminate this 'way', because in normal cases the referent does not represent anything, and because no thinker can think of ordinary referents in non-perspectival, non-representational ways. The stereotype does not illuminate this 'way', because individuals can think of the referent in using a natural kind term (can think of water as water) while wondering whether the stereotype applies, or even believing that it does not apply; and they can think of the referent

The reason why this point is important is that it forces recognition that my thought experiment cannot be taken to bear only on reference. Since relevant natural kind concepts are not indexical, it would be incorrect to construe the thoughts as containing a single concept or 'meaning' or representational content which simply undergoes a contextual shift of referent. The concepts or representational contents are different. This difference marks a difference in the kinds of thought, or the kinds of mental state or event, that occur in the two individuals. It marks a difference in the representative perspectives and epistemic standpoints of the individuals. The difference is ultimately attributable to differences in the causal relations to specific elements in the two environments. Differences in causal relations yield differences in conceptual perspectives on what the causal relations are relations to.

Anti-individualism, often called 'externalism', is commonly misunderstood by philosophers who have some sense of the major changes in linguistic reference, but have not much reflected on my work. It is still common to make the mistake that I criticized in 'Other Bodies' and that Putnam made in "The Meaning of 'Meaning' ". A common line that depends partly on this mistake begins by holding that there are two types of 'content'. Traditional descriptivists are supposed to be right about so-called narrow psychological states or narrow contents, which are supposed to be marked purely by descriptive representational content.[17] Millians are supposed to be right about 'wide psychological states'. These are supposed to be type-identified by relations between the descriptive content and elements in the environment—objects, properties, relations. In effect, 'wide content' is supposed to be simply the referents of the purely descriptive contents. Many people who think rather cursorily about these matters rely mainly on concepts from the philosophy of language. Many even now understand anti-individualism as a thesis that referents go 'into the proposition' expressed by names and natural kind terms.[18]

Much is wrong with this way of thinking. In fact, it completely misconstrues what anti-individualism is, or seriously underestimates its force. 'Other Bodies' was written partly to refute views like this one. The key point is that the relevant concepts (perspectival, representational elements) discussed in its

---

even when the stereotype fails to apply. The view that natural kind terms are indexical is incorrect, for the reasons given in 'Other Bodies'.

From about 1983 onward, Putnam's work becomes genuinely anti-individualist. Cf. 'Computational Psychology and Interpretation Theory', in his *Philosophical Papers*, iii (Cambridge: Cambridge University Press, 1983).

[17] I discussed the notion of narrow content in 'Individualism and the Mental' (Ch. 5). A small industry has emerged elaborating one or another conception. Not all such conceptions insist on narrow content's being descriptive. In some cases the proposed notion does not seem to me to be representational at all. I believe that no one has shown the relevance to psychological explanation of any 'content' that escapes anti-individualist arguments and yet remains representational. Much of the work in this area seems to me to have the status of philosophical game playing without genuine cognitive application.

[18] I was prompted to make these points by Peter Graham.

thought experiment are not context-dependent for their referents. So the idea that there is a constant element that shifts its referent with environmental 'context' does not account for the nature of the mental states or their representational behavior.

Views of this sort tend to have other difficulties. I will mention four. First, they frequently fail to show that the descriptive concepts that are supposed to replace the concepts that the thought experiments deal with are always psychologically available to individuals in the relevant cases. So the descriptive concepts do not in general mark cognitive abilities, as they should. Second, the descriptive concepts (or other supposed narrow contents) are not rationally, psychologically, or epistemically equivalent to the concepts that they are supposed to account for (or replace). This equivalence is not achieved by adverting to the 'wide' contents. For example, it is sometimes thought that the way a thinker thinks of water is fully captured or apriori equivalent to something like *the stuff that occurs in lakes and rivers*. To the contrary, a thinker thinks of water as water, and it is an empirical matter for the thinker whether water is the stuff that occurs in lakes and rivers. Third, these ways of thinking tend not to recognize that the descriptive or supposedly neutral notions in terms of which 'narrow content' is specified are themselves constitutively dependent on relations to a wider environment. Finally, logical, mathematical, and other apriori aspects of thought which are simply assumed to be 'narrow' are themselves dependent on relations to matters beyond the mind of the individual. So 'internal determination' does not correspond to those elements of thought that *are* normally constant among empirically different or contingent 'twin' environments. (I will discuss this matter further below.)

The 'wide' aspects of the view have difficulties as well. No representational content that marks a representational state kind has a non-representational component. Environmental referents of representational states do not by themselves suffice to type-identify any of representational state kinds that are fundamental in psychological explanation or epistemology. Individuals necessarily think about subject matters in certain ways or from certain conceptual perspectives. For example, individuals think about aluminum as aluminum. There are many ways of thinking about aluminum.[19] In fact, there are many ways of thinking about aluminum as aluminum. It will not do to take the referent as capturing any sort of psychological content. Representational content needs to explain or indicate how referents are thought about. Descriptions or other allegedly narrow contents available to the thinker do not suffice to determine the way the individual thinks about aluminum, since they do not determine in themselves (as opposed to contextually or contingently) that they apply to aluminum—as thinking of aluminum as aluminum does. In many of the

---

[19] Thinking about aluminum as aluminum is thinking about aluminum in a way that entails that its denotation or referent is aluminum, if there is any denotation or referent at all. There can be many ways of thinking about aluminum as aluminum that meet these conditions.

relevant cases, indexical devices are demonstrably not how we think about the referents.[20]

As far as I can see, representational content, anti-individualistically individuated, fills the semantical, psychological-explanatory, and epistemic roles that mental-state kinds are supposed to fill. I have seen no grounds to believe in a further sort of representational content, or in a division of representational contents into wide and narrow kinds. Even now, because of compartmentalization in much of philosophy, many philosophers lump the important changes in theory of reference with anti-individualism, failing to appreciate the enormity of the differences, and their implications for our understanding of knowledge and mind.

Although I am emphasizing the fact that relations to entities in the environment play an indispensable role in determining the content of many mental states, I want firmly to insist that these relations are not the only factor in determining mental kinds. There is a large role for the ways that the individual and his cognitive subsystems process information. Different perceptual perspectives on a given property, relation, or kind are at the heart of perceptual representation. These perspectives involve not simply types of causal routes to a represented entity. They involve different ways of processing the information, or different information processed. These help determine different modes of presentation, different types of representational contents.

For example, a given distance can be computed in the visual system in many ways. Each computation utilizes different inputs and yields a different representation, or mode of presentation, of the distance. A given method of computation might compute the same distance from very different angles and with very different proximal stimulation. Each computation that is different in these ways will yield perceptual states with different representational contents. Further, there are different methods for computing distance—different distance cues—in the visual system. These different methods also commonly yield different perceptual representational contents or modes of presentation. Yet further, different perceptual modalities (say, hearing and vision) can represent the same distal property. Again, these differences normally correspond to different representational contents specifying the same property.

What holds for perception holds for other types of representation. Different representational contents referring to a given object, property, kind, or relation can have different inferential potentials, or be affected in different ways by

---

[20] There are a few views that carry over Millian views on linguistic reference to the account of reference in thought. Millian conceptions have some plausibility in accounting for a restricted aspect of language use, though insofar as they omit any meaning or mode of presentation over and above a referent, I am unconvinced that they are correct, even as applied to language. They have no grip on psychological explanation, perceptual theory, or on a reasonable philosophy of mind. It is psychologically incoherent to imagine that we think of referents, but in no way at all–from no representational perspective at all. Anti-individualism specifies representational ways in which relevant referents are thought about, and shows those ways commonly to depend on patterns of relations to the environment.

priming or habituation, or may connect to different files or memories. Thus the individuation of psychological representational kinds does not hinge purely on relations to aspects of the distal environment. Such relations nonetheless anchor individuation and provide a necessary element in it.

I noted that 'Other Bodies' is the best introduction to the series of four thought experiments. But 'Individualism and the Mental' was written first.[21] Both articles show that individual–environment relations constitutively bear on mind as well as language. Both show that those relations help constitutively determine not just reference but the representational natures of mental states and events. That is, each brings its thought experiment to bear on aspects of mind type-identified by representational contents—particularly concepts—not simply referents.

A third primary contribution of 'Individualism and the Mental', not present in 'Other Bodies', concerns the range of concepts that constitutively depend on an individual's non-representational relations to a wider reality. The article shows that the range comprises vastly more representational types than those that correspond to names and natural kind terms. 'Other Bodies' concentrates on natural kind concepts in order to highlight ways in which my anti-individualism differs from Putnam's treatment of the reference and 'meaning' of natural kind terms. 'Individualism and the Mental' brings out how pervasively a wider environment enters into the individuation of mental states. Mental states type-identified by nearly every type of representational content are affected.

I invoke two phenomena to elicit the role of a wider reality in constituting the natures of mental states marked by such a wide range of representational contents. One is incomplete understanding. The other is the role of social relations in mediating between an individual and aspects of the wider reality.[22]

The role of the social in attitude determination seems to me to affect an even wider variety of concepts or terms than are discussed in 'Individualism and the Mental'. For example, I believe that there is a social role for attitude determination in the cases of attitudes marked by certain logical and mathematical concepts.

The standards for understanding vary with the case. A community-wide standard does not apply willy-nilly to all members of the community. There are conditions for minimum mastery, and for dependence or reliance on others. There are various ways of opting out. There are cells of sub-communal interaction that can determine standards for understanding that need not accord with some wider communal practice or understanding.

---

[21] For further discussion of this article, see the Postscript in this volume and 'Davidson and Forms of Anti-Individualism: Reply to Hahn', 'The Thought Experiments: Reply to Donnellan', 'Psychology and the Environment: Reply to Chomsky', all in Hahn and Ramberg (eds.), *Reflections and Replies the Philosophy of Tyler Burge, op. cit.*.

[22] Further discussion of incomplete understanding occurs in 'Intellectual Norms and Foundations of Mind' (Ch. 10), and in 'Frege on Extensions of Concepts, From 1884 to 1903' and 'Frege on Sense and Linguistic Meaning', Chs. 7 and 6 in *Truth, Thought, Reason*.

Actual best understanding in a community may not be complete understanding. Since a role of the social relations is to connect individuals to the referent of a word or concept, the nature of the referent can trump explicational understanding. (This is a primary point of 'Intellectual Norms and Foundations of Mind' Chapter 10.) Standards for understanding are set by a combination of the nature of the referent, the existence of a chain of speakers in connection to the referent, and elements of explicational understanding by participants in the chain.

As I have mentioned, there are opportunities for variations in the ways people conceive a referent, even when they are linked in a communicative chain to it. Nevertheless, there are also strong sources of preservation of representational content among people who communicate with one another. Such communication occurs among people with widely varying linguistic competence, background knowledge, and perspective. One such source of content preservation lies in our common world and our common perceptual equipment. We are molded by the same world; and we have similar perceptual equipment, which yields the first and most dominant base for representing the world. Another source of content preservation lies in the social and normative conditions for agreement, for mutual evaluation, for sharing information, and for relying on one another for knowledge and warrant. Serious reflection on how little knowledge, warrant, agreement, and shared culture would be left if we did not, despite deep differences in understanding and background knowledge, routinely share thoughts will elicit, I think, the pervasiveness of shared representational content. Content preservation lies at the base of a network of conditions that makes a continuous and shared culture possible.[23]

There is still much to be gained from reflecting on mechanisms and norms of social dependence of human language and thought. There remain many interesting questions that I think my initial and subsequent work made progress upon, but which invite further exploration. What types of reliance on others allow a place for social factors in individuation of mental states? What sorts of psychological conditions and attitudes can block or cancel such reliance in individual cases? How do such factors illuminate the nature of language, knowledge, warrant, cooperation, and communication? How do they bear on the transmission of knowledge and culture? In what ways are the relevant social factors distinctive of human beings? In what ways are these factors refinements of social interactions in other animals? What aspects of mind are social conditions necessary to, and in what ways are social conditions merely psychologically, as opposed to constitutively, fundamental? Confronting such questions may

---

[23] I explore aspects of this network in several papers not printed in this volume—particularly, 'Russell's Problem and Intentional Identity', in James Tomberlin (ed.), *Agent, Language, and Structure of the World* (Indianapolis: Hackett Publishing Company, 1983); 'Content Preservation', *The Philosophical Review*, 103 (1993), 457–488; and 'Comprehension and Interpretation', in Lewis Hahn (ed.), *The Philosophy of Donald Davidson* (Chicago: Open Court Publishers, 1999). In these matters, I think, I have hardly scratched the surface.

help carry us beyond the true but overworked bromide that humans are social animals.

In a Postscript to 'Individualism and the Mental', I discuss two main deficiencies in the article that have caused misunderstanding. One is an instability in my early explications of what individualism is. The other is an insufficiently clear distinction between linguistic considerations and considerations regarding the nature of thought. The problem is similar to the unclarity discussed with respect to 'Belief *De Re*'. I try to sort out secondary from primary arguments for anti-individualism by keeping this distinction clearly to the fore. In the latter, more progressive sections of the Postscript, I discuss the implications of the paper for a new sort of rationalism, the nature of incomplete understanding, and the role of norms in our understanding of mind.

'Two Thought Experiments Reviewed' (Chapter 6) is a minor piece that responds to a variety of criticisms by Jerry Fodor of the first two thought experiments. My response sets the first two primary contributions, mentioned earlier, in sharper relief.

For all the importance of the social in our understanding of language and mind, anti-individualism has a deeper root. Environment–individual relations determined the nature of some psychological states before language evolved. Constitutive dependence of perceptual states on the environment is pervasive and inevitable in perception. Environmental relations help constitutively determine the representational content of psychological states in animals that lack language. Here, the mechanisms of content determination do not involve language or other social phenomena.

The phylogenetic priority of perception points toward a more fundamental root of anti-individualism. The basic root lies in the determination of conditions for objectivity. Only through being allied with non-representational relations to a mind-independent reality can an individual have mental or psychological states that represent such a mind-independent reality. The relations not only make intentionality or representation possible. They ground and help establish the specific representational content, or 'meaning', of those states. Having a representational mind requires being embedded in a system of relations to some of the kinds of entities that are represented. Representing mind-independent reality requires bearing further, non-representational relations to that wider reality. Such relations are necessary for having the relevant representative abilities and are partly constitutive of what those abilities are.

The third and fourth thought experiments that helped establish anti-individualism explicitly invoke this connection to objectivity. The third of these thought experiments attempts to elicit the role of individual–environment relations in the determination of the representational nature of *perceptual* states and abilities. Two articles propose this thought experiment, against very different philosophical backgrounds.

One of these articles is 'Cartesian Error and the Objectivity of Perception' (Chapter 7). There I gesture at setting anti-individualism in a larger historical setting. I sketch ways in which anti-individualism is compatible with authoritative self-knowledge and with the thinkability of the Cartesian demon hypothesis. Like Descartes, I think that the hypothesis is ultimately flawed. It assumes an intentionality or representationality some of whose necessary conditions it denies.[24]

The ideas in the article are further articulated in response to a comment on the article by Robert Matthews. In 'Authoritative Self-Knowledge and Perceptual Individualism' (Chapter 8) I reflect on how we might be misled into thinking that the authoritative character of self-knowledge is incompatible with anti-individualism. I also discuss details of the thought experiment that I use to support anti-individualism about perception.

The relevant thought experiment is set out not only in 'Cartesian Error and the Objectivity of Perception', but also in 'Individualism and Psychology' (Chapter 9). Both articles center on showing that anti-individualism applies to perceptual states. In 'Individualism and Psychology' I embed the discussion of anti-individualism regarding perception in a discussion of the method and presuppositions of the science of vision.

Both articles offer an argument that I misleadingly characterize, in two places, as an argument against individualism. The third premise of the argument already entails the positive thesis of anti-individualism—that the natures of perceptual states are partly fixed by relations to the environment. So if this positive thesis was what the thought experiment was trying to establish, the argument would beg the question. What the argument actually attempts to show is that individualist considerations cannot equally fix or co-fix those natures. It thus attempts to block reduction of anti-individualism to individualism.[25] In this respect the point of the thought experiment is different from that of the other three thought experiments in the series.

Even given its limited objective, I believe that the thought experiment is less powerful than the other three, although I continue to stand by it. Unlike the other thought experiments, this one is presented as an instance of general principles. Principles, not examples, lead. The thought experiment is intuitively less powerful because of two features of the example it presents. First, the example centers on a somewhat peripheral type of perceptual state. It does so for reasons that I will soon discuss. Second, the example involves a counterfactual environment in which the laws of optics differ from actual laws. I believe that invoking a case that is incompatible with physical law is legitimate. The point of the thought experiment is to bring out how relations, including lawful relations, between individual and environment help determine what representational

[24] This part of the discussion anticipates later work to be reprinted in a future volume, in particular 'Individualism and Self-knowledge', *The Journal of Philosophy*, 85 (1988), 649–663.

[25] These matters are discussed further in sec. III and note 13 of 'Descartes and Anti-Individualism: Reply to Normore', in Hahn and Ramberg (eds.), *Reflections and Replies*. As the discussion there indicates, my handling of the argument involves some conflation of issues about supervenience with issues about how representational natures of mental states are fixed.

content a perceptual state can have. So imagining those relations co-varying with variations of representational content can help elicit recognition of the role of such relations in determining a perception's content. Nevertheless, these features of the example lessen its intuitive power.

There are two reasons why examples that use twin-earth methodology to support perceptual anti-individualism have these features. One is that an individual's basic perceptual states bear strong law-like relations to proximal stimulation and ultimately, under normal conditions, to distal objects of perception—at least in veridical cases. The other is that an individual's dispositions to bodily movement (for example, in grasping an object of perception, or in tracing its shape) are normally tightly correlated with the perceived properties. Surface stimulation and bodily movement bear close relations to the distal sources or objectives of these movements, at least those guided by basic perceptual states. By contrast, there are no psychologically relevant bodily movements or surface stimulations that normally correlate well, by a relatively circumscribable set of physical laws, with other distal macro-properties. The very tightness of the dependence of perceptual content on relations of one's body to aspects of the environment makes it harder to produce cases in which one varies relations to the environment while holding 'individualist' aspects of the individual's body constant. Thus the very depth of anti-individualism about perception impedes the use of twin-earth methodology to demonstrate it.

Almost inevitably, in applying twin-earth methodology to perceptual cases, one must imagine differences in physical law, not just differences in the kinds of things that occur in the environment. For the effects on an individual's body and the individual's dispositions to bodily movement will be closely tied to the distal objects of perception, if physical law is held constant. These facts make it difficult to hold kinds of bodily states constant in actual and counterfactual circumstances, while varying relevant individual–environment relations. The difficulty of running straightforward twin-earth thought experiments on perceptual cases derives from the fact that the non-representational individual–environment relations that help constitutively to determine the representational nature of perceptual states include physical laws.

The twin-earth method is geared to showing that the psychologically relevant aspects of an individual's body could be constant while associated mental states vary counterfactually, because of variations in individual–environment relations. In some cases, many mental-state kinds could have been different even as the underlying internal physical states and processes remained the same. This latter situation is called a failure of local supervenience of mental states on underlying physical states. Anti-individualism is invoked as explanation of this failure of supervenience.[26] The explanation of the failure lies in the fact that the relevant mental-state kinds are constitutively dependent on relations to the environment

---

[26] The sub-argument for supervenience failure is, I think, relatively powerful in the particular sorts of cases discussed in 'Individualism and the Mental' and 'Other Bodies'. But even in these

beyond the individual's body. The fundamental point of the thought experiments is to argue for anti-individualism, not for local supervenience failure.[27]

So anti-individualism is not rejection of local supervenience of representational states on the individual's underlying bodily physical states.[28] Anti-individualism is constitutive explanation of the representational natures of mental states. Supervenience is a mere modal notion. Failures of local supervenience (supervenience of a representational state on an individual's body) can point toward constitutive explanations. Local supervenience failure, however, is neither constitutive of anti-individualism nor necessary for it.

If one is to apply twin-earth methodology in perceptual cases, one must confine the cases to non-central perceptual states. And one must almost inevitably vary the physical laws in the two environments. The method can invite recognition that laws governing relations to the environment are among the basic factors in understanding the natures of the perceptual states. But the sub-argument for local supervenience is intuitively less powerful.

For these reasons, it came to seem to me that twin-earth thought experiments are not the best basis for arguing for *perceptual* anti-individualism. There are two better bases. One is inference to the best explanation. I think that there is no equally good explanation of the natures and possibility of perceptual representation than one that includes anti-individualism. (I think that this type of argument is sound for nearly all types of representation, not merely perceptual types.) This conclusion derives from reflecting on alternatives and finding them to be patently inadequate or confused. Thus invocations of similarity between perception and

---

cases, one must be willing to discount small gravitational differences on the individual's body caused by remote physical differences in the actual and twin environments.

[27] Putnam's original thought experiment took two people's beliefs about water to differ even as their bodies are type-identical. Putnam assumed he was dealing with living bodies. One of the person's environments is Earth and contains water. The other's environment is Twin-Earth except that it contains no water. Obviously, this set of conditions is not possible. No living body on Earth lacks water. So a duplicate body must contain water. So the twin-earth environment cannot lack water. This infelicity was always recognized to be unimportant. It is unimportant because the main point of the thought experiment was not to establish that local supervenience fails, but to establish that reference and 'meaning' depend not on the character of an individual's body but on relations to the wider environment. It is obvious that what liquid is in an individual's body is not relevant to explaining what the individual's terms 'mean' or what the individual's terms are referring to. Given the thought experiment, it is clear that causal relations between the individual and specific aspects of the wider environment are what matter. So some twin-earth thought experiments might be taken to support rejection of local supervenience, while others need not be. The key point in the use of such experiments is that whatever differences (for example, gravitational differences) there may be in the bodies of the individuals in the respective twin worlds are not relevant to the constitutive determination of the individuals' mental state kinds.

[28] In my early work there are places where this distinction is blurred, though the specific explications of what anti-individualism is tended get the point right. I certainly always thought of anti-individualism as a thesis about the constitutive conditions for being in mental states—about the natures of mental states in this broad sense—and not mainly about supervenience failure. For discussion of reasons for distinguishing the views, see my 'The Indexical Strategy: Reply to Owens', in *Reflections and Replies*, Hahn and Ramberg (eds.), 371–372; see also "Postscript to 'Individualism and the Mental' ", note 2.

perceptual object, appeals to narrow content, postulations of intrinsic intentional-ity, claims that representation derives purely from phenomenality, and so on, can all be shown to be completely inadequate as explanations of perceptual content, or even accounts of its possibility, insofar as they deny anti-individualism. As far as I can see, the basic reasoning underlying this best-explanation justification is apriori. It is supplemented by empirical reflection on cases.

The other basis for arguing for anti-individualism about perception is reflec-tion on ways that it is presupposed, filled in, and developed, in empirical science. Such reflection is the main business of 'Individualism and Psychology'.

I was fortunate to visit MIT in the early 1980s when the approach to the empirical psychology of vision by the then recently deceased psychologist David Marr was being taught and developed by his colleagues. I immediately saw this work as of higher quality, in empirical and methodological respects, than any psychology that I had been exposed to. The work seemed to be the beginning of a mathematically rigorous and empirically well-supported theoretical psychology, not just a compendium of experimental results. I also found that not only Marr's methodological remarks in his book, *Vision*,[29] but the entire approach to the subject in the classes and labs that I attended presupposes and develops anti-individualism. The fundamental theoretical representational kinds postulated by the theory are generically individuated in terms of computational methods for capitalizing on information deriving from causal relations to distal properties and distal regularities in the environment.

In 'Individualism and Psychology' I try to show not only that anti-individualism implicitly guides the empirical psychology of vision. I also try to bring home that the psychological theory indicates *specific* ways in which *specific* perceptual representational states are individuated in terms of relations to *specific* aspects of the distal environment. Of course, the theory is not fun-damentally about individuation. It is about how vision works. Nevertheless, it assumes or presupposes anti-individualism at numerous points, and its empiric-al accounts of how perceptual states work constitute an empirical realization of anti-individualism.

Marr's approach fructified mainstream visual psychology. The psychology of vision surpasses other areas of cognitive psychology in the depth of its empirical support and the mathematical sophistication of its theorizing. Details of Marr's theory have been superseded. The shape of its explanatory strategy and its relation to anti-individualism have remained broadly the same in later empirical developments.

'Individualism and Psychology' was the start, for me, of a long-standing engagement with philosophical issues centered on psychology, especially the psychology of perception.[30] My time at MIT benefited from interaction with

---

[29] David Marr, *Vision* (San Francisco: W. H. Freeman, 1982).

[30] Apart from 'Individualism and Psychology' (Ch. 9) and 'Wherein is Language Social?' (Ch. 11), most of my work in this area is not included in this volume.

the linguist-philosopher Noam Chomsky, the philosophers Ned Block, Jerry Fodor, and Jim Higginbotham, and the psychologists Whitman Richards, Merrill Garrett, and, at greater distance, Shimon Ullman. These engagements sparked an interest in empirical psychology, and philosophy of psychology, that I have maintained ever since.

I believe that there are issues in philosophy of mind that can be fruitfully confronted through reflection on ordinary non-scientific matters. In some areas of philosophy of mind, however, fruitful reflection requires knowing something about empirical science. For the most part, philosophizing about perception seems to me to require such background knowledge. Too much is known about perception that is relevant to nearly any philosophical issue for it to be possible to carry on reasonable philosophical reflection in isolation from science. Unfortunately, quite a lot of philosophical work on perception still does so.

The bulk of the discussion in 'Individualism and Psychology' centers on how anti-individualism is woven into the fabric of the best empirical theory of vision, and indeed best theories of hearing and touch, that we have. It seems to me that its integration into empirical knowledge is strong ground to accept the philosophical doctrine. I believe that this consideration and more general inference-to-the-best-explanation considerations are the main support for anti-individualism about perception.

I said in first introducing the articles on perception that they evoke a connection between objectivity and anti-individualism. This evocation occurs in the general thought experiment whose role in supporting perceptual anti-individualism I have been downplaying. The ideas in the argument seem to me to have a further point. They suggest the fundamental and motivating role of objectivity in a comprehensive understanding of anti-individualism. As the last sentence of 'Cartesian Error and the Objectivity of Perception' indicates, anti-individualism seems to be a necessary condition of representation of an objective mind-independent world.[31]

The thought experiment uses three principles. I want to comment on the relation among these principles, abstracting from the argument that they are used to produce. The principles are:

(1) Our perceptual experience represents or is about objects, properties, and relations that are objective, in the sense that their natures are public—independent of anyone's acts, dispositions, or mental phenomena.

Physical objects, properties, and relations are paradigm cases of objective mind-independent subject matters.

(2) Our perceptual representational contents (and perceptual states with representational contents) specify particular objective types of objects, properties, or relations as such.

---

[31] Essentially the same point is made in the third to last paragraph of 'Individualism and Psychology'.

That is, the representational contents of perceptual states specify such properties or kinds as solidity, color, motion, shape, rigid body, in a way that entails that if the perceptual content is veridical, there are instances of such physical properties or kinds.

(3)　As a constitutive matter, such perceptual representational contents (and perceptual states with representational contents) specify as they do (or are the perceptual states with the representational contents that they have) partly because of non-representational relations that hold between the perceiver, or instances of the type of perceptual system that the perceiver has, and instances of some of the objective properties, relations, and object-kinds that are specified.

Anti-individualism describes the constitutive conditions determining what representational contents our perceptual states have, what our perceptual states are.

I believe that the three premises are not independent. I think that (2) and (3) are consequences of (1).[32] I do not mean that they are logical consequences of (1). I mean that the truth of (2) and (3) are constitutive necessary conditions for the truth of (1).

I will not develop these points in detail here. I will just sketch the ideas. The idea that (1), reference to a mind-independent subject matter, requires (3), the truth of anti-individualism, is outlined in the third paragraph of this Introduction.

The idea that (1), reference in perception to a mind-independent subject matter, requires (2), that perception specify objective properties as the properties that they are, is more complex. It derives from the following considerations. Perceptual reference requires perceptual grouping or attribution of perceivable properties. Such attribution must sometimes be veridical: it must succeed in attributing properties that the subject matter has. The representational content of the attributions sometimes must partly derive from the nature of the relevant perceptible subject matter. So, for example, if perception represents shapes, colors, motion, its content must specify those properties as shapes, colors, motion. Since its subject matter is objective, perceptual reference must be guided by veridical attributive representational contents that derive from objective elements of the subject matter.[33]

The fourth main thought experiment that supports anti-individualism is set out in 'Intellectual Norms and Foundations of Mind' (Chapter 10). This article, too, locates the source of anti-individualism in conditions of objectivity. The thought experiment has an extremely general range of applicability. It centers on the possibility of questioning commonly held explicational beliefs. It exploits the lack of omniscience that is the inevitable consequence of objective reference to

---

[32] In 'Cartesian Error and the Objectivity of Perception' I asserted without argument that (2) is a consequence of (1) in the sixth paragraph of sec. II. As noted, I asserted that (3) is a consequence of (1) in the last sentence of the article and in the last section of 'Individualism and Psychology'.

[33] The first two premises in this argument sketch are discussed in considerable detail in sec. II and III of 'Five Theses on *De Re* States and Attitudes'.

an empirical subject matter. The exploitation of this cognitive distance between thought and subject matter shows, I think, that the first and second thought experiments in the series that I have been discussing are special cases of the phenomena elicited by the fourth, at least with respect to representation of empirical subject matters.[34]

The thought experiment in 'Other Bodies' centers on thinking about natural kinds. It depends on the thinker's having some sensitivity to a distinction between superficial appearances and underlying natures. With respect to natural kinds, the objectivity of empirical reference is at its most dramatic. Still, the distinction between superficial features, which we know easily, and deeper features, which may be harder to know, is just a special case of our lack of omniscience with respect to any objective empirical subject matter, even the superficial features.

The mechanisms driving the thought experiment in 'Individualism and the Mental' are special cases of cognitive distance between individual standpoint and objective subject matter. With regard to empirically accessed subject matters, the cognitive distance between individual and subject matter that is marked by incomplete understanding (and exploited in 'Individualism and the Mental') is again a special case of incomplete knowledge. It is a failure of knowledge mediated by incomplete mastery of one's own cognitive perspective on the world.

'Intellectual Norms and Foundations of Mind' shows that the relevant cognitive distance can be elicited without appeal to incomplete understanding, at least in an ordinary, everyday sense of 'incomplete understanding'. The thought experiment can be made to work for essentially the whole range of concepts applicable to objective, empirically accessible subject matters. The thought experiment both elicits and depends on the fact that most common sense explications of empirically applicable concepts involve empirical commitments. Thus 'sofas are furniture of such and such a size made or meant for sitting' has empirical commitments, even though these commitments seem to be completely safe. The commitments are meant to have constitutive implications. This one is meant to indicate what sofas *are*. They are also summations of empirical belief about the concepts' (or terms') referents. Such summations are fallible and open to question. The natures of the concepts are, in most instances, constrained by the objective referents. These referents are not fixed by the explications. We have partly independent referential access to the referents. We access sofas through perception.

The thought experiment shows that if individuals had never perceived sofas, there are circumstances in which they would not have had beliefs about anything as a sofa. The referent of the individual's concept is not in general fixed by a

---

[34] The thought experiment in 'Individualism and the Mental' (Ch. 5) seems to me to have applications to thought about logic, mathematics, and other apriori accessible subjects that are independent of the applications of this fourth thought experiment. So the relations among the thought experiments are not as simple as the line I am sketching might suggest. Still, I think that this line casts some light on the first two thought experiments.

particular individual's explication, by what the individual believes about the nature of the referent. It is often fixed by causal, perceptual, experimental, or practical relations that the thinker bears to the world.

The relevant concepts would be different if their referents were different. The concepts help type-identify mental states. The referents are partly fixed by non-representational relations between individual and world. So the mental states partly type-identified by the concepts (or representational contents) are partly determined by non-representational relations between individual and world. Thus the thought experiment supports anti-individualism. Of course, the force of the thought experiment lies in its concrete detail, not in this meta-description. For the detail, the reader must reflect on the article 'Intellectual Norms and Foundations of Mind' itself.

The individuals with incomplete understanding, in the thought experiment of 'Individualism and the Mental', are disposed to rely on others with superior understanding. Those with superior understanding have explicational beliefs with fallible commitments.[35] The thought experiment of 'Intellectual Norms and Foundations of Mind' indicates that these commitments commonly do not fix the concepts of the people with superior understanding. The ultimate source of anti-individualism, even in cases of social dependence, is the cognitive distance between individual and subject matter in any objective representation. This distance must be bridged by non-representational relations between individual and objective subject matter. Intellectual norms for application of representational contents are partly grounded on and must accord with these non-representational relations to the subject matter.

Three further articles elaborate ideas in 'Individualism and the Mental' and 'Intellectual Norms and Foundations of Mind'. All give special attention to the status of explicational beliefs, the sorts that have traditionally been thought to give definitions of terms or concepts.

One of these articles is 'Wherein is Language Social?' (Chapter 11) published in a volume on Noam Chomsky.[36] In it I discuss relations between my work on anti-individualism and the sciences of linguistics and cognitive psychology. One of the points of the article is to show that my arguments in 'Individualism and the Mental' do not rely essentially on a generalized notion of a communal language. The social interactions that the arguments cite are much more individualized and fine-grained. I accept Chomsky's conception of linguistics as the study of idiolects and as a part of individual psychology. The article shows how social interaction can bear on the representational contents and structures that occur in idiolects and individual psychologies.

---

[35] Here again, I confine this part of the discussion to cases of beliefs involving empirical commitments. These are the sorts of cases I center on in 'Individualism and the Mental', even though I believe that the basic form of argumentation in that paper applies more widely, to certain cases of beliefs in logic, mathematics, and other apriori disciplines.

[36] Relevant to this article is the exchange between Chomsky and me in Hahn and Ramberg (eds.), *Reflections and Replies*.

The article also shows that even the thought experiments of 'Individualism and the Mental' do not hinge entirely on whether an individual has the same concepts as experts on whom the individual depends. I believe that in the arthritis case, the individual does (or can) have the same concept as his more knowledgeable doctor. But the main point of the argument does not depend on this belief. What is important is that the individual has a non-indexical concept, for whose referent the individual depends on the mediation of others. As long as the individual can share a referent with others, a point that I regard as overwhelmingly plausible, the conclusion of the thought experiment still holds. The root of anti-individualism lies not in the sharing of concepts and transmission of belief or knowledge, but in the objective reference of our thought. Sharing of concepts and transmission of belief are further aspects of this basic phenomenon.

The key idea of 'Wherein is Language Social?' lies in this reasoning: Psychological states involve representational commitments that can be corrected. Individuals often take themselves to be correctable in their explicational beliefs. They are often right to take themselves to be correctable because they have relied on others for being connected to the referents of their concepts—the referents that the explicational beliefs are committed to correctly characterizing. (They have also relied on others for many of their other beliefs about the referents.) Explicational beliefs express individuals' understanding of their own concepts. Others sometimes have better access to or knowledge about the subject matter by reference to which the beliefs can be corrected. So individuals are often beholden to others for refining their understanding of their own idiolects. These points underlie my argument that individual psychology and the study of the semantics of idiolects cannot treat individuals in full isolation from their interactions with others.

A second article that elaborates ideas in 'Individualism and the Mental' and 'Intellectual Norms and Foundations of Mind' is 'Concepts, Definitions, and Meanings' (Chapter 12).[37] This article is less concerned with the impact of the ideas on our understanding of the sciences. It is more concerned with the relation of the ideas to the history of philosophy. I am specifically interested in how the ideas bear on historical conceptions of concepts.

In this article I support some of the traditional assumptions about concepts. I regard concepts as certain components in representational thought contents. I hold that mental abilities are type-identified partly in terms of such contents. Thus concepts are aspects of mental kinds. Concepts are, constitutively, aspects of a thinker's perspective on, or way of representing, a subject matter. Non-indexical, non-demonstrative concepts semantically determine the range of entities that they are about, *modulo* vagueness. All these principles must be

---

[37] In fact, the article also contains a further perspective on Putnam's work and the critical distinctions drawn in 'Other Bodies'. So it presents a more historical angle on ideas in all of the key foundational articles except the ones on perception.

understood in specific ways, but all seem to me to be true and at the heart of traditional conceptions of concepts.

The impact of anti-individualism on traditional conceptions centers on relations among concepts, definitions, and meanings. This impact adds to the impact of other philosophical developments, particularly holism about confirmation and the causal theory of linguistic reference. These developments changed our conceptions of definition and relegated definitions to a lesser place in theories of knowledge and meaning. They also brought out the complexity of relations between thought and various notions of linguistic meaning.

The third article that elaborates issues regarding conceptual explication and social dependence is 'Social Anti-Individualism, Objective Reference' (Chapter 13). This article was written for a symposium on work of Donald Davidson. In it I characterize differences in our approaches regarding the role of the social in language and thought. I hold that dependence on others is more empirical than apriori. I hold that applications of the apriori elements in my thought experiments take various empirical starting points for granted. I also discuss minimal conditions for objective representation and thought. I maintain, contrary to Davidson, that these conditions are fulfilled independently of language use. In fact, the conditions for objective representation are fulfilled by the perceptual systems of numerous animals that are incapable of language. Such representation provides a basis for propositional thought in a smaller group of higher animals that also lack language. This part of the article applies ideas that derive from anti-individualism about perception. The issues about minimal conditions for objective representation are the basis for a substantial body of work that does not appear in this volume. Some of this work will be collected in a further volume of essays.[38] Some of it is yet to be published.

The shape of anti-individualism as mapped by the four basic thought experiments, and associated arguments, is roughly as follows. In cases of nearly all empirically applicable thoughts, the nature of the thoughts is partly determined by non-representational relations to the physical environment.[39] Sometimes these relations are mediated through social relations carried by linguistic communication. However, social relations are not necessary to the basic phenomenon. The fundamental ground for the constitutive dependence of individual thought on a wider environment lies in the distance or 'play' involved in a thinker's relation to a mind-independent reality. In cases of empirical thoughts that do not include the most primitive perceptual concepts, this phenomenon is established through the first, second, and fourth thought experiments. In cases of perception and perceptual belief, anti-individualism still holds. Because of the tight,

---

[38] Cf. e.g. my 'Perception', *International Journal of Psychoanalysis*, 84 (2003), 157–167; 'Perceptual Entitlement', *Philosophy and Phenomenological Research*, 67 (2003), 503–548; 'Five Theses on *De Re* States and Attitudes'.

[39] The 'nearly' allows for certain beliefs about pain and other sensations. There may be other cases.

near law-like connections between the distal properties that are perceived, the operations of the perceptual system, and an individual's dispositions to behavior, twin-earth-based thought experiments do not elicit the point as forcefully with respect to the more primitive types of perception and perceptual belief as they do in other cases of empirical thought. Anti-individualism about perception is supported primarily by general explanatory considerations and by empirical psychology.

I have not much discussed cases of apriori thought in the essays reprinted in this volume. I think that anti-individualism holds in these cases also. For apriori thought, the relevant environment is not the physical environment—at least, not its contingent aspects. Causal relations are not in general the relevant non-representational relations to the subject matter. Despite these differences from the case of empirical thought, I believe that the role of objectivity in our understanding of apriori thought necessarily yields a place for anti-individualism.

The twin-earth methodology does not apply easily in the more basic cases of apriori thought. The reason is that it is often plausible that the relevant (basic, apriori) concepts are universal. At least they can be expected to be shared by individuals that are relevantly twin-like. I believe that social twin-earth thought experiments can evoke the truth of anti-individualism with respect to some types of apriori thoughts—those that are less fundamental and more technical. The main support for anti-individualism in cases of apriori thought lies, however, in more general explanatory considerations and considerations from history. I have sketched some of these considerations elsewhere.[40] The issue invites further development.

Before commenting on other essays in the volume, I want to make some general remarks on the use of thought experiments.[41] Some philosophers deplore the use of thought experiments as a recrudescence of non-scientific, apriori philosophizing that can yield no genuine knowledge. Other philosophers embrace thought experiments as examples of virtually the only sort of contribution that philosophy can make. I think that both positions are extreme.

As regards the negative position, thought experiments have frequently been used in science. Their use in philosophy often contributes to understanding scientific notions, as well as ordinary non-scientific notions. The twin-earth thought experiments have certainly contributed in deep ways to understanding semantics and psychology. Moreover, all the thought experiments that I have used are shot through with broad empirical assumptions. So the simple association of

---

[40] Cf. 'Frege on Extensions of Concepts, from 1884 to 1903', 'Frege on Truth', 'Frege on Sense and Linguistic Meaning', 'Frege on Knowing the Foundation', collected in *Truth, Thought, Reason;* the Introduction of *ibid.* 54–68; 'Logic and Analyticity', *Grazer Philosophische Studien*, 66 (2003), 199–249, and 'Concepts, Conceptions, Reflective Understanding: Reply to Peacocke', in Hahn and Ramberg (eds.), *Reflections and Replies.* See also Postscript to 'Individualism and the Mental' in this volume, the section entitled 'Methodology and Epistemic Implications'.

[41] In the Postscript to 'Individualism and the Mental', I discuss the epistemological implications of the thought experiments in much more detail.

thought experiments with apriori reasoning is a mistake. I do believe that there are apriori elements in the thought experiments. Extracting these elements is, however, neither easy nor straightforward.

The main advantage of thought experiments is that they provide concrete cases that indicate possibilities or relationships that might otherwise go unnoticed, and that either suggest or defeat principles. I think that our judgments about cases tend to be more reliable than our judgments about principles, especially when we get beyond relatively well-known principles. So thought experiments can be evidentially valuable in thinking about abstract, difficult matters. It is true that counterfactual cases can be misleading. It is nonetheless certain that counterfactual cases can be a source of illumination, even new knowledge, if used effectively. Moreover, nearly all the twin-earth cases point toward analogous actual cases that illustrate similar points.

The enthusiast position on thought experiments is often accompanied by injudicious use of them. Thought experiments inevitably leave certain aspects of a case undescribed. Judgment is required to note what matters to a case. Judgment is required to find implicit lessons and project from one case to others. Sometimes arguments from thought experiments are inconclusive or unpersuasive because of under-description. A more common problem is overgeneralization. Since thought experiments are case-based, they do not make evident exactly what principles underlie them. Further considerations, perhaps other thought experiments, are often needed to indicate that the generalizations to be drawn from a case are less neat than one might have hoped. The world is a rich and complicated place.

Anti-individualism seemed at first to some philosophers to conflict with reasonable conceptions of causation or scientific explanation. Many such reactions rested on the simplest of misunderstandings. For example, anti-individualism was accused of invoking action at a distance. Jerry Fodor issued a more interesting type of challenge. Fodor argued that anti-individualism does not individuate psychological states in terms of their causal powers. He held that the causal powers of psychological states cannot differ if the underlying brain states do not differ in their causal powers. Psychological states, anti-individualistically individuated, can be different even though their underlying brain states do not relevantly differ. Psychology, he held, must individuate psychological states in terms of their causal powers. So, he concluded, psychological states must be individuated in 'narrower' ways than those indicated by anti-individualism.[42]

I regard this argument as a virtual *reductio* of its premises. Psychology does individuate many of its explanatory kinds non-individualistically. Any argument that is not itself a piece of science that purports to show that psychology should

---

[42] Fodor would, I think, no longer give this argument, and would no longer support its conclusion. I believe that his current view is clearly anti-individualistic. It should be noted that the argument makes ordinary thoughts causally epiphenomenal on brain states. As further articles in the present volume indicate, this view is, I think, unacceptable on its face.

use different explanatory kinds than those it actually uses has no virtually no chance of being justified. In fact, this argument has a number of difficulties. The most interesting ones center on the notion of causal power.

'Individuation and Causation in Psychology' and 'Intentional Properties and Causation' (Chapters 14 and 15) discuss the notion of causal power in some detail. I argue that the notion must be understood in a way that allows for variations in types of power that the various special sciences are concerned with. I also warn against conflating the non-representational relations that play a constitutive role in determining psychological kinds with the kinds themselves. The former relations are usually not a scientifically recognized kind, and they yield no law-like explanations. The psychological kinds with representational content are, for the most part, not relations at all. They are fitted to causal explanation and causal, law-like explanatory principles. I believe that once one reflects carefully on how to understand causal power in interpreting the special sciences, the idea that anti-individualism is subject to some general difficulty regarding mental causation dissolves.

A third article on mental causation is 'Mind–Body Causation and Explanatory Practice' (Chapter 16). This article raises doubts about how the metaphysics of the mind–body problem and the discussion of mind–body causation have been discussed in much philosophy over the last half-century. These doubts apply to a very wide range of philosophical views. I hold that most mainstream materialist discussion of these issues has relied too much on metaphysical intuitions corrupted by ideology, and not enough on reflecting on the actual explanatory practice of the relevant sciences.

The article uses materialist discussions of epiphenomenalism to illustrate the trend that I deplore. Epiphenomenalism is the view that mental states and their properties have no causal power: all causation in psychology is non-psychological (say, neural) causation; all causal power goes purely through non-psychological events and non-psychological aspects of those events. I think that epiphenomenalism is clearly false. Reflection on explanation in psychology shows it to be. Moreover, epiphenomenalism would make hash of our understanding of ourselves as agents. Nearly all philosophers purport to reject epiphenomenalism.

My complaint is that often both the concern about epiphenomenalism and arguments that purport to disarm it work off metaphysical assumptions that have little genuine justification.[43] Such discussions largely ignore the strongest ground to reject epiphenomenalism—the fact that it is incompatible with actual causal explanations, both in science and in common sense. The metaphysical assumptions lack the epistemic credentials to override or displace these sources of knowledge. More generally, I criticize over-reliance on metaphysical intuitions in discussion of this aspect of the mind–body problem. In a Postscript

---

[43] Also relevant to this work is 'Epiphenomenalism: Reply to Dretske', in Hahn and Ramberg (eds.), *Reflections and Replies*.

I discuss a response to this article by Jaegwon Kim. I take the response to illustrate further the points just outlined.

In my view, the mind–body problem remains difficult, even for representational aspects of the mind. I think that the strong coalescence among American philosophers around materialist solutions—albeit incompatible ones—does not correspond to any epistemic strength in the solutions. I advocate a more modest, more exploratory attitude toward understanding relations between mind and body in general, and toward understanding mind–body causation in particular.

An aspect of mind that I have discussed less than representational states is consciousness. Quite a lot of philosophical discussion over the past two decades has centered on consciousness. Much of the discussion seems to me to have made little progress. Much of it replays issues in other areas—for example, philosophy of language—in only slightly different forms. The first article on consciousness in this volume develops some issues close to work of Ned Block. Block's work does make progress. He develops a distinction between phenomenal consciousness and access consciousness. The former is the sort of consciousness associated with qualitative feel—with the 'what it is like' character of experience.[44] The latter has to do with consciousness that involves the individual's cognitively accessing information of one sort or another.

My article 'Two Kinds of Consciousness' (Chapter 17) makes three points. First, I claim that phenomenal consciousness is the basic type of consciousness. It must be present in an individual for any other type to be present. Second, I hold that Block does not correctly characterize access consciousness. Consciousness is an occurrent feature of mental states or events. Block's characterization leaves it dispositional. I explore ways in which this error might be rectified. Third, I conjecture that phenomenal consciousness might be distinguished from qualitative aspects of mind, which may or may not be conscious. For example, I conjecture that there may be room to distinguish between having a pain and being phenomenally conscious of a pain. Some pain, a qualitative aspect of mind, may not be phenomenally conscious. This is a delicate distinction on which I place no great weight. The allowance for unconscious sensation is, however, a recurrent feature of some traditional psychology. I think that such allowance should not be blocked apriori.

In 'Reflections on Two Kinds of Consciousness', I say more about the second and third issues. I conjecture that there is an important, qualified, constitutive relation between rational-access consciousness and direct cognitive control. I explore some ideas about the form of phenomenal consciousness. I believe that this article provides a unified framework for thinking about all types of phenomenal consciousness.

---

[44] The classic article on this notion is Thomas Nagel's 'What is it Like to Be a Bat?', *Philosophical Review*, 83 (1974), 435–450. Block's original article on the distinction is 'On a Confusion about a Function of Consciousness', *The Behavioral and Brain Sciences*, 18 (1995), 227–247.

The collection concludes with two historical articles. In 'Descartes on Anti-Individualism' (Chapter 19), mentioned earlier, I engage with one of the philosophers I most admire. I discuss how Descartes came to grips with constitutive conditions on representational mind which are broadly parallel to issues I discuss in my own development of anti-individualism.

'Philosophy of Mind: 1950–2000' (Chapter 20) reviews some of the most significant work in philosophy of mind over the last half-century. The article locates anti-individualism in the context of its immediate historical surroundings, and provides an overview of other work in the area.

It will be apparent from these essays that my interest lies in foundations. The foundations that I reflect upon in these essays are not basic truths of a system. I share with traditional philosophers the ideal of finding such truths. But what I have focused on here is more modest—less deductive, less systematic, more preliminary. The foundations I reflect on are broad conditions in the individual or in the wider world that make mental states or events possible–mental states or events in general or ranges of kinds of mental states or events—and that are constitutively associated with them. The conditions include particular sorts of causal conditions, social conditions, psychological conditions, conditions of phenomenal consciousness. I am interested in constitutive conditions under which both representation in general and specific types of representational capacity are possible. Since I believe that mental representation is basic to all representation, I focus on representational mental states, acts, and events. Some of the constitutive conditions that I discuss are certainly among basic conditions under which minds are possible.

I use various methods for understanding such conditions—common sense, general reflection, historical investigation, reflection on scientific theory and practice. The basic impulses are exploratory and constructive, not deflationary or reductionistic. The work in this volume does not constitute a system, either methodologically or doctrinally. The issues are too complex to admit of one method of investigation or to yield a simple set of principles. The work does strive toward whatever principles and system the subject matter allows. I see the articles as pointing toward more systematic work on constitutive conditions for representational and epistemic capacities—on foundations of mind.

1 *On Knowledge and Convention*

Language, we all agree, is conventional. By this we mean partly that some linguistic practices are arbitrary: except for historical accident, they could have been otherwise to roughly the same purposes. Which linguistic and other social practices are arbitrary in this sense is a matter of dispute. Some of the early disputants claimed as nonconventional certain practices which we now consider obvious cases of convention. And such mistakes sometimes held vague but widespread popular sway, owing to provincial or religious prejudices.[1] Whereas it is easy to spot errors of our predecessors, it remains an open question whether some of our own activities are conventional or 'natural'. In short, people sometimes enter into a convention without knowing that it is conventional—even doubting its conventionality.

A principal defect of David Lewis's generally illuminating account of convention is that it controverts these judgments.[2] Lewis defines 'convention' thus:

A regularity *R*, in action or in action and belief, is a *convention* in a population *P* if and only if, within *P*, the following six conditions hold:

(1) Almost everyone conforms to *R*.
(2) Almost everyone believes that the others conform to *R*.
(3) This belief that the others conform to *R* gives almost everyone a good and decisive reason to conform to *R* himself.
(4) There is a general preference for general conformity to *R* rather than slightly-less-than-general conformity—in particular, rather than conformity by all but any one.
(5) There is at least one alternative *R'* to *R* such that the belief that the others conformed to *R'* would give almost everyone a good and decisive practical or epistemic reason to conform to *R'* likewise; such that there is a general preference

I am grateful to John Collier and David Lewis for comments.

[1] Cf. e.g. John Lyons, *Introduction to Theoretical Linguistics* (London, 1968), pp. 4–6; R. H. Robins, *A Short History of Linguistics* (London, 1967), pp. 18 ff.

[2] David K. Lewis, *Convention: A Philosophical Study* (Cambridge, Mass., 1969). Page references in the text are to this work. See also Lewis, 'Language and Languages' (1972), in K. Gunderson. (ed.), *Minnesota Studies in the Philosophy of Science*, vii (Minneapolis: University of Minnesota Press, 1972). The definition given below is from this latter, but the changes from the original definition in the book are not crucial to present considerations.

for general conformity to R' rather than slightly-less-than-general conformity to R'; and such that there is normally no way of conforming to R and R' both.
(6) (1)–(5) are matters of *common knowledge*. (Cf. p. 78.)

On ordinary construals of 'convention' and 'common knowledge' such a definition cannot be right. For participants in a conventional regularity need not know it to be arbitrary. (5) need not be a matter of common knowledge.[3]

To take the most radical case, imagine a small, isolated, unenterprising linguistic community none of whose members ever heard of anyone's speaking differently. It would not be surprising if there were a few such communities in the world today. It would be amazing if there never had been. Such a community would not know—or perhaps even have reason to believe—that there are humanly possible alternatives to speaking their language. If they were sufficiently ignorant of human learning, they might believe that their principal linguistic regularities were immutably determined by natural law. Yet we have no inclination to deny that their language is conventional. They are simply ignorant or wrong about the nature of their activities.

A similar point may be made about more sophisticated naturalists. Kant held that his and Newton's practice of using Euclidean geometry to map physical space was nonconventional (partly) because it had no possible acceptable alternatives. At the time, no one had reason to believe otherwise. Later Poincaré claimed that, in view of Riemannian and other geometries, Kant was mistaken and that the use of Euclidean geometry to map physical space was a convention. It would be strange to cite the lack of common knowledge of alternative geometries in the 18th century as evidence that Poincaré was wrong in calling Newton's practice a convention. (This, regardless of whether Poincaré was in fact right or wrong.) Of course, one might say that the practice became conventional, if at all, only after the alternatives became commonly known. But this would be to use 'conventional' unconventionally.[4]

The point is applicable to our present situation. Linguists are currently fond of claiming that certain rather abstractly described regularities (or certain rules governing the regularities) are necessary to any humanly possible language. Some of these claims are likely to be mistaken, although perhaps we have no sufficient reason to think them so now. The fact that we currently lack reason to believe (or even disbelieve) that a given regularity is a convention does not preclude us from deciding later that it is and was such.

---

[3] Lewis's definition of 'common knowledge' in *Convention*, pp. 52–53, 56, implies that ϕ could be common knowledge and yet be both false and universally disbelieved. The error is implicitly corrected in 'Language and Languages', where 'common knowledge' is taken as a primitive.

[4] There is a similar question—suggested by Quine's view that ordinary translation schemes and ordinary linguistic theories are indeterminate—as to whether or not choosing the ordinary schemes and theories (as opposed to nonequivalent ones) is conventional. Choice of schemes or theories (specifically, choice of analytical hypotheses) is not shown nonconventional simply by the fact that most translators and language theorists think that their choices do not have equally good, nonequivalent alternatives.

It is worth noting that the preceding examples do not depend on whether 'common knowledge' is construed *in sensu composito* or *in sensu diviso* (pp. 64–68). We can imagine participants in a convention who have formulated the mistaken view that their practice per se has no genuine, viable alternative (thus lacking the relevant knowledge *in sensu composito*). We can equally well imagine that the participants mistakenly believe of each instance of their practice that there is no genuine, viable alternative to *it* (thus lacking the relevant knowledge *in sensu diviso*).

The simplest reason why (5) need not be a matter of common knowledge then is that anti-conventionalists may mistakenly (and not unreasonably) believe that there *is* no genuine, humanly possible alternative to their practice. But there are other reasons. And these reasons cast doubt not only on (6) as applied to (5), but on (5) itself.

Members of primitive communities with strong beliefs about the religious power of their words might concede the advantages of human reciprocity but insist that they would retain 'the gods' language' even if the others went astray. Further, they might refuse to entertain the possibility that the gods might switch languages, insisting that nothing could persuade them that this had happened. Although this behavior would probably be unreasonable, the belief that it would be acted upon might not be. Given the inductive standards, background information, and values of such a community, it would not be common knowledge that everyone would have decisive reason to conform to alternative R' if the others did—or that everyone prefers to conform to R' if the others were to. It would not even be *true* that everyone prefers to conform to R' if the others were to. The language of such people, however, would be nonetheless conventional. Thus the second clause in (5) is implausible.

Of course, the preferences of our primitives might be based on mistaken judgments as to what they would do under such bizarre, 'switching' circumstances. Indeed, we might expect that if most people in the community were suddenly to speak in strange tongues, they would be conceived by the rest as divinely inspired. But it is not even clear that such *de facto* (as opposed to self-conceived) adaptability is necessary for a practice to be a convention. (Contrast p. 75.) If the primitives were disposed to stand on the principle that giving up human communication is better than giving up divine communication, it is hard to see why this would affect the conventional character of their actual linguistic practices. Since conventions are arbitrary, they are a poor sort of thing to die for. But stranger choices have been made.

Or consider the mellower example of the sentimental hat tippers. The convention of tipping one's hat to a passing stranger becomes a national trademark. The citizens are sentimentally attached to this mode of greeting and its associations with their culture, to the extent that each would rather fight for the traditional greeting, or give up greeting strangers altogether, than switch to another one, even if the others were to switch. Contrary to (5), and perhaps to (3), this strong traditionalism does not seem to affect the conventionality of the actual practice.

The term 'decisive' in conditions (3) and (5) is multiply ambiguous. If it is taken to bear on motivational efficacy (as distinguished from rational sufficiency), then the examples of the two preceding paragraphs refute the first two clauses of (5). (I return to the 'rational sufficiency' interpretation below.) If 'decisive' in (3) and (5) is meant to imply that belief in others' conformity must give one a reason that is necessary to (as well as efficient in) the agent's motivation, condition (3) falls as well.

What is the picture that led Lewis to a definition that has these difficulties? It is that of a continuing assembly ('convention') of rational agents intent on coordinating, by whatever means, to achieve a recognized end—an end whose achievement they recognize to depend on their coordination. The picture has the advantage of illuminating why it is often reasonable to participate in a convention. But concentrating on the rational underpinnings of conventions carries the dangers as well as advantages of idealization. The 'rational assembly' picture nurtures a feeling that if the parties to a convention were irrational in their actual motives, overly insistent on a particular means, or insufficiently intent on the recognized end, there would be no convention. Such a feeling exaggerates the rationality of human assemblies. (Cf. certain political conventions.) But as applied to social conventions the feeling is even less appropriate. Parties to a convention are frequently confused about the relevant ends (the social functions of their practice); they are often brought up achieving them and do not know the origin of their means; and they sometimes disagree over whether another means is possible, or simply fail to consider the question. In such situations, the reasonable basis for participation may be misconceived; motives may be mixed; and the conventional regularity may be misvalued in relation to its social functions. The stability of conventions is safeguarded not only by enlightened self-interest, but by inertia, superstition, and ignorance. Insofar as these latter play a role, they prevent the arbitrariness of conventional practices from being represented in the beliefs and preferences of the participants.

Thus the arbitrariness of conventions resides somehow in the 'logic of the situation' rather than in the participants' psychological life. But what, more precisely, is it for conventions to be arbitrary? One might be inclined to say that there must be an incompatible alternative regularity R' such that the belief that the others conformed to R' would give almost everyone a rationally sufficient practical or epistemic reason to conform to R' likewise. But this formulation still assumes too much about the participants' preferences. For it is not clear that the sentimental hat tippers would be *irrational* in preferring not to enter into a new way of greeting strangers if everyone else were to switch. (This suggests that the first clause of (5) is vulnerable even if 'decisive' is interpreted in terms of rational sufficiency rather than motivational efficacy.) A less vulnerable formulation would result from conditioning the rationality of conforming to an alternative on willingness to continue to participate in a communal practice that serves substantially the same social functions as the original one.[5]

But this formulation still does not fully explicate the intuition that conventions are arbitrary. The primary hitch is that the alternative regularity (or regularities), though sufficient to fulfill the social functions of the actual practice, may be a significantly inferior means of doing so. In such a case our formulation might be satisfied, but the actual practice would not be arbitrary in the relevant sense. Lewis tries to handle an analogous problem for (5) by invoking his requirement that (5) be common knowledge (pp. 73–74). But as we have seen, this requirement is unattractive on other grounds.

A second difficulty with the formulation is that it presupposes that the participants in a convention *could* switch to an alternative if they believed that the others had done so. But in the case of relatively complicated conventions, the participants might be too set in their ways to learn alternative regularities. For example, the members of a community of old people might be unable to learn alternatives to some of the more complicated conventions of their language.

A requirement that meets these difficulties may be phrased as follows. As a matter of fact—whatever the participants may believe—it is within the power of the participants to have learned an incompatible regularity that would have served substantially the same social functions without demanding significantly greater effort on the part of the participants.[6] This condition does not explicitly mention rationality, nor does it appeal to people's reactions to counterfactual 'switching' circumstances. But it does indicate why we regard it as rational for a participant who is capable of switching to try to do so, given that he believes that the others conform to an alternative regularity (*qua* alternative regularity), given that he is not too ignorant of the consequences of the alternative, and given that his preferences remain in accord with the primary social functions of the actual practice.

On my view, then, the arbitrariness of conventions has two aspects. In the first place, conventions are not determined by biological, psychological, or sociological law: the conventions a given person learns are 'historically

---

[5] Of course, such willingness need not involve an ability to describe the social functions of the practice. I understand the term 'social function' as follows: F is a 'social function' of regularity R in population P iff (1) F results from the mutually expected conformity of almost everyone in P to R, and (2) F fulfills certain needs of most of the members of P. For example, in some groups, shaking hands when being introduced to a stranger might have the social function of reducing the slight apprehension or awkwardness commonly felt in such situations. I shall not worry here over whether the frankly sociological term 'social function' can be replaced by psychological terms. In any case, I do not believe that one need quantify over social functions. But avoiding such quantification is inconvenient for present purposes.

[6] The counterfactual, of course, introduces a certain vagueness into the analysis—a vagueness matched by the notion of convention. I assume it as understood, however, that in considering what a community might have learned, we rule out of consideration extensive knowledge or technological aid that is not available to the community. A similar restriction applies to questions regarding the degree of effort required to carry out alternative practices.

accidental'. In the second, conventions are not uniquely the best means of fulfilling their social functions: other, incompatible means would have done as well.

Lewis has succeeded in freeing the notion of convention from that of explicit agreement, a notion which itself gained purchase from over-literal application of the 'rational assembly' picture. But his account still takes too little note of the extent of the unconscious element in many conventions—and the possibility of their being essentially misconceived or misvalued. The shortcomings stem, I think, from overzealousness in distinguishing human rational systems from mere regularities of nature. Since Descartes, a principal tool in making this important distinction has been the appeal to some psychological element of self-reference in the rational system. (Thus the slogans 'Experience implies self-consciousness,' 'Knowing implies knowing that one knows,' 'Following rules implies tacit knowledge of the rules.') I do not advocate dispensing with such a tool, for I think it has its uses. But overuse of it leads to an exaggerated view of our present self-understanding.

2 Kaplan, Quine, and Suspended Belief

I

In 'Quantifying In', David Kaplan gives an argument that Quine's notation for representing relational contexts is inadequate for certain cases of suspension of belief. The argument has a general interest. For if it were sound, it would undermine any theory which did not represent relational (or *de re*) belief as a special case of notional (or *de dicto*) belief. I think that relational belief is *more* basic than notional belief. But I shall not argue that here. My present purpose is to show that Kaplan's argument is not sound.[1]

Kaplan imagines a case in which Ralph has seen and has beliefs about a certain man (Ortcutt) as he appears in two different guises—wearing a brown hat in suspiciously seditious situations and lounging at the beach in his role as chairman of the chamber of commerce. Ralph does not realize that the man in the brown hat and the man at the beach are one and the same. He believes that the man in the brown hat is a spy. As for the man at the beach, although at first (say, at time t_1) Ralph believed that he was no spy, he has been beset by doubts so that now (time t_2) he does not believe that the man at the beach is a spy in the sense that he cannot make up his mind.

So at time t_1 we want to say both

(1) Ralph believes of Ortcutt that he is a spy

and

(2) Ralph believes of Ortcutt that he is not a spy

I have benefited from conversations with David Kaplan.

[1] W. V. Quine, 'Quantifiers and Propositional Attitudes', *The Journal of Philosophy*, **53** (1956); David Kaplan, 'Quantifying In', in D. Davidson and J. Hintikka (eds.), *Words and Objections* (Dordrecht: D. Reidel, 1969). Other articles on the issue discussed here are Herbert Heidelberger, 'Kaplan on Quine and Suspension of Judgment', *Journal of Philosophical Logic*, **3** (1974), 441–443; Michael Devitt, 'Suspension of Judgment: A Response to Heidelberger on Kaplan', *Journal of Philosophical Logic*, **5** (1976), 17–24. I shall not discuss these latter two articles. In brief, my view is that Devitt's reply to Heidelberger on behalf of Kaplan is correct, except in its assumption that Kaplan's argument is sound.

without imputing any inconsistency to Ralph. I shall assume that both Quine and Kaplan can adequately meet this desideratum. At time t_2 we want to say both (1) and something like

(3) Ralph does not believe of Ortcutt that he is a spy

without involving ourselves in inconsistency. Apart from some qualification or equivocation, (1) and (3), of course, *are* inconsistent. And Kaplan's suggestion is that under one way of representing Ortcutt to himself (e.g. 'The man in the brown hat'), Ralph believes him to be a spy; whereas under another way of representing Ortcutt (e.g. 'The man at the beach'), Ralph does not believe him to be a spy. Thus Kaplan treats (1) as his

(44) $(\exists \alpha)(R(\alpha, \text{Ortcutt}, \text{Ralph}) \wedge B(\text{Ralph}, \ulcorner \alpha \text{ is a spy} \urcorner))$

and the relevant interpretation of (3) as

(46) $(\exists \alpha)(R(\alpha, \text{Ortcutt}, \text{Ralph}) \wedge -B(\text{Ralph}, \ulcorner \alpha \text{ is a spy} \urcorner))$

where 'R' means 'name α represents Ortcutt to Ralph' and 'B' means '(notionally) believes'. The construal of (3) that is inconsistent with (1) is simply the negation of (44).

Now Kaplan's claim is that the relevant distinction cannot be made out in Quine's notation, which does not contain any expression like 'R' and does not derive relational belief from notional belief. But Ralph's suspension of belief with respect to the man at the beach can be expressed in Quine's notation as follows:

(4) $B_r(\text{Ralph}, \text{Ortcutt}, z(z = \text{the man at the beach})) \wedge -B_n(\text{Ralph}, \text{that the man at the beach is a spy})$

where 'B_r' means '(relationally) believes' and 'B_n' means '(notionally) believes'. So (1) and (3) (interpreted as consistent) are parsed as:

(5) $B_r(\text{Ralph}, \text{Ortcutt}, z(z \text{ is not a spy}))$

and

(6) $(\exists \alpha)(B_r(\text{Ralph}, \text{Ortcutt}, z(z = \alpha)) \wedge -B_n(\text{Ralph}, \text{that } \alpha \text{ is a spy}))$

where 'α' ranges over individual concepts—components of intensions. Quine himself does not anywhere quantify over individual concepts, but nothing in his view suggests that doing so is any worse than making reference to intensions (propositions) in the first place.

II

One can get a better sense of the relation between Kaplan's notation and Quine's by translating (6) into Kaplan's language. The translation is

(7) $(\exists \beta)(\exists \alpha)(R(\alpha, \text{Ortcutt}, \text{Ralph}) \wedge B(\text{Ralph}, \ulcorner \alpha = \beta \urcorner) \wedge -B(\text{Ralph}, \ulcorner \beta \text{ is a spy} \urcorner))$.

Kaplan's analysis of (3) is (46). How does (46) compare with (7)? They are logically independent. (7) would entail (46) if we were guaranteed that

(8) $B(\text{Ralph}, \ulcorner \alpha = \beta \urcorner) \rightarrow (B(\text{Ralph}, \ulcorner \beta \text{ is a spy}\urcorner) \leftrightarrow B(\text{Ralph}, \ulcorner \alpha \text{ is a spy}\urcorner))$.

But if Ralph is Everyman, (8) cannot be guaranteed.

The failure of equivalence between (46) and (7) stems from the fact that Kaplan takes relational belief to be defined in terms of notional belief, whereas Quine's notation treats relational belief as primitive. Within Quine's viewpoint, one may regard '$B_r(\text{Ralph}, \text{Ortcutt}, z(z = \alpha))$' as playing the role that '$R(\alpha, \text{Ortcutt}, \text{Ralph})$' plays in Kaplan's. But from Kaplan's viewpoint, relational belief is a special kind of notional belief. So in order for the relational '$B_r(\text{Ralph}, \text{Ortcutt}, z(z = \alpha))$' to be true, there must be some notionally complete name β such that β represents Ortcutt to Ralph and such that Ralph believes (notionally) $\ulcorner \beta = \alpha \urcorner$. (Cf. the first two clauses of (7) and the first clause of (6).) Quine's viewpoint requires no such name β. It is the requirement of this extra representing (in Kaplan's sense of 'representing') name together with the failure of (8) that makes (7) and (46) non-equivalent. Now an obvious candidate for fulfilling the role of β is α itself. If we approve the candidate, and assume that Ralph believes $\ulcorner \alpha = \alpha \urcorner$, then (7) and (46) indeed become strictly equivalent.

In my view, this way of interpreting the Quinean analysis within Kaplan's theory obscures the interesting difference between the two viewpoints. The claim that everyone believes the self-identity statement for each 'representing' singular expression in his repertoire is fairly plausible. Even more plausible—and equally adequate in yielding equivalence between (7) and (46)—is the Frege-like view that everyone believes *some* identity statement for each representing singular expression in his repertoire. The trouble with taking Quine's analysis as thus equivalent to Kaplan's is that Kaplan's analysis is committed to there being a singular expression in the believer's repertoire that *denotes* the object which the *de re* belief is about: A necessary condition for a name β to *represent* an entity for a person, in Kaplan's theory, is that it denote the entity. Kaplan takes representing names to be symbol-types (broadly construed to include conglomerations of images, and the like, as well as linguistic items) or alternatively, abstract meanings. For a symbol-type or abstract meaning to denote an entity, it must individuate the entity in a context-independent manner. If the represented object is not fully determined or individuated by concepts, symbols, or image-types in the believer's cognitive repertoire, then the object is strictly speaking not denoted.[2]

Clearly, the assumption that the believer has a name that denotes the relevant object in all cases of *de re* belief is a strong one. Indeed, I think that it is surely false. I shall not argue this here. My purpose is served by pointing out that Quine's approach, which takes *de re* belief to be primitive rather than defined,

---

[2] Of course, non-conceptual contextual relations enter into Kaplan's analysis of representing names, but they are additional to and independent of the relation of denotation.

is not committed to the assumption. (Whether Quine is himself committed to the assumption on other grounds is, of course, another question.)

One might protest that Kaplan did not intend for his notion of denotation to be taken so strictly. We might hold that the requirement is that there be a singular symbol that denotes the relevant object in the relevant context: The relativity to context might be regarded as simply suppressed. A full answer to this defense involves more discussion of the *de re – de dicto* distinction than I will undertake here. But a short answer is that suppression of the relativity to context can hardly be justified in a project intended to define *de re* notions in terms of *de dicto* notions. For insofar as the believer's conceptual resources only incompletely individuate the relevant object and depend on context to pick out the object in a way analogous to the way we refer with demostratives, the believer's belief is not clearly *de dicto*. For intuitively a *de dicto* attitude is one whose content is completely *expressed* (*dictum*). Insofar as the content of the attitude must be partly *shown*, as opposed to expressed, the attitude is not purely *de dicto* at all.

(6), our Quinean representation of (3), assumes that the 'representing' name occurs in a notional belief. We can eliminate this assumption by revising (6) to

(6′) $(\exists\alpha)(B_r(\text{Ralph, Ortcutt, } z(z = \alpha)) \ \& \ -B_r(\text{Ralph, Ortcutt, } z(\alpha \text{ is a spy})))$.

Here 'α' ranges over intensional entities expressed by singular expressions like 'that man' whose whole scope is governed by a demonstrative construction. (The variable 'z' picks up the demonstrative element in α.) Such entities differ from individual concepts in that their associated denotation is only partially determined apart from context. The important point for present purposes is that Quine's notation can represent Ralph's suspension of judgment while maintaining that relational belief is not to be defined in terms of notional belief.

III

The analyses of (3) that we have so far discussed have a certain air of artificiality about them. (6), (6′), and (46) are longer and conceptually more complex than (3) itself. The source of this incongruity is the fact that the two analyses state matters that (3), on the relevant construal, presupposes. One may simplify the representations of (1) and (3) as follows:

(9) $B_r(\text{Ralph, Ortcutt, } \ulcorner x_1 \text{ is a spy} \urcorner)$

and

(10) $-B_r(\text{Ralph, Ortcutt, } \ulcorner x_2 \text{ is a spy} \urcorner)$.

The free variables in the belief content are distinguished to mark different modes of demonstrative presentation of Ortcutt to Ralph. (9) and (10) are mutually consistent. There is on this approach no need to quantify over the relevant representing name, or individual concept, or other mode of presentation. Of course, in the case of (3), Ralph will have a suspended belief involving the relevant mode of presentation: He will suspend belief about whether *the man at the beach* is a spy. But (3) does not actually make reference to this belief. So its analysis need not. Similarly, (10) does not *say* that Ralph has any relational beliefs about Ortcutt. But then neither does (3). Obviously, these presuppositions may be made explicit in other sentences if the need arises.

Close attention to the role of free variables in the analysis of belief would have simplified another issue between Quine and Kaplan. Quine claimed that the kind of exportation that leads from

(11) Ralph believes that Ortcutt is a spy

to (1) should be viewed 'in general as implicative'. Kaplan noted that although this particular exportation required only that 'Ortcutt' denotes Ortcutt, the exportation from

(12) Ralph believes that the shortest spy is a spy

to

(13) Ralph believes of the shortest spy that he is a spy

requires more than that 'the shortest spy' denote the shortest spy. Kaplan went on to provide a general theory of exportation in terms of the notion of representation.

I do not wish to dispute the obvious interest and fruitfulness of this theory. But I do want to suggest that it blurs a distinction between cases in which exportation is justified (virtually) on the basis of logical form and cases in which it is not. 'Ortcutt', 'the man at the beach', and 'the man in the brown hat' all differ from 'the shortest spy' in containing an indexical construction which governs the whole scope of the expression: Proper names contain implicit demonstratives, and the 'the' beginning the two definite descriptions is playing the role of a demonstrative. On the other hand, the 'the' in 'the shortest spy' functions as a uniqueness operator. Indexical constructions are properly represented as containing free variables, and 'the shortest spy' contains none.[3] We can account for Quine's intuition by noting that terms in a belief content that involve an indexical expression (free variable) governing the whole scope of the term can be exported if (a) the indexical construction is referentially (as opposed to anaphorically) used and (b) the referred-to object satisfies the predicative condition contained in the term.[4] In effect, these two conditions amount to requiring that

---

[3] For discussion of indexical expressions represented by specially indexed free variables, see my 'Reference and Proper Names', *The Journal of Philosophy*, 70 (1973), 425–439 and 'Demonstrative Constructions, Reference, and Truth', *The Journal of Philosophy* 71 (1974), 205–223.

[4] A fuller discussion of this point would show that exportations thus valid on the basis of logical form are always exportations from one relational belief context to another—never exportation from a purely notional context to a relational context. Further discussion of the notional–relational distinction occurs in 'Belief *De Re*', *The Journal of Philosophy*, 74 (1977), 338–362; Ch. 3 below.

the term (relative to a context of use) denote the object. For terms, like 'the shortest spy', which contain no indexical constructions governing their whole scope, exportation cannot be justified on the basis of form. Certain epistemic conditions of the sort sought by Kaplan must be met. But this, I think, is to say that exportation of these terms is not in general 'implicative'.

3 *Belief* De Re

Interest in *de re* belief during this half-century was kindled by W. V. Quine, who focused inquiry on the problem of quantification into belief contexts.[1] In some respects this focus was unfortunate, in that the difficulties, real and imagined, that arose in interpreting quantification tended to suggest that *de re* belief needs to be explained in terms of what came to seem the clearer and more basic notion—*de dicto* belief. The imposition of the methods of modal logic on belief sentences abetted the suggestion by embroiling them in disputes over transworld identity. In fact, *de re* belief is in important ways more fundamental than the *de dicto* variety; and this can be seen if one attends to its role in basic cognitive activities. So I shall argue.

I shall not be discussing the interpretation of quantification. Interesting problems do surround the application conditions of *de re* locutions; but a range of clear-cut, core cases of *de re* belief can, I think, be taken for granted. Problems with the less central cases of belief will stay backstage here. Independently of the problems of quantification, certain epistemic viewpoints have led to the assumption that *de dicto* belief is the fundamental notion. I shall indicate in sections III and IV why these viewpoints do not warrant the assumption. A subsidiary goal will be to show (in section IV) how idealizations stemming from Frege, which were designed to explain intensional phenomena, blur epistemic distinctions that are crucial to explicating the conceptual elements in belief. Some of the arguments I rely on will be familiar. My purpose is to advance a viewpoint which as a whole provides a shift of perspective on *de re* attitudes, and on intensional phenomena generally.

I

Historically, the *de re/de dicto* distinction is more firmly rooted in the logical tradition than in epistemology. The earliest treatments of it all distinguish valid

I have benefited from discussion with Philippa Foot on the topic of sec. II, David Kaplan on sec. III, and Keith Donnellan on sec. IV. I am grateful for support from the National Endowment for the Humanities.

[1] "Quantifiers and Propositional Attitudes", *The Journal of Philosophy*, 53, 5 (1 Mar., 1956), 177–187; repr. in his *The Ways of Paradox* (New York: Random House, 1966).

deductions from fallacies. Most of these bear on modality, but some pertain to knowledge. Aristotle's examples were from the beginning subject to misunderstanding and controversy. But, by the Middle Ages, the grammatical structure relevant to clarifying the examples had been sufficiently articulated to render them beyond reasonable dispute.[2]

As applied to necessity, the grammatical distinction is that between applying the predicate 'is necessary' to a proposition (*dictum*, what is said) and applying a predicate modally—in a qualified way, necessarily—to an entity or entities, typically individuals (*res*). Thus there is a grammatical distinction between

(1) The proposition that every man who steps on the moon steps on the moon, is necessary.

and

(2) Every man who steps on the moon is such that he necessarily steps on the moon.

The distinction clearly affects truth value [(1) is true; (2), on most interpretations of 'necessarily', is false] and, hence, the soundness of inferences.

In epistemic contexts, the grammatical distinction is between belief in a proposition and belief *of* something that it is such and such. Many examples, here as in necessity contexts, are ambiguous. But some are not. Thus

(3) Ortcutt believes the proposition that someone is a spy.

(4) Someone in particular is believed by Ortcutt to be a spy.

So illustrated, the *de re/de dicto* distinction should be uncontroversial. Although there has been some doubt about the very meaningfulness of *de re* locutions, such doubt would be more fruitfully applied to certain explanations of their significance. With respect to modality, the relevant explanation holds that some properties of individuals are necessarily (essentially) had by them, whereas others are had accidentally; that the essential properties are not universal or trivial properties; and that necessity thus resides in the way the world is rather than in the way we talk or think about it. In my view (and contrary to a widespread opinion) the issue over the acceptability of this explanation, with its attendant talk of properties and the way the world is, is not settled or even prejudged by noting the grammatical distinction and defending the truth of certain statements of *de re* modality. Our subject here is belief. But here too it is not the meaningfulness of the grammatical distinction, but the explication of it that is philosophically important.

The surface-level grammatical distinction is the traditional one. But Russell's proposal about the structure of propositions shows that the grammatical

[2] Aristotle, *Prior Analytics* 30ᵃ15–23; *De Interpretatione* 21ᵇ26–22ᵃ13; *De Sophisticis Elenchis* 166ᵃ23–3a; William of Sherwood, *Introduction to Logic*, trans. and ed. Norman Kretzmann (Minneapolis: University of Minnesota Press, 1966), ch. 1, secs. 21–27; W. Kneale, 'Modality De Dicto and De Re', in E. Nagel, P. Suppes, and A. Tarski (eds.), *Logic, Methodology, and the Philosophy of Science* (Stanford, Calif.: Stanford University Press, 1962), 622–633.

distinction does not provide a sufficient condition for drawing the intuitive *de re/de dicto* distinction. (It has never been a necessary condition, on account of ambiguities.) Russell held that sentences containing logically proper names expressed propositions whose components *included* the individuals named by those names. Since he introduced this notion of proposition specifically to account for the notion of *de re* knowledge, I think we should agree that a statement that says that this sort of proposition is necessary, or is believed, is not *de dicto*, but *de re*. Less esoterically, we sometimes say 'He believes the proposition that this is red.' Such sayings are *de re*.

Since Quine's discussion, it has been customary to draw the distinction in terms of a substitutivity criterion. In attributing a *de re* belief about a given object, one is free to substitute any correct description of the relevant object. For example, suppose Alfie believes *de re* that the piano is ugly. Then we could characterize Alfie's attitude by substituting any correct description of the piano—say, 'the 1893 Steinway Grandpa bought for a song'—regardless of whether Alfie could describe the piano in that way. The intuition is that our ascription relates Alfie directly to the piano, without attributing any particular description or conception that Alfie would use to represent it. Quantified cases are analogous. If we say that Alfie believes *de re* something to be ugly, we imply that one existential instantiation is as good as any other that picks out the same entity. By contrast, if we say that Alfie believes *de dicto* (i) that 2 squared is 4, we may refuse to say that Alfie believes (ii) that the only even prime squared is 4. A belief ascription is *de dicto*, on this view, if at every place in the content clause coextensional substitution may fail. Belief *de dicto* essentially involves the believer's conception of the issue at hand, and Alfie may not realize that 2 is the only even prime number. Even if he does, we would say that his believing (i) is one thing, and his believing (ii) another.

The substitutivity criterion has typically been applied to surface-level sentences of natural language. So applied, it does not adequately draw the *de re/de dicto* distinction. The problem is that there are sentences where substitutivity fails at the surface level, but which are nevertheless *de re*. For example, we may say, 'Alfred believes that the man in the corner is a spy.' We may refuse unlimited substitution of terms denoting the man in the corner on the grounds that Alfred's belief involves thinking of the fellow as the man in the corner and not, say, as the firstborn in Kiev in 1942. Yet we may also be intending in our ascription to relate Alfred *de re* to the man to whom we refer with the expression 'the man in the corner'. In short, the term 'the man in the corner' may be doing double duty at the surface level—both characterizing Alfred's conception and picking out the relevant *res*.[3] It would be ill considered to count this simply a case of *de dicto* belief. Cf. (6) below. Even if one wanted to hold

---

[3] The point was first made (though not in this form) by Hector-Neri Castañeda, 'Indicators and Quasi-indicators', *American Philosophical Quarterly*, 4, 2 (Apr. 1967), 85–100; see also Brian Loar, 'Reference and Propositional Attitudes', *The Philosophical Review*, 80 (1972), 43–62.

that the example is both *de re* and *de dicto*, an interpretation I will urge against in section III, the criterion by itself does nothing to explain why the example is partly *de re*.

It should be clear by now that an adequate criterion for drawing the *de re/de dicto* distinction must focus on the meaning, or at least the logical form, of the relevant sentences. Unfortunately, since philosophical issues come thick and fast at the level of logical form, any such criterion is bound to be more controversial than the intuitions it is designed to capture. Instead of proposing a criterion, I shall represent the distinction from a particular semantical and epistemic viewpoint, and then argue that the chief epistemic threat to this viewpoint is impotent. Representations of (3) and (4) (tense ignored) are:

(3′) B_d(Ortcutt, $\ulcorner(\exists x)\mathrm{Spy}(x)\urcorner$)

(4′) $(\exists x)(B_r(\mathrm{Ortcutt}, \langle x\rangle, \ulcorner\mathrm{Spy}(y)\urcorner))$

where 'B_d' and 'B_r' represent *de dicto* and *de re* belief respectively.[4] Alfred's belief about the man in the corner may be represented as

(5) B_r (Alfred, $\langle$the man in the corner$\rangle$, $\ulcorner\mathrm{Spy}(y)\urcorner$)

or as

(6) B_r (Alfred, $\langle$the man in the corner$\rangle$, $\ulcorner\mathrm{Spy}([y](\mathrm{Man}(y) \wedge \mathrm{In}\ C(y)))\urcorner$)

depending on whether we wish to attribute the notion of a man in the corner to Alfred. (6) is a fairly ordinary reading for cases in which Alfred sees the man. And it is this sort of case that motivated rejection of the surface-level substitutivity criterion for the *de re/de dicto* distinction. Proper names are formally analogous to incomplete definite descriptions (singular descriptions containing an indexical element). For example, '*A* believes that Moses had a sister' has readings analogous to (5) and (6):

(7) $B_r(A, \langle\mathrm{Moses}\rangle, \ulcorner(\exists y)\mathrm{Sister}(y, x)\urcorner)$

(8) $B_r(A, \langle\mathrm{Moses}\rangle, \ulcorner(\exists y)\mathrm{Sister}(y, [x]\mathrm{Moses}(x))\urcorner)$[5]

The key to the *de re/de dicto* distinction, as I am representing it, is explicit in these formulations. 'B_d' applies to what is expressed by a closed sentence; 'B_r' applies in part to what is expressed by an open sentence and in part to a *res*.

---

[4] The corner quotes are to be taken literally. For most purposes, however, those who prefer may regard them as a convenience for denoting the proposition, or component of proposition, expressed by the symbols they enclose. The pointed brackets indicate a sequence in the familiar way. Strictly, 'B_r' does not by itself represent 'believes of' since we do not intend in (4′) to be attributing to Ortcutt a belief of a sequence, but rather of a person. 'B_r' together with the pointed brackets represent 'believes of'. The case of 'B_r' is analogous to that of 'satisfies', which does not by itself represent the converse of 'is true of'. I trust that the reader is familiar with the reasons for these niceties. One further point. 'Believes true' and 'believes true of' are, strictly speaking, distinct from 'believes' and 'believes of' in that the former are higher-order.

[5] The square brackets in (6) and (8) serve as scope indicators for the demonstrative. They do not bind the free variables. For details of this sort of formalization, see my 'Reference and Proper Names', *The Journal of Philosophy*, 70, 14 (16 Aug., 1973), 425–439; 'Demonstrative Constructions, Reference and Truth', *The Journal of Philosophy*, 71, 7 (18, Apr. 1974), 205–223; and 'Kaplan, Quine, and Suspended Belief', *Philosophical Studies*, 31 (1977), 197–203 (Ch. 2 above).

More generally, *purely de dicto attributions make reference to complete propositions* — entities whose truth or falsity is determined without being relative to an application or interpretation in a particular context. *De re locutions are about predication broadly conceived.* They describe a relation between open sentences (or what they express) and objects.

This way of making the distinction captures the intuitions of both the previous criteria. It catches the grammatical distinction between modifying a completely expressed statement (*dictum* — what is expressed) and modifying a predication. (In Russellian propositions, the relevant *res* are not expressed but shown.) It catches the intuition behind the substitutivity criterion: any term in the argument place appropriate to the relevant *res* which represents a surface expression at all, represents one that is subject to the usual extensional operations; terms in the 'content' argument place represent expressions in the surface syntax on which extensional substitutions fail.

The representations given so far suggest perhaps that beliefs involving incomplete definite descriptions or proper names are always *de re*. This is not true. For example, beliefs attributed with 'Pegasus' are sometimes not *de re*. Indexical constructions, and so variables, have both deictic and anaphoric uses. Demonstrative constructions may occur in *de dicto* content clauses if they occur anaphorically as pronouns of laziness. If A gullibly believes that Pegasus was a (real) horse, the demonstrative implicit in the name occurs anaphorically, perhaps without A's realizing it, taking as antecedent some description, definite or not, in the repertoire of A or someone else. The name thus has the flavor of 'that Pegasus (whichever one they are talking about)'. The relevant belief could be represented as

$$B_d(A, \ulcorner \text{Horse}([x]\text{Pegasus}(x)) \urcorner)$$

where the antecedent of the pronoun 'x' must be determined by examining a larger containing discourse. Ordinary proper names as well as vacuous names may be expected to occur in purely *de dicto* belief attributions, and with similar explication. Indexicals like 'this' are to be treated as analogous to proper names, except that they do not express a predicative element. (Cf. notes 5 and 17.)

The importance of logical form is widely ignored in discussions of the *de re/de dicto* distinction. For example, attempts to reduce *de re* locutions to *de dicto* ones sometimes appeal to proper names in the allegedly *de dicto* analysans, without seriously defending the view that proper names express *dicta* sufficiently complete to individuate their denotations.[6] Several philosophers have held that proper names do not express anything, but merely tag objects. I think

---

[6] Alvin Plantinga, 'De Dicto et De Re', *Noûs*, 3, **3** (Sept. 1969), 235–258. Examples similar to the one from Plantinga occur in the discussion in Quine, "Quantifiers and Propositional Attitudes", and Kaplan, 'Quantifying In', in D. Davidson and J. Hintikka (eds.), *Words and Objections* (Dordrecht: Reidel, 1969). For discussion of these examples, see sec. III below and my 'Kaplan, Quine, and Suspended Belief', secs. II/III.

this view incorrect.[7] But it is similar to the view I hold in treating proper names as commonly involving indexicals. On both views proper names do not ordinarily express anything sufficiently complete to individuate their denotations. And belief ascriptions containing them will normally be *de re*.

The surface-level grammatical distinction illustrated in (1) (2) and (3) (4) should be innocent of controversy. But our representation of its logical form in (3′) (4′) will be regarded by some as more noxious. There are two viewpoints—one semantic, one epistemic—from which the representations are controversial. The first is the view characteristic of modal and doxastic logics that modal statements or epistemic statements have the logical form of attaching an operator to a sentence, open or closed, rather than that of attaching a predicate to a term denoting a proposition, or component of a proposition. The predicate view is that in terms of which *de re* and *de dicto* were traditionally distinguished. Partly for that reason, the distinction is most naturally explicated from that viewpoint. Although the distinction could be discussed in terms of the operator approach, the discussion would be more complicated, since the analogies between the operator approach and the traditional view are not well established or agreed upon.

The epistemic viewpoint from which (3′) and (4′) may be disputed as representations of the grammatical distinction bears on the relative priority of *de re* and *de dicto* locutions. It has been held that all *de re* locutions may be defined or adequately represented in terms of *de dicto* locutions. I shall be criticizing this view in section III. I tentatively believe that (3) is ultimately best represented

---

[7] For the 'tag' view, see Bertrand Russell, 'The Philosophy of Logical Atomism', in R. C. Marsh (ed.), *Logic and Knowledge* (New York: Capricorn, 1971), pp. 245–246; John Stuart Mill, *A System of Logic*, Book I, ch. II, no. 5; Keith Donnellan, 'Speaking of Nothing', *The Philosophical Review*, 83 (1974), 3–31, esp. pp. 11–12; Saul Kripke, 'Naming and Necessity', in D. Davidson and G. Harman (eds.), *Semantics for Natural Language* (Dordrecht: Reidel, 1972), e.g. p. 322. At least two difficulties beset this sort of view. One is Frege's paradox of identity, which I discuss in sec. IV. As is fairly widely known, this problem seriously undermines the claim made by Russell at one time and articulated by Donnellan: that ordinary proper names make no other contribution to a proposition (what is said or believed) than to import their denotation into it. (Cf. note 17 below.) Russell later restricted his view to 'names' of sense data because of this kind of problem. The remarks by Mill and Kripke seem to be similarly affected; but, since they are vague, it is less clear that this is so. Other 'tag' views less radical than Russell's are imaginable. One assimilates proper names to demonstratives—claiming that neither 'expresses' anything, but that contextually different uses of names (or demonstratives) which refer to a given entity may succeed, in some yet to be specified way, in producing different belief contents. I shall espouse a variant of this view in sec. IV, although I oppose full assimilation of proper names to demonstratives.

The second basic problem for the 'tag' view is that proper names function as predicates, as is indicated by the fact that 'Aristotle is an Aristotle' is a logical truth, modulo an existence assumption. Cf. my 'Reference and Proper Names'. There are, of course, various senses of proper names as predicates—metaphorical uses, aliases, nicknames, 'blood names' (as when Greenberg is a Rothschild because he is descended in the right way) and demonstrative senses (as when we say 'Teddy is a Kennedy' and mean 'Teddy is one of those, contextually delimited, Kennedys'). Mixing these senses to get falsehoods does not suffice to show that proper names are not predicates.

in terms of 'B$_r$' as a variant on (4′).[8] But I suspect that the differences between this representation and the present one are not conceptually deep.

I have expressed the intuitive *de re/de dicto* distinction in terms of the logical form of ascriptions of belief. Before concluding this section, I want to say a word about the intuitive epistemic basis for the distinction. The rough epistemic analogue of the linguistic notion of what is expressed by a semantically significant expression is the notion of a concept. Traditionally speaking, concepts are a person's means of representing objects in thought. For present purposes we may include as concepts other alleged mental entities that the empiricist tradition did not clearly distinguish from them—for example, perceptions or images—so long as these are viewed as types of representations of objects. From a semantical viewpoint, a *de dicto* belief is a belief in which the believer is related only to a completely expressed proposition (*dictum*). *The epistemic analogue is a belief that is fully conceptualized.* That is, a correct ascription of the *de dicto* belief identifies it purely by reference to a 'content' all of whose semantically relevant components characterize elements in the believer's conceptual repertoire.

The analogy between this epistemic characterization of *de dicto* belief and our characterization in terms of logical form is prima facie threatened by certain (possibly deviant) attributions of belief. If Alfie says, 'The most powerful man on earth in 1970 (whoever he is) is a crook,' not having the slightest idea who the most powerful man is, a friend of the potentate may say to him, 'Alfie believes that you are a crook.' The example, if accepted, may seem to present a case in which the belief ascription related Alfie to both an open sentence and the potentate—thus fulfilling the semantical characterization of *de re* belief—even though Alfie's epistemic state depends completely on concepts in his repertoire—thus fulfilling the epistemic characterization of *de dicto* belief. The way to treat such examples is to take the demonstrative pronoun 'you' as not purely deictic. It is at least partly anaphoric, acting as a pronoun of laziness for the description 'the most powerful man on earth'. The logical form of the discourse should reflect this, so that the ascription will ultimately relate Alfie to a closed sentence. Similar remarks apply to cases of 'exportation' of definite descriptions like 'the shortest spy' based purely on the premise that the description denotes. Counting such cases *de re* because of referential occurrence of the surface-level terms 'you' or 'the shortest spy' would mark no epistemically interesting distinction. There is no ascription of a peculiarly *de re* (*en rapport*) attitude. At most, there is a *de re* ascription of a *de dicto* attitude.

What is the appropriate epistemic characterization of *de re* belief? I think one should explicate the notion simply in terms of *the negation of our epistemic*

---

[8] The first to propose the semantical viewpoint I favor was John Wallace, 'Belief and Satisfaction', *Noûs*, 6, 2 (May 1972), 85–95; cf. also Marc Temin, 'The Relational Sense of Indirect Discourse', *The Journal of Philosophy*, 72, 11 (5, June 1975), 287–306. Stephen Schiffer pointed out that someone who held that *de dicto* locutions are basic could accept representations (3′) and (4′), if he (unlike me) regarded them as a step toward a further analysis.

characterization of de dicto belief. But in deference to an issue that will dominate section III, the notion may be explicated more positively, if more vaguely:
A *de re* belief is a belief whose correct ascription places the believer in an
appropriate nonconceptual, contextual relation to objects the belief is about. The
term 'nonconceptual' does not imply that no concepts or other mental notions
enter into a full statement of the relation. Indeed, the relation may well hold
between the object and concepts, or their acquisition or use. The crucial point
is that the relation not be merely that of the concepts' being concepts *of* the
object—concepts that denote or apply to it. For example, although concepts
may inevitably enter into the acquisition of a perceptual belief, the believer's
relation to the relevant object is not merely that he conceives of it or otherwise represents it. His sense organs are affected by it. Perceptual contact is,
of course, not present in every *de re* belief. But it illustrates the sort of element independent of semantical or conceptual application that is essential to
the notion.

II

A sufficient condition for a belief to be *de re* (on the vague, 'neutral' epistemic
construal, as well as on our favored semantical and epistemic construals) is for
it to contain an analog of an indexical expression used deictically, and pick out
a *re*. The first sentences that children actually use or understand are invariably
keyed to their immediate, perceptually accessible surroundings.[9] Attitudes that
accompany such assertions are clearly *de re*. These developmental matters are
closely related to the question of conditions for attributing language use and
understanding. I shall argue that if an entity lacks *de re* attitudes, we would
not attribute to it the use or understanding of language, or indeed propositional
attitudes at all.

   It is hard to imagine how one could learn a language without being exposed
to sentences whose truth-value changed over relatively short periods of time. If
the truth-value of certain sentences were not keyed to salient and changeable
aspects of the immediate environment, the neophyte would have no means of
catching on to the meaning of the sounds he hears—no means of correlating
those sounds with an independently identifiable parameter. Attitudes acquired in
the process of understanding such sounds are *de re*. Still, whereas we ourselves
come to understand language only by understanding indexical sentences, it might
be thought that some organism or robot could be programmed to understand an
indexical-free language, without our attributing any *de re* attitudes to it. The
thought is, I think, mistaken.

---

[9] Cf. Roger Brown, *A First Language: The Early Stages* (Cambridge, Mass.: Harvard University
Press, 1973), e.g. pp. 220 ff.; also Quine, *Word and Object* (Cambridge, Mass.: MIT Press, 1960),
26–39.

It would be widely agreed that current machines that are programmed with indexical-free (mathematical) language do not autonomously use or understand language. What is missing? A major part of what is missing is evidence that the manipulation of symbols is anything more than a mechanical, purely syntactical exercise for the machine. That is, such machines do nothing to indicate that the symbols have any semantical, extralinguistic significance. To indicate this, they should be able, at least sometimes, to recognize and initiate correlations between symbols and what they symbolize. Such correlations may involve nonlinguistic practical activity (finding a ball when someone says he or she wants a ball) or linguistic activity appropriate to one's perceptions (saying 'There's a ball' when one sees one) or some combination. Similarly, if the subject is to be credited with having propositional thoughts, he must indicate some ability to correlate his thoughts with objects those thoughts are thoughts of. Failing evidence of the ability to recognize such correlations, there is no adequate ground for attributing understanding of sentences or propositional attitudes. But any propositional attitudes that accompany such recognition will be *de re*. So attributing an understanding of sentences, or propositional attitudes at all, requires attributing *de re* attitudes.[10]

This argument does not commit one to the view that one must compare a symbol with an entity and come to believe that the symbol applies to the entity. Such a model is implausible for the general case. The recognition should be regarded as a skill rather than a conclusion about the symbol. Further, recognition of a correlation between symbol and entity need not be thought of as a *means* of learning symbols. It need only be regarded as part of what is entailed by understanding and using symbols. The argument does not in itself commit one to the view that all language users must understand some language that contains indexical elements. What the argument requires is that a language user be able to understand referential use (as opposed to attributive use) of his singular terms—to realize what entities some of them apply to—or that he be able to apply some of his predicates to objects or events that he experiences. Thus the argument places requirements on an individual's abilities, not necessarily on the meaning of the sentences he uses.

The argument that having propositional attitudes requires having *de re* attitudes has as corollary the conclusion that having justified empirical beliefs, hence having empirical knowledge, requires having *de re* beliefs—since having

---

[10] I sense a kindred doctrine in Kant, *Critique of Pure Reason*, A51 = B75 and A126. Jonathan Bennett, in *Kant's Analytic* (New York: Cambridge University Press, 1966), 146, criticizes Kant for suggesting that one could have a concept and utilize it in general judgments without being able to apply it under sensorily favorable circumstances. (Cf. A133 = B172.) But Bennett's stricture is far too narrow. I might be able to explain the difference between two kinds of molecule without being able to distinguish them in any sensory (laboratory) conditions; I do not therefore lack the concept of the relevant kinds. The more plausible view is that if we could not apply some concepts under sensorily favorable circumstances, we would have no concepts. Oddly, Frege criticizes Kant for holding the very view Bennett defends. Cf. *The Foundations of Arithmetic*, ed. J. L. Austin (Evanston, Ill.: Northwestern University Press, 1968), 101. Perhaps Kant's view is not fully clear.

justified belief presupposes propositional attitudes. The same conclusion may be reached by a simple variation on the original argument. Justification of empirical beliefs by way of test or evidence depends on having perceptual experiences. But beliefs, 'perceptual beliefs', directly resulting from such experiences are *de re*.

Consider our purely *de dicto* empirical beliefs, where all such beliefs in singular form are nonindexical and where the definite descriptions can be used attributively, but not referentially (and thus are not accompanied by *de re* beliefs). Taken by themselves, these beliefs are clearly lacking in evidential support. The attributively intended singular beliefs have the force of 'the F, whatever object that is, is G'. Justification for the belief that there is an F or that it is G requires some more specific identification. For example, we need to find the F, or else experience circumstances that give ground for believing there is an F. Many of our *de dicto* beliefs are justified because they are based on authoritative hearsay from others. But then, at a minimum, the 'others' must have some *de re* belief in order to ground their authority on the subject. What is more, it is plausible that we must have *de re* beliefs about the person or other source from which we get our information, in order to certify that source as authoritative (or as being in touch with an authoritative source). Intuitively, nonsingular, or general, *de dicto* beliefs are in need of *de re* support in the same way that attributive, nonindexical singular beliefs are.[11]

I claimed at the outset that *de re* belief is in important ways more fundamental than *de dicto* belief. So far, I have argued that having *de re* attitudes is a necessary condition for using and understanding language—in fact for any propositional understanding—and for acquiring empirical knowledge. It remains to argue that having *de dicto* attitudes is not equally necessary to these ends. The most straightforward support for this conclusion is intuitive. To be purely *de dicto* an attitude must be appropriately expressed at bottom by a closed sentence, free of any indexical element. But it does not seem difficult to imagine language users with empirical knowledge whose every attitude contains some such element. One might think that to use a language, one must have general beliefs, counterfactual beliefs, or arithmetical beliefs. But such requirements are compatible with the absence of *de dicto* beliefs. All the relevant generalizations or counterfactuals might be tensed, or restricted by some other indexical element; all the arithmetical beliefs might be applied. Similarly, for other 'conceptual necessities'. These remarks are, of course, only intuitive. But they do suggest that having *de dicto* beliefs is not essential to understanding or to empirical knowledge. I shall now discuss the chief threat to this conclusion.

---

[11] This last argument has a Russellian, as well as a Kantian flavor. Cf. Russell, 'Knowledge by Acquaintance and Knowledge by Description,' in *idem, The Problems of Philosophy* (1912) (London: Oxford University Press, 1982); *idem, Our Knowledge of the External World* (London: Allen & Unwin, 1952), in 65 ff. (first published 1914). Russell, however, thought that *all* singular beliefs are *de re*—on account of his theory of descriptions. This view I do not hold. I am also uncommitted to Russell's foundationalism.

III

The most direct counter to our claims that *de re* beliefs are in certain respects more fundamental than *de dicto* beliefs would be to accept the gist of the arguments given in the previous section, but claim that *de re* beliefs are a mere species of *de dicto*. This claim would be congenial to much that was dear to the British empiricists. It seems to be implicit in views that Frege held. And it has been recently defended by Kaplan, who in fact tried to define *de re* beliefs in terms of *de dicto* ones.[12]

Kaplan represented such sentences as 'Alfred believes of the piano that it is ugly' as follows:

$$(\exists \alpha)(R(\alpha, \text{the piano}, \text{Alfie}) \wedge \text{Bel}(\text{Alfie}, \ulcorner \alpha \text{ is ugly} \urcorner)).$$

As a first approximation 'α' ranges over names or singular terms. 'R' means 'represents'. α represents the piano for Alfie if and only if α denotes the piano, α is vivid for Alfie ('plays a significant role in Alfie's "inner story"'), and α is *of* the piano in the sense that the piano is a crucial factor in Alfie's acquisition of α. The expressions with corners may be thought of as denoting symbols, although it is clear that Kaplan really intends them to denote Fregean senses. α, though a 'name', need not be linguistic in any ordinary sense. α may be a 'conglomeration of images, names, and partial descriptions', 'suitably arranged and regimented'. α may not, and often will not, appear in any sentence that ascribes a *de re* belief: it is enough if there be some such α in the believer's repertoire.

The crucial assumption in Kaplan's analysis that I think mistaken is the view that belief ascriptions containing demonstratives ascribe thought symbols that *denote* the objects demonstrated in the ascription. (I think neither vividness nor ofness is a necessary condition for *de re* belief, but will not discuss these issues.) Kaplan takes belief contents to be sentence types or abstract meanings. In requiring that the representing name type denote an object, one requires that the name itself (given its meaning) individuate the object in a context-independent manner. Of course, it is possible that Kaplan did not specifically intend for his term 'denote' to be taken so strictly. One might say that his 'denotes' was tacitly relativized to a context. But this move would amount to forgoing the attempt to reduce *de re* belief to *de dicto* belief. For, insofar as the thought symbol denotes the relevant object only relative to a context, the content of the believer's attitude does not depend purely on what is expressed (*dictum*) by his symbols, or on the nature of his concepts. Rather the content must be partly shown. But under these circumstances the belief is not purely *de dicto* (purely 'of' something expressed).

---

[12] The position is abetted by, but does not depend on, two Lockean views: representational realism, according to which we see physical objects only indirectly by way of sense data; and the view that images, sense data, and the like are certain sorts of concepts ('concrete' ones) eligible for being expressed by a proposition. I shall not be discussing these views. Frege's position will dominate sec. IV. Kaplan's is set out in 'Quantifying In'. It is doubtful that he still holds the view.

One may, of course, choose to use '*de dicto*' in such a way as to count sentences like (6) and (8), and the examples we give below, *de dicto*. If one did so on the ground that in every case of *de re* belief the believer has *some* means (no matter how sketchy) of representing the relevant *res*, then one would virtually trivialize the reducibility thesis. This trivialization constitutes an objection to the suggested use of '*de dicto*'. Traditionally, it has been assumed that *de re* beliefs are not *de dicto*; the two notions were explained so as to make it appear that their applications are disjoint. But under this liberalized usage, one cannot explain what a *de dicto* belief is without rendering it *obvious* that all or many *de re* beliefs are *de dicto*. All beliefs are *partly* characterizable in terms of the believer's concepts, notions, or *dicta*. To be distinctively *de dicto* a belief should be characterized purely in such terms. Beliefs like those attributed in (6) and (8) are not so characterized or even, sometimes, so characterizable.

Similar objections apply to calling sentences like (6) and (8) *de dicto* as well as *de re* on the following rather mixed criterion: *de dicto* belief ascriptions are those for which surface substitutions fail; *de re* belief ascriptions are those where the believer is taken to be *en rapport* with the relevant *res*. Such a criterion renders it obvious that the categories have considerable overlap, and fails to justify the presumption that indexically infected ascriptions are purely 'of' *dicta*.

To maintain then that Kaplan's theory reduces *de re* belief to *de dicto* belief in an interesting sense, one must use 'denote' strictly. But if one uses 'denote' strictly, it is implausible that in all cases of *de re* belief, one of the believer's beliefs contains a thought symbol or individual concept that denotes the *res*. On seeing a man coming from a distance in a swirling fog, we may plausibly be said to believe of him that he is wearing a red cap. But we do not see the man well enough to describe or image him in such a way as to individuate him fully. Of course, we could individuate him ostensively with the help of the descriptions that we can apply. But there is no reason to believe that we can always describe or conceptualize the entities or spatiotemporal positions that we rely on in our demonstration. Or consider someone who sincerely says, 'I believe of the present moment that it is in the twentieth century,' or 'It hasn't been this cold in ten years.' We cannot assume that the person will always be able to individuate the time or the degree of cold either in some canonical manner or via purely descriptive notions. Even perception under optimal conditions is subject to the point. The perceived object (say, a book) may not be inspected in sufficient detail to distinguish it from all other objects except by reference to spatiotemporal position. And this, as before, will often not be individuatable by the perceiver except by context-dependent, nonconceptual methods. Moreover, though it remains true that one believes of the book that it was, say, rust, one's memory of the details of the particular book's appearance fades.[13]

---

[13] This general style of argument is first explicit in Wittgenstein, whose *Investigations* it permeates. Cf. e.g. § 689. The argument is also highlighted in P. F. Strawson, *Individuals* (Garden

These considerations indicate that there will often be no term or individual concept in the believer's set of beliefs about the relevant object which *denotes* that object. This is not to deny that the believer always has some mental or semantical instrument for picking out the object—a set of concepts, a perceptual image, a demonstrative. But whatever means the believer has often depends for its success partly but irreducibly on factors unique to the context of the encounter with the object, and not part of the mental or linguistic repertoire of the believer.

One might wish to give a Kaplan-type analysis in terms of mental-tokens (e.g. particular sense data) rather than mental entity types. But this move does not circumvent the point of the preceding paragraphs. For features of the mental entity itself (or *dicta* associated with it) are not always sufficient to pick out the relevant object. Some contextual, not purely conceptual relation between mental entity and represented object must still be relied upon to characterize the attitude. Further, such an analysis has the counter-intuitive consequence that it is in principle impossible for different people to have the same *de re* belief.

In the face of the epistemic argument against defining *de re* belief in terms of *de dicto* belief, there are those in the Frege–Carnap tradition who fix the blame on language. True, they say, we cannot express our complete concept of the present moment or the degree of cold or the approaching man in any ordinary terms; but we *have* such a concept nevertheless. Sometimes these alleged concepts or meanings are titled 'nondescriptive'. They are allegedly what we would express if we arbitrarily introduced a name for the relevant *res*. The appeal to incommunicable concepts or meanings here seems to me implausible and obscurantist. There is no intuitive substance to the claim that such names express complete concepts. And there is no likelihood that different believers would 'grasp' the same concept expressed by them. Factors which determine the objects about which the believer holds his beliefs but which are not publicly statable (either 'in principle' or because they are not practically available to either believer or reporter) are appropriately counted nonconceptual—indeed, in most cases, noncognitive. The view that *de re* belief is semantically independent of *de dicto* belief has the fundamental advantage of avoiding unnecessary appeal to the incommunicable.

The considerations that show that *de re* belief sentences are not definable in terms of *de dicto* sentences are equally potent against the view that for every *de re* belief there is an accompanying *de dicto* belief that fully individuates the object the *de re* belief is about. Thus the conceptual priority of *de re* belief seems vindicated.

City, N.Y: Anchor, 1963), 6–9 (originally published, 1959). Cf. also Donnellan, 'Proper Names and Identifying Descriptions', in D. Davidson and G. Harman (eds.), *Semantics for Natural Language* (Dordredit: Reidel, 1972); and Kripke, 'Naming and Necessity', *op. cit.* Kaplan's requirement that a *de re* belief involve a vivid name—a 'conglomeration of images, names and partial descriptions' that gives the relevant *res* a major role in the believer's 'inner story'—may have served as a hedge against these considerations and an implicit defense of the strict use of 'denotes'. Intuitively, the considerations once considered count against the requirement.

Two sorts of consideration might lure one into a position like that which I have been criticizing. One arises from reflecting intuitively on our own cognitive attitudes when, on the basis of a present perceptual experience, we assert sentences like 'That is a piano' or 'That piano is ugly'. It is clear that our perception or conception of the piano is in a sense far richer than the meaning expressed by the words 'That piano'. We view a particular piano of a certain size, shape, and hue, with its idiosyncratic ornaments, scuffs, and scratches. It is easy to conclude that the proposition we believe is conceptually far 'richer' than our words themselves suggest. The 'richness' intuition can be accounted for by noting that we acquire whole sets of beliefs as the result of perceptual experience—all about the relevant object.[14]

IV

The second consideration backing the view that *de re* is a species of *de dicto* is Frege's theory of sense and reference. I shall assume that *de re* beliefs include beliefs about public objects, such as physical things. Now the relevant Fregean viewpoint is as follows. (1) All thought or belief about public objects is from a conceptual perspective—we always think about them from one of a variety of possible standpoints or in one of a variety of possible ways. (2) When we think about particular public objects, this conceptual perspective determines which object we are thinking about. Our initial assumption together with these two plausible principles may seem to assure that *de re* beliefs about public objects will be *de dicto*.[15] The assurance is cancelled by the kind of argument given in Section III. The problem arises with the claim in (2) that the perspective that determines the relevant object is (completely) conceptual. The Fregean viewpoint, however, is worth further discussion, because it bears on the role of *dicta* in *de re* belief.

The first principle is reasonable. Knowledge about public objects is indeed perspectival. Even in direct perception we see physical objects from one side at a time; and so it is in principle possible to fail to realize that an object, when viewed from one perspective is the same object as was just seen from another perspective. Moreover, it is plausible in some loose sense that perceptual beliefs represent the perceived object by means of concepts.

Principle (1) is at the bottom of Frege's basic argument for the postulation of senses—the 'paradox' of identity. The 'paradox' of identity says that, whereas a statement of the form $\ulcorner a = a \urcorner$ is uninformative, a statement of the form $\ulcorner a = b \urcorner$

---

[14] Cf. George Pitcher, *A Theory of Perception* (Princeton: Princeton University Press, 1971), 71 ff.

[15] The first principle is explicit in Frege's 'On Sense and Reference', in P. Geach and M. Black (eds.), *Translations of the Philosophical Writings of Gottlob Frege* (Oxford: Blackwell, 1966), 57–58. Frege suggests that sense is conceptual in character when he says 'The sense of a proper name is grasped by everybody who is sufficiently familiar with the language,' and when he identifies senses with thoughts. The second principle is explicit on p. 58 of the same essay.

may be of considerable empirical significance; but '*a*' and '*b*' are singular terms that refer to the same object; so the difference in the statements must go beyond what is referred to in them. The difference is in the mode with which the denoted object is presented to a thinker by the singular terms '*a*' and '*b*'. And Frege counted this difference a difference in sense. The paradox of identity is closely related to the failure of substitution of coextensive terms in belief contexts. For the point that $\ulcorner a = b \urcorner$ may be informative where $\ulcorner a = a \urcorner$ is not is in effect the point that one may fail to believe that $a = b$ while believing that $a = a$. There is, I think, no denying either of these points. The counterclaim that, where '*a*' and '*b*' are proper names, a belief that $a = b$ is really the same as a belief that $a = a$ (so one believes both or neither) seems to me completely implausible. I shall therefore ignore it.

Propositions are traditionally postulated as the sort of thing that is believed. And Frege's argument refutes any theory that takes singular propositions about public objects of the form Fa, where '*a*' is a proper name, to consist *simply* of a and the attribute expressed or denoted by '*F*'. (Cf. note 6 above.) But Frege's arguments apply to demonstratives as well as to definite descriptions and proper names.[16] We would find boring a claim of the form 'this = this', where 'this' is twice used to refer to some object under the same circumstances (cf. 'this is self-identical'). But we might be surprised by a claim of the form 'this = this', where the first 'this' is used with a nod toward a picture of the Hope diamond, and the second with a gesture to a dirty stone. A similar point holds for proper names. If Alfie knows someone in two different walks of life by 'Bertie', but thinks he knows two Berties, he will be interested if we tell him that Bertie (pointing to the person, or picture of him, in one guise) is identical with Bertie (indicating him in another). Obviously, we can embed these statements in belief sentences and attribute informative and uninformative belief contents by varying the context of use and our intentions as reporters.

For reasons of the sort given in Section III, these considerations should not lead us to postulate complete concepts (or senses) which are expressed by the different tokens of 'this' or 'Bertie' and which completely individuate the relevant referent in different ways. But the considerations do show that, in giving formal representations to these statements, we should distinguish the informative from the uninformative cases. So we should distinguish the two explicit occurrences of 'this' in the informative version of 'this = this', and the two implicit occurrences of a demonstrative in the informative version of 'Bertie = Bertie'. The formal representations of the two occurrences of 'this' in the informative versions will mark different contexts of use, without specifically expressing any particular concepts or *dicta* associated with those uses.[17]

---

[16] This point is due to David Kaplan.

[17] The representations are: $x_1 = x_1$ and $[x_1]\text{Cicero}(x_1) = [x_2]\text{Cicero}(x_2)$, where the variables are specially subscripted to represent indexical constructions. The latter sentence may be parsed by the hybrid, 'That$_1$Cicero = That$_2$Cicero'. Cf. the works cited in note 5. The considerations in the

The notion of sense fills three functions in Frege's theory. One (*sense₁*) is that of representing the mode of presentation to the thinker which is associated with an expression and of accounting for information value. A second (*sense₂*) is that of determining the referent or denotation associated with the expression: for singular terms, senses serve as 'routes' to singling out the unique object, if any, denoted by the term. The third function (*sense₃*) is that of providing entities to be denoted in oblique contexts.[18]

Kripke criticizes Frege for not distinguishing between two senses of 'sense': meaning and means of fixing the referent. This criticism is prima facie related to the distinction between the first two functions of 'sense'. But Kripke's distinction is not really appropriate to any aspect of Frege's notion of sense. Kripke gives three examples of 'fixing the referent'. The first is that of saying that one meter is the length of stick S at time t, where S is the standard meter bar. The second is that of introducing the name 'Hesperus' as applying to the planet in yonder position in the sky. The third is the statement that π is the ratio of the circumference of a circle to its diameter (277 ff.).

In the first and third cases, Frege would not allow that the respective definite descriptions gave the sense of 'one meter' and 'π' in *any* sense of 'sense'. For Frege the fundamental test for determining whether senses differ was the informativeness of the relevant identity statement.[19] *But both of these identity statements are informative.* One might reply that they are uninformative *for the introducer.* But Frege did not intend the sense of such expressions as 'meter' or 'π' to vary from person to person. The respective senses of these expressions as used by their introducers are not different from those of the same expressions for others. So the notion of informativeness that is relevant to Frege's test is more 'public' than this reply would require. As applied to the examples of 'meter' and 'π', Kripke's notion of fixing the referent is pragmatic, having little to do with Frege's second function of sense.

The second example is different. Frege did assume that the sense of ordinary proper names varied from person to person. In the context of the introduction, it

---

text count against any attempt to solve Frege's paradox of identity by simply citing the difference in surface terms (or tags) that are used. Russell tried this in 'Philosophy of Logical Atomism', 245–246. Appeal to different term tokens also will not work, since the uninformative identities also have different term tokens flanking the identity sign.

[18] The three functions emerge in succession in 'On Sense and Reference', 57–58, 58, 58–59, respectively. On the second function, see also the telescope analogy, p. 60. In connection with the first function, Frege remarks that senses are 'grasped' by everyone who understands an expression as it is used in a language. It is not clear how Frege intended to apply this remark to demonstrative constructions, but elsewhere he clearly holds that the sense, mode of presentation, of such constructions varies from thinker to thinker and context to context. (Cf. note 20 below.) Frege's remark has led to the identification of mode of presentation and linguistic meaning. But this identification is not forced by the passage; and in light of Frege's views on demonstrative constructions, the identification is unquestionably mistaken, as I argue below.

[19] Frege believed that the modes of presentation of expressions differed if and only if the relevant individuating features differed. Kripke and I would agree that this biconditional is false. My point is that for Frege the left–right direction is the basic, criterial one for individuating senses.

seems perhaps that the relevant identity is trivial and that the senses of the name 'Hesperus' and the introducing description, on Frege's view, would be the same. The basic weakness of Kripke's criticism of Frege here (and it emerges in the other cases as well) is his widely shared assumption that Fregean sense, in at least the first of its functions, corresponds to the modern notion of linguistic meaning (cf. note 18). The assumption is implausible. In deference to the first function of sense, Frege clearly thought that the sense of a demonstrative like 'this' or 'I', an indexical construction like present tense, or a proper name like 'Aristotle' (even as applied to the philosopher) varied from person to person and context to context. But linguists and philosophers (correctly, I think) regard demonstrative constructions, including proper names, as having a constant meaning, though varying referents. I think it at best rather wooden to regard Frege as simply wrong about this. It is more appropriate to see him as employing a notion close to but distinct from the notion of meaning. Frege was less concerned with linguistic meaning than with how people acquire and pass on knowledge by using language.[20] Thus even though the meaning of 'Hesperus' (if any) and that of the reference-fixing description differ, it remains open whether they differ in sense for the introducer. Nothing Kripke says decides this question.

There is, however, a good objection to Frege's assumption that the first and second functions of the notion of sense coincide—the objection cited in section III.[21] A complete account of the mode in which an object is presented

---

[20] For the remarks on the variations of sense associated with indexical expressions, see Frege, 'The Thought', in E. D. Klemke (ed.), *Essays on Frege* (Urbana, Ill.: University of Illinois Press, 1968), 517–519, 533. Frege repeatedly disavows concern with language, most notoriously in 'On Concept and Object', in Geach and Black (eds.), *Translations*, 54. And he emphasizes that his primary concern is with knowledge and thought. Cf. ibid. 46 n., 59, and in 'The Thought', *passim*, esp. 534. In this connection, the translation of *Gedanke* as 'Thought' seems more appropriate than as 'Proposition'.

I am not sure whether Frege would regard the sense of 'Hesperus' for the introducer at the time of the introduction as the same as that of the description. On the one hand, there will be a *feeling* of uninformativeness in the relevant identity statement. On the other hand, the introducer has means of identifying the planet which are independent of the description (its visual characteristics).

[21] Cf. note 13. The argument from incompleteness of information should be distinguished from the argument (given by numerous people—Wittgenstein, Searle, Donnellan, Kripke) based on the observation that singular sentences whose subject term is a proper name or a demonstrative and whose predicate is an ordinary descriptive expression, are not logical truths. This argument shows that demonstratives and names do not have the same linguistic meaning that definite descriptions have. Its bearing on the notion of sense is more complicated and cannot be discussed here. The 'incompleteness' argument should also be distinguished from an unsound argument that proper names and demonstratives lack sense, or linguistic meaning, because they are rigid designators, designating the same object, if any, in all possible circumstances. Cf. Kripke, "Naming and Necessity", e.g., pp. 276–277. Suppose that proper names were always rigid. The point that they are rigid shows at most that, in necessity contexts, they always have transparent referential position (or from the viewpoint of modal logic, truth conditions analogous to those for definite descriptions with wide scope). But the failures of substitution in belief contexts, show that proper names do not always have transparent reference. And this leaves open the possibility that they have sense (sense$_1$ as well as sense$_3$). Moreover, the paradox of identity requires that to give an adequate theory of linguistic understanding, one say *something* about mode of presentation (sense$_1$) beyond mentioning the name's referent. The rigid designator argument (in contrast to the other arguments) has just as

to us—the effect that it has on our cognitive representations or on our store of information—may be insufficient to determine that one object rather than another is the subject of our beliefs or statements. (Appeal to a community of thinkers here clearly does not change matters.) The individuation of the relevant object depends not only on information the thinker has about it but on his nonconceptual contextual relations to it. These wider relations are necessary to characterize the second function of sense, but they go beyond what the thinker 'grasps' in thought.

It is time now to consider the third function of Frege's notion of sense—that of providing an object of reference for expressions in oblique contexts. Motivating this use of 'sense' was a powerful theory of language according to which the truth-value of any sentence is a function of the denotations of its parts. Here is not the place to defend the principle.[22] I shall simply assume it. It is easy to show that, given this principle, the denotation of expressions in oblique contexts cannot be the denotation they have in transparent contexts. The question then arises whether the oblique denotation ($sense_3$) should be identified with the mode of presentation ($sense_1$) or the mode of designation ($sense_2$), if either.

When A says, 'Aristotle was a philosopher' or 'Sam is a violist', and B says the same, we sometimes want to remark in indirect discourse that they stated, and believed, the same thing. (Let us assume that the proper names do not have purely transparent position. The attributed statements or beliefs may be either *de dicto* or *de re à la* (8).) If in reporting their respective statements, we are making reference to $sense_2$, the mode of designation, we cannot reasonably say that A and B made the same statement. For the way in which the term 'Aristotle' as uttered by A (B) picks out the Stagyrite, rather than some other Aristotle, depends on elements in the context of A's (B's) utterance. But since the contexts differ, the modes of designation ($senses_2$) differ. So in reporting A's statement or belief as being the same as B's (and making reference to $sense_3$), we cannot be making reference to $sense_2$.

No such simple argument shows that $sense_3$ should not be identified with $sense_1$. Much depends on precisely how the $sense_1$ of a name is construed. I think we should ignore suggestions to take the contextual (often 'causal') relation between believer and named object as $sense_1$. In effect these suggestions amount to reidentifying $sense_1$ and $sense_2$. The suggestions are implausible simply because the relevant relation is ordinarily not part of the cognitive world of the believer, so it cannot provide an account of the information value

---

little bearing on meaning as it does on sense. Necessity contexts do not have a definitive position in arguments about either meaning or sense. It is worth noting that the rigid designator argument does not even show that proper names do not have the sense (or even the meaning) of definite descriptions. For a Fregean could reply that the points Kripke cites show only that when the sense of a definite description is expressed by a proper name in a necessity context, the name has its customary reference. It is not hard to think up reasons on behalf of the Fregean as to why this might be the case. But since our subject here is not necessity, I shall not pursue the matter.

[22] Cf. Frege, 'On Sense and Reference', 59 ff. Also Kaplan, "Quantifying In", secs. III–IV.

associated with names. I think it is also clear, for reasons mentioned earlier, that sense$_1$ should not be identified with linguistic meaning, at least for the general case: 'this is this' or 'Bertie is Bertie' might be informative even though the two occurrences of 'this' have the same linguistic meaning.

A touchstone for dealing with the relation between sense$_1$ and sense$_3$ is consideration of when people are said to share a belief. For example, we often want to say that *A, B,* and *C* all believe that Sam Rhodes is a fine fellow, where 'Sam Rhodes' does not have purely transparent position. If the sense$_1$ of the name in a context of potential use is taken to be the descriptions, images, and so forth that the user would associate with it, then sense$_1$ and sense$_3$ must be distinguished. For *A, B,* and *C*'s descriptions and so forth may not coincide. We can even imagine that, although *A* and *B* agree on some descriptions, as do *B* and *C*, the descriptions associated with the name by *A* and *C* are for practical purposes disjoint. Imagine that they agree only on 'living, human male'.[23]

Thinking of sense$_1$ as a set of descriptions 'abroad' in a community provides some relief from this difficulty. In fact, I think the viewpoint (equipped with a sufficiently subtle notion of community) can contribute a partial account of the cognitive value of proper names, although it must give up any ambition to determine the name's referent purely on the basis of the relevant descriptions. Such an account of sense$_1$, however, would at best be partial. For it dramatically fails to account for the cognitive difference among users of names or demonstratives, which Russell and Frege stressed (cf. note 23). Can the 'communal description' account of sense$_1$ be used to account for sense$_3$? I think not. The relevant set of descriptions will change over time, but we will remain willing to ascribe a given belief expressed with the name to people both before and after the change.

Any explication of the informativeness of identity statements is bound to be complex. The account of *public* information will appeal partly to linguistic meaning, partly to communally shared descriptions. The account of an *individual's* information, which is particularly relevant to the informativeness of statements containing demonstratives and many proper names, must discuss matters psychological. That is, I think this latter part of the account will have to treat idiosyncratic associations and connotations—tokens of which Frege called 'ideas'. But none of the aspects of an account of sense$_1$, at least the sense$_1$ of proper names or other demonstrative constructions, is promising as an account of sense$_3$.

I think it would be a mistake to postulate a new intensional entity, sense$_3$. Such postulation will generate little illumination until we better understand the relations between 'sense$_1$', 'meaning', and 'sense$_3$'. As we have seen, much of the trouble with Frege's account, and with objections to it, stems from

---

[23] Frege was probably willing to deny that *A, B,* and *C* share a belief. Cf. 'On Sense and Reference', 58 n., and 'The Thought', 517–519. Russell may have actually urged the denial in 'The Philosophy of Logical Atomism', 195–196. But their authority lends little credence to the view.

commitment to idealization of intensional notions before the phenomena that these idealizations are supposed to explain are adequately sorted out.

Senses$_3$ are roughly the *dicta* that are attributed in ordinary talk about *de re* and *de dicto* beliefs. But, as we have seen, cognitive differences in the *de re* belief content (or a *de re* bearer of truth) are sometimes marked not by reference to different concept expressions, but simply by different free variables. (Cf. notes 5 and 17.) Frege's informative *de re* identities do not demand that a formal representation invoke unapparent concepts or senses that determine the *re*.

Our representation in terms of free variables is flexible as well as spare. We can specify neutral variables for cases in which we want to say that everyone acquainted with Sam believes him to be male (thus attributing a shared *de re* belief). For cases like the surprising *de re* belief that Bertie is Bertie we can utilize different variables representing the implicit 'that' as it is applied in the different contexts. We can distinguish self-knowledge from knowledge about oneself from the third-person viewpoint by variables representing the first-person demonstrative. (Cf. Castañeda, note 3.) And so on. The particular concepts, percepts, images, insights, irritations, or intimations that an individual has of or from the relevant *res* are left unspecified in these cases. The free variables do no more than indicate the not purely conceptual character of these means of identification and mark differences in the contexts in which they are applied.

Thus, senses$_3$ are finer-grained than linguistic meanings for the same reason that sense$_1$ and linguistic meaning are distinct: The linguistic meaning of 'Bertie is Bertie' or 'this is this' is the same whether the sentence is taken as truistic or informative. But one may believe the truism and not believe the informative statement. The different variables in the formal representation mark differences in the context in which the demonstrative construction is used, not differences in linguistic meaning.[24] On the other hand, senses$_3$ sometimes do not characterize (or even involve quantification over) the particular mode of presentation associated with an individual's belief. And in this respect they may be regarded as coarser-grained than senses$_1$.

Full treatment of belief contents is the subject for other occasions. Our discussion, however, has placed limits on such a treatment. I have given reason to believe that sense$_3$ is not in general identifiable with sense$_1$, sense$_2$, or linguistic meaning, on natural construals of these notions. Improving on Frege's view of belief depends partly on attending to the variety of phenomena that he tried to explain with his single idealization, sense, and partly on recognizing the fundamental character of *de re* attitudes.

The lead role of *de re* attitudes is sponsored by a contextual, not purely conceptual relation between thinkers and objects. The paradigm of this relation

---

[24] I discuss senses$_3$ in 'Self-Reference and Translation', in F. Guenthner and M. Guenthner (eds.), in *Translation and Meaning* (London: Duckworth, 1977). I shall discuss the notion further in future papers and will argue that, even in the case of ascriptions of *non*indexical beliefs, senses$_3$ should not be identified with linguistic meaning.

is perception. But projections from the paradigm include memory, many intro-spective beliefs, certain historical beliefs, beliefs about the future, perhaps beliefs in pure mathematics, and so on. There is no adequate general explication of the appropriate nonconceptual relation(s) which covers even the most widely accep-ted projections from the perceptual paradigm. Developing such an explication would, I think, help articulate the epistemic notion of intuition in its broadest, least technical sense, and contribute to our understanding of understanding.

Postscript to "Belief *De Re*"

Although some earlier papers contain elements that became integral to anti-individualism, 'Belief *De Re*' is the main predecessor of 'Individualism and the Mental' and 'Other Bodies' in my work. It begins a shift in my focus of attention. It is also the paper in which I began to find my philosophical voice.

The paper now seems overly technical and too hard to read. There are some emphases in it that I would like to adjust, formulations that I regard as mistaken, and commitments that I no longer maintain. Nevertheless, there are things in the paper that I still like very much. I retain a warm spot for it. In view of the difficulty of the paper, I will go over some of its main points slowly, articulating my current attitudes toward them, cold and warm.

I

'Belief *De Re*' sets out to explicate a *de re*/*de dicto* distinction that respects history and that centers on issues that are of philosophical importance. It focuses on the distinction as applied to propositional attitudes. My counting attitudes, not pieces of language, as the primary domain of the *de re*/*de dicto* distinction is explicit in many places in the paper. I am primarily interested in the logical form of the representational contents of the beliefs themselves, and only secondarily and derivatively interested in the nature of belief ascription in natural language.

There are, however, passages where this idea is not nearly as clear as it should be. Near the end of section I, I write, 'I have expressed the intuitive *de re*/*de dicto* distinction in terms of the logical form of ascriptions of belief.' I then go on to discuss the 'epistemic basis' of the distinction. The epistemic basis has to do with the nature of the attitudes themselves, not anything to do with linguistic ascriptions of the attitudes. What is the relation between these two accounts—linguistic and epistemic?

In the background of this two-pronged approach lay an assumption about a purpose of some ascriptions of propositional attitudes in actual, ordinary language use—and certainly in some scientific language use. I assumed that one purpose of some ascriptions is to describe those attitudes as exactly as possible, consistent with the conventional and practical purposes of language use. I thought that in studying ascriptions that have this purpose, one can gain insight into the nature of the attitudes themselves. I certainly had this methodology in mind when I wrote 'Belief *De Re*'. Yet I did not articulate the methodology or its background assumption as clearly as I should have. As a result, some formulations make it appear that I am primarily concerned with understanding the language of propositional attitude ascriptions *in general*, as opposed to specific uses of propositional attitude ascriptions that shed light on the propositional attitudes themselves.[1]

A reason why it is important to articulate the methodology and background assumption is that significant aspects or uses of many propositional attitude ascriptions do not reflect any particular concern to describe the relevant attitudes at all. Many aspects or uses of ascriptions are aimed simply at communicating something practically relevant to a hearer. Many are aimed at relating the person with the attitudes to an object of interest for the ascriber. Such ascriptions abstract almost entirely from the representational content of the attitudes, from the way that the person thinks about things.

The paper shows awareness of these points. In the penultimate paragraph of section I, I discuss what were sometimes called 'pseudo *de re* ascriptions'. Alfie says, 'The most powerful man on earth in 1970 (whoever he is) is a crook.' Suppose that Alfie has no idea who the most powerful man is, and has only *de dicto* belief regarding that man. A friend of that man, who heard Alfie's claim, says to the man, 'Alfie believes that you are a crook.' The ascription involves a demonstrative ('you') applied to the man. It attributes to Alfie an open content you are a crook, as applied to the powerful man. The ascription is *pseudo de re* because there is no implication that Alfie thinks of the most powerful man in a way that is governed by the demonstrative application, or in any other epistemically special way. The ascriber's demonstrative and application at most preserve the referent of some representation that Alfie used. They do not bear on how Alfie thought about the man at all. I commented that the case is at best an example of a *de re* ascription of a *de dicto* belief, not an example of *de re* belief. This remark seems to me correct.

I also commented that the pronoun 'you' is 'partly anaphoric', picking up the referent of 'the most powerful man'. This point seems correct as well, at least as applied to the particular case. The idea is that the ascriber's demonstrative pronoun has, in addition to its deictic or demonstrating use, a pronominal relation back to some expression used by the person to whom the attitude is ascribed. The demonstrative pronoun does not in itself indicate whether the person's way of thinking was *de re* or not. The ascriber may not care. The ascriber is not ascribing deictic usage. The deictic usage is purely his or her own. Through the expression 'you', the ascriber is 'anaphorically' indicating some singular usage by the subject of the ascription, Alfie.

---

[1] W. V. Quine, in 'Quantifiers and Propositional Attitudes', *The Journal of Philosophy*, 53 (1956), repr. in *Ways of Paradox* (New York: Random House, 1966), is primarily concerned with language. David Kaplan, in 'Quantifying In', in D. Davidson and J. Hintikka (eds.), *Words and Objections: Essays on the Work of W. V. Quine* (Dordrecht: Reidel, 1969), repr. in L. Linsky (ed.), *Reference and Modality* (Oxford: Oxford University Press, 1971), has a dual focus, but certainly makes contributions to understanding the nature of *de re* attitudes themselves. I see my paper as taking a further step away from Quine's purely linguistic focus. However, the interest in natural language was so dominant in those days that separating the issues about the character of language use from issues about the nature of the attitudes as sharply as we would today was not common or easy.

This idea has a chance of being general enough to cover all relevant cases, however, only if 'anaphora' is understood very broadly. The ascriber may not have in mind any definite, antecedent expression used by the subject. In such a case the 'anaphora' would have to purport to go back to some unspecified or unknown singular way of thinking on the part of the individual who has the attitudes. It might, for example, even go back to a definite description used non-referentially, in *pseudo de re* cases. Or the 'anaphora' might go back to a family of ways of thinking—not to any definite *linguistic* antecedent at all.[2] Here again, making explicit what are linguistic claims and what are claims about connections to actual attitudes would have strengthened the paper.

Because the paper was focused on the nature of attitudes, not language, it underplayed the complexities involved in different uses of natural language. The paper acknowledged the existence of these complications. But it did not signal as clearly as it might have how complex these complications are, or how much of ordinary usage is indifferent to describing just what the individual's propositional attitudes are.

II

I turn now to the specifics of the accounts of the *de re/de dicto* distinction. I gave both a semantical account and an epistemic account. The semantical account centers on attitude ascriptions that are meant to characterize or indicate the nature of the attitude, including its representational content. The epistemic account centers on the underlying epistemic and representational capacities of the individual with the attitude.

The epistemic account is squarely aimed at the more fundamental philosophical issues. Kant, in his notion of sensible intuition as a singular capacity, and Russell, in his notion of acquaintance, try to do justice to a common intuition. They believe that we have an epistemically distinctive and important capacity, or set of capacities, to connect our thought to particulars in a singular way. Both philosophers see this sort of capacity as fundamental in understanding human knowledge. Both are opposed to the view that this capacity can be reduced to predicative, attributive capacities. Both seem to be on to something deep about our representational and epistemic relations to objective subject matters. The main reason to reflect on *de re* phenomena is to try to obtain further insight into this 'something'.

Despite my overriding sense that the epistemic issues are the most important ones, I gave a semantical as well as an epistemic account of the distinction. I hoped that the two accounts would reinforce one another.

---

[2] This broad understanding of anaphora is implicit in the discussion of vacuous names in the paragraph in section I that begins 'The representations given so far'. I developed the notion further in 'Russell's Problem and Intentional Identity' in James Tomberlin (ed.), *Agent, Language, and the Structure of the World* (Indianapolis: Hackett Publishing Company, 1983), 79–110.

Let us suppose that we are dealing with ascriptions that are aimed purely at characterizing or indicating the nature of an attitude, including its representational content. Then the semantical account maintains that an ascription ascribes a *de re* attitude if it ascribes the attitude by ascribing a relation between what is expressed by an open sentence, understood as having a free variable marking a demonstrative-like application, and a *re* to which the free variable is referentially related. The semantical account maintains that an ascription ascribes a *de dicto* attitude if it ascribes the attitude by ascribing what is expressed by a closed sentence—roughly one that involves no applied demonstrative or indexical elements.[3] I will return to the points about open sentences, free variables, and applications in section III of this Postscript.

The intuitive idea behind all this *technicalia* is simple. *De re* attitudes are ascribed by indicating representational contents that contain successfully applied demonstrative or indexical elements. *De dicto* attitudes are ascribed by indicating representational contents that contain no demonstratives or indexicals.

There are cases in which an individual thinks in a demonstrative-governed way—for example, in perceptual beliefs—but fails to refer to a *re*. The perceptual belief might derive from a (referential) illusion. There are certain uses of demonstratives that fail reference. An analogous point applies to demonstrative-like applications in thought. A fully informative ascription of such propositional attitudes will ascribe something expressed by a demonstrative-governed open sentence, but will not relate that representational content to a *re*. Strictly speaking, the ascription ascribes an attitude that counts as neither *de re* nor *de dicto*. However, the attitude itself, as distinguished from its referential relation to the world, is more like a *de re* attitude than a *de dicto* attitude. I believe that insofar as one is interested in a taxonomy of mental 'natural' kinds, these non-referring attitudes group with the *de re* attitudes.

The 'epistemic account' of what it is to be *de re* is more basic than the semantical account. In fact, the semantical account points toward an epistemic account inasmuch as the semantical account attempts to explicate ascriptions of belief that are meant to describe the beliefs (as opposed to carrying out other communicative purposes). The epistemic account that I favored at the time directly corresponds to the semantical account: An attitude is *de dicto* if it is completely conceptualized. An attitude is *de re* if it has a content that is not completely conceptualized (and, it should be added, a not completely conceptualized element in the content succeeds in referring to a *re*). That is, the content contains a demonstrative or indexical element successfully applied to a *re*. The application of the demonstrative or indexical element is the element in the content that prevents the content from being completely conceptualized. This

---

[3] The points about anaphora in *pseudo de re* cases are assumed: If the ascription involves anaphora, whether a *de re* or a *de dicto* attitude is ascribed depends on what types of ways of thinking the anaphoric pronoun goes back to. In such cases, the ascription is not aimed purely at describing the attitude, and it may be unclear from the ascription what attitude content is ascribed.

element is formalized by a free variable contextually applied. When successful, such applications are to *res*.

In the last paragraph of section I of 'Belief *De Re*', I gave *two* epistemic accounts of *de re* attitudes. The first is the one just cited. According to the second, which is vaguer, an attitude is *de re* if it involves an appropriate 'not completely conceptual' relation to a *re*. Perception is used as an example of a not completely conceptual relation. Other examples are tentatively suggested in the last paragraph of 'Belief *De Re*'.[4]

The two epistemic accounts are nonequivalent in a subtle but important way. The first account takes successfully applied demonstrative or indexical elements in a belief content to be the hallmark of *de re* attitudes.[5] The second account allows all the cases that the first account allows. It, however, leaves prima facie room for *de re* attitudes to include attitudes that have no demonstrative or indexical element in their representational contents.

The special cases of possible *de re* attitudes mentioned in the last paragraph of 'Belief *De Re*' include beliefs in pure mathematics. I believe—and, I think, believed then—that it is not plausible that demonstratives or indexicals occur in the contents of thoughts in pure mathematics. The representational content $3 + 5 = 8$ does not seem to contain demonstratives or indexicals. So it seems to me that the first account is vulnerable if *de re* attitudes include some thoughts in pure mathematics. The second account is not obviously vulnerable in this regard.

The spirit of the last paragraph of the paper and its relation to the point just made is hard for me to judge at this temporal distance. One might take that spirit to be as follows: The first account of the distinction between *de re* and *de dicto* attitudes takes perceptual beliefs to be the paradigm cases. A range of further cases—perceptual memories, certain historical beliefs, self-ascriptions, and so on—have the relevant features of perceptual beliefs. Beliefs in pure mathematics are a further special case. They do not fit the first account. They do, however, involve other sorts of not completely conceptual relations between attitude and object—sorts other than those involved in perceptual belief. They can be included by a looser criterion of the *de re/de dicto* distinction—that of the second epistemic account.

---

[4] The dialectical point of the second account was not to prejudge the discussion of Kaplan's account—hence the reference, in the last paragraph of sec. I, to sec. III. I wanted to give an account of what it is to be *de re* that did not already entail that a content that denoted its objects noncontextually, purely by way of context-free concepts, was not *ipso facto* ruled out from being *de re*.

[5] Every nonconceptual element in a propositional representational content is associated with a conceptual or other attributive element. There are no unmodified demonstrative applications in thought. The demonstrative referential elements in the contents of *de re* attitudes always have attributive elements that accompany and guide the demonstrative application. All pure indexical applications involve an attributive element—e.g. is a time in now. The key point is that they are not *completely* conceptual. For a discussion of this point see 'Five Theses on *De Re* Attitudes', forthcoming in a volume edited by Paolo Leonardi, honoring David Kaplan (Oxford: Oxford University Press).

This gloss is probably overly generous. As far as I can see, I favor the first epistemic account in the article without explicit reservations. I do not point out any consequences of the difference between the two accounts in the article. I do not indicate the special issues that beliefs in pure mathematics raise. I do remember, however, thinking that such beliefs raise special issues that could not be tackled in the article. And I knew that pure mathematics does not contain demonstratives or indexicals.

How should we see these matters now? Perceptual beliefs do constitute paradigm cases of *de re* attitudes. They surely involve demonstrative-like applications. Most of the other clear types of *de re* attitudes do also. One could draw a *de re/de dicto* distinction so as to exclude the mathematical cases. Drawing such a boundary is not obviously mistaken. Nevertheless, it seems to me that there are epistemic kinds that are more general, that include the mathematical cases, and that can plausibly be associated with the terms '*de re*' and '*de dicto*'. I think it potentially fruitful philosophically to try to understand this broader distinction. The second epistemic account I gave, vague as it was, is more useful than the first as a guide in this enterprise. So I shall take it that at least some simple arithmetic beliefs are singular *de re* attitudes. The *res* are natural numbers. An example might be a belief that $3 + 5 = 8$.

It seems to me that certain specifications of representational *thought contents* are non-demonstrative and non-indexical, but also yield *de re* attitudes. In thinking the thought that snow is white is true, my thought specifies the thought that snow is white in the that-clause way. It seems to me that this thinking is *de re*. Here the *de re* reference feeds directly off immediate understanding of representational contents, the *res*. In this respect the case is different from *de re* beliefs about the numbers. The numbers are not themselves representational contents. They can be understood only by representing them via representational contents.

In neither of these cases—reference to numbers or reference to representational contents—is it plausible that there is an application of a demonstrative or indexical form of representation in the thought contents themselves. In both cases, it appears that the representational thought contents that carry out the *de re* reference are completely conceptualized. If attitudes of these two sorts are to be included among *de re* attitudes, the distinction between *de re* and *de dicto* cannot hinge on whether the representational content itself is completely conceptualized.

The second epistemic account specifies a not completely conceptual relation to the *re*. In both of these cases there is a striking relation to a *re* that goes beyond merely conceiving of it or forming a concept that represents it. I think that these cases satisfy the condition for being *de re* set by the second account, but not the condition set by the first.

Let us first consider the case of that-clause-like reference to representational contents. That-clause forms of representation in thought are individual concepts. They are complex structure- and content-specifying concepts when they name whole representational thought contents. They are simple concepts when they name simple components of the thought contents. Mastery of such an individual concept, of either sort, requires comprehending the representational content that the individual concept names. The 'not completely conceptual' relation to a *re* is comprehending the *re*, not *merely* conceiving of it. Yet the canonical way of thinking about the thought content can itself be fully conceptualized.[6] For example, in an attribution of a belief that $3 + 5 = 8$, the that-clause way of thinking of the thought that $3 + 5 = 8$ is fully conceptualized. There are no demonstratives or indexicals in the that-clause way of naming the thought content. This form of *de re* representation is possible only for *res* that are themselves representational contents.

The canonical concepts for the natural numbers present a somewhat different case. In understanding this case, it seems to me fruitful to consider our actual psychological capacities in thinking about the natural numbers. I think that reflection on these capacities provides a fruitful basis for explicating what it is to be 'directly' or 'immediately' related to a *re*.

Obviously, complex numeral names are formed from simpler ones. I think that the simpler ones are associated with a capacity for immediate, non-inferential, non-computational counting. We have a capacity to count small groups (say, groups of up to about nine) at a glance. We are able to apply the number in counting immediately—non-inferentially through perception. In the arabic system this immediate applicational capacity is at least approximately associated with the non-complexity of the initial canonical names for natural numbers—$\underline{0}$, $\underline{1}$, $\underline{2}$ ... $\underline{9}$. There is psychological evidence that $\underline{2}$ is simple. It is *not* understood as $\underline{1} + \underline{1}$. By contrast, the concept $\underline{12}$ in various contexts is psychologically treated as compound. The capacity to represent the simplest natural numbers (say, those up to about 9) is associated with a perceptual capacity for immediate perceptual application in counting. Thus there is a relation to these smaller numbers in addition to being able to conceive them—being able to apply individual concepts of them noninferentially and noncomputationally in counting perceived groups.

Although unlike Frege, I believe that the numerals are primitive, not defined in terms of sets, classes, or extensions, I think that Frege was correct in thinking of numbers as having a certain second-order status. The equivalences between counting with numerals, on one hand, and quantificational expressions that capture the counting of objects falling under predicates, on the other, is so close that the relation seems to me to be constitutive.[7] The connection suggests a certain second-order status for the numbers. Like the operations expressed by quantifiers, numbers bear an essential relation to predication. Understanding pure

---

[6] The issue is discussed in some detail in 'Frege and the Hierarchy' and especially in the Postscript to that article in *Truth, Thought, Reason: Essays on Frege* (Oxford: Oxford University Press, 2005).

[7] The allusion to the relation between numerals and quantifiers cites the familiar fact that 'there are 3 F's' is equivalent to 'there are F's, x, y, and z, which are not identical to one another, and all F's are identical to x, y, or z'.

arithmetic requires understanding applications of it in counting. Understanding '3' involves understanding 'there are 3 F's', which in turn requires being able to count the F's—put them in one–one relation to the numbers up to 3. Being able to apply a canonical (numeral-like) concept for the number 3 in an immediate perceptual way, without carrying out a discursive figuring, seems to me to constitute a 'not completely conceptual' relation to the number. One can apply a concept of it perceptually and nondiscursively, without conceptual computation or inference.

Canonical concepts for larger natural numbers are the results of computations on the psychologically simple and immediately applicable (applicable, say, in perception-based counting) canonical representations of smaller numbers. Canonical concepts for larger numbers are built by simple recursive rules from the simplest ones. *Perceptual* counting of groups much larger than nine usually involves first factoring the group into smaller groups that can be counted in immediate perceptual apprehension and then adding the numbers numbering the groups.

Understanding what larger numbers are derives from this immediate hold on the applicability of the smaller ones. The concept 547 is formed in simple recursive fashion from the simplest canonical natural number concepts. It seems to me that insofar as the application of these rules invokes an immediately applicable 'non-inferential' computational capacity for comprehending the larger, more complex names, the process is similar to the formation of complex that-clause-like individual concepts for complex representational contents, by grammatical rules, from canonical name-like concepts for the simple contents. Thus the canonical, complex individual concept that writing long papers requires concentration is formed from canonical name-like concepts for the component representational contents (for example, writing) by directly comprehended rules. The canonical individual concept 547 is similar.

The simpler, canonical, numeral-like individual concepts, those that can be immediately applied in perception-based counting, are, I think, the source of *de re* representation of natural numbers. Representation of more complex numbers through canonical numeral individual concepts is *de re* derivatively: Embedded in the content of a complex numeral individual concept (547) are simple individual concepts (5, 4, 7) that involve *de re* application. One may regard the complex name as *de re*. If one does, however, it seems to me a less direct type of *de re* relation to the numbers than that involved in the conceptual counterparts of simple names into which the complex numerals are resolvable.

What is complex and what is simple may vary with individuals. Psychology indicates that for most human beings, the immediately graspable numeral names are very few. They put us in the most direct *de re* touch only with small natural numbers.[8]

---

[8] The foregoing view is a slight elaboration and amendment of an account that I give, with considerably more detail, in 'Five Theses on *De Re* States and Attitudes'. There is a huge psychological

The foregoing account of *de re* representation with canonical individual concepts for natural numbers depends on a very strict view of what counts as immediate, non-inferential, non-computational representation. The *immediacy* lies in non-inferential, paradigmatically perceptual, application in counting. It also lies in the fact that the simple individual concepts, expressed by the numerals, are not products but bases of conceptual computations.

A tenable alternative is to include, as *non-derivatively de re*, representation with the more complex numeral concepts, at least until one gets to canonical representations that require conscious computation, or figuring, for comprehension. The idea is that computation in pure mathematics ultimately comes down to immediate comprehension of canonical names for natural numbers. When one has reduced the answer to a mathematical question to a canonical name for a natural number, one is finished, *unless one needs to do figuring to comprehend the name*. At that point, one knows which number to cite in answering the question—in the most basic sense.

In an unpublished set of lectures on this topic, Saul Kripke argues for an even more liberal conception of (non-derivative) *de re* representation of numbers. He holds that *any* belief involving the conceptual counterparts of numerals is *de re*. So beliefs involving hugely long numerical concepts, expressed with the conceptual counterparts of arabic numerals, will be *de re*. The intuitive idea is that if one has an arabic numeral as a name of a number, it does not make sense to think, the number is *a*, but which number is that? (where '*a*' stands in for the arabic numeral). This very liberal view seems to me also a tenable position. It locates the *de re/de dicto* distinction more in a conscious, commonsense view of the end point of questions than in the more theoretical notion of psychologically and epistemically immediate, non-inferential types of representation.

It does seem to me that Kripke's very liberal conception is fragile, even on its own terms. The underlined question *can* make intuitive sense with extremely long arabic numerals. One needs to do some figuring, calculating, grouping, or simplifying of a thirty-seven-figure numerical name to grasp which number it names.

If one allows evidence from psychology, not merely conscious introspective evidence, I believe that this point can be made to apply even to much smaller numerals (e.g. to '547'). The calculation is so quick psychologically that

literature on animal psychology and human developmental psychology of mental representation relevant to counting and measuring. Issues regarding the relations among different numerically relevant capacities, perceptual and conceptual, are very complex. I am avoiding any precise commitments in this work. In particular, nothing hangs on my writing as if 9 is at the boundary between the simple and complex for both application and conceptual understanding. The example is meant merely to be illustrative and evocative. The general direction of the psychological research seems to me in line with the view that I outline. But I regard the details of the view as inevitably open to empirical specification and refinement. In further work, I hope to discuss in more detail what is known about the psychology of number representation. For an overview and sample, see Stanislas Dehaene, *The Number Sense* (New York: Oxford University Press, 1997); and *idem*, 'Precis of *The Number Sense*', *Mind and Language*, 16 (2001), 16–36.

we do not notice it. But it is part of the psychology of understanding and of representation, nevertheless. Asking 'Which number is 547?' does make sense from this perspective. This consideration points back to the very strict conception of *de re* immediacy that I first outlined above (and employ in 'Five Theses on *De Re* States and Attitudes'). My explication of *de re* mathematical concepts takes seriously the approximate coincidence of the notion of the starting points for calculation with the starting points for non-inferential (say, perception-based) mathematical applications in counting.

A variety of different conceptions of what constitutes *de re* representation in mathematics seem to me to be tenable. What is important is investigation of the different epistemic types, not fixing the meaning of the traditional expression '*de re*'. The very strict construal of that term, however, retains some attraction for me.

I have discussed two types of *de re* representation for abstract *res*. The key idea for both canonical concepts for representational content and canonical concepts for natural numbers is an un-Kantian one. The idea is that individual concepts are among the effectors of *de re* attitudes.[9] The epistemic immediacy that is a hallmark of *de re* reference need not require context dependence, much less perceiving the *re*.

None of the relevant individual concepts are *descriptive*. That-clauses do not describe the representational contents that they specify. Numerals do not describe numbers. Certainly, the non-complex numerals ($\underline{1}$, $\underline{2}$ ... $\underline{9}$) do not. Both of these types of *de re* representation are associated with special immediate, non-descriptive powers—understanding and immediate perceptual applicability.

---

[9] Kant thought that basic (in effect, *de re*) singular representation is effected only by a nonconceptual capacity, intuition. The present view allows basic, *de re*, singular representation to be effected by individual concepts, as long as these concepts are associated with some further appropriate relation to the *re* beyond merely conceiving it. Kant did not discuss canonical that-clause representation of representational contents (backed by understanding the *re*, the represented contents). Perhaps he would have rejected the idea that such contents are *res*. Kant does discuss basic representation of numbers. He sees such representation as derivatively *de re*, but grounded in *de re* representation of time through a nonconceptual capacity—pure sensible intuition. My view is un-Kantian in that the semantics of *de re* singular reference in pure arithmetic is purely conceptual—through individual concepts for the natural numbers. I am inclined to believe that the individual concepts for the numbers are primitively singular. They are not covertly attributive. Kant rejected the very notion of individual concepts. Cf. Charles Parsons, 'The Transcendental Aesthetic', in Paul Guyer (ed.), *The Cambridge Companion to Kant*, (Cambridge: Cambridge University Press, 1992), esp. 63–66, 82. Cf. also my 'Frege on Apriority', in P. Boghossian and C. Peacocke (eds.), *New Essays on the Apriori* (Oxford: Oxford University Press, 2000), repr. in my *Truth, Thought, Reason*, esp. sec. V.

Nevertheless, there is in my position an echo of Kant's view that *de re* conception of the numbers must be 'grounded' in some capacity that goes beyond merely conceiving of them. *De re* representation of the numbers is essentially associated with non-inferential counting, for example through perception. Moreover, as the discussion of sec. II of 'Belief *De Re*' in sec. IV of this Postscript indicates, I believe that all representation requires, as an enabling condition, a capacity for a subset of *de re* representation—*de re* representation that effects a nonconceptual application of representation to subject matter. This is a Kantian thesis, and may capture some of what Kant wanted in his requirement that all representation of objects be grounded in a nonconceptual capacity—intuition.

These powers are not completely conceptual, in that they involve a relation to the *re* that goes beyond its *merely* being conceived.

To review: the second epistemic account of *de re* attitudes in 'Belief *De Re*' takes *de re* representation to be referentially successful representation that involves an appropriate 'not completely conceptual' relation to a *re*. As I have elaborated this account, it grants that in canonical specifications of representational content or the natural numbers, the representational contents themselves are completely conceptualized. The representational contents are supplemented by a not completely conceptual relation to the *re*. The epistemic relation to the canonically named representational contents through understanding the contents is one such relation: We understand the referent as well as conceive of it. Perceptually immediate applicability of the smaller natural numbers is another: We apply the individual concept for the *re* immediately in perception, as well as merely conceive of the *re*. All types of *de re* representation on this conception are marked by a direct, epistemically basic relation to the *re* that goes beyond merely conceiving of it.

III

I want now to discuss one matter that is somewhat obscured in the semi-technical presentation in 'Belief *De Re*'. This matter is crucial for understanding the paradigm cases of *de re* belief. The paradigm cases are those that have a demonstrative or indexical element in the representational thought content. I want to discuss the nature of the relevant representational contents. What is it for a propositional representational content to be incompletely conceptualized?

I have heard interpretations of the paper according to which there is a 'hole' in the representational aspects of the proposition, where the hole corresponds to the object (which completes the proposition). I regard these interpretations as rather silly. But my exposition is partly at fault. In the formalizations of the representational contents of the relevant *de re* beliefs, I formalized the demonstrative or indexical elements as free variables. This formalization may have made it puzzling how the representational contents could in themselves have a truth-value. For open sentences are true of or false of objects, but they are not strictly true or false. One might think that one needs the objects themselves to fill out what is thought in such a way as to make the thought true or false. I did associate the *de re* representational contents with objects, the *re*. I clearly indicated, however, that I was *not* thinking of the contents as having objects 'in the proposition', in what is thought, *à la* Russell. The contents are representational contents through and through. The propositional attitudes are incompletely conceptualized, but they indicate individuals in a way that makes *them* and their representational contents true or false—not just true-of or false-of objects.

Certainly I was thinking too much in terms of formalization and not enough in psychological terms. I expected the talk of free variables to be more informative than it was. Let me say a bit more about free variables. Open sentences are, of course, in themselves neither true nor false. But open sentences can be used or interpreted in such a way as to take on truth or falsity. There are two ways in which they can be thus used or interpreted. One is equivalent to universal quantification on the variable. The other occurs in interpretations of open sentences to form a particular model, assigning particular objects in a domain of discourse to the free variables. I was thinking of this second use.

My idea was that in actual *de re* beliefs the free variables, the formal counterparts of demonstratives and indexicals, are contextually applied, or 'assigned', to an object by the believer. The application or assigning is part of the full representational thought content. The demonstrative or indexical as a *type* cannot fix a referent. It needs an application. Applications are individuated in terms of token acts or events. Ordinary attributions of *de re* beliefs do not specifically refer to such applications, but they presume that they are there.

This idea guides the discussion of deictic *uses* of demonstratives in sections I and II and the discussion of free variables as representing *applied* demonstratives (or indexicals) in the fourth to last paragraph of the paper. I wrote, 'The free variables do no more than indicate the not purely conceptual character of these means of identification and mark differences in the contexts in which they are applied.' Thus, in addition to the demonstrative or indexical *type*, marked by the free variable type, there is an application of the demonstrative analog, or indexical analog, in the believer's thought. Applications are individuated in terms of actual occurrent mental events or acts. Applications are the non-conceptual elements in the propositional representational contents of the relevant *de re* attitudes. These points are developed in greater detail in other papers.[10]

Beliefs are true or false, not merely neutrally true of some objects and false of others. The aspect of a belief that is true or false is its representational content. For a representational content that contains analogs of demonstratives or indexicals to be true or false, the analogs must be applied in a context. So in understanding the relevant representational contents, one must consider the demonstrative or indexical type *and* its contextual application. These two must be distinguished from one another and from any attributive (the 'F' in 'that F') that modifies the demonstrative or indexical and that guides its application.

---

[10] Aspects of applications (and my use of free variables) are also discussed in 'Reference and Proper Names', *The Journal of Philosophy*, 70 (1973), 425–439; 'Demonstrative Constructions, Reference, and Truth', *The Journal of Philosophy*, 71 (1974), 205–223; 'Kaplan, Quine, and Suspended Belief', *Philosophical Studies*, 31 (1977), 197–203 (Ch. 2 in this volume); 'Russell's Problem and Intentional Identity'; 'Vision and Intentional Content', in E. Lepore and R. Van Gulick (eds.), *John Searle and his Critics* (Oxford: Basil Blackwell, 1991); and 'Five Theses on *De Re* States and Attitudes'. The notion of application in 'Belief *De Re*' is the psychological analog of the notion of a linguistic act of reference discussed in the first two articles cited above. Through reflection on perception, I have come to believe that not all applications are acts. But all are individuated in terms of occurrences, some of which are acts.

A second general consideration supports recognition of applications. Inso-far as the beliefs single out a *re*, there must be a singular element in the representational content that does the job. Individuals cannot think (or perceive) objects neat. They must think of them from a perspective — 'intentionally' or representationally. General arguments, discussed in the last section of 'Belief *De Re*', show that individuals cannot always single out objects in context-free ways. So they must do so in context-dependent ways. Context-dependent *types* of reference or representation cannot do the job by themselves. Demonstratives, indexicals, and their analogs as *types* single out no objects at all. The types must be associated with some instantiation, occurrence, or act, in a context, to suc-ceed in representing a *re*. So a full account of the representational content of the relevant thoughts must make a place for the mental instantiations, occurrences, or acts that point context-dependent types, or context-dependent mental abilit-ies, to particular *res*. These occurrences or acts are part of the representational content that is evaluated for successful or unsuccessful reference, for truth or falsity. A fundamental idea of the article is that representational contents include occurrent applications.

IV

Section II of 'Belief *De Re*' contains three general arguments, or argument sketches, that are meant to make plausible a necessary and central role for *de re* attitudes in thought and language. I see these arguments as prefiguring anti-individualism. I think of the second of them as the most broadly interesting feature of the paper.

The argument that *de re* attitudes are necessary for learning language is an adaptation of Quine's point that learning language depends on learning occasion sentences. Occasion sentences are roughly context-dependent sentences, whose truth- and assertability-values vary over relatively short periods of time.[11] I reasoned that such sentences' meaning has to be associated with some true perceptual beliefs about the immediate surroundings, and that perceptual beliefs are, and must be, *de re*. This little argument still seems to me sound.

The second argument, really an argument sketch, is for the conclusion that *de re* attitudes are necessary for having any propositional attitudes at all. This argu-ment is much more ambitious than the first.[12] The idea of the argument is that to

---

[11] W. V. Quine, *Word and Object* (Cambridge, Mass.: MIT Press, 1960), chs. 1 and 2. P. F. Strawson made a similar point earlier in 'Singular Terms, Ontology and Identity', *Mind*, 65 (1956), 433–454; but I believe that I first got the point from Quine.

[12] I want to criticize in this note some of the formulations in the argument sketch in 'Belief *De Re*'. Initially I argue in terms of whether we would *attribute* propositional attitudes under this or that condition. I also discuss *evidence* or *indication* of an ability needed to attribute attitudes. Attribution and evidence are not the heart of the matter. I think I knew better at the time, and the later formulations in the same argument tend to drop these elements. I lapsed into evidential ways of

have attitudes with definite content, an individual must have some supplementary capacity, beyond that of a general conceptual ability to think about the subject matter, to connect the contents to what they are about. The ability can be causal-perceptual or causal-practical. For a robot to have (autonomous) propositional content, it would have to have either perceptual abilities, or practical abilities to do something for itself. (I think that both are required.) Such abilities would entail having *de re* attitudes. So a condition on having attitudes in pure mathematics is an ability to apply it, or at any rate to be able to apply other attitudes in perceptual or practical *de re* ways.

The argument does not specifically require that the capacities to connect contents to what they are about be empirical capacities. The obvious cases—perceptual abilities and abilities to act in the empirical world—are certainly empirical. I left open whether there are non-empirical capacities—for example, in the exercise of memory of one's own thoughts—that determine a thought/subject-matter relation. Since we lack Platonic vision of mathematical or other abstract entities, pure mathematics almost surely requires supplemental singular abilities if it is to have genuine, autonomous, representational content.

Both pure arithmetic and canonical (that-clause-like) specifications of representational content are plausibly second-order enterprises. They hinge on relations to first-order representations. *De re* relations to the numbers hinge on further *de re* relations to objects that one counts with the numbers. The perception-based counting is a necessary condition for both the *de re* relations to the numbers and the comprehension of pure mathematics. *De re* relations to representational contents through that-clause-like specifications hinge on comprehending the representational contents thus specified. Such comprehension depends on further *de re* relations to *res* at the first-order level. So having *de re* attitudes at the first-order level, presumably involving demonstrative or indexical applications, is necessary for having any conceptual content at all. These first-order content-giving abilities involve the 'appropriate not completely conceptual relations to a *re*' that are the mark of *de re* attitudes. As I have intimated, I am inclined to believe that the relevant first-order abilities are marked by representational content that is not completely conceptualized. So I think that the subset of *de re* capacities that are characterized by the first epistemic account of the *de re/de dicto* distinction underlie and make possible the larger set of *de re* capacities characterized by the second epistemic account.

discussing the matter because they were concrete, and probably because straight out 'transcendental' arguments for conditions on the possibility of having some capacity were at the time foreign. These formulations suggest some sort of verificationism that I certainly never held. I believe that it is fairly easy to reformulate what I wrote in such a way as to avoid these formulations. Some of the formulations in the article in terms of abilities an individual must have in order to have propositional attitudes already did so. The argument also waivers between talking purely about propositional attitudes and talking about language use, perhaps in thought. Here is another area where I would make a sharper distinction between discussions of language and discussion of mind—if only to make clear that the argument applies to beings that have propositional attitudes but lack language.

I do not regard the main idea of this argument as self-evident. The main idea is that 'correlational' abilities are a necessary condition on having states or attitudes with propositional representational content. Propositional representational content necessarily includes conceptual content. Concepts are just the standing or ability-general elements in propositional contents. To have states or attitudes with propositional or conceptual content, an individual must have a capacity that supplements mere conceiving of a subject matter. The supplementary capacity must connect at least some concepts—that mark general abilities—to a subject matter by some further occurrent, non-conceptual, non-attributional representational means.[13] It does so through non-attributional applications. Aboutness is fundamentally and constitutively dependent on such 'correlational' connections in use. I think it plausible that the connection must be through action or perception. Although I do not find this idea self-evident, I think it powerful, plausible, unifying, and foundational. I continue to think it a good and fruitful one.

This argument and its key idea provided a framework for anti-individualism. The idea, again, is that successful correlational, nonconceptual, representational abilities must support conceptual abilities. This idea is a short step from the idea that non-representational relations must support representational abilities. For the key nonconceptual abilities, the events or acts of application, depend on context and on causal relations to their objects of reference for their success in representation. Thus the key idea of a dependence of representation on non-representational relations to a wider reality is implicit in the main argument of 'Belief *De Re*'.

A further key idea of anti-individualism is, however, still missing. This is the idea that the *specific* conceptual aspects of propositional attitudes (and specific attributional aspects of perceptual and other lower-level representational states) depend on non-representational relations to *specific* aspects of the wider reality. The specific conceptual contents of an individual's attitudes partly depend, in complex ways, on specific features of that reality.

The third, and last, argument in section II of 'Belief *De Re*' is that having justified (warranted) empirical beliefs, hence having knowledge, requires having *de re* beliefs. Although it is a near corollary of the main argument (the second argument), it can stand on its own. The hard cases for the main argument are non-empirical attitudes. Apart from these cases, the main argument would be relatively uncontroversial. The addition of the idea of justification or warrant seems to me also relatively uncontroversial: Warrant attaches to states or capacities. Empirical warrant derives from perceptual or other sensory-based

---

[13] I now think that the argument generalizes further. A condition on having any representational content at all, perceptual or conceptual, is that one have *de re* perceptual or conceptual states. This point can be made with slightly finer grain. I believe that there are perceptual as well as conceptual attributives. (Cf. 'Five Theses on *De Re* States and Attitudes'.) To have states with attributive representational contents, one must have states that include *de re* applicational contents.

beliefs. Since such beliefs are clearly *de re*, the corollary really should not be controversial, or specially interesting.

V

I will say only little about the remaining elements of the paper. I remain opposed to reducing *de re* to *de dicto*, of course. Thus I resist reducing the epistemology of propositional attitudes to the epistemology of conceptualization. As I pointed out, this resistance is closely associated with the deep changes in our understanding of linguistic reference brought about by Kripke, Putnam, and Donnellan. But it also has a history in the more epistemically oriented conceptions of Russell and Kant.

I have elaborated the discussion of Frege elsewhere.[14] I continue to believe in the distinction among three theoretical functions for his conception of *sense*.

One idea in this discussion seems to me undeveloped, but still worthy of development. It is an idea about the relation between what is normally attributed in the language, even in uses of ordinary language geared to describing propositional attitudes, and what the actual representational contents of an individual's attitudes are. I distinguished $sense_3$—what is attributed in oblique or non-extensional occurrences in attributions of propositional attitudes—from $sense_1$—the way of thinking or cognitive value that a thinker associates with an expression. I suggested that $sense_3$ is coarser-grained than $sense_1$. That is, what is attributed will often be less specific or fine-grained than the actual way of thinking engaged in by the individual thinker to whom the attitude is attributed. This is so *even for correct oblique occurrences in propositional attitude attribution whose purpose is to describe propositional attitudes as fully as ordinary communicational conditions will allow*. What is easily and conventionally attributable as a way of thinking may be unexceptionable as far as it goes. Yet it may fall short of capturing the individual's way of thinking. It may be something common to a class of ways of thinking, which nevertheless is different from another class of ways of thinking about the same object, property, or relation.

The discussion of this issue in 'Belief *De Re*' centers mostly on proper names. I find this discussion on the right track, but rather inconclusive. The simple point is that the attribution of names in propositional attitudes can be expected sometimes to do more than name the bearer. It may attribute to the individual a way of thinking that involves the name. Although the individual's way of thinking may involve the same name (or a contextually appropriate translation of the name) together with some mental file for the name, the public attribution may fail to convey essential specific aspects in the file. Those are often matters that are not easily publicly accessible, or of any special public

---

[14] Cf. the Introduction to *Truth, Thought, Reason*, 29–59. This passage in the last section of 'Belief *De Re*' was my first published interpretative work on Frege.

use. Still, they may be basic to the representational content of the individual's psychology. Scientific attributions may have to be more specific than anything natural language bothers with, if the attributions are to correctly type-identify the individual psychological states, for explanatory purposes.

The point applies more obviously to predicational elements. Suppose that I correctly attribute to Al the occurrent perceptual belief that that square block is blue. Al's way of thinking about squareness incorporates a specific perceptual angle on the squareness, representing it from one of many possible perceptual angles in one of many possible perceptual ways. There is no attempt to express or capture the specific way that Al thinks about squareness (or blueness, or blockness). The attribution may, however, be intended to convey that Al's representational belief content contains a representational content that *entails* that it applies to squareness if to anything. It is understood that Al somehow thinks of something *as square*. Thus the attribution may be intended to be more specific about how Al thought about the block than an attribution of the form: Al believes that that block with the property that Uncle Harry liked most is blue—even assuming that being square *is* the property that Uncle Harry liked most. Thus the ascription is intended not to allow free exchange of coextensional expressions; but it is not intended to specify exactly how Al thought (sense$_1$). It is intended to narrow down Al's way of thinking to a class of concepts of squareness as squareness. I believe that such usage is one standard usage in attributions of propositional attitudes.

I believe that the view of 'meaning' as having a number of different types—sense$_1$, sense$_3$, conventional linguistic meaning—remains attractive. I think that if it were more widely adopted, some of the impasses and ruts that have marked disputes over what is in semantics and what is not would be avoided.

What chiefly interests me is the representational content that corresponds to sense$_1$. This notion derives from Frege. Frege's insight into the structure and general character of thought was profound. But he provided relatively little insight into *de re* phenomena. Russell's general epistemology in terms of infallible and perspective-free acquaintance is, I think, hopeless. Kant's specific account of the epistemology of arithmetic in terms of pure sensible intuition is implausible. But their fascination with *de re* phenomena showed an instinct for an element in mental representation, and the epistemic roots of knowledge and understanding, that is of enduring importance.

4 *Other Bodies*

It is fairly uncontroversial, I think, that we can conceive a person's behavior and behavioral dispositions, his physical acts and states, his qualitative feels and fields (all non-intentionally described) as remaining fixed, while his mental attitudes of a certain kind—his *de re* attitudes—vary.[1] Thus we can imagine Alfred's believing of apple 1 that it is wholesome, and holding a true belief. Without altering Alfred's dispositions, subjective experiences, and so forth, we can imagine having substituted an identically appearing but internally rotten apple 2. In such a case, Alfred's belief differs, while his behavioral dispositions, inner causal states, and qualitative experiences remain constant.

This sort of point is important for understanding mentalistic notions and their role in our cognitive lives. But, taken by itself, it tells us nothing very interesting about mental states. For it is easy (and I think appropriate) to phrase the point so as to strip it of immediate philosophical excitement. We may say that Alfred has the *same* belief content in both situations.[2] It is just that he

---

[1] It is difficult to avoid at least a limited amount of philosophical jargon in discussing this subject. Since much of this jargon is subjected to a variety of uses and abuses, I will try to give brief explications of the most important special terms as they arise. An ordinary-language discourse is *intentional* if it contains *oblique* occurrences of expressions. (Traditionally, the term 'intentional' is limited to mentalistic discourse containing obliquely occurring expressions, but we can ignore this fine point.) An *oblique* (sometimes 'indirect' and, less appropriately, 'opaque' or 'non-transparent') occurrence of an expression is one on which *either* substitution of coextensive expressions may affect the truth-value of the whole containing sentence, *or* existential generalization is not a straightforwardly valid transformation. For example, 'Al believes that many masts are made of aluminum' is intentional discourse (as we are reading the sentence) because 'aluminum' occurs obliquely. If one substituted 'the thirteenth element in the periodic table' for 'aluminum' one might alter the truth-value of the containing sentence.

The characterization of *de re attitudes* (sometimes 'relational attitudes') is at bottom a complex and controversial matter. For a detailed discussion, see my "Belief *De Re*" (Ch. 3 above), esp. sec. I. For present purposes, we shall say that *de re* attitudes are those where the subject or person is unavoidably characterized as being in a not-purely-conceptual, contextual relation to an object (*re*), *of* which he holds his attitude. Typically, though not always, a term or quantified pronoun in non-oblique position will denote the object, and the person having the attitude will be said to believe (think, etc.) that object to be φ (where 'φ' stands for oblique occurrences of predicative expressions). *De re* attitudes may equivalently, and equally well, be characterized as those whose content involves an ineliminable indexical element which is applied to some entity. *De dicto* attitudes (sometimes 'notional attitudes') are those that are not *de re*.

[2] An attitude *content* is the semantic value associated with oblique occurrences of expressions in attributions of propositional attitudes. Actually, there may be more to the content than what is

would be making contextually different applications of that content to different entities. His belief is true of apple 1 and false of apple 2. The *nature* of his mental state is the same. He simply bears different relations to his environment. We do say in ordinary language that one belief is true and the other is false. But this is just another way of saying that what he believes is true of the first apple and would be false of the second. We may call these relational beliefs different beliefs if we want. But differences among such relational beliefs do not entail differences among mental states or contents, as these have traditionally been viewed.

This deflationary interpretation seems to me to be correct. But it suggests an oversimplified picture of the relation between a person's mental states or events and public or external objects and events. It suggests that it is possible to separate rather neatly what aspects of propositional attitudes depend on the person holding the attitudes and what aspects derive from matters external. There is no difference in the obliquely occurring expressions in the content clauses we attribute to Alfred. It is these sorts of expressions that carry the load in characterizing the individual's mental states and processes. So it might be thought that we could explicate such states and processes by training our philosophical attention purely on the individual subject, explicating the differences in the physical objects that his content applies to in terms of facts about his environment.

To present the view from a different angle: *de re* belief attributions are fundamentally predicational. They consist in applying or relating an incompletely interpreted content clause, an open sentence, to an object or sequence of objects, which in effect completes the interpretation. What objects these open sentences apply to may vary with context. But, according to the picture, it remains possible to divide off contextual or environmental elements represented in the propositional attitude attributions from more specifically mentalistic elements. Only the constant features of the predication represent the latter. And the specifically mental features of the propositional attitude can, according to this picture, be understood purely in *individualistic* terms—in terms of the subject's internal acts and skills, his internal causal and functional relations, his surface stimulations, his behavior and behavioral dispositions, and his qualitative experiences, all non-intentionally characterized and specified without regard to the nature of his social or physical environment.

The aim of this paper is to bring out part of what is wrong with this picture and to make some suggestions about the complex relation between a person's mental states and his environment. Through a discussion of certain elements of Putnam's twin-earth examples, I shall try to characterize ways in which identifying a

---

attributed, but I shall be ignoring this point in order not to complicate the discussion unduly. Thus the content is, roughly speaking, the conceptual aspect of what a person believes or thinks. If we exclude the *res* in *de re* attitudes, we may say that the content is what a person believes (thinks, etc.) in *de re* or *de dicto* attitudes. We remain neutral here about what, ontologically speaking, contents are.

person's mental states depends on the nature of his physical environment—or on specification, by his fellows, of the nature of that environment.[3]

Before entering into the details of Putnam's thought experiment, I want to sketch the general position that I shall be defending. What is right and what is wrong in the viewpoint I set out in the third and fourth paragraphs of this paper? I have already given some indication of what seems right: individual entities referred to by transparently occurring expressions, and, more generally, entities (however referred to or characterized) *of* which a person holds his beliefs do not in general play a direct role in characterizing the nature of the person's mental state or event. The difference between apples 1 and 2 does not bear on Alfred's mind in any sense that would immediately affect explanation of Alfred's behavior or assessment of the rationality of his mental activity. Identities of and differences among physical objects are crucial to these enterprises only insofar as those identities and differences affect Alfred's way of viewing such objects.[4] Moreover, it seems unexceptionable to claim that the obliquely occurring expressions in propositional attitude attributions are critical for characterizing a given person's mental state. Such occurrences are the stuff of which explanations of his actions and assessments of his rationality are made.

What I reject is the view that mental states and processes individuated by such obliquely occurring expressions can be understood (or "accounted for") purely in terms of non-intentional characterizations of the *individual subject's* acts, skills, dispositions, physical states, "functional states", and the effects of environmental stimuli on him, without regard to the nature of his physical environment or the activities of his fellows.[5]

In 'Individualism and the Mental' (Chapter 5 below) I presented a thought experiment in which one fixed non-intentional, individualistic descriptions of the physical, behavioral, phenomenalistic, and (on most formulations) functional histories of an individual. By varying the *uses of words* in his linguistic community, I found that the contents of his propositional attitudes varied.[6] I shall draw a parallel conclusion from Putnam's twin-earth thought experiment: We can fix an individual's physical, behavioral, phenomenalistic, and (on some formulations) functional histories; by varying the *physical environment*, one finds that

---

[3] Hilary Putnam, "The Meaning of 'Meaning,' " repr. in *Philosophical Papers*, in (Cambridge: Cambridge University Press, 1975), to which page numbers refer.

[4] This point is entirely analogous to the familiar point that *knowing* is not a mental state. For knowledge depends not only on one's mental state, but on whether its content is true. The point above about indexicals and mental states is the analog for predication of this traditional point about the relation between the mind and (complete) propositions. Neither the truth or falsity of a content nor the 'truth-of-ness' or 'false-of-ness' of a content, nor the entities a content is true of, enters directly into the individuation of a mental state. For more discussion of these points, see Burge, sec. IId.

[5] This rejection is logically independent of rejecting the view that the intentional can be accounted for in terms of the non-intentional. I reject this view also. But here is not the place to discuss it.

[6] Much of the present paper constitutes an elaboration of remarks in 'Individualism and the Mental', note 2.

the contents of his propositional attitudes vary. It is to be re-emphasized that the variations in propositional attitudes envisaged are not exhausted by variations in the entities to which individuals' mental contents are related. The contents themselves vary. At any rate, I shall so argue.

I

In Putnam's thought experiment, we are to conceive of a near duplicate of our planet Earth, called 'Twin-Earth'. Except for certain features about to be noted (and necessary consequences of these features), Twin-Earth duplicates Earth in every detail. The physical environments look and largely are the same. Many of the inhabitants of one planet have duplicate counterparts on the other, with duplicate macro-physical, experiential, and dispositional histories.

One key difference between the two planets is that the liquid on Twin-Earth that runs in rivers and faucets, and is called 'water' by those who speak what is called 'English' is not H_2O, but a different liquid with a radically different chemical formula, XYZ. I think it natural and obviously correct to say, with Putnam, that the stuff that runs in rivers and faucets on Twin-Earth is thus not water. I shall not argue for this view, because it is pretty obvious, pretty widely shared, and stronger than arguments that might be or have been brought to buttress it. I will just assume that XYZ is not water of any sort. Water is H_2O. What the Twin-Earthians call 'water' is XYZ. In translating into English occurrences of 'water' in the mouths of Twin-Earthians, we would do best to coin a new non-scientific word (say, 'twater'), explicated as applying to stuff that looks and tastes like water, but with a fundamentally different chemistry.

It is worth bearing in mind that the thought experiment might apply to any relatively non-theoretical natural kind word. One need not choose an expression as central to our everyday lives as 'water' is. For example, we could (as Putnam in effect suggests) imagine the relevant difference between Earth and Twin-Earth to involve the application of 'aluminum' or 'elm', or 'mackerel'.[7]

A second key difference between Earth and Twin-Earth—as we shall discuss the case—is that the scientific community on Earth has determined that the chemical structure of water is H_2O, whereas the scientific community on Twin-Earth knows that the structure of twater is XYZ. These pieces of knowledge have spread into the respective lay communities, but have not saturated them. In particular, there are numerous scattered individuals on Earth and Twin-Earth untouched by the scientific developments. It is these latter individuals who have duplicate counterparts.

---

[7] Anyone who wishes to resist our conclusions merely by claiming that XYZ is water will have to make parallel claims for aluminum, helium, and so forth. Such claims, I think, would be completely implausible.

We now suppose that Adam is an English speaker and that Adam $_{te}$ is his counterpart on Twin-Earth. Neither knows the chemical properties of what he calls 'water'. This gap in their knowledge is probably not atypical of uneducated members of their communities.[8] But similar gaps are clearly to be expected of users of terms like 'aluminum', 'elm', 'mackerel'. (Perhaps not in the case of water, but in the other cases, we could even imagine that Adam and Adam $_{te}$ have no clear idea of what the relevant entities in their respective environments look like or how they feel, smell, or taste.) We further suppose that both have the same qualitative perceptual intake and qualitative streams of consciousness, the same movements, the same behavioral dispositions and inner functional states (non-intentionally and individualistically described). Insofar as they do not ingest, say, aluminum or its counterpart, we might even fix their physical states as identical.

When Adam says or consciously thinks the words, 'There is some water within twenty miles, I hope,' Adam $_{te}$ says or consciously thinks the same word forms. But there are differences. As Putnam in effect points out, Adam's occurrences of 'water' apply to water and mean *water*, whereas Adam $_{te}$'s apply to twater and mean *twater*. And, as Putnam does not note, the differences affect *oblique* occurrences in 'that'-clauses that provide the contents of their mental states and events. Adam hopes that there is some water (oblique occurrence) within twenty miles. Adam $_{te}$ hopes that there is some twater within twenty miles. That is, even as we suppose that 'water' and 'twater' are not logically exchangeable with coextensive expressions *salva veritate*, we have a difference between their thoughts (thought contents).

Laying aside the indexical implicit in 'within twenty miles', the propositional attitudes involved are not even *de re*. But I need not argue this point. Someone might wish to claim that these are *de re* attitudes about the relevant *properties* —of water (being water? waterhood?) in one case and of twater (etc.) in the other. I need not dispute this claim here. It is enough to note that even if the relevant sentences relate Adam and his counterpart to *res*, those sentences also specify *how* Adam and Adam $_{te}$ think about the *res*. In the sentence applied to Adam, 'water' is, by hypothesis, not exchangeable with coextensive expressions. It is not exchangeable with 'H_2O', or with 'liquid which covers two-thirds of the face of the earth', or with 'liquid said by the Bible to flow from a rock when Moses struck it with a rod'. 'Water' occurs obliquely in the relevant attribution. And it is expressions in oblique occurrence that play the role of specifying a person's mental contents, what his thoughts are.

---

[8] I am omitting a significant extension of Putnam's ideas. Putnam considers "rolling back the clock" to a time when everyone in each community would be as ignorant of the structure of water and twater as Adam and Adam $_{te}$ are now. I omit this element from the thought experiment, partly because arriving at a reasonable interpretation of this case is more complicated and partly because it is not necessary for my primary purposes. Thus, as far as we are concerned, one is free to see differences in Adam's and Adam $_{te}$'s mental states as deriving necessarily from differences in the actions and attitudes of other members in their respective communities.

In sum, mental states and events like beliefs and thoughts are individuated partly by reference to the constant, or obliquely occurring, elements in content clauses. But the contents of Adam's and Adam $_{te}$'s beliefs and thoughts differ while every feature of their non-intentionally and individualistically described physical, behavioral, dispositional, and phenomenal histories remains the same. Exact identity of physical states is implausible in the case of water. But this point is irrelevant to the force of the example—and could be circumvented by using a word, such as 'aluminum', 'elm', etc., that does not apply to something Adam ingests. The difference in their mental states and events seems to be a product primarily of differences in their physical environments, mediated by differences in their social environments—in the mental states of their fellows and conventional meanings of words they and their fellows employ.

II

The preceding argument and its conclusion are not to be found in Putnam's paper. Indeed, the conclusion appears to be incompatible with some of what he says. For example, Putnam interprets the difference between earth and twin-earth uses of 'water' purely as a difference in extension. And he states that the relevant Earthian and Twin-Earthian are 'exact duplicates in ... feelings, thoughts, interior monologue etc.'[a] On our version of the argument, the two are in no sense exact duplicates in their thoughts. The differences show up in oblique occurrences in true attributions of propositional attitudes. I shall not speculate about why Putnam did not draw a conclusion so close to the source of his main argument. Instead, I will criticize aspects of his discussion that tend to obscure the conclusion (and have certainly done so for others).

Chief among these aspects is the claim that natural kind words like 'water' are indexical (pp. 229–235). This view tends to suggest that earth and twin-earth occurrences of 'water' can be assimilated simply to occurrences of indexical expressions like 'this' or 'I'. Adam's and Adam $_{te}$'s propositional attitudes would then be further examples of the kind of *de re* attitudes mentioned at the outset of this paper. Their contents would be the same, but would be applied to different *res*.[9] If this were so, it might appear that there would remain a convenient and natural means of segregating those features of propositional attitudes

[a] Putnam, "The Meaning of 'Meaning' ", in *Philosophical Papers*, ii. 224. Subsequent page numbers of this article are given parenthetically in the text.

[9] This view and the one described in the following sentence were anticipated and "Individualism and the Mental", criticized in Burge, sec. IId and note 2. Both views have been adopted by Jerry Fodor 'Methodological Solipsism Considered as a Research strategy in Cognitive Psychology, *The Behavioral and Brain Sciences*, 3 (1980) 63–73. I believe that these views have been informally held by various others. Colin McGinn, ("Charity, interpretation and Belief", *The Journal of Philosophy*, 74 (1977), 521–535), criticizes Putnam (correctly, I think) for not extending his theses about meaning to propositional attitudes. But McGinn's argument is limited to claiming that the *res* in relational propositional attitudes differ between Earth and Twin-Earth and that these *res* enter into individuating

that derive from the nature of a person's social and physical context, on one hand, from those features that derive from the organism's nature, and palpable effects of the environment on it, on the other. The trouble is that there is no appropriate sense in which natural kind terms like 'water' are indexical.

Putnam gives the customary explication of the notion of indexicality: 'Words like "now", "this" "here", have long been recognized to be *indexical* or *token-reflexive*—i.e. to have an extension which varies from context to context or token to token' (pp. 233–234). I think that it is clear that 'water', *interpreted as it is in English*, or as we English speakers standardly interpret it, does not shift extension from context to context in this way. (One must, of course, hold the language, or linguistic construal, fixed. Otherwise, every word will trivially count as indexical. For by the very conventionality of language, we can always imagine some context in which our word—word form—has a different extension.) The extension of 'water', as interpreted in English in all non-oblique contexts, is (roughly) the set of all aggregates of H_2O molecules, together, probably, with the individual molecules. There is nothing at all indexical about 'water' in the customary sense of 'indexical'.

Putnam suggests several grounds for calling natural kind words indexical. I shall not try to criticize all of these, but will deal with a sampling:

(a) Now then, we have maintained that indexicality extends beyond the *obviously* indexical words ... Our theory can be summarized as saying that words like 'water' have an unnoticed indexical component: 'water' is stuff that bears a certain similarity relation to the water *around here*. Water at another time or in another place or even in another possible world has to bear the relation [same-liquid] to *our* 'water' in order to be water. (p. 234)

(b) 'Water' is indexical. What do I mean by that? If it is indexical, if what I am saying is right, then 'water' means 'whatever is like water, bears some equivalence relation, say the liquid relation, to *our* water.' Where 'our' is, of course, an indexical word. If that's how the extension of 'water' is determined, then the environment determines the extension of 'water'. Whether 'our' water is in fact XYZ or H_2O.[10]

These remarks are hard to interpret with any exactness because of the prima facie circularity, or perhaps ellipticality, of the explications. Water around here, or our water, is just water. Nobody else's water, and no water anywhere else, is any different. Water is simply H_2O (give or take some isotopes and impurities). These points show the superfluousness of the indexical expressions. No shift of extension with shift in context needs to be provided for.

mental states. (The congeniality of this view with Putnam's claim that natural kind terms are indexical is explicitly noted.) Thus the argument supports only the position articulated in the first paragraph of this paper and is subject to the deflationary interpretation that followed (cf. also note 4). McGinn's argument neither explicitly accepts nor explicitly rejects the position subsequently adopted by Fodor and cited above.

[10] Putnam, (1974), 451. Cf. also "Language and Reality" in Philosophical Papers, ii. 277. 'Comment on Wilfrid Sellars', *Synthese*, 27.

Narrower consideration of these 'meaning explanations' of 'water' brings out the same point. One might extrapolate from (a) the notion that 'water' *means* (a′) 'stuff that bears the same-liquid relation to the stuff we call "water" around here'. But this cannot be right. (I pass over the fact that there is no reason to believe that the meaning of 'water' involves reference to the linguistic expression 'water'. Such reference could be eliminated.) For if Adam and his colleagues visited Twin-Earth and (still speaking English) called XYZ 'water', it would follow on this meaning explication that their uses of the sentence 'Water flows in that stream' would be true. They would make no mistake in speaking English and calling XYZ 'water'. For since the extension of 'here' would shift, occurrences on Twin-Earth of 'stuff that bears the same-liquid relation to the stuff we call "water" around here flows in that stream' would be true. But by Putnam's own account, which is clearly right on this point, there is no water on Twin-Earth. And there is no reason why an English speaker should not be held to this account when he visits Twin-Earth. The problem is that although 'here' shifts its extension with context, 'water' does not. 'Water' lacks the indexicality of 'here'.

A similar objection would apply to extrapolating from (b) the notion that 'water' means (b′) 'whatever bears the same-liquid relation to what we call "water" ', or (b″) 'whatever bears the same-liquid relation to this stuff'. 'Water' *interpreted as it is in English* does not shift its extension with shifts of speakers, as (b′) and (b″) do. The fact that the Twin-Earthians apply 'water' to XYZ is not a reflection of a shift in extension of an indexical expression with a fixed linguistic (English) meaning, but of a shift in meaning between one language, and linguistic community, and another. Any expression, indexical or not, can undergo such 'shifts', as a mere consequence of the conventionality of language. The relevant meaning equivalence to (b′) is no more plausible than saying that 'bachelor' is indexical because it means 'whatever social role the speaker applies "bachelor" to' where 'the speaker' is allowed to shift in its application to speakers of different linguistic communities according to context. If Indians applied 'bachelor' to all and only male senators, it would not follow that 'bachelor' as it is used in English is indexical. Similar points apply to (b″).

At best, the term 'water' and a given occurrence or token of (b′) or (a′), say an introducing token, have some sort of deep or necessary equivalence. But there is no reason to conclude that the indexicality of (a′), (b′) or (b″)—which is a feature governing *general use*, not particular occurrences—infects the meaning of the *expression* 'water', as it is used in English.

Much of what Putnam says suggests that the appeal to indexicality is supposed to serve other desiderata. One is a desire to defend a certain view of the role of the natural kind terms in talk about necessity. Roughly, the idea is that 'water' applies to water in all discourse about necessity. Putnam expresses this idea by calling natural kind terms rigid, and seems to equate indexicality and rigidity (p. 234). These points raise a morass of complex issues which I want to avoid getting into. It is enough here to point out that a term can be rigid without being indexical. Structural descriptive syntactical names are examples. Denying that natural kind terms are indexical is fully compatible with holding that they play any given role in discourse about necessity.

Another purpose that the appeal to indexicality seems to serve is that of accounting for the way natural kind terms are introduced, or the way their reference is fixed (p. 234, and (b) above). It may well be that indexicals frequently play a part in the (reconstructed) introduction or reference-fixing of natural kind terms. But this clearly does not imply that the natural kind terms partake in the indexicality of their introducers or reference-fixers. With some stage setting, one could introduce natural kind terms, with all their putative modal properties, by using non-indexical terms. Thus a more general rational reconstruction of the introduction, reference-fixing, and modal behavior of natural kind terms is needed. The claim that natural kind terms are themselves indexical is neither a needed nor a plausible account of these matters.

It does seem to me that there is a grain of truth encased within the claim that natural kind terms are indexical. It is this. *De re* beliefs usually enter into the reference-fixing of natural kind terms. The application of such terms seems to be typically fixed partly by *de re* beliefs we have of particular individuals, or quantities of stuff, or physical magnitudes or properties—beliefs that establish a semantical relation between term and object. (Sometimes the *de re* beliefs are about evidence that the terms are introduced to explain.) Having such beliefs requires that one be in not-purely-context-free conceptual relations to the relevant entities.[b] That is, one must be in the sort of relation to the entities that someone who indexically refers to them would be. One can grant the role of such beliefs in establishing the application and function of natural kind terms, without granting that all beliefs and statements involving terms whose use is so established are indexical. There seems to be no justification for the latter view, and clear evidence against it.

I have belabored this criticism not because I think that the claim about indexicality is crucial to Putnam's primary aims in 'The Meaning of "Meaning"'. Rather, my purpose has been to clear an obstacle to properly evaluating the importance of the twin-earth example for a philosophical understanding of belief and thought. The difference between mistaking natural kind words for indexicals and not doing so—rather a small linguistic point in itself—has large implications for our understanding of mentalistic notions. Simply assimilating the twin-earth example to the example of indexical attitudes I gave at the outset trivializes its bearing on philosophical understanding of the mental. Seen aright, the example suggests a picture in which the individuation of a given individual's mental *contents* depends partly on the nature (or what his fellows think to be the nature) of entities about which he or his fellows have *de re* beliefs. The identity of one's mental contents, states, and events is not independent of the nature of one's physical and social environment.

---

[b] Cf. Burge, "Belief *De Re*" (Ch. 3 above).

To summarize my view: The differences between Earth and Twin-Earth will affect the attributions of propositional attitudes to inhabitants of the two planets, including Adam and Adam $_{te}$. The differences are not to be assimilated to differences in the extensions of indexical expressions with the same constant, linguistic meaning. For the relevant terms are not indexical. The differences, rather, involve the constant context-free interpretation of the terms. Propositional attitude attributions which put the terms in oblique occurrence will thus affect the content of the propositional attitudes. Since mental acts and states are individuated (partly) in terms of their contents, the differences between Earth and Twin-Earth include differences in the mental acts and states of their inhabitants.

III

Let us step back now and scrutinize Putnam's interpretation of his thought experiment in the light of the fact that natural kind terms are not indexical. Putnam's primary thesis is that a person's psychological states—in what Putnam calls the 'narrow sense' of this expression—do not 'fix' the extensions of the terms the person uses. A psychological state in the 'narrow sense' is said to be one which does not 'presuppose' the existence of any individual other than the person who is in that state (p. 220). The term 'presuppose' is, of course, notoriously open to a variety of uses. But Putnam's glosses seem to indicate that a person's being in a psychological state does not presuppose a proposition P, if it does not logically entail P.[11]

Now we are in a position to explore a first guess about what psychological states are such in the 'narrow sense'.[12] According to this interpretation, being in a psychological state in the narrow sense (at least as far as propositional attitudes are concerned) is to be in a state correctly ascribable in terms of a content clause which contains no expressions in a position (in the surface grammar) which admits of existential generalization, and which is not in any sense *de re*. *De dicto*, non-relational propositional attitudes would thus be psychological states in the narrow sense. They entail by existential generalization the

---

[11] In explaining the traditional assumption of 'methodological solipsism', Putnam writes: 'This assumption is the assumption that no psychological state, properly so-called, presupposes the existence of any individual other than the subject to whom that state is ascribed. (In fact, the assumption was that no psychological state presupposes the existence of the subject's *body* even: if P is a psychological state, properly so-called, then it must be *logically possible* for a "disembodied mind" to be in P.)' (p. 220, the second italics mine). He also gives examples of psychological states in the 'wide sense', and characterizes these as *entailing* the existence of other entities besides the subject of the state (p. 220). Although there is little reason to construe Putnam as identifying entailment and presupposition, these two passages taken together suggest that for his purposes, no difference between them is of great importance. I shall proceed on this assumption.

[12] This guess is Fodor's ("Methodological Solipsism"). As far as I can see, the interpretation is not excluded by anything Putnam says. It is encouraged by some of what he says—especially his remarks regarding indexicality and his theory about the normal form for specifying the meaning of 'water'.

existence of no entities other than the subject (and his thought contents). *De re* propositional attitudes—at least those *de re* propositional attitudes in which the subject is characterized as being in relation to some thing other than himself and his thought contents—appear to be psychological states in the 'wide sense'. Having *de re* attitudes of (*de*) objects other than oneself entails the existence of objects other than oneself.

Granted this provisional interpretation, the question arises whether Putnam's twin-earth examples show that a person's psychological states in the narrow sense fail to 'fix' the extensions of the terms he uses. It would seem that to show this, the examples would have to be interpreted in such a way that Adam and Adam $_{te}$ would have the same *de dicto* propositional attitudes while the extensions of their terms differed. This objective would suggest an even stronger interpretation of the thought experiment. Expressions in oblique position in true attributions of attitudes to Adam and Adam $_{te}$ would be held constant while the extensions of their terms varied. But neither of these interpretations is plausible.[13]

Let us see why. To begin with, it is clear that Adam and Adam $_{te}$ will (or might) have numerous propositional attitudes correctly attributable with the relevant natural kind terms in oblique position. The point of such attributions is to characterize a subject's mental states and events in such a way as to take into account the *way* he views or thinks about objects in his environment. We thus describe his perspective on his environment and utilize such descriptions in predicting, explaining, and assessing the rationality and the correctness or success of his mental processes and overt acts. These enterprises of explanation and assessment provide much of the point of attributing propositional attitudes. And the way a subject thinks about natural kinds of stuffs and things is, of course, as relevant to these enterprises as the way he thinks about anything else. Moreover, there is no intuitive reason to doubt that the relevant natural kind terms can express and characterize his way of thinking about the relevant stuffs and things—water, aluminum, elms, mackerel. The relevant subjects meet socially accepted standards for using the terms. At worst, they lack a specialist's knowledge about the structure of the stuffs and things to which their terms apply.

We now consider whether the same natural kind terms should occur obliquely in attributions of propositional attitudes to Adam and Adam $_{te}$. Let us assume, what seems obvious, that Adam has propositional attitudes correctly attributed in English with his own (English) natural kind terms in oblique position. He hopes that there is some water within twenty miles; he believes that sailboat masts are often made of aluminum, that elms are deciduous trees distinct from beeches, that shrimp are smaller than mackerel. Does Adam $_{te}$ have these same

---

[13] Jerry Fodor (ibid.) states that inhabitants of Twin-Earth harbor the thought that water is wet—even granted the assumption that there is no water on Twin-Earth and the assumption that their thought is not 'about' water (H_2O), but about XYZ. Fodor provides no defence at all for this implausible view.

attitudes, or at least attitudes with these same contents? As the case has been described, I think it intuitively obvious that he does not.

At least two broad types of consideration back the intuition. One is that it is hard to see how Adam $_{te}$ could have acquired thoughts involving the concept of water (aluminum, elm, mackerel).[14] There is no water on Twin-Earth, so he has never had any contact with water. Nor has he had contact with anyone else who has had contact with water. Further, no one on Twin-Earth so much as uses a word which means *water*. It is not just that water does not fall in the extension of any of the Twin-Earthians' terms. The point is that none of their terms even translates into our (non-indexical) word 'water'. No English $_{te}$-to-English dictionary would give 'water' as the entry for the Twin-Earthians' word. It would thus be a mystery how a Twin-Earthian could share any of Adam's attitudes that involve the notion of water. They have not had any of the normal means of acquiring the concept. The correct view is that they have acquired, by entirely normal means, a concept expressed in their language that bears some striking, superficial similarities to ours. But it is different. Many people in each community could articulate things about the respective concepts that would make the difference obvious.

There is a second consideration—one that concerns truth—that backs the intuition that Adam $_{te}$ lacks attitudes involving the notion of water (aluminum, elm, mackerel). There is no water on Twin-Earth. If Adam $_{te}$ expresses attitudes that involve the concept of water (as opposed to twater), a large number of his ordinary beliefs will be false—that *that* is water, that there is water within twenty miles, that chemists in his country know the structure of water, and so forth. But there seems no reason to count his beliefs false and Adam's beliefs true (or vice versa). Their beliefs were acquired and relate to their environments in exactly parallel and equally successful ways.

The differences between the attitudes of Adam and Adam $_{te}$ derive not from differences in truth-value, but from differences in their respective environments and social contexts. They give different sorts of entities as paradigm cases of instances of the term. Their uses of the term are embedded in different communal usages and scientific traditions that give the term different constant, conventional meanings, In normal contexts, they can explicate and use the term in ways that are informative and socially acceptable within their respective communities. In doing so, they express different notions and different thoughts with these words. Their thoughts and statements have different truth-conditions and are true of different sorts of entities.

Of course, Adam $_{te}$ believes of XYZ everything Adam believes of water—*if* we delete all belief attributions that involve 'water' and 'twater' in oblique position,

---

[14] More jargon. I shall use the terms '*concept*' and '*notion*' interchangeably to signify the semantical values of obliquely occurring parts of content clauses, parts that are not themselves sentential. Thus a concept is a non-propositional part of a content. The expressions 'concept' and 'notion' are, like 'content', intended to be ontologically neutral. Intuitively, a concept is a context-free way a person thinks about a stuff, a thing, or a group of things.

and assume that there are no relevant differences between uses of others among their natural kind terms. In a sense, they would explicate the terms in the same way. But this would show that they have the same concept only on the assumption that each must have *verbal means besides 'water'* of expressing his concept—means that suffice in every outlandish context to distinguish that concept from others. I see no reason to accept this assumption. Nor does it seem antecedently plausible.

So far I have argued that Adam and Adam $_{te}$ differ as regards the *contents* of their attitudes. This suffices to show that their mental states, ordinarily so-called, as well as the extensions of their terms differ. But the examples we used involved relational propositional attitudes: belief that *that* is water (twater), that some water (twater) is within twenty miles of *this place*, that chemists in *this country* know the structure of water (twater), and so on. Although these do not involve 'water' as an indexical expression and some are not even of (*de*) water (twater), they are, plausibly, propositional attitudes in the wide sense. Thus these examples do not strictly show that Adam and Adam $_{te}$ differ in their *de dicto* attitudes—attitudes in the narrow sense.

But other examples do. Adam might believe that some glasses somewhere sometime contain some water, or that some animals are smaller than all mackerel. Adam $_{te}$ lacks these beliefs. Yet these ascriptions may be interpreted so as not to admit of ordinary existential generalization on positions in the 'that'-clauses, and not to be *de re* in any sense. We can even imagine differences in their *de dicto* beliefs that correspond to differences in truth-value. Adam may believe what he is falsely told when someone mischievously says, 'Water lacks oxygen'. When Adam $_{te}$ hears the same words and believes what *he* is told, he acquires (let us suppose) a true belief: twater does lack oxygen.[15]

I shall henceforth take it that Adam and Adam $_{te}$ have relevant propositional attitudes from whose content attributions no application of existential generalization is admissible. None of these contents need be applied by the subjects—*de re*—to objects in the external world. That is, the relevant attitudes are purely *de dicto* attitudes. Yet the attitude contents of Adam and Adam $_{te}$ differ.

IV

Thus it would seem that on the construal of 'narrow sense' we have been exploring, the twin-earth examples fail to show that psychological states in the narrow

---

[15] As I mentioned earlier, one might hold that 'water' names an abstract property or kind and that attitude attributions typically attribute *de re* attitudes *of* the kind. I do not accept this view, or see any strong reasons for it. But let us examine its consequences briefly. I shall assume that 'kind' is used in such a way that water is the same kind as H_2O. To be minimally plausible, the view must distinguish between kind and concept (cf. note 14)—between the kind that is thought of and the person's way of thinking of it. 'Water' may express or indicate one way of thinking of the kind—'H_2O' another. Given this distinction, previous considerations will show that Adam and Adam $_{te}$ apply different concepts (and contents) to the different kinds. So even though their attitudes are not 'narrow', they still have different mental states and events. For mental states and events are individuated partly in terms of contents.

sense (or the contents of such states) do not 'fix' the extensions of terms that Adam and Adam $_{te}$ use. For different contents and different propositional attitudes correspond to the different extensions. This conclusion rests, however, on a fairly narrow interpretation of 'fix' and—what is equally important—on a plausible, but restrictive application of 'narrow sense'. Let me explain these points in turn.

Propositional attitudes involving non-indexical notions like that of water do 'fix' an extension for the term that expresses the notion. But they do so in a purely semantical sense: (necessarily) the notion of water is true of all and only water. There is, however, a deeper and vaguer sense in which non-relational propositional attitudes do not fix the extensions of terms people use. This point concerns explication rather than purely formal relationships. The twin-earth examples (like the examples from 'Individualism and the Mental') indicate that the order of explication does not run in a straight line from propositional attitudes in the 'narrow sense' (even as we have been applying this expression) to the extensions of terms.[16] Rather, to know and explicate what a person believes *de dicto*, one must typically know something about what he believes *de re*, about what his fellows believe *de re* (and *de dicto*), about what entities they ostend, about what he and his fellows' words mean, and about what entities fall in the extensions of their terms.

A corollary of this point is that one cannot explicate what propositional attitude *contents* a person has by taking into account only facts about him that are non-intentional and individualistic. There is a still flourishing tradition in the philosophy of mind to the contrary. This tradition claims to explain psychological states in terms of non-intentional, functional features of the individual—with no reference to the nature of the environment or the character of the actions, attitudes, and conventions of other individuals.[17] Although there is perhaps something to be said for taking non-intentional, individualistic research strategies as one reasonable approach to explaining the behavior of individuals, the view is hopelessly oversimplified as a philosophical explication of ordinary mentalistic notions.

Even insofar as individualism is seen as a research strategy, like the 'methodological solipsism' advocated by Jerry Fodor, it is subject to limitations. Such strategies, contrary to Fodor's presumptions, cannot be seen as providing a means of individuating ordinary ('non-transparent') attributions of content.

---

[16] I am tempted to characterize this as Putnam's own primary point. What counts against yielding to the temptation is his interpretation of natural kind terms as indexical, his focus on meaning, and his statement that those on Twin-Earth have the same thoughts (p. 224) as those on Earth. Still, what follows is strongly suggested by much that he says.

[17] Works more or less explicitly in this tradition are Putnam, "The Nature of Mental States" in *Philosophical Papers*, ii. 437; Harman, (1973), 43–46, 56–65; D. Lewis, "Psychophysical and Theoretical Identifications", *Australasian Journal of Philosophy* 50 (1972), 249–250 *idem*, "Radical Interpretation", *Synthese*, 27 (1974), 331 ff.; J. A. Fodor, *The Language of Thought* (Cambridge, Mass: Harvard University Press) (1975), ch. 1, and *idem*, "Methodological Solipsism".

Indeed, it is highly doubtful that a psychological theory can treat psychological states as representational at all, and at the same time individuate them in a strictly individualistic, formal, or 'syntactic' way. One could, I suppose, have a theory of behavior that individuated internal states 'syntactically'. Or one could have a representational theory (like most of the cognitive theories we have) which abstracts, in particular attributions to individuals, from the question of whether or not the attributed contents are true. But the latter type of theory, in every version that has had genuine use in psychological theory, relies on individuation of the contents, individuation which involves complex reference to entities other than the individual. Putnam's examples, interpreted in the way I have urged, constitute one striking illustration of this fact.

These remarks invite a reconsideration of the expression 'psychological state in the narrow sense'. Putnam originally characterized such states as those that do not 'presuppose' (entail) the existence of entities other than the subject. And we have been taking the lack of presupposition to be coextensive with a failure of existential generalization and an absence of *de re* attitudes. Thus we have been taking psychological states in the 'narrow sense' to be those whose standard 'that'-clause specification does not admit of existential generalization on any of its expressions, and is not in any sense *de re*. But our weakened construal of 'fix' suggests a correction in the application of the notion of presupposition. One might say that Adam's *de dicto* attitudes involving the notion of water *do* presuppose the existence of other entities. The conditions for individuating them make essential reference to the nature of entities in their environment or to the actions and attitudes of others in the community. Even purely *de dicto* propositional attitudes presuppose the existence of entities other than the subject in this sense of presupposition. On this construal, *none* of the relevant attitudes, *de re* or *de dicto*, are psychological states in the narrow sense.

I want to spend the remainder of the section exploring this broadened application of the notion of presupposition. The question is what sorts of relations hold between an individual's mental states and other entities in his environment by virtue of the fact that the conditions for individuating his attitude contents—and thus his mental states and events—make reference to the nature of entities in his environment, or at least to what his fellows consider to be the nature of those entities.

We want to say that it is logically possible for an individual to have beliefs involving the concept of water (aluminum, elm, mackerel) even though there is no water (and so on) of which the individual holds these beliefs. This case seems relatively unproblematic. The individual believer might simply not be in an appropriately direct epistemic relation to any of the relevant entities. This is why existential generalization can fail and the relevant attitudes can be purely *de dicto*, even though our method of individuating attitude contents makes reference to the entities.

I think we also want to say something stronger: it is logically possible for an individual to have beliefs involving the concept of water (aluminum, and so on), even though there exists no water. An individual or community might (logically speaking) have been wrong in thinking that there was such a thing as water. It is epistemically possible—it might have turned out—that contrary to an individual's beliefs, water did not exist.

Part of what we do when we conceive of such cases is to rely on actual circumstances in which these illusions do not hold—rely on the actual existence of water—in order to individuate the notions we cite in specifying the propositional attitudes. We utilize—must utilize, I think—the actual existence of physical stuffs and things, or of other speakers or thinkers, in making sense of counterfactual projections in which we think at least some of these surroundings away.

But these projections are not unproblematic. One must be very careful in carrying them out. For the sake of argument, let us try to conceive of a set of circumstances in which Adam holds beliefs he actually holds involving the notion of water (aluminum, etc.), but in which there is no water and no community of other speakers to which Adam belongs. Adam may be deluded about these matters: he may live in a solipsistic world. What is problematic about these alleged circumstances is that they raise the question of how Adam *could* have propositional attitudes involving the notion of water. How are they distinguished from attitudes involving the notion of twater, or any of an indefinitely large number of other notions?

In pressing this question, we return to considerations regarding concept acquisition and truth. How, under the imagined circumstances, did Adam acquire the concept of water? There is no water in his environment, and he has contact with no one who has contact with water. There seems no reason derivable from the imagined circumstances (as opposed to arbitrary stipulation) to suppose that Adam's words bear English interpretations instead of English $_{te}$ interpretations, since there are no other speakers in his environment. Nothing in Adam's own repertoire serves to make 'water' mean *water* instead of *twater*, or numerous other possibilities. So there seems no ground for saying that Adam *has* acquired the concept of water.

Considerations from truth-conditions point in the same direction. When Adam's beliefs (as held in the putative solipsistic world) are carried over to and evaluated in a 'possible world' in which twater (and not water) exists, why should some of the relevant beliefs be false in this world and true in a world in which water exists, or vice versa? Nothing in the solipsistic world seems to ground any such distinction. For these reasons, it seems to me that one cannot credibly imagine that Adam, with his physical and dispositional life history, could have beliefs involving the notion of water, even though there were no other entities (besides his attitude contents) in the world.

We have now supported the view that the point about explication and individuation brings with it, in this case, a point about entailment. Adam's psychological states in the narrow sense (those that do not entail the existence of other entities) do not fix (in either sense of 'fix') the extensions of his terms. This is so not because Adam's beliefs involving the notion of water are indexical or *de re*, and not because he has the same propositional attitudes as Adam $_{te}$ while the extensions of his terms differ. Rather it is because all of Adam's attitude contents involving relevant natural kind notions—and thus all his relevant attitudes (whether *de re* or *de dicto*)—are individuated, by reference to other entities. His having these attitudes in the relevant circumstances entails (and thus presupposes in Putnam's sense) the existence of other entities.

The exact nature of the relevant entailment deserves more discussion than I can give it here. As I previously indicated, I think that Adam's having attitudes whose contents involve the notion of water does not entail the existence of water. If by some wild communal illusion, no one had ever really seen a relevant liquid in the lakes and rivers, or had drunk such a liquid, there might still be enough in the community's talk to distinguish the notion of water from that of twater and from other candidate notions. We would still have our chemical analyses, despite the illusoriness of their object. (I assume here that not *all* of the community's beliefs involve similar illusions.[18]) I think that Adam's having the relevant attitudes probably does not entail the existence of other speakers. Prima facie, at least, it would seem that if he did interact with water and held a few elementary true beliefs about it, we would have enough to explain how he acquired the notion of water—enough to distinguish his having that notion from his having the notion of twater. What seems incredible is to suppose that Adam, in his relative ignorance and indifference about the nature of water, holds beliefs whose contents involve the notion, even though neither water nor communal cohorts exist.

V

It should be clear that this general line promises to have a bearing on some of the most radical traditional sceptical positions. (I think that the bearing of the argument in 'Individualism and the Mental' is complementary and more comprehensive.) The line provides fuel for the Kantian strategy of showing that at least some formulations of traditional scepticism accept certain elements of our ordinary viewpoint while rejecting others that are not really separable. Exploring the epistemic side of these issues, however, has not been our present task.

Our main concern has been the bearing of these ideas on the philosophy of mind. What attitudes a person has, what mental events and states occur in him, depends on the character of his physical and social environment. In some instances, an individual's having certain *de dicto* attitudes *entails* the existence of entities other than himself and his attitude contents. The twin-earth

---

[18] Thus I am inclined to think that, if one is sufficiently precise, one could introduce a 'natural kind' notion, like water without having had any causal contact with instances of it. This seems to happen when chemical or other kinds are anticipated in science before their discovery 'in nature'. The point places a prima facie limitation on anti-sceptical uses of our argument. Thus I have been careful to emphasize Adam's relative ignorance in our criticism of solipsistic thought experiments.

thought experiment may work only for certain propositional attitudes. Certainly its clearest applications are to those whose contents involve non-theoretical natural kind notions. But the arguments of 'Individualism and the Mental' suggest that virtually no propositional attitudes can be explicated in individualistic terms. Since the intentional notions in terms of which propositional attitudes are described are irreducibly non-individualistic, no purely individualistic account of these notions can possibly be adequate.

Although most formulations of the lessons to be learned from twin-earth thought experiments have seemed to me to be vague or misleading in various ways, many of them indicate a broad appreciation of the general drift of the argument just presented. In fact, as I indicated earlier, the general drift is just beneath the surface of Putnam's paper. A common reaction, however, is that if our ordinary concept of mind is non-individualistic, so much the worse for our ordinary concept.

This reaction is largely based on the view that if mentalistic notions do not explain 'behavior' individualistically, in something like the way chemical or perhaps physiological notions do, they are not respectable, at least for 'cognitive' or 'theoretical' as opposed to 'practical' purposes. I cannot discuss this view in the detail it deserves here. But it has serious weaknesses. It presupposes that the only cognitively valuable point of applying mentalistic notions is to explain individual 'behavior'. It assumes that the primary similarities in 'behavior' that mentalistic explanations should capture are illustrated by Adam's and Adam $_{te}$'s similarity of physical movement. It assumes that there are no 'respectable' non-individualistic theories. (I think evolutionary biology is a counterexample—not to appeal to much of cognitive psychology and the social sciences.) And it assumes an unexplicated and highly problematic distinction between theoretical and practical purposes. *All* of these assumptions are questionable and, in my view, probably mistaken.

The non-individualistic character of our mentalistic notions suggests that they are fitted to purposes other than (or in addition to) individualistic explanation. The arguments I have presented, here and earlier, challenge us to achieve a deeper understanding of the complex system of propositional attitude attribution. The purposes of this system include describing, explaining, and assessing people and their historically and socially characterized activity against a background of objective norms—norms of truth, rationality, right. Some form of fruitful explanation that might reasonably be called 'psychological' could, conceivably, ignore such purposes in the interests of individualistic explanation. But animus against mentalistic notions because they do not meet a borrowed ideal seems to me misplaced. That, however, is a point for sharpening on other occasions.

5 *Individualism and the Mental*

Since Hegel's *Phenomenology of Spirit*, a broad, inarticulate division of emphasis between the individual and his social environment has marked philosophical discussions of mind. On one hand, there is the traditional concern with the individual subject of mental states and events. In the elderly Cartesian tradition, the spotlight is on what exists or transpires 'in' the individual—his secret cogitations, his innate cognitive structures, his private perceptions and introspections, his grasping of ideas, concepts, or forms. More evidentially oriented movements, such as behaviorism and its liberalized progeny, have highlighted the individual's publicly observable behavior—his input–output relations and the dispositions, states, or events that mediate them. But both Cartesian and behaviorist viewpoints tend to feature the individual subject. On the other hand, there is the Hegelian preoccupation with the role of social institutions in shaping the individual and the content of his thought. This tradition has dominated the Continent since Hegel. But it has found echoes in English-speaking philosophy during this century in the form of a concentration on language. Much philosophical work on language and mind has been in the interests of Cartesian or behaviorist viewpoints that I shall term 'individualistic'. But many of Wittgenstein's remarks about mental representation point up a social orientation that is discernible from his flirtations with behaviorism. And more recent work on the theory of reference has provided glimpses of the role of social cooperation in determining what an individual thinks.

In many respects, of course, these emphases within philosophy—individualistic and social—are compatible. To an extent, they may be regarded simply as different currents in the turbulent stream of ideas that has washed the intellectual landscape during the last hundred and some odd years. But the role of the social environment has received considerably less clear-headed philosophical attention (though perhaps not less philosophical attention) than the role of the states, occurrences, or acts in, on, or by the individual. Philosophical

I am grateful to participants at a pair of talks given at the University of London in the spring of 1978, and to Richard Rorty for discussions earlier. I am also indebted to Robert Adams and Rogers Albritton whose criticisms forced numerous improvements. I appreciatively acknowledge support of the John Simon Guggenheim Foundation.

discussions of social factors have tended to be obscure, evocative, metaphorical, or platitudinous, or to be bent on establishing some large thesis about the course of history and the destiny of man. There remains much room for sharp delineation. I shall offer some considerations that stress social factors in descriptions of an individual's mental phenomena. These considerations call into question individualistic presuppositions of several traditional and modern treatments of mind. I shall conclude with some remarks about mental models.

I. TERMINOLOGICAL MATTERS

Our ordinary mentalistic discourse divides broadly into two sorts of idiom. One typically makes reference to mental states or events in terms of sentential expressions. The other does not. A clear case of the first kind of idiom is 'Alfred thinks that his friends' sofa is ugly'. A clear case of the second sort is 'Alfred is in pain'. Thoughts, beliefs, intentions, and so forth are typically specified in terms of subordinate sentential clauses, that-clauses, which may be judged as true or false. Pains, feels, tickles, and so forth have no special semantical relation to sentences or to truth or falsity. There are intentional idioms that fall in the second category on this characterization, but that share important semantical features with expressions in the first—idioms like 'Al worships Buicks'. But I shall not sort these out here. I shall discuss only the former kind of mentalistic idiom. The extension of the discussion to other intentional idioms will not be difficult.

In an ordinary sense, the noun phrases that embed sentential expressions in mentalistic idioms provide the *content* of the mental state or event. We shall call that-clauses and their grammatical variants *'content clauses'*. Thus the expression 'that sofas are more comfortable than pews' provides the content of Alfred's belief that sofas are more comfortable than pews. My phrase 'provides the content' represents an attempt at remaining neutral, at least for present purposes, among various semantical and metaphysical accounts of precisely how that-clauses function and precisely what, if anything, contents are.

Although the notion of content is, for present purposes, ontologically neutral, I do think of it as holding a place in a systematic *theory* of mentalistic language. The question of when to count contents different, and when the same, is answerable to theoretical restrictions. It is often remarked that in a given context we may ascribe to a person two that-clauses that are only loosely equivalent and count them as attributions of the 'same attitude'. We may say that Al's intention to climb Mt. McKinley and his intention to climb the highest mountain in the United States are the 'same intention'. (I intend the terms for the mountain to occur obliquely here. See later discussion.) This sort of point extends even to content clauses with extensionally non-equivalent counterpart notions. For contextually relevant purposes, we might count a thought that the glass contains some water as 'the same thought' as a thought that the glass contains some thirst-quenching liquid, particularly if we have no reason to attribute either content as opposed to the other, and distinctions between them are contextually irrelevant. Nevertheless, in both these examples, every systematic theory I know of would want to represent the semantical contribution of the content clauses in distinguishable ways—as 'providing different contents'.

One reason for doing so is that the person himself is capable of having different attitudes described by the different content clauses, even if these differences are irrelevant in a particular context. (Al might have developed the intention to climb the highest mountain before developing the intention to climb Mt. McKinley—regardless of whether he, in fact, did so.) A second reason is that the counterpart components of the that-clauses allude to distinguishable elements in people's cognitive lives. 'Mt. McKinley' and 'the highest mountain in the U.S.' serve, or might serve, to indicate cognitively different notions. This is a vague, informal way of generalizing Frege's point: the thought that Mt. McKinley is the highest mountain in the U.S. is potentially interesting or informative. The thought that Mt. McKinley is Mt. McKinley is not. Thus when we say in a given context that attribution of different contents is attribution of the 'same attitude', we use 'same attitude' in a way similar to the way we use 'same car' when we say that people who drive Fords (or green 1970 Ford Mavericks) drive the 'same car'. For contextual purposes different cars are counted as 'amounting to the same'.

Although this use of 'content' is theoretical, it is not, I think, theoretically controversial. In cases where we shall be counting contents different, the cases will be uncontentious: On any systematic theory, differences in the *extension*—the actual denotation, referent, or application—of counterpart expressions in that-clauses will be semantically represented, and will, in our terms, make for differences in content. I shall be avoiding the more controversial, but interesting, questions about the general conditions under which sentences in that-clauses can be expected to provide the same content.

I should also warn of some subsidiary terms. I shall be (and have been) using the term '*notion*' to apply to components or elements of contents. Just as whole that-clauses provide the content of a person's attitude, semantically relevant components of that-clauses will be taken to indicate notions that enter into the attitude (or the attitude's content). This term is supposed to be just as ontologically neutral as its fellow. When I talk of understanding or mastering the notion of contract, I am not relying on any special epistemic or ontological theory, except insofar as the earlier mentioned theoretical restrictions on the notion of content are inherited by the notion of notion. The expression, '*understanding (mastering) a notion*' is to be construed more or less intuitively. Understanding the notion of contract comes roughly to knowing what a contract is. One can master the notion of contract without mastering the term 'contract'—at the very least if one speaks some language other than English that has a term roughly synonymous with 'contract'. (An analogous point holds for my use of 'mastering a content'.) Talk of notions is roughly similar to talk of concepts in an informal sense. 'Notion' has the advantage of being easier to separate from traditional theoretical commitments.

I speak of *attributing* a content, or notion, and of *ascribing* a that-clause or other piece of language. Ascriptions are the linguistic analogs of attributions. This use of 'ascribe' is nonstandard, but convenient and easily assimilated.

There are semantical complexities involving the behavior of expressions in content clauses, most of which we can skirt. But some must be touched on. Basic to the subject is the observation that expressions in content clauses are often not intersubstitutable with extensionally equivalent expressions in such a way as to maintain the truth-value of the containing sentence. Thus from the facts that water is H_2O and that Bertrand thought that water is not fit to drink, it does not follow that Bertrand thought that H_2O is not fit to drink. When an expression like 'water' functions in a content clause so that it is not freely exchangeable with all extensionally equivalent expressions, we shall say that it has *oblique occurrence*. Roughly speaking, the reason why 'water' and 'H_2O' are not interchangeable in our report of Bertrand's thought is that 'water' plays a role in characterizing a different mental act or state from that which 'H_2O' would play a role in characterizing. In this context at least, thinking that water is not fit to drink is different from thinking that H_2O is not fit to drink.

By contrast, there are non-oblique occurrences of expressions in content clauses. One might say that some water—say, the water in the glass over there—is thought by Bertrand to be impure; or that Bertrand thought that *that* water is impure. And one might intend to make no distinction that would be lost by replacing 'water' with 'H_2O'—or 'that water' with 'that H_2O' or 'that common liquid', or any other expression extensionally equivalent with 'that water'. We might allow these exchanges even though Bertrand had never heard of, say, H_2O. In such purely non-oblique occurrences, 'water' plays *no role* in providing the *content* of Bertrand's thought, *on our use of 'content'*, or (in any narrow sense) in characterizing Bertrand or his mental state. Nor is the water part of Bertrand's thought content. We speak of Bertrand *thinking his content of* the water. At its non-oblique occurrence, the term 'that water' simply isolates, in one of many equally good ways, a portion of wet stuff to which Bertrand or his thought is related or applied. In certain cases, it may also mark a context in which Bertrand's thought is applied. But it is expressions at oblique occurrences within content clauses that primarily do the job of providing the content of mental states or events, and in characterizing the person.

Mentalistic discourse containing obliquely occurring expressions has traditionally been called *intentional discourse*. The historical reasons for this nomenclature are complex and partly confused. But roughly speaking, grammatical contexts involving oblique occurrences have been fixed upon as specially relevant to the representational character (sometimes called 'intentionality') of mental states and events. Clearly, oblique occurrences in mentalistic discourse have something to do with characterizing a person's epistemic perspective—how things seem to him, or in an informal sense, how they are represented to him. So without endorsing all the commitments of this tradition, I shall take over its terminology.

The crucial point in the preceding discussion is the assumption that obliquely occurring expressions in content clauses are a primary means of identifying a person's intentional mental states or events. A further point is worth remarking here. It is normal to suppose that those content clauses correctly ascribable to a person that are not in general intersubstitutable *salva veritate*—and certainly those that involve extensionally non-equivalent counterpart expressions—identify different mental states or events.

I have cited contextual exceptions to this normal supposition, at least in a manner of speaking. We sometimes count distinctions in content irrelevant for purposes of a given attribution, particularly where our evidence for the precise content of a person or animal's attitude is skimpy. Different contents may contextually identify (what amount to) the 'same attitude'. I have indicated that even in these contexts, I think it best, strictly speaking, to construe distinct contents as describing different mental states or events that are merely equivalent for the purposes at hand. I believe that this view is widely accepted. But nothing I say will depend on it. For any distinct contents, there will be imaginable contexts of attribution in which, even in the loosest, most informal ways of speaking, those contents would be said to describe different mental states or events. This is virtually a consequence of the theoretical role of contents, discussed earlier. Since our discussion will have an 'in principle' character, I shall take these contexts to be the relevant ones. Most of the cases we discuss will involve *extensional* differences between obliquely occurring counterpart expressions in that-clauses. In such cases, it is particularly natural and normal to take different contents as identifying different mental states or events.

II. A THOUGHT EXPERIMENT

IIa. First Case

We now turn to a three-step thought experiment. Suppose first that:

> A given person has a large number of attitudes commonly attributed with content clauses containing 'arthritis' in oblique occurrence. For example, he thinks (correctly) that he has had arthritis for years, that his arthritis in his wrists and fingers is more painful than his arthritis in his ankles, that it is better to have arthritis than cancer of the liver, that stiffening joints is a symptom of arthritis, that certain sorts of aches are characteristic of arthritis, that there are various kinds of arthritis, and so forth. In short, he has a wide range of such attitudes. In addition to these unsurprising attitudes, he thinks falsely that he has developed arthritis in the thigh.

Generally competent in English, rational, and intelligent, the patient reports to his doctor his fear that his arthritis has now lodged in his thigh. The doctor replies by telling him that this cannot be so, since arthritis is specifically an inflammation of joints. Any dictionary could have told him the same. The patient is surprised, but relinquishes his view and goes on to ask what might be wrong with his thigh.

The second step of the thought experiment consists of a counterfactual supposition. We are to conceive of a situation in which the patient proceeds from birth through the same course of physical events that he actually does, right to and including the time at which he first reports his fear to his doctor. Precisely the same things (non-intentionally described) happen to him. He has the same physiological history, the same diseases, the same internal physical occurrences. He goes through the same motions, engages in the same behavior, has the same sensory intake (physiologically described). His dispositions to respond to stimuli are explained in physical theory as the effects of the same proximate causes. All of this extends to his interaction with linguistic expressions. He says and hears the same words (word forms) at the same times he actually does. He develops the disposition to assent to 'Arthritis can occur in the thigh' and 'I have arthritis in the thigh' as a result of the same physically described proximate causes. Such dispositions might have arisen in a number of ways. But we can suppose that in both actual and counterfactual situations, he acquires the word 'arthritis' from casual conversation or reading, and never hearing anything to prejudice him for or against applying it in the way that he does, he applies the word to an ailment in his thigh (or to ailments in the limbs of others) which seems to produce pains or other symptoms roughly similar to the disease in his hands and ankles. In both actual and counterfactual cases, the disposition is never reinforced or extinguished up until the time when he expresses himself to his doctor. We further imagine that the patient's non-intentional, phenomenal experience is the same. He has the same pains, visual fields, images, and internal verbal rehearsals. The *counterfactuality* in the supposition touches only the patient's social environment. In actual fact, 'arthritis', as used in his community, does not apply to ailments outside joints. Indeed, it fails to do so by a standard, non-technical dictionary definition. But in our imagined case, physicians, lexicographers, and informed laymen apply 'arthritis' not only to arthritis but to various other rheumatoid ailments. The standard use of the term is to be conceived to encompass the patient's actual misuse. We could imagine either that arthritis was not singled out as a family of diseases, or that some other term besides 'arthritis' was applied, though not commonly by laymen, specifically to arthritis. We may also suppose that this difference and those necessarily associated with it are the only differences between the counterfactual situation and the actual one. (Other people besides the patient will, of course, behave differently.) To summarize the second step:

> The person might have had the same physical history and non-intentional mental phenomena while the word 'arthritis' was conventionally applied, and defined to apply, to various rheumatoid ailments, including the one in the person's thigh, as well as to arthritis.

The final step is an interpretation of the counterfactual case, or an addition to it as so far described. It is reasonable to suppose that:

> In the counterfactual situation, the patient lacks some—probably *all*—of the attitudes commonly attributed with content clauses containing 'arthritis' in oblique occurrence. He lacks the occurrent thoughts or beliefs that he has arthritis in the thigh, that he has had arthritis for years, that stiffening joints and various sorts of aches are symptoms of arthritis, that his father had arthritis, and so on.

We suppose that in the counterfactual case we cannot correctly ascribe any content clause containing an oblique occurrence of the term 'arthritis'. It is hard to see how the patient could have picked up the notion of arthritis. The word 'arthritis' in the counterfactual community does not mean *arthritis*. It does not apply only to inflammations of joints. We suppose that no other word in the patient's repertoire means *arthritis*. 'Arthritis', in the counterfactual situation, differs both in dictionary definition and in extension from 'arthritis' as we use it. Our ascriptions of content clauses to the patient (and ascriptions within his community) would not constitute attributions of the same contents we actually attribute. For counterpart expressions in the content clauses that are actually and counterfactually ascribable are not even extensionally equivalent. However we describe the patient's attitudes in the counterfactual situation, it will not be with a term or phrase extensionally equivalent with 'arthritis'. So the patient's counterfactual attitude contents differ from his actual ones.

The upshot of these reflections is that the patient's mental contents differ, while his entire physical and non-intentional mental histories, considered in isolation from their social context, remain the same. (We could have supposed that he dropped dead at the time he first expressed his fear to the doctor.) The differences seem to stem from differences 'outside' the patient considered as an isolated physical organism, causal mechanism, or seat of consciousness. The difference in his mental contents is attributable to differences in his social environment. In sum, the patient's internal qualitative experiences, his physiological states and events, his behaviorally described stimuli and responses, his dispositions to behave, and whatever sequences of states (non-intentionally described) mediated his input and output—all these remain constant, while his attitude contents differ, even in the extensions of counterpart notions. As we observed at the outset, such differences are ordinarily taken to spell differences in mental states and events.

IIb. Further Exemplifications

The argument has an extremely wide application. It does not depend, for example, on the kind of word 'arthritis' is. We could have used an artifact term, an ordinary natural kind word, a color adjective, a social role term, a term for a historical style, an abstract noun, an action verb, a physical movement

verb, or any of various other sorts of words. I prefer to leave open precisely
how far one can generalize the argument. But I think it has a very wide scope.
The argument can get under way in any case where it is intuitively possible to
attribute a mental state or event whose content involves a notion that the subject
incompletely understands. As will become clear, this possibility is the key to
the thought experiment. I want to give a more concrete sense of the possibility
before going further.

It is useful to reflect on the number and variety of intuitively clear cases in
which it is normal to attribute a content that the subject incompletely understands. One need only thumb through a dictionary for an hour or so to develop
a sense of the extent to which one's beliefs are infected by incomplete understanding.[1] The phenomenon is rampant in our pluralistic age.

a. Most cases of incomplete understanding that support the thought experiment will be fairly idiosyncratic. There is a reason for this. Common linguistic
errors, if entrenched, tend to become common usage. But a generally competent
speaker is bound to have numerous words in his repertoire, possibly even common words, that he somewhat misconstrues. Many of these misconstruals will
not be such as to deflect ordinary ascriptions of that-clauses involving the incompletely mastered term in oblique occurrence. For example, one can imagine a
generally competent, rational adult having a large number of attitudes involving
the notion of sofa—including beliefs that *those* (some sofas) are sofas, that
some sofas are beige, that his neighbors have a new sofa, that he would rather
sit in a sofa for an hour than on a church pew. In addition, he might think
that sufficiently broad (but single-seat) overstuffed armchairs are sofas. With
care, one can develop a thought experiment parallel to the one in section IIa, in
which at least some of the person's attitude contents (particularly, in this case,
contents of occurrent mental events) differ, while his physical history, dispositions to behavior, and phenomenal experience—non-intentionally and asocially
described—remain the same.

b. Although most relevant misconstruals are fairly idiosyncratic, there do seem
to be certain types of error which are relatively common—but not so common
and uniform as to suggest that the relevant terms take on new sense. Much of
our vocabulary is taken over from others who, being specialists, understand our
terms better than we do.[2] The use of scientific terms by laymen is a rich source

---

[1] Our examples suggest points about learning that need exploration. It would seem naive to think
that we first attain a mastery of expressions or notions we use and then tackle the subject matters we
speak and think about in using those expressions or notions. In most cases, the processes overlap.
But while the subject's understanding is still partial, we sometimes attribute mental contents in
the very terms the subject has yet to master. Traditional views take mastering a word to consist
in matching it with an already mastered (or innate) concept. But it would seem, rather, that many
concepts (or mental content components) are like words, in that they may be employed before they
are mastered. In both cases, employment appears to be an integral part of the process of mastery.

[2] A development of a similar theme may be found in Hilary Putnam's notion of a division
of linguistic labor. Cf. "The Meaning of 'Meaning' ", in *Philosophical Papers*, ii (Cambridge:

of cases. As the arthritis example illustrates, the thought experiment does not depend on specially technical terms. I shall leave it to the imagination of the reader to spin out further examples of this sort.

c. One need not look to the laymen's acquisitions from science for examples. People used to buying beef brisket in stores or ordering it in restaurants (and conversant with it in a general way) probably often develop mistaken beliefs (or uncertainties) about just what brisket is. For example, one might think that

Cambridge University Press, 1975), 227 ff. Putnam's imaginative work is in other ways congenial with points I have developed. Some of his examples can be adapted in fairly obvious ways so as to give an argument with different premises, but a conclusion complementary to the one I arrive at in Sec. IIa.

Consider Alfred's belief contents involving the notion of water. Without changing Alfred's (or his fellows') non-intentional phenomenal experiences, internal physical occurrences, or dispositions to respond to stimuli on sensory surfaces, we can imagine that not water (H_2O), but a different liquid with different structure but similar macro-properties (and identical phenomenal properties) played the role in his environment that water does in ours. In such a case, we could ascribe no content clauses to Alfred with 'water' in oblique position. His belief contents would differ. The conclusion (with which I am in sympathy) is that mental contents are affected not only by the physical and qualitatively mental way the person is, but by the nature of his *physical environment*.

Putnam himself does not give quite this argument. He nowhere states the first and third steps, though he gives analogs of them for the meaning of 'water'. This is partly just a result of his concentration on meaning instead of propositional attitudes. But some of what he says even seems to oppose the argument's conclusion. He remarks in effect that the subject's *thoughts* remain constant between his actual and counterfactual cases (p. 224). In his own argument he explicates the difference between actual and counterfactual cases in terms of a difference in the extension of terms, not a difference in those aspects of their meaning that play a role in the cognitive life of the subject. And he tries to explicate his examples in terms of indexicality—a mistake, I think, and one that tends to divert attention from major implications of the examples he gives. (Cf. Sec. IId.) In my view, the examples do illustrate the fact that all attitudes involving natural kind notions, including *de dicto* attitudes, presuppose *de re* attitudes. But the examples do not show that natural kind linguistic expressions are in any ordinary sense indexical. Nor do they show that beliefs involving natural kind notions are always *de re*. Even if they did, the change from actual to counterfactual cases would affect oblique occurrences of natural kind terms in that-clauses—occurrences that are the key to attributions of cognitive content. (Cf. above and note 3.) In the cited paper and earlier ones, much of what Putnam says about psychological states (and implies about mental states) has a distinctly individualistic ring. Below in Sec. IV, I criticize viewpoints about mental phenomena influenced by and at least strongly suggested in his earlier work on functionalism. (Cf. note 9.)

On the other hand, Putnam's articulation of social and environmental aspects of the meaning of natural kind terms complements and supplements my viewpoint. For me, it has been a rich rewarder of reflection. More recent work of his seems to involve shifts in his viewpoint on psychological states. It may have somewhat more in common with my approach than the earlier work, but there is much that I do not understand about it.

The argument regarding the notion of water that I extracted from Putnam's paper is narrower in scope than my argument. The Putnam-derived argument seems to work only for natural kind terms and close relatives. And it may seem not to provide as direct a threat to certain versions of functionalism that I discuss in Sec. IV: At least a few philosophers would claim that one could accommodate the Putnamian argument in terms of *non*-intentional formulations of input–output relations (formulations that make reference to the specific nature of the physical environment). My argument does not submit to this maneuver. In my thought experiment, the physical environment (sofas, arthritis, and so forth in my examples) and the subject's causal relations with it (at least as these are usually conceived) were held constant. The Putnamian argument, however, has fascinatingly different implications from my argument. I have not developed these comparisons and contrasts here because doing justice to Putnam's viewpoint would demand a distracting amount of space, as the ample girth of this footnote may suggest.

brisket is a cut from the flank or rump, or that it includes not only the lower part of the chest but also the upper part, or that it is specifically a cut of beef and not of, say, pork. No one hesitates to ascribe to such people content clauses with 'brisket' in oblique occurrence. For example, a person may believe that he is eating brisket under these circumstances (where 'brisket' occurs in oblique position); or he may think that brisket tends to be tougher than loin. Some of these attitudes may be false; many will be true. We can imagine a counter-factual case in which the person's physical history, his dispositions, and his non-intentional mental life, are all the same, but in which 'brisket' is commonly applied in a different way—perhaps in precisely the way the person thinks it applies. For example, it might apply only to beef and to the upper and lower parts of the chest. In such a case, as in the sofa and arthritis cases, it would seem that the person would (or might) lack some or all of the propositional attitudes that are actually attributed with content clauses involving 'brisket' in oblique position.

d. Someone only generally versed in music history, or superficially acquainted with a few drawings of musical instruments, might naturally but mistakenly come to think that clavichords included harpsichords without legs. He may have many other beliefs involving the notion of clavichord, and many of these may be true. Again, with some care, a relevant thought experiment can be generated.

e. A fairly common mistake among lawyers' clients is to think that one cannot have a contract with someone unless there has been a written agreement. The client might be clear in intending 'contract' (in the relevant sense) to apply to agreements, not to pieces of paper. Yet he may take it as part of the meaning of the word, or the essence of law, that a piece of formal writing is a neces-sary condition for establishing a contract. His only experiences with contracts might have involved formal documents, and he undergeneralizes. It is not ter-ribly important here whether one says that the client misunderstands the term's meaning, or alternatively that the client makes a mistake about the essence of contracts. In either case, he misconceives what a contract is; yet ascriptions involving the term in oblique position are made anyway.

It is worth emphasizing here that I intend the misconception to involve the subject's attaching counterfactual consequences to his mistaken belief about con-tracts. Let me elaborate this a bit. A common dictionary definition of 'contract' is 'legally binding agreement'. As I am imagining the case, the client does not explicitly define 'contract' to himself in this way (though he might use this phrase in explicating the term). And he is not merely making a mistake about what the law happens to enforce. If asked why unwritten agreements are not contracts, he is likely to say something like 'They just aren't' or 'It is part of the nature of the law and legal practice that they have no force'. He is not disposed without prodding to answer, 'It would be possible but impractical to give unwritten agreements legal force'. He might concede this. But he would add that such agreements would not be contracts. He regards a document as inseparable from contractual obligation, regardless of whether he takes this to be a matter of meaning or a metaphysical essentialist truth about contracts.

Needless to say, these niceties are philosophers' distinctions. They are not something an ordinary man is likely to have strong opinions about. My point is that the thought experiment is independent of these distinctions. It does not depend on misunderstandings of dictionary meaning. One might say that the client understood the term's dictionary meaning, but misunderstood its essential application in the law—misconceived the nature of contracts. The thought experiment still flies. In a counterfactual case in which the law enforces both written and unwritten agreements and in which the subject's behavior and so forth are the same, but in which 'contract' *means* 'legally binding agreement based on written document', we would not attribute to him a mistaken belief that a contract requires written agreement, although the lawyer might have to point out that there are other legally binding agreements that do not require documents. Similarly, the client's other propositional attitudes would no longer involve the notion of contract, but another more restricted notion.

f. People sometimes make mistakes about color ranges. They may correctly apply a color term to a certain color, but also mistakenly apply it to shades of a neighboring color. When asked to explain the color term, they cite the standard cases (for 'red', the color of blood, fire engines, and so forth). But they apply the term somewhat beyond its conventionally established range—beyond the reach of its vague borders. They think that fire engines, including *that* one, are red. They observe that red roses are covering the trellis. But they also think that *those* things are a shade of red (whereas they are not). Second looks do not change their opinion. But they give in when other speakers confidently correct them in unison.

This case extends the point of the contract example. The error is linguistic or conceptual in something like the way that the shopper's mistake involving the notion of brisket is. It is not an ordinary empirical error. But one may reasonably doubt that the subjects misunderstand the dictionary meaning of the color term. Holding their non-intentional phenomenal experience, physical history, and behavioral dispositions constant, we can imagine that 'red' were applied as they mistakenly apply it. In such cases, we would no longer ascribe content clauses involving the term 'red' in oblique position. The attribution of the correct beliefs about fire engines and roses would be no less affected than the attribution of the beliefs that, in the actual case, display the misapplication. Cases bearing out the latter point are common in anthropological reports on communities whose color terms do not match ours. Attributions of content typically allow for the differences in conventionally established color ranges.

Here is not the place to refine our rough distinctions among the various kinds of misconceptions that serve the thought experiment. Our philosophical purposes do not depend on how these distinctions are drawn. Still, it is important to see what an array of conceptual errors is common among us. And it is important to note that such errors do not always or automatically prevent attribution of mental content provided by the very terms that are incompletely understood or misapplied. The thought experiment is nourished by this aspect of common practice.

IIc. Expansion and Delineation of the Thought Experiment

As I have tried to suggest in the preceding examples, the relevant attributions in the first step of the thought experiment need not display the subject's error. They may be attributions of a true content. We can begin with a propositional attitude that involved the misconceived notion, but in a true, unproblematic application of it: for example, the patient's belief that he, like his father, developed arthritis in the ankles and wrists at age 58 (where 'arthritis' occurs obliquely).

One need not even rely on an underlying *mis*conception in the thought experiment. One may pick a case in which the subject only partially understands an expression. He may apply it firmly and correctly in a range of cases, but be unclear or agnostic about certain of its applications or implications which, in fact, are fully established in common practice. Most of the examples we gave previously can be reinterpreted in this way. To take a new one, imagine that our protagonist is unsure whether his father has mortgages on the car and house, or just one on the house. He is a little uncertain about exactly how the loan and collateral must be arranged in order for there to be a mortgage, and he is not clear about whether one may have mortgages on anything other than houses. He is sure, however, that Uncle Harry paid off his mortgage. Imagine our man constant in the ways previously indicated and that 'mortgage' commonly applied only to mortgages on houses. But imagine banking practices themselves to be the same. Then the subject's uncertainty would plausibly not involve the notion of mortgage. Nor would his other propositional attitudes be correctly attributed with the term 'mortgage' in oblique position. Partial understanding is as good as misunderstanding for our purposes.

On the other hand, the thought experiment does appear to depend on the possibility of someone's having a propositional attitude despite an incomplete mastery of some notion in its content. To see why this appears to be so, let us try to run through a thought experiment, attempting to avoid any imputation of incomplete understanding. Suppose the subject thinks falsely that all swans are white. One can certainly hold the features of swans and the subject's non-intentional phenomenal experience, physical history, and non-intentional dispositions constant, and imagine that 'swan' meant 'white swan' (and perhaps some other term, unfamiliar to the subject, meant what 'swan' means). Could one reasonably interpret the subject as having different attitude contents without at some point invoking a misconception? The questions to be asked here are about the subject's dispositions. For example, in the actual case, if he were shown a black swan and told that he was wrong, would he fairly naturally concede his mistake? Or would he respond, 'I'm doubtful that that's a swan,' until we brought in dictionaries, encyclopedias, and other native speakers to correct his usage? In the latter case, his understanding of 'swan' would be deviant. Suppose then that in the actual situation he would respond normally to the counterexample. Then there is reason to say that he understands the notion of swan correctly; and his error is not conceptual or linguistic, but empirical in an ordinary and narrow sense. (Of course, the line we are drawing here is pretty fuzzy.) When one comes to the counterfactual stage of the thought experiment, the subject has the same dispositions to respond pliably to the presentation of a black specimen. But such a response would suggest a misunderstanding of the term 'swan' as counterfactually used. For in the counterfactual community, what they call 'swans' could not fail to be white. The mere presentation of a black swan would be irrelevant to the definitional truth 'All swans are white'. I have not set this case up as an example of the thought experiment's going through. Rather I have used it to support the conjecture that *if* the thought experiment is to work, one must at some stage find the subject believing (or having some attitude characterized by) a content, despite an incomplete understanding or misapplication. An ordinary empirical error appears not to be sufficient.

It would be a mistake, however, to think that incomplete understanding, in the sense that the argument requires, is in general an unusual or even deviant phenomenon. *What I have called 'partial understanding' is common or even normal in the case of a large number of expressions in our vocabularies.* 'Arthritis' is a case in point. Even if by the grace of circumstance a person does not fall into views that run counter to the term's meaning or application, it would not be in the least deviant or 'socially unacceptable' to have no clear attitude that would block such views. 'Brisket', 'contract', 'recession', 'sonata', 'deer', 'elm' (to borrow a well-known example), 'pre-amplifier', 'carburetor', 'gothic', 'fermentation', probably provide analogous cases. Continuing the list is largely a matter of patience. The sort of 'incomplete understanding' required by the thought experiment includes quite ordinary, nondeviant phenomena.

It is worth remarking that the thought experiment as originally presented might be run in reverse. The idea would be to start with an ordinary belief or thought involving no incomplete understanding. Then we find the incomplete understanding in the second step. For example, properly understanding 'arthritis', a patient may think (correctly) that he has arthritis. He happens to have heard of arthritis only occurring in joints, and he correctly believes that that is where arthritis always occurs. Holding his physical history, dispositions, and pain constant, we imagine that 'arthritis' commonly applies to rheumatoid ailments of all sorts. Arthritis has not been singled out for special mention. If the patient were told by a doctor 'You also have arthritis in the thigh', the patient would be disposed (as he is in the actual case) to respond, 'Really? I didn't know that one could have arthritis except in joints'. The doctor would answer, 'No, arthritis occurs in muscles, tendons, bursas, and elsewhere.' The patient would stand corrected. The notion that the doctor and patient would be operating with in such a case would not be that of arthritis.

My reasons for not having originally set out the thought experiment in this way are largely heuristic. As will be seen, discussion of the thought experiment will tend to center on the step involving incomplete understanding. And I wanted to encourage you, dear reader, to imagine actual cases of incomplete understanding in your own linguistic community. Ordinary intuitions in the domestic case are perhaps less subject to premature warping in the interests of theory. Cases involving not only mental content attribution, but also translation of a foreign tongue, are more vulnerable to intrusion of side issues.

A secondary reason for not beginning with this 'reversed' version of the thought experiment is that I find it doubtful whether the thought experiment always works in symmetric fashion. There may be special intuitive problems in certain cases—perhaps, for example, cases involving perceptual natural kinds. We may give special interpretations to individuals' misconceptions in imagined foreign communities, when those misconceptions seem to match our conceptions. In other words, there may be some systematic intuitive bias in favor of at least certain of our notions for purposes of interpreting the misconceptions of imagined foreigners. I do not want to explore the point here. I think that any such bias is not always crucial, and that the thought experiment frequently works 'symmetrically'. We have to take account of a person's community in interpreting his words and describing his attitudes—and this holds in the foreign case as well as in the domestic case.

The reversal of the thought experiment brings home the important point that *even those propositional attitudes not infected by incomplete understanding* depend for their content on social factors that are independent of the individual, asocially and non-intentionally described. For if the social environment had been appropriately different, the contents of those attitudes would have been different.

Even *apart* from reversals of the thought experiment, it is plausible (in the light of its original versions) that our well-understood propositional attitudes depend partly for their content on social factors independent of the individual, asocially and non-intentionally construed. For each of us can reason as follows. Take a set of attitudes that involve a given notion and whose contents are well-understood by me. It is only contingent that I understand that notion as well as I do. Now holding my community's practices constant, imagine that I understand the given notion incompletely, but that the deficient understanding is such that it does not prevent my having attitude contents involving that notion. In fact, imagine that I am in the situation envisaged in the first step of one of the original thought experiments. In such a case, a proper subset of the original set of my actual attitude contents would, or might, remain the same—intuitively, at least those of my actual attitudes whose justification or point is untouched by my imagined deficient understanding. (In the arthritis case, an example would be a true belief that many old people have arthritis.) These attitude contents remain constant despite the fact that my understanding, inference patterns, behavior, dispositions, and so on would in important ways be different and partly inappropriate to applications of the given notion. What is it that enables these unaffected contents to remain applications of the relevant notion? It is not *just* that my understanding, inference patterns, behavior, and so forth are enough like my actual understanding, inference patterns, behavior, and so forth. For if communal practice had *also* varied so as to apply the relevant notion as I am imagining I misapply it, then my attitude contents would not involve the relevant notion at all. This argument suggests that communal practice is a factor (in addition to my understanding, inference patterns, and perhaps behavior, physical activity, and other features) in fixing the contents of my attitudes, even in cases where I fully understand the content.

IId. Independence from Factive-Verb and Indexical-Reference Paradigms

The thought experiment does not play on psychological 'success' verbs or 'factive' verbs—verbs like 'know', 'regret', 'realize', 'remember', 'foresee', 'perceive'. This point is important for our purposes, because such verbs suggest an easy and clearcut distinction between the contribution of the individual subject and the objective, 'veridical' contribution of the environment to making the verbs applicable. (Actually the matter becomes more complicated on reflection, but we shall stay with the simplest cases.) When a person knows that snow is common in Greenland, his knowledge obviously depends on more than the way the person is. It depends on there actually being a lot of snow in Greenland. His mental state (belief that snow is common in Greenland) must be successful in a certain way (true). By changing the environment, one could change the truth-value of the content, so that the subject could no longer be said to know the content. It is part of the burden of my argument that even intentional mental states of the individual like beliefs, which carry no implication of veridicality or success, cannot be understood by focusing purely on the individual's acts, dispositions, and 'inner' goings on.

The thought experiment also does not rest on the phenomenon of indexicality, or on *de re* attitudes, in any direct way. When Alfred refers to an apple, saying to himself, 'That is wholesome,' what he refers to depends not just on the content of what he says or thinks, but on what apple is before him. Without altering the meaning of Alfred's utterance, the nature of his perceptual experiences, or his physical acts or dispositions, we could conceive an exchange of the actual apple for another one that is indistinguishable to Alfred. We would thereby conceive him as referring to something different and even as saying something with a different truth-value.

This rather obvious point about indexicality has come to be seen as providing a model for understanding a certain range of mental states or events—*de re* attitudes. The precise characterization of this range is no simple philosophical task. But the clearest cases involve non-obliquely occurring terms in content clauses. When we say that Bertrand thinks of some water that it would not slake his thirst (where 'water' occurs in purely non-oblique position), we attribute a *de re* belief to Bertrand. We assume that Bertrand has something like an indexical relation to the water. The fact that Bertrand believes something of some water, rather than of a portion of some other liquid that is indistinguishable to him, depends partly on the fact that it is water to which Bertrand is contextually, 'indexically' related. For intuitively we could have exchanged the liquids without changing Bertrand and thereby changed what Bertrand believed his belief content *of* —and even whether his belief was true of it.[3] It is easy to interpret such cases by holding that the subject's mental states and contents (with allowances for brute differences in the contexts in which he applies those contents) remain the same. The differences in the situations do not pertain in any fundamental way to the subject's mind or the nature of his mental content, but to how his mind or content is related to the world.

I think this interpretation of standard indexical and *de re* cases is broadly correct, although it involves oversimplifications and demands refinements. But what I want to emphasize here is that it is inapplicable to the cases our thought experiment fixes upon.

It seems to me clear that the thought experiment need not rely on *de re* attitudes at all. The subject need not have entered into special *en rapport* or quasi-indexical relations with objects that the misunderstood term applies to in order for the argument to work. We can appeal to attitudes that would usually be regarded as paradigmatic cases of *de dicto*, non-indexical, *non-de-re*, mental attitudes or events. The primary mistake in the contract example is one such, but we could choose others to suit the reader's taste. To insist that such attitudes must all be indexically infected or *de re* would, I think, be to trivialize and emasculate these notions, making nearly all attitudes *de re*. All *de dicto* attitudes presuppose *de re* attitudes. But it does not follow that indexical or *de re* elements survive in every attitude. (Cf. notes 2 and 3.)

I shall not, however, argue this point here. The claim that is crucial is not that our argument does not fix on *de re* attitudes. It is, rather, that the social differences between the actual and counterfactual situations affect the *content* of the subject's attitudes. That is, the difference affects standard cases of obliquely occurring, cognitive-content-conveying expressions in content clauses. For example, still with his misunderstanding, the subject might think that this (referring to his disease in his hands) is arthritis. Or he might think *de re* of the disease in his ankle (or of the disease in his thigh) that his arthritis is painful. It does not really matter whether the relevant attitude is *de re* or purely *de dicto*. What is crucial to our argument is that the occurrence of 'arthritis' is oblique and

---

[3] I have discussed *de re* mental phenomena in 'Belief *De Re*', *The Journal of Philosophy*, 74 (1977), 338–62 (Ch. 3 above). There I argue that all attitudes with content presuppose *de re* attitudes. Our discussion here may be seen as bearing on the details of this presupposition. But for reasons I merely sketch in the next paragraph, I think it would be a superficial viewpoint that tried to utilize our present argument to support the view that nearly all intentional mental phenomena are covertly indexical or *de re*.

contributes to a characterization of the subject's mental content. One might even hold, implausibly I think, that all the subject's attitudes involving the notion of arthritis are *de re*, that 'arthritis' in that-clauses *indexically* picks out the property of being arthritis, or something like that. The fact remains that the term occurs obliquely in the relevant cases and serves in characterizing the *dicta* or contents of the subject's attitudes. The thought experiment exploits this fact.

Approaches to the mental that I shall later criticize as excessively individualistic tend to assimilate environmental aspects of mental phenomena to either the factive-verb or the indexical-reference paradigm. (Cf. note 2.) This sort of assimilation suggests that one might maintain a relatively clearcut distinction between extra-mental and mental aspects of mentalistic attributions. And it may encourage the idea that the distinctively mental aspects can be understood fundamentally in terms of the individual's abilities, dispositions, states, and so forth, considered in isolation from his social surroundings. My argument undermines this latter suggestion. Social context infects even the distinctively mental features of mentalistic attributions. No man's intentional mental phenomena are insular. Every man is a piece of the social continent, a part of the social main.

III. REINTERPRETATIONS

IIIa. Methodology

I find that most people unspoiled by conventional philosophical training regard the three steps of the thought experiment as painfully obvious. Such folk tend to chafe over my filling in details or elaborating on strategy. I think this naivete appropriate. But for sophisticates the three steps require defense.

Before launching a defense, I want to make a few remarks about its methodology. My objective is to better understand our common mentalistic notions. Although such notions are subject to revision and refinement, I take it as evident that there is philosophical interest in theorizing about them as they now are. I assume that a primary way of achieving theoretical understanding is to concentrate on our *discourse* about mentalistic notions. Now it is, of course, never obvious at the outset how much idealization, regimentation, or special interpretation is necessary in order to adequately understand ordinary discourse. Phenomena such as ambiguity, ellipsis, indexicality, idioms, and a host of others certainly demand some regimentation or special interpretation for purposes of linguistic theory. Moreover, more global considerations—such as simplicity in accounting for structural relations—often have effects on the cast of one's theory. For all that, there is a methodological bias in favor of taking natural discourse literally, other things being equal. For example, unless there are clear reasons for construing discourse as ambiguous, elliptical, or involving special idioms, we should not so construe it. Literal interpretation is *ceteris paribus* preferred. My defense of the thought experiment, as I have interpreted it, partly rests on this principle.

This relatively non-theoretical interpretation of the thought experiment should be extended to the gloss on it that I provided in Section IIc. The notions of misconception, incomplete understanding, conceptual or linguistic error, and ordinary empirical error are to be taken as carrying little theoretical weight. I assume that these notions mark defensible, commonsense distinctions. But I need not take a position on available philosophical interpretations of these distinctions. In fact, I do not believe that understanding, in our examples, can be explicated as independent of empirical knowledge, or that the conceptual errors of our subjects are best seen as 'purely' mistakes about concepts and as involving no 'admixture' of error about 'the world'. With Quine, I find such talk about purity and mixture devoid of illumination or explanatory power. But my views on this matter neither entail nor are entailed by the premises of the arguments I give (cf. e.g. Sec. IIId). Those arguments seem to me to remain plausible under any of the relevant philosophical interpretations of the conceptual-ordinary–empirical distinction.

I have presented the experiment as appealing to ordinary intuition. I believe that common practice in the attribution of propositional attitudes is fairly represented by the various steps. This point is not really open to dispute. Usage may be divided in a few of the cases in which I have seen it as united. But broadly speaking, it seems to me undeniable that the individual steps of the thought experiment are acceptable to ordinary speakers in a wide variety of examples. The issue open to possible dispute is whether the steps should be taken in the literal way in which I have taken them, and thus whether the conclusion I have drawn from those steps is justified. In the remainder of Section III, I shall try to vindicate the literal interpretation of our examples. I do this by criticizing, in order of increasing generality or abstractness, a series of attempts to reinterpret the thought experiment's first step. Ultimately, I suggest (Secs. IIId and IV) that these attempts derive from characteristically philosophical models that have little or no independent justification. A thoroughgoing review of these models would be out of bounds, but the present paper is intended to show that they are deficient as accounts of our actual practice of mentalistic attribution.

I shall have little further to say in defense of the second and third steps of the thought experiment. Both rest on their intuitive plausibility, not on some particular theory. The third step, for example, certainly does not depend on a view that contents are merely sentences the subject is disposed to utter, interpreted as his community interprets them. It is compatible with several philosophical accounts of mental contents, including those that appeal to more abstract entities such as Fregean thoughts or Russellian propositions, and those that seek to deny that content clauses indicate any *thing* that might be called a content. I also do not claim that the fact that our subject lacks the relevant beliefs in the third step follows from the facts I have described. The point is that it is plausible, and certainly possible, that he would lack those beliefs.

The exact interpretation of the second step is relevant to a number of causal or functional theories of mental phenomena that I shall discuss in Section IV. The intuitive idea of the step is that none of the different physical, non-intentionally described causal chains set going by the differences in communal practice need affect our subjects in any way that would be relevant to an account of their mental contents. Differences in the behavior of other members of the community will, to be sure, affect the gravitational forces exerted on the subject. But I assume that these differences are irrelevant to macro-explanations of our subjects' physical movements and inner processes. They do not relevantly affect ordinary non-intentional physical explanations of how the subject acquires or is disposed to use the symbols in his repertoire. Of course, the social origins of a person's symbols do differ between actual and counterfactual cases. I shall return to this point in Sections IV and V. The remainder of section III will be devoted to the first step of the thought experiment.

IIIb. Incomplete Understanding and Standard Cases of Reinterpretation

The first step, as I have interpreted it, is the most likely to encounter opposition. In fact, there is a line of resistance that is second nature to linguistically oriented philosophers. According to this line, we should deny that, say, the patient really believed or thought that arthritis can occur outside of joints because he misunderstood the word 'arthritis'. More generally, we should deny that a subject could have any attitudes whose contents he incompletely understands.

What a person understands is indeed one of the chief factors that bear on what thoughts he can express in using words. If there were not deep and important connections between propositional attitudes and understanding, one could hardly expect one's attributions of mental content to facilitate reliable predictions of what a person will do, say, or think. But our examples provide reason to believe that these connections are not simple entailments to the effect that having a propositional attitude strictly implies full understanding of its content.

There are, of course, numerous situations in which we normally reinterpret or discount a person's words in deciding what he thinks. Philosophers often invoke such cases to bolster their animus against such attributions as the ones we made to our subjects: 'If a foreigner were to mouth the words "arthritis may occur in the thigh" or "my father had arthritis", not understanding what he uttered in the slightest, we would not say that he believed that arthritis may occur in the thigh, or that his father had arthritis. So why should we impute the belief to the patient?' Why, indeed? Or rather, why do we?

The question is a good one. We do want a general account of these cases. But the implied argument against our attribution is anemic. We tacitly and routinely distinguish between the cases I described and those in which a foreigner (or anyone) utters something without any comprehension. The best way to understand mentalistic notions is to recognize such differences in standard practice and try to account for them. One can hardly justify the assumption that full understanding of a content is in general a necessary condition for believing the content by appealing to some cases that tend to support the assumption in order to reject others that conflict with it.

It is a good method of discovery, I think, to note the sorts of cases philosophers tend to gravitate toward when they defend the view that the first step in the thought experiment should receive special interpretation. By reflecting on the differences between these cases and the cases we have cited, one should learn something about principles controlling mentalistic attribution.

I have already mentioned foreigners without command of the language. A child's imitation of our words and early attempts to use them provide similar examples. In these cases, mastery of the language and responsibility to its precepts have not been developed; and mental content attribution based on the meaning of words uttered tends to be precluded.

There are cases involving regional dialects. A person's deviance or ignorance judged by the standards of the larger community may count as normality or full mastery when evaluated from the regional perspective. Clearly, the regional standards tend to be the relevant ones for attributing content when the speaker's training or intentions are regionally oriented. The conditions for such orientation are complex, and I shall touch on them again in Section V. But there is no warrant in actual practice for treating each person's idiolect as always analogous to dialects whose words we automatically reinterpret—for purposes of mental content attribution—when usage is different. People are frequently held, and hold themselves, to the standards of their community when misuse or misunderstanding are at issue. One should distinguish these cases, which seem to depend on a certain *responsibility* to communal practice, from cases of automatic reinterpretation.

Tongue slips and Spoonerisms form another class of example where reinterpretation of a person's words is common and appropriate in arriving at an attribution of mental content. In these cases, we tend to exempt the speaker even from commitment to a homophonically formulated assertion content, as well as to the relevant mental content. The speaker's own behavior usually follows this line, often correcting himself when what he uttered is repeated back to him.

Malapropisms form a more complex class of examples. I shall not try to map it in detail. But in a fairly broad range of cases, we reinterpret a person's words at least in attributing mental content. If Archie says, 'Lead the way and we will precede', we routinely reinterpret the words in describing his expectations. Many of these cases seem to depend on the presumption that there are simple, superficial (for example, phonological) interference or exchange mechanisms that account for the linguistic deviance.

There are also examples of quite radical misunderstandings that sometimes generate reinterpretation. If a generally competent and reasonable speaker thinks that 'orangutan' applies to a fruit drink, we would be reluctant, and it would unquestionably be misleading, to take his words as revealing that he thinks he has been drinking orangutans for breakfast for the last few weeks. Such total misunderstanding often *seems* to block literalistic mental content attribution, at least in cases where we are not directly characterizing his mistake. (Contrary to philosophical lore, I am not convinced that such a man cannot correctly and literally be attributed a belief that an orangutan is a kind of fruit drink. But I shall not deal with the point here.)

There are also some cases that do not seem generally to prevent mental content attribution on the basis of literal interpretation of the subject's words in quite the same way as the others, but which deserve some mention. For almost any content except for those that directly display the subject's incomplete understanding, there will be many contexts in which it would be misleading to attribute that content to the subject without further comment. Suppose I am advising you about your legal liabilities in a situation where you have entered into what may be an unwritten contract. You ask me what Al would think. It would be misleading for me to reply that Al would think that you do not have a contract (or even do not have any legal problems), if I know that Al thinks a contract must be based on a formal document. Your evaluation of Al's thought would be crucially affected by his inadequate understanding. In such cases, it is incumbent on us to cite the subject's eccentricity: '(He would think that you do not have a contract, but then) he thinks that there is no such thing as a verbally based contract.'

Incidentally, the same sort of example can be constructed using attitudes that are abnormal, but that do not hinge on misunderstanding of any one notion. If Al had thought that only traffic laws and laws against violent crimes are ever prosecuted, it would be misleading for me to tell you that Al would think that you have no legal problems.

Both sorts of cases illustrate that in reporting a single attitude content, we typically suggest (implicate, perhaps) that the subject has a range of other attitudes that are normally associated with it. Some of these may provide reasons for it. In both sorts of cases, it is usually important to keep track of, and often to make explicit, the nature and extent of the subject's deviance. Otherwise, predictions and evaluations of his thought and action, based on normal background assumptions, will go awry. When the deviance is huge, attributions demand reinterpretation of the subject's words. Radical misunderstanding and mental instability are cases in point. But frequently, common practice seems to allow us to cancel the misleading suggestions by making explicit the subject's deviance, retaining literal interpretation of his words in our mentalistic attributions all the while.

All of the foregoing phenomena are relevant to accounting for standard practice. But they are no more salient than cases of straightforward belief attribution where the subject incompletely understands some notion in the attributed belief content. I think any impulse to say that common practice is *simply* inconsistent should be resisted (indeed, scorned). We cannot expect such practice to follow general principles rigorously. But even our brief discussion of the matter should have suggested the beginnings of generalizations about differences between cases where reinterpretation is standard and cases where it is not. A person's overall linguistic competence, his allegiance and responsibility to communal standards, the degree, source, and type of misunderstanding, the purposes of the report—all affect the issue. From a theoretical point of view, it would be a mistake to try to assimilate the cases in one direction or another. We do not want to credit a two-year-old who memorizes 'e $=$ mc^2' with belief in relativity theory. But the patient's attitudes involving the notion of arthritis should not be assimilated to the foreigner's uncomprehending pronunciations.

For purposes of defending the thought experiment and the arguments I draw from it, I can afford to be flexible about exactly how to generalize about these various phenomena. The thought experiment depends only on there being some cases in which a person's incomplete understanding does not force reinterpretation of his expressions in describing his mental contents. Such cases appear to be legion.

IIIc. Four Methods of Reinterpreting the Thought Experiment

I now want to criticize attempts to argue that even in cases where we ordinarily do ascribe content clauses despite the subject's incomplete understanding of expressions in those clauses, such ascriptions should not be taken literally. In order to overturn our interpretation of the thought experiment's first step, one must argue that none of the cases I have cited is appropriately taken in the literal manner. One must handle (apparent) attributions of unproblematically true contents involving incompletely mastered notions, as well as attributions of contents that display the misconceptions or partial understandings. I do not doubt that one can erect logically coherent and metaphysically traditional reinterpretations of all these cases. What I doubt is that such reinterpretations taken *in toto* can present a plausible view, and that taken individually they have any claim to superiority over the literal interpretations—either as accounts of the language of ordinary mentalistic ascription, or as accounts of the evidence on which mental attributions are commonly based.

Four types of reinterpretation have some currency. I shall be rather short with the first two, the first of which I have already warned against in Section IId. Sometimes relevant mentalistic ascriptions are reinterpreted as attributions of *de re* attitudes *of* entities not denoted by the misconstrued expressions. For example, the subject's belief that he has arthritis in the thigh might be interpreted as a belief *of* the non-arthritic rheumatoid ailment that it is in the thigh. The subject will probably have such a belief in this case. But it hardly accounts for the relevant attributions. In particular, it ignores the oblique occurrence of 'arthritis' in the original ascription. Such occurrences bear on a characterization of the subject's viewpoint. The subject thinks of the disease in his thigh (and of his arthritis) in a certain way. He thinks of each disease that it is arthritis. Other terms for arthritis (or for the actual trouble in his thigh) may not enable us to describe his attitude content nearly as well. The appeal to *de re* attitudes in this way is not adequate to the task of reinterpreting these ascriptions so as to explain away the difference between actual and counterfactual situations. It simply overlooks what needs explication.

A second method of reinterpretation, which Descartes proposed (cf. Sec. IV) and which crops up occasionally, is to claim that in cases of incomplete understanding, the subject's attitude or content is indefinite. It is surely true that in cases where a person is extremely confused, we are sometimes at a loss in describing his attitudes. Perhaps in such cases, the subject's mental content *is* indefinite. But in the cases I have cited, common practice lends virtually no support to the contention that the subject's mental contents are indefinite. The subject and his fellows typically know and agree on precisely *how to confirm or infirm* his beliefs—both in the cases where they are unproblematically true (or just empirically false) and in the cases where they display the misconception. Ordinary attributions typically specify the mental content without qualifications or hesitations.

In cases of partial understanding—say, in the mortgage example—it may indeed be unclear, short of extensive questioning, just how much mastery the subject has. But even this sort of unclarity does not appear to prevent, under ordinary circumstances, straightforward attributions utilizing 'mortgage' in oblique position. The subject is uncertain whether his father has two mortgages; he knows that his uncle has paid off the mortgage on his house. The contents are unhesitatingly attributed and admit of unproblematic testing for truth-value, despite the subject's partial understanding. There is thus little prima facie ground for the appeal to indefiniteness. The appeal appears to derive from a prior assumption that attribution of a content entails attribution of full understanding. Lacking an easy means of attributing something other than the misunderstood content, one is tempted to say that there *is* no definite content. But this is unnecessarily mysterious. It reflects on the prior assumption, which so far has no independent support.

The other two methods of reinterpretation are often invoked in tandem. One is to attribute a notion that just captures the misconception, thus replacing contents that are apparently false on account of the misconception, by true contents. For example, the subject's belief (true or false) that that is a sofa would be replaced by, or reinterpreted as, a (true) belief that that is a *chofa*, where 'chofa' is introduced to apply not only to sofas, but also to the armchairs the subject thinks are sofas. The other method is to count the error of the subject as purely metalinguistic. Thus the patient's apparent belief that he had arthritis in the thigh would be reinterpreted as a belief that 'arthritis' applied to something (or some disease) in his thigh. The two methods can be applied simultaneously, attempting to account for an ordinary content attribution in terms of a reinterpreted object-level content together with a metalinguistic error. It is important to remember that in order to overturn the thought experiment, these methods must not only establish that the subject held the particular attitudes that they advocate attributing; they must also justify a *denial* of the ordinary attributions literally interpreted.

The method of invoking object-level notions that precisely capture (and that replace) the subject's apparent misconception has little to be said for it as a natural and generally applicable account of the language of mentalistic ascriptions. We do not ordinarily seek out true object-level attitude contents to attribute to victims of errors based on incomplete understanding. For example, when we find that a person has been involved in a misconception in examples like ours, we do not regularly reinterpret those ascriptions that involved the misunderstood term, but were intuitively unaffected by the error. An attribution to someone of a true belief that he is eating brisket, or that he has just signed a contract, or that Uncle Harry has paid off his mortgage, is not typically reformulated when it is learned that the subject had not fully understood what brisket (or a contract, or a mortgage) is. A similar point applies when we know about the error at the time of the attribution—at least if we avoid misleading the audience in cases where the error is crucial to the issue at hand. Moreover, we shall frequently see the subject as sharing beliefs with others who understand the relevant notions better. In counting beliefs as shared, we do not require, in every case, that the subjects 'fully understand' the notions in those belief contents, or understand them in just the same way. Differences in understanding are frequently located as differences over other belief contents. We agree that you have signed a contract, but disagree over whether someone else could have made a contract by means of a verbal agreement.

There are reasons why ordinary practice does not follow the method of object-level reinterpretation. In many cases, particularly those involving partial understanding, finding a reinterpretation in accord with the method would be entirely non-trivial. It is not even clear that we have agreed upon means of pursuing such inquiries in all cases. Consider the arthritic patient. Suppose we are to reinterpret the attribution of his erroneous belief that he has arthritis in the thigh. We make up a term 'tharthritis' that covers arthritis and whatever it is he has in his thigh. The appropriate restrictions on the application of this term and of the patient's supposed notion are unclear. Is just any problem in the thigh that the patient wants to call 'arthritis' to count as tharthritis? Are other ailments covered? What would decide? The problem is that there are no recognized standards governing the application of the new term. In such cases, the method is patently *ad hoc*.

The method's willingness to invoke new terminology whenever conceptual error or partial understanding occurs is *ad hoc* in another sense. It proliferates terminology without evident theoretical reward. We do not engender better understanding of the patient by inventing a new word and saying that he thought (correctly) that tharthritis can occur outside joints. It is simpler and equally informative to construe him as thinking that arthritis may occur outside joints. When we are making other attributions that do not directly display the error, we must simply bear the deviant belief in mind, so as not to assume that all of the patient's inferences involving the notion would be normal.

The method of object-level reinterpretation often fails to give a plausible account of the evidence on which we base mental attributions. When caught in the sorts of errors we have been discussing, the subject does not normally respond by saying that his views had been misunderstood. The patient does not say (or think) that he had thought he had some-category-of-disease-like-arthritis-and-including-arthritis-but-also-capable-of-occurring-outside-of-joints   in   the thigh *instead* of the error commonly attributed. This sort of response would be disingenuous. Whatever other beliefs he had, the subject thought that he had arthritis in the thigh. In such cases, the subject will ordinarily give no evidence of having maintained a true object-level belief. In examples like ours, he typically admits his mistake, changes his views, and leaves it at that. Thus the subject's own behavioral dispositions and inferences often fail to support the method.

The method may be seen to be implausible as an account of the relevant evidence in another way. The patient knows that he has had arthritis in the ankle and wrists for some time. Now with his new pains in the thigh, he fears and believes that he has got arthritis in the thigh, that his arthritis is spreading. Suppose we reinterpret all of these attitude attributions in accord with the method. We use our recently coined term 'tharthritis' to cover (somehow) arthritis and whatever it is he has in the thigh. On this new interpretation, the patient is right in thinking that he has tharthritis in the ankle and wrists. His belief that it has lodged in the thigh is true. His fear is realized. But these attributions are out of keeping with the way we do and should view his actual beliefs and fears. His belief is not true, and his fear is not realized. He will be relieved when he is told that one cannot have arthritis in the thigh. His relief is bound up with a network of assumptions that he makes about his arthritis: that it is a kind of disease, that there are debilitating consequences of its occurring in multiple locations, and so on. When told that arthritis cannot occur in the thigh, the patient does not decide that his fears were realized, but that perhaps he should not have had those fears. He does not think: Well, my tharthritis *has* lodged in the thigh; but judging from the fact that what the doctor called 'arthritis' cannot occur in the thigh, tharthritis may not be a single kind of disease; and I suppose I need not worry about the effects of its occurring in various locations, since evidently the tharthritis in my thigh is physiologically unrelated to the tharthritis in my joints. There will rarely if ever be an empirical basis for such a description of the subject's inferences. The patient's behavior (including his reports, or thinkings-out-loud) in this sort of case will normally not indicate any such pattern of inferences at all. But this is the description that the object-level reinterpretation method appears to recommend.

On the standard attributions, the patient retains his assumptions about the relation between arthritis, kinds of disease, spreading, and so on. And he concludes that his arthritis is not appearing in new locations—at any rate, not in his thigh. These attributions will typically be supported by the subject's behavior. The object-level reinterpretation method postulates inferences that are more complicated and different in focus from the inferences that the evidence supports. The method's presentation in such a case would seem to be an *ad hoc* fiction, not a description with objective validity.

None of the foregoing is meant to deny that frequently when a person incompletely understands an attitude content he has some other attitude content that more or less captures his understanding. For example, in the contract example, the client will probably have the belief that if one breaks *a legally binding agreement based on formal documents*, then one may get into trouble. There are also cases in which it is reasonable to say that, at least in a sense, a person has a notion that is expressed by his dispositions to classify things in a certain way—even if there is no conventional term in the person's repertoire that neatly corresponds to that 'way'. The sofa case may be one such. Certain animals as well as people may have non-verbal notions of this sort. On the other hand, the fact that such attributions are justifiable *per se* yields no reason to deny that the subject (also) has object-level attitudes whose contents involve the relevant incompletely understood notion.

Whereas the third method purports to account for the subject's thinking at the object level, the fourth aims at accounting for his error. The error is construed as purely a metalinguistic mistake. The relevant false content is seen to involve notions that denote or apply to linguistic expressions. In examples relevant to our thought experiment, we ordinarily attribute a metalinguistic as well as an object-level attitude to the subject, at least in the case of non-occurrent propositional attitudes. For example, the patient probably believes that 'arthritis' applies in English to the ailment in his thigh. He believes that his father had a disease called 'arthritis'. And so on. Accepting these metalinguistic attributions, of course, does nothing *per se* toward making plausible a denial that the subjects in our examples have the counterpart object-level attitudes.

Like the third method, the metalinguistic reinterpretation method has no prima facie support as an account of the language of mentalistic ascriptions. When we encounter the subject's incomplete understanding in examples like ours, we do not decide that all the mental contents which we had been attributing to him with the misunderstood notion must have been purely metalinguistic in form. We also count people who incompletely understand terms in ascribed content clauses as sharing true and unproblematic object-level attitudes with others who understand the relevant terms better. For example, the lawyer and his client may share a wish that the client had not signed the contract to buy the house without reading the small print. A claim that these people share *only* attitudes with metalinguistic contents would have no support in linguistic practice.

The point about shared attitudes goes further. If the metalinguistic reinterpretation account is to be believed, we cannot say that a relevant English speaker shares a view (for example) that many old people have arthritis, with *anyone* who does not use the English word 'arthritis'. For the foreigner does not have the word 'arthritis' to hold beliefs about, though he does have attitudes involving the notion arthritis. And the attribution to the English speaker is to be interpreted metalinguistically, making reference to the word, so as not to involve attribution of the notion arthritis. This result is highly implausible. Ascriptions of such that-clauses as the above, regardless of the subject's language, serve to provide single descriptions and explanations of similar patterns of behavior, inference, and communication. To hold that we cannot accurately ascribe single content clauses to English speakers and foreigners in such cases would not only accord badly with linguistic practice. It would substantially weaken the descriptive and explanatory power of our common attributions. In countless cases, unifying accounts of linguistically disparate but cognitively and behaviorally similar phenomena would be sacrificed.

The method is implausible in other cases as an account of standard evidence on which mental attributions are based. Take the patient who fears that his arthritis is spreading. According to the metalinguistic reinterpretation method, the patient's reasoning should be described as follows. He thinks that the word 'arthritis' applies to a single disease in him, that the disease in him called 'arthritis' is debilitating if it spreads, that 'arthritis' applies to the disease in his wrists and ankles. He fears that the disease called 'arthritis' has lodged in his thigh, and so on. Of course, it is often difficult to find evidential grounds for attributing an object-level attitude *as opposed* to its metalinguistic counterpart. As I noted, when a person holds one attitude, he often holds the other. But there are types of evidence, in certain contexts, for making such discriminations, particularly contexts in which *occurrent* mental events are at issue. The subject may maintain that his reasoning did not fix upon words. He may be brought up short by a metalinguistic formulation of his just-completed ruminations, and may insist that he was not interested in labels. In such cases, especially if the reasoning is not concerned with linguistic issues in any informal or antecedently plausible sense, attribution of an object-level thought content is supported by the relevant evidence, and metalinguistic attribution is not. To insist that the occurrent mental event really involved a metalinguistic content would be a piece of *ad hoc* special pleading, undermined by the evidence we actually use for deciding whether a thought was metalinguistic.

In fact, there appears to be a general presumption that a person is reasoning at the object level, other things being equal. The basis for this presumption is that metalinguistic reasoning requires a certain self-consciousness about one's words and social institutions. This sort of sophistication emerged rather late in human history. (Cf. any history of linguistics.) Semantical notions were a product of this sophistication.

Occurrent propositional attitudes prevent the overall reinterpretation strategy from providing a plausible total account which would block our thought experiment. For such occurrent mental events as the patient's thought that his arthritis is especially painful in the knee this morning are, or can be imagined to be, clear cases of object-level attitudes. And such thoughts may enter into or connect up with pieces of reasoning—say the reasoning leading to relief that the arthritis had not lodged in the thigh—which cannot be plausibly accounted for in terms of object-level reinterpretation. The other reinterpretation methods (those that appeal to *de re* contents and to indefiniteness) are non-starters. In such examples, the literally interpreted ascriptions appear to be straightforwardly superior accounts of the evidence that is normally construed to be relevant. Here one need not appeal to the principle that literal interpretation is, other things equal, preferable to reinterpretation. Other things are not equal.

At this point, certain philosophers may be disposed to point out that what a person says and how he behaves do not infallibly determine what his attitude contents are. Despite the apparent evidence, the subject's attitude contents may in all cases I cited be metalinguistic, and may fail to involve the incompletely understood notion. It is certainly true that how a person acts and what he says, even sincerely, do not determine his mental contents. I myself have mentioned a number of cases that support the point. (Cf. Sec. IIIb.) But the point is often used in a sloppy and irresponsible manner. It is incumbent on someone making it (and applying it to cases like ours) to indicate considerations that override the linguistic and behavioral evidence. In section IIId, I shall consider intuitive or apriori philosophical arguments to this end. But first I wish to complete my evaluation of the metalinguistic reinterpretation method as an account of the language of mentalistic ascription in our examples.

In this century philosophers have developed the habit of insisting on meta-linguistic reinterpretation for any content attribution that directly *displays* the subject's incomplete understanding. These cases constitute but a small number of the attributions that serve the thought experiment. One could grant these reinterpretations and still maintain our overall viewpoint. But even as applied to these cases, the method seems dubious. I doubt that any evidentially sup-ported account of the language of these attributions will show them in general to be attributions of metalinguistic contents—contents that involve denotative reference to linguistic expressions.

The ascription 'He believes that broad overstuffed armchairs are sofas', as ordinarily used, does not in general *mean* 'He believes that broad, overstuffed armchairs are covered by the expression "sofas"' (or something like that). There are clear grammatical and semantical differences between

(i) broad, overstuffed armchairs are covered by the expression 'sofas'

and

(ii) broad, overstuffed armchairs are sofas.

When the two are embedded in belief contexts, they produce grammatically and semantically distinct sentences.

As noted, ordinary usage approves ascriptions like

(iii) He believes that broad, overstuffed armchairs are sofas.

It would be wildly *ad hoc* and incredible from the point of view of linguistic theory to claim that there is *no* reading of (iii) that embeds (ii). But there is no evidence from speaker behavior that *true* ascriptions of (iii) always (or perhaps even *ever*) derive from embedding (i) rather than (ii). In fact, I know of no clear evidence that (iii) is ambiguous between embedding (i) and (ii), or that (ii) is ambiguous, with one reading identical to that of (i). People do not in general seem to regard ascriptions like (iii) as elliptical. More importantly in most cases no amount of non-philosophical badgering will lead them to withdraw (iii), under some interpretation, *in favor of* an ascription that clearly embeds (i). At least in the cases of *non-occurrent* propositional attitudes, they will tend to agree to a clearly metalinguistic ascription—a belief sentence explicitly embedding something like (i)—in cases where they make an ascription like (iii). But this is evidence that they regard ascriptions that embed (i) and (ii) as both true. It hardly tells against counting belief ascriptions that embed (ii) as true, or against taking (iii) in the obvious, literal manner. In sum, there appears to be no ordinary empirical pressure on a theory of natural language to represent true ascriptions like (iii) as *not* embedding sentences like (ii). And other things being equal, literal readings are correct readings. Thus it is strongly plausible to assume that ordinary usage routinely accepts as true and justified even ascriptions like (iii), literally interpreted as embedding sentences like (ii).

There are various contexts in which we may be indifferent over whether to attribute a metalinguistic attitude or the corresponding object-level attitude. I have emphasized that frequently, though not always, we may attribute both. Or we might count the different contents as describing what contextually 'amount to the same attitude'. (Cf. Sec. I.) Even this latter locution remains compatible with the thought experiment, as long as both contents are *equally attributable* in describing 'the attitude'. In the counterfactual step of the thought experiment, the metalinguistic content (say, that broad, overstuffed armchairs are called 'sofas') will still be attributable. But in these circumstances it contextually 'amounts to the same attitude' as an object-level attitude whose content is in no sense equivalent to, or 'the same as', the original object-level content. For they have different truth values. Thus, assuming that the object-level and metalinguistic contents are equally attributable, it remains informally plausible that the person's attitudes are different between actual and counterfactual steps in the thought experiment. This contextual conflation of object-level and metalinguistic contents is not, however, generally acceptable even in describing non-occurrent attitudes, much less occurrent ones. There are contexts in which the subject himself may give evidence of making the distinction.

IIId. Philosophical Arguments for Reinterpretation

I have so far argued that the reinterpretation strategies that I have cited do not provide a plausible account of evidence relevant to a theory of the language of mentalistic ascriptions or to descriptions of mental phenomena themselves. I now want to consider characteristically philosophical arguments for revising ordinary discourse or for giving it a non-literal reading, arguments that rely purely on intuitive or apriori considerations. I have encountered three such arguments, or argument sketches.[4]

One holds that the content clauses we ascribed must be reinterpreted so as to make reference to words because they clearly concern linguistic matters—or are about language. Even if this argument were sound, it would not affect the thought experiment decisively. For most of the mental contents that vary between actual and counterfactual situations are not in any intuitive sense 'linguistic'. The belief that certain armchairs are sofas is intuitively linguistic. But beliefs that some sofas are beige, that Kirkpatrick is playing a clavichord, and that Milton had severe arthritis in his hands are not.

But the argument is unpersuasive even as applied to the contents that, in an intuitive sense, do concern linguistic matters. A belief that broad, overstuffed armchairs are sofas is linguistic (or 'about' language) in the same senses as an 'analytically' true belief that no armchairs are sofas. But the linguistic nature of the latter belief does not make its logical form metalinguistic. So citing the linguistic nature of the former belief does not suffice to show it metalinguistic. No semantically relevant component of either content applies to or denotes linguistic expressions.

Both the 'analytically' true and the 'analytically' false attitudes are linguistic in the sense that they are tested by consulting a dictionary or native linguistic intuitions, rather than by ordinary empirical investigation. We do not scrutinize pieces of furniture to test these beliefs. The pragmatic focus of expressions of these attitudes will be on usage, concepts, or meaning. But it is simply a mistake to think that these facts entail, or even suggest, that the relevant contents are metalinguistic in form. Many contents with object-level logical forms have primarily linguistic or conceptual implications.

A second argument holds that charitable interpretation requires that we not attribute to rational people beliefs like the belief that one may have arthritis in the thigh. Here again, the argument obviously does not touch most of the attitudes that may launch the thought experiment; for many are straightforwardly true, or false, on ordinary empirical grounds. Even so, it is not a good argument. There is nothing irrational or stupid about the linguistic or conceptual errors we attribute to our subjects. The errors are perfectly understandable as results of linguistic misinformation.

---

[4] Cf. my 'Belief and Synonymy', *The Journal of Philosophy*, 75 (1978), 119–138, sec. III, where I concentrate on attribution of belief contents containing 'one criterion' terms like 'vixen' or 'fortnight' which the subject misunderstands. The next several pages interweave some of the points in that paper. I think that a parallel thought experiment involving even these words is constructible, at least for a narrowly restricted set of beliefs. We can imagine that the subject believes that some female foxes—say, those that are virgins—are not vixens. Or he could believe that a fortnight is a period of ten days. (I believed this for many years.) Holding his physical history, qualitative experience, and dispositions constant, we can conceive of his linguistic community defining these terms as he actually misunderstands them. In such a case, his belief contents would differ from his actual ones.

In fact, the argument makes sense only against the background of the very assumption that I have been questioning. A belief that arthritis may occur in the thigh appears to be inexplicable or uncharitably attributed only if it is assumed that the subject must fully understand the notions in his attitude contents.

A third intuitive or apriori argument is perhaps the most interesting. Sometimes it is insisted that we should not attribute contents involving incompletely understood notions because *the individual must mean something different by the misunderstood word than what we non-deviant speakers mean by it.* Note again that it would not be enough to use this argument from deviant speaker meaning to show that the subject has notions that are not properly expressed in the way he thinks they are. In some sense of 'expressed', this is surely often the case. To be relevant, the argument must arrive at a negative conclusion: that the subject cannot have the attitudes that seem commonly to be attributed.

The expression 'the individual meant something different by his words' can be interpreted in more than one way. On one group of interpretations, the expression says little more than that the speaker incompletely understood his words: The patient thought 'arthritis' meant something that includes diseases that occur outside of joints. The client would have misexplained the meaning, use, or application of 'contract'. The subject applied 'sofa' to things that, unknown to him, are not sofas. A second group of interpretations emphasizes that not only does the speaker misconstrue or misapply his words, but he had *in mind* something that the words do not denote or express. The subject sometimes had in mind certain armchairs when he used 'sofa'. The client regarded the notion of legal agreement based on written documents as approximately interchangeable with what is expressed by 'contract', and thus had such a notion in mind when he used 'contract'. A person with a problem about the range of red might sometimes have in mind a mental image of a non-red color when he used 'red'.

The italicized premise of the argument is, of course, always true in our examples under the first group of interpretations, and often true under the second. But interpreted in these ways, the argument is a *non sequitur*. It does not follow from the assumption that the subject thought that a word means something that it does not (or misapplies the word, or is disposed to misexplain its meaning) that the word cannot be used in literally describing his mental contents. It does not follow from the assumption that a person has in mind something that a word does not denote or express that the word cannot occur obliquely (and be interpreted literally) in that-clauses that provide some of his mental contents. As I have pointed out in Section IIIb, there is a range of cases in which we commonly reinterpret a person's incompletely understood words for purposes of mental-content attribution. But the present argument needs to show that deviant speaker meaning always forces such reinterpretation.

In many of our examples, the idea that the subject has some deviant notion *in mind* has no intuitively clear application. (Consider the arthritis and mortgage examples.) But even where this expression does seem to apply, the argument does not support the relevant conclusion. At best it shows that a notion deviantly associated with a word plays a role in the subject's attitudes. For example, someone who has in mind the notion of an agreement based on written documents when he says 'I have just entered into a contract', may be correctly said to believe that he has just entered into an agreement based on written documents. It does not follow from this that he *lacks* a belief or thought that he has just entered into a contract. In fact, in our view, the client's having the deviant notion in mind is a *likely consequence* of the fact that he believes that contracts are impossible without a written document.

Of course, given the first, more liberal set of interpretations of 'means something different', the fact that in our examples the subject means something different by his words (or at least applies them differently) is *implied* by certain of his beliefs. It is implied by a belief that he has arthritis in the thigh. A qualified version of the converse implication also holds. Given appropriate background assumptions, the fact that the subject has certain deviant (object-level) beliefs is implied by his meaning something different by his words. So far, no argument has shown that we cannot accept these implications and retain the literal interpretation of common mentalistic ascriptions.

The argument from deviant speaker meaning downplays an intuitive feature that can be expected to be present in many of our examples. The subject's willingness to submit his statement and belief to the arbitration of an authority suggests a willingness to have his words taken in the normal way—regardless of mistaken associations with the word. Typically, the subject will regard recourse to a dictionary, and to the rest of us, as at once a check on his usage and his belief. When the verdict goes against him, he will not usually plead that we have simply misunderstood his views. This sort of behavior suggests that (given the sorts of background assumptions that common practice uses to distinguish our examples from those of foreigners, radical misunderstandings, and so forth) we can say that in a sense our man meant by 'arthritis' *arthritis*—where '*arthritis*' occurs, of course, obliquely. We can say this despite the fact that his incomplete understanding leads us, in one of the senses explicated earlier, to say that he meant something different by 'arthritis'.

If one tries to turn the argument from deviant speaker meaning into a valid argument, one arrives at an assumption that seems to guide all three of the philosophical arguments I have discussed. The assumption is that what a person thinks his words mean, how he takes them, fully determines what attitudes he can express in using them: the contents of his mental states and events are strictly limited to notions, however idiosyncratic, that he understands; a person cannot think with notions he incompletely understands. But supplemented with this assumption, the argument begs the question at issue.

The least controversial justification of the assumption would be an appeal to standard practice in mentalistic attributions. But standard practice is what brought the assumption into question in the first place. Of course, usage is not sacred if good reasons for revising it can be given. But none have been.

The assumption is loosely derived, I think, from the old model according to which a person must be directly acquainted with, or must immediately apprehend, the contents of his thoughts. None of the objections explicitly invokes this model—and many of their proponents would reject it. But I think that all the objections derive some of their appeal from philosophical habits that have been molded by it. I shall discuss this model further in Section IV.

One may, of course, quite self-consciously neglect certain aspects of common mentalistic notions in the interests of a revised or idealized version of them. One such idealization could limit itself to just those attitudes involving 'full understanding' (for some suitably specified notion of understanding). This limitation is less clearcut than one might suppose, since the notion of understanding itself tends to be used according to misleading stereotypes. Still, oversimplified models, idealizations, of mentalistic notions are defensible, as long as the character and purpose of the oversimplifications are clear. In my opinion, limiting oneself to 'fully understood' attitudes provides no significant advantage in finding elegant and illuminating formal semantical theories of natural language. Such a strategy has perhaps a better claim in psychology, though even there its propriety is controversial. (Cf. Sec. IV.) More to the point, I think that models that neglect the relevant social factors in mentalistic attributions are not likely to provide long-run philosophical illumination of our actual mentalistic notions. But this view hardly admits of detailed support here and now.

Our argument in the preceding pages may, at a minimum, be seen as inveighing against a long-standing philosophical habit of denying that it *is* an oversimplification to make 'full understanding' of a content a necessary condition for having a propositional attitude with that content. The oversimplification does not constitute neglect of some quirk of ordinary usage. Misunderstanding and partial understanding are pervasive and inevitable phenomena, and attributions of content despite them are an integral part of common practice.

I shall not here elaborate a philosophical theory of the social aspects of mentalistic phenomena, though in Section V I shall suggest lines such a theory might take. One of the most surprising and exciting aspects of the thought experiment is that its most literal interpretation provides a perspective on the mental that has received little serious development in the philosophical tradition. The perspective surely invites exploration.

IV. APPLICATIONS

I want to turn now to a discussion of how our argument bears on philosophical approaches to the mental that may be termed *individualistic*. I mean this term to be somewhat vague. But roughly, I intend to apply it to philosophical treatments that seek to see a person's intentional mental phenomena ultimately and purely in terms of what happens to the person, what occurs within him, and how he responds to his physical environment, without any essential reference to the social context in which he or the interpreter of his mental phenomena is situated. How I apply the term 'individualistic' will perhaps become clearer by reference to the particular cases that I shall discuss.

a. As I have already intimated, the argument of the preceding sections affects the traditional intro-(or extro-)spectionist treatments of the mind, those of Plato, Descartes, Russell, and numerous others. These treatments are based on a model that likens the relation between a person and the contents of his thought to seeing, where seeing is taken to be a kind of direct, immediate experience. On the most radical and unqualified versions of the model, a person's inspection of the contents of his thought is infallible: the notion of incompletely understanding them has no application at all.

The model tends to encourage individualistic treatments of the mental. For it suggests that what a person thinks depends on what occurs or 'appears' within his mind. Demythologized, what a person thinks depends on the power and extent of his comprehension and on his internal dispositions toward the comprehended contents. The model is expressed in perhaps its crudest and least qualified form in a well-known passage by Russell:

> Whenever a relation of supposing or judging occurs, the terms to which the supposing or judging mind is related by the relation of supposing or judging must be terms with which the mind in question is acquainted. ... It seems to me that the truth of this principle is evident as soon as the principle is understood.[5]

Acquaintance is (for Russell) direct, infallible, non-propositional, non-perspectival knowledge. 'Terms' like concepts, ideas, attributes, forms, meanings, or senses are entities that occur in judgments more or less immediately before the mind on a close analogy to the way sensations are supposed to.

The model is more qualified and complicated in the writings of Descartes. In particular, he emphasizes the possibility that one might perceive the contents of one's mind unclearly or indistinctly. He is even high-handed enough to write, 'Some people throughout their lives perceive nothing so correctly as to be capable of judging it properly.'[6] This sort of remark appears to be a concession to the points made in Sections I and II about the possibility of a subject's badly understanding his mental contents. But the concession is distorted by the underlying

---

[5] Bertrand Russell, *Mysticism and Logic* (London: Unwin Hyman, 1959), 221. Although Russell's statement is unusually unqualified, its kinship to Descartes's and Plato's model is unmistakable. Cf. Plato, *Phaedrus* 249b–c, *Phaedo* 47b6–c4, both in *The Collected Dialogues of Plato*, trans. E. Hamilton and H. Cairus (New York: Pantheon Books, 1961); Descartes, *Philosophical Works*, ed. E. Haldane and G. R. T. Ross, 2 vols. (New York Dover, 1955), *Rules for the Direction of the Mind*, sec. XII, i. 41–42, 45; *Principles of Philosophy*, Part I, XXXII–XXXV, i. 232–233; *Replies*, ii. 52; Hume, *A Treatise of Human Nature*, ed. L. A. Selby-Bigge (Oxford: Clarendon Press, 1965), I. 3 5; II, 2 6; Kant, *Critique of Pure Reason*, trans. N. K. Smith (New York: St Martin's Press, 1965), A7–B11; Frege, *The Foundations of Arithmetic*, ed. J. L. Austin (Evanston, Ill.: Northwestern University Press, 1968), sec. 105; G. E. Moore, *Principia Ethica* (Cambridge: Cambridge University Press, 1966), 86.

[6] Descartes, *Principles of Philosophy*, XLV–XLI.

introspection model. On Descartes's view, the person's faculty of understanding, properly so-called, makes no errors. Failure to grasp one's mental contents results from either blind prejudice or interference by 'mere' bodily sensations and corporeal imagery. The implication is that with sufficiently careful reflection on the part of the individual subject, these obstacles to perfect understanding can be cleared. That is, one need only be careful or properly guided in one's introspections to achieve full understanding of the content of one's intentional mental phenomena. Much that Descartes says suggests that where the subject fails to achieve such understanding, no definite content can be attributed to him. In such cases, his 'thinking' consists of unspecifiable or indeterminate imagery; attribution of definite conceptual content is precluded. These implications are reinforced in Descartes's appeal to self-evident, indubitable truths:

There are some so evident and at the same time so simple that we cannot think of them without believing them to be true. ... For we cannot doubt them unless we think of them; and we cannot think of them without at the same time believing them to be true, i.e. we can never doubt them.[7]

The self-evidence derives from the mere understanding of the truths, and fully understanding them is a precondition for thinking them at all. It is this last requirement that we have been questioning.

In the Empiricist tradition Descartes's qualifications on the direct experience model—particularly those involving the interfering effects of sensations and imagery—tend to fall away. What one thinks comes to be taken as a sort of impression (whether more imagistic or more intellectual) on or directly grasped by the individual's mind. The tendency to make full comprehension on the part of the subject a necessary condition for attributing a mental content to him appears both in philosophers who take the content to be a Platonic abstraction and in those who place it, in some sense, inside the individual's mind. This is certainly the direction in which the model pulls, with its picture of immediate accessibility to the individual. Thus Descartes's original concessions to cases of incomplete understanding became lost as his model became entrenched. What Wölfflin said of painters is true of philosophers: they learn more from studying each other than from reflecting on anything else.

The history of the model makes an intricate subject. My remarks are meant merely to provide a suggestive caricature of it. It should be clear, however, that in broad outline the model mixes poorly with the thought experiment of Section II, particularly its first step. The thought experiment indicates that certain 'linguistic truths' that have often been held to be indubitable can be thought yet doubted. And it shows that a person's thought *content* is not fixed by what goes on in him, or by what is accessible to him simply by careful reflection. The reason for this last point about 'accessibility' need not be that the content lies too deep in the unconscious recesses of the subject's psyche. Contents are sometimes

---

[7] Descartes, *Philosophical Works*, ii: *Replies*, 42.

'inaccessible' to introspection simply because much mentalistic attribution does not presuppose that the subject has fully mastered the content of his thought.

In a certain sense, the metaphysical model has fixed on some features of our use of mentalistic notions to the exclusion of others. For example, the model fastens on the facts that we are pretty good at identifying our own beliefs and thoughts, and we have at least a prima facie authority in reporting a wide range of them. It also underlines the point that for certain contents we tend to count understanding as a sufficient condition for acknowledging their truth. (It is debatable, of course, how well it explains or illumines these observations.) The model also highlights the truism that a certain measure of understanding is required of a subject if we are to attribute intentional phenomena on the basis of what he utters. As we have noted, chance or purely rote utterances provide no ground for mental content attributions; certain verbal pathologies are discounted. The model extrapolates from these observations to the claim that a person can never fail to understand the content of his beliefs or thoughts, or that the remedy for such failure lies within his own resources of reflection (whether autonomous and conscious, or unconscious and guided). It is this extrapolation that requires one to pass over the equally patent practice of attributing attitudes where the subject incompletely understands expressions that provide the content of those attitudes. Insistence on metalinguistic reinterpretation and talk about the indefiniteness of attitude contents in cases of incomplete understanding seem to be rearguard defenses of a vastly overextended model.

The Cartesian–Russellian model has few strict adherents among prominent linguistic philosophers. But although it has been widely rejected or politely talked around, claims that it bore and nurtured are commonplace, even among its opponents. As we have seen in the objections to the first step of the argument of section II, these claims purport to restrict the contents we can attribute to a person on the basis of his use of language. The restrictions simply mimic those of Descartes. Freed of the picturesque but vulnerable model that formed them, the claims have assumed the power of dogma. Their strictures, however, misrepresent ordinary mentalistic notions.

b. This century's most conspicuous attempt to replace the traditional Cartesian model has been the behaviorist movement and its heirs. I take it as obvious that the argument of Section II provides yet another reason to reject the most radical version of behaviorism—'philosophical', 'logical', or 'analytical' behaviorism. This is the view that mentalistic attributions can be 'analytically' defined, or given strict meaning equivalences, purely in non-mental, behavioral terms. No analysis resting purely on the individual's dispositions to behavior can give an 'analytic' definition of a mental content attribution, because we can conceive of the behavioral definiens applying while the mentalistic definiendum does not. But a new argument for this conclusion is hardly needed, since 'philosophical' behaviorists are, in effect, extinct.

There is, however, an heir of behaviorism that I want to discuss at some-what greater length. The approach sometimes goes by the name 'functionalism', although that term is applied to numerous slogans and projects, often vaguely formulated. Even views that seem to me to be affected by our argument are frequently stated so sketchily that one may be in considerable doubt about what is being proposed. So my remarks should be taken less as an attempt to refute the theses of particular authors than as an attack on a way of thinking that seems to inform a cluster of viewpoints. The quotations I give in footnotes are meant to be suggestive, if not always definitive, of the way of thinking the argument tells against.[8]

The view affected by the argument of Section II attempts to give something like a philosophical 'account' of the mental. The details and strategy—even the notion of 'account'—vary from author to author. But a recurrent theme is that mental notions are to be seen ultimately in terms of the individual subject's input, output, and inner dispositions and states, where these latter are character-ized purely in terms of how they lead to or from output, input, or other inner states similarly characterized. Mental notions are to be explicated or identified in functional, non-mentalistic, non-intentional terminology. Proponents of this sort of idea are rarely very specific about what terms may be used in describing input and output, or even what sorts of terms count as 'functional' expressions. But the impression usually given is that input and output are to be specified in terms (acceptable to a behaviorist) of irritations of the subject's surfaces and move-ments of his body. On some versions, neurophysiological terms are allowed. More recently, there have been liberalized appeals to causal input and output relations with particular, specified physical objects, stuffs, or magnitudes. Func-tional terms include terms like 'causes', 'leads to with probability n', and the like. For our purposes, the details do not matter much, as long as an approach allows no mentalistic or other intentional terms (such as 'means' or that-clauses) into its vocabulary, and as long as it applies to individuals taken one by one.

A difference between this approach and that of philosophical behaviorism is that a whole array of dispositional or functional states—causally or probabilist-ically interrelated—may enter into the 'account' of a single mental attribution. The array must be ultimately secured to input and output, but the internal states need not be so secured one by one. The view is thus not immediately vulnerable to claims against simplistic behaviorisms, that a *given* stimulus–response pattern

---

[8] Certain movements sometimes called 'functionalist' are definitely not my present concern. Nothing I say is meant to oppose the claim that hypotheses in psychology do and should make ref-erence to 'sub-personal' states and processes in explaining human action and ordinary mental states and processes. My remarks may bear on precisely how such hypotheses are construed philosoph-ically. But the hypotheses themselves must be judged primarily by their fruits. Similarly, I am not concerned with the claim that computers provide an illuminating perspective for viewing the mind. Again, my view may bear on the interpretation of the computer analogy, but I have no intention of questioning its general fruitfulness. On the other hand, insofar as functionalism is merely a slogan to the effect that 'once you see how computers might be made to work, you realize such and such about the mind', I am inclined to let the cloud condense a little before weighing its contents.

may have different contents in different social contexts. Such claims, which hardly need a defender, have been tranquilly accepted on this view. The view's hope is that differences in content depend on functional differences in the individual's larger functional structure. From this viewpoint, analytical behaviorism erred primarily in its failure to recognize the interlocking or holistic character of mental attributions and in its oversimplification of theoretical explanation.

As I said, the notion of an account of the mental varies from author to author. Some authors take over the old-fashioned ideal of an 'analysis' from philosophical behaviorism and aim at a definition of the meaning of mentalistic vocabulary, or a definitional elimination of it. Others see their accounts as indicating a series of scientific hypotheses that identify mental states with causal or functional states, or roles, in the individual. These authors reject behaviorism's goal of providing meaning equivalences, as well as its restrictive methods. The hypotheses are supposed to be type or property identities and are nowadays often thought to hold necessarily, even if they do not give meaning relations. Moreover, these hypotheses are offered not merely as speculation about the future of psychology, but as providing a philosophically illuminating account of our ordinary notion of the mental. Thus if the view systematically failed to make plausible type identities between functional states and mental states, ordinarily construed, then by its own lights it would have failed to give a philosophical 'account' of the mental. I have crudely over-schematized the methodological differences among the authors in this tradition. But the differences fall roughly within the polar notions of *account* that I have described. I think my discussion will survive the oversimplifications.[9]

---

[9] A representative of the more nearly 'analytical' form of functionalism is David Lewis, 'Psychophysical and Theoretical Identifications', *Australasian Journal of Philosophy*, 50 (1972), 249–258: 'Applied to common-sense psychology—folk science rather than professional science, but a theory nonetheless—we get the hypothesis ... that a mental state M ... is definable as the occupant of a certain causal role R—that is, as the state, of whatever sort, that is causally connected in specified ways to sensory stimuli, motor responses, and other mental states' (pp. 249–250). Actually, it should be noted that the argument of sec. I applies to Lewis's position less directly than one might suppose. For reasons unconnected with matters at hand, Lewis intends his *definition* to apply to relational mentalistic predicates like 'thinks' but not to complex predicates that identify actual mental states or events, like 'thinks that snow is white'. Cf. ibid., 256 n. 13. This seems to me a puzzling halfway house for some of Lewis's philosophical purposes. But our argument appears to apply anyway, since Lewis is explicit in holding that physical facts about a person taken in isolation from his fellows 'determine' all his specific intentional events and states. Cf. "Radical Interpretation", *Synthese*, 27 (1974), 331 ff. I cite Lewis's definitional approach because it has been the most influential recent piece of its genre, and many of those influenced by it have not excluded its application to specific intentional mental states and events. Other representatives of the definitional approach are J. J. C. Smart, 'Further Thoughts on the Identity Theory', *The Monist*, 56 (1972), 149–162; D. W. Armstrong, *A Materialist Theory of Mind* (London: Routledge & Kegan Paul, 1968), pp. 90–91 and *passim*; Sidney Shoemaker, 'Functionalism and Qualia', *Philosophical Studies*, 27 (1975), 306–307. A representative of the more frequently held 'hypothesis' version of functionalism is Hilary Putnam, 'The Mental Life of Some Machines', in *Philosophical Papers*, ii (Cambridge: Cambridge University Press, 1975), and 'The Nature of Mental States', ibid., cf. p. 437: '... if the program of finding psychological laws that are not species specific ... ever succeeds, then it will bring in its wake a delineation of the kind of functional organization that is

Any attempt to give an account of specific beliefs and thoughts along the lines I have indicated will come up short. For we may fix the input, output, and total array of dispositional or functional states of our subject, as long as these are non-intentionally described and are limited to what is relevant to accounting for his activity taken in isolation from that of his fellows. But we can still conceive of his mental contents as varying. Functionally equivalent people—on any plausible notion of functional equivalence that has been sketched—may have non-equivalent mental state and event contents, indicated by obliquely non-equivalent content clauses. The argument indicates a systematic inadequacy in attempts of the sort I described.

Proponents of functionalist accounts have seen them as revealing the true nature of characteristic marks of the mental and as resolving traditional philosophical issues about such marks. In the case of beliefs, desires, and thoughts, the most salient mark is intentionality—the ill-specified information-bearing, representational feature that seems to invest these mental states and events.[10] In my terminology, accounting for intentionality largely amounts to accounting for the content of mental states and events. (There is also, of course, the application of content in *de re* cases. But let us put this aside here.) Such content is clearly part of what the functional roles of our subjects' states fail to determine.

It is worth re-emphasizing here that the problem is unaffected by suggestions that we specify input and output in terms of causal relations to particular

necessary and sufficient for a given psychological state, as well as a precise definition of the notion "psychological state".' In more recent work, Putnam's views on the relation between functional organization and psychological (and also mental) states and events have become more complicated. I make no claims about how the argument of sec. II bears on them. Other representatives of the 'hypothesis' approach are Gilbert Harman, 'Three Levels of Meaning', *The Journal of Philosophy*, 65 (1968); 'An Introduction to "Translation and Meaning"', in D. Davidson and I. Hintikka (eds.), *Words and Objections* (Dordrecht: Reidel, 1969), 21; and *Thought* (Princeton: Princeton University Press, 1973), 43–46, 56–65, e.g., p. 45: '... mental states and processes are to be functionally defined (by a psychological theory). They are constituted by their function or role in the relevant programme'; Jerry Fodor, *The Language of Thought* (New York: Cravell, 1975), ch. 1; Armstrong, *A Materialist Theory of Mind*, 84. An attempt to articulate the common core of the different types of functionalist 'account' occurs in Ned Block and Jerry Fodor's 'What Psychological States are Not', *Philosophical Review*, 81 (1972), 173: '... functionalism in the broad sense of that doctrine which holds that type identity conditions for psychological states refer only to their relations to inputs, outputs and one another.'

[10] Often functionalists give mental contents only cursory discussion, if any at all. But claims that a functional account explains intentionality by accounting for all specific intentional states and events in non-intentional, functional language occur in the following: Daniel Dennett, *Content and Consciousness* (London: Rontledge & Kegan Paul, 1969), ch. 2 and *passim*; Harman, *Thought*, e.g. p. 60: 'To specify the meaning of a sentence used in communication is partly to specify the belief or other mental state expressed; and the representative character of that state is determined by its functional role'; Fodor, *Language of Thought*, ch. 1 and 2 e.g. p. 75: 'The way that information is stored, computed ... or otherwise processed by the organism explains its cognitive states and in particular, its propositional attitudes'; Smart, 'Further Thoughts on the Identity Theory'; Hartry Field, 'Mental Representation', *Erkenntnis*, 13 (1978), 9–61. I shall confine discussion to the issue of intentionality. But it seems to me that the individualistic cast of functionalist accounts renders them inadequate in their handling of another major traditional issue about intentional mental states and events—first-person authority.

objects or stuffs in the subject's physical environment. Such specifications may be thought to help with some examples based on indexicality or psychological success verbs, and perhaps in certain arguments concerning natural kind terms (though even in these cases I think that one will be forced to appeal to intentional language). (Cf. note 2.) But this sort of suggestion has no easy application to the argument. For the relevant causal relations between the subject and the physical environment to which his terms apply—where such relations are non-intentionally specified—were among the elements held constant while the subject's beliefs and thoughts varied.

The functionalist approaches I have cited seem to provide yet another case in which mental contents are not plausibly accounted for in non-intentional terms. They are certainly not explicable in terms of causally or functionally specified states and events of the *individual* subject. The intentional or semantical role of mental states and events is not a function merely of their functionally specified roles in the individual. The failure of these accounts of intentional mental states and events derives from an underestimation of socially dependent features of cognitive phenomena.

Before extending the application of the argument, I want briefly to canvass some ways of being influenced by it, ways that might appeal to someone fixed on the functionalist ideal. One response might be to draw a strict distinction between mental states, ordinarily so-called, and psychological states. One could then claim that the latter are the true subject matter of the science of psychology and may be identified with functional states functionally specified, after all. Thus one might claim that the subject was in the same psychological (functional) states in both the actual and the imagined situations, although he had different beliefs and thoughts ordinarily so-called.

There are two observations that need to be entered about this position. The first is that it frankly jettisons much of the philosophical interest of functionalist accounts. The failure to cope with mental contents is a case in point. The second observation is that it is far from clear that such a distinction between the psychological and the mental is or will be sanctioned by psychology itself. Functionalist accounts arose as philosophical interpretations of developments in psychology influenced by computer theory. The interpretations have been guided by philosophical interests, such as throwing light on the mind–body problem and accounting for mentalistic features in non-mentalistic terms. But the theories of cognitive psychologists, including those who place great weight on the computer analogy, are not ordinarily purified of mentalistic or intentional terminology. Indeed, intentional terminology plays a central role in much contemporary theorizing. (This is also true of theories that appeal to 'sub-personal' states or processes. The 'sub-personal' states themselves are often characterized intentionally.) Purifying a theory of mentalistic and intentional features in favor of functional or causal features is more clearly demanded by the goals of philosophers than by the needs of psychology. Thus it is at least an open question whether functional approaches of the sort we have discussed give a satisfactory account of *psychological* states and events. It is not evident that psychology will ever be methodologically 'pure' (or theoretically purifiable by some definitional device) in the way these approaches demand. *This* goal of functionalists may be simply a meta-psychological mistake.

To put the point another way, it is not clear that functional states, characterized purely in functional, non-intentional terms (and non-intentional descriptions of input and output) are the natural subject matter of psychology. Psychology would, I think, be an unusual theory if it restricted itself (or could be definitionally restricted) to specifying abstract causal or functional structures in purely causal or functional terms, together with vocabulary from other disciplines. Of course, it *may* be that functional states, functionally specified, form a psychological natural kind. And it is certainly not to be assumed that psychology will respect ordinary terminology in its individuation of types of psychological states and events. Psychology must run its own course. But the assumption that psychological terminology will be ultimately non-intentional and purely functional seems without strong support. More important from my viewpoint, if psychology did take the individualistic route suggested by the approaches I have cited, then its power to illumine the everyday phenomena alluded to in mentalistic discourse would be correspondingly limited.

These remarks suggest a second sort of functionalist response to the argument of Section II, one that attempts to take the community rather than the individual as the object of functional analysis. One might, for example, seek to explain an individual's responsibility to communal standards in terms of his having the right kind of interaction with other individuals who collectively had functional structures appropriate to those standards. Spelling out the relevant notions of interaction and appropriateness is, of course, anything but trivial. (Cf. Section V.) Doing so in purely functional, non-intentional terms would be yet a further step. Until such a treatment is developed and illustrated in some detail, there is little point in discussing it. I shall only conjecture that, if it is to remain non-intentional, such a treatment is likely to be so abstract—at least in our present state of psychological and sociological ignorance—that it will be unilluminating from a philosophical point of view. Some of the approaches we have been discussing already more than flirt with this difficulty.

c. Individualistic assumptions about the mental have infected theorizing about the relation between mind and meaning. An example is the Gricean project of accounting for conventional or linguistic meaning in terms of certain complex intentions and beliefs of individuals.[11] The Gricean program analyzes

---

[11] H. P. Grice, 'Meaning', *The Philosophical Review*, 66 (1957), 377–388; 'Utterer's Meaning, Sentence-Meaning, and Word-Meaning', *Foundations of Language*, 4 (1968), 225–242; Stephen Schiffer, *Meaning* (Oxford: Oxford University Press, 1972), cf. esp. pp. 13, 50, 63. ff.; Jonathan Bennett, 'The Meaning-Nominalist Strategy', *Foundations of Language*, 10 (1974), 141–168. Another example of an individualistic theory of meaning is the claim to explicate all kinds of meaning ultimately in psychological terms, and these latter in functionalist terms. See e.g. Harman, 'Three Levels of Meaning'. This project seems to rest on the functionalist approaches just criticized.

conventional meaning in terms of subtle 'mutual knowledge', or beliefs and intentions about each others' beliefs and intentions, on the part of most or all members of a community. Seen as a quasi-definitional enterprise, the program presupposes that the notion of an individual's believing or intending something is always 'conceptually' independent of the conventional meaning of symbols used to express that something. Insofar as 'conceptually' has any intuitive content, this seems not to be the case. Our subject's belief or intention contents can be conceived to vary simply by varying conventions in the community around him. The content of individuals' beliefs seems sometimes to depend partly on social conventions in their environment. It is true that our subjects are actually rather abnormal members of their community, at least with respect to their use and understanding of a given word. But normality here is judged against the standards set by communal conventions. So stipulating that the individuals whose mental states are used in defining conventional meaning be relevantly normal will not avoid the circularity that I have indicated. I see no way to do so. This charge of circularity has frequently been raised on intuitive grounds. The argument gives the intuitions substance. Explicating convention in terms of belief and intention may provide various sorts of insight. But it is not defining a communal notion in terms of individualistic notions. Nor is it reducing, in any deep sense, the semantical, or the intentional generally, to the psychological.

d. Individualistic assumptions have also set the tone for much discussion of the ontology of the mental. This subject is too large to receive detailed consideration here. It is complicated by a variety of crosscurrents among different projects, methodologies, and theses. I shall only explore how the argument affects a certain line of thinking closely allied to the functionalist approaches already discussed. These approaches have frequently been seen as resuscitating an old argument for the materialist identity theory. The argument is three-staged. First, one gives a philosophical 'account' of each mentalistic locution, an account that is prima facie neutral as regards ontology. For example, a belief or a thought that sofas are comfortable is supposed to be accounted for as one functionally specified state or event within an array of others—all of which are secured to input and output. Second, the relevant functionally specified states or events are expected to be empirically correlated or correlatable with physiological states or events in a person (states or events that have those functions). The empirical basis for believing in these correlations is claimed to be provided by present or future physical science. The nature of the supposed correlations is differently described in different theories. But the most prevalent views expect only that the correlations will hold for each organism and person (perhaps at a given time) taken one by one. For example, the functionally specified event type that is identified with a thought that sofas are comfortable may be realized in one person by an instance (or 'token') of one physiological event type, and in another person by an instance of another physiological event type. Third, the ('token') mental state or event in the person is held to be identical with the relevant ('token') physiological state or event, on general grounds of explanatory simplicity and scientific method. Sometimes, this third stage is submerged by building uniqueness of occupancy of functional role into the first stage.[12]

I am sceptical about this sort of argument at every stage. But I shall doubt only the first stage here. The argument I gave in Section II directly undermines the attempt to carry out the first stage by recourse to the sort of functionalist approaches that we discussed earlier. Sameness of functional role, individual-istically specified, is compatible with difference of content. I know of no better non-intentional account of mentalistic locutions. If a materialist argument of this genre is to arrive, it will require a longer first step.

I shall not try to say whether there is a philosophically interesting sense in which intentional mental phenomena are physical or material. But I do want to note some considerations against materialist *identity* theories.

State-like phenomena (say, beliefs) raise different problems from event-like phenomena (say, occurrent thoughts). Even among identity theorists, it is some-times questioned whether an identity theory is the appropriate goal for material-ism in the case of states. Since I shall confine myself to identity theories, I shall concentrate on event-like phenomena. But our considerations will also bear on views that hope to establish some sort of token identity theory for mental states like beliefs.

One other preliminary. I want to remain neutral about how best to describe the relation between the apparent event-like feature of occurrent thoughts and the apparent relational feature (their relation to a content). One might think of there being an event, the token thought event, that is in a certain relation to a content (indicated by the that-clause). One might think of the event as consisting—as not being anything 'over and above'—the relevant relation's holding at a certain time between a person and a content. Or one might prefer some other account. From the viewpoint of an identity theory, the first way of seeing the matter is most advantageous. So I shall fit my exposition to that point of view.

Our ordinary method of identifying occurrent thought events and differenti-ating between them is to make reference to the person or organism to whom the thought occurs, the time of its occurrence, and the content of the thought. If person, time, and content are the same, we would normally count the thought event the same. If any one of these parameters differs in descriptions of thought events (subject to qualifications about duration), then the events or occurrences described are different. Of course, we can differentiate between events using descriptions that do not home in on these particular parameters. But these

---

[12] Perhaps the first reasonably clear modern statement of the strategy occurs in J. J. C. Smart, 'Sensations and Brain Processes', *The Philosophical Review*, 68 (1959), 141–156. This article treats qualitative experiences; but Smart is explicit in applying it to specific intentional states and events in 'Further Thoughts on the Identity Theory'. Cf. also David Lewis, 'An Argument for the Identity Theory', *The Journal of Philosophy*, 63 (1966), 17–25; 'Psychophysical and Theoretical Identi-fications'; Armstrong, *A Materialist Theory of Mind, passim*; Harman, *Thought*, 42–43; Fodor, *Language of Thought*, Introduction.

parameters are dominant. (It is worth noting that differentiations in terms of causes and effects usually tend to rely on the content of mental events or states at some point, since mental states or events are often among the causes or effects of a given mental event, and these causes or effects will usually be identified partly in terms of their content.) The important point for our purposes is that in ordinary practice, sameness of thought content (or at least some sort of strong equivalence of content) is taken as a necessary condition for sameness of thought occurrence.

Now one might codify and generalize this point by holding that no occurrence of a thought (that is, no token thought event) could have a different (or extensionally non-equivalent) content and be the very same token event. If this premise is accepted, then our argument of Section II can be deployed to show that a person's thought event is not *identical* with any event in him that is described by physiology, biology, chemistry, or physics. For let b be any given event described in terms of one of the physical sciences that occurs in the subject while he thinks the relevant thought. Let 'b' be such that it denotes the same physical event occurring in the subject in our counterfactual situation. (If you want, let 'b' be rigid in Kripke's sense, though so strong a stipulation is not needed.) The second step of our argument in Section II makes it plausible that b need not be affected by counterfactual differences in the communal use of the word 'arthritis'. Actually, the subject thinks that his ankles are stiff from arthritis, while b occurs. But we can conceive of the subject's *lacking* a thought event that his ankles are stiff from arthritis, while b occurs. Thus in view of our initial premise, b is not identical with the subject's occurrent thought.[13]

Identity theorists will want to reject the first premise—the premise that no event with a different content could be identical with a given thought event. On such a view, the given thought event that his ankles are stiff from arthritis might well have been a thought that his ankles are stiff from tharthritis,

---

[13] The argument is basically Cartesian in style, (cf. *Meditations* II), though the criticism of functionalism, which is essential to its success, is not in any obvious sense Cartesian. (Cf. note 14.) Also the conclusion gives no special support to Cartesian ontology. The terminology of rigidity is derived from Saul Kripke, 'Naming and Necessity', in D. Davidson and G. Harman (eds.), *Semantics of Natural Language* (Dordrecht: Reidel, 1972), though as mentioned above, a notion of rigidity is not essential for the argument. Kripke has done much to clarify the force of the Cartesian sort of argument. He gives such an argument aimed at showing the non-identity of sensations with brain processes. The argument as presented seems to suffer from a failure to criticize materialistic accounts of sensation language and from not indicating clearly how token physical events and token sensation events that are prima facie candidates for identification could have occurred independently. For criticism of Kripke's argument, see Fred Feldman, 'Kripke on the Identity Theory', *The Journal of Philosophy*, 71 (1974), 665–676; William G. Lycan, 'Kripke and the Materialists', *The Journal of Philosophy*, 71 (1974), 677–689; Richard Boyd, 'Materialism without Reductionism: What Physicalism Does Not Entail', in N. Block (ed.), *Readings in the Philosophy of Psychology*, i (Cambridge, Mass.: Harvard University Press, 1980); Colin McGinn, 'Anomalous Monism and Kripke's Cartesian Intuitions', *Analysis*, 37 (1977), 78–80. It seems to me, however, that these issues are not closed.

yet be precisely the same token thought event. Such a view is intuitively very implausible. I know of only one reasonably spelled-out basis of support for this view. Such a basis would be provided by showing that mentalistic phenomena are causal or functional states, in one of the strong senses discussed earlier, and that mental events are physical tokens or realizations of those states. If 'that thought that his ankles are stiff from arthritis' could be accounted for in terms like 'that event with such and such a causal or functional role' (where 'such and such' does not itself involve intentional terminology), and if independently identified physical events systematically filled these roles (or realized these states), we could perhaps see a given thought event as having a different role—and hence content—in different possible situations. Given such a view, the functional specification could perhaps be seen as revealing the contingency of the intentional specification as applied to mental event tokens. Just as we can imagine a given physiological event that actually plays the role of causing the little finger to move two inches, as playing the role of causing the little finger to move three inches (assuming compensatory differences in its physiological environment), so we could perhaps imagine a given thought as having a different functional role from its actual one—and hence, assuming the functionalist account, as having a different content. But the relevant sort of functionalist account of intentional phenomena has not been made good.[14]

The recent prosperity of materialist-functionalist ways of thinking has been so great that it is often taken for granted that a given thought event might have been a thought with a different, obliquely non-equivalent content. Any old event, on this view, could have a different content, a different significance, if its surrounding context were changed. But in the case of occurrent thoughts—and intentional mental events generally—it is hardly obvious, or even initially plausible, that

---

[14] It is important to note that our argument against functionalist specifications of mentalistic phenomena did not depend on the assumption that no occurrent thought could have a different content from the one it has and be the very same occurrence or event. If it did, the subsequent argument against the identity theory would, in effect, beg the question. The strategy of the latter argument is rather to presuppose an independent argument that undermines non-intentional functionalist specifications of what it is to be *a* thought that (say) sofas are comfortable; then to take as plausible and undefeated the assumption that no occurrent thought could have a different (obliquely non-equivalent) content and be the same occurrence or event; and, finally, to use this assumption with the modal considerations appealed to earlier, to arrive at the non-identity of an occurrent thought event with any event specified by physical theory (the natural sciences) that occurs within the individual.

Perhaps it is worth saying that the metaphorical claim that mental events are identified by their *role* in some 'inference-action language game' (to use a phrase of Sellars's) does not provide a plausible ground for rejecting the initial premise of the argument against the identity theory. For even if one did not reject the 'role-game' idea as unsupported metaphor, one could agree with the claim on the understanding that the roles are largely the intentional contents themselves and the same event in *this* sort of 'game' could not have a different role. A possible view in the philosophy of mathematics is that numbers are identified by their role in a progression and such roles are essential to their identity. The point of this comparison is just that appeal to the role metaphor, even if accepted, does not settle the question of whether an intentional mental event or state could have had a different content.

anything is more essential to the identity of the event than the content itself. Materialist identity theories have schooled the imagination to picture the content of a mental event as varying while the event remains fixed. But whether such imaginings are possible fact or just philosophical fancy is a separate question.[15]

At any rate, functionalist accounts have not provided adequate specification of what it is to be a thought that——, for particular fillings of the blank. So a specification of a given thought event in functionalist terms does not reveal the contingency of the usual, undisputed intentional specifications.

Well, *is* it possible for a thought event to have had a different content from the one it has and be the very same event? It seems to me natural and certainly traditional to assume that this is not possible. Rarely, however, have materialists seen the identity theory as natural or intuitive. Materialists are generally revisionist about intuitions. What is clear is that we currently do identify and distinguish thought events primarily in terms of the person who has them, the rough times of their occurrence, and their contents. And we do assume that a thought event with a different content is a different thought event (insofar as we distinguish at all between the thinking event and the person's being related to a thought content at a time). I think these facts give the premise prima facie support and the argument against the identity theory some interest. I do not claim that we have '*apriori*' certainty that no account of intentional phenomena will reveal intentional language to be only contingently applicable to belief states or thought events. I am only dubious.

---

[15] There are prima facie viable philosophical accounts that take sentences (whether tokens or types) as truth-bearers. One might hope to extend such accounts to mental contents. On such treatments, contents are not things over and above sentences. They simply *are* sentences interpreted in a certain context, treated in a certain way. Given a different context of linguistic interpretation, the content of the same sentence might be different. One could imagine mental events to be analogous to the sentences on this account. Indeed, some philosophers have thought of intentional mental events as being inner, physical sentence (or symbol) tokens—a sort of brain writing. Here again, there is a picture according to which the same thought event might have had a different content. But here again the question is whether there is any reason to think it is a true picture. There is the prior question of whether sentences can reasonably be treated as contents. (I think sentence types probably can be; but the view has hardly been established, and defending it against sophisticated objections is treacherous.) Even if this question is answered affirmatively, it is far from obvious that the analogy between sentences and contents, on the one hand, and thought events and contents, on the other, is a good one. Sentences (types or tokens) are commonly identified independently of their associated contents (as evidenced by inter- and intra-linguistic ambiguity). It is *relatively* uncontroversial that sentences can be identified by syntactical, morphemic, or perceptual criteria that are in principle specifiable independently of what particular content the sentence has. The philosophical question about sentences and contents is whether discourse about contents can be reasonably interpreted as having an ontology of nothing more than sentences (and intentional agents). The philosophical question about mental events and contents is 'What is the nature of the events?' 'Regardless of what contents are, could the very same thought event have a different content?' The analogous question for sentences—instead of thought events—has an uncontroversial affirmative answer. Of course, we know that when and where non-intentionally identifiable physical events have contents, the same physical event could have had a different content. But it can hardly be *assumed* for purposes of arguing a position on the mind–body problem that mental events are non-intentionally identifiable physical events.

One might nurture faith or hope that some more socially oriented functionalist specification could be found. But no such specification is ready to hand. And I see no good reason to think that one must be found. Even if such a specification were found, it is far from clear that it would deflect the argument against the identity theory just considered. The 'functional' states envisaged would depend not merely on what the individual does and what inner causal states lead to his activity—non-intentionally specified—but also on what his fellows do. The analogy between functional states and physiological states in causing the individual's internal and external activity was the chief support for the view that a given token mental event might have been a token of a different content. But the envisaged socially defined 'functional states' bear no intuitive analogy to physiological states or other physical causal states within the individual's body. Their function is not simply that of responding to environmental influences and causing the individual's activity. It is therefore not clear (short of *assuming* an identity theory) that any event that is a token of one of the envisaged socially defined 'functional states' could have been a token of a different one. The event might be essentially identified in terms of its social role. There is as yet no reason to identify it in terms of physically described events in the individual's body. Thus it is not clear that such a socially oriented functional account of thought contents would yield grounds to believe that the usual intentional specifications of mental events are merely contingent. It is, I think, even less clear that an appropriate socially oriented functional account is viable.

Identity theories, of course, do not exhaust the resources of materialism. To take one example, our argument does not speak directly to a materialism based on composition rather than identity. On such a view, the same physical material might compose different thoughts in different circumstances. I shall say nothing evaluative about this sort of view. I have also been silent about other arguments for a token identity theory—such as those based on philosophical accounts of the notions of causality or explanation. Indeed, my primary interest has not been ontology at all. It has been to identify and question individualistic assumptions in materialist as well as Cartesian approaches to the mental.

V. MODELS OF THE MENTAL

Traditional philosophical accounts of mind have offered metaphors that produce doctrine and carry conviction where argument and unaided intuition flag. Of course, any such broad reconstructions can be accused of missing the pied beauties of the natural article. But the problem with traditional philosophy of mind is more serious. The two overwhelmingly dominant metaphors of the mental—the infallible eye and the automatic mechanism—have encouraged systematic neglect of prominent features of a wide range of mental phenomena: broadly speaking, social features. Each metaphor has its attractions. Either can be elaborated or doctored to fit the facts that I have emphasized. But neither illumines those facts. And both have played some part in inducing philosophers to ignore them.

I think it optimistic indeed to hope that any one picture, comparable to the traditional ones, will provide insight into all major aspects of mental phenomena. Even so, a function of philosophy is to sketch such pictures. The question arises whether one can make good the social debts of earlier accounts while retaining at least some of their conceptual integrity and pictorial charm. This is no place to start sketching. But some summary remarks may convey a sense of the direction in which our discussion has been tending.

The key feature of the examples of Section II was the fact that we attribute beliefs and thoughts to people even where they incompletely understand contents of those very beliefs and thoughts. This point about intentional mental phenomena is not everywhere applicable: non-linguistic animals do not seem to be candidates for misunderstanding the contents of their beliefs. But the point is certainly salient and must be encompassed in any picture of intentional mental phenomena. Crudely put, wherever the subject has attained a certain competence in large relevant parts of his language and has (implicitly) assumed a certain general commitment or responsibility to the communal conventions governing the language's symbols, the expressions the subject uses take on a certain inertia in determining attributions of mental content to him. In particular, the expressions the subject uses sometimes provide the content of his mental states or events even though he only partially understands, or even misunderstands, some of them. Global coherence and responsibility seem sometimes to override localized incompetence.

The detailed conditions under which this 'inertial force' is exerted are complicated and doubtless more than a little vague. Clearly, the subject must maintain a minimal internal linguistic and rational coherence and a broad similarity to others' use of the language. But meeting this condition is hardly sufficient to establish the relevant responsibility. For the condition is met in the case of a person who speaks a regional dialect (where the same words are sometimes given different applications). The person's aberrations relative to the larger community may be normalities relative to the regional one. In such cases, of course, the regional conventions are dominant in determining what contents should be attributed. At this point, it is natural to appeal to etiological considerations. The speaker of the dialect developed his linguistic habits from interaction with others who were a party to distinctively regional conventions. The person is committed to using the words according to the conventions maintained by those from whom he learned the words. But the situation is more complicated than this observation suggests. A person born and bred in the parent community might simply decide (unilaterally) to follow the usage of the regional dialect or even to fashion his own usage with regard to particular words, self-consciously opting out of the parent community's conventions in these particulars. In such a case, members of the parent community would not, and should not, attribute mental contents to him on the basis of homophonic construal of his words. Here the individual's

intentions or attitudes toward communal conventions and communal conceptions seem more important than the causal antecedents of his transactions with
a word—unless those intentions are simply included in the etiological story.

I shall not pursue these issues here. The problem of specifying the conditions under which a person has the relevant general competence in a language
and a responsibility to its conventions is obviously complicated. The mixture of
'causal' and intentional considerations relevant to dealing with it has obvious
near analogs in other philosophical domains (etiological accounts of perception, knowledge, reference). I have no confidence that all of the details of the
story would be philosophically interesting. What I want to stress is that to a
fair degree, mentalistic attribution rests not on the subject's having mastered
the contents of the attribution, and not on his having behavioral dispositions
peculiarly relevant to those contents, but on his having a certain responsibility
to communal conventions governing, and conceptions associated with, symbols
that he is disposed to use. It is this feature that must be incorporated into an
improved model of the mental.

I think it profitable to see the language of content attribution as constituting a
complex *standard* by reference to which the subject's mental states and events
are estimated, or an abstract grid on which they are plotted. Different people may
vary widely in the degree to which they master the elements and relations within
the standard, even as it applies to them all. This metaphor may be developed in
several directions and with different models: applied geometry, measurement of
magnitudes, evaluation by a monetary standard, and so forth. A model I shall
illustrate briefly here borrows from musical analysis.

Given that a composer has fulfilled certain general conditions for establishing
a musical key, his chordal structures are plotted by reference to the harmonic system of relations appropriate to the tonic key. There is vast scope for
variation and novelty within the harmonic framework. The chords may depart
widely from traditional 'rules' or practices governing what count as interesting or
'reasonable' chordal structures and progressions. And the composer may or may
not grasp the harmonic implications and departures present in his composition.
The composer may sometimes exhibit harmonic incompetence (and occasionally harmonic genius) by radically departing from those traditional rules. But
the harmonic system of relations applies to the composition in any case. Once
established, the tonic key and its associated harmonic framework are applied
unless the composer takes pains to set up another tonic key or some atonal
arrangement (thereby intentionally opting out of the original tonal framework),
or writes down notes by something like a slip of the pen (suffering mechanical
interference in his compositional intentions), or unintentionally breaks the harmonic rules in a massive and unprincipled manner (thereby indicating chaos or
complete incompetence). The tonic key provides a standard for describing the
composition. The application of the standard depends on the composer's maintaining a certain overall coherence and minimal competence in conforming to
the standard's conventions. And there are conditions under which the standard

would be replaced by another. But once applied, the harmonic framework—its formal interrelations, its applicability even to deviant, pointless progressions—is partly independent of the composer's degree of harmonic mastery.

One attractive aspect of the metaphor is that it has some application to the case of animals. In making sounds, animals do sometimes behave in such a way that a harmonic standard can be roughly applied to them, even though the standard, at least in any detail, is no part of what they have mastered. Since they do not master the standard (though they may master some of its elements), they are not candidates for partial understanding or misunderstanding. (Of course, this may be said of many people as regards the musical standard.) The standard applies to both animals and people. But the conditions for its application are sensitive in various ways to whether the subject himself has mastered it. Where the subject does use the standard (whether the language, or a system of key relationships), his uses take on special weight in applications of the standard to him.

One of the metaphor's chief virtues is that it encourages one to seek social explications for this special weight. The key to our attribution of mental contents in the face of incomplete mastery or misunderstanding lies largely in social functions associated with maintaining and applying the standard. In broad outline, the social advantages of the 'special weight' are apparent. Symbolic expressions are the overwhelmingly dominant source of detailed information about what people think, intend, and so forth. Such detail is essential not only to much explanation and prediction, but also to fulfilling many of our cooperative enterprises and to relying on one another for second-hand information. Words interpreted in conventionally established ways are familiar, palpable, and public. They are common coin, a relatively stable currency. These features are crucial to achieving the ends of mentalistic attribution just cited. They are also critical in maximizing interpersonal comparability. And they yield a bias toward taking others at their word and avoiding *ad hoc* reinterpretation, once overall agreement in usage and commitment to communal standards can be assumed.

This bias issues in the practice of expressing even many differences in understanding without reinterpreting the subject's words. Rather than reinterpret the subject's word 'arthritis' and give him a trivially true object-level belief and merely a false metalinguistic belief about how 'arthritis' is used by others, it is common practice, and correct, simply to take him at his word.

I hardly need re-emphasize that the situation is vastly more complicated than I have suggested in the foregoing paragraphs. Insincerity, tongue slips, certain malapropisms, subconscious blocks, mental instability all make the picture more complex. There are differences in our handling of different sorts of expressions, depending, for example, on how clear and fixed social conventions regarding the expressions are. There are differences in our practices with different subject matters. There are differences in our handling of different degrees of linguistic error. There are differences in the way meaning-, assertion-, and mental-contents are attributed. (Cf. note 4.) I do not propose ignoring these points. They are all parameters affecting the inertial force of 'face value' construal. But I want to keep steadily in mind the philosophically neglected fact about social practice: Our attributions do not require that the subject always correctly or fully understand the content of his attitudes.

The point suggests fundamental misorientations in the two traditional pictures of the mental. The authority of a person's reports about his thoughts and beliefs (*modulo* sincerity, lack of subconscious interference, and so forth) does not issue from a special intellectual vision of the contents of those thoughts and beliefs. It extends even to some cases in which the subject incompletely understands those contents. And it depends partly on the social advantages of maintaining communally established standards of communication and mentalistic attribution. Likewise, the descriptive and explanatory role of mental discourse is not adequately modeled by complex non-intentional mechanisms or programs for the production of an individual's physical movement and behavior. Attributing intentional mentalistic phenomena to individuals serves not only to explain their behavior viewed in isolation but also to chart their activity (intentional, verbal, behavioral, physical) by complex comparison to others—and against socially established standards.[16] Both traditional metaphors make the mistake, among others, of treating intentional mental phenomena individualistically. New approaches must do better. The sense in which human beings are social animals runs deeper than much mainstream philosophy of mind has acknowledged.

---

[16] In emphasizing social and pragmatic features in mentalistic attributions, I do not intend to suggest that mental attributions are any the less objective, descriptive, or on the ontological up and up. There are substantial arguments in the literature that might lead one to make such inferences. But my present remarks are free of such implications. Someone might want to insist that from a 'purely objective viewpoint' one can describe 'the phenomena' equally well in accord with common practice, literally interpreted, or in accord with various reinterpretation strategies. Then our arguments would, perhaps, show only that it is 'objectively indeterminate' whether functionalism and the identity theory are true. I would be inclined to question the application of the expressions that are scare-quoted.

Postscript to "Individualism and the Mental"

'Individualism and the Mental' has been reprinted and anthologized so frequently, and so much more prominently than some of my closely related papers, that its place in my work is often misunderstood. Sometimes misunderstanding has stemmed from superficial reading of the essay itself. Often it has derived from reading only it, and not recognizing the background from which it developed, or the qualifications, supplements, and initiatives that came later. Here I want to reframe some of the key points in the article.

The main idea of the article is that the natures and correct individuation of many of an individual person's intentional, or representational, mental states and events commonly depend in a constitutive way on relations that the individual bears to a wider social environment. In the article, I support this idea by a family of thought experiments. In all these thought experiments, I describe a situation in which an individual has certain thoughts, but has certain misconceptions about the subject matter of the thoughts. Then I describe a counterfactual situation in which another individual is supposed to have substantially the same bodily history—including physical dispositions and proximal stimulations—but in which the social environment with which the individual has normal interactions is different. The second individual's bodily history is described in such a way that any differences from the original individual's body are, in themselves, intuitively irrelevant to the individual's psychology or mental states. The differences in the social environment bear on the meanings of words and the ways words are connected through social chains to their subject matters. This second individual does not have any misconception at all. Finally, I point out that in the counterfactual situation the second individual does not have the same types of thoughts that the first one has in the original situation. This is the structure of the thought experiments. The detailed content is what carries persuasion.

The main idea, again, is that differences in types or natures of thoughts depend on the individuals' different social relations in the two situations. In particular, the different ways in which the social chains connect the individuals to different subject matters bear on the differences in their thoughts. The upshot is that the natures of the individuals' thoughts, as marked by the representational contents of their thoughts, constitutively depend on the social environment. The individuals themselves may not know enough to describe the elements in the social environment or subject matter that constitutively determine the natures of their thoughts.

I believe that these ideas and the lines of thought that support them have held up well in the intervening years. I would like to set them in a wider context.

WHAT 'INDIVIDUALISM' MEANS

The title of the article contains the term 'individualism'. The term has been used in various ways, by myself and others. I see in retrospect that I changed my construal, though my understanding of the range of phenomena broadly associated with the term remained the same.

The term is introduced on the first page by reference to a contrast between the individual subject and the *social* environment. The last sentence of the article cites the same contrast. The term (or its cousin 'individualistic') is given a rough gloss at the beginning of Section IV. It is said to apply, roughly, to views that 'seek to see a person's intentional mental phenomena ultimately and purely in terms of what happens to the person, what occurs within him, and how he responds to his physical environment, without any essential reference to the social context in which he or the interpreter of his mental phenomena are situated'. The relevance of the term 'individualism' to issues about an individual's relations to a *social* surround is reinforced by the fact that the term has a similar use in discussions of the nature of social science. All of these considerations support interpreting my uses of 'individualism' in 'Individualism and the Mental' as bearing specifically on whether there is ever a constitutive relation between an individual's thoughts and the individual's *social* environment.

On the other hand, I recognized from the beginning that the role of social relations in determining the natures of mental states and events was one part of a larger order. I make this very clear in footnote 2 of 'Individualism and the Mental'. This footnote argues that the natures of many mental states are partly determined by relations to the *physical environment*. I expanded this sort of argument in subsequent work. The footnote emphasizes a point that I developed later in 'Other Bodies' (Ch. 4 above): Putnam did not use his own imaginative arguments about language, 'meaning', and reference to support the view that the natures of most ordinary non-factive *mental* states and events (as ordinarily understood and in addition to their mere referential relations) are partly determined by relations to the physical environment.

Putnam mistakenly took natural kind terms to be indexical. Such a view naturally supports the idea that the mental state and its distinctively representational content or 'meaning' are constant between the actual individual and the counterfactual individual, even as the referents of their shared thought content differ. The *representational* content of the mental states, on this view, remains the same. This idea no doubt played a role in Putnam's missing the import of his twin-earth arguments for mind. In Section IId of 'Individualism and the Mental', I make this point again. The thought experiments cannot be glossed as involving reference shifts in context-dependent thoughts.[1]

---

[1] These points are discussed in the Introduction. My criticism is also elaborated in greater detail and applied specifically to Putnam in 'Other Bodies' (Ch. 3 above). Putnam's original discussion

At the time, I regarded the physical environment as more fundamental than the social environment in determining the natures of mental states. It is more fundamental psychologically, ontogenetically, and phylogenetically. I focused first on the social environment because I thought that its role was less close to the surface, less easily recognized.

In later work I developed the role of the physical environment—especially in 'Other Bodies', 'Individualism and Psychology', 'Cartesian Error and the Objectivity of Perception', and 'Intellectual Norms and Foundations of Mind' (Chs. 4, 9, 7, 10 in this volume). Each of these articles produced arguments that brought out ways in which non-social factors beyond the cognitive purview of the individual help determine the natures of his or her mental states and events.

In the course of this later development, certainly by the mid-1980s, I came consistently to use the term 'individualism' to apply to any view that takes *the nature of mental states to depend entirely on physical factors in the individual or psychological resources cognitively available to the individual*. On this understanding of the term, individualism is not concerned purely with denying a role for social relations beyond the individual. It is concerned with denying a constitutive role to any factors beyond the individual. Although I see that in 'Individualism and the Mental' my usage and contextual explication is the narrower one, I think that I always understood the general phenomenon in the broader way. My use of the term 'anti-individualism' came firmly to reflect this broader understanding.[2]

---

occurs in "The Meaning of 'Meaning'" in *Philosophical Papers*, ii (Cambridge: Cambridge University Press, 1975). Putnam's acknowledgment of the correctness of my criticism occurs in Andrew Pessin and Sanford Goldberg (eds.), *The Twin Earth Chronicles* (London: M. E. Sharpe, 1996), p. xxi.

[2] I am taking it for granted that individualism is not the claim of local supervenience of an individual's mental states on the individual's physical states. In the first place, I take a dualism that maintains that mental states do not depend in any way on anything outside what is both internal to the individual's mind and available by reflection to the individual to be individualistic. Such an individualism would reject local supervenience. In the second place, anti-individualism is compatible with maintaining local supervenience of the mental on the physical. It could hold that the individual's bodily states are individuated only through relations to the wider environment. Or it could hold that any difference in the environment that helps determine the mental states will have some impact on the individual's bodily states in such a way as to preserve local supervenience. In the third place (and most importantly), individualism and anti-individualism are not fundamentally about supervenience, but about the natures of mental states, their correct individuation conditions. They are about the explanatory conditions associated with those natures, not about a mere modal relation. Cf. my 'The Indexical Strategy: Reply to Owens', in Martin Hahn and Bjorn Ramberg (eds.), *Reflections and Replies: Essays on the Philosophy of Tyler Burge*, (Cambridge, Mass.; MIT Press, 2003), 371–372. All my explicit, set-piece formulations of what anti-individualism is focused on the natures of mental states, not on supervenience. Some careless writing in my earliest papers mistakenly implies that anti-individualism *is* the rejection of local supervenience. I have, however, long disavowed this identification, and do so again here.

Some of the thought experiments do reject local supervenience. But the main point of the thought experiments is independent. It is to call attention to the relevance of relations to matters beyond the individual in the determination of what representational contents mental states have (and what types of mental states are in play)—regardless of whether these matters vary with differences in the individuals' bodies.

Some authors came to use the term 'internalism' for the broader phenomenon, confining 'individualism' to a claim about social relations. By now, I think, more authors take the terms to be approximately interchangeable, as I do. Usage here is obviously a matter of taste. I have preferred not to use 'internalism' and 'externalism' for a number of reasons. One is that my broader usage of 'individualism' is as early as similar uses of 'internalism'. Individualism in this broad sense rules out relations to a social, physical, or mathematical environment as constitutive factors in determining mental kinds.

A second reason for my preferring 'individualism' is that the terms 'internalism' and 'externalism' are already used in philosophy for a related but quite distinct issue in epistemology.

A third reason is that 'internalism' and 'externalism' are not specific about what constitutes the inside–outside border. The terms have been used to draw this border in many ways, not all of which have to do with a distinction between the individual and a wider reality.[3]

My primary reason is that the term 'externalism' suggests to many that the main issue is essentially concerned with spatial location. It has also suggested to many that mental states and events are themselves 'outside the head' or are relations to something outside the individual. Both suggestions are mistaken.

First, as I understand anti-individualism, the doctrine applies to some cases in which no spatial relations are at issue. I think that the natures of mathematical thoughts are determined by relations to an abstract subject matter that is not only not in the individual, but it is not anywhere. The point is that the mental kinds are not understandable by focusing entirely on the individual—not that the constitutively relevant relations are spatially external to the individual.

As to the second suggestion, anti-individualism certainly does not entail that thoughts are 'outside the head' or are themselves relations to something external. Neither thoughts themselves nor their representational contents are relations to something outside the individual. Their natures constitutively *depend* on relations that are not reducible to matters that concern the individual alone. But the natures are not themselves relations, and their representational contents are not themselves (in general) relational.[4]

Psychological explanations normally do not take mental states or events to be relations to the distal environment. They are psychological kinds that represent that environment. To be the kinds that they are, I claim, there must be an underlying network of relations to the environment. These are constitutive enabling conditions. Referring to those relations occurs in a different sort of explanation—a constitutive or philosophical explanation—than psychological

---

[3] For a useful discussion of the enormous variation in ways in which an internal–external division has been drawn in biology and psychology, see Peter Godfrey-Smith, *Complexity and the Function of Mind in Nature* (Cambridge: Cambridge University Press, 1996), ch. 2.

[4] These points are often obscured by philosophers who use the term 'intrinsic property'. Some of these writers claim, without explication, that mental contents are intrinsic properties of the mind. This sort of writing tends to be obfuscatory. There are many uses of 'intrinsic'.

explanations. The psychological explanations, in effect, take the natures of mental states for granted. They make reference to kinds that are dependent on relations. But the relations are usually not appealed to in psychological explanations; nor do they enter into psychological laws. I conjecture, with some confidence, that often the relations that constitutively determine or enable a psychological kind to be what it is are not natural or psychological kinds at all.

The idea that a nature or kind depends on relations beyond entities that are of that kind is a relatively modest claim—arguably applicable to most or all physical kinds. A physical body's shape and rest mass, for example, arguably depend on the body's being in space. Space is something beyond the individual. Shape and rest mass are not themselves relations to anything external. Similarly, being the number 3 depends for being what it is on relations to other numbers, but it does not follow that being the number 3 is itself a relation.[5]

Avoiding these suggestions is compatible with using the terms 'internalism' and 'externalism'. Nevertheless, I find these terms less appropriate to the main issue than 'individualism' and 'anti-individualism'. The main issue concerns the role of the individual and the individual's relations to a wider order in the constitutive conditions for the individual's being in specific representational mental states, or engaging in specific representational mental events or acts.

So anti-individualism concerns a variety of ways in which the natures of an individual's mental states and events are determined by relations between the individual and a wider order or environment. The wider order or environment is not in general in the individual's body or mind, or subject to reflective cognitive control by the individual, or explicable purely in terms of the individual's functional, causal, or dispositional capacities. Relations to a *social* environment are a prominent subclass among the relevant relations to a wider order.

THE NATURE OF MIND AND THE NATURE OF CONTENT

Let me turn to another way in which anti-individualism has been misunderstood. It is common to take anti-individualism as a theory of content. This take is understandable. 'Individualism and the Mental' has a lot to say about content. It derives its conclusions from reflection on what the representational contents of particular mental states and events are. Nevertheless, anti-individualism is not fundamentally about the nature of content. It is about the nature of representational mental states and events. It is about constitutive or essential conditions

---

[5] I make this point in 'Phenomenality and Reference: Reply to Loar', in Hahn and Ramberg (eds.), *Reflections and Replies*, 435–436. The point can easily be inferred from numerous passages in 'Individualism and the Mental'. The point is fully understood and incisively developed in Robert Stalnaker, 'On What's in the Head', in James Tomberlin (ed.), *Philosophical Perspectives*, iii (Atascadero, Calif.: Ridgeview Publishing Company, 1989), repr. in Pessin and Goldberg (eds.), *Twin Earth Chronicles*.

on an individual's having the kinds of mental states and events that the individual has.

In the thought experiments I maintained that the individuals in the original and counterfactual situations have thoughts with different representational contents. Since representational contents help type-identify thoughts, the thoughts are of different types or kinds. The conclusion is about the thoughts themselves. It is about how *having* certain thoughts constitutively depends on relations to the environment. It is not about the nature of the thought contents themselves.

The talk of representational contents was not strictly necessary to the arguments at all. It served to ward off philosophical misunderstandings—such as assimilating the differences in original and counterfactual situations to differences in the referents of terms or in the subject matter of the thoughts. The arguments center on the point that in the original situation an individual has one set of thoughts, and in the counterfactual situation the individual cannot have those same thoughts. The kinds of mental states and events differ in the two situations. So what kinds of mental states and events the individual has depends essentially on relations to the different environments.

I emphasize that anti-individualism is about the nature of the mental, not about the nature of representational content. The latter subject seems to me to be a relatively *recherché* ontological topic. For me it has substantially fewer interesting philosophical consequences. Moreover, the thought experiments are compatible with the Fregean–Platonic view that the natures of representational contents are completely independent of relations to anything else. On such a view, different thought contents mark different kinds of thought events or mental states in the original and counterfactual situations. Still, the contents themselves are independent of anything in space or time, including social relations. I think that this view, at least in any general form, is implausible. It is not, however, the objective of anti-individualism *per se* to defeat it.[6]

Representational contents and mental states and events are ontologically different topics. Determining constitutive conditions for being a representational content is a different enterprise from determining constitutive conditions for being a particular kind of belief or thought. Nevertheless, representational contents are to this degree central to the natures of mental states and events. Representational contents are aspects of the fundamental or constitutive kinds (natures) of representational mental states and events. Anti-individualism is about the conditions under which mental states and events can have the representational contents that they have, not about the nature of the contents themselves.

This point figures in my argument in Section d of Section IV against materialist token identity theories of mental events. The first premise in that argument is that a thought event *a* is necessarily distinct from a thought event *b* if *a* and *b* have different representational contents. (This principle is compatible with a

---

[6] These issues are discussed further in my *Truth, Thought, Reason: Essays on Frege* (Oxford: Oxford University Press, 2005), Introduction, esp. pp. 54–68.

variety of ontologies of representational contents.) I defended this principle by appeal to the centrality of representational contents in the explanatory enterprises in which mentalistic notions fit. I stand by this relatively pragmatic defense. In retrospect, I see it as overly modest. It seems to me that denying the principle is really quite evidently and apriori unacceptable. An account of thoughts that allows that a given thought could have either of two different representational contents while remaining the same thought event amounts to changing the subject. Thought events are partly type- or kind-identified by their contents. They are partly individuated by their contents. It seems to me that a philosophy that denies this principle has lost its way in ungrounded ideology.

LANGUAGE AND MIND

If I were to rewrite 'Individualism and the Mental', what I would change most is some of its emphasis on issues in the philosophy of language.[7] This emphasis was a sign of the times. It was partly necessary for clarifying exactly what I was claiming. Sometimes it did not distinguish issues about natural-language ascriptions of propositional attitudes from issues about the nature of the attitudes as sharply as I now would.

The article is explicitly about the nature of mental states and events—the nature of thoughts, or propositional attitudes. A strategy for reflecting on a subject matter that has yielded some insight, especially over the last century, is to begin by reflecting on aspects of language that we take to describe a subject matter veridically and systematically. By understanding such linguistic aspects, one then gains insight into structures and other large features of the subject matter. Although the language is one level removed from the subject matter, the language's concreteness and structure often enable one to recognize features of the subject matter that would otherwise be missed.[8]

This linguistic approach has special advantages when the subject matter is mind. A good bit of our thinking depends on language, both in the sense that without language we would never have been able to think many of our thoughts and in the sense that many of the structures of thought—for example, logical structures—are also structures of language.

On the other hand, this strategy has obvious limitations. In the first place, it can never supplant direct exploration of the subject matter, whether by science or by common sense. The knowledge about mind that reposes in common sense and in psychology is more extensive and, in a sense, more nearly final than any

---

[7] For parallel points about 'Belief *De Re*', see the Postscript to that article above.

[8] The methodology derives, of course, from Frege. For fuller explication of the methodology, see Section I of Postscript to 'Belief *De Re*' above. It is clear that the methodology is better suited to some subject matters than to others. Reflecting on language promises much less insight with respect to astronomy and molecular biology than it does with respect to formal logical consequence or the grammar module in the mind.

knowledge gained by reflecting on language. In the second place, language is used for many other purposes besides those of limning the nature of a subject matter. It has metaphorical, rhetorical, emotional, and other broadly communicative functions as well. One cannot simply assume that all aspects of language mirror or correspond to aspects of its subject matters.

In writing 'Individualism and the Mental', I self-consciously followed this strategy and was thoroughly aware of its limitations. I thought that the limitations could be mitigated by acknowledging them and by being sensitive to the various purposes for which language is used. I believed then, and believe now, that commonsense is close enough to psychology, certainly to what is now known in psychology, that one can learn things from reflecting on common sense talk about mental states and events. Although later work of mine reflects on psychology directly, 'Individualism and the Mental' stayed close to ordinary intuitive reflection. As to sensitivity to the different purposes of ordinary language, I think that, for the time at which it was written, the article shows, especially in Sections IIc–d, IIIa–c, a fairly sophisticated sensitivity to different ways in which language can be taken or used. I tried to indicate that the thought experiments in Sections IIa–b avoid depending on uses of language that do not reflect anything significant about the mentalistic subject matter.

Most of the discussion of language in the article was intended to be defensive and clarificatory. I wanted to show that common philosophical assumptions about automatically reinterpreting a person's language and mental states, when the person does not fully understand a term, fail to accord with common practice and fail to issue from any strong rationale. I wanted to distinguish my points about the natures of mental states and events from points that had already been made about the reference of certain terms and concepts. I wanted to show that the thought experiments apply to nearly all mental states, not simply to factive mental phenomena (knowing, seeing, being jealous of) that obviously depend on some relation to the subject matter. And I wanted to distinguish the phenomena that interested me from indexical phenomena that were easily conflated with them. All of these points were facilitated by employing terminology and reasoning from the philosophy of language. I stand by the points that I made then, and I believe that my way of making them was correct.

Still, there are scattered remarks in the article about contributing to a theory of language about propositional attitudes (Sections I, IIId). And some of the strategy of argumentation moves back and forth between discussing ascriptions of propositional attitudes and discussing the nature of the attitudes themselves. Some of this shuttling back and forth failed to keep it completely clear that ascriptions are simply evidence or a diagnostic device, not the primary subject matter. In fact, some responses to the article maintained that I had given a reasonable account of ordinary language use, but that ordinary language is simply misleading about the natures of mental states and events. I believe that such responses missed the real force of the thought experiments. I think that some of what I wrote anticipated such responses and did a lot to rebut them in advance.

(Cf. the sections mentioned above: IIc–d, IIIa–c, but also Section b of IV.) There is no question that the article is fundamentally about mind, not fundamentally about mentalistic language. I also believe that the methodology of the thought experiments and of the discussions of language could have been more sharply delineated. I think that the article does contribute to an understanding of language. Nonetheless, I think that this is a secondary contribution.

There are more specific, more technical assumptions about language that enter into the argumentation of the article. In order to show that my thought experiments bear on the natures of mental states, and not merely on ascriptions of mental states that overtly relate the states to aspects of the environment, I emphasized that the points are supported by 'oblique occurrences' in content clauses of mental-state ascriptions. I wanted to bring out that my claims bore not only on *'de re'* aspects of mental states and events, but also on *'de dicto'* aspects. More accurately, I wanted to bring out that the claims bore not only on demonstrative-like aspects of the content of mental states, but also on constant, non-indexical, non-demonstrative concepts.

We can say 'Alfred believes that that X-ray machine is blocking his way'. If Alfred is a chimp, it is obvious that Alfred has no thoughts about X-ray machines as such. The term 'that X-ray machine' is not used to even suggest anything about *how* Alfred thinks about anything. The ascription is just a loose way of indicating that Alfred has some thought about the physical object that is (or constitutes) the machine, and that the thought is to the effect that that thing is in his way. Any other expression that picked out roughly the same thing—such as 'that big contraption' or 'the biggest artifact in the room' or 'that hunk of metal' (recognizing that these expressions do not really denote the same objects)—would have served communicative purposes about as well, and would have produced a sentence that is roughly true. Any other singular expression that picked out even *roughly* the same object would do as well. The purpose of the ascription is not primarily to indicate the nature of Alfred's mental state, or even exactly what object Alfred has a belief about. It indicates almost nothing about how he is thinking. (Even the predication 'is blocking his way' is pretty loose.) The main point is simply to relate Alfred to some hunk or artifact in the world and say that Alfred believed it to be some sort of obstacle.

I meant to contrast this sort of case with ascriptions that had more the point of indicating something about how an individual is thinking—what the individual's concepts or representational contents are, what kinds of mental states the individual is in. I took it that there are ascriptions of propositional attitudes in which certain expressions in content clauses cannot be exchanged with any old coextensive expression without changing the truth-value of the whole sentence. The reason that they cannot be exchanged is that the expression in the content clause has partly the role of signifying something (perhaps exactly, perhaps approximately) about the individual's way of thinking, or equivalently, about the representational content of his or her thought.

Thus, Bert may believe that mercury is in the thermometer without believing that quicksilver is in the thermometer, even though mercury is quicksilver. Or Cary may believe that Mohammed Ali was a great fighter without believing that Cassius Clay was a great fighter, even though Cassius Clay is Mohammed Ali. Or child Dirk might believe that three-quarters of the milk was spilt without believing that 75 percent of the milk was spilt, even though three-quarters and 75 percent are the same proportion. In each case, the key term—'mercury', 'Mohammed Ali', 'three-quarters'—plays a role not only in indicating some kind, property, individual, proportion, or relation. It also signifies a particular way of thinking, or a class of ways of thinking, about the entity. One can think of someone as Mohammed Ali without thinking of him as Cassius Clay. One can think of a material as mercury without realizing that mercury is quicksilver. And so on.

I summed up these sorts of points by saying that the relevant expressions in the content clauses occur obliquely and would not undergo exchange with coextensive expressions without risking affecting the truth-value of the whole sentence. I believe that there are uses of the language according to which these points are correct.

Subsequent to the time when I wrote 'Individualism and the Mental', some philosophers of language have maintained that these kinds of point about language are incorrect. They hold that, always, if an individual believes that mercury is in the thermometer, the individual believes that quicksilver is in the thermometer, even if the individual thinks of quicksilver as a kind of silver, or is unsure what quicksilver is. They maintain that there may be a pragmatic implicature in the sentence 'Bert believes that mercury is in the thermometer'. The implicature would be that the individual uses 'mercury' and not 'quicksilver', or appropriate cognates. They hold that it might be contextually misleading to say 'Bert believes that quicksilver is in the thermometer'. They hold that the terms are nevertheless inter-substitutable without risk of change of truth-value of the whole sentence. So they hold, 'Bert believes that quicksilver is in the thermometer' is true if and only if 'Bert believes that mercury is in the thermometer' is true. And similarly for all the other examples that I cited or gestured at: If one believes that mercury is in the thermometer, one believes that quicksilver is in the thermometer—full stop.

I find this sort of view implausible, or at best incomplete. There are certainly standard uses of these sentences on which coextensive expressions are inter-substitutable *salve veritate*.[9] There are also standard uses on which the exchanges

---

[9] A *de re* ascription that does not purport to be relevant to how the individual is thinking of the *re* simply specifies a referent and implies that the individual had some *de re* attitude toward it. A *pseudo de re* ascription simply specifies an object that the attributer of the attitude takes to be a denotation of some component in the individual's thought, without implying that the specification is relevant to how the individual thought of the object, or even to whether the individual's thought is *de re* at all. There are cases in which even the attributer may not have a *de re* attitude toward the denoted (perhaps merely described) object.

will lead to false sentences, not just misleading ones. There is a systematic point to refusing exchange—that of indicating something about the way an individual is thinking. The fact that this point is systematic, and well understood among language users, indicates that it is not merely a matter of contextual implicature. The fact that it is expressed in systematic structural ways, independently of particular lexical items, indicates that it is not analogous to standard examples of conventional implicature.

The differences in the sentences that derive from such substitutions can bear on differences in the individual thinker's point of view. I think that when we allow free substitution, we are engaging in a standard use in which we do not care about such differences. What proponents of the relevant pragmatic theory count as cancellations of implicatures are in fact switches from one standard usage to the other.

So I stand by my original arguments. In those arguments I pointed out that the thought experiments apply just as much to an ascription 'Al believes that he has arthritis' if 'arthritis' is understood to occur obliquely (in a way that does not admit free interchange of coextensive expressions *salve veritate*) as it does if 'arthritis' is understood to occur transparently (in a way that admits of free interchange with coextensive expressions *salve veritate*). The purpose of this point was, again, to emphasize that the thought experiments bear not just on what the individual's beliefs refer to (or to what *we* refer to in ascribing the beliefs). They bear primarily on the way the individual thinks, what kinds of mental states he has.

This issue about the semantics of natural language is not, however, of central importance for my primary purposes. Whether exchange of what are normally coextensive expressions in ordinary belief ascriptions can yield changes in truth-value is a relatively technical issue in the philosophy of language. I believe that two other points are primary.

One is that the force and purpose of my linguistic argument is unaffected by the outcome of the dispute just described. Even if there is merely a pragmatic difference between the two ascriptions, the pragmatic difference bears on a difference in mental state, or point of view in the individual to whom the mental state is ascribed. This is the point at issue. It does not matter whether the difference is indicated semantically or pragmatically. My argument was supposed to bring out that the thought experiments bear on differences in mental state, not merely differences in mental reference (or reference by the ascriber). That fact stands whether the differences are actually denoted semantically in natural-language ascriptions, or are only pragmatically implicated in such ascriptions. My primary interest lay not in the character of natural-language ascriptions, but in the nature of mental states. The ascriptions played merely the role of clarification and evidence for a conclusion about mind.

I believe that it is obvious that even if the pragmatic account of the natural-language phenomena were correct, we could explain a language of psychological ascription in which the representational contents of mental states, and relevant differences among them, would be denoted in ascriptions, not merely implicated. I believe that such a language would be useful in psychological description and explanation. In fact, I believe that our natural language closely approximates such a language in *some* of its uses.

The other primary point is really the fundamental one. The thought experiments in 'Individualism and the Mental' do not rely primarily or essentially on argumentation about the nature of *ascriptions* of mental states at all. Although discussion of ascriptions looms large in the article—too large—it is not essential to the force or purpose of the main line of the argument. The fundamental reasoning in 'Individualism and the Mental', and in subsequent thought experiments that support anti-individualism, is not reasoning about language. The fundamental reasoning concerns conditions under which one can be in certain sorts of mental states, or have certain concepts. The intuitions on which the thought experiments rely center on conditions under which it is possible or impossible to have certain thoughts or perceptions.

This approach to the issues is evident in the extensive discussion of incomplete understanding of concepts or notions, where understanding a notion X is explicated roughly as knowing what an X is (Sections I, IIc–d). It is present in the various non-meta-linguistic formulations of the thought experiments, and in such remarks as that it is hard to see how the patient (in the third step of the arthritis thought experiment) 'could have picked up the notion of arthritis' (end of Section IIa). It is present in the persistent reasoning about the subject's viewpoint (Sections IIIc–d) and about the contents of states, which I take to help mark or type-identify the basic mental-state kinds (*passim*).

The arthritis thought experiment is this simple: The first stage illustrates that it is possible for an individual to have thoughts about arthritis as such even if one does not realize that arthritis must occur in joints. Other people on whom the individual partly relies in communication for connection to arthritis do know this. The second stage sets out a possible situation in which a similar individual, is, in ways relevant to understanding his psychology, a duplicate of the original individual, from the skin inwards. The second individual is in a different social situation. In this situation, neither the individual nor anyone else has isolated arthritis as a syndrome of diseases. In this situation, the individual's and community's word form 'arthritis' is standardly used to apply to some syndrome that includes rheumatoidal ailments that occur outside joints. The third stage indicates that in such a situation it is not possible for the individual to have thoughts about arthritis as such. So the first and second individuals have different kinds of thoughts.

METHODOLOGY AND EPISTEMIC IMPLICATIONS

The thought experiments center on examples. In philosophy, at least philosophy that is not explicitly philosophy of science, it seems to me that there is commonly more epistemic power and persuasiveness in examples than in principles. One aim of philosophy is to find principles. Finding them is often surer through reflection on cases than through trying to think up principles directly. The examples test and provide counterexamples for putative principles. They also stimulate discovery. The thought experiments proposed in 'Individualism and the Mental' are intended to be counterexamples to individualist principles. They are also intended to suggest directions for finding positive principles about constitutive factors involved in determining mental states, or in determining what representational contents an individual's mental states can have.

The steps of the thought experiments are not principles, it must be stressed.[10] They are judgments about hypothetical cases. How to generalize from a case is usually not evident. Usually, one has to consider more cases.

My thought experiments suggest some epistemic lessons. One of the broadest lessons is that conceptual and linguistic understanding commonly do not rest on the stable mastery of self-evident principles governing use of concepts or terms. One can master a concept well enough to think with it without understanding constitutive principles that govern its usage. Broadly, the reason for this is that constitutive principles depend on the nature of the subject matter of the concept. Normally, we do not have infallible insight into the nature of the subject matter. Sufficient mastery to think with a concept commonly resides in a know-how ability to apply the concept to cases and in mastery of a few members from a large family of rules of thumb and forms of inference, perhaps in association with some perceptual presentations. The rules of thumb need not be distinctive to the concept or sufficient to fix its range of application. They need not even be veridical. We may be vague as to how to apply a concept even though our concept is not itself vague, or is less vague. The natural commitments of our usage may be fuller than we realize.

In what follows I will be using the terms 'explicational principle', 'conceptual understanding', 'explicational understanding', and 'explicational belief'. I intend these expressions in very broad senses. I do not think that there is a sharp line between what constitutes understanding a concept and what constitutes using a concept while presupposing comprehension of it. Examples of explicational principles are 'Atoms are indivisible particles', 'Atoms are particles with a nucleus of protons and neutrons surrounded by electrons in orbits', 'Genes are the basic biological unit-determiners of heredity', 'Arthritis occurs only in joints', 'Contracts can be oral as well as written', 'Water is H_2O', 'To be an artifact is to bear some relation to an individual's intention or use', 'Sets are identical if and only if they have the same members', 'A function is an abstract law of correlation which given an input yields a unique output, if any output at all'. Such principles, true or false, purport to bear on what it is to be the sort of

---

[10] Among my thought experiments, the one exception to this claim is the thought experiment common to 'Cartesian Error and the Objectivity of Perception' and 'Individualism and Psychology' (Chs. 7 and 9 below). See the discussion of this exception in the Introduction.

thing indicated by the concept being explicated. The principles bear both on the nature of the thing—what it is to be that sort of thing—and the nature of the concept. Conceptual understanding is purportedly deepened when one comes to believe such principles. The relevant cases that I discuss are intuitively central to deepening understanding, or making it fuller or more nearly complete. They are relevant to conditions that bear on the nature of the concept by bearing on the nature of the subject matter that it specifies.

I shall be discussing cases in which I believe that concepts are *shared* among individuals some of whom understand the concept better than others. Much of what I say does not depend on this belief. What is important is that the relevant explications provide constitutive conditions on the application of the concept, or concepts, to a shared referent (or range of application). I believe that the stronger description in terms of shared concepts is nevertheless often correct. It is part of the best explanation of the transmission of knowledge. It is also often psychologically, culturally, historically, and epistemically illuminating.

It will be apparent, both from the examples and from what follows, that I do not believe that all explications of concepts are analytic, in any sense of 'analytic'. Many are empirically warranted. Even those beliefs in conceptual explications that are apriori warranted are normally not analytic in any sense. I reject as altogether without application the notion of analyticity that entails that an analytic truth is vacuous or not made true by a subject matter. I also believe that relatively few concepts are best regarded as having any extensive internal conceptual structure, which would allow other concepts to be 'contained' in them. So I think that there are very few analytic truths of containment.[11] Most of the apriori beliefs that I discuss that bear on conceptual understanding are synthetic apriori, in every normal sense of 'synthetic'.

The notions of conceptual understanding and conceptual explication that I employ are meant to be intuitive, relatively non-technical notions. I do not assume that there is, in general, a sharp line between what constitutes an explicational principle and what constitutes a non-constitutive fact about a subject matter. Still, in the cases I discuss, I do assume that it is intuitively correct to regard the identity or nature of a concept to be purportedly illuminated by explicational principles. I also take the notions of conceptual understanding and explicational principle to be illuminated by the cases to which they seem to apply. I do not associate these notions with a worked-through theory. I intend

---

[11] The rejection of the sort of analyticity that claims that analytic truths are vacuous and not made true by a subject matter derives, of course, from W. V. Quine. Cf. his 'Carnap and Logical Truth' (1954), repr. in *Ways of Paradox* (New York: Random House, 1960). The rejection of all but a few cases of the sort of analyticity that claims that analytic truths enunciate containment relations among concepts derives from Hilary Putnam, 'The Analytic and the Synthetic' (1962), repr. in *Philosophical Papers*, ii (Cambridge: Cambridge University Press, 1975). Discussion of the these different conceptions of analyticity, and one other, occurs in my 'Philosophy of Language and Mind: 1950–1990', *The Philosophical Review*, 100 (1992), 3–51 (Cf. Ch. 20 below); and in my 'Logic and Analyticity', *Grazer Philosophische Studien*, 66 (2003), 199–249, secs. I–II.

the remarks that follow to point toward a better understanding of the terms, and perhaps ultimately toward something resembling theory.

I think that one can distinguish four types of cases that bear on conceptual understanding. These cases delineate conditions under which reflection can or cannot yield fuller understanding of our concepts and conceptual abilities.[12]

In the first type of case, conceptual understanding of an explicational principle is dependent for its warrant on empirical information. The explicational principle can be understood implicitly and brought to explicit consciousness through reflection. Or it can be constructed through providing empirical explanations. The second, third, and fourth types of case involve different forms of apriori explicational understanding.[13] The second type involves apriori implicit understanding of a principle that can be brought to the surface by reflection. The idea is that an apriori warranted implicit belief in an explicational principle guides the individual's employment of a concept even though reflection or dialectic is necessary if the implicitly understood principle is to be brought to consciousness. The third type involves implicit understanding of materials from which the relevant explicational principle can be constructed. But the principle itself is not implicitly believed. It does not implicitly guide the individual's employment of the concept, at least until the individual comes to believe the principle explicitly. Eventual belief in the principle is apriori warranted. In this case, reflection does not simply clarify and make distinct something that is already unconsciously present in the individual's psychology and guiding the individual's judgments about cases. Reflection puts together the explicational principle for the first time within the individual's psychology. The fourth type of case involves coming to recognize, with apriori warrant, a principle that intuitively bears on the correct explication of a concept, at least partly from materials that were *not* all available in earlier uses of the same concept. In this case, at a certain time, reflection alone would not have sufficed for recognition of the principle, for some users of the concept. Further education, perhaps even new concepts, would be necessary.[14]

---

[12] In this section of the Postscript, I draw on all the thought experiments, not just those in 'Individualism and the Mental'. For further discussion of these methodological and epistemic matters, see my 'The Thought Experiments: Reply to Donnellan' and 'Concepts, Conceptions, Reflective Understanding: Reply to Peacocke', both in Hahn and Ramberg (eds.), *Reflections and Replies*, and my replies to the essays by Martin Davies and Antoni Gomila Benejam in Maria J. Frapolli and Esther Romero (eds.), *Meaning, Basic Self-Knowledge, and Mind: Essays on Tyler Burge* (Stanford, Calif.: CSLI Publications, 2003).

[13] It will be seen that the three types of apriori understanding could be taken to have three counterparts as sub-cases of empirically warranted understanding of explicational beliefs. I give four cases instead of six only because I think that separating the sub-cases is philosophically and historically more illuminating in cases of apriori explicational understanding.

[14] Delicate issues hover over these points. Some kinds of reflection, especially in the third type of case, yield new knowledge for the individual. This can be seen as a sort of self-education. Nevertheless, I think that we have a rough, at least case-based, sense of a distinction between when the individual uses materials already available to work out new knowledge, and when the individual gains further knowledge that is not simply derived from putting things together that he already knew. Sometimes new concepts or techniques are needed. Sometimes communication with others

The last three types of case bear on apriori warranted understanding, and thus on the limited rationalism that I maintain. The last type of case was not recognized by traditional rationalists, and the next to last was not high-lighted. It is therefore, I think, of some interest to mark their possibility.[15]

In all four cases, the principle that is taken to explicate the concept and illuminate its application conditions could be false. This is an important point. All explication is eventually responsible to an objective subject matter to which the concepts purportedly apply. In view of our fallibility, explications can be mistaken, even those that are taken to be definitional. I shall, however, assume in this discussion that the relevant explicative principles are true.

Let me turn to concrete examples of the four types of cases. In the thought experiments that I have given, the most common type of belief that expresses conceptual understanding is empirical.[16] For example, the belief that a contract can be oral as well as written has empirical warrant. The belief that water is H_2O clearly empirical. The thought experiment from 'Intellectual Norms and Foundations of Mind' (Ch. 10 below) suggests that the belief that sofas are artifacts made or meant for sitting has partly empirical sources of warrant and is vulnerable to empirically based doubt.

Similarly, Dalton's false explicational belief that atoms are indivisible and our (presumably true) explicational belief that atoms have a nucleus surrounded by electrons in orbits are, respectively, empirically disconfirmed and warranted. The empirical explication does not, of course, give conceptual 'definitions' of the empirical concept, conceptually guaranteed to be true, although perhaps Dalton mistakenly thought that his did. It is nevertheless relevant to understanding basic, constitutive matters about the concept's application.

---

is essential. The distinction between synthetic apriori knowledge gained by reflection and synthetic apriori knowledge gained by other means is delicate. I think, however, that there is no reason simply to ignore the distinction. Rather we should use cases and reflection to try to understand it better.

[15] I believe that Frege had a conception of apriori knowledge that in effect acknowledges these last two sorts of cases. My conception of apriority has been substantially influenced by Frege. Aspects of the ideas that follow, together with their relations to anti-individualism, are discussed in much greater detail in 'Frege on Extensions of Concepts, from 1884 to 1903', 'Frege on Truth', 'Frege on Sense and Linguistic Meaning', 'Frege on Knowing the Foundation', 'Frege on Apriority', collected in Burge, *Truth, Thought, Reason*, the Introduction, *ibid.* 54–68; and 'Logic and Analyticity'.

The key difference between my conception of rationalism and classical rationalism is the main point of an exchange between me and Christopher Peacocke. Peacocke advances a fairly standard, Leibnizian version of the traditional rationalist view. I point to ways in which such a view misses the resources that anti-individualism provides to expand the range of possibilities for understanding the nature of reflection. Cf. Christopher Peacocke, 'Implicit Conceptions, Understanding, and Rationality' and Burge, 'Concepts, Conceptions, Reflective Understanding: Reply to Peacocke' both in Hahn and Ramberg (eds.), *Reflections and Replies*.

[16] The general point about the extreme fallibility and empiricality of most explications of empirically applicable words, in both science and common sense, is a major theme, developed repeatedly and well, in the work of Hilary Putnam. His development of the point is much earlier than my development of the anti-individualistic framework. I think that that framework helps explain several of Putnam's insights. See numerous articles in his *Philosophical Papers*, I and II. See esp. 'An Examination of Grünbaum's Philosophy of Geometry' (1963), 'A Memo on Conventionalism' (1963) (vol. i), and 'The Analytic and the Synthetic' (1962), 'Is Semantics Possible?' (1970) (vol. ii).

There are cases of empirically warranted beliefs or presuppositions that are relevant to conceptual understanding and that are more 'meta'. For example, the fact that having the concept <u>aluminum</u> is constitutively dependent on either theorizing about the structure of aluminum in a way that is approximately correct or bearing some causal relation to something with the chemical structure of aluminum, depends on <u>aluminum</u>'s being a natural kind concept and aluminum's being a natural kind. An individual does not have to believe that aluminum is a natural kind, or that <u>aluminum</u> is a natural kind concept, if the individual is to have the concept <u>aluminum</u>. But I think that the individual must have some notion of what a natural kind is, and must not be closed to the possibility that aluminum might be a natural kind. Understanding that aluminum is a natural kind or that <u>aluminum</u> is a natural kind concept is relevant to fully understanding the concept <u>aluminum</u>. Understanding these two truths is warranted only empirically. Similarly, our theoretical meta-knowledge that having the concept <u>aluminum</u> requires bearing some causal or correct theoretical relation to something with the chemical structure of aluminum is warranted only empirically.

The second type of case is the sort emphasized by the classical rational- ists—Descartes, Leibniz, Kant. The idea is that embedded in an individual's psychology is an implicit understanding of a principle that explicates the relev- ant concept. The understanding is implicit in that it is unconscious and available to conscious belief only through reflection. It is present in the individual's psy- chology in that belief in the principle helps explain the individual's application of the concept to cases, or in other less general applications. The job of reflec- tion is to make one's conceptual understanding consciously explicit, partly by making one's ideas clear and distinct.

My thought experiments have not centered on cases of this sort. But those experiments, and earlier ones by Kripke, Donnellan, and Putnam, brought back to philosophical prominence the classical rationalist view of reflection. They did so because the classical rationalists reflected more on reflection, and had a fuller story about it, than other philosophers in the history of philosophy. And these thought experiments clearly utilize some sort of reflection—even though there are clearly empirical aspects to all of these thought experiments. For example, they make such assumptions as that Jonah, Aristotle, aluminum, arthritis, and so on, exist.

An example that I believe illustrates the classical rationalist view is Zermelo's formulation of the principles of extensionality and grounding for the (iterative) concept of set. These principles, or approximations to them, are fundamental to anyone's understanding of the iterative concept of set. They are so well known now that they do not illustrate implicit knowledge for many of us. However, an intelligent novice in set theory who has been given a few examples of sets and then given the principles might well, on reflection, explicitly recognize the truth of the principles for the first time. It might well be correct that the principles implicitly guided the individual's use of the concept in reasoning about particular sets, before the principles were formulated for him or her.

It is important in understanding the classical rationalist view that one not assume that the concept being explicated, or the concepts used in the explication, must be non-empirical. Some of the applications of the concept of set to cases in pure mathematics are not empirical at all. But not all concepts used in apriori conceptual explications need be of this sort.

For example, the concepts <u>natural kind</u> and <u>chemical structure</u> are empirical in two ways. First, the concepts were probably acquired through empirical experience.[17] Second, all applications of them to instances that they are true of are warranted empirically. Acceptance of certain principles that are part of explicational understanding of the concept <u>natural kind</u> nevertheless seems to be apriori warranted. Consider the principles:

> If something is a natural kind concept, an individual could use the concept without being able to tell definitively by correct observation whether something is an instance of the natural kind: instances of natural kinds admit of look-alikes in normal conditions.

> If something is a natural kind concept, and the relevant natural kind is individuated by its chemical structure, then an individual could have that natural kind concept without knowing the kind's chemical structure.

It seems to me that belief in these principles is apriori warranted, even though the concepts <u>natural kind</u> and <u>chemical structure</u> are acquired only through experience, and even though any warrants for identifying instances of these kinds are certainly empirical.

As regards the first principle, knowing what a natural kind is requires being open to perception's not determining whether something is an instance of a natural kind. Whether something is an instance of the natural kinds water, gold, fruit, and so on depends on facts that may not be immediately evident to perception. What determines an instance of a natural kind to *be* an instance may be a fact about the thing that is hidden from view, and discoverable only through further investigation. Answers to which things are natural kinds are warranted only empirically. Whether a concept is a natural kind concept is similarly dependent on these empirical matters. But warrant for believing the principle

---

[17] Probably all concepts are 'acquired' through experience, at least in that they are triggered and become available through perceptual stimulation. Some conceptual development is, however, the result of normal human maturation, rather than the product of being taught through the transmission of history and culture, or dependent on any particular range of experiences for acquisition. It is common in current developmental psychology to consider concepts that are acquired in this weak sense as innate, not learned. So for such concepts, the sense in which their acquisition is empirical is very weak. In fact, there is a spectrum of cases on this issue. The concept <u>natural kind</u> is, at least in Western culture, acquired by human children at a fairly regular time of life, about 3 or 4 years old. Cf. S. A. Gelman and E. M. Markham, 'Young Children's Inductions from Natural Kinds: The Role of Categories and Appearances', *Child Development*, 58 (1987), 1532–1541. It would be interesting to know whether the concept is universal among human beings. It would also be interesting to know whether particular sorts of experiences, and if so which, are necessary to its being acquired. The same questions arise for the concept <u>chemical structure</u>.

itself seems to me to be apriori. Understanding the principle, or some dumbed-down approximation to it, is part of distinguishing natural kind concepts from observational concepts. Similar remarks apply to the second principle.

Lower-order versions of these principles can, and probably often do, implicitly guide an individual's application of natural kind concepts. To have the concept natural kind, much less to have natural kind concepts, an individual need not have the concept natural kind concept. So only lower-order analogs of these principles are likely to be psychologically in play in early uses of natural kind concepts. But once the individual believes, on empirical grounds, that something is a natural kind, or uses a natural kind concept, the individual will be open to allowing that whether something is an instance of the kind can be determined by more than meets the eye. If an individual has the concept natural kind concept, and the other concepts in the principles, the individual will probably also be guided in applications of his or her natural kind concepts by something like the principles. Of course, even so, the individual might fail to assent to them. The individual might require dialectic or reflection to make the principles explicit and convincing. And of course, individuals, not excluding philosophers(!), can mistakenly deny the principles, because of bias or interference in their understanding.

Similarly, acquisition of a concept like arthritis depends on experience. Application of the concept to cases rests on empirical warrant. An appreciation of the ways that people depend on one another in language use derives from experience of specializations, differences of positioning, and differences in background knowledge among people within a culture. Consider the principle:

> If an individual relies on others in certain ways for acquisition of the concept arthritis and for correction in its use and application, the referent (or range of correct application) of the individual's concept can depend partly on what others count as arthritis, and on others' connecting the individual to the referent (or denotation) of the concept through causally mediated chains.

I think that this principle, like an analogous principle for the referents of proper names, is apriori warranted. It is apriori warranted even though acquisition of concepts in the principle is empirical. This principle may guide recognition of examples of reference for a concept of arthritis, even though an individual may not recognize the principle immediately when presented with it—and even though an individual may deny the principle when presented with it.[18]

The third type of case is also relevant to understanding apriori conceptual understanding. This type of case is incompatible with doctrines of classical rationalists. Or at least those doctrines commonly neglect such cases. Some explicational principles whose recognition derives from reflection make use only

---

[18] It was part of classical rationalism to hold that apriori knowable principles may not be known, even on reflection, because some prejudice may block clear and distinct understanding of principles that implicitly guide usage.

of matters that are already known or are at least implicitly available to reflection. Yet some of those principles are in no sense implicit in the psychology of the individual before reflection. They are not part of the explanation of the individual's previous uses of the concept. Implicit belief in them does not guide the individual's application of the concept. The principle is arrived at synthetically, through apriori theory building. It goes beyond anything that the individual implicitly knew, believed, or had 'as a unit' in his or her psychology prior to reflection. It yields new conceptual understanding.[19]

Many cases may be indeterminate, or at least difficult to determine. I believe it plausible and certainly coherent to take Newton's notion of limit to be what Weierstrass's definition of limit explicates. Weierstrass's explication gives the best unifying explication of Newton's primary uses of a concept of limit in his calculus. It gives a constitutive explication of what Newton's concept applies to. The explication plausibly provides deeper understanding of a concept that was used prior to its recognition. Acceptance of the explication is apriori warranted. Newton's actual uses need not have been guided by unconscious belief in the explication. I think it plausible that they were not. Newton's uses were, or might have been, guided only by a grab-bag of applications to cases, rules of thumb, partial explications, idealized geometrical diagrams, and so on. Nevertheless, Newton could have understood Weierstrass's explication and could have recognized it to be true. The main point here is that this description of the case is coherent and possible.[20]

---

[19] I develop these points for empirical as well as apriori cases in 'Concepts, Conceptions, Reflective Understanding: Reply to Peacocke'.

[20] The historical cases that I discuss are meant to be illustrative of epistemic possibilities. I recognize that a full treatment of cases, and making them plausible to historians, would require much more development. This particular case is especially complex. Newton also had the concept of limits as infinitesimals. This idea is, however, more central to Leibniz's treatment of the calculus. (See the discussion of Leibniz below.) As I understand the history, from the early 1670s onward, Newton came to think that his use of the concept of motion in his application of the calculus was in some tension with the more static/geometrical notion of infinitesimal. He tried to develop his theory of 'fluxions' in a way that freed it from reliance on the notion of infinitesimal. In an unpublished treatise *De Methodis* (probably 1671–2), he wrote of quotients of affected equations extended in an infinite series that they 'ever more closely approach the root till finally they differ from it by less than any given quantity and so, when they are infinitely extended, differ from it not at all.' Newton developed this conception during the next fifteen years, into the work of *Principia*. This way of thinking is different from thinking of limits in terms of infinitesimals. Although in later published work he mixes talk of infinitesimals with this idea of approaching a root, there are unpublished passages in which he scorns the idea of infinitesimals and takes his fluxion method to be superior. Newton was clearly aware that he had (at least) two concepts. I take the latter fluxion concept to be dominant in guiding Newton's main conception and use of the calculus. I take the quoted passage to be suggestive of Weierstrass's intuitive idea, and quite different from Leibniz's (and Newton's own) infinitesimal conception. Of course, Newton probably saw the idea of approaching a limit literally in dynamical terms, and in this respect his view differs from Weierstrass's. I regard this aspect of Newton's position as a mistaken conflation of dynamical ideas with an underlying, partially understood, purely mathematical concept. Of course, we now understand Weierstrass's conception of limit in terms of the notions of function and operator. Newton had only a partial understanding of these notions. They too did not become clarified until centuries later. As with Weierstrass's definition of limit, Newton had the conceptual materials to understand the later explications, even though

Similarly, pre-Fregean nineteenth-century logicians made judgments about one proposition or thought following, as a logical consequence, from others. Such logicians could have understood, with minimal explanation, the general explications that were given of logical consequence by Tarski and others. It is extremely implausible to think that the earlier logicians' judgments about cases were guided by an implicit understanding of the general explications. They were guided in their judgments by particular understandings of logical constants in particular arguments, and perhaps by vague middle-level principles. It is not, however, plausible that the generalizations that are required to yield a systematic account of logical consequence were embedded in their psychologies—even though such generalizations were both comprehensible to the nineteenth-century logicians and correct general meta-logical explications of their intuitive concept of logical consequence.[21]

Although the third principle that I blocked off in discussing the second case of conceptual understanding may often implicitly guide individuals' judgments about instances, I think that this need not be so. An individual can be persuaded by the principle because it accounts well for remembered cases. For example, an individual can remember particular cases in which he or she did not know enough about arthritis to determine its range of application by description, but in which he or she was thinking about arthritis. Then it could be noticed that the thinking must have succeeded through reliance on others who knew more and who could better distinguish arthritis from other possible or actual diseases. The individual need not, even unconsciously, have put together the generalization. But the individual can understand the principle and recognize its truth, at least arguably with apriori warrant, once given a few cases to reflect upon.

I turn now to a fourth case of conceptual explication. Here again belief in the explication can be apriori warranted. The case differs from the third case in that an individual may not be in a position, even in principle, to put together the explication and recognize its truth without very substantial additional education. Some apriori warranted belief can constitute fuller understanding of a concept than employers of the concept had before, even though the explicating principle does not derive fully from material accessible to those who had thought with the concept.

almost surely they had not been put together as a unit in his psychology, in a way that implicitly guided his own understanding. Still, it seems plausible to say that he had a concept of limit that Weierstrass explicated, and a concept of function, or one concept of function, that later became clarified. I hope to write more fully on these cases. For material on Newton's mathematical views on which I have drawn, see D. T. Whiteside (ed.), *The Mathematical Works of Isaac Newton*, 2 vols. (New York: Johnson Reprint Corporation, 1964), Introduction; D. T. Whiteside, *The Mathematical Principles Underlying Newton's Principia* (Glasgow: University of Glasgow Press, 1970); Richard S. Westfall, *Never at Rest: A Biography of Isaac Newton* (Cambridge: Cambridge University Press, 1980); the quote is from page 228 of this work.

[21] Cf. my 'Logic and Analyticity', esp. secs. IV–VI.

In the third case, we assumed that a correct explicational principle of an individual's concept had not coalesced and had not been put together at any level of the individual's psychology. So the principle did not implicitly guide his or her usage. Still, the individual could in principle have come to recognize the truth of the principle by putting together materials already at his or her disposal. Thus, although it would have been too much to expect, Newton could in principle have thought up Weierstrass's definition of limit, from conceptual materials and mathematical principles already available to him. Such thinking-up may have required putting together conceptual materials that Newton had not put together in his uses of his concept limit. Newton nevertheless had the background knowledge and conceptual wherewithal to have understood the definition, and to have even produced it, if he had exercised sufficient reflection.

In this fourth case, an individual whose concept is explicated in a constitutively relevant way might not be in a position to recognize the truth of the principle, no matter how much reflection he or she exercised on available material. A plausible example of this sort of case is Leibniz's use of a notion of infinitesimal in his development of the calculus. The notion received a rigorous and stable explication by Abraham Robinson three centuries later. Robinson used mathematical concepts and techniques that simply were not available to Leibniz. Yet Robinson's account through non-standard analysis plausibly gives a mathematically correct explication of the concept that Leibniz employed. The explication bears on constitutive application conditions of the concept. Robinson was apriori warranted in his acceptance of the explication. And Leibniz might have been warranted if he had been brought to understand it. But he could not have understood it without substantial further education and new mathematical concepts. Reflection on what he already knew and understood could not have sufficed to give Leibniz an adequate understanding of the constitutively relevant explication of his own concept.[22]

---

[22] Although Leibniz and his followers on the Continent tended to employ the notion of infinitesimal in their use of the calculus, complications in Leibniz's work parallel those noted in Newton's. (Cf. note 20.) Leibniz was aware of metaphysical doubts about his notion of infinitesimal. In a letter to Varignon, 1702, he cites a work of his own in which he claims: 'my intention was to point out that it is unnecessary to make mathematical analysis depend on metaphysical controversies or to make sure that there are lines in nature which are infinitely small in a rigorous sense in contrast to ordinary lines.' He continues: 'it would suffice here to explain the infinite through the incomparable, that is, to think of quantities incomparably greater or smaller than ours.' He seems to mean these incomparable quantities to be finite. For he claims further: 'we must consider that these incomparable magnitudes themselves, as commonly understood, are not at all fixed or determined but can be taken to be as small as we wish.' Leibniz remarks that infinitesimals may be taken as ideal concepts which shorten reasoning in the same way that imaginary numbers do. Although imprecisely stated, the remarks about taking magnitudes to be incomparable and as small as one wishes seem to be in the direction of the limit concept. Both Newton and Leibniz knew that they had (at least) two concepts that could be used in differentiation. Newton's dominant concept is on track toward Weierstrass's explication of limits. Leibniz's dominant concept is on track toward Robinson's explication of infinitesimals. But each had at least some approximation to the other's dominant concept. Cf. G. W. Leibniz, *Philosophical Papers and Letters*, trans. and ed. L. Loemker (Chicago: University of

A humbler instance of this same sort of case is present in the thought experiments about arthritis and brisket. The individual Al is in no position to recognize through reflection that arthritis is a disease that can only occur in joints. Al cannot recognize through reflection alone that brisket is a cut from the breast, or lower part of the chest, of certain quadrupeds. Al must learn new information to be in a position to obtain full explicational understanding of the implications of his own conceptual usage. The information might be obtained through empirical experience.[23] Belief in the relevant explicational principle is nevertheless apriori knowable. Al's own acceptance of it can be apriori warranted once he is apprised of his own incomplete understanding. Here again we see the importance of distinguishing dependence on experience to *acquire the means to understand* a concept, or to think an explicational principle, from dependence on experience for being *warranted in believing* an explicational principle.

Sometimes <u>arthritis</u> is called a 'deferential concept'. This phrase seems to me very misleading. Nearly any concept can be employed in such a way that the employer depends on others for the range of the concept's application, and even for instruction on explicational principles and other norms governing the concept. Our reliance on others places us under standards and norms that we may not have fully mastered. Moreover, we cannot in general tell by simple reflection whether and how we depend on others. The dependence commonly is buried in the history of one's usage and in dispositions not all of which are open to reflective recognition. The main issue has to do with what objective reality we are connected to and what standards for full understanding apply to those aspects of our usage that rely on such connection.

Other instances of this fourth case may be present in standard philosophical explications. It may be that the correct account of justice, for example, requires knowledge of matters that will emerge only with experience of a variety of communities and institutions. Such information may be needed to indicate certain possibilities that the concept must accommodate. Perhaps a given individual can think about justice as such without having the experience, or even the concepts, necessary for giving a fully adequate explication of the notion. The eventual explication might nonetheless be apriori warranted.

The fourth case brings out that coming to fuller understanding of one's concepts and their constitutive application conditions may require obtaining new information, or new concepts. This point is fairly obvious in the case of empirically warranted constitutive explications. It is of some interest that it can apply to apriori warranted constitutive explications as well.

Chicago Press, 1956), ii, 881–883 I am indebted to Sheldon Smith for finding this passage and for general discussion on these issues in the history of the calculus.

[23] In my view, warrant for believing the information is usually empirical. But it need not be. Cf. my 'Content Preservation', *The Philosophical Review*, 103 (1993), 457–488.

Anti-individualism indicates that the conditions that determine what concepts one has are not fully determined by definitions that the individual has mastered, or by any other set of conditions immediately available to the individual's reflection. Conceptual abilities are not in general, or even often, made what they are by mastery of explicational principles. They are determined partly by perception and dispositions that we may not have fully conceptualized or understood. They are determined by relations to a wider order, the objective subject matter, about which our knowledge and understanding may be quite limited. The thought experiments awake us to the limits of our conceptual mastery.

This point holds even in cases of apriori knowable conditions. Anti-individualism leads one to expect that finding principles that govern conditions for having thoughts will not be easy. Of course, traditional rationalists emphasized the difficulty of successful reflection. Anti-individualism demonstrates that the dependence on empirical conditions that determine what concept an individual has may vastly outrun the individual's own awareness of those conditions. And it shows that even where reflection is an appropriate method for gaining explicational knowledge relevant to the individuation of one's concepts and mental states, and even where the resulting knowledge is apriori, the individual doing the reflecting may not have the principles or all their components, explicitly or implicitly, within his psychology. The individual may lack the resources, informational or conceptual, to gain apriori warranted understanding of apriori knowable principles governing conditions on *having* the concepts that he or she has. This situation is possible because the natures of an individual's thoughts are determined by matters that need not be cognitively available, implicitly or explicitly, to the individual.

We still have much to learn about basic anti-individualist principles themselves. Some learning may be open to present reflection, pushed further. There is, however, no guarantee that we are in a position even now to learn by reflection all general principles, even apriori principles, governing conditions of having the representational content that we have. New knowledge may be necessary. Here philosophy has led to an improved explanation of why it is so difficult.

INCOMPLETE UNDERSTANDING

Early in Section IIc, I write: 'the thought experiment does appear to depend on the possibility of someone's having a propositional attitude despite an incomplete mastery of some notion in its content.' The relevant incomplete understanding need not be a failure to know the sort of explication codified in a dictionary. As I point out near the end of Section IIb, incomplete understanding of observation concepts, such as color concepts, or of concepts like <u>contract</u>, can yield thought experiments analogous to the <u>arthritis</u> thought experiment, without centering on failure to comprehend dictionary meaning. Incomplete understanding can involve any failure to understand some condition that is constitutively necessary to the application range of a concept.

Incomplete understanding is not the key to all the thought experiments that support anti-individualism. The thought experiments that center on perception, on natural kind concepts, and on questioning of fundamental explicational beliefs do not require any incomplete understanding—in any ordinary sense of the phrase—on the part of the protagonists. In those cases, certain limitations of perspective or failures of omniscience suffice.

Incomplete understanding is, however, the pivot on which the particular thought experiments of 'Individualism and the Mental' turn. Reflection on incomplete understanding seems to me valuable in eliciting, through the thought experiments, a social factor in the determination of an individual's mental states. Having concepts can depend partly on reliance on others for possible correction of explications. The corrections make reference to facts about the subject matter to which the concepts apply.

Incomplete understanding is also a key element in understanding such historical cases as those of Newton and Leibniz. In those cases, the incomplete understanding is not a matter of knowing less than other experts in the community. Their explications of their concepts failed to accord with their applications of the concepts and with the nature of the reality to which they applied their concepts. Their explications were corrected only later.

What explains their having the relevant concepts is their ability to apply them veridically to cases, and their having paradigms and rules of thumb that were approximately veridical. This partial understanding—this inadequacy of understanding both to usage and to subject matter—motivated explications by subsequent thinkers. The subsequent explications clarified and unified the usage. In these respects, the cases of Newton and Leibniz are similar to the case of Dalton.

Reading 'Individualism and the Mental' again, I was struck by my insistent emphasis on the idea that one can have thoughts that one incompletely understands. This emphasis had an autobiographical root. A primary impetus for my discovering the thought experiments was recognizing how many words or concepts I went around using which I found, on pressing myself, that I did not fully understand. I came to realize that this was not just a personal weakness. It was part of the human condition, at least in complex societies.

In the article, I paid special attention to criticizing a near-automatic response to the first stage of the thought experiments. The near-automatic response was that if an individual incompletely understands a word, the individual's word meaning—and the concept that the individual associates with the word—must be reconstrued. If a foreigner uses one of our words without understanding it, we reconstrue the foreigner's word. We take the foreigner to be using a concept different from any concept that we would express if we used the word. A readiness to invoke reconstrual to interpret incomplete understanding was part of the elementary toolkit of every mainstream philosopher of the time. Automatic reinterpretation is certainly less widely taken as gospel nowadays. Yet it is still fairly common.[24]

Of course, there are many situations in which reconstrual is appropriate. But neither reconstrual nor 'homophonic' interpretation is automatically correct. Reconstrual is correct in many fewer instances than the common philosophical wisdom maintained three decades ago.

Reinterpretation picks up on something in ordinary practice. Misuses or failures of understanding exemplified by malapropisms, tongue slips, extreme 'category' misuses, the first uses of words by very young children, and the fumblings of foreigners, all normally and rightly occasion reinterpretation. Most other cases are more complex.

Individuals can fashion idiosyncratic uses of communal words. If their usage corresponds to their own understanding, and they do not rely in unconscious ways on others for fixing the applications of their words or concepts, individuals can cut themselves off from communal usage. It is no part of my view that just because a person is using the same word forms as others in a given social network, the person's words express the same concepts that his fellows' words do. Any dependence on others for linguistic or psychological content derives from reliance on others through certain types of causal relations to them.

Neither reconstrual nor standard construal is automatic. The relevant conditions governing each are extremely complex and varied. As the thought experiments suggest, however, reinterpretation is less often correct than was commonly supposed when the article was written.

The motivations for invoking automatic reconstrual are varied. Some lie deeply embedded in certain forms of individualism. If one thinks that the constitutive conditions for being in a mental state are limited to what is in the individual, one might take this 'being in' to be *being in the individual's understanding, or at least available to it*. The various views according to which having a concept is being able to give a definition, or a criterion for application, are ways of expressing this idea. A more sophisticated expression is an over-generalization of the insight that an individual's representational content depends (partly) on a web of inferential connections with other representational contents. The idea is that the constitutive conditions for understanding a concept cannot outrun the network of inferences that the individual can draw.

---

[24] Two esteemed former colleagues, Keith Donnellan and Donald Davidson, appealed to it right to the ends of their careers. Cf. Keith Donnellan, 'Burge Thought Experiments' in Hahn and Ramberg (eds.), *Reflections and Replies*; Donald Davidson, 'Knowing One's Own Mind' and 'Epistemology Externalized', collected in his *Subjective, Intersubjective, Objective* (Oxford: Oxford University Press, 2001). These responses to my work by Davidson and Donnellan seem to me to be vulnerable to replies that amount to repeating Sec. IIIb–d. Cf. also parts of Sec. V. My response to Donnellan is in 'The Thought Experiments: Reply to Donnellan', in Hahn and Ramberg (eds.), *Reflections and Replies*. My response to Davidson is in 'Social Anti-Individualism, Objective Reference' (Ch. 13 below).

A psychological state's representational content cannot be explained fully in terms of confirmation procedures, or any other transitions among psychological states. The errors of these views are clear from reflecting on the anti-individualist thought experiments, and not just those experiments that invoke incomplete understanding. Representational content is determined partly by causal relations to actual aspects of the environment. Sometimes these relations run through other people. In either case, they run beyond what must show up in the individual's inferences.

The still broader idea that meaning is use is sometimes invoked to motivate automatic reconstrual. There are two difficulties with such invocation. There is no evident reason why an individual cannot fail to understand his or her own use. And use cannot be separated from relations to kinds, properties, and relations in a subject matter. One can fail to understand the subject matter in a way that limits one's understanding of one's use.

The programmatic character of these doctrines leaves them vulnerable to over-generalization. The cases that I discuss in 'Individualism and the Mental' show that ordinary practice simply does not accord with automatic reconstrual in the face of a person's incomplete understanding. There is a complex terrain here. Automatic reconstrual is a revisionist position, not a piece of common sense or philosophical wisdom.

I want to discuss one other rationale for automatic reconstrual in the face of incomplete understanding. The idea is that individuals with psychologies must be guided by rules and principles in their representational processes. To be guided by a rule or principle (goes the reasoning), an individual must be capable of accessing it. Any difference in rule must be accessible to the individual. So incomplete understanding not remediable by reflection is impossible. So any supposed incomplete understanding that depends for completion on matters inaccessible to the individual must be illusory. Supposed incomplete understanding of rule or principle is really understanding of some other rule or principle.

This reasoning informs not only views that try to block the thought experiments. It also informs some views that nominally accept them, but use the reasoning to motivate an underlying level of content that is common to the twins in the thought experiments and that guides our intuitions about the cases. The idea is that only by being guided by rules or principles that explain how content is established (perhaps by reference to a social or physical environment) can an individual have the environment-dependent content that the thought experiments postulate. So a level of 'narrow content' must underlie and supplement the level of 'wide' or 'broad' content.[25]

---

[25] For further, brief discussion of other aspects or versions of such a distinction, see the Introduction. The presumption that any principle that guides intuitions about the thought experiments is made up of concepts that can be 'narrowly' individuated is itself without foundation. An individual's having notions like <u>cause</u>, <u>environment</u>, <u>social</u>, <u>physical</u>, <u>natural kind</u>, and so on is itself constitutively dependent on the individual's relations to a wider order beyond him-or herself. There are other

Regardless of whether the reasoning is used to resist the thought experiments or to motivate a new layer of representational content, I believe that this line of reasoning constitutes a fundamental misunderstanding of the implications of all the thought experiments, not just those of 'Individualism and the Mental'. The individuating principles that govern relations between representational activity and the environment are not in general implicit in the psychologies of individuals governed by the principles. Moreover, such principles need not be and often are not accessible to the individual. Relevant individuals need not be able to understand or follow the thought experiments. A very young language user might not be able to follow the thought experiment of 'Individualism and the Mental'. An animal perceiver need not be able to understand the considerations that support anti-individualism about perception. Even for adult sophisticates whose judgments regarding the thought experiments are presumably partly guided by an implicit understanding of some principles, not all details of the principles need be accessible. An individual may have to obtain new information about social or physical matters to see the truth of some constitutive principles.

The thought experiments in 'Individualism and the Mental' elicit the intuitive point that partial understanding need not be fully remediable by reflection, and need not be merely a matter of not having brought to consciousness an implicit full understanding. It begs the question against the thought experiments simply to invoke the negation of this point in motivating some contrary or supplemental view.

In 'Individualism and the Mental' I several times indicate in passing that a requirement of infallible and indubitable explicational understanding—even implicit understanding—is surely odd. I want to emphasize this point here. The view that incomplete understanding requires reconstrual really rests on such a requirement. A little reflection shows the requirement to be wildly implausible. Representational content is, broadly speaking, fixed by usage. Regardless of how usage is specified, it is surely a hyper-intellectualized conceit to think that the user *must* have (implicitly) an understanding that exactly reflects the nature of this usage—in such a way as to be able to have an infallible general explicational mastery.[26]

The main upshot of the thought experiments in 'Individualism and the Mental' is that individuals have far less cognitive control over discursive accounts of the natures of their mental states and the contents of those states than it has been common to concede in philosophy. The prevalence of incomplete understanding, even incomplete understanding that cannot be remedied by mere reflection, is one significant sign of this limitation. This limitation on cognitive omnipotence

difficulties with the view. For example, the conception of 'wide' content commonly misconstrues what width amounts to.

[26] Belief in simple mathematical or logical truths and belief in the purest cases of *cogito* can perhaps count as infallible and indubitable. Sufficient misunderstanding to yield apparent disbelief perhaps requires reconstrual in these cases. But explicational understanding of the sort that my discussions have centered upon seems to me clearly very different.

over one's own mind is in retrospect not so surprising. I believe that it puts us in a better position to understand the sorts of cognitive control and insight that we do have.

NORMS AS NATURAL STANDARDS

In Section V of 'Individualism and the Mental' I discuss certain models for understanding the representational content of mental states. The model I outline is that of the set of key relationships set up by a composition's tonic key. The model was meant to bring out ways in which standards of evaluation allow for quite a lot of individual variation but are independent of the individual's attitudes toward those standards, once the individual has the competence to write music or make sounds that establish a set of key relationships.

This metaphor was, of course, never meant to be more than suggestive. I would like to comment on it a bit further, however, partly to reinforce its main points, partly to highlight ways in which the metaphor is deficient.

The system of key relationships is like the logical relations among representational contents, and the semantical relations between such contents and the world, in one respect. Both are what they are independently of the individual's particular attitudes or understanding regarding what they are. Both allow for a lot of individual variation even as the system applies equally to all. This is the basic point of the metaphor.

The metaphor's main deficiency lies in there being no analog in the musical case to the representationality of representational content. Representational content entails or sets conditions for veridicality—truth or correctness. In helping to type-identify mental states, it entails certain fundamental goods of those states. Veridicality is a representational good, a type of representational success. Representational content sets conditions for the representational success of mental states. The system of key relations has no implications for representational correctness or success.

Although the point is obvious, some of its implications are perhaps less so. There are two sorts of doing well or badly in the making of sounds. First, animals can do well or badly insofar as making the sounds fulfills a biological function. The bird's singing loudly enough and according to some appropriate template enables it to attract a mate. Success normally has nothing to do with according with key relationships *per se*. All the bird needs is some distinctive sequence of sounds that can yield an uptake appropriate to the bird's needs. By contrast, representational contents set veridicality conditions, and veridicality is a type of representational success.

Second, human makers of music can do well or badly insofar as the sounds that they make or compose fulfill their intentions, or meet some historical and partly conventional standard of beauty, ingenuity, or coherence with respect to key relationships. Issues of genuine evaluation arise for these sound makers only insofar as they intend to make music. Good music making may be an objective matter, but it depends on some combination of individual intention and historical norms. By contrast, veridicality as a standard of representational success is not set by social activity or historical conventions. Nor does its being a standard of representational success depend on the individual's aiming to achieve it. Veridicality is set as a standard for representational success necessarily and apriori. It is a standard constitutively present in the very having of representational content. Given that a creature has states with representational content, in particular those like perception or belief, it follows that a type of success (representational success!) is inherent in being veridical; and a kind of failure resides in being non-veridical.

Further standards for *achieving* representational success—including epistemic norms—are also set by the psychological capacities and informational resources of the individual, not by any aim to meet the norms. Thus some standards governing how well an individual or representational system is doing at achieving veridicality are natural norms. They are part of the terms of being in the psychological states.[27] The terms for achieving harmonically successful compositions are not set purely by the terms of being a composer. They depend on the composer's aims and on historical-conventional understandings of what count as better or worse harmonic figurations, given those aims.

In both musical composition and representational state cases, meeting standards for success can depend on relations to others: in composition, through intended relations to the examples set by predecessors and contemporaries; in thought, through reliance on others for connection to the subject matter. The terms of this reliance differ greatly, however. As noted, the composer's intentions help to set what standards apply. By contrast, the veridicality conditions and content of an individual's psychological states mostly depend on factors over which the individual has very little control. So what counts as representational success and what norms apply are much less under the control of intentional activity by the individual.

RETROSPECTIVE

I think that 'Individualism and the Mental' made four main contributions in its historical context. One is the shift of focus in understanding reference and 'meaning' from language to mind. The article takes mind to be a distinct subject matter for which issues of reference, dependence on causal chains, sharing and transmitting of cognition, arise. I believe that the roots of linguistic representation—reference and meaning—lie at least initially in perceptual and conceptual representation. Language and mind inevitably become intertwined at relatively sophisticated levels. At that point, aspects of each depend psychologically, and

---

[27] For more on these points, see 'Perceptual Entitlement', *Philosophy and Phenomenological Research*, 67 (2003), Secs. I and II, pp. 503–548.

perhaps even constitutively, on aspects of the other. But at primitive levels, including primitive perception and perceptual belief, mental representation precedes and helps explain language, both idiolectic and public. The role of perception and perceptual belief in accounts of linguistic reference is partly independent of anything about the role of linguistic reference in perception and perceptual belief. So the shift in focus is toward part of the ground underlying the work on linguistic representation. 'Individualism and the Mental' started this shift, although only later did I center on perceptual aspects of mental representation.

A second contribution is the concentration not primarily on reference (linguistic or mental), or on *de re* aspects of mental states, but on the nature of representational states, and on how their *representational* content is determined. Reference plays a role in the article insofar as it helps illumine constitutive conditions that determine the nature of mental states themselves.[28] The arguments of the article show that the natures of certain mental states and events, understood as centering on the explanatory kind and epistemic perspective associated with the mental state, constitutively depend on relations to a broader environment.

A third contribution is to show that the mental states and events whose natures depend on relations to an environment constitute a much wider range than the conceptual counterparts of demonstratives, proper names, and natural kind terms, which the revolutionary theory of linguistic reference had centered upon. This is the main point of Section IIb. I later extended the range of application of anti-individualism yet further—particularly to perceptions and perception-based thoughts. I also showed later that the width of the range does not depend purely on reliance on others in a linguistic community.

A fourth contribution, the one most often recognized, is that of showing how the natures of an individual's representational states can depend on the individual's relation to a *social* environment. Our dependence on others to connect our words to a subject matter and to correct our beliefs about the subject matter helps constitutively to determine what attitudes we have. Certain representational and epistemic norms derive from these socially determined relations.

'Individualism and the Mental' was the first modern work to formulate anti-individualism clearly and to give specific convincing arguments for it. Anti-individualism is, however, very old—almost a commonplace in the history of philosophy. There remains much to be understood by reflecting on this old idea, developing it, and exploring its consequences. Fuller understanding of it would enrich understanding of many other philosophical matters.

---

[28] Many philosophers still do not appreciate the importance and distinctiveness of this point. Many still run together referential 'content' — the referents of linguistic terms, or mental states — with representational content. Different types of mental state can make reference to the same objects and properties. The differences are differences of perspective in a broad sense. They are differences in psychological and epistemic point of view. These differences are fundamental to epistemic evaluation and psychological explanation. They are not merely differences in reference. They are fundamental to both common sense and scientific understanding, to explanation, to epistemology, and to other evaluation of mental states and events.

6 *Two Thought Experiments Reviewed*

The issues raised by the arguments in Hilary Putnam's "The Meaning of 'Meaning' " and my 'Individualism and the Mental' (Ch. 5 above) are various and complicated. I shall be able to touch on only a few of these issues in this space. What makes matters more complicated is that Putnam's interests and viewpoint differ from mine. Although a comparison of our views would be useful, I will have to concentrate entirely on those of Fodor's remarks that concern my work. I begin by setting out two thought experiments, which I formulate in ways that raise a minimum of issues that are extraneous to my primary interests. Then I will state what I take the thought experiments to show. Finally, I will discuss Fodor's criticisms.[1]

The first thought experiment is a variant on Putnam's original twin earth case. For our purposes, the differences are significant. Assume that Al has a variety of beliefs and occurrent thoughts involving the notion of aluminum. He thinks that aluminum is a light, flexible metal, that many sailboat masts are made out of aluminum, that someone across the street recently bought an aluminum canoe. These occurrent and state-like attitudes are correctly (truly) described with that-clauses containing 'aluminum' in oblique, not purely transparent position. That is, exchanges of expressions that are coextensive with 'aluminum' (apply to exactly the same quantities of aluminum) do not in general preserve the truth-value of these original attitude ascriptions.

Now, as a second step in the thought experiment, conceive of a physical duplicate of Al who lives on a fraternal twin of Earth. Call him Al$_i$. Al$_i$ is bodily identical with Al. He undergoes the same stimulations on his bodily surfaces, excepting minor micro- and gravitational differences, engages in the same motions, utters the same sounds, has the same experiences—insofar as

---

[1] The reader is to be warned that an accurate assessment of the present discussion cannot dispense with a careful reading of the original papers in which the thought experiments are given. The two thought experiments that follow are set out in Burge, "Other Bodies", in A. Woodfield (ed.), *Thought and Object* (Oxford: Oxford University Press, 1982) and *idem*, "Individualism and the Mental," *Midwest Studies of Philosophy*, 4 (1979), respectively (Chs. 4 and 5 above). Actually both are stated in "Individualism and the Mental", but only the second is discussed in detail; the first occurs only in note 2. Putnam's argument appears in "The Meaning of 'Meaning' " in *Philosophical Papers*, ii (Cambridge: Cambridge University Press, 1975).

these stimulations, motions, and experiences are nonintentionally described. This physical and phenomenal similarity—virtual type-identity—is preserved from birth to the present. I will suppose also that there are internal-causal, functional, and syntactical similarities as long as they are specified nonintentionally and defined on the individual in isolation from his social and physical environment. Twin Earth looks very much like Earth to the naked eye. But on Twin Earth there is no aluminum. There is, however, a metal, not occurring on Earth that looks like aluminum and is put to many of the uses aluminum is put to here. The sign 'aluminum' is assigned to this stuff on Twin Earth (we shall use the sign 'aluminum$_2$' for it). And wherever Al encounters aluminum, Al$_i$ encounters this other stuff.

To sharpen certain contrasts, I want to introduce some further differences between Earth and Twin Earth. Laymen like Al and Al$_i$ know of no features that could in principle be used to differentiate between aluminum and its look-alike, if the issue were ever to arise (it doesn't). But there are substantial differences in the actions and attitudes in their respective communities toward the respective metals. Scientists here know aluminum to be an element; scientists on Twin Earth know the complicated formula, ZYX, of the look-alike. Differences in physical properties, including subtle macro-differences are reflected in the attitudes of the respective scientific, technological, and business communities. Differences also occur in some industrial uses. One can ramify the differences through the community as much as one wants, as long as they do not produce significantly different physical impacts on Al's and Al$_i$'s bodily surfaces. Al$_i$ remains surface-identical and movement-identical with Al.[2]

The thought experiment concludes with an observation. Al$_i$ does not think that aluminum is a light, flexible metal; he does not think that sailboat masts are made of aluminum; and so forth. He lacks attitudes that can be correctly (truly) described with 'aluminum' in oblique position. I take this to be obvious. Al$_i$ has never had contact with aluminum, nor contact with anyone who had contact with aluminum … ; and no one in his community uses a word that means what the word 'aluminum' means in English. Under these circumstances, we do not attribute thoughts like those we attributed to Al. We attribute different thoughts. So despite their physical similarities, Al and Al$_i$ have different propositional attitudes—differences that affect obliquely occurring terms in propositional attitude ascriptions.

We turn now to a second thought experiment. Assume that Bert has arthritis, knows it, and has a variety of occurrent and state-like attitudes truly describable with 'arthritis' in oblique position. He thinks his Aunt Mary's arthritis was more severe than his own, that arthritis has crippled many people, and so on. At a certain time t, he mistakenly thinks that he has got arthritis in the thigh as well as in the fingerjoints and knee. Later he is apprised of the fact that arthritis is an inflammation of joints and cannot occur in the thigh.

---

[2] As far as I can see, it does not matter whether twin earth scientists know that aluminum exists. Suppose that they do not.

Next conceive of a counterfactual situation in which Bert is identical to his actual self up through time t in all the ways we took Al and Al$_i$ to be. In the counterfactual situation, the community has not isolated arthritis for any special mention. (Incidentally, the disease is in actual fact not a physiological kind.) Counterfactually, the sign 'arthritis' applies to certain rheumatoid ailments, including forms of arthritis, but also including certain ailments of the muscles and tendons. Not only specialists but many laymen use the sign in this way.

The thought experiment concludes with the observation that in the counterfactual situation, Bert lacks attitudes truly describable with 'arthritis' in oblique position. When he utters the signs 'arthritis seems to have lodged in my thigh', he expresses a belief that may be true, not one that is false. When before t, he compares his disease with Aunt Mary's, he is not thinking of his disease as arthritis (even though the disease he is thinking of is arthritis). No one in the counterfactual community thinks of any disease as arthritis.

What do the thought experiments show? They show that the intentional content of ordinary propositional attitudes, as indicated by obliquely occurring expressions in that-clauses, cannot be accounted for in terms of physical, phenomenal, causal-functional, computational, or syntactical states or processes that are specified nonintentionally and are defined purely on the individual in isolation from his physical and social environment. Intentional content, in the aforesaid sense, is not even supervenient on the nonintentional processes and states of an individual, insofar as these processes and states are 'individualistically' described. Thus individualistic, functionalist, computationalist, or physicalist accounts of ordinary intentional content fail in a systematic manner.

The thought experiments also strongly suggest that conventional meaning is not illuminatingly seen as a 'logical construct', to use Fodor's phrase, out of individuals' propositional attitudes. They suggest that what a person's propositional attitudes are is neither determined nor explicable independently of the socially determined meaning of his words. This is not to say that one could not fix social meaning given the propositional attitudes of all members of a community, together with their linguistic behavior. But note carefully that such 'fixing' does not yield a logical construct. It is not yet a construction, and it yields no insight into 'conceptual priority'. The propositional attitudes of the individuals in a community do not seem to be individuated independently of publicly accessible meaning. Meaning and propositional attitudes seem to be coordinate notions. In view of Quine's work, this conclusion does not seem surprising. Nor do I think it should be rued. Philosophical attempts at logical constructions that reveal conceptual priorities seem to me to have yielded little insight. They represent, I think, an unpromising way of doing philosophy.[3]

---

[3] There may be projects that could be called 'Gricean', but that do not involve attempts at 'logical construction', with which I could have more sympathy. They would have to be specified more

The thought experiments are not incompatible with the idea that there are token mental representations, unique to the individual thinker, in every case of an occurrent propositional attitude. They are also not incompatible with the view that such tokens enter into causal relations in virtue of their 'syntax', as opposed to their intentional features. These views constitute the principal tenets of what Fodor calls 'Cognitive Science'. (In my view, the term is best taken to be like 'Christian Science' not only in denoting a doctrine rather than a discipline, but also in being a proper name rather than a description.) These tenets are variants on a very old, very resilient philosophical interpretation of mentalistic ascriptions. I think that Fodor has provided a challenging defense of this philosophical viewpoint in earlier writing.[a] As I said, the thought experiments are compatible with these tenets. I do doubt their truth. And these doubts are not unrelated to the thought experiments. But the relations are too complex to discuss here.

The two tenets of Cognitive Science make an ontological claim and a claim about the form of causal mechanism. Neither claim is incompatible with the thought experiments—which refute a view about how intentional content in ordinary propositional attitudes is determined and how it is to be explicated. Fodor does, however, appear to hold such a view. He often writes that he expects computational relations among inner syntactical tokens to 'explain' the content of propositional attitudes.[b] At the very least, Fodor fails to clearly distinguish a claim about what 'accounts for' the causal efficacy of propositional attitudes (which I think is his primary concern) from a claim about what determines or 'accounts for' their (opaquely, or obliquely specified) intentional content. Moreover, in his present piece, he resists the view that 'the content of a mental representation is not a function of *psychological* variables as cognitive scientists understand such variables'. (Although he does not say so, he seems to assume that such psychological variables must be individualistically specified.) And he seems to want to find some way of reinterpreting the thought experiments so as to avoid their anti-reductive, anti-individualistic consequences. On the other hand, much of his animus seems to be directed against inferences from the thought experiments, or closely related thought experiments, that I do not draw.

Let me make a very abbreviated pass at sorting some of this out. In practice, cognitive psychologists, including those who embrace the tenets of Cognitive

precisely before they could be fruitfully discussed. I do not see why Fodor is attracted to Gricean 'logical construction'. It does not seem to be needed by Cognitive Science, as he explains it. Nor do I see any strong motivation for it. There is the point that some (animal) propositional attitudes are independent of socially accessible meaning. There is the point that people normally know their own intentions (obliquely specified). And there is the point that propositional attitudes serve in the explanation of behavior. But I do not think that these points support the logical construction view. Fodor does not say how they, or other points, might be supposed to.

[a] [J. Fodor, *The Language of Thought* (Cambridge, Mass.: Harvard University Press, 1979); *idem*, "Methodological Solipsism Considered as a Research Strategy in Cognitive Psychology", in *Representations* (Cambridge, Mass.: MIT Press, 1981).]

[b] See Fodor, *Language of Thought*, 75–77, and *idem*, "Methodological Solipsism", 231, 234–235, 239–240.

Science, make nontrivial use of intentional attributions. They attribute propositional attitudes. So one would think that intentional states and processes would count as psychological variables. But since such states and processes are specified by reference to intentional content (i.e. in terms of obliquely occurring terms in that-clauses), content is trivially a function of psychological variables. It is only if one invests 'psychological variable' with some special, philosophical, individualistic meaning that the thought experiments show that content is not a function of psychological variables. Insofar as that content is what is adverted to in use of ordinary English discourse about propositional attitudes, it is not individualistically determined.

From here, the issues become complicated. For one may or may not take different views toward ordinary propositional attitude discourse and *idealized* psychological ascriptions. One might hold that some idealized psychological explanation uses nonindividualistic notions. I am sympathetic with this view, but only given a certain reservation: nonintentional specifications of computational relations are parasitic on ordinary intentional attributions. I see no clear reason to believe that this parasitism will ideally be dispensed with. Alternatively, one might hold that idealized psychology must purge nonindividualistic elements from current psychology. Having taken this position, one might either seek some individualistic revision of ordinary intentional discourse or claim that intentional explanation must be dispensed with altogether in psychology.

I think that Fodor is right in seeing this last eliminationist alternative as poorly motivated. Thus I do not take the thought experiments to place the notion of intentional content 'in jeopardy'—even in psychology, much less for ordinary, macro-descriptive purposes. At the very least, Fodor is right in holding that the eliminationist viewpoint cannot reasonably argue from the theory or practice of 'computational psychology'.

The other 'individualistic' strategy for interpreting idealized psychology is revisionist rather than eliminationist. Fodor does not explicitly adopt this strategy either. Those philosophical attempts in this vein that have so far appeared strike me as patently inadequate. Perhaps, though, psychology—or some important part of it, such as a descendent of 'computational' approaches—will yield individualistic notions that are both intentional and adequate to sophisticated explanatory purposes. I believe, however, that much of cognitive psychology will remain intentional, nonindividualistic, and intellectually worthwhile.[4]

All of these remarks about idealized psychology are rather speculative. My original claim about what the thought experiments show is, I think, not speculative. The intentional content of ordinary propositional attitudes cannot be accounted for in terms of physical, phenomenal, causal-functional, or syntactical

---

[4] In making this remark, I must issue a caution about it. A lot of philosophy hangs on what one expects from psychology and what one takes to be intellectually worthwhile. I cannot undertake to develop my views on these issues here, except to say that I am not monistic about either 'science' or the tasks of the intellect.

states or processes that are specified nonintentionally and individualistically. Cognitive psychology, including computational approaches, now makes non-trivial use of ordinary intentional language (somewhat refined and made more precise). So the same point holds for intentional content, as specified in *actual* psychological theory.

Fodor does not adopt either of the individualistic responses to the thought experiments that I mentioned four paragraphs back. He appears to question parts of the thought experiments themselves. But the issue is somewhat unclear. He concentrates on Putnam's counterpart of the first thought experiment and criticizes inferences from it that I am not concerned to defend. Moreover, he is none too careful in his reading of the argument of my 'Individualism and the Mental' (Ch. 5 above). And he significantly misconstrues my background assumptions. In the remainder of this paper I will try to set forth the basics of my position by reference to some of Fodor's remarks.

In the first place, my thought experiments are not primarily about meaning. They are about propositional attitudes. Here they differ from Putnam's first thought experiment. Considerations about meaning play a role in setting the circumstances in which we say what the protagonists think. But I do not know a precisely formulable inference from a general principle about meaning to our conclusions about attitudes. For example, I am not assuming, absurdly, that whenever someone sincerely utters words that mean that p, he believes that p. The thought experiments depend on no such inference. Nor do they depend on an antecedently formulated theory of 'concepts'. Our judgments about attitudes stand on their own. If one (nontheoretically) understands propositional-attitude discourse and knows how to apply it, one should realize that, in the situations we specify, it is plausible and certainly possible that the protagonists have the attitudes I say they have.[5]

We turn now to Fodor's central question: 'What *de dicto* belief is a speaker of Twin English expressing when he says, "water$_2$ is wet" ["aluminum$_2$ is flexible", "cancer is worse than arthritis$_2$"]?' Fodor puts this question to Putnam. I shall presume to answer it from my viewpoint. There is great potential in the expression '*de dicto*' for misunderstanding. For present purposes, I think Fodor would agree that we could replace the expression with the stipulation that we are interested in oblique, or not purely transparent, occurrences in belief ascriptions.[6]

---

[5] To be sure, one might ask for a fuller description of the situations. I have tried to comply, at probably unnecessary length, in "Individualism and the Mental" (Ch. 5 above).

[6] The problem is that a belief may be *de re*, with respect to either some aluminum or some other entity, yet the term 'aluminum' may still occur obliquely. ('Aluminum' may do double duty both as a referring term and as an attitude characterizer.) The argument in Fodor's note 11 seems to me to be flawed because it overlooks this point. I agree, however, that 'water', 'aluminum', 'arthritis', and so forth are not indexical, and have so argued in "Other Bodies", 103–107. There are other things that Fodor says about *de dicto* attitudes that I do not accept, although some of these differences are terminological. (Cf. Burge, "Belief *De Re*", *The Journal of Philosophy*, 74 (1977), 338–362—

So understood, the question should be answered by Fodor's 'first gambit': Al_i believes that aluminum$_2$ (oblique occurrence) is flexible. The protagonist Twin Earthian lacks the thought that aluminum [oblique occurrence] is flexible. He lacks any scientific competence, or (we may suppose) any exposure to a term like 'ZYX' that is closely associated with scientific usage. So it would be wrong to take him to be expressing the belief that ZYX [oblique occurrence] is flexible. Insofar as we lack a term that has the uses of 'aluminum$_2$', we should introduce one—'aluminum$_2$' would do—making sure that these uses are understood.

Fodor replies to the 'first gambit' by saying that we do not know which belief the belief that [aluminum$_2$ is flexible] is.[7] It seems to me that this reply does not raise any real problem for my point of view. One needs only to master Twin Earthians' usage to know which beliefs they express. I have set out the thought experiments in such a way as to suggest that this usage might be as rich and different from our use of the Earthian counterpart term as one likes. For example, 'water$_2$' or 'aluminum$_2$' might differ from 'water' or 'aluminum' not only in their referents, but also in their usage among businessmen, laymen, and so forth. I do not think it necessary to describe details of twin earthian usage to make it clear that the meaning and use of these terms differ from those of 'water' and 'aluminum'—and that we could master this usage and meaning, and associate them with 'water$_2$' or 'aluminum$_2$' for our own purposes. Similar points apply to 'arthritis$_2$'. Under these circumstances, I see no philosophically relevant problem in understanding what beliefs we attribute with propositional attitude discourse that places 'aluminum$_2$' (etc.) in oblique position.

This answer seems to me to need no further defense at present. But since Fodor's other 'gambits' may be a source of distraction I will remark on them. I am in broad agreement with his rejection of the third gambit, the invocation of indexicality (cf. note 6). What of the second?

The idea is that Twin Earthians believe that sailboat masts (on Twin Earth) are made of aluminum; Bert counterfactually believes that arthritis has lodged in his thigh. This line may have had some initial plausibility in reference to Putnam's original twin earth experiment, though it seems to me quite mistaken there too. But it lacks any plausibility as applied to my thought experiments. One only needs to understand how we use propositional attitude discourse to realize this. Bear in mind here that we are discussing ordinary propositional attitude notions. One can go on later to inquire 'what to do about them'.

There is no ordinary means of explaining how Twin Earthians might have acquired the beliefs attributed by the 'second gambit'. No one on Twin Earth has ever had contact with aluminum. No word on Twin Earth, at least no word used by the protagonist, means what 'aluminum' does. In the arthritis case, it

---

(Ch. 3 above); *idem*, "Individualism and the Mental"; *idem*, "Other Bodies".) I will not go into these matters here.

[7] This reply is backed by a criticism of Putnam's lexical theory that I do not fully understand. But since I need not defend that theory, I shall ignore the criticism.

is again hard to see why Bert, in his counterfactual situation, could be seen as having acquired the relevant beliefs, since no one on Twin Earth ever isolated arthritis for special consideration.

Further, there are no grounds for attributing to the Twin Earthian what are patently false beliefs. There are no aluminum sailboat masts on Twin Earth; and arthritis can no more occur in the thigh in the counterfactual situation than it can actually. There is no ground for seeing Al_i or 'counterfactual' Bert as being mistaken about these matters.

The second gambit is no better off if one claims that Al_i thinks (*de re*) *of* ZYX that it is aluminum, or *of* ZYX that sailboat masts are made of aluminum (oblique occurrence). Under the circumstances I described, we just do not attribute these false beliefs, or indeed any attitudes by using discourse that places 'aluminum' or 'arthritis' in oblique position. What is more, in the arthritis case, there is no difference in the *res* that Bert holds beliefs *of*, between actual and counterfactual circumstances. So there should be no temptation to think that the difference between actual and counterfactual situations can be explicated purely by reference to differences in the *res* that his attitudes apply to.

Fodor's own positive solution to the twin earth problems, in terms of pragmatically governed shifts in the domain of discourse, is a variant of the view discussed in the previous paragraph. The proposal is subject to the same criticisms. It is not plausible, when one considers the actual sentences of propositional-attitude attribution that would have to be asserted, that the same terms ('aluminum', 'arthritis', etc.) can remain in oblique position when we attribute propositional attitudes to the protagonists in actual and counterfactual situations. I also think that the modal problems Fodor raises for his view are more serious than his replies indicate. Moreover, the proposal will not apply to the second thought experiment, since there is no shift in the domain of discourse. The change is in the language spoken, and in the usage and attitudes among those in the protagonist's social environment.[8]

We turn now to the 'fourth gambit'. I find it quite baffling that Fodor attributes to me the view that on Twin Earth 'water$_2$ is wet' is used to express the belief that XYZ is wet, or the 'corresponding solution' for the examples I discuss. I have never held or expressed such a view of Putnam's thought experiment, or of any of the cases I constructed. I take it that if the protagonist lacks a term that is closely associated with specialized knowledge and lacks the specialized knowledge, we do not attribute attitudes using the term in oblique position. Since the protagonist on Earth in Putnam's example lacks the term 'H_2O' and lacks

---

[8] I think that Fodor is calling attention to an interesting and genuine pragmatic phenomenon, but that he is misapplying it to the cases at hand. There are other misapplications as well. The Marco Polo example is easily accounted for in terms of underlying tense constructions. The John the Baptist example (note 18) is best accounted for in terms of the indexicality of proper names (cf. Burge, "Reference and Proper Names", *The Journal of Philosophy*, 70 (1973), 425–439). I believe that indexicality is also involved in the Chinese cookie example (note 18). In order to understand the pragmatic phenomenon, we need a more careful discussion of its scope and limits.

knowledge of chemistry, we should not attribute the belief that H_2O (oblique occurrence) fills rivers and streams. Similar remarks apply to 'XYZ' and the twin earthian counterpart.

Perhaps the misunderstanding derives somehow from Fodor's misstatement of my contract example. This example was one of many, and in some respects it is not a central case. But Fodor's criticisms largely rest on a misreading of it. So I shall discuss it. The root of the trouble lies in the statement that I assume (or ask someone to assume) that the fact that contracts need not be written is constitutive of our concept of contract. In fact, I assumed only that it is not 'constitutive of our concept' of contract that contracts must be written. (I use the scare-quoted terms only in a loose nontheoretical way, and gave similar warning in "Individualism and the Mental", 81.) I explicitly disavowed any reliance on a philosophical view of concept-constitution (Ibid. 88). I share Quine's distaste for using such notions for philosophical gain. What I did claim was that a person who thought that contracts must be written would be mistaken and that we could imagine a society, where the word 'contract$_2$' was explicitly and strictly confined to written agreements, in which a physically identical person, described individualistically, would not hold that mistaken belief.

The rest of Fodor's criticism flows from this initial mistake and is made irrelevant by it. The claim that, on my view, Jones' denial that verbal contracts bind is 'explicitly contradictory', the points about the principle of charity, the substitutivity of identity, and so forth, all miss the mark because of the initial misstatement of my view. Similarly, his claim that I place excessive weight on the notion of same language is misdirected, or at least needs sharpening. I nowhere make heavy use of the notion of same language or same language community. I am quite free to allow considerable pragmatic latitude in using these notions (cf. ibid. 91–92). All I rely on is the fact that individuals actually regard themselves as responsible to linguistic or conceptual norms that might be applied to them by others. This much seems implicit in the notion of interpersonal agreement and disagreement.

I shall conclude by briefly discussing Fodor's claim that I cannot reasonably maintain the five assumptions he lists. I think that this claim is right. But I do not find it a source of discomfort.

1. I reject the first assumption. I agree with Fodor that it is untrue that *verbal contracts bind* is constitutive of the meaning of 'contract'. More generally, as I have said, the thought experiments do not depend on any philosophical views about concepts or concept constitution.

2. I am not happy with the second assumption. I doubt that the meaning of a word is rightly seen as a construct out of anything, and I would not take the notion *concept* as a good starting point for a construction in any case. I do suppose that there is something commonsensical and right about saying that two words that express the same concept are synonymous, as long as the saying is not pressed. (The converse is more problematic.) But synonymy does not play a critical role in the thought experiments, nor does 'same concept'. I rely only on

judgments about nonsynonymy, and nonequivalence among obliquely occurring expressions.

3. I would not accept without serious qualification the statement that when Jones says 'contract' he expresses the same concept that we do when we say 'contract'. This is partly because of wariness about 'same concept'. But it is partly because, on a perfectly ordinary reading, the statement is not true. I have discussed parallel subtleties, ibid. 100–102. What I do accept as true is that Jones might really believe (mistakenly) that there are no verbal contracts (oblique occurrence)—and that he might have other, true beliefs specified with 'contract' in oblique position (such as that one should not sign a contract without reading the fine print) that we share with him.

4. I accept the principle of charity in the form: Do not attribute simple, explicitly contradictory beliefs (like a belief that contracts are sometimes verbal and are never verbal). But this form of the charity principle is not relevant to our thought experiments. The mistake Jones is charged with in the previous paragraph is not an explicit contradiction. It is a mistake any rational person could make. I discussed just these matters, ibid. 100.[c] As far as I can see, Fodor overlooked this discussion. The crux of my view is that there is nothing impossible about certain sorts of ignorance. One can believe that aluminum occurs in masts without knowing about features of aluminum that would distinguish it from other metals that one does not often encounter. One can believe that arthritis is lodged in one's thigh, even though occurrence in joints is a distinguishing feature of arthritis. One can think that contracts must necessarily be written, even though being written is not a fundamental feature of contracts. I find these claims rather humdrum. But they do run against a very comprehensively articulated and deeply entrenched philosophical tradition.[d] The suggestion that alternatives to this tradition be pursued is the thought experiments' main claim to philosophical interest.

5. In earlier work,[e] I have explicitly rejected assumption 5, the general intersubstitutability of synonymous expressions in oblique belief contexts.[f] This rejection is abetted by giving up the traditional viewpoint challenged by the thought experiments. But it is not essential to my view of the thought experiments, since they nowhere rely on pairs of synonyms.

Attention to basics has prevented my discussing the relevance of the thought experiments to idealized cognitive psychology, except by the way. Although I see this matter differently from Fodor, I have some sympathy with his resistance to what I regard as too cavalier a rejection of (or instrumentalism about) propositional-attitude discourse. My aim here has been to give some sense of the power and simplicity of the thought experiments and to point out their effect on certain reductionistic philosophical programs.

---

[c] [See also Burge, "Belief and Synonymy", *The Journal of Philosophy*, 75 (1978), 119–138.]

[d] Cf. Burge, "Individualism and the Mental".

[e] Burge, "Belief and Synonymy".

[f] Burge, "Individualism and the Mental", n. 4.

7 *Cartesian Error and the Objectivity of Perception*

Individualism as a theory of mind derives from Descartes. It dominates the post-Cartesian tradition—Locke, Berkeley, Leibniz, Hume—up until Kant. And it has re-emerged in the writings of Husserl and of many English-speaking behaviorists and functionalists. Although a generic similarity of standpoint is discernible in this motley, it is difficult to state clearly and succinctly what these philosophers hold in common. Roughly, they all think that the nature and individuation of an individual's mental kinds are 'in principle' independent of the nature and individuation of all aspects of the individual's environment.

A more precise characterization of individualism that captures the position of many modern functionalists is

> Individualism is the view that if one fixes those non-intentional physical and functional states and processes of a person's body whose nature is specifiable without reference to conditions beyond the person's bodily surfaces, one has thereby fixed the person's intentional mental states and processes—in the sense that they could not be different intentional states and processes from the ones that they are.

This characterization is useful. But it is not directly relevant to the non-materialist tradition. Perhaps for some in this tradition (most plausibly, Berkeley and Hume), one could alter the characterization by referring to the person's phenomenological mental phenomena instead of to the person's physical states and processes. So for them individualism would be the thesis that a person's phenomenological, qualitative mental phenomena fix all the person's mental states, including those (like thoughts, desires, intentions) with intentionality or representational characteristics.

But now the characterization seems strained. It depends on distinguishing two aspects of the mental: phenomenological and intentional. I think it hard to maintain that traditional philosophers were drawing such a distinction cleanly enough to use it as the foundation for a major assumption. In retrospect we can see philosophers in this tradition as tending to assimilate concepts or even

I am indebted to John McDowell, Robert Matthews, and group discussion during the Colloquium at Oberlin College in 1985.

thoughts to (sometimes rarefied) percepts, and as regarding percepts as having their referential or intentional features intrinsically, as a result of their non-relational, qualitative, phenomenological natures. But it is doubtful that these philosophers can be seen as having made the distinctions necessary to be attributed a supervenience thesis of the sort just proposed. Moreover, the rationalists purported to lay little weight at all on the phenomenological character of our intentional states.

One could say that

> Individualism is the view that a person's mental states and processes have intrinsic natures, in the strong sense that the nature and correct individuation of those states and processes (including individuation of their intentional content) is independent of any conditions that obtain outside that person's mind.

Although this characterization does better for Descartes, it has its own difficulties. These center on the term "outside". It is not just that the term is vague as applied to the mind. The primary problem is that the characterization trades on a crucially unclear point in most idealist, especially most pre-Kantian idealist, theories. With Leibniz and Berkeley (and, on some interpretations, Hume), it is a subtle matter to say what is "outside" an individual's mind. Of course, in solipsistic theories nothing is outside the individual's mind in any sense. One may argue over whether the theories of Leibniz, Berkeley, or Hume are in some sense "ultimately" solipsistic. But regardless of what one thinks on this matter, the present characterization is crude at just the wrong point.

Still, the idea that the mind is somehow self-contained seems common to individualists. The idea can be refined, at least somewhat. Although it is difficult to generalize smoothly across Descartes, idealists, and various materialist reductionists, we shall characterize individualism, for our purposes, in roughly the way we began:

> Individualism is the view that an individual person or animal's mental state and event kinds—including the individual's intentional or representational kinds—can in principle be individuated in complete independence of the natures of empirical objects, properties, or relations (excepting those in the individual's own body, on materialist and functionalist views)—and similarly do not depend essentially on the natures of the minds or activities of other (non-divine) individuals. The mental natures of all an individual's mental states and events are such that there is no necessary or other deep individuative relation between the individual's being in states, or undergoing events, with those natures, and the nature of the individual's physical and social environments.

Individualism has been motivated in a variety of ways. Explanatory or reductionistic strategies, ontological preconceptions, and various epistemic intuitions have provided undeveloped but nonetheless deep conviction in the truth of the doctrine. The epistemic intuitions, however, were the original ones, deriving as they do from Descartes. They retain considerable power, I think, even among philosophers who instinctively avoid resting weight on Cartesian thought experiments. In the first section of this paper, I shall discuss these intuitions in a sketchy and preliminary way. In the second, I shall propose an argument against individualism that bears fairly directly on those intuitions. The argument centers on perception. The issues at stake here are of some moment; and the present brief discussion should be construed as a sketch, not an appropriately scaled treatment.[1]

1. Descartes imagined himself thoroughly mistaken about the nature and even existence of the empirical world. The thought experiments that he proposed are exceptionally vivid and powerful, at least on first encounter. And they have suggested to many—as they suggested to Descartes—that one's mental phenomena are in certain fundamental ways independent of the nature of the empirical and social worlds.

When one considers the thought experiments in any depth, one comes to realize that their details bear heavily on precisely what philosophical theses can be supported by reference to them. This generalization applies with undiminished force to attempts to use Cartesian thought experiments to support individualism. For example, the case for individualism based on the dreaming hypothesis is immediately affected (undermined, I believe) by the fact that an interpretation of dreams presupposes thoughts in a wakeful state. And the fact that it is part of the demon hypothesis that one is being deceived or fooled is of critical importance to any discussion of the relevance of the hypothesis to individualism. But I want to cut through such subtleties as much as possible. The "Cartesian" cases that I will be imagining make no use of dreams and make no assumptions about demonic deception. I think that laying these aspects of the thought experiments aside strengthens their prima facie usefulness for individualist purposes. I will construe Descartes as capitalizing on the causal gap that we tend to assume there is between the world and its effects on us: different causes could have produced "the same" effects, certainly the same physical effects on our sense organs. I will interpret him as conceiving a person as radically mistaken about the nature of the empirical world. I shall see him as imagining that there is something

---

[1] I have discussed individualism in several other papers: "Individualism and the Mental", *Midwest Studies*, 4 (1979), 73–121; "Other Bodies", in Andrew Woodfield (ed.), *Thought and Object* (Oxford: Oxford University Press, 1982); "Two Thought Experiments Reviewed", *Notre Dame Journal of Formal Logic*, 23 (1982), 284–93; "Intellectual Norms and Foundations of Mind", *The Journal of Philosophy*, 83 (1986), 697–720, and 'Individualism and Psychology', *The Philosophical Review*, 95 (1986), 3–45. (Chs. 5, 4, 6, 10, 9, this volume). There are significant differences among the various arguments against individualism in these papers. Some center on the role of the linguistic environment, some on the objectivity of theoretical discussion, some on the role of the physical environment. "Individualism and Psychology" contains the argument that I shall present here in sec. 2. But the argument in this other paper is given in a substantially different context. I think that ultimately the greatest interest of the various arguments lies not in defeating individualism, but in opening routes for exploring the concepts of objectivity and the mental, and more especially those aspects of the mental that are distinctive of persons.

causing the given person's mental goings on, but as imagining that the entities that lie at the ends of relevant causal chains (and perhaps the causal laws) are very different from what the person thinks.

The Cartesian hypotheses gain considerable power if one places oneself in the position of the person under the delusion. From the "inside", from a "first-person" point of view, one develops an impression of the independence of the nature of one's mental life from outside determining factors. One has a vivid sense of how the world seems; but one remains conscious of the contingency of the relation between the way the objective world is and its effects on us. That is, the same sensory effects could seemingly have been systematically produced by a variety of different sets of causes-cum-laws. Then our vividly grasped thoughts would be mistaken. These sorts of considerations have led many to conclude that individualism must be true.

But let us consider more closely. As I have stated the Cartesian hypothesis, it contains two elements: some epistemic remarks and some remarks about causation.

The causal elements by themselves do not support the individualist position. The possibility that very different causal antecedents could issue in the same physical effects on the individual's body, and perhaps even issue in the same phenomenological mental phenomena, is used as a component in my previous arguments against individualism. (See n. 1.) The strategy of the arguments is to conceive of a person's having certain thoughts (for example, a belief that aluminum is a light metal used in making airplanes). Then, holding the history of the person's body—and perhaps non-intentionally specified, qualitative experiences—constant, one conceives of a relevantly different environment's having substantially the same physical effects on the person's surfaces. (For example, one may conceive of an environment that lacks aluminum altogether, and contains some superficially similar metal instead, but in such a fashion that the person's body is not differently affected in any relevant way.) In such a case, the person plausibly lacks some of the originally specified thoughts. (The person lacks beliefs involving a concept of aluminum.) Differences in the nature of the environment with which the person interacts seem to affect the individuation of a person's thoughts, even though there is no difference in the way the person's surfaces, individualistically and non-intentionally described, are affected.

Thus both the Cartesian thought experiments and my anti-individualistic arguments make use of the possibility that different causal antecedents could have the same effects on the person's surfaces. The Cartesian might want to describe the causal elements in his thought experiments more richly: relevantly different causal antecedents have the same effects on the person's mind. But such a description would blatantly beg the question at issue. Whatever force the Cartesian thought experiments lend to individualism must lie elsewhere.

The epistemic observations center on the point that one could be drastically wrong about the nature of the empirical world around one. Until this point is made into a claim about the difficulty of justifying one's beliefs, it has no sceptical force. But even in its present form, the point is hardly uncontroversial. It tends to be the target of transcendental arguments. I shall accept it here for heuristic purposes, however, since my immediate aims are not epistemic. I want to grant a fairly strong epistemic conclusion from the thought experiments (one that I would not accept outright), and show, in a setting where scepticism is not at issue, that the conclusion by itself does not support individualism in the slightest.

So let us assume that we know or have reasonable beliefs about what the empirical world is like. And let us grant that the Cartesian thought experiments show that we could be radically wrong in these beliefs. That is, it is epistemically possible that the world be, or have been, very different from the way we reasonably think it is, or even know it is. This may be seen as a concession that we are deeply fallible. We can imagine being, and perhaps even being shown to be, pretty spectacularly wrong. But it is not a concession that there is reason to think that the beliefs, which we are conceding might "in principle" be wrong, really are wrong, or even are unjustified.

So what follows from this concession of the Cartesian epistemic possibility? Nothing immediate that favors individualism. We took our thoughts about the world as a *given* and conceded that they might be radically mistaken. But we conceded nothing about how our thoughts about the world are determined to be what they are. That is the issue before us. To assume that the epistemological intuitions occasioned by the Cartesian thought experiments support individualism is to make a step that needs justification. It is to beg precisely the question at issue.

It is a well-known point that in considering counterfactual situations we hold constant the interpretation of the language whose sentences we are evaluating in the counterfactual situations. It is quite possible to consider the truth or falsity of interpreted sentences even in counterfactual situations where those sentences could not be used or understood. Similarly for our thoughts when we are considering the Cartesian situations. We hold our thoughts constant. We consider situations in which the thoughts that we have would be false. And we concede that we could in principle be mistaken in thinking that the world is not arranged in one of the ways that would make our thoughts radically false. We do not ask how our thoughts' being false in certain ways would affect our thinking them. To ask what language or what thoughts would be possible if the world were in a given counterfactual state is to raise a question different from those raised in the Cartesian thought experiments. Thus there is some tendency for a Cartesian to move without argument from the counterfactual features of the thought experiments to the conclusion that the individuation of thoughts is unaffected by any possible differences in the environment. The move, or conflation, begins with: "Things might have been radically otherwise without our surfaces being differently affected; and relative to these imagined circumstances, our (actual) thoughts would be subject to numerous and radical errors." It concludes with: "Things might have been radically otherwise and our thoughts and minds would remain just as they are." Taken by itself, the transition is completely without justification.

There is, of course, another factor in the transition. Descartes's individualism rests primarily on his view of the special authoritative character of our knowledge of (some of) our own thoughts. A reconstructed Cartesian argument for individualism might follow these lines: (a) Suppose that one imagines that one's thoughts are subject to error in one of the Cartesian ways. (b) One knows what one's thoughts are, and they would be mistaken. But (c) an anti-individualist position holds that in some of the Cartesian cases we would think thoughts different from those we actually think—we would be in different mental states. (d) This conflicts with our authoritative knowledge about what (some of) our thoughts are and would be: we know authoritatively that our present thoughts would be the same.

This argument equivocates between considering what our thoughts are and what they would be. We can imagine that our thoughts are radically mistaken. So we accept (a) for present purposes. (b) is correct: we know what our thoughts are and we can see that in the counterfactual circumstances, those thoughts would be mistaken. (c) is also correct. I think it true, and compatible with (a), that in some of the Cartesian situations in which our actual thoughts about the empirical world would be mistaken, we would not be thinking the thoughts that we actually are thinking. But contrary to (d) there is no conflict with reasonable characterizations of first-person authority. We are authoritative about some of our actual thoughts about the empirical world; and we can imagine those very thoughts being quite mistaken. Moreover, whatever our thoughts would be if the counterfactual situation were to obtain, we would be authoritative about some of them. But we are *not* authoritative about what our thoughts about the empirical world would be if the counterfactual cases were actual. That is a philosophical issue, not a matter of what one's present mental events actually are. Although it may be settled by special, "apriori" means, it is not an issue over which anyone has first-person (singular) authority. First-person authority presupposes our thoughts as given; we are then authoritative about those thoughts. But our thoughts are determined to be what they are partly by the nature of our environment. And we are authoritative about neither our environment nor the nature of that determination.

The problem of explicating the nature and source of the authoritative knowledge that we have of some of our present mental phenomena is close to the heart of the larger problem of explicating what is distinctive about persons. Here is not the place to elaborate a position on these matters. In opposing individualism, however, I am opposing the traditional rationalist assumption that in order to be authoritative about one's thoughts, one must be authoritative about (or at least be able to know apriori) all conditions for determining or individuating the nature of those particular thoughts. I believe that there is no simple, cogent defence of this assumption, certainly none that is immediately sustained by the Cartesian thought experiments.

Although all of these points demand development, what I have said so far seems to me to undermine the sense that the Cartesian thought experiments provide simple, direct support for individualism. It is easy to see how we might be involved in either or both of the two conflations that I have just warned against: conflating questions of counterfactually evaluating one's thoughts with questions of what thoughts one would think if one were in the counterfactual situation; and conflating the fact that we are authoritative about our actual thoughts, and would be authoritative about what our thoughts would be in any (relevant) counterfactual situation, with the claim that we are actually authoritative about certain thoughts that we would be thinking regardless of what actual or counterfactual situation we would be in. I think that the belief that the Cartesian cases support individualism usually rests on one or both of these conflations. The individualist needs arguments beyond what the intuitive thought experiments yield.

I want to close this section by mentioning a very common argument for individualism that involves a crude version of the sort of thinking that infers the doctrine directly from the Cartesian thought experiments. It begins by noting that we could have the same perceptual experiences, same perceptual representations, whether these were veridical perceptions, misperceptions, or hallucinations. Similar points can be made for other intentional mental phenomena. The argument concludes from these observations that perceptual experiences are independent, for their intentional natures, of the perceiver or thinker's environment. This inference has no force. Questions of veridicality are judged with respect to given mental states. It is a further question how those states are determined to be what they are. The natures of such states are determined partly by normal relations between the person or organism and the environment. Error is determined against a background of normal interaction. I will develop this idea in the next section.

2. It seems to me that a deeper consideration of perceptual error and veridicality provides powerful grounds for rejecting individualism. I begin with the premise that our perceptual experience represents or is about objects, properties, and relations that are *objective*. That is to say, their nature (or essential character) is independent of any one person's actions, dispositions, or mental phenomena. An obvious consequence is that individuals are capable of having perceptual representations that are misperceptions or hallucinations: a person may have a perceptual representation even though he or she is perceiving nothing of the kind that is perceptually represented. A stronger consequence of the premise is that, in any given case, all of a person's perceptual capacities, and indeed cognitive capacities, could in principle be mistaken about the empirically perceivable property (object, relation) being perceptually presented. To put this consequence with some gesture at precision: for any given person at any given time, there is no necessary function from all of that person's abilities, actions, and representations up to that time to the natures of those entities that

that person perceptually interacts with at that time (and is capable of perceiving at that time and earlier).

Our second premise is that we have perceptual representations (or perceptual states with contents) that *specify* particular objective types of objects, properties, or relations *as such*. Representations specify such objective entities as blobs, bars, boundaries, convexity, cones, rough texturedness, being farther from x than from y; and they specify them *as* blobs, bars, boundaries, and so on. The "logical form" of such perceptual representations is not particularly important to our argument. I am inclined to think that some have the form of "that boundary". But as far as our argument is concerned, all could have the form "that is a boundary", or "there is a boundary there", or even (what I consider quite implausible) "there is a boundary there causing this perceptual experience".[2] The important thing is that the representations specify some particular objective entities (e.g. a boundary) as such (e.g. as a boundary). They do not simply describe those entities in terms of their role in causing perceptual states of a certain kind. For example, I assume that perceptual representations do not all have contents like those of 'whatever normally causes this sort of perceptual representation'—or "whatever normally has this sort of perceptual appearance", where the description denotes some objective property.

There are a variety of reasons why this latter sort of perceptual representation is not fundamental or canonical. The idea that our perceptual representations make primary reference to themselves is an old philosopher's tale with little or no genuine plausibility. I take it that attribution of such complicated perceptual representations is implausible on its face. And to get the description to apply

---

[2] The second premise is in conflict with Descartes's view that one cannot make perceptual errors because one perceives only one's own mental phenomena. According to this view one infers (wills to infer) the existence of objective properties causing those phenomena. Cf. *The Principles of Philosophy*, Pt. II, Principle III; *Meditations* VI. A similar view was embraced by Russell. Cf. *The Problems of Philosophy* (London: Oxford University Press, 1912), ch. 3; *The Analysis of Matter* (New York: Dover, 1954). I have discussed these sorts of views briefly in "Individualism and Psychology" (Ch. 9 below). John Searle, *Intentionality* (Cambridge: Cambridge University Press, 1983), ch. 2, argues that the content of perceptual states is always self-referential, in the last of the ways listed in the text. I find the argument unpersuasive, in that it depends on an undefended conception of "conditions of satisfaction". I do not think that there is strong reason to think that perceptual experiences have as complicated contents as he claims, and do not think that those contents are self-referential. (Searle's examples all concern recognition—a very late stage of perception. Cf. David Marr, *Vision* (San Francisco: W. H. Freeman and Company, 1982).) Still, these disagreements are not crucial to my argument. Searle's purportedly individualistic contents contain specifications of objective entities as such—for example, "a yellow station wagon". So such contents satisfy the requirements of my argument.

Perhaps this is a good place to emphasize that neither this premise nor any other part of the argument relies essentially on any particular notion of content or representation. I use these notions without apology, but I am aware that there are those who think they see something wrong with this sort of talk. For purposes of the argument this language may be regarded as a variant on talk about the type of intentional state. Clearly perceptual experiences are properly specified and individuated in such intentional terms. The argument concerns the nature and preconditions for the states and events thus individuated.

to appropriate entities (as opposed to antecedent or intermediate occurrences, such as arrays of light striking the retina), the descriptions would have to be complicated in ways that have never been fully articulated. Such complications make a bad case worse. There is no reason to think that notions like normality, or causation as a relation between objects and perceivers, or appearance, enter into primary perceptual experience. These notions are developed from meta-reflection on that experience.

Moreover, to be appropriately informative, the perceptual representation would have to specify the *sort* of phenomenological type that it itself instantiated: "this sort" is simply too unspecific to account for the reticulated array of perceptual types that we recognize and discriminate. But the idea that we classify our perceptual phenomenology without specifying the objective properties that occasion it is wildly out of touch with actual empirical theories of perception as well as with common sense. The sorts of complicated representations that we have been discussing seem to me to have little place in perception at all (as opposed to sophisticated, self-conscious, discursive reflection on perception—where they presuppose classifications of perceptual types in terms of public entities). But our argument requires only that they not be the only sorts of perceptual representations that we have.

In a sense, this second premise is a rejection of what used to be called the representational theory of perception. According to that theory, we primarily perceive, or at least primarily make reference to, *representations* of objective entities; we make reference to objective entities *only* indirectly—by assuming or inferring that there are objective counterparts or causes of the representations that we make direct perceptual reference to. I take it that this theory is discredited and rarely defended nowadays. It is implausible for the reasons I have mentioned. Among our perceptual representations are surely specifications, not merely role descriptions, of objective entities.

Although this second premise is worth articulating, I think that at a deeper level of argument, it can be dispensed with. I believe that the second premise is ultimately a necessary consequence of the first: we can make veridical perceptual reference to objective entities of a given type only if we can make perceptual reference to them as such. But I shall not take on the burden of arguing that here.

My final premise is that some perceptual types that specify objective types of objects, properties, and relations as such do so partly because of relations that hold between the perceiver (or at least members of the perceiver's species) and instances of those objective types. These relations include causal interaction.[3]

---

[3] I think that these relations always include intentional application—a notion that I have discussed elsewhere in some detail. Cf. "Belief *De Re*", *The Journal of Philosophy*, 74 (1977), 338–362 (Ch. 3 above); and "Russell's Problem and Intentional Identity", in J. Tomberlin (ed.), *Agent, Language, and the Structure of the World* (Indianapolis: Hackett Publishing Company, 1983). The relation of application to the present set of issues is in fact complex and worth pursuing. But pursuit is inappropriate here.

If there were no such relations, a perceiver would lack at least some perceptual intentional types that he or she has.

The premise derives from the fact that perceptual experience, and the formation of perceptual representation, is *empirical*. The intentional nature of some of our perceptual representations—what information they carry, what they mean—depends partly on the way epistemically contingent aspects of the world that occasion them actually are. Our perceptual information and our informational and representational states are worked up out of empirical interaction with an objective world.

The force of this point was obscured in the Locke-to-Hume tradition by a peculiar distortion. The empirical character of perception was depicted as if it were (at most) a purely causal affair. The perceptual types were considered to carry information about the world intrinsically—because of their shape in the image, for example. The role of the objective world was simply to cause appropriate ones among these information-bearing percepts to pop into the mind at appropriate moments.

Behind this distortion was the intuitively powerful but primitive idea (deriving from pre-Cartesian Aristotelians and prominent among post-Cartesian empiricists) that perceptual representations represented by virtue of similarity with their objects. This idea seems now to have little explanatory value. How could similarity alone (even assuming that the relevantly similar respects were articulated) explain perceptual representation? Among post-Cartesian empiricists the answer sometimes relied on the representational theory of perception, which we have just discussed: we represent objective empirical entities by representing subjective counterparts that are similar and by representing or inferring a relation between subjective and objective correlates.

Descartes and his rationalist successors either rejected or laid little weight on explanations in terms of similarity. But they tended to retain the view that perceptual representational types carry information or have their representational characters in complete independence of the way the empirical world is. Theological and idealist considerations were imported to shore up the objectivity and cognitive value of perceptual representation. And the whole tradition fell prey to Humean scepticism.

In retrospect, this set of ideas seems strange. Not only do our perceptual presentations or experiences have the qualitative features that they have because of the law-governed ways that our sense organs and neural system interact with the physical environment. But their giving empirical information to conscious beings about the environment—their representing it—depends on their qualitative features being regularly and systematically related to objective features of the environment. No matter what their phenomenological character, perceptual presentations can represent objective empirical features beyond themselves as such only through having instances stand in regular causal relations to instances of those objective features.

Granted, certain of our visual representations may be attributed attributes that are the same as or at least analogous to attributes of the objective entities that they represent. Our perceptual representation-in-the-image of a straight line may perhaps itself be said to be "straight". The image may be thought of as like a picture with some elements that have properties (for example, geometrical ones) that correspond to some of those that it depicts. (Of course, this line has been vociferously doubted by many philosophers; but I shall grant it for present purposes. Doubters have one less obstacle to agreement with my primary position.) Even where such analogies hold, they do so at least partly because of the laws of optics, the natures of our bodies, and the geometrical characteristics of physical objects. And similarities in the perceptual image are of representational significance only because and only insofar as they are formed through regular interactions with objective entities.

It must also be noted that any such similarities are limited in scope. Whatever similarities perceptual representations of three-dimensional orientations, or of three-dimensional shapes, or of occluding edges, bear to their objects are certainly not sufficient even to suggest a unique match. In such cases, which surely include the bulk of our perceptual representations, there is no other natural way to specify the intentional content of the perceptual experiences than by reference to the types of objective entities that they are normally applied to.

The third premise states that some of a perceiver's perceptual types take on their representational characters partly because their instances interact in certain ways with the objective entities that are represented. It does not claim that all do. It is plausible that many perceptions are composites of others. In some few cases, the whole may be representational, though it is *never* formed by interaction with actual objects. One thinks of hallucinations of pink elephants or unicorns. Moreover, some representations at the level of recognitional capacity (beyond the level of early vision) may be heavily informed by background theory, in such a way as to acquire representational character independently of any interaction. Again, these cases seem very much the exception. Still, it would be a mistake not to allow for them.

There are other ways that perceptual states may acquire their representational characteristics. Sometimes the evolutionary history of a species may form a perceptual tendency in members of the species that has representational characteristics that depend in some way on interaction between an individual's ancestors and objects of a relevant sort. The intentional content of a perceptual state may be independent of the individual's learning history. Instances of the state could, in an individual, be occasioned in an abnormal way, yielding misperceptions not preceded in that individual by veridical perceptions. My premise could be complicated to accommodate such possibilities explicitly. But the basic anti-individualistic thrust of the argument that follows would be unaffected.

The empirical character of perceptual representation formation is evinced in our common methods of interpreting a creature's perceptual experience. When we seek to determine the intentional content or representational types in a creature's perceptual experience, we determine what objective properties are discriminated by its perceptual apparatus. That is, we build up intentional type attributions by determining the types of objective entities whose instances regularly causally affect the creature's sense organs and are normally discriminated perceptually by the creature—or at least by creatures of the same species.

This fact about perception constitutes, I think, a qualified basis for the oft-repeated slogan that error presupposes a background of veridicality.[4] I think that this slogan is sometimes misused. I think that we are not immune from fairly dramatic and wholesale error in characterizing the nature of the empirical world. But I do think that we are nearly immune from error in asserting the existence of instances of our perceptual kinds, and of other kinds that are taught by more or less immediate association with perceptually based applications. I think that (induced) massive perceptual hallucination or a total lack of regularity between an individual's experience and his or her environment are the only possible explanations for an individual's perceptual experiences *always* systematically failing to apply to the world.

Most perceptual representations are formed and obtain their content through regular interaction with the environment. They represent what, in some complex sense of "normally", they normally stem from and are applied to. It makes no sense to attribute systematic perceptual error to a being whose perceptual representations can be explained as the results of regular interaction with a physical environment and whose discriminative activity is reasonably well adapted to that environment.

So there are the three premises: our perceptual experience represents objective entities; perceptual experience specifies objective entities as such; and the formation of perceptual representation (of perceptual intentional types) is empirical. We are now in a position to argue that individualism is not true for perceptual representation.

We begin with an individual with perceptual experience of objective entities. The person normally perceives instances of a particular type of objective entity (call it "O") correctly (as Os). But imagine that one or more of his or her perceptual experiences involves misperception. At time t, the person misperceives an instance of another type of objective entity (call it "C") as an O. That is, an instance of C is present and is causing the perceptual experience. Since C and

---

[4] The slogan has roots, I think, in Kant's point that the concept of seeming makes sense only in contrast to the concept of being. Cf. *Critique of Pure Reason*, "The Refutation of Idealism". The point regained prominence in Quine's "Principle of Charity", *Word and Object* (Cambridge, Mass.: MIT Press, 1960), ch. 2; and it has been employed in different ways by Donald Davidson, for example, in "On the Very Idea of a Conceptual Scheme", in his *Inquiries into Truth and Interpretation* (Oxford: Clarendon Press, 1984). I am inclined to believe that Quine and Davidson sometimes use this important idea with insufficient discrimination. But the issues here are again complex, and require more development than I can undertake. I should note, however, that in the remarks that follow my terms "characterization" and "application" are terms of art. Cf. "Intellectual Norms and Foundations of Mind", and the works cited in n. 3.

its instance are objective, it is in principle possible that all the given person's sensory modalities together might be fooled. In fact, we may imagine that given what the person knows and can do at the time of the misperception, he or she cannot discriminate the actual situation, at that time, from the one he or she represents. We may even imagine that nothing the person does or is disposed to do up until time t would (on this particular occasion) have discriminated between this instance of C and an instance of O.[5] My first premise gives us this much. The objectivity of the objects of perception entails that there is always a possible gap between the proximal effects of those objects on an individual's mind or body (and the sum of what the person represents, thinks, and can do), on one hand, and the nature of the objects themselves, on the other. The same proximal effects, representations, thought, and activity could in certain instances derive from different objective entities.

The first premise also yields the following counterfactual. We fix those of our person's physical states and discriminative abilities that can be specified non-intentionally and independently of the nature of his or her environment. But we conceive of a counterfactual environment in which the sort of entity O that the person actually represents never occurs. Instead, the sort of proximal stimulations that are actually normally caused by instances of O are counterfactually normally caused by instances of C (or at any rate by something other than instances of O). We may further imagine that members of our person's species have evolved so as to adapt to this situation. They regularly obtain information about instances of C; and we may imagine that their physical movements and discriminative abilities are quite different from the ones they have in the actual circumstances. Only the protagonist's body, non-intentionally and individualistically specified, need remain the same.

We assume, using the second premise, that in both actual and counterfactual situations, our person has perceptual experiences that are or include specific specifications of the relevant objective entities. For example, if in the actual situation, P correctly perceives an instance of O, the person perceives it as an O. By the third premise, since the objective entities that the person normally interacts with—and perceives as such—differ between actual and counterfactual situations, and since the laws explaining these interactions differ, the perceptual intentional types of the person also differ. Counterfactually, he or she perceives a C as a C, not as an O. Our protagonist's perceptual experience at t in the counterfactual situation is not a misperception, but is in fact veridical. (What

---

[5] There is no need to assume that the instance of C is in principle unverifiable or indiscernible as an instance of C. Another person with relevant background information might be able to infer that the instance of C would produce a perceptual illusion. Another person with different dispositions might even be able to perceive the difference between the instance of C and an instance of O. It need not be that all instances of C always look like instances of O to other members of the species. It is enough for the argument that instances of C that our protagonist is exposed to not be discriminable by him or her from the instances of O that he or she has been exposed to.

is important is only that the perceptual state does not specify anything as an
O.) But the person's physical states, discriminative abilities, and perhaps purely
phenomenological (non-intentional) states remain the same between the two
situations. So the person's intentional perceptual types are not individualistically
individuated.

It is easiest to imagine an example concretely if the case is taken from
the more primitive (but still conscious) stages of vision. For then elaborate
conceptual or verbal dispositions associated with the visual state need not be
brought into consideration. More dispositions complicate the attempt to imagine
a case in detail. But they do not affect the logic or soundness of the argument
already given. As long as the first assumption about objectivity is in place, there
is the guarantee that there is no unique fit between non-intentional dispositions
and the represented environment.

To fix an example, we may imagine that the sort of entities being perceived
are very small and are not such as to bear on the individual's success in adapting to the environment. An *O* may be a shadow of a certain small size on a
gently contoured surface. A *C* may be a similarly sized crack. The individual *P*
encounters several *O*s, and they are commonly seen in the environment. In the
only case(s) in which *P* encounters a *C, P* may have no dispositions that would
discriminate the instance of *C* from an instance of *O*—although *P* might in
principle have been taught such procedures, and although other individuals may
have them. For example, *P* may have no dispositions involving touch that could
be used to discriminate them, perhaps because the relevant entities are too small,
or because *P* is not disposed to rely on non-visual modalities in such cases, or
because touch itself is fooled. Still, if only *O*s normally cause visual representations of the sort *P* has, if *P*'s having those representations is explained in terms
of their relation to *O*s (characterized as *O*s), if *P* can discriminate *O*s from
relevantly different things in the environment, and if *P*'s visual or cognitive
systems have some means of distinguishing objective entities from subjective
ephemera (most of the time), then *P*'s visual representation may specify *O*s as
such. The misperception of a relevant sort of crack as a relevant sort of shadow
may be a result of a one-time causal aberration.

We may assume, if we wish, that in the actual situation—given *P*'s abilities,
and the actual laws of optics—*P* would be capable of visually discriminating
some instances of *C* (cracks of the relevant sort) from some instances of *O* in
ideal circumstances. But we are supposing that *P* is confronted by only one or
a few instances of *C*; and in those cases, circumstances are sufficiently non-
ideal so that all *P*'s abilities would not succeed, in those circumstances, in
discriminating those instances of *C* from instances of *O*. *P* misperceives the
relevant cracks as shadows.

Now imagine a counterfactual case. Owing to peculiar optical laws or effects,
there are no visible *O*s—no shadows (visible to *P*'s species) of relevantly
similar shape and size on gently contoured surfaces. The optical laws are also

such that all the visual impressions caused by and explained in terms of Os in the actual situation are counterfactually caused by and explained in terms of Cs—relevantly sized cracks. The cracks are where the shadows were in the actual case. Suppose also that at the (few) time(s) when in the actual situation P is confronted with a C, P is also counterfactually confronted with a C. None of the differences relevantly affects the physical history of P's visual system or any of P's other physical stimulations, physical dispositions, or physical activity.[6] In such a counterfactual situation, P would normally be visually representing Cs—relevantly small cracks—as Cs. P would never be visually representing, or misrepresenting, anything as an O. One can imagine that in the counterfactual case, even if there *were* appropriately sized shadows on relevant surfaces, the different laws of optics in that counterfactual case would not enable P ever to see them. If this were so, one could hardly take P's visual impressions (physically and perhaps phenomenologically the same as in the actual case—but explained as *normally* caused by cracks) to be misrepresentations of things as the relevant sort of shadows. For we imagine P's visual impressions to be caused in a regular way by the objects P is looking at. The visual impressions provide as sound a basis for learning about the environment in the counterfactual case as they do for learning about the (different) environment in the actual case. Counterfactually, P's intentional perceptual states are different: P sees Cs as Cs.

The general strategy of the argument is simple. The first premise notes a possible gap between a person's physical states and intentional states, on one hand, and the state of the world that is seen, on the other. Holding the relevant physical effects constant, we imagine different visible objects in the world, and different optical laws normally and regularly relating those objects to the person's physical states. In such a case, it is clear that some of the person's intentional visual states, at least some of those that specify objective entities as such, would be different. The second and third premises of my argument already jointly indicate that a person's intentional perceptual states are in fact not individuated individualistically. These premises presuppose the first. The first premises makes explicit the possibility of error, and thereby indicates that the non-individualist methods of individuation, indicated by the second and third premises, do not "in principle" have counterpart methods that are individualistic.

If one relinquishes the claim that a person's perceptions represent objective entities, then the argument collapses. All three premises are undermined. So as

---

[6] One may imagine that the dispositions that would, in the actual case under ideal circumstances, have visually discriminated Cs from Os would, in the counterfactual case, be activated in circumstances that provide discrimination of some other type of thing from Cs. Given the very different physical environment and laws, one can imagine these dispositions to have almost any visual meaning that one likes.

applied to a solipsistic thinker, the argument is powerless.[7] On the other hand, the objective and empirical character of perceptual representation seems to guarantee non-individualistic intentional perceptual states, and non-individualistic methods of individuating them.

---

[7] Perhaps one should see in this light the fanciful examples of beings that are bodily identical to us over a period of time, but that are extended quantum accidents with no regular relations to their physical environment. There is perhaps enough in the mental events of such beings to count them thinkers. (Actually, this seems to me problematic: there are problems about dispositions; but let them pass.) Whatever thoughts they entertain have no determinate *objective* reference. Their mental goings on and their physical movements are compatible with successful adaptation to and regular causation by any one of an infinity of possible environments. Such intentionality as their phenomenological states have should perhaps be seen as making reference to qualitative phenomenological types, not to objects that are in principle independent of the individual's thought and perception. For such a being, individualism is perhaps true. But its truth would be bought at the price of interpreting the thinker as a solipsist unawares. I leave the ultimate coherence of such a description an open question.

8 *Authoritative Self-Knowledge and Perceptual Individualism*

In 'Cartesian Error and the Objectivity of Perception' (Ch. 7 above) I discussed three issues: the nature of individualism, the role of first-person authority in traditional Cartesian individualist views, and the way that considerations of objectivity support a non-individualist view of perception. I treated each of these issues only in a brief and preliminary way. Professor Matthews concentrates on the latter two. Here I hope to clarify some of the points I made on these two issues by responding to his criticisms, and by developing some of my points further.

I

Let us begin with the matter of first-person authority. I centered the discussion on Descartes, attempting to understand a traditional, Cartesian motivation for accepting individualism. I took the notion of first-person authority in an intuitive way. I did not provide an account of the phenomenon since I conceive of that task as requiring very substantial systematic development. But I did make certain commitments regarding it.

Matthews holds that the two conflations I cite are not sufficient by themselves to lead to individualism. The second conflation is (in my words):

> conflating the fact that we are authoritative about our actual thoughts and would be authoritative about what our thoughts would be in any (relevant) counterfactual situation, with the claim that we are actually authoritative about certain thoughts that we would be thinking regardless of what actual or counterfactual situation we would be in.

The idea was that in this conflation, the Cartesian moves without argument from what I call a fact in this quotation to what I call a claim. Matthews maintains that this and the first conflation carry us only to the conclusion that we know what thoughts we would think if we were in the imagined counterfactual situation. He thinks that something more is needed if we are to draw the conclusion that

This was written in reply to Robert J. Matthews, "Comments", in R. Grimm and D. Merrill (eds.), *The Contents of Thought* (Tucson: University of Arizona Press, 1985); Page references in the text are to this article.

the thoughts we would think in the counterfactual situation are the very same thoughts that we are thinking now.

But this conclusion is already contained in the statement of the second conflation: There are *certain* thoughts that we are actually authoritative about (and, of course, actually thinking since authority applies paradigmatically to actual present thoughts) and would be thinking in the counterfactual situation as well. I think that there is no other way to read the expression 'certain'. It is a 'wide scope' expression *par excellence*. The expression attaches the authority to particular thoughts in the actual situation that are held in relevant counterfactual situations as well. There is no gap in the reasoning.

The conflations are to be understood as leading to individualism in the context of reflection on our authoritative knowledge of some of our present mental events. Descartes was impressed with this sort of knowledge. I think that he was right to be impressed. He was further right in thinking that we have a special, strong, intuitively direct, authoritative (though I think not infallible) knowledge of certain of our present mental events. He was on to something real and profound. The difficult philosophical problem—still unsolved in my opinion—is coming to a deep and accurate understanding of this sort of knowledge. My claim is that the conflations seduced traditional individualists like Descartes into implicitly construing this authority in a way that has no intuitive warrant and that led to stronger epistemic conclusions than it can really support.

Suppose that one thinks that one has a peculiarly direct knowledge of particular thoughts one is thinking. And suppose that one is involved in the relevant conflations. One slides easily between evaluating thoughts counterfactually and determining what thoughts would be thought in counterfactual circumstances. One does not reflect on the difference between, on one hand, the necessity that one *has* the relevant sort of authority (if one is a certain sort of self-conscious being) and, on the other, a putative power to extend one's authority about certain thoughts one actually has to the counterfactual cases—giving one the right to claim that one would have authoritative knowledge of *those same thoughts* even though the counterfactual circumstances in which one would be thinking are entirely different.

Then it is easy to see how one could conclude that the nature of one's thoughts is independent of one's environment. One simply performs a thought experiment. One fixes on some empirical contingent thoughts that one is presently thinking and imagines that causal antecedents of one's thoughts were very different. The causal antecedents of those particular thoughts would seem to be contingently related to those thoughts. This is suggested by the fact that even if they are veridical, they could have been non-veridical. It would appear that one could just fix those thoughts authoritatively and hold them in mind even as the background scenery is changed. The conclusion is that one's authoritative and direct knowledge is supposed to show that no change in background scenery could affect the nature of the thoughts that are under one's authoritative control. My view is that no intuitively plausible conception of first-person authority warrants so strong a conclusion. Apart from the conflations, even Descartes's conception of authority does not warrant individualism.

Matthews offers an alternative argument that may have led some to embrace individualism. I do not doubt that his argument has had some influence. I do doubt that it has much to do with first-person authority. For purposes of the diagnostic argument, Matthews glosses authority twice. Once our being authoritative about our thoughts is glossed: 'we know what we believe, desire, and so on.' Once it is counted equivalent to our knowing what we believe, desire, intend, and so on, in both actual and counterfactual circumstances.

These characterizations are certainly not Cartesian. They do not suggest anything special about some of our knowledge of our mental events. They apply to all our self-knowledge. Much of the knowledge that we have of our own beliefs, desires, and so on, is not special, and is similar to the knowledge that we have of others' mental states. Matthews's glosses do not speak to traditional intuitions that some of our self-knowledge is fundamentally first-person singular, applies paradigmatically to present occurrent conscious mental events, and is in some sense peculiarly immediate, authoritative, certain, or central to personhood. In short, the glosses ignore the apparently special character of first-person authoritative knowledge. So I think that the argument based on this conception of knowledge is not a serious contender for explaining the Cartesian motivations for individualism.

The argument Matthews offers is as follows. (1) We are 'authoritative' about our thoughts in the senses that Matthews lays down. Hence, (2) we can ascertain by empirical observation the type-stability of our tokened thoughts in the face of actual changes in the environment. (3) When we undertake such observations we discover that our tokened thoughts are type-invariant in the face of changes in the environment. (4) But if our tokened thoughts are thus type-invariant, individualism is true, since individualism is the view that an individual's mental state and event kinds can in principle be individuated in complete independence of that individual's physical and social environments.

In my view, the failure of the argument lies primarily in steps (3) and (4). (1) is defective only in its inadequacy as a conception of first-person authority. We surely know what some of our thoughts are and would know what some of our thoughts were in the relevant counterfactual circumstances. (2) does not *follow* from (1), as the argument claims. (There is nothing in (1) about type-stability or empirical observation.) But apart from the fact that the sort of knowledge described in (2) is more complex than 'empirical observation' suggests (an interesting conjunction of first-person and third-person points of view is involved), (2) seems to me acceptable. (3) is also acceptable if it is clearly understood to apply to an 'observation' of type-stability in the face of *(some) actual* changes in the environment—the condition laid down in (2). Of course, our thoughts frequently do shift under actual changes in the environment. We change our minds. But sometimes our thoughts remain stable, and frequently we know this.

As stated, however, (3) does not clearly confine itself to such actual changes. It may be read as a generalization over *any* 'changes' in the environment—counterfactual variations as well as actual ones. On this more general reading, (3) directly contradicts the results of the anti-individualist thought experiments that I have set out. But it does so without offering any interesting support for itself. It certainly gains no support from the relatively modest claims about knowledge set out in (1) and (2).

(4) takes up this generalized reading of (3). Unless (4) is applied to all possible variations in the individual's environment (laying aside again variations that would lead the individual to change his or her mind), it is irrelevant to a defense of individualism. Type-stability of some of our thoughts under some actual and counterfactual changes in the environment is compatible with both individualism and its denial. So either (3) or (4)—depending on where the implicit move from 'some actual changes' to 'all relevant counterfactual changes' is made—begs the question.

Matthews conjectures at one point that I may accept the view that there can be no empirical warrant for counterfactual conclusions. I do not accept this view. And nothing in my position commits me to it. The problem with the argument he develops and criticizes is that it rests on counterfactual conclusions for which the argument gives no warrant at all—empirical, first-person authoritative, apriori, or otherwise. I see no argument for the transition from some empirical cases to all relevant counterfactual cases. The argument appears to fall into a variant of the second conflation that I cited. Since the conclusions are also incompatible with intuitions on which I rest the non-individualist thought experiments, they beg the question.

Matthews's own criticism of the argument centers on (1). He thinks we are authoritative about our thoughts, but 'not in the sense that the above argument requires if it is to go through'. He holds,

We are authoritative about the tokening of thoughts, but not about the types to which tokened thoughts belong. Or, to put it another way, we are authoritative in the sense that we can *express* our beliefs, desires, etc. Thus, I can express what I would describe as my belief that water is wet by saying 'water is wet.' Yet the fact that we can so express our thoughts does *not* entail that we know what thoughts we have thereby expressed. (p. 80)

As support for this view, Matthews cites the Twin Earth cases in which the twins do not share certain beliefs. He holds that they could not know that they do not share beliefs. He quotes me with approval: 'our thoughts are determined to be what they are partly by the nature of our environment. And we are authoritative about neither our environment nor about the nature of that determination.'

Although I share Matthews's opposition to the argument, I do not accept his mode of criticizing it. I stand by the view that we appear to agree upon: that we are authoritative neither about the environment nor about the principles that govern the individuation of our thoughts. But my formulation of this view involves the intuitive, relatively pre-theoretic conception of authority that interested Descartes. It is obvious that we do not have special authoritative first-person (-singular) knowledge of the environment. It is nearly as obvious that we do not have such knowledge of the general principles that govern the individuation of thought—or the general principles governing the individuation of anything else. Matthews's explications of 'authority' make it clear that he is not operating with this conception. If I understand it correctly, his criticism of the argument depends on claims that seem to me to be very implausible—certainly stronger than any I would make. This takes some explaining.

I do not know what Matthews means by saying that we are authoritative about our thought tokens, 'in the sense that we can express our beliefs and desires'. But this does not seem to me to be a sense of either authority or knowledge. Perhaps he is getting at the important though rather vague point, found in Wittgenstein, that part of our authority over our thoughts involves some sort of proprietary right to initiate them and express them. If this is what Matthews means, I think that he is touching on a significant *element* in the understanding of first-person authority. But whatever this comes to, it is not all there is to first-person authority. In my view, first-person authority primarily concerns knowledge, not expression. And it does not reduce merely to the knowledge that one has initiated some particular thought token or other.

Matthews's central negative point in his criticism of the argument seems to go beyond a view that I think is already deeply implausible: that we lack any sort of *authoritative knowledge* of what thoughts we think. The further claim seems to be that in view of the twin earth thought experiments we do not even *know* what thoughts we think or express: 'The authoritative knowledge that we lack is precisely the knowledge that would enable us to correctly individuate our thoughts.' This suggests that we do not know our own thoughts because we cannot correctly and knowledgeably individuate them—cannot know which thoughts they are.

I do not accept these claims. I think that we do individuate our thoughts. That is, we know them as the particular types of thoughts that they are. We know which thoughts we think. I think it completely unacceptable to hold that we do not know what our thoughts are. When I occurrently and consciously think that water is wet at a given time, I typically know that I think that water is wet. Denying this would, in my opinion, be a *reductio* of one's own position. Moreover, I hold the further view that this knowledge is authoritative and distinctive in *something like* the way Descartes held that it was, even though it is not infallible, and does not involve the powers of counterfactual discrimination that he attributed to it.

There are, of course, those influenced by Wittgenstein who hold that the proprietary right to avowals is all that first-person authority comes to: no knowledge at all (much less a distinct and interesting sort of knowledge) is involved. I find the reasons given for this view quite unpersuasive. But I have not undertaken to discuss them. The issues involved resist brief treatment. It suffices for my present purposes to emphasize that this sort of view is not mine, and that the view is not entailed or, as far as I can see, made more plausible by my rejection of individualism.

The point that I emphasized in the paper is that first-person authoritative knowledge does not give one special insight into the principles underlying the individuation of our thoughts. We typically know our current, conscious thoughts. We individuate them in the sense that we know what thoughts we think. But we do not do so by knowing (much less by knowing in the way we know our own occurrent thoughts) general principles and environmental facts that conspire to make the thoughts what they are.

There is, of course, a sense in which we cannot—using phenomenological, explicational, or inferential abilities—discriminate thoughts that we actually have from thoughts that we might have had if the environment were relevantly different. None of our abilities that do not already presuppose the exercise of the relevant actual thoughts suffice to discriminate for us those thoughts from counterfactual alternatives. We cannot discriminate by introspection the actual situation from the various 'twin' counterfactual situations. I mean by this that we cannot use our authoritative self-knowledge to pick out some feature of our actual thoughts that distinguishes them from the counterfactual thoughts and that enables us (authoritatively) to give some ground for thinking that our thoughts are not the counterfactual ones but the actual ones. Our authority is over our actual thoughts, not over some comparison between them and non-actual thoughts.

But this state of affairs would undermine knowledge of our own thoughts only if our only means of identifying our own thoughts were to bring to bear phenomenological, explicational, or inferential abilities (specified independently of those thoughts) to distinguish them from every such alternative. Our self-knowledge would be undermined by the anti-individualist point of view only if we could know our actual thoughts only by being uniquely sensitive to their uniquely distinguishing features.

What reason is there to accept this condition on self-knowledge? I see no reason. And there are considerations to the contrary. It is extremely implausible to think that our knowledge of our own thoughts always depends purely on such abilities. We do not have to reason to the identity of our thoughts. We do not base the relevant self-knowledge on phenomenological accessories, or indeed on any sort of recognition.

This is not to say that we have an infallible access to our present conscious mental events. It is just to say that we do not gain the knowledge by exercising the sort of discursive abilities involved in discriminating our actual thoughts from counterfactual alternatives. Nor do we exercise special introspective recognitional abilities. Explicating the nature of the 'directness' involved in first-person knowledge is a complex problem. I intend to confront it elsewhere. But it is implausible, from the start and independently of any philosophical theory, to think that self-knowledge depends on our discriminating our actual thoughts from all counterfactual alternatives that are compatible with those of our powers of discrimination that are independent of those actual thoughts.

I think that the analogous position does not even hold for the knowledge we have of particular observable physical entities. We can know things about certain observables without being able to discriminate them from all possible duplicates (except by seeing them rather than their duplicates). That is, we can have such knowledge even though if we were in a situation in which a duplicate were substituted for the object we actually observe, we could not discriminate the duplicate from the actual entity. I take it that the possibility that we could not discriminate such duplicates is entailed by the objectivity of perception, discussed in the last part of my paper. This objectivity hardly undermines empirical knowledge.

But the requirement that to know what thoughts we are thinking, we must have the ability to discriminate our thoughts from those of a Doppelganger (in some way that does not presuppose the thinking of our actual thoughts) is, I think, even more implausible than this analogous position regarding perception.

The idea that we can attempt to determine what our thoughts are from a vantage point that is neutral as to which of various alternative thoughts we are thinking seems to me to be not only deeply implausible but incoherent. (I believe it also incoherent to think that we always find out what our thoughts are by purely empirical means—that is, in a way similar to the way we gain knowledge of our own and others' thoughts through observation of our behavior. I cannot, however, argue either of these points here.) These points are related to the special character of first-person authoritative knowledge. I freely concede that these matters are complex and difficult. A deeper explication of first-person authority is needed, and I shall have more to say about the matter elsewhere. But it seems clear from the outset that such an account must not require that one discriminate one's actual thoughts from counterfactual alternatives, from a vantage point that is independent of what thoughts one is actually thinking. One's first-person standpoint is inseparable from the thoughts that one actually thinks.

II

In the last section of 'Cartesian Error and the Objectivity of Perception', I gave a general argument against individualism about perceptual states. Professor Matthews raises some objections which he takes to undermine the argument. I think that these objections are off the mark. They fail to come to grips with the argument as it was presented. I am glad to have the opportunity to make its strategy clearer.

Matthews expounds the argument correctly. But I will repeat its premises for convenience: (i) Our perceptual experience represents or is about objects, properties, and relations that are objective in a sense that entails the following: for any given person at any given time, there is no necessary function from all of that person's abilities, actions, and presentations up to that time to the natures of those entities that that person perceptually interacts with at that time (and is capable of perceiving at that or some prior time). (ii) We have perceptual representations (or perceptual states with contents) that specify particular objective types of objects, properties, or relations as such—not merely in terms of their relation to the perceiver. (iii) Some perceptual types that specify objective types of objects, properties, and relations as such, do so partly because of relations that hold between the perceiver (or at least members of the perceiver's species) and instances of those objective types. If there were no such relations, a perceiver would lack at least some perceptual intentional types that he or she has.

I provided an example that was supposed to illustrate how the argument worked. A person might have seen instances of certain small shadows and then come to misperceive a similarly sized crack as a shadow. In accord with the first premise, I stipulate that none of the person's representations or abilities could discriminate this particular crack from the sort of shadow that is visually represented. I assumed in accord with the second premise that the person's perceptual state was to be specified as of a shadow. Then I considered a counterfactual situation in which the person's environment never involved shadows of the relevant sort in the etiology of the person's (or his fellows') perceptual states. I imagined that the counterfactual environment has compensating, but different, optical and other laws that enable the perceiver's physical dispositions to be just as adaptive in the counterfactual environment as they are in the actual environment. I imagined that relevantly sized cracks were the source (by different causal processes than are common in the actual situation) of his and his fellows' perceptual states. I stipulated that the person's physical history, described in isolation from the environment, was to be held constant between actual and counterfactual situations. I concluded that whereas it is perfectly possible for the person to have perceptual states as of the relevant shadows in the actual situation, it is not possible for the person to have those same intentional perceptual states in the counterfactual situation. In view of the symmetries that I built into the thought experiment, a further view—unnecessary to the argument—seemed plausible. It seemed (and still seems) to me that the person would, and certainly could, have perceptions as of cracks.

Matthews concentrates on the example instead of the argument. He questions the supposition that the organism in the counterfactual environment perceives cracks as cracks. After considering an example other than the one I discussed, he concludes:

Burge's argument against individualism fails, I believe, not because he has seized on an inappropriate example, but rather because his claim about what perceptual representations represent fails to provide anything like a sufficient condition for individuating an organism's perceptual types. In particular, it fails to preclude the possibility that an organism's perceptual types may properly include more than a single type of objective entity, so that an organism may represent entities of different objective types as instances of one and the same perceptual type. (p. 83)

The idea is that in my example, cracks and shadows may be instances of one and the same type of entity, and that the organism has perceptions as of this entity alone, in both actual and counterfactual cases. So there is no difference in the organism's intentional perceptual state between actual and counterfactual situations.

As criticism, these remarks come up short. In the first place, there is no discussion of the premises of my argument. There is no discussion of the reasoning that leads from them to my conclusion. It is unclear to me what Matthews questions in the argument I actually gave.

In the second place, my argument in no way depends on stating a sufficient condition for individuating an organism's perceptual types. I never attempted to state a sufficient condition, and I think it a *strength* of the argument that it is independent of any such attempt. I stand by my example. But nothing in the argument depends on attributing any specific perceptual states to the organism in the counterfactual situation. All that is important is that it be plausible that the counterfactual perceptual states are different from those in the actual situation. So the question about whether, in the illustration, the organism perceives cracks as cracks in the counterfactual situation is not directly relevant to the argument.

The argument depends primarily on commitment to a certain *necessary* condition, stated in the third premise, and on a general conception of objectivity, stated in the first. According to the third premise, some intentional perceptual types that specify objective types of entities do so *partly* because of relations between the perceiver, or members of the perceiver's species, and instances of those objective types.

There is no reliance on and no need for a sufficient condition here. The only claim I need and make is that, for some perceptual states, it is necessary that there be some interaction between the perceiver, or other members of the species, and some objective entities in order for those perceptual states to be typed in terms of those objective entities. In the illustrative example, the function of the premise is to prevent one from specifying the perceiver's counterfactual perceptual types in terms of shadows. (Matthews seems to concede this: 'Of course, there is no reason to suppose that in the counterfactual environment the organism perceives cracks as shadows. ...') More generally, the premise blocks attribution, in the counterfactual situation, of intentional perceptual states that specify the objective entities which the perceiver's actual perceptual states are about. In the counterfactual case, the necessary causal relations are missing.

These points shift the question from the counterfactual to the actual stage of the thought experiment. There remains Matthews's charge that the argument 'fails to preclude the possibility that an organism's perceptual types may properly include more than a single type of objective entity, so that an organism may represent entities of different objective types as instances of one and the same perceptual type'. In the illustrative example, the perceiver might be thought to perceive both shadows and cracks as instances of the same more inclusive sort of objective entity.

Now it is not my intention to preclude such a possibility. As far as I am concerned, the possibility may obtain in every case to which my argument would apply. What I must preclude is that this possibility *always excludes the possibility that the perceiver also has different intentional perceptual states in the actual and counterfactual cases*. So, in the illustrative example, it is important that if the organism lacks 'shadow' perceptions in the counterfactual case, it be possible that it have them in the actual case. Whether the perceiver has in addition other more inclusive perceptions that are common between actual and counterfactual cases does not really matter.[1]

How does my argument insure that the perceiver could have states in the actual situation which—by the third premise—it must lack in the counterfactual situation? And how does it do this without giving sufficient conditions for having particular intentional perceptual states? The argument is not committed to any particular attribution of perceptual states. But the first premise about objectivity sets a boundary on attribution. It prevents one from always adjusting the account of the organism's perceptual states in the actual situation so as to fit what is (by the third premise) possible in the counterfactual case. I will explain in more detail how this works.

The first premise has two functions in the argument. One is to entail that any series of perceptual effects on the body (and any series of non-intentional phenomenological effects, assuming there are such) might have had an entirely different series of objective entities as causal antecedents. This point is especially easy to concede if one considers the possibility of different physical (including, but not restricted to, optical) laws. Thus the same bodily effects could have been occasioned by different sorts of sources. The alternative sources might even have been in the same positions as the objective entities that we actually perceive. This traditional point is entailed by the first premise.

The second function of the first premise is to entail the possibility, in the actual situation, of a certain sort of misperception. As long as perception is objective in our sense, the organism must be capable of a certain sort of misperception. This is a misperception where the organism is unable in the context—using all its bodily, perceptual, and cognitive capacities—to discriminate the thing as it perceives it from the thing as it actually is. Call this '*fundamental misperception*'. I think it clear that the possibility of such misperception is part of our assumption that our perception is objective.

---

[1] Similarly, it does not matter whether the organism has 'crack' perceptions in the counterfactual case. In my view, it is intuitively clear that it could. If anything, this is more obvious than the perceptual attributions as of shadows in the actual case. But the main point is that the argument does not depend on this aspect of the example. Indeed, it does not rest on the example at all.

Since fundamental misperception is possible, imagine that it is actual at some time *t* for some organism. (We are assuming throughout, in accord with the second premise, that the perceptual content, or perceptual state, specifies objective entities as such.) Then utilizing the first function of the first premise, imagine counterfactually that the same organism is bodily identical from an individualistic point of view. But we vary the environmental antecedents of all the organism's perceptual states. Imagine that the organism never interacted in the appropriate way with the entities (relevant to the case) that it actually interacts with in acquiring the perceptions it actually acquires. (But imagine that it is reasonably well adapted to the environment anyway.) By the third premise, it must lack the intentional perceptual states that it actually has: In the counterfactual case, it fails to meet a necessary condition for having the same perceptual content it has in the actual situation. This is because, counterfactually, the entities specified in the actual misperception are not only not present at *t*; they are not present in the counterfactual 'world' at all. So they never interacted with the organism or any member of the organism's species. (We assume, of course, that perceptual types and entities are chosen so as to meet the condition of the third premise. We need not assume that the third premise holds for all perceptual types.) So whatever perceptual states the organism has in the counterfactual case, it cannot there undergo the same misperception at *t* that it actually undergoes.

The appeal to the possibility of fundamental misperception in the argument obviates the need to state sufficient conditions for having any particular perceptual content. Whatever the sufficient conditions are, they must allow a loose enough fit between perceptions and the entities perceived, to allow for the objectivity of perception—for fundamental misperception.

The possibility of fundamental misperception precludes one from *always* adjusting the account of the organism's actual perceptions so as to make them veridical in both actual and counterfactual situations. One is precluded from always substituting for the perceptual states needed by the argument some inclusive objective perceptual states that are veridical and invariant between actual and counterfactual situations. The argument forces one to begin with a non-veridical perception. (It can force such a beginning on the mere assumption that fundamental misperception is possible.) Then environmental conditions are varied, without varying the organism's physical equipment. They are varied in ways that go beyond the individual instance and that affect the normal patterns of interaction between organism and environment. The variations make it obvious that the organism has not met a necessary condition, stated in the third premise, for being in the original non-veridical perceptual states. In the counterfactual situation, *that* sort of error is not possible. So the perceptual states differ.

Some arguments in philosophy rest on examples. Others rest primarily on more general principles, utilizing examples in a more supplementary way. Still others appeal to the practices of a science. My earlier arguments against individualism were of the first type.[2] The examples were primary. They were seen as a source for the development of more general principles. The present argument from visual perception is of the second type. It derives from more general principles.

But the example does play a supplementary role. And considerations of the third type—the practice of science—are also relevant. The example I gave accords not only with common sense but with scientific practice.[3] We do attribute visual representations of cracks or shadows, even where—in a given instance—the perceiver is fundamentally unable to discriminate the one from the other.

---

[2] I have in mind the argument in 'Individualism and the Mental', in *Midwest Studies in Philosophy, Studies in Metaphysics*, ed. Peter A. French *et al.* (Minneapolis: University of Minnesota Press, 1979); and the argument in 'Other Bodies', in Andrew Woodfield (ed.), *Thought and Object*, (Oxford: Oxford University Press, 1982) (Chs. 5 and 4 in this volume).

[3] I discuss how and why the scientific study of vision attributes perceptual states of the relevant sort in 'Individualism and Psychology', *The Philosophical Review*, 95 (1986): 3–45 (Ch. 9 in this volume). I take it as fully in accord with common sense that someone could have fundamental misperceptions of the sort I used in the illustrative example.

I shall not discuss all of Matthews's examples. But I do want to remark on two. I am not deeply concerned exactly how to specify the perceptual states of frogs. I think that this is a complex empirical issue. *If* frogs have objective perceptions and are capable of fundamental misperceptions, then our argument will apply to them. I do think that in a laboratory *some* individual organisms (not necessarily frogs) could be induced to have systematic misperceptions, in such a way that they never come in direct causal relation to the sorts of entities that their perceptions specify. The appeal to other members of the organism's species in the third premise of my argument was partly motivated by just such considerations. As noted, there are complex problems in specifying perceptual states of particular lower animal species (although I am not at all persuaded by the various attempts to show that these problems are in principle beyond solution). It seems to me very plausible that a reasonable theory for frogs will attribute fundamental mistakes in those cases where the frog gulps down BBs. It is clear that the frog has made some sort of mistake, assuming that it is attributed intentional states at all. Whether it is a mistake of the frog's visual system, or some higher-level mistake is, for me, an open question. In any case, the example of the BBs does not serve to vary the frog's intentional states between normal and laboratory conditions. The frog has a constant intentional state that is correct in the wild and mistaken in the laboratory.

In Matthews's last section there is a misunderstanding of the twin-earth examples regarding water. (Cf. 'Other Bodies', note 2 above.) Where water and some other visually similar substance are exchanged between actual and counterfactual cases, it is no essential part of my view that the *perceptual* experiences of the protagonists are different. I take it that there is a perfectly good sense in which water and twater (the other substance on Twin Earth) are perceptually identical for the protagonists. So I can assume that the perceptual experiences in this case are invariant. The differences that interest me, in such a case, are cognitive, not perceptual. (This allows for the view that although we see water, we do not have perceptual states that are distinctively as of water, as opposed to being as of some other relatively clear liquid. Perhaps this is controversial. The main point is that my argument regarding water is independent of any controversy about perceptual states. The argument centers on cognitive states.) The present argument against perceptual individualism is thus different from the earlier argument against (conceptual) individualism that centers on natural kinds.

And scientific theories of vision make similar attributions. Neither the phenomenology of the visual image, nor the individual perceiver's discriminative abilities are decisive, in every case, in determining what perceptual state the perceiver is in. Thus it seems to me that the example I gave has some force in itself, and can be overturned only by appeal to general considerations. But the general considerations in favor of allowing such attributions—those set out in my argument—are, in my view, even stronger than the force of example.

9   *Individualism and Psychology*

Recent years have seen in psychology—and overlapping parts of linguistics, artificial intelligence, and the social sciences—the development of some semblance of agreement about an approach to the empirical study of human activity and ability. The approach is broadly mentalistic in that it involves the attribution of states, processes, and events that are intentional, in the sense of 'representational'. Many of these events and states are unconscious and inaccessible to mere reflection. Computer jargon is prominent in labeling them. But they bear comparison to thoughts, wants, memories, perceptions, plans, mental sets, and the like—ordinarily so-called. Like ordinary propositional attitudes, some are described by means of that-clauses and may be evaluated as true or false. All are involved in a system by means of which a person knows, represents, and utilizes information about his or her surroundings.

In the first part of this paper, I shall criticize some arguments that have been given for thinking that explanation in psychology is, and ought to be, purely 'individualistic'. In the second part of the paper, I shall discuss in some detail a powerful psychological theory that is not individualistic. The point of this latter discussion will be to illustrate a non-individualistic conception of explanatory kinds. In a third section, I shall offer a general argument against individualism, that centers on visual perception. What I have to say, throughout the paper, will bear on all parts of psychology that attribute intentional states. But I will make special reference to explanation in cognitive psychology.

Individualism is a view about how kinds are correctly individuated, how their natures are fixed. We shall be concerned primarily with individualism about the individuation of mental kinds. According to individualism about the mind, the mental natures of all a person's or animal's mental states (and events) are such that there is no necessary or deep individuative relation between the individual's being in states of those kinds and the nature of the individual's physical or social environments.

A version of this paper was given at the Sloan Conference at MIT in May 1984. I have benefited from the commentaries by Ned Block, Fred Dretske, and Stephen Stich. I have also made use of discussion with Jerry Fodor, David Israel, Bernie Kobes, and Neil Stillings; and I am grateful to the editors of *The Philosophical Review* for several suggestions.

This view owes its prominence to Descartes. It was embraced by Locke, Leibniz, and Hume. And it has recently found a home in the phenomenological tradition and in the doctrines of twentieth-century behaviorists, functionalists, and mind–brain identity theorists. There are various more specific versions of the doctrine. A number of fundamental issues in traditional philosophy are shaped by them. In this paper, however, I shall concentrate on versions of the doctrine that have been prominent in recent philosophy of psychology.

Current individualistic views of intentional mental states and events have tended to take one of two forms. One form maintains that an individual's being in any given intentional state (or being the subject of such an event) can be *explicated* by reference to states and events of the individual that are specifiable without using intentional vocabulary and without presupposing anything about the individual subject's social or physical environments. The explication is supposed to specify—in non-intentional terms—stimulations, behavior, and internal physical or functional states of the individual. The other form of individualism is implied by the first, but is weaker. It does not attempt to explicate anything. It simply makes a claim of *supervenience*: an individual's intentional states and events (types and tokens) could not be different from what they are, given the individual's physical, chemical, neural, or functional histories, where these histories are specified non-intentionally and in a way that is independent of physical or social conditions outside the individual's body.

In other papers I have argued that both forms of individualism are mistaken. A person's intentional states and events could (counterfactually) vary, even as the individual's physical, functional (and perhaps phenomenological) history, specified non-intentionally and individualistically, is held constant. I have offered several arguments for this conclusion. Appreciating the strength of these arguments, and discerning the philosophical potential of a non-individualist view of mind, depend heavily on reflecting on differences among these arguments. They both reinforce one another and help map the topography of a positive position.

For present purposes, however, I shall merely sketch a couple of the arguments to give their flavor. I shall not defend them or enter a variety of relevant qualifications. Consider a person *A* who thinks that aluminum is a light metal used in sailboat masts, and a person *B* who believes that he or she has arthritis in the thigh. We assume that *A* and *B* can pick out instances of aluminum and arthritis (respectively) and know many familiar general facts about aluminum and arthritis. *A* is, however, ignorant of aluminum's chemical structure and micro-properties. *B* is ignorant of the fact that arthritis cannot occur outside of joints. Now we can imagine counterfactual cases in which *A* and *B*'s bodies have their same histories considered in isolation of their physical environments, but in which there are significant environmental differences from the actual situation. *A*'s counterfactual environment lacks aluminum and has in its places a similar-looking light metal. *B*'s counterfactual environment is such that no one has ever isolated arthritis as a specific disease, or syndrome of diseases. In these cases, *A* would lack 'aluminum thoughts' and *B* would lack 'arthritis thoughts'. Assuming natural developmental patterns, both would have different thoughts. Thus these differences from the actual situation show up not only in the protagonists' relations to their environments, but also in their intentional mental states and events, ordinarily so-called. The arguments bring out variations in obliquely (or intensionally) occurring expressions in literal mental state and event ascriptions, our primary means of identifying intentional mental states.[1]

I believe that these arguments use literal descriptions of mental events, and are independent of conversational devices that may affect the form of an ascription without bearing on the nature of the mental event described. The sort of argument that we have illustrated does not depend on special features of the notions of arthritis or aluminum. Such arguments go through for observational and theoretical notions, for percepts as well as concepts, for natural kind and non-natural kind notions, for notions that are the special preserve of experts, and for what are known in the psychological literature as 'basic categories'. Indeed, I think that, at a minimum, relevantly similar arguments can be shown to go through with any notion that applies to public types of objects, properties, or events that are typically known by empirical means.[2]

I shall not elaborate or defend the arguments here. In what follows, I shall presuppose that they are cogent. For my purposes, it will be enough if one bears firmly in mind their conclusion: mental states and events may in principle vary with variations in the environment, even as an individual's physical (functional, phenomenological) history, specified non-intentionally and individualistically, remains constant.

A common reaction to these conclusions, often unsupported by argument, has been to concede their force, but to try to limit their effect. It is frequently held that they apply to commonsense attributions of attitudes, but have no application to analogous attributions in psychology. Non-individualistic aspects of mentalistic attribution have been held to be uncongenial with the purposes and requirements of psychological theory. Of course, there is a tradition of holding that ordinary intentional attributions are incapable of yielding any knowledge at all. Others have held the more modest view that mentalistic attributions are

[1] 'Individualism and the Mental,' *Midwest Studies of Philosophy*, 4 (1979), 73–121; 'Other Bodies', in A. Woodfield (ed.), *Thought and Object* (Oxford: Oxford University Press, 1982); 'Two Thought Experiments Reviewed', *Notre Dame Journal of Formal Logic*, 23 (1982), 284–293; 'Cartesian Error and the Objectivity of Perception', in MacDowell and P. Pettit (eds.), *Subject, Thought, and Context* (Oxford: Oxford University Press, 1986); 'Intellectual Norms and Foundations of Mind', *The Journal of Philosophy*, 83 (1986), 697–720 (Chs. 5, 4, 6, 7, 10 in this volume). The aluminum argument is adapted from an argument in Hilary Putnam, "The Meaning of 'Meaning' ", in *Philosophical Papers*, ii (Cambridge: Cambridge University Press, 1975). What Putnam wrote in his paper was, strictly, not even compatible with this argument. (Cf. the first two cited papers in this note for discussion.) But the aluminum argument lies close to the surface of the argument he does give. The arthritis argument raises rather different issues, despite its parallel methodology.

[2] On basic categories, cf., e.g., E. Rosch, C. B. Mervis, W. Gray, O. Johnson, and P. Boyes-Graem, 'Basic Objects in Natural Categories', *Cognitive Psychology*, 8 (1976), 382–439. On the general claim in the last sentence, cf. 'Intellectual Norms', and the latter portion of this paper.

capable of yielding only knowledge that could not in principle be systematized in a theory.

I shall not be able to discuss all of these lines of thought. In particular I shall ignore generalized arguments that mentalistic ascriptions are deeply indeterminate, or otherwise incapable of yielding knowledge. Our focus will be on arguments that purport to show that non-individualistic mentalistic ascriptions cannot play a systematic role in psychological explanation—*because* of the fact that they are not individualistic.

There are indeed significant differences between theoretical discourse in psychology and the mentalistic discourse of common sense. The most obvious one is that the language of theoretical psychology requires refinements on ordinary discourse. It not only requires greater system and rigor, and a raft of unconscious states and events that are not ordinarily attributed (though they are, I think, ordinarily allowed for). It also must distill out descriptive-explanatory purposes of common attributions from uses that serve communication at the expense of description and explanation. Making this distinction is already common practice. Refinement for scientific purposes must, however, be systematic and meticulous—though it need not eliminate all vagueness. I think that there are no sound reasons to believe that such refinement cannot be effected through the development of psychological theory, or that effecting it will fundamentally change the nature of ordinary mentalistic attributions.

Differences between scientific and ordinary discourse survive even when ordinary discourse undergoes the refinements just mentioned. Although commonsense discourse—both about macro-physical objects and about mental events—yields knowledge, I believe that the principles governing justification for such discourse differ from those that are invoked in systematic scientific theorizing. So there is, prima facie, room for the view that psychology is or should be fully individualistic—even though ordinary descriptions of mental states are not. Nevertheless, the arguments for this view that have been offered do not seem to me cogent. Nor do I find the view independently persuasive.

Before considering such arguments, I must articulate some further background assumptions, this time about psychology itself. I shall be taking those parts of psychology that utilize mentalistic and information-processing discourse pretty much as they are. I assume that they employ standard scientific methodology, that they have produced interesting empirical results, and that they contain more than a smattering of genuine theory. I shall not prejudge what sort of science psychology is, or how it relates to the natural sciences. I do, however, assume that its cognitive claims and, more especially, its methods and presuppositions are to be taken seriously as the best we now have in this area of inquiry. I believe that there are no good reasons for thinking that the methods or findings of this body of work are radically misguided.

I shall not be assuming that psychology *must* continue to maintain touch with commonsense discourse. I believe that such touch will almost surely be maintained. But I think that empirical disciplines must find their own way according to standards that they set for themselves. Quasi-apriori strictures laid down by philosophers count for little. So our reflections concern psychology as it is, not as it will be or must be.

In taking psychology as it is, I am assuming that it seeks to refine, deepen, generalize, and systematize some of the statements of informed common sense about people's mental activity. It accepts, for example, that people see physical objects with certain shapes, textures, and hues, and in certain spatial relations, under certain specified conditions. And it attempts to explain in more depth what people do when they see such things, and how their doing it is done. Psychology accepts that people remember events and truths, that they categorize objects, that they draw inferences, that they act on beliefs and preferences. And it attempts to find deep regularities in these activities, to specify mechanisms that underlie them, and to provide systematic accounts of how these activities relate to one another. In describing and, at least partly, in explaining these activities and abilities, psychology makes use of interpreted that-clauses and other intensional constructions—or what we might loosely call 'intentional content'.[3] I have seen no sound reason to believe that this use is merely heuristic, instrumentalistic, or second class in any other sense.

I assume that intentional content has internal structure—something like grammatical or logical structure—and that the parts of this structure are individuated finely enough to correspond to certain individual abilities, procedures, or perspectives. Since various abilities, procedures, or perspectives may be associated with any given event, object, property, or relation, intentional content must be individuated more finely than the entities in the world with which the individual interacts. We must allow different ways (even, I think, different primitive ways) for the individual to conceive of, or represent any given entity. This assumption about the fine-grainedness of content in psychology will play no explicit role in what follows. I note it here to indicate that my scepticism about individualism as an interpretation of psychology does not stem from a conception of content about which it is already clear that it does not play a dominant role in psychology.[4]

---

[3] Our talk of intentional 'content' will be ontologically colorless. It can be converted to talk about how that-clauses (or their components) are interpreted and differentiated—taken as equivalent or non-equivalent—for the cognitive purposes of psychology. Not all intentional states or structures that are attributed in psychology are explicitly propositional. My views in this paper apply to intentional states generally.

[4] Certain approaches to intensional logic featuring either 'direct reference' or some analogy between the attitudes and necessity have urged that this practice of fine-structuring attitudinal content be revised. I think that for purely philosophical reasons these approaches cannot account for the attitudes. For example, they do little to illumine the numerous variations on Frege's 'paradox of identity'. They seem to have even less to recommend them as prescriptions for the language of psychology. Some defenses of individualism have taken these approaches to propositional content to constitute the opposition to individualism. I think that these approaches are not serious contenders as accounts of propositional attitudes and thus should be left out of the discussion.

Finally, I shall assume that individualism is prima facie wrong about psychology, including cognitive psychology. Since the relevant parts of psychology frequently use attributions of intentional states that are subject to our thought experiments, the language actually used in psychology is not purely individualistic. That is, the generalizations with counterfactual force that appear in psychological theories, given their standard interpretations, are not all individualistic. For ordinary understanding of the truth conditions, or individuation conditions, of the relevant attributions suffices to verify the thought experiments. Moreover, there is at present no well-explained, well-understood, much less well-tested, individualistic language—or individualistic reinterpretation of the linguistic forms currently in use in psychology—that could serve as surrogate.

Thus individualism as applied to psychology must be revisionistic. It must be revisionistic at least about the language of psychological theory. I shall be developing the view that it is also revisionistic, without good reason, about the underlying presuppositions of the science. To justify itself, individualism must fulfill two tasks. It must show that the language of psychology should be revised by demonstrating that the presuppositions of the science are or should be *purely* individualistic. And it must explain a new individualistic language (attributing what is sometimes called 'narrow content') that captures genuine theoretical commitments of the science.

These tasks are independent. If the second were accomplished, but the first remained unaccomplishable, individualism would be wrong; but it would have engendered a new level of explanation. For reasons I will mention later, I am skeptical about such wholesale supplementation of current theory. But psychology is not a monolith. Different explanatory tasks and types of explanation coexist within it. In questioning the view that psychology is individualistic, I am not *thereby* doubting whether there are some sub-parts of psychology that conform to the strictures of individualism. I am doubting whether all of psychology as it is currently practiced is or should be individualistic. Thus I shall concentrate on attempts to fulfill the first of the two tasks that face someone bent on revising psychology along individualistic lines. So much for preliminaries.

I

We begin by discussing a general argument against non-individualistic accounts. It goes as follows. The behavior of the physiologically and functionally identical protagonists in our thought experiments is identical. But psychology is the science (only) of behavior. Since the behavior of the protagonists is the same, a science of behavior should give the *same* explanations and descriptions of the two cases (by some Ockhamesque principle of parsimony). So there is no room in the discipline for explaining their behavior in terms of different mental states.[5]

The two initial premises are problematic. To begin with the first: it is not to be assumed that the protagonists are behaviorally identical in the thought experiments. I believe that the only clear, general interpretation of 'behavior' that is available and that would verify the first premise is 'bodily motion'. But this construal has almost no relevance to psychology as it is actually practiced. 'Behavior' has become a catch-all term in psychology for observable activity on whose description and character psychologists can reach quick 'pre-theoretical' agreement. Apart from methodological bias, it is just not true that all descriptions that would count as 'behavioral' in cognitive (social, developmental) psychology would apply to both the protagonists. Much behavior is intentional action; many action specifications are non-individualistic. Thought experiments relevantly similar to those which we have already developed will apply to them.

For example, much 'behavioral' evidence in psychology is drawn from what people say or how they answer questions. Subjects' utterances (and the questions asked them) must be taken to be interpreted in order to be of any use in the experiments; and it is often assumed that theories may be checked by experiments carried out in different languages. Since the protagonists' sayings in the thought experiments are different, even in non-transparent or oblique occurrences, it is prima facie mistaken to count the protagonists 'behaviorally' identical. Many attributions of non-verbal behavior are also intentional and non-individualistic, or even relational: she picked up the apple, pointed to the square block, tracked the moving ball, smiled at the familiar face, took the money instead of the risk. These attributions can be elaborated to produce non-individualist thought experiments. The general point is that many relevant specifications of behavior in psychology are intentional, or relational, or both. The thought experiments indicate that these specifications ground non-individualist mental attributions. An argument for individualism cannot reasonably *assume* that these specifications are individualistic or ought to be.

Of course, there are non-individualistic specifications of behavior that are unsuitable for any scientific enterprise ('my friend's favorite bodily movement'). But most of these do not even appear to occur in psychology. The problem of providing reasonable specifications of behavior cannot be solved from an armchair. Sanitizing the notion of behavior to meet some antecedently held methodological principle is an old game, never won. One must look at what psychology actually takes as 'behavioral' evidence. It is the responsibility of

---

[5] Stephen Stich, *From Folk Psychology to Cognitive Science* (Cambridge, Mass.: MIT Press, 1983), ch. 8. Although I shall not discuss the unformulated Ockhamesque principle, I am skeptical of it. Apart from question-begging assumptions, it seems to me quite unclear why a science should be required to explain two instances of the same phenomenon in the same way, particularly if the surrounding conditions that led to the instances differ.

the argument to show that non-individualistic notions have no place in psychology. Insofar as the argument assumes that intentional, non-individualistic specifications of behavior are illegitimate, it either ignores obvious aspects of psychological practice or begs the question at issue.

The second step of the argument also limps. One cannot assume without serious discussion that psychology is correctly characterized as a science (only) of behavior. This is, of course, particularly so if behavior is construed in a restrictive way. But even disregarding how behavior is construed, the premise is doubtful. One reason is that it is hardly to be assumed that a putative science is to be characterized in terms of its evidence as opposed to its subject matter. Of course, the subject matter is to some extent under dispute. But cognitive psychology appears to be about certain molar abilities and activities some of which are propositional attitudes. Since the propositional attitudes attributed do not seem to be fully individuable in individualistic terms, we need a direct argument that cognitive psychology is not a science of what it appears to be a science of.

A second reason for doubting the premise is that psychology seems to be partly about relations between people, or animals, and their environment. It is hard to see how to provide a natural description of a theory of vision, for example, as a science of behavior. The point of the theory is to figure out how people do what they obviously succeed in doing—how they see objects in their environment. We are trying to explain relations between a subject and a physical world that we take ourselves to know something about. Theories of memory, of certain sorts of learning, of linguistic understanding, of belief formation, of categorization, do the same. It is certainly not obvious that these references to relations between subject and environment are somehow inessential to (all parts of) psychological theory. They seem, in fact, to be a large part of the point of such theory. In my view, these relations help motivate non-individualistic principles of individuation (cf. Section II). In sum, I think that the argument we have so far considered begs significant questions at almost every step.

There is a kindred argument worth considering: the determinants of behavior supervene on states of the brain. (If one is a materialist, one might take this to be a triviality: 'brain states supervene on brain states.') So if propositional attitudes are to be treated as among the determinants of behavior, they must be taken to supervene on brain states. The alternative is to take propositional attitudes as behaviorally irrelevant.[6]

---

[6] I have not been able to find a fully explicit statement of this argument in published work. It seems to inform some passages of Jerry Fodor's 'Methodological Solipsism Considered as a Research Strategy in Cognitive Psychology', in *Representations* (Cambridge, Mass.: MIT Press, 1981), e.g. 228–232. It lies closer to the surface in much work influenced by Fodor's paper. Cf., e.g., Colin McGinn, 'The Structure of Content', in A. Woodfield (ed.), *Thought and Object* (Oxford: Oxford University Press, 1982), 207–216. Many who like McGinn concede the force of the arguments against individualism utilize something like this argument to maintain that individualistic 'aspects' of intentional states are all that are relevant to psychological explanation.

This argument can, I think, be turned on its head. Since propositional attitudes are among the determinants of our 'behavior' (where this expression is as open-ended as ever), and since propositional attitudes do not supervene on our brain states, not all determinants of our 'behavior' supervene on our brain states. I want to make three points against the original argument, two metaphysical and one epistemic or methodological. Metaphysics first.

The ontological stakes that ride on the supervenience doctrine are far less substantial than one might think. It is simply not a 'trivial consequence' of materialism about mental states and events that the determinants of our behavior supervene on the states of our brains. This is because what supervenes on what has at least as much to do with how the relevant entities are individuated as with what they are made of. If a mental event *m* is individuated partly by reference to normal conditions outside a person's body, then, regardless of whether *m* has material composition, *m* might vary even as the body remains the same.

Since intentional phenomena form such a large special case, it is probably misleading to seek analogies from other domains to illustrate the point. To loosen up the imagination, however, consider the Battle of Hastings. Suppose that we preserve every human body, every piece of turf, every weapon, every physical structure, and all the physical interactions among them, from the first confrontation to the last death or withdrawal on the day of the battle. Suppose that, counterfactually, we imagine all these physical events and props placed in California (perhaps at the same time in 1066). Suppose that the physical activity is artificially induced by brilliant scientists transported to earth by Martian film producers. The distal causes of the battle have nothing to do with the causes of the Battle of Hastings. I think it plausible (and certainly coherent) to say that in such circumstances, not the Battle of Hastings, but only a physical facsimile would have taken place. I think that even if the location in Hastings were maintained, sufficiently different counterfactual causal antecedents would suffice to vary the identity of the battle. The battle is individuated partly in terms of its causes. Though the battle does not supervene on its physical constituents, we have little hesitation about counting it a physical event.

Our individuation of historical battles is probably wrapped up with intentional states of the participants. The point can also be made by reference to cases that are clearly independent of intentional considerations. Consider the emergence of North America from the ocean. Suppose that we delimit what count as constituent (say, micro-) physical events of this larger event. It seems that if the surrounding physical conditions and laws are artfully enough contrived, we can counterfactually conceive these same constituent events (or the constituent physical objects' undergoing physically identical changes in the same places) in such a way that they are embedded in a much larger land mass, so that the physical constituents of North America do not make up any salient part of this larger mass. The emergence of North America would not have occurred in such a case, even though its 'constituent' physical events were, in isolation, physically identical with the actual events. We individuate the emergence of continents or other land masses in such a way that they are not supervenient on their physical constituents. But such events are nonetheless physical.

In fact, I think that materialism does not provide reasonable restrictions on theories of the role of mentalistic attributions in psychology. The relation of physical composition presently plays no significant role in any established scientific theory of mental events, or of their relations to brain events. The restrictions that physiological considerations place on psychological theorizing, though substantial, are weaker than those of any of the articulated materialisms, even the weak compositional variety I am alluding to. My point is just that rejecting individualistic supervenience does not entail rejecting a materialistic standpoint. So materialism *per se* does nothing to support individualism.[7]

The second 'metaphysical' point concerns causation. The argument we are considering in effect simply assumes that propositional attitudes (type and token) supervene on physico-chemical events in the body. But many philosophers appear to think that this assumption is rendered obvious by bland observations about the etiology of mental events and behavior. It is plausible that events in the external world causally affect the mental events of a subject only by affecting the subject's bodily surfaces; and that nothing (not excluding mental events) causally affects behavior except by affecting (causing or being a causal antecedent of causes of) local states of the subject's body. One might reason that in the anti-individualistic thought experiments these principles are violated insofar as events in the environment are alleged to differentially 'affect' a person's mental events and behavior without differentially 'affecting' his or her body: only if mental events (and states) supervene on the individual's body can the causal principles be maintained.

The reasoning is confused. The confusion is abetted by careless use of the term 'affect', conflating causation with individuation. Variations in the environment that do not vary the impacts that causally 'affect' the subject's body may 'affect' the individuation of the information that the subject is receiving, of the intentional processes he or she is undergoing, or of the way the subject is acting.

---

[7] In 'Individualism and the Mental', 109–113 (and Ch. 5 above), I argue that token *identity* theories are rendered implausible by the non-individualistic thought experiments. But token identity theories are not the last bastion for materialist defense policy. Composition is what is crucial.

It is coherent, but I think mistaken, to hold that propositional-attitude attributions non-rigidly pick out physical events: so the propositional attributions vary between the actual and counterfactual protagonists in the thought experiments, though the ontology of mental event tokens remains identical. This view is compatible with most of my opposition to individualism. But I think that there is no good reason to believe the very implausible thesis that mental events are not individuated ('essentially' or 'basically') in terms of the relevant propositional-attitude attributions. (Cf. ibid.) So I reject the view that the same mental events (types or tokens) are picked out under different descriptions in the thought experiments. These considerations stand behind my recommending, to the convinced materialist, composition rather than identity as a paradigm. (I remain unconvinced.)

It does not follow that the environment causally affects the subject in any way that circumvents its having effects on the subject's body.

Once the conflation is avoided, it becomes clear that there is no simple argument from the causal principles just enunciated to individualism. The example from geology provides a useful countermodel. It shows that one can accept the causal principles and thereby experience no bewilderment whatsoever in rejecting individualism. A continent moves and is moved by local impacts from rocks, waves, molecules. Yet we can conceive of holding constant the continent's peripheral impacts and chemically constituent events and objects, without holding identical the continent or certain of its macro-changes—because the continent's spatial relations to other land masses affect the way we individuate it. Or take an example from biology. Let us accept the plausible principle that nothing causally affects breathing except as it causally affects local states of the lungs. It does not follow, and indeed is not true, that we individuate lungs and the various sub-events of respiration in such a way as to treat those objects and events as supervenient on the chemically described objects and events that compose them. If the same chemical process (same from the surfaces of the lungs inside, and back to the surfaces) were embedded in a different sort of body and had an entirely different function (say, digestive, immunological, or regulatory), we would not be dealing with the same biological states and events. Local causation does not make more plausible local individuation, or individualistic supervenience.

The intended analogy to mental events should be evident. We may agree that a person's mental events and behavior are causally affected by the person's environment only through local causal effects on the person's body. Without the slightest conceptual discomfort we may individuate mental events so as to allow distinct events (types or tokens) with indistinguishable chemistries, or even physiologies, for the subject's body. Information from and about the environment is transmitted only through proximal stimulations, but the information is individuated partly by reference to the nature of normal distal stimuli. Causation is local. Individuation may presuppose facts about the specific nature of a subject's environment.

Where intentional psychological explanation is itself causal, it may well presuppose that the causal transactions to which its generalizations apply bear some necessary relation to some underlying physical transactions (or other). Without a set of physical transactions, none of the intentional transactions would transpire. But it does not follow that the kinds invoked in explaining causal interactions among intentional states (or between physical states and intentional states—for example, in vision or in action) supervene on the underlying physiological transactions. The same physical transactions in a given person may in principle mediate, or underlie, transactions involving different intentional states—if the environmental features that enter into the individuation of the intentional states and that are critical in the explanatory generalizations that invoke those states vary in appropriate ways.

Let us turn to our epistemic point. The view that propositional attitudes help determine behavior is well entrenched in common judgments and in the explanatory practices of psychology. Our arguments that a subject's propositional attitudes are not fixed purely by his or her brain states are based on widely shared judgments regarding *particular* cases that in relevant respects bring out familiar elements in our actual psychological and common sense practices of attitude attribution. By contrast, the claim that none of an individual's propositional attitudes (or determinants of his behavior) could have been different unless some of his brain states were different is a metaphysical conjecture. It is a modal generalization that is not grounded in judgments about particular cases, or (so far) in careful interpretation of the actual explanatory and descriptive practices of psychology. Metaphysical ideology should either conform to and illuminate intellectual praxis, or produce strong reasons for revising it.

What we know about supervenience must be derived, partly, from what we know about individuation. What we know about individuation is derived from reflecting on explanations and descriptions of going cognitive practices. Individuative methods are bound up with the explanatory and descriptive needs of such practices. Thus justified judgments about what supervenes on what are *derivative* from reflection on the nature of explanation and description in psychological discourse and common attitude attributions. I think that such judgments cannot be reasonably invoked to restrict such discourse. It seems to me therefore that, apart from further argument, the individualistic supervenience thesis provides no reason for requiring (pan-) individualism in psychology. In fact, the argument from individualistic supervenience begs the question. It *presupposes* rather than establishes that *individuation—hence explanation and description*—in psychology should be fully individualistic. It is simply the wrong sort of consideration to invoke in a dispute about explanation and description.

This remark is, I think, quite general. Not just questions of supervenience, but questions of ontology, reduction, and causation generally, are epistemically posterior to questions about the success of explanatory and descriptive practices.[8] One cannot reasonably criticize a purported explanatory or descriptive practice primarily by appeal to some prior conception of what a 'good entity' is, or of what individuation or reference should be like, or of what the overall structure of science (or knowledge) should turn out to look like. Questions of what exists,

---

[8] The points about ontology and reference go back to Frege, *Foundations of Arithmetic*, trans. J. L. Austin (Evanston, Ill: Northwestern University Press, 1968). The point about reduction is relatively obvious, though a few philosophers have urged conceptions of the unity of science in a relatively aprioristic spirit. At least as applied to ontology, the point is also basic to Quine's pragmatism. There are, however, strands in Quine's work and in the work of most of his followers that seem to me to let a preoccupation with physicalism get in the way of the Fregean (and Quinean) pragmatic insight. It is simply an illusion to think that metaphysical or even epistemic preconceptions provide a standard for judging the ontologies or explanatory efforts of particular sciences, deductive or inductive.

how things are individuated, and what reduces to what, are questions that arise by reference to going explanatory and descriptive practices. By themselves, proposed answers to these questions cannot be used to criticize an otherwise successful mode of explanation and description.[9]

Of course, one might purport to base the individualist supervenience principle on what we know about good explanation. Perhaps one might hope to argue from inference to the best explanation concerning the relations of higher-level to more basic theories in the natural sciences that the entities postulated by psychology should supervene on those of physiology. Or perhaps one might try to draw analogies between non-individualistic theories in psychology and past, unsuccessful theories. These two strategies might meet our methodological strictures on answering the question of whether non-individualistic explanations are viable in a way that an unalloyed appeal to a supervenience principle does not. But philosophical invocations of inference to the best explanation tend to conceal wild leaps supported primarily by ideology. Such considerations must be spelled out into arguments. So far they do not seem very promising.

Take the first strategy. Inductions from the natural sciences to the human sciences are problematic from the start. The problems of the two sorts of sciences look very different, in a multitude of ways. One can, of course, reasonably try to exploit analogies in a pragmatic spirit. But the fact that some given analogy does not hold hardly counts against an otherwise viable mode of explanation. Moreover, there are non-individualistic modes of explanation even in the natural sciences. Geology, physiology, and other parts of biology appeal to entities that are not supervenient on their underlying physical makeup. Kind notions in these sciences (plates, organs, species) presuppose individuative methods that make essential reference to the environment surrounding instances of those kinds.

The second strategy seems even less promising. As it stands, it is afflicted with a bad case of vagueness. Some authors have suggested similarities between vitalism in biology, or action-at-a-distance theories in physics, and non-individualist theories in psychology. The analogies are tenuous. Unlike vitalism, non-individualist psychology does not ipso facto appeal to a new sort of force. Unlike action-at-a-distance theories, it does not appeal to action at a distance. It is true that aspects of the environment that do not differentially affect the physical movement of the protagonists in the thought experiments do differentially affect the explanations and descriptions. This is not, however, because

---

[9] Even more generally, I think that epistemic power in philosophy derives largely from reflections on particular implementations of successful cognitive practices. By a cognitive practice, I mean a cognitive enterprise that is stable, that conforms to standard conditions of intersubjective checkability, and that incorporates a substantial core of agreement among its practitioners. Revisionistic philosophical hypotheses must not, of course, be rejected out of hand. Sometimes, but rarely nowadays, such hypotheses influence cognitive practices by expanding theoretical imagination so as to lead to new discoveries. The changed practice may vindicate the philosophical hypothesis. But the hypothesis waits on such vindication.

some special causal relation is postulated, but rather because environmental differences affect what kinds of laws obtain, and the way causes and effects are individuated.

Let us now consider a further type of objection to applying the thought experiments to psychology. Since the actual and counterfactual protagonists are so impressively *similar* in so many psychologically relevant ways, can a theoretical language that cuts across these similarities be empirically adequate? The physiological and non-intensional 'behavioral' similarities between the protagonists seem to demand similarity of explanation. In its stronger form this objection purports to indicate that non-individualistic mentalistic language has no place in psychology. In its weaker form it attempts to motivate a new theoretical language that attributes intensional content, yet is individualistic. Only the stronger form would establish individualism in psychology. I shall consider it first.

The objection is that the similarities between the protagonists render implausible any theory that treats them differently. This objection is vague or enthymemic. Filling it out tends to lead one back toward the arguments that we have already rejected. On any view, there are several means available (neurophysiology, parts of psychology) for explaining in similar fashion those similarities that are postulated between protagonists in the thought experiments. The argument is not even of the right form to produce a reason for thinking that the differences between the protagonists should not be reflected somewhere in psychological theory—precisely the point at issue.

The objection is often coupled with the remark that non-individualistic explanations would make the parallels between the behavior of the protagonists in the thought experiments 'miraculous': explaining the same behavioral phenomena as resulting from different propositional attitudes would be to invoke a 'miracle'. The rhetoric about miracles can be deflated by noting that the protagonists' 'behavior' is not straightforwardly identical, that non-individualistic explanations postulate no special forces, and that there are physical differences in the protagonists' environments that help motivate describing and explaining their activity, at least at one level, in different ways.

The rhetoric about miracles borders on a fundamental misunderstanding of the status of the non-individualistic thought experiments, and of the relation between philosophy and psychology. There is, of course, considerable empirical implausibility, which we might with some exaggeration call 'miraculousness', in two persons' having identical individualistic physical histories but different thoughts. Most of this implausibility is an artifact of the two-person version of the thought experiments—a feature that is quite inessential. (One may take a single person in two counterfactual circumstances.) This point raises a caution. It is important not to think of the thought experiments as if they were describing actual empirical cases. Let me articulate this remark.

The kinds of a theory, and its principles of individuation, evolve in response to the world as it is actually found to be. Our notions of similarity result from attempts to explain actual cases. They are not necessarily responsive to preconceived philosophical ideals.[10] The kind terms of propositional attitude discourse are responsive to broad, stable similarities in the actual environment that agents are taken to respond to, operate on, and represent. If theory had been frequently confronted with physically similar agents in different environments, it might have evolved different kind terms. But we are so far from being confronted by even rough approximations to global physical similarities between agents that there is little plausibility in imposing individual physical similarity by itself as an ideal sufficient condition for sameness of kind terms throughout psychology. Moreover, I think that local physical similarities between the psychologically relevant activities of agents are so frequently intertwined with environmental constancies that a psychological theory that insisted on entirely abstracting from the nature of the environment in choosing its kind terms would be empirically emasculate.

The correct use of counterfactuals in the thought experiments is to explore the scope and limits of the kind notions that have been antecedently developed in attempts to explain actual empirical cases. In counterfactual reasoning we assume an understanding of what our language expresses and explore its application conditions through considering non-actual applications. The counterfactuals in the philosophical thought experiments illumine individuative and theoretical principles to which we are already committed.

The empirical implausibility of the thought experiments is irrelevant to their philosophical point—which concerns possibility, not plausibility. Unlikely but limiting cases are sometimes needed to clarify the modal status of presuppositions that govern more mundane examples. Conversely, the highly counterfactual cases are largely irrelevant to *evaluating* an empirical theory—except in cases (not at issue here) where they present empirical possibilities that a theory counts impossible. To invoke a general philosophical principle, like the supervenience principle, or to insist in the face of the thought experiments that only certain sorts of similarity can be relevant to psychology—without criticizing psychological theory on empirical grounds or showing how the kind notions exhibited by the thought experiments are empirically inadequate—is either to treat counterfactual circumstances as if they were actual, or to fall into apriorism about empirical science.

Let us turn to the weaker form of the worry that we have been considering. The worry purports to motivate a new individualistic language of attitude attribution. As I have noted, accepting such a language is consistent with rejecting (pan-) individualism in psychology. There are a variety of levels or kinds of explanation in psychology. Adding another will not alter the issues at stake here. But let us pursue the matter briefly.

---

[10] For an interesting elaboration of this theme in an experimental context, see Amos Tversky, 'Features of Similarity', *Psychological Review*, 84 (1977), 327–352. Cf. also Rosch *et al.*, "Basic Objects".

There are in psychology levels of individualistic description above the physiological but below the attitudinal that play a role in systematic explanations. Formalistically described computational processes are appealed to in the attempt to specify an algorithm by which a person's propositional information is processed. I think that the protagonists in our thought experiments might, for some purposes, be said to go through identical algorithms formalistically described. Different information is processed in the 'same' ways, at least at this formal level of description. But then might we not want a whole level of description, between the formal algorithm and ordinary propositional attitude ascription, that counts 'information' everywhere the same between protagonists in the thought experiments? This is a difficult and complex question, which I shall not attempt to answer here. I do, however, want to mention grounds for caution about supplementing psychology wholesale.

In the first place, the motivation for demanding the relevant additions to psychological theory is empirically weak. In recent philosophical literature, the motivation rests largely on intuitions about Cartesian demons or brains in vats, whose relevance and even coherence have been repeatedly challenged; on preconceptions about the supervenience of the mental on the neural that have no generalized scientific warrant; on misapplications of ordinary observations about causation; and on a sketchy and unclear conception of behavior unsupported by scientific practice.[11] Of course, one may reasonably investigate any hypothesis on no more than an intuitively based hunch. What is questionable is the view that there are currently strong philosophical or scientific grounds for instituting a new type of individualistic explanation.

In the second place, it is easy to underestimate what is involved in creating a relevant individualistic language that would be of genuine use in psychology. Explications of such language have so far been pretty make-shift. It does not suffice to sketch a semantics that says in effect that a sentence comes out true in all worlds that chemically identical protagonists in relevant thought experiments cannot distinguish. Such an explication gives no clear rules for the *use* of the language, much less a demonstration that it can do distinctive work in psychology. Moreover, explication of the individualistic language (or language component) only for the special case in which the language-user's physiological or (individualistically specified) functional states are held constant, is psychologically useless since no two people are ever actually identical in their physical states.

To fashion an individualist language it will not do to limit its reference to objective properties accessible to perception. For our language for attributing

---

[11] The most careful and plausible of several papers advocating a new language of individualist explanation is Stephen White, 'Partial Character and the Language of Thought', *Pacific Philosophical Quarterly*, 63 (1982), 347–365. It seems to me, however, that many of the problems mentioned in the text here and below, beset this advocacy. Moreover, the positive tasks set for the new language are already performed by the actual non-individualist language of psychology. The brain-in-vat intuitions raise very complex issues that I cannot pursue here. I discuss them further in 'Cartesian Error and the Objectivity of Perception' (Ch. 7 above).

notions of perceptually accessible physical properties is not individualistic. More generally, as I have argued elsewhere, any attitudes that contain notions for physical objects, events and properties are non-individualistic.[12] The assumptions about objective representation needed to generate the argument are very minimal. I think it questionable whether there is a coherent conception of objective representation that can support an individualistic language of intentional attitude attribution. Advocates of such a language must either explain such a conception in depth, or attribute intentional states that lack objective physical reference.

II

I have been criticizing arguments for revising the language of psychology to accord with individualism. I have not tried to argue for non-individualistic psychological theories from a standpoint outside of psychology. The heart of my case is the observation that psychological theories, taken literally, are not purely individualistic, that there are no strong reasons for taking them non-literally, and that we currently have no superior standpoint for judging how psychology ought to be done than that of seeing how it *is* done. One can, of course, seek deeper understanding of non-individualistic aspects of psychological theory. Development of such understanding is a multi-faceted task. Here I shall develop only points that are crucial to my thesis, illustrating them in some detail by reference to one theory.

Ascription of intentional states and events in psychology constitutes a type of individuation and explanation that carries presuppositions about the specific nature of the person's or animal's surrounding environment. Moreover, states and events are individuated so as to set the terms for specific evaluations of them for truth or other types of success. We can judge directly whether conative states are practically successful and cognitive states are veridical. For example, by characterizing a subject as visually representing an X, and specifying whether the visual state appropriately derives from an X in the particular case, we can judge whether the subject's state is veridical. Theories of vision, of belief formation, of memory, learning, decision making, categorization, and perhaps even reasoning all attribute states that are subject to practical and semantical evaluation *by reference to standards partly set by a wider environment*.

Psychological theories are not themselves evaluative theories. But they often individuate phenomena so as to make evaluation readily accessible *because* they are partly motivated by such judgments. Thus we judge that in certain delimitable contexts people get what they want, know what is the case, and perceive what is there. And we try to frame explanations that account for these successes, and correlative failures, in such a way as to illumine as specifically as possible the mechanisms that underlie and make true our evaluations.

I want to illustrate and develop these points by considering at some length a theory of vision. I choose this example primarily because it is a very advanced and impressive theory, and admits to being treated in some depth. Its information-processing approach is congenial with mainstream work in cognitive psychology. Some of its intentional aspects are well understood—and indeed are sometimes conceptually and mathematically far ahead of its formal (or syntactical) and physiological aspects. Thus the theory provides an example of a mentalistic theory with solid achievements to its credit.

The theory of vision maintains a pivotal position in psychology. Since perceptual processes provide the input for many higher cognitive processes, it is reasonable to think that if the theory of vision treats intentional states non-individualistically, other central parts of cognitive psychology will do likewise. Information processed by more central capacities depends, to a large extent, on visual information.

Certain special aspects of the vision example must be noted at the outset. The arguments that I have previously published against individualism (cf. note 1) have centered on 'higher' mental capacities, some of which essentially involve the use of language. This focus was motivated by an interest in the relation between thought and linguistic meaning and in certain sorts of intellectual responsibility. Early human vision makes use of a limited range of representations—representations of shape, texture, depth and other spatial relations, motion, color, and so forth. These representations (percepts) are formed by processes that are relatively immune to correction from other sources of information; and the representations of early vision appear to be fully independent of language. So the thought experiments that I have previously elaborated will not carry over simply to early human vision. (One would expect those thought experiments to be more relevant to social and developmental psychology, to concept learning, and to parts of 'higher' cognitive psychology.) But the case against individualism need not center on higher cognitive capacities or on the relation between thought and language. The anti-individualistic conclusions of our previous arguments can be shown to apply to early human vision. The abstract schema which those thought experiments articulate also applies.

The schema rests on three general facts. The first is that what entities in the objective world one intentionally interacts with in the employment of many representational (intentional) types affects the semantic properties of those representational types, what they are, and how we individuate them.[13] A near consequence of this first fact is that there can be slack between, on the one

---

[13] 'Representational type' (also 'intentional type') is a relatively theory-neutral term for intentional content, or even intentional state-kinds. Cf. note 3. One could about as well speak of concepts, percepts, and the representational or intentional aspects of thought contents—or of the counterpart states.

hand, the way a subject's representational types apply to the world, and on the other, what that person knows about, and how he or she can react to, the way they apply. It is possible for representational types to apply differently, without the person's physical reactions or discriminative powers being different. These facts, together with the fact that many fundamental mental states and events are individuated in terms of the relevant representational types, suffice to generate the conclusion that many paradigmatic mental states and events are not individualistically individuated: they may vary while a person's body and discriminative powers are conceived as constant. For by the second fact one can conceive of the way a person's representational types apply to the objective world as varying, while that person's history, non-intentionally and individualistically specified, is held constant. By the first fact, such variation may vary the individuation of the person's representational types. And by the third, such variation may affect the individuation of the person's mental states and events. I shall illustrate how instances of this schema are supported by Marr's theory of vision.[14]

Marr's theory subsumes three explanatory enterprises: (a) a theory of the computation of the information, (b) an account of the representations used and of the algorithms by which they are manipulated, and (c) a theory of the underlying physiology. Our primary interest is in the first level, and in that part of the second that deals with the individuation of representations. Both of these parts of the theory are fundamentally intentional.

The theory of the computation of information encompasses an account of what information is extracted from what antecedent resources, and an account of the reference-preserving 'logic' of the extraction. These accounts proceed against

---

[14] In what follows I make use of the important book *Vision*, by David Marr (San Francisco: W. H. Freeman and Company, 1982). Marr writes:

The purpose of these representations is to provide useful descriptions of aspects of the real world. The structure of the real world therefore plays an important role in determining both the nature of the representations that are used and the nature of the processes that derive and maintain them. An important part of the theoretical analysis is to make explicit the physical constraints and assumptions that have been used in the design of the representations and processes ... (p. 43)

It is of critical importance that the tokens [representational particulars] one obtains [in the theoretical analysis] correspond to real physical changes on the viewed surface; the blobs, lines, edges, groups, and so forth that we shall use must not be artifacts of the imaging process, or else inferences made from their structure backwards to the structures of the surface will be meaningless. (p. 44)

Marr's claim that the structure of the real world figures in determining the nature of the representations that are attributed in the theory is tantamount to the chief point about representation or reference that generates our non-individualist thought experiments—the first step in the schema. I shall show that these remarks constitute the central theoretical orientation of the book.

Calling the theory Marr's is convenient but misleading. Very substantial contributions have been made by many others; and the approach has developed rapidly since Marr's death. Cf. O. H. Ballard, G. E. Hinton, and T. J. Sejnowski, 'Parallel Vision Computation', *Nature*, e.g. 306 (1983), 21–26. What I say about Marr's book applies equally to more recent developments.

a set of biological background assumptions. It is assumed that visual systems have evolved to solve certain problems forced on them by the environment. Different species are set different problems and solve them differently. The theory of human vision specifies a general information processing problem—that of generating reliable representations of certain objective, distal properties of the surrounding world on the basis of proximal stimulations.

The human visual system computes complex representations of certain visible properties, on the basis of light intensity values on retinal images. The primary visible properties that Marr's theory treats are the shapes and locations of things in the world. But various other properties—motion, texture, color, lightness, shading—are also dealt with in some detail. The overall computation is broken down into stages of increasing complexity, each containing modules that solve various sub-problems.

The theory of computation of information clearly treats the visual system as going through a series of intentional or representational states. At an early stage, the visual system is counted as representing objective features of the physical world.[15] There is no other way to treat the visual system as solving the problem that the theory sees it as solving than by attributing intentional states that represent objective, physical properties.

More than half of Marr's book is concerned with developing the theory of the computation of information and with individuating representational primitives. These parts of the theory are more deeply developed, both conceptually and mathematically, than the account of the algorithms. This point is worth emphasizing because it serves to correct the impression, often conveyed in recent philosophy of psychology, that intentional theories are regressive and all of the development of genuine theory in psychology has been proceeding at the level of purely formal, 'syntactical' transformations (algorithms) that are used in cognitive systems.

I now want, by a series of examples, to give a fairly concrete sense of how the theory treats the relation between the visual system and the physical environment. Understanding this relation will form essential background for understanding the non-individualistic character of the theory. The reader may skip the detail and still follow the philosophical argument. But the detail is there to support the argument and to render the conception of explanation that the argument yields both concrete and vivid.

Initially, I will illustrate two broad points. The *first* is that the theory makes essential reference to the subject's distal stimuli and makes essential assumptions

---

[15] It is an interesting question when to count the visual system as having gone intentional. I take it that information is, in a broad sense, carried by the intensity values in the retinal image; but I think that this is too early to count the system as intentional or symbolic. I'm inclined to agree with Marr that where zero-crossings from different-sized filters are checked against one another (cf. Example 1), it is reasonable to count visual processes as representational of an external physical reality. Doing so, however, depends on seeing this stage as part of the larger system in which objective properties are often discriminated from subjective artifacts of the visual system.

about contingent facts regarding the subject's physical environment. Not only do the basic questions of the theory refer to what one sees under normal conditions, but the computational theory and its theorems are derived from numerous explicit assumptions about the physical world.

The *second* point to be illustrated is that the theory is set up to explain the reliability of a great variety of processes and sub-processes for acquiring information, at least to the extent that they are reliable. Reliability is presupposed in the formulations of the theory's basic questions. It is also explained through a detailed account of how in certain specified, standard conditions, veridical information is derived from limited means. The theory explains not merely the reliability of the system as a whole, but the reliability of various stages in the visual process. It begins by assuming that we see certain objective properties and proceeds to explain particular successes by framing conditions under which success would be expected (where the conditions are in fact typical). Failures are explained primarily by reference to a failure of these conditions to obtain. To use a phrase of Bernie Kobes, the theory is not success-neutral. The explanations and, as we shall later see, the kinds of theory presuppose that perception and numerous subroutines of perception are veridical in normal circumstances.

Example 1: In an early stage of the construction of visual representation, the outputs of channels or filters that are sensitive to spatial distributions of light intensities are combined to produce representations of local contours, edges, shadows, and so forth. The filters fall into groups of different sizes, in the sense that different groups are sensitive to different bands of spatial frequencies. The channels are primarily sensitive to sudden intensity changes, called 'zero-crossings', at their scales (within their frequency bands). The theoretical question arises: How do we combine the results of the different-sized channels to construct representations with physical meaning—representations that indicate edge segments or local contours in the external physical world? There is no apriori reason why zero-crossings obtained from different-sized filters should be related to some one physical phenomenon in the environment. There is, however, a physical basis for their being thus related. This basis is identified by *the constraint of spatial localization*. Things in the world that give rise to intensity changes in the image, such as changes of illumination (caused by shadows, light sources) or changes in surface reflectance (caused by contours, creases, and surface boundaries), are spatially localized, not scattered and not made up of waves. Because of this fact, if a zero-crossing is present in a channel centered on a given frequency band, there should be a corresponding zero-crossing at the same spatial location in larger-scaled channels. If this ceases to be so at larger scales, it is because a) two or more local intensity changes are being averaged together in the larger channel (for example, the edges of a thin bar may register radical frequency changes in small channels, but go undetected in larger ones); or b) because two independent physical phenomena are producing intensity changes in the same area but at different scales (for example, a shadow superimposed on a sudden reflectance change; if the shadow is located in a certain way, the positions of the zero-crossings may not make possible a separation of the two physical phenomena). Some of these exceptions are sufficiently rare that the visual system need not and does not account for them—thus allowing for possible illusions; others are reflected in complications of the basic assumption that follows. The spatial coincidence constraint yields *the spatial coincidence assumption*:

> If a zero-crossing segment is present in a set of independent channels over a contiguous range of sizes, and the segment has the same position and orientation in each channel, then the set of such zero-crossing segments indicates the presence of an intensity change in the image that is due to a single physical phenomenon (a change in reflectance, illumination, depth, or surface orientation).

Thus the theory starts with the observation that physical edges produce roughly coincident zero-crossings in channels of neighboring sizes. The spatial coincidence assumption asserts that the coincidence of zero-crossings of neighboring sizes is normally sufficient evidence of a real physical edge. Under such circumstances, according to the theory, a representation of an edge is formed.[16]

Example 2: Because of the laws of light and the way our eyes are made, positioned, and controlled, our brains typically receive similar image signals originating from two points that are fairly similarly located in the respective eyes or images, at the same horizontal level. If two objects are separated in depth from the viewer, the relative positions of their image signals will differ in the two eyes. The visual system determines the distance of physical surfaces by measuring the angular discrepancy in position (disparity) of the image of an object in the two eyes. This process is called stereopsis. To solve the problem of determining distance, the visual system must select a location on a surface as represented by one image, identify the same location in the other image, and measure the disparity between the corresponding image points. There is, of course, no apriori means of matching points from the two images. The theory indicates how correct matches are produced by appealing to three *Physical Constraints* (actually the first is not made explicit, but is relied upon): (1) the two eyes produce similar representations of the same external items; (2) a given point on a physical surface has a unique position in space at any given time; (3) matter is cohesive—separated into objects, the surfaces of which are usually smooth in the sense that surface variation is small compared to overall distance from the observer. These three physical constraints are rewritten as three corresponding *Constraints on Matching:* (1) two representational elements can match if and only if they normally could have arisen from the same physical item (for

---

[16] Marr, vision, 68–70; cf. also D. Marr and E. Hildreth, 'Theory of Edge Detection', *Proceedings of the Royal Society of London*, B207 (1980), 187–217, where the account is substantially more detailed.

example, in stereograms, dots match dots rather than bars); (2) nearly always, each representational element can match only one element from the other image (exceptions occur when two markings lie along the line of sight of one eye but are separately visible by the other—causing illusions); (3) disparity varies smoothly almost everywhere (this derives from physical constraint (3) because that constraint implies that the distance to the visible surface varies, approximately continuously except at object boundaries, which occupy a small fraction of the area of an image). Given suitable precisifications, these matching constraints can be used to prove the *Fundamental Theorem of Stereopsis*:

> If a correspondence is established between physically meaningful representational primitives extracted from the left and right images of a scene that contains a sufficient amount of detail (roughly 2% density for dot stereograms), and if the correspondence satisfies the three matching constraints, then that correspondence is physically correct—hence unique.

The method is again to identify general physical conditions that give rise to a visual process, then to use those conditions to motivate constraints on the form of the process that, when satisfied, will allow the process to be interpreted as providing reliable representations of the physical environment.[17]

These examples illustrate theories of the computation of information. The critical move is the formulation of general physical facts that limit the interpretation of a visual problem enough to allow one to interpret the machinations of the visual system as providing a unique and veridical solution, at least in typical cases. The primary aim of referring to contingent physical facts and properties is to enable the theory to explain the visual system's reliable acquisition of information about the physical world: to explain the success or veridicality of various types of visual representation. So much for the first two points that we set out to illustrate.

I now turn to a *third* that is a natural corollary of the second, and that will be critical for my argument that the theory is non-individualistic: the information carried by representations—their intentional content—is individuated in terms of the specific distal causal antecedents in the physical world that the information is about and that the representations normally apply to. The individuation of the intentional features of numerous representations depends on a variety of physical constraints that our knowledge of the external world gives us. Thus the individuation of intentional content of representational types, presupposes the veridicality of perception. Not only the explanations, but the intentional kinds of the theory presuppose contingent facts about the subject's physical environment.

Example 3: In building up informational or representational primitives in the primal sketch, Marr states six general physical assumptions that constrain the

---

[17] Marr, *Vision*, 111–116; D. Marr and T. Poggio, 'A Computational Theory of Human Stereo Vision', *Proceedings of the Royal Society of London*, B204 (1979), 301–328. Marr, *Vision*, 205–212; Shimon Ullman, *The Interpretation of Visual Motion* (Cambridge, Mass.: MIT Press, 1979).

choice of primitives. I shall state some of these to give a sense of their character: (a) the visible world is composed of smooth surfaces having reflectance functions whose spatial structure may be complex; (b) markings generated on a surface by a single process are often arranged in continuous spatial structures—curves, lines, etc.; (c) if direction of motion is discontinuous at more than one point—for example, along a line—then an object boundary is present. These assumptions are used to identify the physical significance of—the objective information normally given by—certain types of patterns in the image. The computational theory states conditions under which these primitives form to carry information about items in the physical world.[a] The theory in Example 1 is a case in point: conditions are laid down under which certain patterns may be taken as representing an objective physical condition; as being edge, boundary, bar, or blob detectors. Similar points apply for more advanced primitives.

Example 4: In answering the question 'what assumptions do we reasonably and actually employ when we interpret silhouettes as three-dimensional shapes?' Marr motivates a central representational primitive by stating physical constraints that lead to the proof of a theorem. *Physical Constraints.* (1) Each line of sight from the viewer to the object grazes the object's surface at exactly one point. (2) Nearby points on the contour in an image arise from nearby points on the contour generator on the viewed object. (That is, points that appear close together in the image actually are close together on the object's surface.) (3) The contour generator lies wholly in a single plane. Obviously, these are conditions of perception that may fail, but they are conditions under which we seem to do best at solving the problem of deriving three-dimensional shape descriptions from representations of silhouettes. *Definition.* A *generalized cone* is a three-dimensional object generated by moving a cross-section along an axis; the cross-section may vary smoothly in size, but its shape remains the same. (For example, footballs, pyramids, legs, stalagmites are or approximate generalized cones.) *Theorem.* If the surface is smooth and if physical constraints (1)–(3) hold for all distant viewing positions in any one plane, then the viewed surface is a generalized cone. The theorem indicates a natural connection between generalized cones and the imaging process. Marr infers from this, and from certain psycho-physical evidence, that representations of generalized cones—that is, representations with intentional content concerning generalized cones—are likely to be fundamental among our visual representations of three-dimensional objects.[b]

Throughout the theory, representational primitives are selected and individuated by considering specific, contingent facts about the physical world that typically hold when we succeed in obtaining veridical visual information about that world. The information or content of the visual representations is always

---

[a] Marr, *Vision*, 44–71.
[b] Ibid. 215–225.

individuated by reference to the physical objects, properties, or relations that are seen. In view of the success-orientation of the theory, this mode of individuation is grounded in its basic methods. If theory were confronted with a species of organism reliably and successfully interacting with a different set of objective visible properties, the representational types that the theory would attribute to the organism would be different, regardless of whether an individual organism's physical mechanisms were different.

We are now in a position to argue that the theory is not individualistic: (1) The theory is intentional. (2) The intentional primitives of the theory and the information they carry are individuated by reference to contingently existing physical items or conditions by which they are normally caused and to which they normally apply. (3) So if these physical conditions and, possibly, attendant physical laws were regularly different, the information conveyed to the subject and the intentional content of his or her visual representations would be different. (4) It is not incoherent to conceive of relevantly different physical conditions and perhaps relevantly different (say, optical) laws regularly causing the same non-intentionally, individualistically individuated physical regularities in the subject's eyes and nervous system. It is enough if the differences are small; they need not be wholesale. (5) In such a case (by (3)) the individual's visual representations would carry different information and have different representational content, though the person's whole non-intentional physical history (at least up to a certain time) might remain the same. (6) Assuming that some perceptual states are identified in the theory in terms of their informational or intentional content, it follows that individualism is not true for the theory of vision.

I shall defend the argument stepwise. I take it that the claim that the theory is intentional is sufficiently evident. The top levels of the theory are explicitly formulated in intentional terms. And their method of explanation is to show how the problem of arriving at certain veridical representations is solved.

The second step of the argument was substantiated through Examples 3 and 4. The intentional content of representations of edges or generalized cones is individuated in terms of *specific* reference to those very contingently instantiated physical properties, on the assumption that those properties normally give rise to veridical representations of them.

The third step in our argument is supported both by the way the theory individuates intentional content (cf. the previous paragraph and Examples 3 and 4), and by the explanatory method of the theory (cf. the second point illustrated above, and Examples 1–2). The methods of individuation and explanation are governed by the assumption that the subject has adapted to his or her environment sufficiently to obtain veridical information from it under certain normal conditions. If the properties and relations that *normally* caused visual impressions were regularly different from what they are, the individual would obtain different information and have visual experiences with different intentional content. If the regular, law-like relations between perception and the environment were different, the visual system would be solving different information-processing problems; it would pass through different informational or intentional states; and the explanation of vision would be different. To reject this third step of our argument would be to reject the theory's basic methods and questions. But these methods and questions have already borne fruit, and there are presently no good reasons for rejecting them.

I take it that step four is a relatively unproblematic counterfactual. There is no metaphysically necessary relation between individualistically individuated processes in a person's body and the causal antecedents of those processes in the surrounding world.[18] (To reject this step would be self-defeating for the individualist.) If the environmental conditions were different, the same proximal *visual* stimulations could have regularly had different distal causes. In principle, we can conceive of some regular variation in the distal causes of perceptual impressions with no variation in a person's individualistically specified physical processes, even while conceiving the person as *well adapted* to the relevant environment—though, of course, not uniquely adapted.

Steps three and four, together with the unproblematic claim that the theory individuates some perceptual states in terms of their intentional content or representational types, entail that the theory is non-individualistic.

Steps two and three are incompatible with certain philosophical approaches that have no basis in psychological theory. One might claim that the information content of a visual representation would remain constant even if the physical conditions that lead to the representation were regularly different. It is common to motivate this claim by pointing out that one's visual representations remain the same, whether one is perceiving a black blob on a white surface or having an eidetic hallucination of such a blob. So, runs the reasoning, why should changing the distal causes of a perceptual representation affect its content? On this view, the content of a given perceptual representation is commonly given as that of 'the distal cause of *this* representation', or 'the property in the world that has *this* sort of visual appearance'. The content of these descriptions is intended to remain constant between possible situations in which the micro-physical events of a person's visual processes remain the same while distal causes of those processes are regularly and significantly different. For it is thought that the representations themselves (and our experiences of *them*) remain constant under these circumstances. So as the distal antecedents of one's perceptual representations vary, the reference of those representations will vary, but their intentional content will not.[19]

---

[18] As I have intimated above, I doubt that all biological, including physiological, processes and states in a person's body are individualistically individuated. The failures of individualism for these sciences involve different, but related considerations.

[19] Descartes went further in the same direction. He thought that the perceptual system, and indeed the intellect, could not make a mistake. Mistakes derived from the will. The underlying view is that we primarily perceive or make perceptual reference to our own perceptions. This position fails to account plausibly for various visual illusions and errors that precede any activity of the will, or even

There is more wrong with this line than I have room to develop here. I will mention some of the more straightforward difficulties. In the first place, the motivation from perceptual illusion falls far short. One is indeed in the same perceptual state whether one is seeing or hallucinating. But that is because the intentional content of one's visual state (or representation) is individuated against a background in which the relevant state is *normally* veridical. Thus the fact that one's percepts or perceptual states remain constant between normal perception and hallucinations does not even tend to show that the intentional visual state remains constant between circumstances in which different physical conditions are the normal antecedents of one's perceptions.

Let us consider the proposals for interpreting the content of our visual representations. In the first place both descriptions ('the distal cause of *this* representation' *et al.*) are insufficiently specific. There are lots of distal causes and lots of things that might be said to appear 'thus' (for example, the array of light striking the retina as well as the physical surface). We identify the relevant distal cause (and the thing that normally appears thus and so) as the thing that we actually see. To accurately pick out the 'correct' object with one of these descriptions would at the very least require a more complex specification. But filling out the descriptive content runs into one or both of two difficulties: either it includes kinds that are tied to a specific environment ('the convex, rough textured object that is causing this representation'). In such a case, the description is still subject to our argument. For these kinds are individuated by reference to the empirical environment. Or it complicates the constraints on the causal chain to the extent that the complications cannot plausibly be attributed to the content of processes in the early visual system.

Even in their unrevised forms, the descriptions are over-intellectualized philosophers' conceits. It is extremely implausible and empirically without warrant to think that packed into every perceptual representation is a distinction between distal cause and experiential effect, or between objective reality and perceptual appearance. These are distinctions developed by reflecting on the ups and downs of visual perception. They do not come in at the ground, animal level of early vision.

A further mistake is the view that our perceptual representations never purport to specify particular physical properties *as such*, but only via some relation they bear to inner occurrences, which are directly referred to. (Even the phrase 'the convex object causing this percept' invokes a specification of objective convexity as such.) The view will not serve the needs of psychological explanation as actually practiced. For the descriptions of information are too unspecific to

intellect. And the idea that perceptions are in general what we make perceptual reference to has little to recommend it and, nowadays, little influence. The natural and, I think, plausible view is that we have visual representations that specify external properties specifically, that these representations are pre-doxastic in the sense they are not themselves objects of belief, and that they sometimes fail to represent correctly what is before the person's eyes: when they result from abnormal processes.

account for specific successes in solving problems in retrieving information about the actual, objective world.

The best empirical theory that we have individuates the intentional content of visual representations by specific reference to specific physical characteristics of visible properties and relations. The theory does not utilize complicated, self-referential, attributively used role descriptions of those properties. It does not individuate content primarily by reference to phenomenological qualities. Nor does it use the notions of cause or appearance in specifying the intentional content of early visual representations.[20]

The second and third steps of our argument are incompatible with the claim that the intentional content of visual representations is determined by their 'functional role' in each person's system of dispositions, non-intentionally and individualistically specified. This claim lacks any warrant in the practice of the science. In the first place, the theory suggests no reduction of the intentional to the non-intentional. In the second, although what a person can do, non-visually, constitutes evidence for what he or she can see, there is little ground for thinking that either science or common sense takes an individual person's non-visual abilities fully to determine the content of his or her early visual experience. A person's dispositions and beliefs develop by adapting to what the person sees. As the person develops, the visual system (at least at its more advanced stages—those involving recognition) and the belief and language systems affect each other. But early vision seems relatively independent of these non-visual systems. A large part of learning is accommodating one's dispositions to the information carried by visual representations. Where there are failures of adaptation, the person does not know what the visual apparatus is presenting to him or her. Yet the presentations are there to be understood.

III

There is a general argument that seems to me to show that a person's non-intentional dispositions could not fix (individuate) the intentional content of

---

[20] Of course, at least in the earliest stages of visual representation, there are analogies between qualitative features of representations in the experienced image and the features that those representations represent. Representations that represent bar segments are bar-shaped, or have some phenomenological property that strongly tempts us to call them 'bar-shaped'. Similarly for blobs, dots, lines and so forth. (Marr and Hildreth, "Theory of Edge Detection", 211, remark on this dual aspect of representations.) These 'analogies' are hardly fortuitous. Eventually they will probably receive rigorous psycho-physical explanations. But they should not tempt one into the idea that visual representations in general make reference to themselves, much less into the idea that the content of objective representation is independent of empirical relations between the representations and the objective entities that give rise to them. Perhaps these qualitative features are constant across all cases where one's bodily processes, non-intentionally specified, are held constant. But the information they carry, their intentional content, may vary with their causal antecedents and causal laws in the environment.

the person's visual presentations. The argument begins with a conception of objectivity. As long as the person's visual presentations are of public, objective objects, properties, or relations, it is possible for the person to have mistaken presentations. Such mistakes usually arise for a single sensory modality—so that when dispositions associated with other modalities (for example, touch) are brought into play, the mistake is rectified. But as long as the represented object or property is objective and physical, it is in principle possible, however unlikely, that there be a confluence of illusions such that all an individual person's sensory modalities would be fooled and all of the person's non-intentional dispositions would fail to distinguish between the normal condition and the one producing the mistaken sensory representations. This is my first assumption. In the argument, I shall employ a corollary: my concept of objectivity is such that no one objective entity that we visually represent is such that it must vary with, or be typed so as necessarily to match exactly, an individual's proximal stimuli and discriminative abilities. The point follows from a realistic, and even from a non-subjectivistic, view of the objects of sight.[21]

I argued earlier that intentional representational types are not in general individuated purely in terms of an attributive role-description of a causal relation, or a relation of appearance-similarity, between external objects and qualitative perceptual representatives of them. For present purposes, this is the second assumption: some objective physical objects and properties are visually represented as such; they are specifically specified.

Third, in order to be empirically informative, some visual representations that represent objective entities as such must have the representational characteristics that they have partly *because* instances regularly enter into certain relations with those objective entities.[22] Their carrying information, their having objective intentional content, consists partly in their being the normal causal products of objective entities. And their specific intentional content depends partly on their being the normal products of the specific objective entities that give rise to

---

[21] There is no need to assume that the abnormal condition is unverifiable. Another person with relevant background information might be able to infer that the abnormal condition is producing a perceptual illusion. In fact, another person with different dispositions might even be able to perceive the difference.

[22] Not all perceptual representations that specify objective entities need have their representational characteristics determined in this way. The representational characters of *some* visual representations (or states) may depend on the subject's background theory or primarily on interaction among other representations. There are hallucinations of purple dragons. (Incidentally, few if any of the perceptual representations—even the conscious perceptual representations—discussed in Marr's theory depend in this way on the subject's conceptual background.) Here, I assume only that *some* visual representations acquire their representational characters through interaction. This amounts to the weak assumption that the formation of some perceptual representations is *empirical*.

Some of the interaction that leads to the formation and representational characters of certain innate perceptual tendencies (or perhaps even representations) may occur in the making of the species, not in the learning histories of individuals. Clearly this complication could be incorporated into a generalization of this third premise—without affecting the anti-individualistic thrust of the argument.

them. That is why we individuate intentional visual representations in terms of the objective entities that they normally apply to, for members of a given species. This is the core of truth in the slogan, sometimes misapplied, I think, that mistakes presuppose a background of veridicality.

The assumptions in the three preceding paragraphs make possible the statement of a general argument against individualism regarding visual states. Consider a person P who normally correctly perceives instances of a particular objective visible property O. In such cases, let the intentional type of P's perceptual representation (or perceptual state) be O'. Such perceptual representations are normally the product of interaction with instances of O. But imagine that for P, perceptual representations typed O' are on some few occasions the product of instances of a different objective property C. On such occasions, P mistakenly sees an instance of C as an O; P's perceptual state is of type O'. We are assuming that O' represents any instance of O as such (as an O), in the sense of our second premise, not merely in terms of some attributive role description. Since O' represents an objective property, we may, by our first premise, conceive of P as lacking at his or her disposal (at every moment up to a given time) any means of discriminating the instances of C from instances of O.

Now hold fixed both P's physical states (up to the given time) and his or her discriminative abilities, non-intentionally and individualistically specified. But conceive of the world as lacking O altogether. Suppose that the optical laws in the counterfactual environment are such that the impressions on P's eyes and the normal causal processes that lead to P's visual representations are explained in terms of C's (or at any rate, in terms of some objective, visible entities other than instances of O). Then by our third premise, P's visual representation (or visual state) would not be of intentional type O'. At the time when in the actual situation P is misrepresenting a C as an O, P may counterfactually be perceiving something (say, a C) correctly (as a C)—if the processes that lead to that visual impression are normal and of a type that normally produces the visual impression that P has on that occasion. So the person's intentional visual states could vary while his or her physical states and non-intentionally specified discriminative abilities remained constant.

The first premise and the methodology of intentional content individuation articulated in the third premise entail the existence of examples. Since examples usually involve shifts in optical laws, they are hard to fill out in great detail. But it is easiest to imagine concrete cases taken from early but still conscious vision. These limit the number of an individual's dispositions that might be reasonably thought to bear on the content of his or her visual states. Early vision is relatively independent of linguistic or other cognitive abilities. It appears to be relatively modular.

Suppose that the relevant visible entities are very small and not such as to bear heavily on adaptive success. An O may be a shadow of a certain small size and shape on a gently contoured surface. A C may be a similarly sized, shallow crack. In the actual situation P sees O's regularly and correctly as O's: P's visual

representations are properly explained and specified as shadow representations of
the relevant sort. We assume that P's visual and other discriminative abilities are
fairly normal. P encounters C's very rarely and on those few occasions not only
misperceives them as O's, but has no dispositions that would enable him or her
to discriminate those instances from O's. We may assume that given P's actual
abilities and the actual laws of optics, P would be capable, in ideal circumstances,
of visually discriminating some instances of C's (relevantly similar cracks) from
instances of O (the relevant sort of shadows). But our supposition is that in the
actual cases where P is confronted by instances of C's, the circumstances are
not ideal. All P's abilities would not succeed in discriminating those instances
of relevant cracks, in those circumstances, from instances of relevant shadows.
P may not rely on touch in cases of such small objects; or touch may also
be fooled. P's ability to have such mistaken visual states is argued for by the
objectivity premise.

In the counterfactual case, the environment is different. There are no instances
of the relevant shadows visible to P; and the laws of optics differ in such a way
that P's physical visual stimulations (and the rest of P's physical makeup) are
unaffected. Suppose that the physical visual stimulations that in the actual case
are derived from instances of O—the relevant sort of shadows—are counterfactually caused by and explained in terms of C's, relevantly sized cracks.
Counterfactually, the cracks take the places of the shadows. On the few occasions
where, in the actual case, P misperceives shadows as cracks, P is counterfactually confronted with cracks; and the optical circumstances that lead to the visual
impressions on those occasions are, we may suppose, normal for the counterfactual environment.[23] On such counterfactual occasions, P would be visually
representing small cracks as small cracks. P would never have visual representations of the relevant sort of shadows. One can suppose that even if there were
the relevant sort of shadows in the counterfactual environment, the different
laws of optics in that environment would not enable P ever to see them. But
since P's visual states would be the normal products of normal processes and
would provide as good an empirical basis for learning about the counterfactual
environment as P has for learning about the actual environment, it would be
absurd to hold that (counterfactually) P misperceives the prevalent cracks as
shadows on gently contoured surfaces. Counterfactually, P correctly sees the
cracks as cracks. So P's intentional perceptual states differ between actual and

---

[23] What of the non-intentionally specified dispositions that in the actual environment (given the
actual laws of optics) would have enabled P to discriminate C's from O's in ideal circumstances? In
the counterfactual environment, in view of the very different optical laws and different objects that
confront P, one can suppose that these dispositions have almost any visual meaning that one likes.
These dispositions would serve to discriminate C's from some other sort of entity. In view of the
objectivity premise, the non-intentional dispositions can always be correlated with different, normal
antecedent laws and conditions—in terms of which their intentional content may be explained.

The argument of this section is developed in parallel but different ways in 'Cartesian Error and
the Objectivity of Perception' (Ch. 7 above).

counterfactual situations. This general argument is independent of the theory of vision that we have been discussing. It supports and is further supported by that theory.

IV

Although the theory of vision is in various ways special, I see no reason why its non-individualistic methods will not find analogs in other parts of psychology. In fact, as I noted, since vision provides intentional input for other cognitive capacities, there is reason to think that the methods of the theory of vision are presupposed by other parts of psychology. These non-individualistic methods are grounded in two natural assumptions. One is that there are psychological states that represent, or are about, an objective world. The other is that there is a scientific account to be given that presupposes certain successes in our interaction with the world (vision, hearing, memory, decision, reasoning, empirical belief formation, communication, and so forth), and that explains specific successes and failures by reference to these states.

The two assumptions are, of course, interrelated. Although an intention to eat meat is 'conceptually' related to eating meat, the relation is not one of entailment in either direction, since the representation is about an objective matter. An individual may be, and often is, ignorant, deluded, misdirected, or impotent. The very thing that makes the non-individualistic thought experiments possible—the possibility of certain sorts of ignorance, failure, and misunderstanding—helps make it possible for explanations using non-individualistic language to be empirically informative. On the other hand, as I have argued above, some successful interaction with an objective world seems to be a precondition for the objectivity of some of our intentional representations.

Any attempt to produce detailed accounts of the relations between our attitudes and the surrounding world will confront a compendium of empirically interesting problems. Some of the most normal and mundane successes in our cognitive and conative relations to the world must be explained in terms of surprisingly complicated intervening processes, many of which are themselves partly described in terms of intentional states. Our failures may be explained by reference to *specific* abnormalities in operations or surrounding conditions. Accounting for environmentally specific successes (and failures) is one of the tasks that psychology has traditionally set itself.

An illuminating philosophy of psychology must do justice not only to the mechanistic elements in the science. It must also relate these to psychology's attempt to account for tasks that we succeed and fail at, *where these tasks are set by the environment and represented by the subject him or herself.* The most salient and important of these tasks are those that arise through relations to the natural and social worlds. A theory that insists on describing the states of human beings *purely* in terms that abstract from their relations to any specific environment cannot hope to provide a completely satisfying explanation of our accomplishments. At present our best theories in many domains of psychology do not attempt such an abstraction. No sound reason has been given for thinking that the non-individualistic language that psychology now employs is not an appropriate language for explaining these matters, or that explanation of this sort is impossible.

10 Intellectual Norms and Foundations of Mind

Two paramount tasks for philosophy are articulating the nature of propositional attitudes and articulating the nature of the intellectual norms that govern thinking about objective matters. The first task is fundamental to explicating the notion of mind. The second is fundamental to saying what is significant and distinctive about being human.

With respect to the first task, I have previously argued that propositional mental-state and event kinds are *nonindividualistically individuated*. The mental natures of many of an individual's mental states and events are dependent for their individuation on the individual's physical and social environments.[1] The arguments I have given indicate that a person's mental-state and event kinds might, in principle, vary with variations in the environment, even as the person's physical history and constitution, described nonintentionally and individualistically (without relation to the physical and social environments), remain constant.

A deep source of interest in these arguments lies in the help they provide with the second of the two tasks I described. They sharpen our conception of intellectual responsibility. This notion undergirds the proprietary concepts of dialectic, rationality, understanding, spirit, and rule-following that Plato, Aristotle, Kant, Hegel, and Wittgenstein, respectively, tried to explicate. The conditions under which people become responsible to intellectual norms are complicated. They involve considerations regarding etiology, minimum competence, and intention. I will not be concerned here with these conditions or with implications of the

I have benefited from conversation with Rogers Albritton and Keith Donnellan at early stages of this project and with Willi Vossenkuhl at a later stage. I have also learned from discussion at Berkeley, Konstanz, Munich, Stanford, and Tucson, where I gave talks based on the paper.

[1] One such argument occurs in 'Individualism and the Mental', *Midwest Studies of Philosophy*, 4 (1979), 73–121 (Ch. 5 above). A second occurs in note 2 of the same article and in 'Other Bodies', in Andrew Woodfield (ed.), *Thought and Object* (New York: Oxford University Press, 1982). (Ch. 4 above.) Aspects of both arguments are further discussed in 'Two Thought Experiments Reviewed', *Notre Dame Journal of Formal Logic*, 23, 3 (July 1982), 284–293 (Ch. 6 above). A third argument occurs in 'Individualism and Psychology', *The Philosophical Review*, 45, 1 (Jan. 1986), 3–45, and in 'Cartesian Error and the Objectivity of Perception', John McDowell and Philip Pettit (eds.), *Subject, Thought, and Context* (Oxford: Oxford University Press, 1986) (Chs. 9 and 7 above). As is usually the case in philosophy, the important thing is less the conclusion itself than the routes that lead to it.

notions of agency and responsibility. I shall discuss rather the nature and source of the norms' authority and the role of those norms in constituting the notion of mind.

In this paper I propose a new argument for the view that mental-state and event kinds are nonindividualistically individuated. The argument uses the basic strategy of its predecessors, but provides a different perspective on the factors that underlie the conclusion.

The argument proceeds on two levels. At the more general level the key idea is that some necessarily true thoughts or statements can be doubted.[2] A few philosophers have rejected this idea. Perhaps some rationalists and certainly some positivists and possible-worlds semanticists have maintained that one cannot believe an impossibility. Most of these would add that one cannot doubt a necessary truth. I find these positions antecedently implausible, and I do not find their motivations compelling. (In some cases the motivations involve implicit commitment to individualism.) Moreover, these positions account poorly, in my view, for the epistemology of logic, mathematics, analyses of meaning, and aposteriori necessary truths. They do raise interesting issues. But I shall not confront them in detail here.[3]

I take it that most thoughts that are necessarily true are dubitable. The anti-individualistic argument I propose in section II is perhaps most clearly applicable to empirical necessary truths (e.g. that water is H_2O). I shall say little about these truths or about their role in the argument because they fit so straightforwardly into the scheme.[4] Thus the most general level of argument will largely stay backstage, with occasional bit appearances.

Most of the paper will proceed at a more specific level. At this level the key idea is that a particular subclass of necessary truths is dubitable. The subclass is made up of those necessary truths which are intuitively central to giving the meaning of an empirically applicable term or to providing an explicit general understanding of such a concept. I concentrate on this subclass because the ramifications of the more general argument against individualism are richest and least obvious for this case.

In Section I I provide a rationale for the fact that this subclass of necessary truths can be doubted. In Section II I lay out a thought experiment which anchors

---

[2] Actually, the argument need not rest on an assumption about necessity. What we need are general thoughts or statements so central to the correct identification of a type of thing, property, or event, that, under ordinary conditions, if the thought failed to apply to some given entity x, we would correctly and almost automatically refuse to count x an instance of the type. For expositional convenience, I shall write in terms of necessity, without further qualification. I shall use the term 'doubt' in the weak sense of 'withhold belief' (analogously, for cognates like 'dubitable')—except where the context indicates some different usage.

[3] For a motivated development of the opposing semantical view, see Robert Stalnaker, *Inquiry* (Cambridge, Mass.: MIT Press, 1984). Positivist motivations will be discussed briefly in sec. I.

[4] For a different reason, I shall not discuss logical and mathematical truths. Nearly all these are both necessary and dubitable. But the issues involved in relating them to my overall view are complex and require special attention.

the argument against individualism. Section III is devoted to a brief discussion of alternative construals of the thought experiment. Section IV introduces a distinction, implicit in the argument, between cognitive value and conventional or idiolectic linguistic meaning. In Section V I use this distinction to sketch an argument to the effect that even nonindividualistic 'use-based' theories of mind (in senses to be specified) cannot be correct.

I

My aim in this section is to explain why necessary truths that intuitively give the meaning of an empirically applicable term (or purport to provide general understanding of such a concept) are dubitable.

As a preliminary, let us review some recent history. The most significant source of appeals to indubitability in this century has been a set of assumptions about meaning, understanding, and belief which emerged in positivist theories of knowledge. Some positivists counted logical and mathematical truths 'true by convention' or 'true purely in virtue of meaning' in order to protect empiricism against the charge that it could not account for knowledge in the deductive sciences. Propositions of logic and mathematics and truths that have criterial status (such as 'Sofas are pieces of furniture made or meant for sitting') were held to express not knowledge, but convention. In effect they were counted indubitable. This conclusion could be drawn in either of two ways. One could reason that doubting something requires understanding it; but criterial truths are true in virtue of meaning, so understanding them entails realizing that they are true; so it is impossible to doubt them. Alternatively, one could emphasize the allegedly degenerate nature of criterial truths: since such truths express only convention or fiat, anyone who understands them must realize that doubting them is pointless or meaningless; and doubt requires understanding; so doubt is impossible.

Neither argument would be given today. But their assumptions are worth making explicit. They assume that doubt requires complete understanding of what is doubted; that criterial truths are true by fiat or convention, or meaning alone; and that understanding these truths requires realizing this (alleged) connection between their meaning and their truth.

All these assumptions are unacceptable. The argument that I shall develop in Section II does not attribute incomplete understanding. But I shall develop reasons for doubting the first assumption shortly.[a] W. V. Quine's work long ago threw the second into deserved disrepute.[5] There is no explanatory use for

---

[a] [Cf. Burge, "Individualism and the Mental", note 1.]

[5] I do not back all elements in Quine's attack on the view that there are truths that are true purely in virtue of meaning (in particular, his empiricism and some of his attacks on the notion of meaning itself). But I think that his earliest criticisms of analyticity are sound: see 'Carnap and

claiming that the relevant truths are true purely in virtue of meaning, as opposed to partly in virtue of meaning and partly in virtue of (perhaps 'obvious') ways the world is. That is, there is no reason to see them as degenerately true. The third assumption is clearly vulnerable to the same Quinean considerations.

Taken as self-conscious academic doctrine, positivist theories have not survived the century's sixth decade. But the general picture they offer of the relation between the meaning, understanding, and truth of 'criterial' statements still informs much philosophical common sense. The first and third premises just discussed come closest to painting the general picture: the idea is that *in the cases at issue, understanding sufficient for carrying on responsible ratiocination—which is identified with understanding ordinary linguistic meaning—necessarily requires recognition of truth.*

Substantially the same picture has been painted by some self-styled Wittgensteinians. It has been assumed that belief entails full understanding, and claimed that a 'criterion' of understanding is recognition of the truth of the relevant statements. The attempt of the positivists to provide a theoretical ground for this connection between understanding and belief (second assumption above) is dismissed as quixotic. Of course, we often do use apparent disbelief as ground for attributing failure of understanding, and even sometimes for reconstruing a person's words to avoid attributing disbelief. But these criteria are defeasible, as the cases we shall later discuss indicate. Sometimes the criterion is mechanically invoked in philosophical discussion as if it mirrored some absolute practice that we all recognize. Such invocation often serves to undergird the picture inherited from positivism.

There is a common enthymematic argument which also serves this picture. It goes as follows: The meaning of (say) 'sofa' is the same as the meaning of 'piece of furniture [of such and such a construction] meant or made for sitting'; but, if one understands both phrases, one cannot doubt that sofas are pieces of furniture ... meant or made for sitting, since the expressions, meaning the same, are interchangeable; such a doubt would be a doubt that sofas are sofas; but *that* is not a doubt that anyone could be thought to have. So anyone who *appears* to be doubting that sofas are pieces of furniture ... meant or made for sitting, cannot really be doing so.[6] This reasoning again assumes that doubt

Logical Truth', secs. I–V, X; 'Truth by Convention', both in *Ways of Paradox* (New York: Random House, 1966). I take it that Quine's challenge to justify a disjoint distinction between 'truths of fact' (possibly including, so far as this argument is concerned, necessary facts and facts known by reason) and *mere* 'truths purely by virtue of meaning'—has gone unmet. This section supplements Quine's view by showing in some detail why certain 'truths of meaning' are simultaneously 'truths of fact', or better—why they are not degenerately true. Cf. also Sec. IV below. Nothing I argue in this paper depends on acceptance of any particular theoretical conception of meaning. I merely make use of an untendentious intuitive notion of meaning to isolate a rough class of statements or thoughts.

[6] The argument from the substitutivity of synonyms, at least in embedded cases, received considerable discussion in the 1950s. The discussion was started by a different argument in Benson Mates, 'Synonymity', in Leonard Linsky (ed.) *Semantics and the Philosophy of Language* (Urbana, Ill.: University Press Illinois, 1952), 215. The points at issue in Mates's discussion are developed in some

requires full understanding; and it again assumes that understanding the relevant meaning entails recognizing truth. The reasoning, however, will provide a basis for exploring why these two assumptions are mistaken in cases relevant to the issues at hand, and thereby explain why necessarily true, 'meaning-giving' statements involving many empirically applicable terms are dubitable.

My strategy will be to consider in some detail how synonymies are grounded and how we come to affirm them. I shall develop the view that the role of examples in the cases of the relevant synonymies guarantees that the relevant object-level statements or thoughts are dubitable.

What does *having the same meaning* involve in the cases of empirically applicable terms? Synonymies are grounded in practice: *the most competent speakers would use the two relevant expressions interchangeably.*

The notions of interchangeability and competence, which are central to this characterization, require discussion. First, interchangeability. Competent speakers are normally willing to exchange synonymous expressions in extensional, counterfactual, and many other contexts *salve veritate;* they use one expression as a means of identifying entities to which the other applies and as the primary and sufficient explanation of the other, apart from any particular perceptual context. This is a rough, minimal characterization; but it will serve.

One should not interpret 'interchangeability' more strictly than our practices warrant. Abbreviative definition in formal systems is in most cases a misleading model. It is simply not the case that the only hold competent speakers have on one of a pair of synonymous expressions is always through the other. As any book on synonyms will show, there are many reasons for this. One example will suffice here. Sometimes there are syntactical differences between the relevant expressions which occasion differences in the ties they have to perceptual experiences. Thus 'sofa' is commonly applied, defeasibly but directly, to objects that look a certain way. The components of 'pieces of furniture of such and such construction meant or made for sitting' have independent perceptual and conceptual ties. The application of the longer expression to sofas often seems to involve a kind of computation.

Let us turn to 'competence'. The language does not present a standard of competence independent of individuals' activity. Minimal competence consists in conformity to the practice of others. 'Greatest competence' consists in abilities to draw distinctions, to produce precisifications, to use numerous linguistic resources, to offer counterexamples to proposed equivalences—that elicit the reflective agreement of other competent speakers. We may imagine a vast, ragged network of interdependence, established by patterns of deference which lead

detail in my 'Belief and Synonymy'. *The Journal of Philosophy*, 75, 3 (Mar. 1978), 119–138. These issues have antecedents in earlier discussions of the 'paradox of analysis'. It should be emphasized that we are concerned with whether substitutivity of all ordinary synonyms is guaranteed necessarily or logically. In *most contexts*, of course, exchanges preserve the point and certainly the truth-value of the report.

back to people who would elicit the assent of others. (Of course, we idealize from this network; a person's degree of competence may vary over time and with the case at hand, and may develop or regress.) To put it crudely, a person counts as among the *most competent* if he or she would be *persuasive* to other competent speakers in the use and explication of the language. The point about persuasion is fundamental. I shall develop it by considering the dialectic that commonly leads to statements that explicate meaning.[7]

It is obvious that few, even among the competent, can quickly and accurately hit upon meaning-giving characterizations for ordinary terms. Usually they need thought or discussion to improve their initial attempts. Beliefs about *what Xs are* typically contain minor errors, often because of over- or undergeneralization from common examples of Xs. This fact already motivates some distinction between the sort of competence necessary to engage in ratiocination involving use of the term or notion, and the sort necessary to have an accurate understanding of the conventional meaning of the term. For a person may, in the course of the dialectic, have thoughts involving the concept X, and yet have beliefs about what Xs are which are incompatible with the conventional normative characterization or with the characterization he or she would regard on reflection as correct. Thus I may have numerous ordinary chair beliefs (that that is a chair), yet believe incorrectly that chairs must have legs. Such a belief betrays an incomplete understanding of the conventional meaning-giving characterization of chairs, but does nothing to exempt me from responsibility to communal norms of evaluation when I have or express my chair beliefs.

The dialectic attempts to arrive at what might be called *normative characterizations*. These are statements about *what Xs are* that purport to give basic, 'essential', and necessarily true information about Xs. They are used as guides to certifying the identity of entities: something that is cited as an X but does not fulfill the condition laid down by the normative characterization will not normally be counted an X. A subclass of normative characterizations not only purport to state facts that set norms for identification; they also provide linguistic meaning—set a norm for conventional linguistic understanding ('A knife is an instrument consisting of a thin blade with an edge for cutting, fastened to a handle'; 'To walk is to move on foot at a natural unhurried gait'; 'A baby is a very young child or very young higher animal'). Not all normative characterizations provide meaning in this sense ('Water is H_2O'). But my primary interest is in cases where they do.

Meaning-giving characterizations, for ordinary terms, are usually arrived at through reflection on *archetypical applications*. These are perceptually backed,

---

[7] My characterization of dialectic will overschematize enormously. I shall ignore the variety of types of synonyms (some of which would require different treatment) in order to concentrate on certain types that will further my purposes most directly. And I ignore many cases of explaining meaning that do not aim at synonymy in any sense. Such cases are rife, and important to my view. But I must omit discussing them here.

indexically mediated applications (or imagined projections from these) to 'normal' or 'good' examples ('That's a knife'; 'That woman is walking'). The dialectic consists of an attempt to find a fit between such examples and the characterizations that are dominant in selecting them. To provide meaning, a proposed normative characterization must accord with archetypical applications and must treat the characterizations that competent users actually give, as at least approximations to the norm. The conventional linguistic meaning of a term has been correctly specified when, under these restrictions, the most competent speakers have reached equilibrium on a characterization.

I have pointed up the central role of persuasion in the dialectic. To understand the dialectic one must understand the nature of the persuasion. Sometimes we see the most competent speakers as creating new uses through impressive employment of verbal resources. In such cases, persuasion in the strict sense need not be involved. Imitation may be based primarily on the attractiveness of the style of speech, the power or status of the speaker, or the impressionability of the hearer. But often when someone is seen as more competent it is because he or she is persuasive on matters about which there are objective rights and wrongs and on which substantive reasons have a bearing. The agreement reached is not to a decree, nor is it merely the result of practical reasoning about how to adjust our usage for smoothest communication. The agreement concerns the proper ordering of applications of a term which we have already made or are disposed to make and, ultimately, the correct characterization of the examples that those applications pick out. In the course of the dialectic, we *stand corrected*: we recognize ourselves as convicted of *mistakes*, not merely infelicitous strategies for communication. We come to know something that characterizes empirical entities and sets standards for characterizations to which we regard *ourselves* as antecedently committed. Thus the most competent speakers are pre-eminent not merely because they impress the impressionable. Their influence is based on persuasion that is subject to dispute and cognitive checks.[8]

These disputes usually concern two matters at once. One is how correctly to characterize the relevant entities: whether all chairs have legs or must have legs.

---

[8] Of course, there is nothing about the signs or about the most competent speakers *per se* that makes it right for others to use the signs 'interchangeably'. This point has encouraged the claim that some people's using expressions interchangeably *does not ever* signal that it is cognitively correct for other people to do so. Cases of linguistic correction are assimilated to cases of strategic accommodation for achieving a common communicative purpose. This position is part of Donald Davidson's theory of linguistic interpretation. Cf. his *Inquiries into Truth and Interpretation* (New York: Oxford University Press, 1984), e.g. 'Radical Interpretation'. It is also implicit in Quine's views about translation. Cf. e.g., *Theories and Things* (Cambridge, Mass.: Harvard University Press, 1981), 49–50, and the role of stimulus meaning in the translation theory of *Word and Object* (Cambridge, Mass.: MIT Press, 1960). It seems to me that this position is mistaken. It gives no plausible account of the fact that people frequently do stand corrected for not using (or for using) expressions interchangeably, for making nonmetalinguistic, cognitive mistakes expressed in their own terms. And it has certainly not explained why they ought not stand corrected, or why they are immune from that sort of error. For further discussion, cf. 'Individualism and the Mental', 89–103. (See also note 10 below.)

The other is how to state the meaning of the term as such: whether according to (by) definition chairs have legs, whether according to the standard accepted meaning of 'chair', chairs have legs. The second question is higher-order: either it is explicitly about words, or it otherwise contains an extra intensional context ('according to'). The first question is formulated more directly about extralinguistic entities (chairs). Later I will indicate that these questions are not equivalent. Their answers can come apart. But for now, what is important is that, even where there is no practical point in distinguishing the questions, the second is typically pursued by trying to answer the first. Questions of meaning are pursued by attempting to arrive at factually correct characterizations of empirically accessible entities, the examples.

This point rests on two features of the dialectic which I have already noted. One is the central role that *examples* play in arriving at meaning-giving characterizations for ordinary terms ('Here is a chair and it lacks legs', 'That man is pulling'). The dialectic aims at capturing archetypical applications in a way that sharpens explications that competent speakers naturally give. In being responsible for correctly characterizing core examples, explications of meaning are sensitive to empirically available facts. Examples are ineliminable from our procedures of meaning-giving. For where expressions are regularly and nondelusively applied to perceivable extralinguistic reality, examples necessarily tend to be created and legitimated. (Cf. note 16 below.) If some terms were not so applied, no terms would have objective, empirical meaning.[9]

The second notable feature of the dialectic is that, as the participants work toward an expression of communal meaning, they typically do not discuss the matter as outsiders. Usually, all participants begin the discussion without being able to give a precisely correct normative characterization; all or most would make minor errors in attempting to do so. But this does not entail that any lack object-level thoughts expressible, by the rest of us, with the term whose meaning is in question. If it did, most people would have few if any object-level thoughts so expressible—an absurdity. Participants commonly regard their object-level thoughts (thoughts about, say, chairs) as undergoing correction in the course of the inquiry. They stand corrected on substantive matters. This is exactly what one would expect in view of the role of examples in the discussion.[10]

---

[9] Cf. my 'Belief *De Re*', *The Journal of Philosophy*, 74 6 (June 1977), 338–362, sec. II (Ch. 3 above).

[10] I have conducted the discussion on what seems to me to be the natural and correct view that an individual's terms' meanings sometimes are dependent on commitment to standards for understanding that others can hold him to. (Cf. note 8.) But the argument for the dubitability of 'meaning characterizations' that follows still works if one assumes that only the individual can criticize his or her own characterizations. For the dialectic of persuasion can be seen as carried out purely by oneself. Each characterization one gives oneself could be corrected or come to be doubted because of examples to which one is antecedently committed. The rest of the paper can be preserved, under fairly simple qualifications and transpositions, if one maintains this antisocial picture of meaning. But it seems to me that there is no good reason to maintain it. In fact, if an individual can correct him or herself by reference to publicly available examples, it is hard to see

We may now return to the argument for indubitability from the substitutivity of synonyms (seventh paragraph of this section). Suppose that a given normative characterization is both true and expressive of communal meaning. What would make it indubitable? The answer is alleged to derive from the synonymy of the relevant expressions. The expressions' synonymy is grounded—indeed in a sense consists in—their being treated as interchangeable by the most competent speakers.

Now it is true, as noted, that in ordinary cases synonymy provides a rough norm for understanding and belief: apparent rejection of the relevant statements derived from synonymies is usually a sign of mistake resulting from incomplete understanding. But the nature of authority developed and manifested in the course of the dialectic indicates that criterial statements derived from synonymies are (typically) not indubitable. Authority derives in part from an ability to answer doubts—to persuade oneself and others that erstwhile beliefs do not accord with facts about core examples or with usage to which the participants hold themselves responsible.

The norms for *understanding* provided by synonymies take their force from actual or potential agreement partly stemming from persuasion. But the *truth* of normative characterizations does not rest primarily on agreement. In the first place, agreement is elicited through a process that involves reasoning and citations of extralinguistic fact. In the second place, even when equilibrium is reached—even when one arrives at a complete expression of and agreement on relevant norms, at complete understanding of linguistic meaning—there is no transcendental guarantee that people cannot agree in making mistakes. The authority of the 'most competent' rests on an ability to turn back challenges. But usually there is no method for demonstrating that every possible relevant challenge has been answered. The role of examples in the dialectic makes such assurance impossible. I conclude that our reflective conception of synonymy not only does not support the indubitability of meaning-giving normative charac-terizations for many empirically applicable terms; it actually underwrites and makes inevitable their dubitability.

II

The dubitability of meaning-giving normative characterizations can be con-verted into a demonstration that social practices are not the only or ultimate nonindividualistic factor in individuating mental states and events. I have else-where argued for this view on other grounds. Some mental states (for example, some perceptual states) depend for their identity on the nature of the physical

why the individual should not stand corrected by others using similar considerations. Although each person participating in the dialectic is reflecting on his or her *own language*, there is a willingness to take criticism from others.

environment, in complete independence of social practices. What I want to show here is that, even where social practices are deeply involved in individuating mental states, they are often not the final arbiter. This is because the sort of agreement that fixes a communal meaning and norms for understanding is itself, in principle, open to challenge. The argument that follows articulates this fact.

We begin by imagining a person *A* in our community who has a normal mastery of English. *A*'s early instruction in the use of 'sofa' is mostly ostensive, though he picks up the normal truisms. *A* can use the term reliably. At some point, however, *A* doubts the truisms and hypothesizes that sofas function not as furnishings to be sat on, but as works of art or religious artifacts. He believes that the usual remarks about the function of sofas conceal, or represent a delusion about, an entirely different practice. *A* admits that some sofas have been sat upon, but thinks that most sofas would collapse under any considerable weight and denies that sitting is what sofas are pre-eminently *for*. *A* may attack the veridicality of many of our memories of sofas being sat upon, on the grounds that the memories are products of the delusion.

A is willing to test his hypothesis empirically, and the sociological tests he proposes are reasonable. *A* also offers to demonstrate by experiment how the delusive memories are produced. He is sophisticated, and the tests would require elaborate controls. We can even imagine that the theory is developed so as to be compatible with all past experience that might be thought to have falsified his theory. Thus a normal but sophisticated conception of confirmation accompanies *A*'s unusual theory. We may imagine that if we were to carry out his proposed experiments, *A* would come to admit that his theory is mistaken.

As a second step, imagine a person *B* (or *A* in nonactual circumstances) who is, for all intents and purposes, physically identical to *A*. He has the same physical dispositions, receives substantially the same physical stimulations, produces the same motions, utters the same sounds. Like *A*, *B* hears, though seldom, word forms that are counterparts to the truisms that *A* hears. But in *B*'s situation, these word forms are not taken as truisms; they are contextually appropriate remarks that do not purport to convey a general meaning. (They could be lies or jokes, but it is more natural to take them as not-completely-general contingent truths.) The objects that *B* is confronted with are objects that look like sofas, but are, and are widely known to be, works of art or religious artifacts sold in show-rooms and displayed in people's houses. Many of these objects would collapse under a person's weight. There are no sofas in *B*'s situation, and the word form 'sofa' does not mean *sofa*. Call the relevant objects 'safos'. *B* assumes that most people would take these objects to function primarily as seats and that the remarks he hears are communally accepted truisms. But, like *A*, *B* develops doubts. At least by the time *B* expresses his scepticism and his theory, he is correctly doubting that safos function as furniture to be sat upon. Thus *B*'s thoughts differ from *A*'s.

The self-proclaimed sceptics face different responses when they express their views. *A*'s view is resisted. Although *B* thinks he is opposing received opinion, his claim about what safos are is taken as a matter of course. *A* mistakenly thinks that sofas do not function primarily to be sat upon. *B*'s counterpart thoughts do not involve the notion of sofa and could not correctly be ascribed with 'sofa' in oblique position. He correctly thinks that safos are works of art or religious artifacts. There are numerous correlative differences in the thoughts of the two people which I shall not spell out. *A* is right about the sociolinguistic practice of his comrades, but wrong in the relevant sofa thoughts. *B* is right about safos and wrong about the surrounding sociolinguistic practice (though his usage and beliefs may accord with it perfectly).

The conclusion is that *A* and *B* are physically identical until the time when they express their views. But they have different mental states and events. *A* has numerous mental events involving the notion of sofa. *B*'s scepticism does not involve thinking of anything as a sofa. I do not assume that what I have said about the case in non-propositional-attitude terms *entails* that *A* and *B* have different thoughts. I think, however, that it is overwhelmingly plausible that they do and, more importantly, that there is no general objection to the natural view that they do.

The arguments of 'Individualism and the Mental' and 'Other Bodies' ascribe incomplete linguistic understanding and ignorance of expert knowledge (respectively) to the relevant protagonists. By contrast, *A* may be a sophisticate. He need not lack linguistic understanding or be unapprised of expert or common opinion. The present argument features not incomplete understanding or ignorance of specialized knowledge, but nonstandard theory.

This orientation makes the argument extremely comprehensive in its application and very resistant to objection. Nearly anything can be the topic of nonstandard theorizing. Similar thought experiments apply to knives, clothing, rope, pottery, wheels, boats, tables, watches, houses. Both technical and everyday natural-kind notions clearly fall within the domain of the argument. (Science has generated nonstandard theory with respect to most such notions.) Concepts of other ordinary objects and stuffs, which are not natural kinds, are equally good examples: earth, air, fire, mountains, rivers, bread, food, dung. Notions associated with common verbs are also subject to our argument. What it is to eat, to talk, to sing, to own, to walk, to sleep, to fight, to hunt, to have intercourse can each be subjected to strange theory. The last already has been.

I claim that the argument can be adapted to any substantive notion that applies to physical objects, events, stuffs, properties. The point I wish to press is that the notions may be as ordinary and as observational as one likes. They may be the basic tools of common sense and child rearing.

The thought experiments instantiate three general points. The first is that propositional mental-state and event kinds are individuated by reference to intentional notions. The second is that there are certain relations between an individual and the environment that are necessary to the individual's having certain intentional notions. If one conceives the environment—or the individual's relations to the environment—as varying in certain ways, one must conceive of the individual's intentional notions as varying. The third point is that there is possible slack between the relevant environmental facts and relations to the environment, on one hand, and what the individual knows and can discriminate, on the other. The sort of slack relevant to the present argument is the dubitability of our beliefs about individuation. Clearly this third point applies not only to the special case of meaning-giving normative characterizations, but also at the more general level mentioned in the introduction.

These points schematize the thought experiments. The third point functions in the argument in two ways. It allows ascription of error, ignorance, incomplete understanding, or nonstandard theory in the first stage of the thought experiment. And it allows us to conceive of the relevant environmental facts or the individual's environmental relations as varying without varying the individual's individualistically described nonintentional discriminatory powers. The second point indicates that these variations prevent the ascription of error or ignorance which was possible in the first stage of the thought experiment. Under certain conditions one cannot have acquired certain thoughts. And the first point indicates that mental-state and event kinds have varied between the two stages because intentional notions have varied.

The iconoclastic theory will often require ingenuity. But we can draw upon traditional scepticism to elaborate cases. To discourage attempts to show by transcendental arguments that the protagonist's doubt is incoherent or impossible, I have made the scepticism testable. By traditional standards, the sort we require is quite modest. The protagonist need not believe it; he or she may simply consider it. It need not be possibly true. It is enough that it be epistemically possible in the weak sense that it is thinkable.

III

I now want to defend the argument briefly against some possible rejoinders.[11] Since we shall mainly discuss the first step, let us look briefly at the second in order to lay it aside. Consider a parallel case. Suppose that someone, who can recognize sofas as well as anyone, told us, 'These things, sofas, are not art objects, contrary to what you think; they are pieces of furniture commonly made, intended, and used to be sat upon.' We might regard the person as having delusions about our views. But, barring further evidence, we would regard the opinions about sofas as unproblematic and would concentrate on the sociological perversity. I believe that the point is fairly obvious. Rather than belabor it, I turn to the first step.

---

[11] I discuss related objections in a different context in 'Individualism and the Mental', sec. III (Ch. 5 above).

That step presupposes that widely accepted thoughts about what *X*s are are not indubitable: that it is possible to be uncertain about them. I believe that a claim that *A* literally cannot doubt what he appears to doubt is obviously implausible. But I will consider some ways of making the claim.

It would be unacceptably superficial to gloss the case by claiming that *A* is refusing to speak our language. We have no difficulty understanding that he is raising questions about what sofas really are. The proposals for deciding the question are exactly what we would expect, given a literal interpretation of what he says.

One could claim that, whatever he says, *A* has no thoughts literally attributable to him by using 'sofa' in oblique position, but only metalinguistic thoughts about the word 'sofa'. The metalinguistic maneuver is even less plausible as applied to the present argument than it is as applied to the argument of 'Individualism and the Mental'. *A*'s doubts focus on empirical facts and are to be tested by empirical methods. The metalinguistic maneuver is appropriate when the speaker has no minimal competence. But there need not be any failure or incompleteness of understanding on *A*'s part, much less a lack of minimal competence.

A related objection would hold that *A* thinks only that *what most people think of as sofas* are works of art or religious artifacts. The word 'sofa' should, on this view, be reinterpreted in terms of the italicized phrase. Of course, we must ask how to interpret 'sofa' *in* the italicized phrase. Answering this question will lead to complications that favor my view. But there is a simple reply to the suggestion. We may assume that *A* would say that what most people think of as sofas are sofas. If he makes the distinction between meta- and object-level, we cannot collapse it in interpreting him. What he questions, quite explicitly we may imagine, is not whether these things—or what people think of as sofas—are sofas, but *whether sofas are what people think they are*.

One might hold that the protagonist is to be attributed a 'reduced' notion of sofa, like one an anthropologist might employ on coming into a society that uses a term for objects that he or she can recognize, but whose use he or she has not yet determined. The key to understanding this objection lies in being scrupulous with the term 'reduced notion'. *A* is not an outsider; he has fully learned communal usage. *A* does use 'sofa' in a 'reduced' way in that he prescinds from assuming as true the 'truisms' that explicate the term's communal meaning. But it does not follow that 'sofa' should be re- or de-interpreted in literal attributions of *A*'s propositional attitudes. When one tries to be more specific about what the 'reduced' notion is, difficulties emerge.

Suppose, for example, that the 'reduced' notion were tied to perceptual aspects of sofas. Sofas in the 'reduced' sense are just things that look like those things (where sofas are indicated). Clearly, this notion need not be what *A* utilizes. He may be unwilling to commit himself to how all sofas look or to there being no counterfeits. He may rely on others in determining whether some samples are sofas. In the interests of brevity, I shall not pursue alternative 'reduced' interpretations. I think it is always possible to show, compatibly with the thought experiments, that revised construals of 'sofa' need not capture the protagonist's way of thinking.[12]

One might claim that two ways of describing the dispute must be 'equivalent'. *A* could be said to doubt whether sofas are really such and such, agreeing that *these* are sofas. Or *A* could be said to agree that sofas must be such and such, and doubt whether these are sofas. I think that any claim of this sort is quite mistaken. There may be such cases of descriptive equivalence, but I see no reason or plausibility for the claim that our attributions to *A* are necessarily descriptively equivalent with different ones. In view of the way *A* expresses his reasoning—agreeing that these are sofas, acknowledging the communal agreement on the defining condition, but questioning that condition by attacking its empirical presuppositions—it is difficult to imagine an equally good redescription of the case that would have him accepting the defining condition but doubting alleged exemplifications of it. The reasons that *A* gives support one description rather than the other (cf. note 16).

I think that it must be admitted that the various maneuvers for blocking the first step in the thought experiments, taken as claims about our common conceptions, are not very plausible. There is simply nothing in our ordinary practices that precludes our taking *A* as literally entertaining the doubts I have attributed. Whatever impetus there is behind the objections derives not from antecedent practice, but from the feeling that there must be some way of resisting the attributions. This feeling derives from habits that stem from background philosophical doctrine. The main sources of philosophical opposition to the thought experiment's first step are the claims about indubitability discussed in Section I. These views provide no good reason for regarding our common cognitive practices as in need of revision.[13]

---

[12] This sort of dialectic can be pursued at considerable length. Another possibility for a 'reduced' sense of 'sofa' in attributions to *A* is *thing of a kind relevant to understanding what those things are* (where some sofas are indicated). This sort of suggestion again (at best) confuses reference fixing and way of thinking. If one takes the proposal literally, the italicized phrase expresses a way of thinking of things which is indexical; it will shift its application or referent from occasion to occasion. 'Sofa' in our attributions to *A* is not indexical. (Cf. 'Other Bodies', sec. II (Ch. 4 above).) We can build into the thought experiments behavioral tests to help establish the point. For example, it could emerge under questioning that *A* would regard himself as subject to correction if he were to allow the referent of 'sofa' to shift with context. One could perhaps modify the italicized phrase to *thing of a kind relevant to understanding what I (or we) usually refer to when I have this sort of experience (or, alternatively, when I use 'sofa')*. But now it is clear that no one but a philosopher would think of sofas in that complex, meta-level way. A complex analysis or theory of reference should not be conflated with the way *A* thinks of sofas. The counterfeit is recognized by Frege's test. Such analyses, even if true, are informative. *A* might have to reason to decide whether they are true. So the analysans need not yield the way *A* thinks of sofas. *A* might even lack notions that occur in the analysans without lacking his notion of sofa. No version of the reduced-sense line of objection that I know of is acceptable.

[13] There are, of course, the indeterminacy theses of Quine and Davidson and other views that challenge the objectivity and cognitive status of mentalistic attributions. For the indeterminacy theses, see Quine, *Word and Object*, and Davidson, *Inquiries into Truth and Interpretation*. These views are somewhat orthogonal to our primary theses here, since they bear more directly on the

IV

The story inherited from positivism holds that understanding sufficient for responsible ratiocination—which is identified with understanding ordinary linguistic meaning—necessarily requires recognizing the truth of normative statements derived from synonymies. There are two things wrong with the story: the two sorts of understanding should not be identified; and neither sort necessarily requires belief in the relevant statements.

Consideration of the dialectic for arriving at meaning-giving characterizations (Section I) indicates different types or levels of understanding. There is, first, understanding sufficient to engage in responsible ratiocination with a notion expressed by a term.[14] We presuppose that a person has this sort of understanding when we use the term in oblique position literally to specify attitudes—when we treat the person as responsible to cognitive criticism by reference to the relevant normative characterizations. Such responsibility is usually incurred before normal competence is achieved. But even normal competence—the sort of understanding that one can reasonably expect of a person who is a member of the community—typically throws up mistaken explications that meaning-giving normative characterizations must correct. Finally, there is full understanding of the meaning-giving normative characterization—the ideal, articulable mastery achieved by the most competent speakers or by an individual who fully understands his or her own idiolectic usage. The critical point is that neither understanding sufficient for ratiocination nor normal competence requires full understanding.

Moreover, understanding the meaning-giving characterization for a term does not necessitate acknowledging it as true. It is sufficient to be able to apply the term correctly and to give approximations to standard characterizations that may be adjusted under reflection, criticism, or new information. There is a potential gap between even the best understanding of accepted usage and belief. The consensus of the most competent speakers can be challenged. Usually such challenges stem from incomplete understanding. But, as our arguments in Sections I and II indicate, they need not. One may always ask whether the most competent speakers' characterizations of examples (or one's own best characterizations)

---

status of our conceptions than on their character. (It is doubtful, incidentally, that Davidson's view is individualistic.) However, I find unpersuasive all current doctrines that hold that mentalistic discourse is noncognitive or even (as a matter of principle) less cognitive or 'factual' than physicalistic discourse. Some of what I say here and in 'Individualism and Psychology' (Ch. 9 above) is material for supporting this view. In this latter article I argue that nonindividualistic, mentalistic methods of individuation are legitimate for and present in scientific explanation.

[14] Animal ratiocination is ontogenetically prior to any use or understanding of linguistic symbols. In omitting animal thought from the present discussion I am not overlooking or denigrating it. I think, however, that it does not involve certain sorts of intellectual responsibility, the norms for which are my present concern.

are *correct*, and whether all examples usually counted archetypical *should* be so counted.

The impetus to accept these conclusions, and their anti-individualistic corollaries, already lies implicit, I think, in Quine's first point against positivism. I have in mind his point that there is no separating truths of meaning or truths of logic (or criterial truths, or truths of reason, or necessary truths) from truths of fact. (Cf. note 5.) In stating a truth of meaning (however one construes the notion), one is not stating a degenerate truth. To put this crudely: in explicating one's 'meanings', one is equally stating nondegenerate truths—'facts'. So giving a true explication is not separable from getting the facts right. It is a short step from this point to the observation that truths of meaning are dubitable.

Of course, the key idea is much older. Our cases develop a theme from the Socratic dialogues: Thought can correct meaning. Although dialectic typically serves to correct wayward belief and incomplete understanding, there remains the possibility that the discussion will overflow the boundaries of the established norms. A conventional norm is nearly always subject to the most general evaluative question: 'Is it true?' If new empirical facts or new insights are imported into the discussion, the background assumptions of normative characterizations may be undermined, and the characterizations themselves may be shown to be mistaken.

The fact that thought can correct meaning has significant consequences for a philosophy of mind. A consequence I shall develop is a distinction between cognitive value and conventional (or idiolectic) linguistic meaning. There are two closely related arguments for this distinction. One derives from the possibility of doubt. The other issues from reflection on the epistemic possibility of radical theoretical change.

We must be able to specify a person's thoughts in situations where meaning-giving normative characterizations come under fire. Since it is possible to doubt such characterizations (and their logical consequences), it is possible to find them informative. Doubts of such characterizations ('Sofas are pieces of furniture ... meant for sitting') are supported by publicly recognized means different from those which would support doubt of the corresponding identity judgment (say, the judgment that sofas are sofas). In short, such characterizations have different cognitive values from those of the corresponding identity judgments. So in interpreting a specification of a belief that sofas are pieces of furniture ... meant for sitting, one must assign different cognitive values or units of potential information—to the conventionally synonymous phrases ('sofa' and 'piece of furniture ... meant for sitting') as they occur in such specifications. Thus cognitive value and conventional meaning should be distinguished.[15]

---

[15] The argument, of course, is a variant of Frege's for distinguishing senses from one another and from denotation. The argument should not be construed in a narrowly linguistic manner. Its aim is to illumine the cognitive phenomena underlying the language about belief. Cf. 'On Sense and Reference', in P. T. Geach and Max Black (eds.), *Translations from the Philosophical Writings of*

The same conclusion can be derived from considering possible linguistic or conceptual change pursuant to disagreement over meaning-giving normative characterizations. For example, it is possible to doubt that sofas are all and only pieces of furniture of a certain construction meant or made for sitting. If the doubt were to prove well founded, the conventional meaning of 'sofa' would be forced to change. But despite the change, it might remain appropriate, before and after the change, to attribute propositional attitudes involving the notion of sofa. Both before and after, *A* and his opponents would agree that *these are sofas*. Before and after, they would be characterized as having disagreed over whether all and only *sofas* are furnishings of a certain structure made or meant for sitting.

This situation bears some analogy to cases of theoretical change in science. Dalton and his predecessors *defined* 'atom' (and its translations) in terms of indivisibility. Major theoretical changes intervened. The definition was discarded. Despite the change, we want to say, Dalton wrongly thought that *atoms* were indivisible: despite his erroneous definition, he had the 'concept' of atom (not merely the referent of 'atom'). I think that this sort of attribution is defensible in a wide variety of central examples of scientific developments, even in the light of Kuhnian insights into scientific revolutions. Although I cannot develop the point here, the distinction between theoretical meaning and cognitive value is in many ways analogous to that between conventional meaning and cognitive value.

It would be a mistake, however, to assimilate commonsense notions to a theoretical paradigm. Although meaning-giving characterizations from ordinary terms or notions are vulnerable to theoretical change, they differ from theoretical definitions of terms whose original home is a systematic theory, not only in that they are more stable and in that sense less vulnerable to theoretical criticism. They also differ in the means by which they are known and checked and in the ways in which they are vulnerable. (This is one durable element in the problematic observational/theoretical distinction.) The dialectic that we have been exploring seeks to derive characterizations from reflection

---

Gottlob Frege (Oxford: Basil Blackwell, 1966). Although there are differences between my view of 'cognitive value' and Frege's, the conclusion of my argument as so far stated is also Fregean in spirit. In Frege's view, what sense an expression expressed was fixed by a deep rationale underlying the expression's use and understanding—a rationale that might not have been understood by anyone. Cf. my 'Frege on Extensions of Concepts, from 1884 to 1903', *The Philosophical Review*, 93, (1984), 3–34, esp. 3–12, 30–34; repr. as ch. 7 in *Truth, Thought, Reason*; and 'Frege on Sense and Conventional Meaning', in David Bell (ed.), *The Analytical Tradition in Contemporary Philosophy* (New York: Cambridge University Press, 1986). Other, lesser reasons for distinguishing meaning and cognitive value appear in my 'Sinning against Frege', *The Philosophical Review*, 88, 3 (July 1979), 398–432; repr. as ch. 5 in *Truth, Thought, Reason*. I might add here that, although I have been speaking of cognitive value and conventional linguistic meaning as if they were different *entities*, nothing so far said commits me to regarding them in this way. One might take the expressions as labels for different methods of interpretation. The pressure to speak of entities, which is I think more insistent in the case of cognitive value, derives from providing a systematic semantical interpretation of the relevant discourse.

on perceived examples picked out by common indexical usage. By contrast, the natural sciences, whose methodology we best understand, do not expect to reach their normative characterizations through simple reflection on usage or common perceptual experiences. Theoretical terms are not indexically applied to perceived objects. ('This is a quark; see the quark'—not kosher.) Ordinary words (or notions) for ordinary entities are given their life and meaning through such applications. Not only meaning-giving characterizations for these words but also doubts about these characterizations must accord with the bulk of ordinary, indexically aided, perception-based uses of these words—uses which yield the archetypical examples. This fact is part of what underlies the relative security of commonsense notions for observables.[16]

On the other hand, the fact that ordinary conceptions are more familiar and less embedded in a systematic theory does not indicate that normative characterizations involving them are indubitable or immune from theoretical intrusion. Criticism can emerge unforeseen from almost any quarter. This open-endedness is a matter of principle. It motivates the distinction between cognitive value and conventional linguistic meaning.

There was never any obvious reason why the two notions should coincide. They are responsible to different paradigms, and their explanatory purposes are distinct. Cognitive value is fitted to explicating possible differences in attitudes—cognitive perspective. Such differences are invoked to explain action and epistemic inquiry. Frege's test for differential dubitability, when accompanied with requirements that doubt be supportable by publicly recognized methods, is a defeasible but profoundly valuable tool in individuating cognitive values. Attributions of continuity through changes of conventional or theoretical meaning provide another touchstone for cognitive value. Conventional meaning, by contrast, is fitted to describing reflective agreement on the means of conveying, in short order, accepted usage. Dialectic ending in reflective equilibrium among competent speakers is a defeasible but reliable tool for individuating conventional meanings.

The two notions differ not only in their explanatory or descriptive purposes but in the ways they provide a basis for applying norms in our linguistic and cognitive practice. Conventional meaning provides norms for ideal competence by reference to which a person's usage and beliefs may be corrected. The normative function of cognitive value is more complex. On one hand, the notion

[16] It is, for example, appropriate (as distinguished from merely possible) to doubt the existence of entities categorized by an ordinary notion, like *sofa*, only by appealing to doubts about the veridicality (referentiality) of typical perceptual experiences of entities so categorized. 'Ordinary' notions are those, unlike *phlogiston* or *witch*, which in an ordinary sense and in ordinary circumstances are thought to apply to entities that are perceived and are not taught or applied by reference to a theory that depends heavily on assumptions about events or powers that are not commonly perceived. As long as archetypical perceptual applications ('That's a sofa') are not criticized wholesale, doubts about normative characterizations of such entities categorized by ordinary notions can be quite radical without undermining the basic usefulness of the categorizing notion.

marks the minimum competence necessary for ratiocination specifiable with the term. To be attributed the 'concept' of sofa—and to have one's attitudes literally and correctly specified with 'sofa' in oblique occurrence—one must be able to use the term 'sofa' sufficiently well to be attributed mistakes and true beliefs about what sofas are. On the other hand, the notion of cognitive value marks the openness of established normative characterizations to correction by reference to nonconventional theory. One may use one's concept of sofa to criticize conventional meaning.

Earlier in this section we distinguished different levels of understanding, culminating in ideal, articulable mastery of a conventional normative characterization. Is there a further sort of ideal understanding associated with cognitive value? There is no simple answer. In order to think with a given cognitive value (or concept), one need only attain the minimal level of understanding mentioned earlier. Usually, the best understanding one can achieve of a cognitive value is that offered by accepted normative characterizations and whatever background information accompanies them. Thus full understanding of cognitive value is normally not distinct from ideal understanding of ordinary usage and meaning. (In such cases, the cognitive value expressed by a term is, however, still individuated differently from its linguistic meaning.) When thought does correct meaning, one may achieve a revised understanding of cognitive value based on theoretical realization that goes beyond ordinary usage and meaning. Understanding of this sort bears comparison with the sort of ultimate insight, championed by the rationalist tradition, that was regarded as concomitant with deep foundational knowledge. Perhaps foundations and ultimacy are not to be expected. But our cognitive commitments and potential go beyond the boundaries set by conventional (or idiolectic) linguistic meaning.

V

A central aim, some have said the central aim, of the analytic tradition has been to give an account of thought and meaning by reference to some pattern of activity by language-users or thinkers. There are various positions on the relative priority of thought and meaning. One approach, distinctive of this century, is to explicate thought in terms of linguistic meaning and thinking in terms of using symbols with such meaning. A more traditional view is to explicate linguistic meaning in terms of thought. A third view, which I regard as correct, is that the two notions are interwoven in complex ways which render it impossible fully to analyze one in terms of the other. But with all these approaches, a syndrome of philosophizing characteristic of the analytic tradition has been to explicate both mind and meaning in terms of some pattern of activity: behavior, use, functional role, verification or confirmation procedure, computational role, subjective probability metric, teaching or interpretation procedure, illocutionary or perlocutionary act potential—and so on.

Surely, some pattern of actual physical, linguistic, or mental activity is essential to investing any given act with linguistic meaning or cognitive value. Such activity is even, I think, necessary to making meaning and cognitive value possible. Several of the use-based accounts have illumined and deepened this point. But, when these accounts have posed as reductive explanations, they have been notably unilluminating. Most have been extremely programmatic. And where they have become more specific, they have become clearly implausible. Ironically, these implausibilities have often been made the basis of sceptical attack on intentional notions. I think the proper object of blame is the assumption that a reduction must be possible.

One significant obstacle to reduction is the complexity forced on reductive accounts by the failure of individualism. Both the conventional linguistic meaning and the cognitive value expressed by an individual may vary with the individual's environment, even as the individual's activities, individualistically and nonintentionally specified, are held constant.

Despite these similarities, conventional linguistic meaning and cognitive value relate to use, or nearly any actual pattern of activity, in significantly different ways. I shall first sketch an application of the point to linguistic use, and then generalize it.

Schematically, our thesis is that in certain senses, 'use', socially conceived, necessarily 'fixes' conventional linguistic meaning; but 'use' (individualistically or socially conceived) does not necessarily 'fix' cognitive value. This general schema comprehends a variety of specific instantiations. I shall try to articulate two.

The most straightforward specification of the thesis proceeds from an intentional conception of use and an epistemic conception of fixing. Ordinary, thorough, unimpeded, rational reflection by members of a community on the totality of their actual communal practices—all patterns of assertion, deference, teaching, persuasion—would necessarily suffice to yield a characterization that in fact gives the term's conventional meaning. This fact reflects the common observation that there can be nothing hidden or esoteric about the public conventional meaning of an expression. Such meaning derives from ideal projections from what people do and what people believe about what they do.

But this limitative point does not apply to the relation between 'use' and cognitive value. Reflection on and analysis of linguistic use at any given time need not suffice to explicate cognitive value correctly. For the question of whether communally (or individually) acceptable normative characterizations *should be accepted*—whether the totality of communal (or individual) practices *should be revised*—can always be raised. Such questions may survive reflection on actual usage and may lead, by means of new theory, to changed practice. Cognitive value partly functions to make such questions possible and to interpret cases where their answer forces revisions in conventional meaning and actual use.

A second version of my thesis employs a noncognitive conception of fixing. Hold constant all discriminations that members of a person's community make, or are disposed to make, with a given term at a given time. (One may *include* among these discriminations all beliefs and assertions expressed with help of the term, with the proviso that one leaves unspecified the meaning and cognitive value of the term.) Then the linguistic meaning of the term at the given time could not possibly vary; but its cognitive value could—if the nature of the environment, or the subjects' relations to it, were in certain ways varied.

These points about the distinction between conventional meaning and cognitive value generalize to nearly all other conceptions of meaning that are similarly explicated or 'fixed' in terms of conformity to some actual pattern of activity or dispositions to activity. For insofar as meaning is representational or purports to convey information, the question of whether the information has been correctly identified or characterized can be raised. One can thereby question whether the relevant underlying pattern of activity *should be as it is*. Cognitive values are individuated in such a way as to allow such radical questions to be raised.

Intentional mental states and events are individuated in terms of cognitive value. We have no other systematic, cognitively informative way of individuating them. Since communally accepted characterizations as well as expert opinion can be doubted, the ultimate authority regarding the application, explication, and individuation of a subject's intentional mental events does not derive solely from the actual motions, behavior, actions, usage, practices, understanding, or even (except trivially) thoughts of any person or social group. Our conception of mind is responsive to intellectual norms which provide the permanent possibility of challenge to any actual practices of individuals or communities that we could envisage.

11 *Wherein is Language Social?*

In this paper I will develop two limited senses in which the study of language, specifically semantics, is the study of a partly social phenomenon. These senses are compatible with the idea that the study of language is a part of individual psychology. I will argue for this standpoint from some obvious facts about human interaction together with elements from a view, which I have supported elsewhere, that the semantics of a language is partly dependent on relations between individual speakers and their physical environments. Most of what I say about language will apply to individual psychology. I begin by discussing two background senses in which language is social.

Language is social in that interaction with other persons is psychologically necessary to learn language. Some philosophers have made the further claim that there is some conceptually necessary relation between learning or having a language and being in a community. I do not accept this view. I assume only that it is a psychologically important fact that we cannot learn language alone.

Language is social in another sense. There is a rough, commonsensical set of languages—English, German, and so on—and dialects of these languages, that are in some vague sense shared by social groups. Of course, problems attend taking commonsense languages to be objects of systematic study. The normal divisions among languages correspond to no significant linguistic distinctions.

But this issue is really quite complex. In studying language or dialect in a systematic way, we commonly do not specify who uses the construction at issue, and we commonly assume that there is common ground among a large number of speakers—even though we are studying matters that are not species-wide. In historical studies, for example, we must abstract from individual usage in order to get any generality at all. We simply do not know enough about the quirks of individual usage to make an interesting subject matter: one must study such things as the history of a word, understood more or less in the commonsensical, trans-individual way. In semantics, one provides theories of reference or meaning in natural language again in nearly total disregard of individual variations, even for phenomena that are by no means universal or species-wide.

These facts of theoretical usage suggest that there is some theoretical point to taking dialects or other linguistic units as abstractions from some sorts of social patterns. Perhaps the abstractions warrant thinking of individual variation as an interference to be accounted for after the primary theorizing is done. I think that there is something to this point of view. Nothing that I will say contradicts it. But the point of view is limited. It cannot provide anything like a complete picture.

One source of limitation derives from the wide variation among any group of individuals on numerous non-universal aspects of language use. People do not share exactly the same vocabulary, for example. People often use words in idiosyncratic ways that exempt them from evaluation by any socially accepted standard. Such quirks motivate the bromide that one should not invoke majority usage "imperialistically" to fit individual variations into a standardized mold. These two points alone make it likely that no two people speak the same "version" of any natural language or dialect.

There is a general reason for variation among individuals' language use. Languages depend on the experiences, usage, and psychological structures of individuals. Variation in individuals' word meaning, for example, is the natural result of the close relation between meaning and belief. Although the precise character of this relation is controversial and although intuitively meaning does not vary as freely as belief, some variation in meaning with individual belief is inevitable. The interplay between meaning and belief is a special case of the interplay between actual languages and psychology—about which similar points regarding individual variation could be made. It is therefore plausible that in studying language one must study the languages of individuals, idiolects.

These considerations suggest aiming for a science of universal aspects of language and for a study of non-universal aspects of language, both of which are tailored to the usage and psychology of individual speakers. I accept this much. Some have drawn the further inference that such a program's method of kind-individuation is independent of any considerations of social interaction among individuals. I will argue that this inference is unsound.

The inference just cited may be suggested by Chomsky's methodology for studying syntax. Actually, Chomsky is more cautious. What he is firm about is that there is a study of *universal grammar* which can be investigated independently of the diversity among individuals, and that linguistics (at least the sort of linguistics he pursues)—both universal and individual—is a part of individual psychology.[1] I shall argue that social factors may enter in complex ways into individual psychology and the semantics of idiolects.

Unlike many philosophers, I do not find Chomsky's methodology misguided. His views that linguistic structures are real, that some of them are universal, and that they are mental structures seem to me substantially more plausible than

---

[1] Noam Chomsky, *Knowledge of Language: Its Nature, Origin, and Use* (New York: Praeger, 1986), 18. Chomsky recognizes the possibility of "other kinds of study of language that incorporate social structure and interaction". Chomsky's methodology for studying language goes back to *Aspects of the Theory of Syntax* (Cambridge, Mass.: MIT Press, 1965).

alternatives.[2] Arguments that we may speak merely in accidental accord with the structures postulated in linguistics, or that there is no scientific way to investigate universality of syntax, or that generative linguistics has no direct place in psychology, seem to me unconvincing and indicative of mistaken methodology. I shall not review these arguments.

The study of universal grammar is informed by certain simplifying idealizations. The idealization most relevant to this discussion attempts to cut through the variation and "noise" associated with usage in a community. The linguist considers an idealized "speech community" that is "uniform"—internally consistent in its linguistic practice (cf. n. 1). Without denying that individuals are members of a community, and without denying that they could develop into mature language-users only because they are, the idealization attempts to study an individual in complete abstraction from the actual presence of others. Any given individual is taken as a representative having universal linguistic abilities or cognitive structures. The assumption is that underlying the variation among individuals, there is a common initial linguistic capacity that is specific enough to have certain definite structural features and that is capable of further linguistic development in certain delimited and specifiable ways. Variations in individual grammar are taken to be results of a fixing of parameters from a set of delimited alternatives.

For present purposes, I accept this idealization regarding universal grammar. It has received substantial support through its fruitful application both in pure linguistics and in developmental psycho-linguistics. (I will conjecture about a qualification on the idealization as applied to individual syntax later; cf. n. 4.) I believe that the methodology accompanying this idealization has some application to universal and individual aspects of semantics. But here the situation is, I think, more complex. In particular, I think that relations to others do affect the individuation of some semantical kinds. To consider the role of social elements in semantics, I want to start further back.

In recent years I have argued that the natures of many of our thoughts are individuated *non-individualistically*. I shall have to presuppose these arguments. But according to their common conclusion, the individuation of many thoughts, of intentional kinds, depends on the nature of the environment with which we interact. What information we process—for example, what perceptions we have—is dependent on the properties in the empirical world that members of our species normally interact with when they are having perceptual experiences. What empirical concepts we think with are fixed partly through relations to the kinds of things we think about.[3]

---

[2] This view hinges not only on intuitive linguistic data but on studies of development, learning, psychological simplicity, language deficit, psychological processing, and so on. See, e.g., Noam Chomsky, *Lectures on Government and Binding* (Dordvecht: Foris, 1982), ch. 1.

[3] "Non-individualistic" in this context does not entail "social". The environment can be either physical surroundings or social surroundings. I begin with physical surroundings alone.—

It is easy to confuse this view with another more obvious one. It is obvious that if we did not interact with the empirical or social worlds, we would not have the thoughts we do. Our thoughts and perceptions are causally dependent on the environment. My view concerns not merely causation; it concerns individuation.

Distinguishing the point about individuation from the point about causation is easiest to do by putting the point about individuation in terms of supervenience. Our thoughts do not supervene on the nature and history of our bodies, considered in isolation from the environment, in the following sense: It is in principle possible for one to have had different thoughts from one's actual thoughts, even though one's body had the same molecular history, specified in isolation from its relations to a broader physical environment. The same chemical effects on our bodies might have been induced by different antecedent conditions (perhaps, but not necessarily, including different causal laws). The point about individuation is not only that actual thoughts (like actual chemical effects) depend on the actual nature of the environment. Even if the effects had been chemically the same, it is possible in some cases for the thoughts, the information about the environment carried in our mental states, to have been different—if the environmental antecedents of those effects had been relevantly different. The kind of thought that one thinks is not supervenient on the physical make-up of one's body, specified in isolation from its relations to the environment. Thought kinds are individuated in a way that depends on relations one bears to kinds in one's physical environment. On this view individual psychology itself is not purely individualistic.

The failure of supervenience in no ways casts doubt on investigations of neural or biological realizations of mental structures. The failure of supervenience requires only that the identity of certain mental structures be dependent on relations between the individual and the environment. The identity of a heart depends on its function in the whole body—on its relations to parts of the body outside the heart. In a crudely analogous way, the identities of some mental kinds depend on those kinds' relations to entities beyond the individual's body. They depend on cognitive function, on obtaining information, in an environment in something like the way the kind *heart* depends for its individuation on the function of the heart in the body that contains it.

The failure of supervenience also does not entail that an individual psychology that takes its kinds not to be supervenient on an individual's body must study—or make theoretical reference to—the relations between individual and

---

The arguments against individualism that I shall be presupposing may be found in Tyler Burge, "Individualism and the Mental", *Midwest Studies of Philosophy*, 4 (1979), 73–121; *idem*, "Other Bodies", in A. Woodfield (ed.), *Thought and Object* (Oxford: Oxford University Press, 1982); *idem*, "Individualism and Psychology", *Philosophical Review*, 95 (1986), 3–45; *idem*, "Cartesian Error and the Objectivity of Perception", in P. Pettit and J. McDowell (eds.), *Subject, Thought, and Context* (Oxford: Oxford University Press, 1986); *idem*, "Intellectual Norms and Foundations of Mind", *The Journal of Philosophy*, 83 (1986), 697–720 (Chs. 5, 4, 9, 7, 10 in this volume.) Different arguments bring out different environmental interdependencies.

environment that are presupposed in the individuation of its kinds. It is open to psychology to take such kinds as primitive, leaving their presupposed individuation conditions to some other science or to philosophy. I believe this often to be the right course.

The arguments for anti-individualistic individuation of mental kinds can be extended in relatively obvious ways to show that much of semantics is not purely individualistic.[4]

The claim that semantics is non-individualistic is not merely a claim that the *referents* of an individual's words could in principle vary even though the history of the individual's body, considered in isolation from the environment, were held constant.[5] The claim is more comprehensive. The empirical referents

---

[4] Are syntactical elements and structures individualistically individuated? This question is close to the issue regarding the autonomy of syntax. But one should not identify the two questions. The discussions of the autonomy of syntax concern whether some non-syntactical parameter must be mentioned in stating syntactical generalizations. Our question concerns not the parameters mentioned in stating rules of syntax, but the individuation of the syntactical elements. Syntax could be non-individualistic and yet be autonomous (see the preceding paragraph in the text). Evidence has been suggesting that syntax is much more nearly autonomous than common sense might have realized. My reasons for thinking that individual psychology is non-individualistic in its individuation of some thought kinds have nothing directly to do with syntax. They derive purely from considerations that, within the study of language, would be counted semantic. What is at issue then is whether because of some functional relation to semantics, some syntactical kinds are non-individualistically individuated.

I think it arguable that much of syntax is individualistically individuated, or at least no less individualistically individuated than ordinary neural or biological kinds are. But it seems likely that lexical items are individuated in a content-sensitive way. Words or morphemes with the same phonetic and structural-syntactic properties are distinguished because of etymological or other semantical differences. Even if it turned out that every such lexical difference were accompanied by other syntactic or phonological differences, it would seem plausible that the latter differences were dependent on the former. So it seems plausible that the lexical differences do not supervene (in our specified sense) on other syntactic or phonological differences.

Although most philosophers write as if only word types are ambiguous, it is clear that word tokens are often ambiguous. It is arguable that *only* word tokens, never word types, are ambiguous. I do not find this view plausible: words with different but etymologically and semantically related senses are individuated as the same word type. But the view is a useful antidote to habits in the philosophy of language. In any case, word individuation appears to be semantically dependent.

Assuming this to be true, and assuming that semantics is non-individualistic, it follows that what it is to be a given word sometimes depends (in the way that what it is to be a given meaning or concept depends) on relations between the individual and the objective, empirical world. *Whether* this is true about lexical items, and how far it might extend beyond the individuation of lexical items, is a question I leave open here. The answer will not very much affect the practice of generative grammar, since environmental relations need not be mentioned in syntax. But it will affect our understanding of the place of syntax in our wider theorizing about the world.

Similar issues might be raised about some universal syntactic categories (animate, agent, etc.). And as James Higginbotham has pointed out to me, analogous questions may be raised about the relation between phonology and ordinary perception. Ordinary perceptual kinds are not individualistically individuated (see n. 6). It may be that this fact should affect our understanding of perception studies in phonology.

[5] This view, though not trivial, is a consequence of a view that is widely accepted. It is a consequence of the work of Donnellan and Kripke, and indeed Wittgenstein, on reference. I will not defend it here. But I will develop a reason for its inevitability below. Numerous examples indicate that an individual's proper names, kind terms, demonstratives, and various other parts of speech

of an individual's word are obviously not themselves part of the individual's psychology, or point of view. Thoughts are the individual's perspective on the world. And meanings or senses are, very roughly speaking, a speaker's way of expressing such perspective in language. They are what an individual understands and thinks in the use of his words. My thesis is that even (many of) those aspects of semantics that would be reflected in meaning or sense, and that would be represented in an individual's thought processes, in his psychology, are non-individualistically individuated. What a word means, even in an individual's idiolect, can depend on environmental factors, beyond an individual's body, considered as a molecular structure.

I think it plausible that some meanings of words are universal to the species in that if a person has the requisite perceptual experience and acquires language normally, the person will have words with those meanings. A likely source of such universality is perceptual experience itself. It appears that early vision is language-independent and constant for the species. Because of the evolution of our species, we are fashioned in such a way that perceptual experience will automatically trigger the application of perceptual notions associated with innate dispositions. Linguistic expressions for such perceptual notions as edge, surface, shadow, under, curved, physical object, and so on, are likely to be tied to elementary, universal perceptual experience, or to innate states fixed by species-ancestors' perceptual interactions with the world.

Many such notions can be shown to be non-individualistically individuated. It is possible to construct hypothetical cases in which the optical laws of the world are different, and the interactions of one's species with elements of the world are different, so that different perceptual notions, carrying different perceptual information, are innate or universally acquired. But in these same cases, one can coherently conceive an individual whose bodily history is molecularly identical to one whose perceptual notions are like ours. (The optical differences need not prevent, in certain special cases, a given individual from being affected in the same chemical way by different causal antecedents in the empirical world.) So the perceptual content or information of his experience is different—he has different perceptions—even though his body is, individualistically specified, the same. In such a case, it is clear that the meanings or senses of his words for objective, perceptual properties will also be different.[6]

have definite referents even though the individual could not, by other means, discriminate the referent from other possible or actual entities that might have been in an appropriate relation to the individual's words—other entities that might have been the referent even though the individual's body could have remained molecularly the same. See Saul Kripke, *Naming and Necessity* (Cambridge, Mass.: Harvard University Press, 1980); Keith Donnellan, "Proper Names and Identifying Descriptions", in D. Davidson and G. Harman (eds.), *Semantics of Natural Languages* (Dordrecht: Reidel, 1972); Hilary Putnam, "Is Semantics Possible?" and "The Meaning of 'Meaning' ", in *Philosophical Papers*, ii (Cambridge: Cambridge University Press, 1975); and numerous other works.

[6] See David Marr, *Vision* (San Francisco: W. H. Freeman and Co., 1982) for a very explicit statement of the non-individualistic methodology. For a more general review of the point that anti-individualistic individuation is implicit in all scientific theories of perception, see Neil Stillings,

Thus the view that certain concepts and meanings are non-individualistically individuated is compatible with those concepts and meanings being innate. The effect of the environment in determining psychological kinds may occur in the evolution of the species as well as in the experiential history of the individual.

Whether or not they are universal, virtually all concepts and meanings that are applied to public objects or events that we know about empirically are non-individualistically individuated. Such meanings attributed by semantics, and such concepts attributed by individual psychology, are non-individualistic to the core.

So far I have stated an anti-individualistic view of psychology and semantics that is entirely independent of social considerations. The failure of individualism derives, at this stage, purely from relations between the individual and the empirically known physical world. Now I want to use considerations that underlie this non-social anti-individualism to show how social elements enter the individuation of linguistic and psychological kinds. In a sense I will derive principles underlying social anti-individualistic thought experiments (see my "Individualism and the Mental") from obvious facts, together with some of the principles underlying non-social anti-individualistic thought experiments.

As a means of setting background, I begin with Chomsky's suggestion for incorporating social elements into semantics. Responding to Putnam's "division of linguistic labor", he writes.[7]

In the language of a given individual, many words are semantically indeterminate in a special sense: The person will defer to 'experts' to sharpen or fix their reference. ... In the lexicon of this person's language, the entries [for the relevant words] will be specified to the extent of his or her knowledge, with an indication that details are to be filled in by others, an idea that can be made precise in various ways but without going beyond the study of the system of knowledge of language of a particular individual. Other social aspects of language can be regarded in a like manner—although this is not to deny the possibility or value of other kinds of study of language that incorporate social structure and interaction.

Chomsky's proposal is certainly part of a correct account of the individual's reliance on others. I do not want to dispute the cases that he specifically discusses. I think, however, that the proposal cannot provide a complete

"Modularity and Naturalism in Theories of Vision", in. L. Garfield (ed.), *Modularity in Knowledge Representation and Natural-Language Understanding* (Cambridge, Mass.: MIT Press, 1987). For the cited philosophical arguments, see Burge, "Individualism and Psychology", and "Cartesian Error". The former article discusses Marr's theory. For perception, the point is really pretty obvious even apart from philosophical argument: perceptual states are individuated by reference to physical properties that bear appropriate relations to the subjects' states or those of his species-ancestors.

Although Chomsky does not discuss non-individualistic features of the visual system, he clearly makes a place for psychological states that have a different genesis and different conditions for individuation from those psychological states that constitute the structures of universal grammar. He counts such states part of the 'conceptual system', and uses vision as a prime example (see Chomsky, *Rules and Representations*).

[7] Chomsky, *Knowledge of Language*, 18. The relevant articles by Hilary Putnam are "Is Semantics Possible?" and "The Meaning of 'Meaning'".

account. My first concern is that it might be read to imply that in all relevant cases, the reference of an individual's own word is semantically indeterminate: determinateness only appears in the idiolects of the "experts". (I am not sure whether Chomsky intends the proposal in this way.) Sometimes the reference of a relevant term is incomplete or vague. But sometimes, even in cases where the individual's substantive *knowledge in explicating* features of the referent is vague, incomplete, or riddled with false belief, the reference is as determinate as anyone else's. The reference of an individual's word is not always dependent on what the individual knows or can specify about the referent. When the individual defers to others, it is not in all cases to sharpen or fix the reference, but to sharpen the individual's explicative knowledge of a referent that is already fixed. Our and the individual's own attitudes toward the specification of the reference often makes this clear (see n. 5).

For present purposes, brief reflection on various natural kind terms that we use without expert knowledge should make the point intuitive. One might use 'feldspar', 'tiger', 'helium', 'water', 'oak', or 'spider', with definite referents even though one cannot oneself use one's background knowledge to distinguish the referent from all possible counterfeits. Knowledge obtained from better-informed people—they need not be experts—often tells one more about the standard kinds we all refer to with these words. It does not *in general* change the referents of our words. (This is not to deny that sometimes experts' terms have different, more technical meaning than lay usage of the same word forms.) The referents of such kind terms is simply not fixed entirely by the individual's background knowledge. Individuals often recognize this about their own terms. Although this point could be supported through numerous cases, and through more general considerations, I think that it is fairly evident on reflection. I shall assume it in what follows.

Even granted this qualification, Chomsky's proposal will not provide a complete account of the individual's own language—or even of the individual's knowledge of his or her idiolect. For in some cases, an individual's explicational ability not only does not suffice to fix the referent of the individual's word; it does not exhaust the meaning expressed by a word in the individual's idiolect.

I distinguish between a lexical item and the explication of its meaning that articulates what the individual would give, under some reflection, as his understanding of the word. Call the former "the word" and the latter "the entry for the word". I also distinguish between the concept associated with the word and the concept(s) associated with the entry. Call the former "the concept" and the latter "the conceptual explication". Finally, I distinguish between a type of meaning associated with the word, "translational meaning", and the meaning associated with its entry, "explicational meaning". For our purposes, the explicational meaning is the semantical analog of the conceptual explication. The translational meaning of a word can be articulated through exact translation and sometimes through such trivial thoughts as *my word 'tiger' applies to tigers*, but need not be exhaustively expressible in other terms in an idiolect.

A traditional view in semantics is that a word's explicational meaning and its translational meaning are, for purposes of characterizing the individual's idiolect, always interchangeable; and that the individual's conceptual explication always completely exhausts his or her concept. This view is incorrect. It is incorrect because of the role that the referent plays in individuating the concept and translational meaning, and because of the role that non-explicational abilities play in the individual's application of the word and concept. Accounting for a person's lexical entry or conceptual explication is relevant to determining the nature of a person's meaning or concept. But the two enterprises are not the same. I will try to give some sense for why this is so.

Let us begin by concentrating on the large class of nouns and verbs that apply to everyday, empirically discernible objects, stuffs, properties, and events. I have in mind words like 'tiger', 'water', 'mud', 'stone', 'tree', 'bread', 'knife', 'chair', 'edge', 'shadow', 'baby', 'walk', 'fight', and so on. Except for tense, these words are not and do not contain indexicals in any ordinary sense. Given only that their meaning in the language is fixed, their applications or referents are fixed. They do not depend for their applications on particular contexts of use; not do they shift their applications systematically with context or with the referential intentions of speakers. Without contextual explication or relativization, we can trivially, but correctly, state their ranges of applications: 'tiger' applies to tigers; 'walk' applies to instances of walking; and so on. Contrast: 'then' applies to then. This latter explication requires a particular context to do its job, a particular, context-dependent application of 'then' to a salient time. The constancy of application of non-indexical words, within particular idiolects, is a feature of their meaning and of the way that they are understood by their users.

Although the reference of these words is not all there is to their semantics, their reference places a constraint on their meaning, or on what concept they express. In particular, any such word w has a different meaning (or expresses a different concept) from a given word w' if their constant referents, or ranges of application, are different. That is part of what it is to be a non-indexical word of this type.[8]

The individual's explicational beliefs about the referents of such words, his conceptual explications, do not always fix such words' referents, even in his idiolect. So, by the considerations of the previous paragraph, they do not always fix such words' meanings or concepts in the individual's idiolect.

---

[8] The ontology of meanings or concepts is unimportant for these purposes. But I assume the standard view that the meaning or concept should not be identified with the word—since different words could express the same meaning or concept, and the same word can express different meanings or concepts. I assume also that the meaning or concept should not be identified with the referent, since a meaning or concept is a way of speaking or thinking about the referent. Of course, sometimes words express meanings or concepts that have no referent. And meanings or concepts normally have vague boundaries of application.

The point about non-indexicality can be established on purely linguistic grounds. I discuss the non-indexicality of the relevant words in more detail in Burge, "Other Bodies" (Ch. 4 above).

The point that explicational beliefs do not always fix reference is substantiated not only through the examples that have dominated the theory of reference for the last forty years (see n. 5). It is also supported by considering the dialectic by which we arrive at conceptual explications, or lexical entries.

Sometimes such explications are meant to produce approximate synonymies (as in the explication of 'knife'). Other times, not ('tiger', 'water'). In the cases we are discussing, applications of the words are backed by and learned through perceptual experience. Perceptually fixed examples typically determine the application of the word before conceptual explications do.[9]

Conceptual explications are typically inferences from these perceptual experiences, or general epithets derived from the remarks of others, or both. In attempting to articulate one's conception of one's concept, one's conceptual explication, one naturally alternates between thinking of examples and refining one's conceptual explication in order to accord with examples that one recognizes as legitimate. It is crucial here to note that the legitimacy of examples does not in general derive from one's attempts at conceptual explication. Although sometimes examples are shown to be legitimate or illegitimate by reference to such explications, the normal order—in the class of words that we are discussing—is the other way around. The examples, first arrived at through perception, tend to be the touchstone for evaluating attempts at conceptual explication.

Consider the sort of dialectic in which people try to arrive at an explication of the meanings of their words. First attempts are usually seen to be mistaken. Reflection on examples leads to improvements. The altered characterizations improve on one's characterization of a referent that is assumed to have been fixed. (They are not normally mere sharpenings of reference, or changes in the meanings of one's word.) They are equally improvements in one's conceptual understanding of one's own concept or meaning.

Such dialectic typically adds to one's knowledge. Suppose I explicate my word 'chair' in a way that requires that chairs have legs, and then come to realize that beach chairs, or deck-chairs bolted to a wall, or ski-lift chairs, are counterexamples. Or suppose that I learn more about how to discriminate water from other (possible or actual) colorless, tasteless, potable liquids. In such cases, I learn something about chairs or water that I did not know before. In these cases it is simply not true that the reference of my words 'chair' and 'water' must change. Although it is true that my conception—my explication—changes, it remains possible for me to observe (with univocal use of 'chair'): "I used to think chairs had to have legs, but now know that chairs need not have legs." It

---

[9] This point is now common not only in the philosophical literature (see Putnam, "Is Semantics Possible?" and "The Meaning of 'Meaning' " and Burge, "Other Bodies"), but also in the psychological literature. Cf. Eleanor Rosch and Barbara Lloyd, *Cognition and Categorization* (Hillsdale, NJ: Erlbaum, 1978); Edward Smith and Douglas Medin, *Categories and Concepts* (Cambridge, Mass.: Harvard University Press, 1981). For excellent philosophical discussion of this literature, with criticism of some of its excesses, see Bernard Kobes, "Individualism and the Cognitive Sciences" (unpub-diss., UCLA, 1986), ch. 6.

remains possible for me to have thoughts about water as water, knowing that there might be other liquids that I could not, by means other than use of my concept *water*, discriminate from it. Thus there is a sense in which the concept, and the translational meaning of the word in the idiolect, remain the same despite the changed discriminating ability, or change in explication.

Of course, my ability to come up with better explications by considering examples with which I am already familiar indicates that I have more to go on than my initial explications suggest. Perhaps I have "tacitly cognized" more than what I give as my reflective explication, before I arrive consciously at a better explication.

I think that this view is right. But it would be a mistake to infer that I always already know the correct explication in some suppressed way. It would be an even more serious mistake to infer that our tacit conceptual explications exhaust our concepts. There are several reasons why these moves are unsound.

In the first place, the dialectic involves genuine reasoning—using materials at hand to form a better conception. Granting that we have the materials in our mental repertoires to form a better conception does not amount to granting that we have already put them together. Reflection on the examples seems to play a role in doing this. When I give a mistaken explication of 'chair', I may have failed to hold empirical information in my memory, or failed to put together things that I knew separately. I may have failed to believe at the time of the explication that there were legless chairs, even though I had experience and even perhaps knowledge from which I could have derived this belief. Thus the sort of unconscious or tacit cognition that is involved is not just an unconscious analog of having reflective knowledge of the proposition formed by linking the concept and the improved conceptual explication. Attribution of tacit cognition entails only that the mental structures for deriving the recognition of examples are in place and will (ideally) lead to such recognition, when examples are presented.

In the second place, there is substantial evidence that some of the "underlying" materials are stored in our perceptual capacities and are not, properly speaking, conceptualized (see n. 9). We are often able to project our concept (e.g. *chair*) to new cases never before considered. Often this projection seems to be based on perceptual capacities that are modular and preconceptual. Thus the "materials" that are put together and worked up into conceptual explications through the process of dialectic sometimes do not, before reflection begins, appear to be the right sort to count as criterial knowledge, even unconscious criterial knowledge.

In the third place, even the perceptual abilities need not suffice to discriminate instances of the concept from every possible look-alike—from look-alikes that might have been normal in other environments, and which in that case might have determined other concepts, but which play no role in the formation of concepts in the speaker's actual environment. The explicated concepts are determined to be what they are by the actual nature of objects and events that we can perceptually discriminate from other relevantly similar things in the same environment. Thus even our perceptual abilities and our conceptual explications combined need not provide necessary and sufficient conditions for the correct application of our concepts in all possible environments in which the concepts have a definite application. They therefore need not fully exhaust the content of our concepts.

There is a more general reason why our explicational abilities, including our unconscious ones, do not in general and necessarily suffice to exhaust the concepts that they serve to explicate. One's cognitive relation to the examples that played an initial role in fixing one's concept is perceptual. That relation inherits the fallibility of perceptual experience. Since the concepts under discussion are not merely given by conceptual explications, but are partly fixed through examples in the environment, their conceptual explications must correctly describe the examples. Conceptual explications (and dictionary entries) are not normally true by logic and stipulation. They are true because they capture examples that are fixed partly through perceptual experience. But our cognitive relations to the examples are fallible. So the conceptual explications and dictionary entries that sum up our current discriminative abilities are fallible. The things that we perceive and that fix our concepts may not be just as we see and characterize them. Yet they may be genuine instances of the concepts. And we are subject to misidentifying other things that fit our perceptual schemas and conceptual explications as instances of our concepts, when they are not. So those schemas and explications do not necessarily exhaust the concepts or meanings that they explicate.[10]

Our commitment to getting the examples right is part of our understanding of the relevant class of words and concepts. This commitment is illustrated in, indeed explains, many cases of our *standing corrected* by others in our attempts to explicate our own words and concepts. Such correction, by oneself or by others, is common in the course of the dialectic. One sees oneself as having made a mistake about the meaning of one's own word, in one's explication of one's own concept.

Some philosophers have characterized all cases of standing corrected as pliant shifts of communicative strategy. According to this view, I previously used 'chair' in my idiolect with a meaning that did in fact exclude legless chairs. But on encountering resistance from others, I tacitly shift my meaning so as to surmount practical obstacles to communication or fellowship that would result from maintaining an idiosyncratic usage.[11]

I agree, of course, that such practically motivated changes occur. But they cannot explain all cases of our standing corrected. For such correction is often—I would say, typically—founded on substantive, empirical matters about which

---

[10] I have discussed other problems with exhaustive conceptual explications: "Other Bodies", "Intellectual Norms" (Chs. 4, 10 above).

[11] See Donald Davidson, "Knowing one's own Mind", *Proceedings and Addresses of the American Philosophical Association*, 60 (1987).

there are cognitive rights and wrongs. We make mistakes, sometimes empirically correctable mistakes, that others catch, and that bear on the proper explication of the meaning of words in our idiolects. In such cases we come to understand our idiolects better.

Others are sometimes better placed than we are to judge the fit between our proposed lexical entries, or our conceptual explications, and the examples to which our words or concepts apply. Thus we may correctly see others as sometimes understanding our own idiolects better than we do. When we defer to someone else's linguistic authority, it is partly because the other person has superior empirical insight, insight that bears on the proper characterization of examples to which our words or concepts apply. The reason for their insight is not that they have made a study of us. It is also not that they are foisting some foreign, socially authorized standard on us. It is that they understand their idiolects better than we understand ours, and they have a right to assume that our idiolects are in relevant respects similar, or the same.

The justification of this assumption, also fallible, has two main sources. One is the publicity of the examples and our shared perceptual and inferential equipment. Given that we have been exposed to substantially similar knives, chairs, water, trees, mud, walkings, and fightings, and have heard these associated with the same words, it is to be expected that we project from actual examples in similar ways. Although our kind-forming abilities may differ in some instances, it is reasonable to expect that they will typically be the same, especially with concepts that apply to entities of common perceptual experience. Normally we will be committed to the legitimacy of the same examples, and will be committed to characterizing those examples, correctly. Given that the examples are public, no one has privileged authority about their characteristics.

A second source of the assumption that others can correct one's explications is that a person's access to the examples—to the applications that help fix the relevant concept—is partly or fully through others. Words are initially acquired from others, who are already applying those words to cases. Word acquisition occurs in conjunction with acquisition of information, information from testimony or communication with others, about those cases.

Of course, until the learner develops some minimal amount of background knowledge and likeness of application, he or she cannot be said to have acquired the word in the predecessor's sense, or with the predecessor's range of applications. But as we have seen in the preceding paragraphs, possession of an infallible explication is not required—because it is not possible.

The dependence on others for access to examples grows as one's linguistic and cognitive resources widen. In some cases we depend heavily on the perceptual experience of others (as with 'tiger', 'penguin', and 'rain', for those of us in California). In other cases we depend on theoretical background knowledge ('gene', 'cancer') or on more ordinary expertise ('arthritis', 'carburetor'). In many such cases, we intentionally take over the applications that others have made. We rely on their experience to supplement our own. And we accept corrections of our explications from them because they have better access to the examples which partly determine the nature of our concepts. Although the function of explication varies significantly in these various cases, the main points of the argument for social dependence apply equally, indeed even more obviously, to terms that are less closely associated with direct perception.

Since fixing examples—or more broadly, referents—that partly determine an individual's concept or translational meaning is sometimes dependent on the activity of others with whom he interacts, the individuation of an individual's concepts or translational meanings is sometimes dependent on his interaction with others. Even where the individual has epistemic access to the examples independently of others (for example, where he perceives instances directly), others may have superior knowledge of the examples. They may therefore have superior insight into the proper explication of the individual's words and concepts: they may have put together relevant cognitive materials in a way that provides standards for understanding the individual's words and concepts. In such cases, the individual's deference may be cognitively appropriate.

The cases in which the individual does and does not have independent access to the examples might seem to be significantly different. The former case might be seen as showing only that others may know more about the explication of the individual's meanings and concepts than he does, and that it is easier to understand an individual's idiolect by studying idiolects and attitudes of others. One might still insist, relative to this case, that the materials for determining the individual's concepts or meanings do not involve the individual's relations to others.

Though I need not contest this point for the sake of present argument, I doubt that it is correct. It is metaphysically possible for an individual to learn his idiolect in isolation from a community. But it is no accident, and not merely a consequence of a convenient practical strategy, that one obtains insight into an idiolect by considering the usage and attitudes of others. In learning words, individuals normally look to others to help set standards for determining the range of legitimate examples and the sort of background information used in explicating a word or concept. I believe that this is a psychological necessity for human beings.

The second case, where the individual has had limited relevant access to the examples independently of others, provides independent ground for thinking that individuation of an individual's concepts or meanings is sometimes dependent on the social interactions that the individual engages in. If others had provided access to a different range of examples, compatible with one's minimal background information, one would have had different meanings or concepts.

Let me summarize the argument that an individual's idiolect and concepts cannot be fully understood apart from considering the language and concepts of others with whom he interacts. Numerous empirically applicable words are non-indexical. Non-indexical words must have different translational meanings, and express different concepts, if their referents are different. Our explicational abilities, and indeed all our cognitive mastery, regarding the referents of such words and concepts do not necessarily fix the referents. Nor therefore (by the first premise) do they necessarily fix the translational meanings or concepts associated with the words. To be correct, our lexical entries and conceptual explications are subject to correction or confirmation by empirical consideration of the referents. Since such empirical consideration is fallible, our cognitive relations to the referents are fallible. Others are often in a better position to arrive at a correct articulation of our word or concept, because they are in a better position to determine relevant empirical features of the referents. This, for two reasons: the referents are public, so no one has privileged authority regarding their properties; and we are frequently dependent on others for linking our words to the referents and for access to the referents. Since the referents play a necessary role in individuating the person's concept or translational meaning, individuation of an individual's concepts or translational meanings may depend on the activity of others on whom the individual is dependent for acquisition of and access to the referents. If the others by acting differently had put one in touch with different referents, compatibly with one's minimum explicational abilities, one would have had different concepts or translational meanings.[12] Although I have argued only that this conclusion derives from obvious facts of social interaction, I have conjectured that it derives from psychological necessities for human beings.

The argument does not depend on assuming that people ever share the same concepts or translational meanings.[13] However, the argument makes it plausible that people in a community do often share concepts and translational meanings, despite differences in their beliefs about the world, and even differences in their explications of the relevant terms. Most empirically applicable concepts are fixed by three factors: by actual referents encountered through experience—one's own, one's fellows', or one's species ancestors', or indirectly through theory; by some rudimentary conceptualization of the examples—learned or innately

[12] I think that this argument admits of an important extension. The argument derives non-individualistic variation in an individual's meanings or concepts from variation in empirical referents to which the community provides access. But the variation need not occur in the referents. It may depend on the nature of our cognitive access through the community to the examples. The variation may occur in the way the referents are approached in the community. Thus it may be that the referents are held fixed, but the community's cognitive access to them may vary in such a way as to vary the concept, without varying the effect on the individual's body or rudimentary explicational abilities. This extension is, I think, a corollary of the Fregean observation that referents (or examples) do not determine meanings or concepts. Since my purpose has been to establish a minimal sense in which language is social, I shall not illustrate or develop this extension here.

[13] This is also true of the argument in Burge, "Individualism and the Mental" (Ch. 5 above). The conclusion can rest on the mere assumption that the referents of the concepts in the actual and counterfactual communities are different. (Brian Loar, "Social Content and Psychological Contents", in R. Grimm and D. Merrill (eds.), *Contents of Thought* (Tucson: University of Arizona Press, 1988) seems mistakenly and crucially to assume the contrary in his critical discussion of "Individualism and the Mental".) For all that, I know of no persuasive reason for thinking that in every relevant case the person in the actual community cannot share his concept or meaning (e.g. *arthritis*) with his fellows.

possessed by virtually everyone who comes in contact with the terms; and by perceptual information, inferential capacities, and kind-forming abilities, that may be pre-conceptual. The referents are often shared, because of similarity of experience and because of intentional reliance on others for examples. So the concepts and translational meanings associated with many words will be shared. Shared idiolectal meanings and shared concepts derive from a shared empirical world and shared cognitive goals and procedures in coming to know that world.[14]

Traditional philosophy tended to ignore the first and third factors in concept determination, and to expand the second into the requirement of necessary and sufficient conditions that 'define' the meaning or concept and that must be believed if one is to have the relevant concept at all. The dissolution of this picture makes possible an appreciation of the dependence of the individuation of our empirical concepts on direct or indirect perceptual relations to our empirical environment.

Drawing on these ideas, together with obvious facts about social interaction, I have tried to show that idiolects are social in two senses. First, in many cases we must, on cognitive grounds, defer to others in the explication of our words. Second, the individuation of our concepts and meanings is sometimes dependent on the activity of others from whom we learn our words and on whom we depend for access to the referents of our words. The second sense grounds the view that individual psychology and the study of the semantics of idiolects are not wholly independent of assumptions of interaction among individuals.

---

[14] So it appears that there is an element of meaning that can remain constant and common across individuals, despite the interdependence of meaning and belief noted at the outset. It is notable that this constancy in no way depends on the assumption of a distinction between sentences that are *true* purely by virtue of their meaning and sentences that depend for their truth on the way the subject matter is. (Like Quine, I find this distinction empty.) See Burge, "Intellectual Norms". Belief in the relevant element of meaning does not even depend on invocation of a distinction between criterial or linguistic truths and other sorts of truths (although like Chomsky and unlike Quine, I think that this latter distinction, commonly conflated with the previous one, is clearly defensible).

Another point about the semantics of word meaning bears emphasizing. There is a relevant semantical distinction between cases in which the individual has sufficient materials in his conceptual repertoire to construct a given lexical entry, maximally faithful to the range of applications or examples that he recognizes as legitimate, and cases in which the individual's dependence on others is such that his repertoire allows only entries that are less full than those of others. In the latter cases, it is *not true*, on my view, that the "communal" entry is the "correct" entry within the person's idiolect. I take it that lexical entries sum up an idealized conceptual understanding. If the person lacks resources to arrive at some given entry, the entry is not a part of his idiolect.

But it does not *follow* from this difference that the person does not have the same concept, or the same translational meaning, that others have. To think this would be to confuse concept and conceptual explication, or translational meaning and explicational understanding. In not sharing this explication with others, the person will not fully share an understanding of the word (or the conception of the concept) with others. But lexical entries (conceptual explications) do not determine the translational meaning (concepts); they may even be mistaken, and only contingently related to it. The person still has his or her perceptual abilities for picking out referents, and the relevant referents may still be partly fixed by the person's reliance on others. Thus as far as present considerations go, the person's concept may be shared with others even though his or her conceptual explication or lexical entry may differ.

12 *Concepts, Definitions, and Meaning*

The Aristotelian tradition produced many of the elements of what is widely thought of as 'the traditional view' of concepts. I begin by attempting to summarize this view. The summary runs roughshod over numerous distinctions that were dear to various thinkers who contributed to this general conception of concepts. I sacrifice historical accuracy in favor of an idealized type that, I hope, will serve despite its crudity to further understanding.

Although I shall be criticizing natural and traditional readings of the principles that follow, there are readings, which should become clear as we proceed, under which I accept all the principles but the last, (4c). My objective is to show how two important contemporary doctrines—holism about confirmation and anti-individualism about the individuation of mental states—affect our understanding of this traditional view of concepts.

Here are the main principles that delineate the idealized traditional conception of concepts that I wish to discuss. Principles (1)–(1b) concern the relation between concepts, thought contents, and propositional attitudes.

(1) Concepts are sub-components of thought contents. Such contents type propositional mental events and abilities that may be common to different thinkers or constant in one thinker over time. Having a concept is just being able to think thoughts that contain the concept.[1]

(1a) Propositional mental abilities are type-individuated in terms of concepts partly because concepts enable one to capture a thinker's ability to relate different thoughts to one another according to rational inferential patterns.

Thus we count a thought that all dogs are animals and a thought that Fido is a dog as sharing a concept in order to capture a thinker's ability to infer, according to the obvious deductive pattern, that Fido is an animal.

I am indebted to David Charles for valuable comments.

[1] Georges Rey discusses misconstruals within empirical psychology of concepts, and of philosophical work relevant to them, in his excellent articles 'Concepts and Stereotypes', *Cognition*, 15 (1983), 237–262; 'Concepts and Conceptions: A Reply to Smith, Medin and Rips', *Cognition*, 19 (1985), 297–303. Although my account of the traditional view differs from his, many of the fundamental points are similar.

(1b) In being components of thought contents, concepts constitute ways a thinker thinks about things, properties, relations, and so on. A concept of these things is a way of thinking of these things.

Principles numbered (2)–(2b) concern the referential functions of concepts—or relations between concepts and the world that they purport to be about.

(2) In being components of thought contents, and ways of thinking, concepts are representational or intentional (I make no distinction here). They need not apply to actual objects, but their function is such that they purport to apply; they have intentional or referential functions.

(2a) Concepts' identities are inseparable from their specific intentional properties or functions.

Thus a concept of an eclipse could not be the concept that it is if it did not represent, or if it were not about, eclipses. If a concept were found to apply to things in the world that were not eclipses, it would not be the concept *eclipse*. Traditionally, the principle also applied to vacuous concepts. So the concept of a unicorn could not be the concept that it is if it were not about unicorns.

This principle may appear trivial, and it certainly is virtually undeniable as applied to concepts. But it is notable that an analog of the principle does not apply to other types of representation. Thus the word form 'eclipse' would be the same word form even if it were not about eclipses; and an image of a tower on a screen could be the same image even if it were not an image of a tower—if, say, it had been produced in response to something other than a tower.

(2b) Many concepts fix the things that they are about in the sense that given the concept and given the world, the concept, of its nature, referentially determines the range of entities that it is about.

Some traditionalists recognized that this principle does not apply to indexical concepts like *now*, or demonstrative concepts like *that*, or a variety of other context-dependent notions.[2] There are also role or office concepts that have implicit tensed elements—like *the president*—for which the principle needs obvious modifications. Moreover, it requires some qualification for vagueness. But it was taken to be true—and I think is obviously true—of many concepts for empirical and mathematical objects, properties and relations. For example, given the concept *dog* or *chair* and given the elements of the world, the concept will referentially apply to exactly the dogs or chairs in the world.

---

[2] Since indexical notions like *now* do constitute ways of thinking, I think it appropriate to think of them as concepts. But the concepts are general in that they are common to any application of 'now'. According to (2a) they are inseparable from their particular intentional functions. (Roughly in this case, to pick out the time of a thought or utterance.) But they do not fix the things that they referentially determine except relative to the existence of the thought or utterance in which they are contained (or more broadly, relative to context). Thus there is a natural awkwardness in speaking of the concept of *now*, since such an occurrence suggests misleadingly a particular time that is associated with all occurrences of the concept.

I take it that the principles numbered (1)–(2) are more fundamental to the traditional view than those numbered (3)–(4). Principles (3)–(3a) concern the relation between concepts and definitions. Principles (4)–(4c) govern the relation between concepts, meaning, and language.

(3) Definitions associated with concepts fix necessary and sufficient conditions for falling under the concept. They give the essence, or if not essence at least the most fundamental individuating conditions, of the entities that the concept applies to.

Not just any set of necessary and sufficient conditions were seen as essential or fundamental individuating conditions. A definition captured something peculiar to conditions for individuation associated with the concept. It was supposed to say something illuminating about what it is to be the relevant kind.

(3a) Definitions also state basic epistemic conditions that the individual has for applying the concept, or the individual's best understanding of conditions for falling under the concept.

Commonly a distinction was made between adventitious and inessential methods of application and fundamental or essential ones. Only the latter belong in the definition.

Different thinkers seem to have taken different views about the relation between what one might call metaphysical or essence-determining definitions and epistemic definitions—definitions that capture what is epistemically prior when one sets out to discover what something's essence is. Aristotle seems to have distinguished the two. Others, such as Hume and the Logical Positivists, drew no such distinction.[3]

(4) Concepts are commonly expressed in language. They constitute meanings of the speaker's words.

When we say 'That's a chair', we express a thought that that's a chair; we express the concept *chair* with the word 'chair'. The concept is not to be distinguished from the meaning of the word 'chair'.

(4a) Just as concepts, as ways of thinking, are to be distinguished from the range of entities thought about, so the sort of meaning that is expressed in language as concepts is to be distinguished from the sort of 'meaning' that is constituted by the range of entities which the words and concepts signify, apply to, or refer to.

---

[3] Aristotle conceived definitions primarily as attempts at codifications of the essence of what terms or concepts apply to. See, e.g., Aristotle *Topics* VII, 5, 30 and *Posterior Analytics* II, 10. But for some purposes he did distinguish between definitions that articulated essence and definitions that articulated epistemic procedures. He seems to have thought, in the cases of concepts like *eclipse* or *thunder*, that the essence could be discovered only through empirical investigation; the epistemic conditions for applying the concept seem to precede and underdetermine the outcome of the investigation. Cf. *Posterior Analytics* II, 8.

The general idea that I have summarized in (4a) and (2b) was variously expressed in terms of a distinction between two kinds of meaning: concept and kind, objective reality and reality, idea and nature, connotation and denotation, intension and extension, sense and reference. But the common theme was that the former element in each pair fixed the latter; a word that expressed the former applied to the latter.

(4b) Definitions of words articulate conceptual meanings.

(4c) Concepts are prior to language in the sense that language is to be understood as functioning to express thought; but thought is never fundamentally individuated in terms of language.

A traditional consideration in favor of this view was expressed by Aristotle: thoughts are the same for all men, but language varies.[4]

Although the Logical Positivists maintained a version of this view of concepts, much subsequent mainstream work in philosophy in this century has attacked various elements in it. Behaviorism and Quinean eliminationism attack the very idea of an idea or concept, or indeed the very idea of mental events and kinds. I shall not discuss these general forms of hostility to mentalistic notions. I want to discuss two other doctrines that have been used to attack the traditional view—holism and anti-individualism. Unfortunately, I will largely ignore (4c), an element in the traditional view that has received very considerable discussion in this century. I think that this omission will leave us with more than enough to think about.

Quine pointed out that sentences are not confirmed or disconfirmed one by one. Only whole theories, or at least large bodies of theory, face experience. Quine joined Duhem in further indicating that there is no set formula for saying which sentences within the theory might be revised, and which still assented to, when new experience is out of step with the theory's pronouncements. In fact, the practice of empirical science suggests that virtually any scientific claim, including one that serves as a definition, is subject to possible revision in the interests of accounting for new findings. These points apply to beliefs as well as sentences, to definitions of concepts as well as to definitions of terms.[5]

The claim that theoretical definitions are revised is supportable by numerous cases from the history of science. Definitions of mass, momentum, atom, gene, and so on have been rejected for theoretical reasons. Subsequent discussion has made it seem hopeless to claim that in every one of these cases the old definition remains true (because it is a definition!) and a new theoretical notion (e.g. a new notion of atom or momentum) is introduced with the new definition. Rather it is often the case that the old definitions are false; and the new ones are better

---

[4] Aristotle, *De Interpretatione* I, 5–9.

[5] W. V. Quine, 'Two Dogmas of Empiricism', in *From a Logical Point of View* (Cambridge, Mass.: Harvard University Press, 1953).

accounts of how to understand the defined notion, as well as better accounts of what the defined notion applies to.[6]

How do these considerations affect the traditional view? Some, including Quine, have taken them to undermine the belief that there are concepts at all. This line of reasoning is directed against the idea that there is clear sense to the notion of a constituent of a propositional content. An oversimplified version of the reasoning is as follows: concepts and word meanings are if anything procedures used to determine whether something falls under the concept, or satisfies the meaning. But no such procedure can be associated with any unit as 'small' as a concept or a word meaning would have to be. Such procedures can be associated only with blocks of sentences. So there is no determinate entity that is a concept or a word meaning.

Another argument, again oversimplified, proceeds similarly: The only ground for attributing concepts lies in accounting for a person's linguistic and cognitive procedures in assenting to or dissenting from sentences. But one can always attribute *systematically* different concepts and come out with equally good overall accounts of such procedures. So there is no reasonable ground for attributing any particular set of concepts to anyone.

Each argument's first premise seems to me vulnerable. I think concepts are not merely procedures for finding a referent or merely elements in procedures for determining responses to sentences. The second argument's second premise—the claim that equally good, systematically different attributions of concepts are always available—also is questionable.

I will not undertake to discuss these and allied arguments here. Instead, I will proceed on the invidious assumption that such arguments are unsound, making up slightly for this high-handed policy by later advancing considerations that count against the first premise of each argument. That is, I will later raise considerations for thinking that one should not conceive of confirmation procedures and patterns of assent and dissent as the only grounds for individuating or attributing concepts. I think that holism has been thought to undermine the notion of a concept because holism about confirmation is equated or conflated with holism about the nature of meaning or propositional content.[7]

Holistic considerations can seem to threaten aspects of the traditional view even when they are not taken to undermine the very applicability of the notion of a concept. Holism bears most specifically on the principles in the traditional view that are concerned with definition—(3) and (3a).

---

[6] The view that new definitions sometimes produce deeper understanding of the original concepts is expressed, without any special philosophical motivation, over and over in scientific writings. For example, see Robert Geroch, *General Relativity, From A to B* (Chicago: University of Chicago Press, 1978), 4–5.

[7] An example of the slide from holism about confirmation to holism about meaning without any explicitly connecting premise is Putnam's otherwise excellent summary discussion of the force of the Quine–Duhem thesis in Hilary Putnam, *Representation and Reality* (Cambridge, Mass.: MIT Press, 1988), 8–9.

Take (3a) first. It seems reasonable to think of definitions as sometimes artic-ulating the epistemic conditions that a thinker *treats* as most basic for applying the concept. Scientific practice indicates, however, that a definition that functions as the most basic explanation of a concept at one time can later be displaced and even seen to be false. This is possible because the thinker, or theory, has, besides the definition, other epistemic hooks on the entities that the concept applies to—for example, other theoretical characterizations that had seemed less fundamental; or experimental identifications that are not fully dependent on the definition. What the thinker treats as fundamental in his own epistemic practice may have to defer to other epistemic means of access that turn out to have been more accurate or basic. Thus a given concept can have a succession of definitions, each of which functions as a fundamental epistemic tool, only to be seen to be mistaken, or adventitious, and replaced.

Turning to (3): it is not in general true that statements that actually func-tion as definitions fix necessary and sufficient conditions for falling under the concept. A definition may not even be true of things that fall under the concept. Thus (3) must be seen as stating an ideal for definitions. Or it may be seen as applying not (or not necessarily) to definitions that are actually in use, but to something that is yet to be discovered—either the end result of ideal inquiry, or simply the true account of necessary and sufficient conditions, whether it has been discovered or not. Either way, this idealized notion of definition must be distinguished from the notion of definition that applies to whatever is functioning as a definition in the thinker's current repertoire.

A metaphysically correct definition—one that states actual necessary and sufficient conditions, indeed essential or fundamental individuating conditions for instantiating a kind—need not be known, or knowable on mere reflection, by someone who has the concept. This is clearly true in empirical cases. I think it true in other cases as well. Finding 'the definition' in this idealized sense may require acquisition of new knowledge or even new concepts. As I noted earlier, there is reason to suppose that Aristotle already made something like the distinction between metaphysical definitions, yet to be discovered, and definitions that guide one's current investigations. So these remarks about (3) are not meant as criticism of all versions of 'the traditional view'. They do, however, bring out points that are not emphasized and developed in the tradition. There is little reflection before this century on how what a thinker treats as his most fundamental means of applying a concept can be displaced by other means that are in fact more fruitful and accurate.

These effects of holism on the traditional principles governing definition also affect our understanding of traditional principles governing the relation between concepts and meaning. According to (4), concepts are commonly expressed in lan-guage; in being so expressed they constitute word meanings. So far there is nothing more to the notion of meaning than 'what is expressed' by words. I will explicate some restrictions on notions of linguistic meaning that have become standard in modern thinking. Then I will try to show how (4) and (4b) are affected.

On most modern conceptions, linguistic meaning is a complex idealization of use and understanding. The meaning of a term is revealed in its use and articulated in reflective explanations of its use by competent users. The meaning of a term at a given time is fixed by what an ideally reflective speaker would articulate by reflecting on all his intuitions, beliefs, dispositions to apply a term, and so on, with no reliance on advances in non-linguistic knowledge. This point applies both to communal and idiolectic linguistic meaning. Communal meaning is fixed by the reflective understanding and use of the 'most competent' speakers or by some idealized rendering of normal usage. Idiolectic meaning is fixed by the individual's idealized use and understanding.

There are many problems with the full specification of this conception, but let us take it as a familiar and rather deeply entrenched restriction on a notion of meaning, which will help us interpret (4). Let us now add (4b) to this conception of meaning. Interpreted in the light of my assumptions about meaning, this principle maintains that the content of a concept—and hence the meaning of a term—is codified in ideal lexical entries that capture the cognitive condition under which the speaker would apply the term. Thus if a fundamental reflective explication of the meaning of a word is changed, because of acquisition of new non-linguistic information, the meaning of the term changes.

Holism notes that the definitions that capture the conditions that the speaker treats in his usage as most fundamental for applying the term may be false. They may be false of what the term, and the concept it expresses, apply to. This shows, contrary to what some traditionalists presumed, that the definition cannot exhaust the significance of the term or the associated concept.

Of course, a number of other developments besides holism have conspired to demote the role of definitions in accounting for meaning. Wittgenstein's discussion of family resemblances, his insistence on the contextual complexity of language use, his and Austin's emphasis on the wide variety of word function, and Davidson and Quine's theories of interpretation, have all reduced the prominence of definition in thinking about language. Many words and concepts are not susceptible to definition at all, whether epistemic or metaphysical.

On the other hand, I think that it would be a mistake simply to reject (4b). Where they are possible, epistemic definitions do articulate the meanings of a speaker's words in one important sense. They articulate what the word means for the speaker, and what conception he associates with his concept. They constitute a summary or explanation of speaker usage that provides the speaker's most considered explication of his term.

The points I am making here do not depend on just what sort of function the definition fulfills. Different words, and perhaps different conceptions of meaning, allow for variation here. I have been assuming that the definition fulfills the function of trying to state the conditions most fundamental to the speaker under which something satisfies the concept. For example, take Dalton's definition of an atom, near enough: 'An atom is the smallest indivisible particle, out of which all other bodies are made.' Dalton assumed that atoms fall into a scheme of atomic weights, in something like the way his experimental evidence suggested. The definition turned out to be false, but the approximately true scheme of atomic weights turned out to anchor the concept. Some definitions are like this in reaching for fundamental characteristics. Others function differently. Some seem to provide a short account of the application of the concept that meets the practical interests of someone else likely to use the term. (E.g. 'Tigers are big, normally orange and black, striped cats.') I think that the primary points that I am making apply to these sorts of definitions as well.

Thus one should distinguish between two sorts of meaning: the meaning of the term that would remain constant even as one definition is replaced by another, and the articulations of what the term means for the speaker—which might undergo change. The former might be called 'translational meaning'; the latter will be called 'lexical meaning'. Similarly, the thinker's concept must be distinguished from the conception that the thinker associates with the concept.

A corollary of this point is that one must distinguish the sort of understanding of a word in being able to use it to express a concept or translational meaning from the sort of understanding that is involved in being able to give a correct and knowledgeable explication of it. One may think with a concept even though one has incompletely mastered it, in the sense that one associates a mistaken conception (or conceptual explication) with it.

The need for these distinctions is most straightforward in instances in which the definition actually turns out to be false. But I think that the distinctions should be drawn in any case. One argument for drawing the distinction in either case derives from Frege's test. The definitions ('force is mass times acceleration') are informative in a way that identity statements ('force is force') are not. So there is some difference in the significance of the defined word from the definition; definitions are usually not simply abbreviatory. Yet there remains the sense we discussed in which the definition does give the (lexical) meaning of the term.

Another argument for drawing the distinction derives from considerations of dynamic potential. It is not incoherent to conceive of there being a discovery that would lead to our counting the definitions false, even though the defined term succeeds in referring. In such a case the definition would be given up, but the term would continue to be used to pick out the same entity. And we would continue to interpret our past attitudes making use of the term. The mere fact that these changes are conceivable indicates that we attach some difference in significances of the defined term and the definition. Thus there is a need to have some way of conceptualizing this type of difference, even as we recognize that such definitions do provide 'the meaning' of the term in the sense that I have indicated.

I think that the distinction is largely independent of the role of definition in accounting for 'meaning'. There is a notion of meaning that is dependent on use and understanding, where these are cashed out in terms of some idealization of some of the speaker's considered beliefs and his normal practice. Such a notion of meaning is more subject to change under radical changes in belief than translational meaning or concepts. These latter notions are grounded as much in the reference of the term and the way that the speaker's practices are actually connected to that referent, as in the speaker's beliefs and understanding. (Cf. principles 2–2b.)[8] The upshot of all this for the traditional view is that the sense in which concepts *are* (sometimes) the meanings of a speaker's words (cf. (4)) is different from the sense in which definitions constitute or 'provide' the meaning of the word (cf. (4b)). Neither epistemic nor metaphysical definitions exhaust the significance of a word (the word's translational meaning). Nor are they merely re-expressions of the concept that they provide a conception of.

I want to turn now from holism to a second putative threat to the traditional view, anti-individualism. Modern anti-individualism has its roots in the theory of reference. Donnellan, Kripke, and Putnam showed that proper names and natural kinds in ordinary discourse could succeed in referring even though the speaker's knowledge of the referent is incomplete or defective.[9] Reference depends not just on background descriptions that the speaker associates with the relevant words, but on contextual, not purely cognitive relations that the speaker bears to entities that a term applies to.

The work on reference bears on the meaning of terms and on the identity of concepts. For the meaning of a wide range of non-indexical terms and the nature of a wide range of concepts are dependent on the referent or range of application in the sense that if the referent were different, the meaning of the term, and the associated concept, would be different. (Cf. principles 2a–b.) For example, different meanings or concepts would be expressed by the word forms 'chair' and 'arthritis' if the word forms did not apply exactly to chairs and to instances of arthritis. The points about reference can be shown to carry over to many such terms and concepts. That is, an individual can think of a range of entities via such terms and concepts even though the thinker's knowledge of the entities is not complete enough to pick out that range of entities except through the employment of those terms and concepts. What the individual knows about the range of entities—and hence, by (2a)–(2b)–(4), about the meanings or concepts—need not provide a definition that distinguishes them from all other (possible) meanings or concepts. So the meanings of many terms—and the identities of many concepts—are what they are even though what the individual knows about the meaning or concept may be insufficient to determine it uniquely. Their identities are fixed by environmental factors that are not entirely captured in the explicatory or even discriminatory abilities of the individual, unless those discriminatory abilities include application of the concept itself.

---

[8] Cf. my 'Intellectual Norms and Foundations of Mind', *The Journal of Philosophy*, 83 (1986), 697–720, and 'Wherein is Language Social?', in Alexander George (ed.), *Reflections on Chomsky* (Oxford: Basil Blackwell, 1989) (Chs. 10 and 11 above).

[9] Keith Donnellan, 'Proper Names and Identifying Descriptions', in D. Davidson and G. Harman (eds.), *Semantics of Natural Language* (Dordrecht: D. Reidel, 1972); Saul Kripke, 'Naming and Necessity', in ibid. also reprinted in book form by Harvard University Press, Cambridge, Mass., 1980; Hilary Putnam, 'Is Semantics Possible?', in *Philosophical Papers* ii (Cambridge: Cambridge University Press, 1975).

Anti-individualism is the view that not all of an individual's mental states and events can be type-individuated independently of the nature of entities in the individual's environment to which the individual bears not purely conceptual relations. There is a deep individuative relation between the individual's being in mental states of certain kinds and the nature of the individual's physical or social environments. Anti-individualism can be supported by numerous specific thought experiments, but can also be derived by reflecting on the foregoing points about reference and its relation to our conceptions of meanings and concepts.[10]

Hilary Putnam has in effect sought to turn the sorts of considerations that support anti-individualism into an argument against the conjunction of (1), (2b), and (4). He maintains that one cannot hold both that knowing the meaning of a term is a matter of being in a certain psychological state and that the meaning of a term fixes its reference or extension. The argument is that one cannot hold these two principles because the reference of the term may be fixed even though the speaker's knowledge of the referent is incomplete. The reference depends on non-cognitive relations between the speaker and the referents of his terms that are beyond anything the speaker knows. So the speaker's psychological state cannot suffice to fix the referents of his terms in the relevant cases, as the conjunction of (1), (2b), and (4) requires.[11]

This argument is unsound. The argument would succeed if the meaning of a speaker's term or concept were reducible to what he believed, knew, or understood about its meaning, content, or referent; or if a speaker's psychological state consisted in elements of his psychology that could be described independently of relations to the environment or of what concepts he has. But neither of these conditions holds. As regards the first, anti-individualism reinforces the point derived from holism that there must be a notion of meaning—associated, I think, with the traditional notion of concept—that is distinct from the notion of meaning that is fixed by what the speaker can articulate as his understanding. As regards the second, anti-individualism underwrites a notion of psychological state that is not describable independently of an individual's concepts, or of the relations the speaker bears to his environment.[12]

So the considerations that support anti-individualism, far from undermining the conjunction of the three principles that Putnam discusses, show their

---

[10] Cf. my 'Individualism and the Mental', *Midwest Studies in Philosophy*, 4 (1979), 73–121; 'Other Bodies', in A. Woodfield (ed.), *Thought and Object* (New York: Oxford University Press, 1982); 'Intellectual Norms and Foundations of Mind'; 'Individualism and Psychology', *The Philosophical Review*, 95 (1986), 3–45 (Chs. 5, 4, 10, 9 above).

[11] Putnam, *Representation and Reality*, 19–24. Putnam's argument goes back to his "The Meaning of 'Meaning' ", in *Philosophical Papers*, ii. I discuss the argument critically in 'Other Bodies'.

[12] I think that the ordinary notion of psychological state is typed in terms of concepts and their demonstrative or perceptual applications. One need not appeal to environmental relations to describe ordinary psychological states. The mind, or the psychological state, is not normally itself a relation to the environment. But the individuative conditions for the psychological states involve relations to the environment.

compatibility. In one sense of 'knowing the meaning', one knows the meaning of the term 'arthritis'—even though one's knowledge of the nature of arthritis may be defective—if one can use the term to express thoughts involving the concept arthritis: if one can express such beliefs as that arthritis is a painful disease. One's term 'arthritis' applies to arthritis. One's belief that arthritis is a painful disease contains a concept, that of arthritis, that fixes its referent. One's belief and one's concepts are part of one's psychological state. So one's psychological state of believing that arthritis is a painful disease (or the psychological state of having the concept *arthritis*) and one's understanding of the term 'arthritis' suffice to fix the referent of the concept *arthritis* and the term 'arthritis'. All these points are compatible with the individual's making mistakes about the nature of arthritis or about the definition of the word.

Putnam's error is historical as well as substantive. He attributes to the tradition stemming from Aristotle the conjunction of (1), (2b), and (4).[13] This much seems right. But he interprets concepts as mental representations and interprets mental representations as signs that can be individuated independently of their intentional properties—in the cases we are dealing with, independently of their referents. Thus he underestimates the centrality of (2a) in the traditional view. He writes,

... the Aristotelian model is what I spoke of ... as a Cryptographer model of the mind. ... No thinker has ever supposed that sameness and difference of meaning are the same thing as sameness and difference of the syntactic properties ... of the sign. But the Cryptographer model—the model of sign understanding as 'decoding' into an innate *linqua mentis*—postulates that at a deeper level there is an identity between sign and meaning (this is the fundamental idea of the model, in fact). The idea is that in the *linqua mentis* each sign has one and only one meaning. ... By this point we should be quite suspicious. What makes it plausible that the mind (or brain) thinks (or 'computes') using representations is that all the thinking we know about uses representations. But none of the methods of representation that we know about—speech, writing, painting, carving in stone, etc.—has the magical property that there *cannot be* different representations with the same meaning. None of the methods of representation that we know about has the property that the representations *intrinsically* refer to whatever it is that they are used to refer to.[14]

This construal seems to me inapposite to the way thoughts and concepts were conceived by most philosophers from Aristotle to Frege.[15] It is directly relevant

---

[13] Putnam, *Representation and Reality*, 19. Putnam's attribution is slightly different. But except for his interpretation of concepts as a certain sort of mental representation, which I shall discuss, I think the differences are not significant in the present context. He actually attributes these three principles: (1) Every word a person uses is associated in the mind of the speaker with a certain mental representation. (2) Two words are synonymous (have the same meaning) just in case they are associated with the *same* mental representation by the speakers who use those words. (3) The mental representation determines what the word refers to, if anything.

[14] Ibid. 20–21.

[15] Much of what Putnam goes on to say in criticism of the Cryptographer model seems to me to be true, if one abstracts from the historical attribution. Indeed, in fairness to Putnam, there are elements in the tradition that suggest approximations to the attribution. Some empiricists, for example,

to syntactic theories of mind recently proposed by Jerry Fodor and others. But Fodor is hardly a stereotypical representative of the tradition. I do not see the Cryptographer model as central to the philosophical tradition at all. It is not 'the fundamental idea' of the traditional view of concepts that at some deep level there is an identity between sign and meaning. Traditionally, concepts were not seen as signs in Putnam's sense. Unlike sounds in speech or signs in writing, or paintings, or stone carvings, concepts were not seen as entities whose identities are independent of their intentional functions, independent of the sorts of things they represent. So questions about how they *relate* to their intentional properties did not arise. The identity of sign and meaning was not a hypothesis of the traditional view because concepts were not construed as signs. Concepts' identities were seen as inseparable from their specific intentional properties or functions—(2a).

There is no reason for the Traditional view to deny that the mind makes use of signs or mental representations in Putnam's sense. But concepts are not to be identified with such signs. (Cf. the remark about Frege in note 15.) Insofar as concepts are construed as signs in the mind like images or words, it may indeed appear 'magical', as Putnam implies, that they intrinsically refer to whatever they are used to refer to, or even that they always have one and only one meaning. But there is no invocation of magic in the traditional view. I see no reason to construe an explanatory scheme that identifies mental abilities in terms of their specific intentional functions (concepts) as 'magical'.

Many modern philosophers—inspired by the idea that thought is just use of an inner language or that the mind is just a computer—begin by assuming that mental activity must be construed as the manipulation of inner signs. Intentional aspects of the mental are seen as interpretations or meanings of the manipulations of these signs. This approach seems to have borne some fruit, although I am agnostic about whether it is a good general model of the propositional attitudes. But many philosophers go further. They assume that attributing inner signs is theoretically more basic and somehow ontologically more secure than attributing intentional items like concepts or thought contents. They see it as a theoretical advance to 'identify' concepts with inner signs. (And if the identification cannot be effected, then so much the worse for concepts.) This assumption is rather like the older view, common among the British Empiricists, that images are theoretically and ontologically basic, and thought contents must be identified with or constructed out of them.

---

conflated images and concepts, thinking of all mental representations as inner pictures, though these pictures are not very language-like. The historical issues are, of course, extremely complex. But I think that the role of (2a) remains dominant even in many of those thinkers who tend to give images a prominent place in their accounts of thought. Moreover, the rationalist tradition—from Descartes, Leibniz, and Kant through Frege—drew a sharp distinction between signs and concepts. These thinkers give almost no ground for attributing the Cryptographer model. Frege's distinction between ideas (which might pass for inner signs or images) and senses (which are the analogs of concepts in his scheme) is an especially refined example of the rationalist point of view.

I think that these assumptions about theoretical and ontological priority are mistaken. Understanding of propositional mental activity—and even, I think, most mental signs—is fundamentally dependent on attributing intentional notions whose identities depend on their intentional properties or functions. (Cf. (2a).) That is the traditional view. Here I agree with it. Anti-individualism concerns how intentional function itself is to be explicated.[16]

Modern anti-individualism makes it clear that, why, and to some extent how, the nature of our meanings, concepts, and mental states are dependent on the individual's relations to the environment. The explanation of kind-determination, at least for many mental states and intentional contents about the empirical world, is from the environment to the mind. This point does not show that concepts do not fix their referents in the semantical or logical sense that 'fix' is intended by the traditional view—from Aristotle to Frege: the sense intended in (2b). This sense of 'fix' is neutral as regards explanatory or individuative priority.[17]

The main effect of anti-individualism on the traditional view of concepts lies in its contribution to our understanding of the relations between concepts, definitions, and meaning. It forces essentially the same qualifications of (3), (3a), (4), and (4b) that holism about confirmation does. One must distinguish the concept (and an associated notion of meaning) from a definition that captures the individual's explication or construal of the concept. One must realize that the latter does not in general individuate what the concept applies to. And one must distinguish between concepts (and the sort of meaning associated with them), on one hand, and the sort of meaning associated with explication and understanding, on the other.

What does anti-individualism contribute to our understanding of the traditional account of the relations between concepts, definitions, and meaning, that holism does not? I think that it makes three main additional contributions. It broadens the applicability of the points about definition and meaning beyond theoretical notions of science to an extremely wide range of notions in ordinary discourse. It points toward an understanding of the factors in concept-determination that supplement definition and user-explication. And it indicates that procedural, understanding-based, or use-based accounts of intentional notions—often associated with holism about confirmation—cannot be completely satisfactory. Let me comment briefly on these points in turn.

---

[16] In characterizing the traditional view I have left it open whether concepts are to be seen as abstractions that are independent of minds, as Frege saw them (or rather as he saw their analogs—thought components); or as abstractions that are though mind-dependent nevertheless not dependent on any individual mind, as Aristotle and Kant saw them; or as particulars 'in' individual minds, as Leibniz seems to have seen them. These differences are compatible with agreement on the priority of intentional properties in individuating concepts.

[17] I think that most philosophers before the British Empiricists, including all Aristotelians, were anti-individualists. Even Descartes is not a clear case of an individualist, although his initial statement of scepticism involves dramatic individualistic presuppositions.

The lessons drawn from holism depended on the possibility of fundamental changes in scientific outlook. Such changes are not common in ordinary discourse. We use definitions for many artifact terms, for example, that are not at all likely to be overturned. So it is less clear that the Duhem–Quine points about the falsifiability of definitions extend to ordinary discourse.

But the thought experiments that fueled the advances in the theory of reference indicate how individual user-explications of non-scientific kind terms can be inadequate to fix the reference and can undergo change even as the referent remains the same. Thought experiments that support anti-individualism go further. They indicate how the same phenomenon can occur in individuals' use of other ordinary terms. Someone can think of arthritis as arthritis and think mistakenly that it can occur outside joints. Someone can think that chairs must have legs—having seen ski-lift chairs and counted them chairs, but under circumstances in which icicles hanging from the bottom of the chairs appeared to be legs.[18] In these cases an individual's best reflective explication of a concept can come to be recognized by the individual as mistaken. The individual continues to think of arthritis as arthritis and chairs as chairs, even though his epistemically primary definition—his best means of identifying these entities—is out of step with their individuating conditions. In such cases, the individual's understanding and lexical meaning may change even as the concept or translational meaning remains the same. Anti-individualism uncovers this sort of phenomenon and extensions of it for most notions that apply to empirically discernible entities. Typically, such notions are not introduced through theories or definitions, but through exposure to examples. Relation to the examples may remain constant even when one learns that some of one's fundamental beliefs about the examples are mistaken, or not as general as one might have thought.

A second contribution of anti-individualism, derivative from the work on reference, is that it points toward certain thinker–environmental relations that play a fundamental role in concept determination. Holism suggested that one can rely on one characterization to correct another. This is true. But one's ability to maintain a concept of something even while one changes one's putatively fundamental beliefs about it is grounded in more than alternative descriptions. It is partly grounded in relations to the environment that are not purely descriptive.

The simplest sort of relation is the causal-perceptual relation to instances of the kind to which the concept applies. But this is supplemented by discourse with others who have had perceptual relations to such instances, by inference or imagination about putative instances of one kind based on perception of instances of other kinds, by the inheritance of innate perceptual or conceptual categories from ancestors who have had evolutionarily relevant, cognitive relations to instances of the kind—and so on. These sorts of thinker–environmental relations help fix the identity of a thinker's concepts. They may do so even where the individual's

---

[18] Cf. my 'Individualism and the Mental' and 'Wherein is Language Social?' (Chs. 5 and 11 above).

explicational abilities or other epistemic procedures fail in themselves to distinguish the entities to which the concept is applicable from other entities which (in especially unfortunate circumstances) the thinker might mistake for those entities.[19]

An individual's concepts for empirically discernible entities are not fully captured by the individual's explications, by his dominant epistemic procedures, by referentially accurate indexical expressions, or by specification of the individuating environmental relations. All of these conceptual elements are significantly, in some cases even constitutively, related to having the ordinary empirical concepts. But the concepts are not to be reduced to them.

This point is in effect the third contribution of anti-individualism to our understanding of the traditional notion of concepts. One of the dominant themes of twentieth-century philosophy has been the idea that intentional notions—thoughts, concepts, meaning—are to be accounted for in terms of an individual's procedures for applying those notions. What is understood or thought has been thought to be reducible to actual understanding, which is in turn reducible to actual articulateable abilities or experiences. The Positivistic view that meaning is confirmation procedure, the Wittgensteinian slogan that meaning is use, Quine's argument for the indeterminacy of meaning based on his combination of holism about confirmation with the view that meaning must reduce to confirmation, the attempts to account for conceptual content in terms of inferential or functional role—all develop this theme.

Anti-individualism shows, in a way that holism about confirmation does not, that having certain intentional notions is not thus reducible to an individual's discriminative abilities or procedures. Of course, an individual can discriminate arthritis from any other thing simply by employing his concept of arthritis.

---

[19] In the absence of a distinctive definition or explication that individuates a concept's range of application, the individual might in principle use expressions like 'That sort of thing' or 'The kind of thing with such and such characteristics which bears relation R to my present thought about it', where R is the relevant environmental relation that fixes the application of the concept. These indexical specifications, however, do not suffice to explicate, much less provide a surrogate for, the individual's concept. Expressions like 'That sort of thing' are indexical—undergo shifts of reference with context—in a way that concepts like *water, aluminum, arthritis, edge, chair*, are not. So the ordinary meaning of the indexical expressions does not articulate the character of the relevant concepts. It is clear that the ordinary indexical expression might be used to fix the referents, or ranges of application, of any number of different concepts. The perceptual or other contextual mode of presentation associated with 'that' at a particular occurrence is not in every case a 'defining' characteristic, much less the concept itself. In any case, the contextually relevant conceptual backing for the demonstrative would have to be made explicit if philosophical weight were to be placed on it.

The expressions that involve specification of the relevant individuating environmental relation R also fail to provide concept-surrogates. They clearly express different concepts from those they purport to explicate; they do not come close to expressing the way that the individual thinks with concepts like the ones mentioned above, or to typing the same mental abilities. In some cases, the individual may lack the concepts to think about the complex R relation. Cf. 'Other Bodies' and my 'Vision and Intentional Content', in R. LePore and R. Van Gulick (eds.), *John Searle and His Critics*, (Cambridge, Mass.: Basil Blackwell, 1991).

Having such concepts requires having certain associated discriminating abilities. But having the concept is not exhausted by those associated abilities. Thus the individual must be able to discriminate arthritis from such things as animals, trees, and numbers, and from certain other diseases, in order to have the concept. But he need not be able to discriminate it from all other rheumatoidal diseases, actual or possible—except insofar as he does so by employing the concept *arthritis*. This is a point that nearly all individuals can be brought to recognize about their own concepts. Having the concept does not depend purely on associated discriminative procedures. It normally depends partly on causally mediated relations to actual instances of arthritis.

Holism and anti-individualism have forced refinement of the traditional view of the role of definition in constituting concepts and of the sense in which concepts are expressed by language. These changes do not 'overturn' the tradition, as philosophers fond of the revolutionary model of philosophy sometimes claim. But the changes are of fundamental importance in understanding thought and language. I think that they constitute genuine progress in philosophy.

13 *Social Anti-individualism, Objective Reference*

Donald Davidson taught me in graduate school. I have learned from him ever since. Quine and Hempel dealt the deathblows to the restricted approach to philosophy embodied in logical positivism. Davidson helped show how philosophy can say new and valuable things about traditional philosophical problems, including issues of fundamental human concern. His work is systematic and subtle. I think that on many basic matters it is right. Disagreement will occupy most of my remarks. But agreement looms largest in the broader scheme of things.

So first, agreement. I am in substantial agreement with Donald's discussion of the subjective—particularly our knowledge of our propositional attitudes as being authoritative and non-evidential. I also agree on what he calls perceptual externalism, and on its compatibility with authoritative self-knowledge. I agree that perceptual knowledge is non-evidential, and that it is fundamentally and directly about the physical world, not about sense-data. I see knowledge of other minds somewhat differently. I think that, like perceptual knowledge and self-knowledge, it can be direct and non-evidential.[1] But I agree in holding that self-knowledge and knowledge of other minds normally stand in a reciprocal relation.

Our disagreements lie primarily in our understanding of the role of the social in anti-individualism (or externalism) and in our understanding of the nature of objectivity.

First, let me characterize differences in our versions of social anti-individualism. We surely agree that as a matter of psychological necessity, we must communicate with others to learn a language. Davidson further argues that, as a constitutive matter, having thoughts and having language are dependent on relations to another person. My social anti-individualism is less global. I argue apriori that given that certain contingent matters are fixed, certain types of

All page numbers in parentheses in the text refer to Donald Davidson, *Subjective, Intersubjective, Objective* (Oxford: Clarendon Press, 2001).

[1] Cf. my 'Content Preservation', *The Philosophical Review*, 102 (1993), 457–488, and 'Reason and the First-Person', in C. Wright, B. C. Smith, and C. Macdonald (eds.), *Knowing Our Own Minds* (Oxford: Clarendon Press, 1998).

thoughts necessarily depend for their individuation on an individual's relations to others. For example, it is metaphysically or constitutively contingent that an individual allows that norms governing the use of his words partly depend on others' usage. It is contingent that some particular individual lacks sufficient background knowledge to distinguish arthritis from other rheumatoidal diseases. Given that these contingent matters are in place, and given that *arthritis* is a non-indexical notion, it is metaphysically or constitutively *necessary* that in order to have a thought about arthritis, one be in certain relations to others who are in a better position to specify the disease. I believe that these arguments bear both on concept possession (the ability to think about arthritis as such) and on reference through thought (the ability to make reference to arthritis at all), whether or not one's thought contains some familiar way of thinking about arthritis. I do not hold that social relations are necessary for having thoughts. My apriori arguments for necessities of social anti-individualism presuppose that certain contingent matters are fixed.

Despite the fact that my arguments are more modest, more concrete, and I think more compelling than Davidson's, he rejects them. One ground Davidson gives is that the incomplete understanding that they invoke—an individual's inability to distinguish arthritis from other rheumatoidal diseases—conflicts with first-person authority about attitudes involving the incompletely under-stood concept (pp. 26–27).[2] I cannot find a clear and cogent explanation of the supposed conflict. I suspect that the point rests on not distinguishing, as I do, between knowing what one's thoughts are in the sense of having the compet-ence required to think them and knowledgeably attribute them to oneself, on one hand, and knowing what one's thoughts are in the sense of being able to give correct explications of them, on the other (pp. 27–28).[3] This difference may connect to further differences between us regarding the specific ways hav-ing a thought depends on inferential relations that connect that thought to other thoughts. I believe that Davidson may be relying on a more restrictive view of these matters than I think tenable. But the view is not explicit in this context.

Another ground Davidson gives for his rejection is the proposal of a different interpretation of the particular cases. Where I held that a person could believe that arthritis occurs in the thigh, Davidson maintains that any such interpreta-tion of a person's belief could not be right.[4] He maintains that the error is a meta-linguistic one about the dictionary meaning of the word 'arthritis'. I do

---

[2] Donald Davidson, 'Knowing One's Own Mind', *Proceedings and Addresses of the American Philosophical Association*, 60 (1987), 448–449.

[3] I emphasize this distinction in various places. Cf. 'Individualism and Self-Knowledge', *The Journal of Philosophy*, 85 (1988), 662. Davidson's claim that on my view the relevant agents do not know what they mean or think suggests failure to draw this distinction. Cf. his 'Knowing One's Own Mind', 449–450.

[4] He appeals to holism about belief and the uncontroversial point that such a person would associate arthritis with different background beliefs and inferences from someone who knows that arthritis can occur only in joints.

not, as Davidson charges, insist that 'we are bound to give a person's words the meaning they have in his linguistic community' (28).[5] My account is based on details particular to the case. I built into the case various facts that I believe make the meta-linguistic move unacceptable. Davidson does not discuss these.

Davidson's critical remark 'we understand a speaker best when we interpret him as he intended to be interpreted' (p. 199) tells, I think, in favor of my view, not against it: Speakers commonly intend to be interpreted according to standards of usage that are in some respects better understood by others.[6] But this is not the crux of the disagreement. For my social anti-individualist thought experiment does not even depend on my view that an expert and an individual with a misconception of the nature of a disease can share beliefs. It is enough if they share reference with non-indexical concepts.[7] I believe it evident, from many other thought experiments in addition to mine, that partial dependence on others for securing the reference of one's words and concepts is a common and well-entrenched phenomenon. Non-indexical concepts (non-indexical predicational elements in propositional representational contents) must differ if their referents, or ranges of application, differ. Thus since the relevant concepts are non-indexical and their referents or ranges of application differ, the patients in the earth and twin-earth situations have different concepts or intentional thought contents, regardless of whether they share concepts or thoughts with their respective doctors.

Finally, Davidson expresses a distrust of thought experiments that center on conditions that in fact never arise. It is true that the twin-earth aspects of the thought experiment never arise. But these aspects are again inessential. The phenomena of shared reference and shared thoughts despite differences in explicational understanding, and the phenomenon of relying on others for fixing reference and for fixing standards of use, are ubiquitous in social life. The argument can work directly off these facts. I will not defend my view further here. I turn to Davidson's social anti-individualism.

As I noted, Davidson's version is very global. He holds that there are no beliefs without language, no language without an actual interpreter, and hence no beliefs without an actual interpreter. This very global social anti-individualism is linked to a set of further theses. He further claims that having beliefs constitutively depends on having a concept of objectivity, on having intentions to be interpreted as one intends to be interpreted, and on having knowledge of one's

---

[5] Davidson, 'Knowing One's Own Mind', 449.

[6] I believe that there is a network of principles, with many escape clauses, that carry a bias in favor of preservation of meaning and thought content between people who communicate with one another. Cf. my 'Content Preservation'; 'Interlocution, Perception, and Memory', *Philosophical Studies*, 86 (1997), 21–47; 'Computer Proof, Apriori Knowledge, and Other Minds', *Philosophical Perspectives*, 12 (1998), 1–37; and 'Comprehension and Interpretation', in L. Hahn (ed.), *The Philosophy of Donald Davidson* (Chicago: Open Court Publishers, 1999).

[7] Cf. my 'Wherein is Language Social?', in Alexander George (ed.), *Reflections on Chomsky* (Oxford: Basil Blackwell, 1989), (Ch. 11 above).

own thoughts. I doubt all of these theses. Detailed criticism of all of them here would be impossible. The systematic character of Davidson's work precludes it. I will fix on a pair of central points.

Davidson's triangulation thesis holds that to have thoughts, an individual must have a language that is actually interpreted by someone else. Davidson surely realizes that this thesis is unintuitive. But it is motivated by the plausible view that in order for an individual to have definite thoughts, there must be some non-arbitrary fact or ground that fixes what those thoughts are about. We can assume that something that regularly causes perceptual beliefs and which is discriminable for the individual gives one a start at finding a referent. But this consideration does not distinguish among, for example, light frequencies, retinal surface stimulations, various distal types of stimulations in the environment—such as physical surfaces, physical objects, properties of the objects—and various other elements in the causal chains leading to a purported perceptual belief. The fact that a speaker and an interpreter both respond to the same objects and properties in the distal environment, even though they respond to different light frequencies, different surface stimulations, and so on, gives a non-arbitrary basis for attributing referents to the thoughts. These referents provide a starting point for attributing concepts about those referents. Davidson holds that in the absence of such triangulation in the context of actual linguistic interpretation, there is no non-arbitrary ground for attributing what thoughts are about. Similarly, Davidson holds that in the absence of an interpreter, there is no non-arbitrary way to fix what would count as similarity of response to a purported cause.

I do not find it plausible that the presence of an interpreter, who need bear no causal relation to the interpreted individual, could play any role in constituting the nature of an individual's mental states. I believe that any interpreter must try to interpret mental states whose natures are independent of his or her interpretation. I will not develop this general doubt. I will also lay aside considerations about whether by memory and self-criticism an individual could develop triangulation on his own linguistic practice. I have never been convinced by arguments that hold that this is impossible in any deeper sense than that human children cannot do it.

The ground for doubt that I want to highlight stems from my view that the role that Davidson gives triangulation is filled much earlier in the ontogeny and phylogeny of the mental. Perceptual representation is individuated not only in terms of what an animal can discriminate.[8] It is individuated by reference to how perception figures in the animal's basic activities and functions. The first thing that a psychologist of animal vision asks is how vision aids the animal in coping with its particular environment. Perceptual representation is always individuated with an eye not only to what the animal or its systems can discriminate, but also to how the discriminations are used by the animal on the environment. The

---

[8] Cf. my 'Perception', *International Journal of Psychoanalysis*, 84 (2003), 157–167; and 'Perceptual Entitlement', *Philosophy and Phenomenological Research*, 67 (2003), 503–548.

relevant functions and activities are broadly biological and ecological. They are activities like navigating around obstacles, finding home, catching prey, foraging for food, escaping predators, linking up with a mate, and so forth. Relevant objects and properties in the distal environment are those that the animal uses perception to deal with. *Insofar as there is perception*, these are the objects of perceptual representation, other things equal. Similarity of response is also understood in terms of responses (across comparable animals and within an individual animal's own life) appropriate to these activities. The relevant distal objects, properties, and relations are further narrowed down by considering what features are accessible through the sensory receptors. For vision, these would be fundamentally features like color, shape, motion, distance, moving physical bodies, and so on. Other perceptual representations—those of food, danger, or shelter—would have to be explained in terms of their relations to representations of properties like these.

I said 'insofar as there is perception'. Not all sensory systems are perceptual systems. Perceptual systems link directly to animal activity—unlike servo-regulator sensory systems for regulating heartbeat, digestion, or even most mech-anisms for balance. Perceptions—at least many perceptions—are functionally available to the whole animal. Moreover, perceptual systems exhibit perceptual constancies. There are principles or mechanisms in the systems for representing properties or other entities as the same even as proximal stimulation and per-spective or mode of presentation vary. For example, a perceptual system might enable an animal to treat an object as stationary even as its retinal image grows dramatically and as its percepts of the object, its shape, and its position change. Or a perceptual system might enable an animal to treat a color as the same even though the illumination (hence the light intensity available to the retina and the perceptual mode of presentation) vary dramatically. Treating entities as the same is responding to them in ways that are functionally the same relative to the animal's basic activities. The science of vision has gone very far in providing rigorous explanations, in these terms, of perception in a wide range of animals.

In my view, the triangulation problem—often called the 'disjunction prob-lem'—that Davidson discusses to motivate appeal to linguistic communication in the triangulation thesis is no longer a serious problem. A solution is open to reflection. The same solution has long been exploited in psychology—especially animal psychology and visual psychology. Discriminated elements in the distal environment are the objects of perceptual representation because the distal envir-onment is what enters into animal activity, and because triangulation already occurs within genuine perceptual systems. Given this framework, just which properties and objects are perceptually represented can be determined by empir-ical testing. Triangulations offered by interpreters in linguistic communication are not needed to provide a non-arbitrary ground that fixes what perceptual representation is about.

Perception is not thought. As a matter of terminology, I take concepts to be certain elements in the representational contents of propositional attitudes.

I take thought to be a generic category for propositional attitudes. To think, an animal must have more than perception. As Davidson rightly emphasizes (pp. 98–101, 124 ff.), it must engage in inferences that tie different beliefs together; it must have intentions connected to beliefs; and so on. Independently of the triangulation thesis, Davidson claims that a creature without language cannot have beliefs. One argument is that without a language an animal cannot have the holistic interconnection among beliefs necessary to give the beliefs definite representational identities.

I believe that Davidson is correct to insist that to have propositional attitudes, an individual must be capable of connecting any given attitude with a range of others through capacities for propositional inference. But I see no apriori ground to think that in the absence of language, an animal's psychology cannot have requisite holistic connections. I want to enter two caveats here. One is that holistic, inferential connections do not do all of the work in determining propositional content. Perceptual beliefs have conceptual representational content that is parasitic on the representational content of perceptions. Perception-dependent concepts have quite definite representational identities that depend not only on their role in simple propositional inferences (a role necessary to enable them to be concepts), but also on their relation to perceptual representations, which have their own definite representational, though non-conceptual, identities. The other caveat is that the nature and extent of the requisite holism should not be assumed apriori. There may be areas of propositional inference for an animal or young child that are relatively specialized in the sense that principles and concepts appropriate to a given domain or type of enterprise are not transferred to other domains. Cognitive specialization seems to be a natural product of evolution, and I see no apriori reason why it should not apply to propositional attitudes as well as more primitive action sets and perceptual representations—as long as beliefs and intentions of any given sort are connected to some others by a range of inferential capacities—deductive, inductive, categorizational.

Davidson sometimes lists concepts that cannot be correctly attributed to animals. There are, of course, many concepts for which there is no empirical ground to believe an animal has them. It is extremely plausible that many concepts could not mark abilities in an individual's psychology if that individual did not have language. But listing such concepts does not show that attributing simple logical constants, perceptual concepts, and other primitive concepts fitted to an animal's basic activities and abilities is mistaken.

Sometimes Davidson claims that to have concepts and propositional attitudes, a being must have many *general* beliefs, or beliefs about *natures*, or beliefs about *what it is to be* an F (pp. 98, 101, 124, 195). I am not sure whether having a language is necessary to having such beliefs.[9] I think we need a much

---

[9] I think that simple quantification is probably available to non-linguistic higher animals, though I have never been convinced by (Quinean) arguments that quantification is constitutively necessary for objective reference.

richer analysis of purported internal connections between having a language and having explicational and explanatory abilities. But I also see no reason why an animal must have beliefs about natures or essences, or a conception of laws or criteria, to have beliefs. I am not even sure that it is necessary that an animal have non-modal general beliefs, as long as it makes inferences according to general principles.[10]

Davidson does not defend these claims about the need for general beliefs and beliefs about natures. I am aware that others have. I believe that such defenses as have been mounted do not survive close scrutiny. What is needed to have propositional attitudes is an interconnected set of capacities for propositional inference in the formation of belief and in intentional activity—all making use of definite representational contents. The attribution of such abilities should yield genuine, non-otiose explanations of the individual's or species' activities. In the last two or three decades, I believe that empirical explanations of the behavior of very young children and higher, pre-linguistic animals have met these constraints. There is evidence that higher animals use simple reasoning about perceivable objects and events to carry out plans, including long-term plans involving adaptable, flexible, multi-form relations between means and ends, that are illuminatingly explained only in terms of inferences among simple propositional attitudes. In the case of many non-human species, it seems to me an open empirical question whether they have propositional attitudes. I think that there is empirical ground, however, to think that non-human apes are among those that do. No apriori argument that I know of preempts or rules out these apparent empirical grounds.

Davidson also claims that to have beliefs, a being must be capable of surprise, in the particular sense that it has a *conception of a mistaken belief and a conception of objective truth* (p. 102). I do not find this claim persuasive. In my view, there is a persistent tendency in twentieth-century philosophy to move too easily between requirements on having propositional attitudes with objective reference and requirements on attitudes involving a *conception* of objectivity. In the work of some very fine philosophers, the move is just conflation. Davidson does not conflate the two levels. He makes the move quite explicitly.

But I see no impressive justification for it. I think the claim that to have a belief, one must have beliefs about beliefs—and about their objective truth or falsity—is not a conceptually compelling claim. I think it quite implausible.

---

[10] Cf. note 9. The very having of concepts requires associated inferential capacities. Inferential capacities are general. I believe that an animal need not be capable of representing logical truths associated with the relevant inference rules. Whether an animal must be capable of *representing* some sort of generality (that is, have quantifiers) if it is to have propositional attitudes seems to me less obvious. One can certainly imagine inferences involving propositional connectives among singular perceptual thoughts, following inference rules for the connectives together with substitution of identities. I believe that certain types of animal memory introduce generality in ways that go beyond perception and that higher animals may have simple beliefs in quantified form. These issues need more exploration.

I believe that this claim, and its attendant background considerations, are not nearly strong enough to oppose an increasingly sophisticated and well-entrenched body of empirical explanation. Empirical evidence suggests that there are animals and very young children with beliefs, but no beliefs about beliefs.[11]

A *conception* of objectivity does require the interconnected set of abilities that Davidson lays out in many subtle and compelling ways. A conception of objectivity is perhaps intimately connected with having a language. A conception of objectivity may well be distinctive of human beings, at least on our planet. But having simple capacities for propositional inference among perceptual beliefs, memories, intentions, and plans that represent a world that is objectively independent of those beliefs does not require a *conception* of objectivity. Having such beliefs perhaps requires a capacity for learning and for surprise in the ordinary sense. It certainly requires a system of first-level beliefs and intentions and first-level capacities for propositional inferences, which are subject to norms for veridicality, correctness, error, entitlement, and so on. But meta-conceptions of these matters are not constitutively necessary.

The notions of correctness and error in representation already have a grip on perceptual representation. They gain grip in the context of the perceptual constancies embedded in animal perceptual systems and in the context of the use of perception to fulfill animal needs and functions in the animal's normal environment. Notions of (propositional) truth and falsity become applicable when representation is embedded in a system of propositional inference, and when questions of rational and other epistemic norms for inference and belief formation are apropos. This system necessarily involves at least limited inferential holisms, and it again serves the animal's functions in its normal environment. Such a system does require certain capacities to represent independently of the immediate perceptual context which I will not detail here. But having a language and having a concept of objectivity are not necessary conditions on having propositional attitudes. They are conditions on various types of understanding. Propositional abilities emerge before any capacity to understand them.

I have other differences with Davidson. I differ on what it takes to answer the sceptic. I differ on important details of the epistemology of perceptual belief.[12] But I want to conclude on a harmonious note. Excellence in philosophy is not fundamentally a matter of getting things just right. It is a matter of richness in argumentation. It is a matter of depth and breadth of insight. It is a matter of opening new subjects for reflection and of reorienting reasoning about old

[11] Cf., e.g., Daniel Povanelli, *Folk Physics for Chimps* (Oxford: Oxford University Press, 2000); Michael Tomasello and Josep Call, *Primate Cognition* (Oxford: Oxford University Press, 1997).

[12] On the former, see my 'Some Reflections on Scepticism: Reply to Stroud' in M. Hahn and B. Ramberg (eds.), *Reflections and Replies: Essays on the Philosophy of Tyler Burge* (Cambridge, Mass.: MIT Press, 2003). On the latter, see my 'Perceptual Entitlement'.

subjects. It is sometimes a matter of developing new truths or approximate truths. Donald has done all these things, and in good measure. We do not pause frequently enough to celebrate, admire, and praise achievement in philosophy. Here is a case and an occasion where we should do so. Let us hope that we will be given even more from this rich source of philosophical wisdom.[13]

---

[13] This comment is a lightly edited and lightly supplemented version of my oral comments on Donald Davidson's *Subjective, Intersubjective, Objective* at the convention of the Pacific Division of the American Philosophical Association in Spring of 2002. I have retained some of the informality of the occasion—using 'Davidson' in passages of discord and 'Donald' where the cadences express harmony.

14   *Individuation and Causation in Psychology*

Over the last decade I have argued that certain relations between an individual and his environment are partly determinative of what it is for the individual to have certain kinds of mental states and events. In any full explication of the nature of such mental states, such relations will be cited. I call this view 'anti-individualism'.

I have grounded this view on a series of thought experiments. I will provide a crude sketch of one of them. One imagines someone *A* with a general familiarity with aluminum but without an ability to provide an account of the nature of aluminum that would distinguish it from every other actual or possible metal. *A* is aware that he is unable to do this, and allows that there might be other metals that would not be aluminum, but which he would be at a loss to distinguish practically or theoretically from aluminum. Nevertheless, *A* does often see, talk about, think about aluminum—as aluminum. He thinks that aluminum is a light metal, for example. *A* is like most of us.

Next one imagines a counterfactual environment in which there is no aluminum and no colleagues of *A* who think or talk about aluminum. This environment contains in aluminum's place one of those actual or possible metals that *A* could not distinguish from aluminum. Call this metal 'twalum'. The environment also contains either *A* or a counterpart of *A* that is for our purposes physiologically identical with *A*, throughout his history. Call this individual '*B*'. (Insofar as there are minor gravitational differences between aluminum and the other metal, I assume that they need not affect *B*'s physiology in any way that is relevant to accounting for his mental states.)

In such a case, *B* clearly does not have any thoughts about aluminum. He does not, for example, think that aluminum is a light metal. He thinks rather that twalum is a light metal. The difference in thoughts clearly depends on differences in the two individuals' relations to their environments. *A* grew up seeing and otherwise interacting with aluminum. The kinds of thoughts that he can think are determined by these interactions. *B*'s counterpart grew up interacting with twalum, and acquired thoughts grounded in these interactions. Thus the

I am grateful to Ned Block and David Braun for valuable criticisms.

individuation of thought kinds sometimes depends on one's relations to one's environment.

The original thought experiments concerned mental states and events, ordinarily understood. More recently, I showed that non-individualistic modes of individuation can be clearly discerned in the method and theory of cognitive psychology—in particular, the psychology of vision. I think that nearly all parts of psychology that attribute intentional mental states presuppose such modes of individuation for some of their explanatory kinds.[1]

I find this view about psychology natural and unmomentous, once it is realized that intentional states as specified in ordinary mentalistic discourse are individuated non-individualistically. Cognitive psychology makes extensive use of intentional idiom. Nothing critical to the scientific purposes of cognitive psychology seems to be at odds with its sharing with common sense a presupposition of non-individualistic kind individuation. Such individuation supports some of the primary aims of psychology.

Many philosophers do not agree. Although most have conceded the non-individualistic character of mental states as specified in ordinary discourse, many are convinced that psychology cannot reasonably individuate mental states in the same way. Most of the writing from this point of view has not bothered to defend this conviction in any detail. It is devoted to attempts to specify individualistic conceptions of content—'narrow content'. These conceptions are not employed outside philosophical circles. Their potential interest derives from the conviction that cognitive psychology (unbeknownst to itself) needs them as surrogates for more ordinary, non-individualistic conceptions. I shall ignore them here, the better to concentrate on the conviction.

I want to discuss a line of objection to my views, developed by Jerry Fodor, that features causation.[2] I hope that this parochial exercise will serve two more general purposes. It will indicate how a common but mistaken view of the special sciences can underlie reasoning about causation. And it will motivate an alternative view of the relation between causation and individuation in psychology.

I

Fodor's line of objection is very general. It purports to appeal to such general features of science that, were it sound, there would be no need to discuss

[1] Cf. my 'Individualism and the Mental', *Midwest Studies of Philosophy*, 4 (1979), 73–121; 'Other Bodies', in A. Woodfield (ed.), *Thought and Object* (Oxford: Oxford University Press, 1982); 'Cartesian Error and the Objectivity of Perception', in P. Pettit and J. McDowell (eds.), *Subject, Thought, and Context* (Oxford: Oxford University Press, 1986); 'Intellectual Norms and Foundations of Mind'. *The Journal of Philosophy*, 83 (1986), 697–720; 'Individualism and Psychology', *The Philosophical Review*, 95 (1986), 3–45 (Chs. 5, 4, 7, 10, 9 above).

[2] Jerry A. Fodor, *Psychosemantics*, (Cambridge, Mass.: MIT Press, 1987), ch. 2. I will cite page numbers from this work in the text.

specific theories in psychology. In keeping with the cast of his objection, Fodor has nothing to say to my arguments that the psychology of vision is non-individualistic. The objection begins with a simple argument, and proceeds with some intricate considerations in favor of one of the argument's premises.

The argument is as follows: (1) Psychological explanation is causal explanation. (2) States and processes appealed to in psychological explanation should be type-individuated in terms of their causal powers. (3) The anti-individualistic conception postulates the possibility of differences in mental states and processes between two individuals without any corresponding differences in their brain states. (4) But individuals cannot differ in their causal powers if they do not differ in their brain states. So: (5) Psychological explanation should not type-individuate states and processes anti-individualistically.

I will concentrate on step (4), but first a word about the other steps. Step (3) is acceptable for the sake of argument, but it is not strictly true. The anti-individualistic conception claims that in many cases what it is to be in a certain kind of mental state depends on relations between an individual and his environment. This conception does not entail that two individuals' mental kinds might differ while relevantly corresponding brain states and events remain type-identical.[3] Failure of supervenience of an individual's mental kinds on his neural kinds follows only if relevant differences in the environment do not necessitate differences in the individual's underlying brain states. Now I do reject mind–brain supervenience. I think it 'metaphysically possible' for two people with the same brain state kinds (over their whole histories) to have different kinds of mental states. Mental states depend for their natures on relations to the environment in ways that are different from the ways brain states do.[4] I think that the aluminum example can be used to undermine mind–brain supervenience as well as individualism. Thus step (3) is sound, at least *ad hominem*.

Fodor's construal of steps (1) and (2) ignores a widely held position associated with Davidson. According to this position, although psychological explanation is causal in the sense that it makes reference to causal relations, psychological states are not type-individuated to fit causal laws. Psychological explanation

---

[3] Here and elsewhere, I understand the notion of 'might' or possibility involved in step (3) to be not scientific or physical possibility but something like what is commonly called 'metaphysical possibility'. (Similarly for 'cannot' in step (4).) My views do not depend on exactly how one construes this notion as long as one allows possibilities or illustrative stories that allow conditions of individuation to vary, where these conditions may include physical law. I think that some psychological kinds depend for their natures on physical laws relating individual to environment. In testing this view, one must consider 'possibilities' in which physical laws are not held fixed. It is not strictly necessary that one consider such variations of physical law 'possible' (although I do incline toward thinking of them as possible) as long as one allows oneself heuristic devices that enable one to bring out the sensitivity of psychological kinds to environmental conditions, including environmental laws. I use the phrase 'metaphysical possibility' with these qualifications in mind.

[4] I take it that to *be* a brain involves evolving in a certain way and having certain functions within the environment of the rest of the body, and probably within a larger environment. So an entity that coalesced by quantum accident but which was atomically homologous to a brain would not be a brain. So the natural kind *brain* is itself not supervenient on the atomic make-up of a brain.

provides loose law-like generalizations about events whose causal efficacy is best accounted for only in non-psychological terms.[5]

For the sake of argument I will grant steps (1) and (2) with two qualifications. One is that I will not assume that Fodor and I understand 'causal power' in the same way. The other is that I do not agree that causally relevant type-individuation always focuses on *effects*. The causal *antecedents* of instances of a type (or of events explanatorily associated with instances of a type) are sometimes more significant. Types of rock in geology, species in biology, indicator instruments in science and engineering, optical fibers in physiology, perceptual states in psychology are clearly typed more with a view to causal antecedents than with a view to causal consequents.

The crux of the dispute is step (4) and its notion of 'causal power'. Before considering Fodor's arguments for step (4), I want to make some background remarks. I assume with Fodor that individuals with the same brain states will make the same movements. I also assume that there are no gaps (into which mental events might swoop) among the events described by the physical sciences. I further assume that if causal chains as described in the physical sciences ('physical causation') did not occur, causal chains as described by psychology ('psychological causation') would not occur.

If one thinks about psychological causation purely from the point of view of 'physiological causation' (causation as described by physiology)—or more generally, causation as described in the physical sciences—one is likely to settle on a use of 'causal power' according to which step (4) is unproblematic. Considered apart from individuation in psychology, (4) can certainly seem plausible. But Fodor's notion of causal power is developed in the context of steps (1) and (2). The causal powers of an individual must be understood to be properties that determine how *psychology* individuates its kinds. This restriction is critical in evaluating (4). I shall invoke it repeatedly.

The following point of view motivates accepting (4) in the light of the restriction: Physiological processes are where the 'real' causation in psychology goes on. Psychology should concern itself with 'real' causation. So psychology should adopt a taxonomic scheme that does not distinguish psychological causes or

[5] Cf. Donald Davidson, 'Mental Events', in *Essays on Actions and Events* (Oxford: Oxford University Press, 1980). This view seems to lie behind the excellent discussion of Fodor's argument in Robert Van Gulick, 'Metaphysical Arguments for Internalism and Why They Don't Work', in S. Silvers (ed.), *ReRepresentation*, Synthese Philosophy Series (Dordrecht: Kluwer, 1988). I agree with much of Van Gulick's discussion. In particular, we agree that Fodor provides no good reason to believe that individuation of psychological kinds must supervene on individuation of neural kinds. But I want to mention a point of difference. Van Gulick apparently holds that physical descriptions are the primary ones in indicating causal relations. He apparently does not see psychological principles as causal principles but calls them psychologically interesting generalizations that, in some unspecified way throw light on causal patterns. This view may be correct. But I do not myself embrace it because I do not think that there is any clear, well-established sense in which physical descriptions of mental–physical causal relations provide the primary insight into causal relations. Cf. sec. V.

effects unless there is a distinction in physiological causes or effects. I believe that this point of view drives Fodor's intuitions.

The point of view is certainly odd. It is a precarious strategy to abstract from the aims and practice of psychology in trying to understand psychological kind individuation. Fodor thinks that he can assume a notion of causal power that is independent of issues regarding psychology and then use it to place restrictions on kind individuation in psychology. I will explain in the following sections why I find this approach hopeless.

II

I turn now to Fodor's arguments for step (4)—the view that it is impossible for individuals with the same brain states to have mental states with different causal powers. I shall divide the arguments into two stages, letting exposition precede evaluation.

(I) Fodor considers the following view: *A* and *B* have different causal powers because when *A* says the word forms 'Bring aluminum', he causes someone to bring him aluminum; whereas when *B* says 'Bring aluminum', he causes someone to bring him twalum (since in his environment, those word forms mean to bring twalum).[6]

Fodor replies that identity of causal powers must be assessed across 'contexts', not within 'contexts'. As an analogy he considers testing the causal powers of his and his reader's biceps: 'Roughly, our biceps have the same causal powers if the following is true: For any thing x and any context C, if you can lift x in C, then so can I; and if I can lift x in C, then so can you.' If in a context in which a chair is nailed to the floor Fodor cannot lift it, and in another context in which the chair is not nailed to the floor his reader can lift it—that difference does not show that their biceps have different causal powers; for they have been tested in 'different contexts'. Fodor concedes that when *A* and *B* say the word forms 'Bring aluminum', they get different sorts of things in their respective environments. But he claims that this difference is irrelevant to testing their causal powers, because their utterances occur in different contexts. He holds that if the causal powers of *A* and *B* were tested in the same contexts, they would always be the same [pp. 34–35]. I think these claims mistaken. I shall return to them after setting out the second stage of the argument.

(II) Fodor next imagines his opponent's conceding that the causal powers of physiological twins are always the same when tested against effects that are non-intentionally individuated. He considers the view that such twins still differ in their intentionally individuated behavior. One might add that they also differ

---

[6] Fodor discusses other examples I have given. I will key his discussion to the aluminum example. I think that this will not affect the substance of the discussion.

in numerous other mental effects—including those thoughts, desires, intentions that involve the concept *aluminum*. Fodor offers two replies.

(IIA) He finds it hard to see why the position would not be committed to holding that *A* and *B*'s brain states differ as well as their mental states (pp. 37–38): *A* is in a brain state that eventuates in his uttering the form of words 'Bring aluminum'; so is *B*. If their uttering these forms of words counts as their behaving differently, it looks as though their brain states differ in their behavioral consequences—hence in their causal powers, hence in the brain state types of which they are tokens. But it seems clear that *A* and *B* need not differ in their brain states.

(IIB) Fodor's primary reply rests on an example that he appeals to repeatedly. He defines 'is an H-particle at time t' so that this phrase applies to a particle at t if and only if Fodor's dime is heads-up at t. He defines 'is a T-particle at time t' analogously for tails-up. He points out that whether particles are H-particles has nothing to do with their causal powers. [p. 33]

Fodor thinks that the view that psychology might treat *A* and *B* as differing in their intentionally specified behavior (and mental states) is analogous to the view that physics might distinguish H-particles from T-particles. But it is hardly obvious that the analogy holds. What Fodor needs to show is that there are no laws or law-like generalizations, of the sort psychology provides, that describe actual causal patterns and that are formulable in the ordinary non-individualistic vocabulary.[7]

Fodor's remarks to this end are not very concise. I will try to summarize them fairly. Fodor states that the trouble with the H-particle method of individuation is that the relations between the coin and the particles are not the right kind to 'affect the causal powers' of the latter:[8] 'Effects on causal powers require mediation by laws and/or mechanisms; and, in the Twin cases, there are no such mechanisms and no such laws.' He supports this claim as follows: For any causal relation between *A*'s mental states and instances of aluminum, there must be a corresponding relation that holds between *A*'s *neurological* states and instances of aluminum—a sort of causal relation which *B*'s neurological states do not enter. Despite this difference, *A*'s and *B*'s neurological states are type-identical. This is because 'the difference in causal *histories* of their brain states is not of the right sort to effect a difference in the causal *powers* of their brains.' He concludes, 'Parallelism of argument surely requires us to hold that the differences between the causal histories of the mental states [of *A* and *B*] are

---

[7] I am using my terminology here rather than Fodor's. Oddly, he characterizes individualism as the view that psychological states are individuated with respect to their causal powers [p. 42]. I agree with this view, with the provisos about the understanding of 'causal power' and about the role of causal antecedents in individuation that I have indicated.

[8] Elsewhere, Fodor seems to suggest this definition: 'x's having property P affects x's causal powers just in case x wouldn't have caused the same events had it not been P' [p. 38]. He seems to interpret 'x wouldn't have caused the same events had it not been P' as 'in some possible context, if x had not been P, x would not cause some kinds of events that it now would cause in that context'.

not of the right sort to effect differences in the causal powers of their minds.'
[p. 39, note 6]

This supporting argument does not advance the discussion. It simply begs the
question. I accept everything in the argument up to the conclusion, but I deny
the conclusion. Psychology does not and need not individuate mental states in
parallel with brain states.

Fodor says more. He says that on my view about the individuation of psychological kinds, there must be some mechanism that connects the causal powers
of an individual's mental states with his environment and that it does so without
affecting his physiology. But he claims it is impossible to affect the causal
powers of a person's mental states without affecting his physiology:

God made the world such that the mechanisms by which environmental variables
affect organic behaviors run via their effects on the organism's nervous system.
[pp. 39–40]

You can affect the relational properties of things in all sorts of ways—including by
stipulation. But for one thing to affect the causal powers of another, there must be a
mediating law or mechanism. It's a mystery what this could be in the Twin ... cases;
not surprisingly, since it's surely plausible that the only mechanisms that can mediate environmental effects on the causal powers of mental states are neurological.
The way to avoid making this mystery is to count the mental states—and mutatis
mutandis, the behaviors—of Twins ... as having the same causal powers, hence as
taxonomically identical. [p. 41]

These remarks risk conflating the question whether causal claims of events
that run from the environment to behavior necessarily run 'via' neural chains
of events, with the question whether *patterns* of causal relation between the
environment and the individual could bear on the *individuation* of psychological
kinds in a different way from the way they bear on the individuation of neural
kinds.[9]

The first quote urges the view that the environment has effects on organic
behavior only if it has effects on the organism's nervous system. This view is
no objection, since I accept it.

The second passage is hard to interpret. Insofar as it differs from the first, it
claims that only a neurological law or pattern can connect environmental effects
on an individual with those causal properties of mental states that are relevant
to the individuation of mental states. I suspect that if Fodor were not conflating

---

[9] Fodor's terms 'mechanism' and 'affect the causal powers' tend to engender the conflation
described above. Sometimes 'mechanism' can mean 'causal chain of particular events'; sometimes
it can mean 'law' or 'law-governed pattern of causally related events.' 'Affect the causal powers'
can seem to describe a relation between particular events that are the effects of the environment
on the individual and particular states or properties that are further effects of these effects. But
insofar as it is relevant to individuation, it must be used to describe the bearing of patterns of causal
relations (e.g. between the environment and the individual) on the individuation of kinds relevant
to causal explanation in psychology.

chains of individual events with patterns—chains of types of events—or with laws, he would not have made this claim. For there is no reason why a psychological law or pattern cannot make the connection. Nor is there any reason why a law or pattern involving psychological kinds cannot relate the individual to his environment. Fodor suggests that there is some mystery about failures of supervenience between psychological and physiological kinds, without explaining what it is.

In order to understand better how failures of supervenience of the mental on the physiological are compatible with psychology's assumption that gapless neurological chains must connect stimulus with response, let us set psychology aside for a moment and look at some other sciences. In geology, land masses are typed as plates because of their relations to other land masses. If there were no sliding of land masses across the face of the earth, land masses would not have been typed as plates. Moreover, the causal powers associated with these land masses would have been differently described by geology. But the chemistry and physics of the relevant land masses need not (metaphysically need not) have been affected. A land mass with substantially the same non-relational physical features could—because of its different relations to the environment—be of a different geological kind. Thus geological kinds do not supervene on the kinds of masses that are described by physics and that constitute the geological entities.

Similarly in biology, organs in the body are typed because of their function in the 'bodily environment' that surrounds them. Something is a heart because its organic function is to pump blood in a circulatory system that extends beyond the surfaces of the heart. One can imagine an organ in a different sort of body with a totally different function (it might pump waste for example). The causal powers attributed to such an organ by biology would be different from those attributed to a heart. Such an organ would not be a heart, but it might be chemically and structurally homologous to a heart. The biological kind *heart* does not supervene on the chemical structures of material that constitutes hearts.

The special sciences track causal patterns that cut across one another. One science's typology may be more 'environmentally' dependent than another's, or dependent on a different sort of environment. In such cases, it is possible for that science (geology, biology) to make its methods of kind individuation sensitive to possible differences in individual environmental patterns of interaction, while the typology of a science (chemistry, physics) that deals with the underlying physical constitution of the individual remains insensitive to those possible differences.

In my view, despite significant differences between psychology and the natural sciences, psychology's relation to neurophysiology is similar, in the relevant respects, to the just mentioned relations between natural sciences. There are causal patterns between environment and individual that warrant typing certain psychological states in terms of aspects of the environment. Psychology may try to explain such environment–individual interaction. Or it may presuppose such causal relations in its typology, using this typology in explaining the individual's behavior and formation of mental states. (For more on this distinction, see

Section IV.) Whenever psychology attempts to explain an individual's behavior on the basis of such a typology, there must be neurologically typed causal chains connecting stimulations of bodily surfaces and bodily motions.

But these typologies cut across one another. If the environment has been relevantly different, the patterns of interaction between individual and environment—which are either explained or presupposed—would have been different. The psychological kinds that the individual would instantiate would have been different. But there is no reason in metaphysical principle why these differences must affect the typology of neurophysiology. The patterns of causation that neurophysiology deals with have less to do with individual–environmental relations than those that concern psychology.[10]

---

[10] I made these points in 'Individualism and Psychology' (Ch. 9 above). (The quote that I take from this article below is on pp. 230–231, this volume.) I warned against confusing causation—a relation among particular events or states—and individuation, which is based on patterns among causal relations. I pointed out that there is a *non sequitur* in the following reasoning: the world is so constituted that the only way that the environment can have effects on an organism's behavior is to have effects on its nervous system, which in turn produce bodily motions that constitute behavior. So any difference in the typology of mental states or behavior must have a corresponding difference in the typology of neural states. This reasoning leaps from necessary dependence of psychological causation on neural causation and continuity of causation at the neural level, to supervenience of psychological kind on neural kinds. The gap in reasoning is illustrated in the examples from other sciences that I provided.

I had written, 'Variations in the environment that do not vary the impacts that causally 'affect' the subject's body may 'affect' the individuation of the ... intentional processes he or she is undergoing. ... It does not follow that the environment causally affects the subject in any way that circumvents its having effects on the subject's body'. Fodor replies:

But it looks to me like that's precisely what *does* follow, assuming that by 'causally affecting' the subject Burge means to include determining the causal powers of the subject's psychological states. You can't both individuate behaviors in Burge's way (viz. *non*locally) and hold that the causal powers of mental states are locally supervenient. [p. 41]

This reply is confused. I meant by 'causally affects the subject' *'bears causal relations to events or states in the subject's mind or body'*. I do individuate some behavior nonlocally, but I take it that the causal powers of mental states—and more generally the sorts of properties that psychology is concerned with when it gives causal explanations—are also not locally supervenient; the individuation of the mental states and their causal powers presupposes certain relations between the individual and his environment. Causation is local in the sense that each causal series of particular events between the environment and the individual's mental states necessarily 'runs via', or presupposes the existence of, some causal relations (causal series of particular events) between the environment and the surfaces of the individual's body; and each causal relation between the individual's mental states and his behavior is necessarily associated with some causal series between the individual's neural states and his bodily motions (ignoring behavior that does not involve motion). But individuation of mental kinds and behavioral kinds, and individuation of those causal powers associated with these kinds, are nonlocal.

Fodor does get around to questioning this position. But his questioning amounts to unsupported expostulation: 'But is Burge seriously prepared to give up the local supervenience of causal powers? *How could* differences of context affect the [individuation of] causal powers of one's mental states without affecting the [individuation of] states of one's brain?' [pp. 41–42]. (I have interpolated the phrases in the brackets to guard against further confusion of causation with individuation.) The answer to the first question is 'yes'. As regards the second, the examples from other sciences show how differences in environmental 'context' could affect psychology's individuation of kinds and causal powers without affecting the individuation of kinds or causal powers by a science concerned with the physical constitution of the individual.

This completes my discussion of Fodor's defense of line (IIB). It also constitutes a reply to his line (IIA). Brain sciences are concerned with patterns that are not as sensitive to individual–environmental relations as the patterns that concern psychology.

III

I turn now to Fodor's first (I) line of defense of the idea that individuals cannot differ in their causal powers if they have the same brain states—step (4) in his argument. It will be recalled that Fodor claimed that causal powers of two individuals must be tested by considering effects of their activities in the same contexts. He further claimed that if the twins were tested in the same contexts, they would always produce the same effects. He took this result to indicate that they have the same causal powers—powers in terms of which psychology individuates its kinds. So the twins are supposed to be psychologically identical.[11]

The appropriate applications of the notions of causal power and context are, however, less obvious than Fodor supposes. In the first place, there are clearly 'contexts' in which the twins' utterances would produce different non-intentionally specified effects in the physical world. Suppose a context in which hearers understand what both *A* and *B* say, wish to comply with their requests, and are in a position to do so. (For no explicit reason, Fodor uses only contexts in which the remarks by exactly one of the twins will be misunderstood by his hearers.) When *A* makes a request with the sounds 'Bring aluminum', he is brought aluminum. When *B* makes a request with the sounds 'Bring aluminum', he is brought twalum. Since the individuals have different physical effects in the same context, by Fodor's own test they have different causal powers.

The case relies on hearers' understanding. I think that this reliance is appropriate. Hearer understanding is the normal situation when the effects of speech are being considered. Regularities associated with successful communication are presupposed in most experiments in cognitive psychology.

This reliance is, however, inessential. There could be a device that traced the histories of individuals, recording whether they had been in causal contact with aluminum. Such a device could bring aluminum to an individual with such a causal history when he made the sounds 'Bring aluminum'—and not otherwise. In such a context, *A* would have different effects from *B*. Once again, there is a possible context in which the twins' acts produce different effects. Unless some restriction is placed on admissible contexts, Fodor's test will count any

---

[11] The mental events of the twins in the relevant thought experiments cause different mental events and intentional actions. Our discussion has shown how this is possible. But for purposes of criticizing this line of objection, I shall not rely on this view.

two individuals with any differences at all in their physical histories as having different causal powers.

Of course, one might justly protest that many such devices will not be keyed to the sort of causal powers that are relevant to causal explanation in science. But this protest brings out a weakness in Fodor's test. The test does not provide an independent check on whether two individuals will fall under the same explanatory kinds for any given science. Interpreting the test in such a way as to make it individuate those causal powers that are relevant to scientific typology requires that one already know what counts as an admissible kind. But that is precisely the point at issue. Not all historical considerations are irrelevant to typing in the sciences. Whether a rock is igneous, whether an organ is a heart, whether a neural fiber is optical depends on how it was formed and/or what its evolved function is—not merely on how it will respond physically to any conceivable stimulus. Similarly, it is hardly obvious that a context in which a speaker's utterances are understood is an inappropriate context for checking causal powers relevant to psychological explanation. By itself Fodor's test provides no restriction at all on kind individuation in the sciences.

There is another thing wrong with the test. It is insensitive to differences among the typologies of different sciences. So it is insensitive to the different ways in which sciences recognize causal powers. Consider the case of a heart again. To be a heart, an entity has to have the normal, evolved function of pumping blood in a body's circulatory system. One can conceive of a physically homologous organ whose function is to pump waste—or even a physically homologous entity that came together accidentally and lacks a function. Such entities would not be hearts.

The causal powers of a heart that are relevant to its being typed a heart concern its role in circulating blood. Similarly, many of the physiological laws that govern a heart have to do with its relations to its environment—the relation between heart pressure and pressure in the blood vessels, the relation between regulatory systems in the brain and pumping action by the heart, and so on.

We can imagine that a physically homologous organ whose function is to pump waste is surgically replaced by a heart. This is a physically and perhaps even biologically possible situation. In such a context, the heart would have the same physical effects as its physically homologous counterpart. We can also imagine a heart being surgically replaced by the organ for pumping waste; again that organ would pump blood in the same way that the heart would.

But it would be ludicrous to argue from these cases that the heart and its counterpart have the same causal powers *as typed by physiology* and that there is therefore no difference in kind. From the point of view of some sciences, the two entities would indeed count as type-identical. But the physiological differences are patent. Physiology recognizes causal powers of the heart which are exercised in its functionally normal environment. It individuates its kinds with a view to understanding regularities in an actual environment. Of course, other 'environments' for the heart, in which it would have very different sorts of effects, are metaphysically possible. The surgical example indicates such possibilities. Physiology may explain how the heart would act in some of these environments. But these environments are irrelevant to the scheme of kind individuation that physiology actually uses. Fodor's test is insensitive to this dependence of many special sciences on a normal environment for picking out those causal powers that are relevant to an explanatory typology in those sciences.

The analogy to psychology should be obvious. Psychological states are type-individuated to account for causal patterns that are played out in the environment of the individual subject. The fact that from the point of view of physics or physiology, the bodies of *A* and *B* may have the same effects if each were transplanted into the other's context does not show that those causal powers that are of interest to psychology should be counted the same. Insofar as Fodor's test ignores the environmental background against which the individuals' psychological states are type-individuated, it is useless as a test for those causal powers that are relevant to type individuation in psychology.

I conclude that Fodor's line of defense (I) for step (4), like the lines (IIA) and (IIB), fails. I see no other arguments in favor of this step, nor does the step seem plausible in view of the anti-individualistic considerations that count against it.

IV

An implicit source of the conviction that there is something scientifically impossible about the individuation of psychological states in an environmentally sensitive way is a misconception about the relation between individuation and environment–individual causal interaction. It is often thought that since bearing some complicated causal relation to aluminum or to water is clearly not a property cited in psychology and is not something that psychology is likely to try to explain, the anti-individualist view must be mistaken.[12]

But a conflation underlies this reasoning. Not every relation between individual and environment that is necessary, sufficient, or importantly contributory to the individuation of mental kinds is itself a candidate for a scientifically useful kind or relation. It is one thing to presuppose a property or relation in one's

---

[12] Fodor seems to reason this way. He ridicules the anti-individualist conception by repeatedly comparing the property of being an H-particle with that of being a mental state of a person who lives in a world where there is XYZ rather than H_2O in the puddles [p. 34]. He then points out that living in a world where there is H_2O in puddles is clearly not a scientific kind. A boring mistake in this reasoning is that, on my view (as on virtually anyone's), just living somewhere has nothing directly to do with having any particular concept, and thus is irrelevant to psychology. (Fodor knows this—cf. p. 39, note 6; but he backslides in the interests, I suspect, of rhetorical point-making—cf. p. 40 and p. 40, note 7.) A more interesting reason for the failure of this sort of objection is the subject of the ensuing paragraphs. The sort of conflation that I shall be discussing also dominates Fodor's 'Methodological Solipsism Considered as a Research Strategy in Cognitive Psychology', in *Representations* (Cambridge, Mass.: MIT Press, 1981), 246–252.

typology. It is another to use it in one's explanations. Thus a full philosophical understanding of what it is to have the concept of water might refer to causal relations between individuals and their environments. But it is not incumbent on psychology, or any other science, to cite those relations as explanatory kinds. The property *bears such and such causal relation to H_2O* is not the sort of property that is appropriate for purposes of scientific explanation. The relevant psychological kind is *having the concept water*.

This conflation of scientific kinds with properties that figure in the explication of what is involved in being an instance of those kinds plays a part in an argument originally put forward by Ned Block and repeated by Fodor.[13] Block describes a psychology of individual differences regarding taste. In accordance with one of my examples, we are to imagine twins with different concepts—someone who mistakenly thinks that brisket can only be beef, and a twin who has a concept other than brisket (call it *tw-brisket*) that correctly applies only to beef brisket. Fodor and Block lampoon the view that a psychology of individual differences would attribute a difference between the twins and ascribe the difference to a difference in 'linguistic affiliation', which is the putative source of their conceptual differences. They hold that the science would attribute any differences either to genetic endowment or to early learning.

I see no reason to disagree. The objection does not clearly conflict with anything I hold. Let us grant, what seems dubious, that this branch of psychology is acceptably clear about how it should treat the case. There is no reason to think that the science makes full use of intentional notions. The science appears to be aimed at something like individuals' *de re* preferences among tastes, regardless of the details of how individuals conceptually associate those tastes with food types. Presumably, any given piece of food, regardless of whether it is thought of as brisket or as tw-brisket, would taste the same to the twins. I do not doubt that the individual's precise way of thinking about the food taste is a matter of indifference to the science. In such a case, the individuals would be treated as having the same preferences. Some aspects of psychology will be insensitive to some or all the twin-earth thought experiments. Parts of psychology that make do with limited or no intentional notions will fall in this category.

My main reason for discussing the objection derives from another problem with it. Suppose (I do not know how plausibly) a science that concerned itself with distinctively *intentional* differences among food preferences. Thus it would recognize the possibility that an individual might prefer *A* to *B* even though, unbeknownst to him, *A* and *B* were the same food or food taste. Suppose that in such a case, the twins were treated as having different preferences. Contrary to Block's objection, it is not a consequence of my view that such a science need cite linguistic affiliation as the explanatory source of the difference. One would

[13] Ned Block, 'Advertisement for a Semantics for Psychology', in P. French *et al.* (eds.), *Midwest Studies in Philosophy* (Minneapolis: University of Minnesota Press, 1986). Fodor's discussion of the argument occurs in *Psychosemantics*, 40.

think that it is a consequence only if one conflated scientific explanatory kinds with relations that figure in the account of how those kinds are type-individuated. Linguistic affiliation (or the like)[14] need not compete as an explanatory kind with the kinds cited by Block. Innate equipment and early training are the rather crude explanatory categories cited. If the conceptual difference is innate, it would be attributed to innate conceptual endowment; if the difference is learned, it would be attributed to differences in early training. Differences in idiolect might well be associated with individual conceptual differences deriving from early training; they reflect underlying differences in causal patterns. But they need not be cited as an explanatory kind. Whether a property is cited depends on the explanatory objectives of the science, not merely on its presupposed methods of individuation.

Block's objection may suggest the following reasoning: cognitive psychology does not make reference to social relations and does not attempt to explain linguistic or other social interaction; so it cannot make use of intentional kinds that are individuated by reference to social interaction. As I have indicated, the inference is mistaken. Cognitive psychology can presuppose social interaction in the explication of what it is to have a given propositional attitude without making use of explanatory kinds or relations that refer to social matters, and without attempting to explain social interaction. Dependence on others in learning language may be so inescapable that it is a factor in the individuation of intentional states. Yet the details of causal relations, involving interlocutors, that determine the reference and identity of a person's concepts may not be appropriate for any scientific study, much less the study of psychology. Individual psychology can idealize away from these interactions and make use of unreduced intentional notions as explanatory kinds, while it presupposes the existence of such interactions in the individuation of these kinds.[15]

Even where psychology does attempt to explain individual–environment relations, it need not explain the individuation conditions of its non-individualistic explanatory kinds. This may be seen in the theory of perception, whose concern with such relations is comparatively straightforward. Perceptual theory is

---

[14] 'Linguistic affiliation', like Fodor's 'living in a world where there is H_2O' (cf. note 12) is rather misleading as an indicator of the sort of property I would cite in an explication of what in early training is relevant to conceptual differences. The way that interaction with other people affects one's idiolect is a complex matter. Cf. my 'Wherein is Language Social?', in A. George (ed.), *Reflections on Chomsky* (Oxford: Blackwell, 1989) (Ch. 11 above). 'Linguistic affiliation' suggests primitive ways of thinking about linguistic community.

[15] Several philosophers have held that my anti-individualistic views may be applicable to cognitive psychology, but only insofar as they do not appeal to social interaction. I find this distinction misconceived. It is true that cognitive psychology may attempt to explain (say) perceptual interaction with the environment and may avoid concerning itself with social interaction. But this distinction in explanatory objectives does not entail that there is a parallel distinction in the presuppositions of the explanatory typologies. An individual's thoughts about arthritis can be cited in explanations that idealize away from social interaction, even though an individual's having those thoughts may be explicable partly in terms of his dependence on others. Cf. my 'Individualism and the Mental' and 'Wherein is Language Social?' (Chs. 5 and 11 above).

largely motivated by explaining the conditions under which perceptions present the physical world veridically (and those under which illusions are created). But perceptual theory does not explain the conditions under which its intentional perceptual kinds are individuated. That enterprise cuts across various scientific disciplines—optics, evolutionary biology, cognitive psychology, and common sense remarks about physical properties and the behavior of observers. Very likely it will remain an enterprise for philosophy and for schematic background remarks within the sciences, rather than for rigorous special-science theorizing.

The general point is hardly peculiar to psychology. The special sciences parcel out their domains of explanation in ways that do not necessarily treat the background conditions that govern their modes of individuation. The physiology of the human heart presupposes but does not explain all the biological conditions that go into making an organ count as a heart. An account of the conditions under which words are individuated may go into historical matters; yet generative linguistics may simply assume words for a lexicon as already individuated. The social sciences cite psychological kinds, without explaining the individuating conditions for such kinds.

Psychology is partly concerned with how individuals function in the world—how they get around in it; how they act in accord with their conceptions of it; how they perceive it, learn from it, and form certain true beliefs about it; and how they relate to others who function similarly. These individual–environment relations help motivate the explanatory typology of intentional psychology. But psychological explanations of individual–environment relations need not recapitulate, or provide an explication of, the individuation conditions of the kinds cited in those explanations. Scientific explanation and philosophical explication are different enterprises. Philosophers are more likely to forget this than scientists.

V

I want to close by reflecting briefly on the notions of causal power and causation in psychology. I have argued that insofar as we associate a conception of causal power with individuation of psychological kinds, we get that conception not from some model drawn from other sciences, but from the explanations that psychology provides. This point generalizes to other special sciences.

Not all the causal powers of an entity, considered in the abstract or from the point of view of physics, are relevant to typing it. The heart has numerous 'causal powers' that are irrelevant to its being a heart. It will color a surface red if dropped from a given height; it will damage an eye if it is used to skeet certain solutions at it; it would pump waste if inserted into certain organic systems. None of these powers is relevant to typing something as a heart. None are causal powers recognized by biology or physiology. What are relevant are those causal and receptive powers exercised by the heart that yield the patterns of causation studied in physiology—the powers exhibited when it carries out its basic function, pumping blood in the circulatory system of an organism.

Many of the special sciences, including psychology, study patterns of causation that involve relations between entities and other entities in their normal 'environments'. Their explanatory kinds are individuated in a way that presupposes such relations. Astronomy studies the motions of the planets; geology studies land masses on the surface of the earth; physiology studies hearts or optic fibers in the environment of a larger organism; psychology studies activity involving intentional states in an environment about which those states carry information; the social sciences study patterns of activity among persons.

Because the kinds recognized by these sciences are individuated by reference to patterns in a normal environment that reaches beyond the surfaces of individuals typed by those kinds, the kinds are not in general supervenient on the constituents of those individuals. It follows that the causal powers *relevant to type-individuating the explanatory kinds of a special science* need not be 'locally supervenient' on causal powers recognized by sciences that deal with underlying constituents. It also follows that there are imaginable cases in which two entities with the same causal powers recognized by the latter sciences, or by physics, may have different causal powers recognized by a higher-level special science. The heart and the organ that pumps waste, and the twins with different psychological states, provide examples.

It is true that entities studied in the special sciences may act or react in certain ways when they are transported outside their normal environments. A heart is still a heart when it is in free fall, or hooked up in a body in order to pump waste. A person would still act on his beliefs and desires on Twin Earth. Sometimes the relevant special science will have nothing to say about how the entity will behave in the 'abnormal' environment: Physiology has nothing to say about gravitational forces on a heart in free fall. In these cases, one can perhaps infer the entity's would-be behavior from the laws of other sciences, together with descriptions of relevant properties of the entities. In other such cases, the special science might have something to say. Physiology could predict how much liquid waste the heart could pump, given information about input and assuming that the heart's anatomical condition were not otherwise altered. Psychology can predict how someone will act on Twin Earth, given appropriate descriptions of the stimuli. But these fanciful situations do not affect the typology of the special science. The typology is fitted to capture actual patterns, actual law-like regularities, into which the relevant entities enter.

The point that those causal powers relevant to individuating the explanatory kinds of a special science cannot be identified independently of the science's modes of explanation is fairly obvious on reflection. I am inclined to think that the point applies not only to kind-relevant causal powers, but also to causation. Here, however, the issues are more complicated and less clear-cut. Many philosophers have thought that the best strategy for understanding causation involving psychological events is to assume a notion of causation that is derived from other sciences, and then to shape the interpretation of psychological causation to fit that notion.

The most deeply imaginative execution of this strategy is Donald Davidson's.[16] Davidson holds that attribution of causal relations entails commitment to a certain sort of explanatory law, a sort of law that has properties (those of being exceptionless and of forming a closed system of explanation) that one cannot reasonably expect the principles of psychology to exhibit. Mind–body causation is then interpreted in the light of this assumption. Such causation is held to fall under purely physical laws. I think that there is no such entailment. Insofar as causal ascriptions entail commitment to any sort of law, it is an empirical question what sort. Indeed, what counts as a law is filled out partly through scientific practice. One cannot know apriori that every causal relation, regardless of domain, must fall under laws that have any particular form. So Davidson's argument that physical descriptions provide the fundamental insight into causal relations involving psychological events seems to me unpersuasive.

Earlier I cited a cruder version of the same strategy. The argument went: Physiological processes are where the 'real' causation in psychology goes on. Psychology should concern itself with 'real' causation. So psychology should adopt a taxonomy that distinguishes psychological causes or effects only if in all possible circumstances there are associated differences in physiological causes or effects. In Sections I–IV I argued that the inference in the last step is faulty. (Davidson would agree.) But the first premise is doubtful as well. What is true is that physiological processes are *sine qua non* for psychological processes. But atomic and quantum processes are *sine qua non* for physiological processes. Few would advance the view that atomic or quantum processes are where the 'real' causation goes on in physiology.[17] Is there any strong ground for thinking that the 'true nature' of causation involving psychological events is better revealed in physiology than in psychology?

Our knowledge of mental-physical causation derives primarily from mentalistic explanation. I think that it may be a mistake to seek to reinterpret psychological causation in non-psychological terms. The relations between mental and physical descriptions are more a subject of speculation than of scientific certainty. It is an empirical question what sorts of laws or principles are to be associated with attributions of causal relations. Understanding psychological causation is at least as dependent on what sorts of explanations we achieve in psychology, and how they are related to explanations in the biological sciences, as it is on any antecedent conception of causation. It is therefore an open question

[16] Donald Davidson, 'Mental Events'.

[17] Ned Block makes substantially the same point in 'Can the Mind Change the World?', in George Boolos (ed.), *Meaning and Method: Essays in Honor of Hilary Putnam* (Cambridge: Cambridge University Press, 1990). John Heil and Alfred Mele also make the point in 'Mental Causation', unpublished. Incidentally, one should not infer that psychology cannot provide a notion of causation because it does not promise the bump and grind conception suggested by classical mechanics. Such a conception is inapplicable to large reaches of physics.

whether it will ever be illuminating and correct to count relations between neural events (tokens) as revealing the nature of causal relations involving intentional psychological events. The anti-individualistic position does not depend on rejecting this common view of psychological causation. But I think that the view warrants scepticism.

It is usually a mistake to allow ontological preconceptions that have primarily philosophical underpinning to affect one's interpretation of scientific enterprises. It is almost always a mistake, and a larger one, to allow them to dictate the sorts of explanatory kinds that are deemed admissible for explanation. I think that many of the objections to anti-individualistic modes of kind individuation in psychology rest on these mistakes. Mentalistic explanations dominate large reaches of psychology. Certainly our notion of psychologically relevant causal power, and probably even our notion of psychological causation, are best illuminated by reflecting on these explanations. Most intentional kinds attributed in these explanations are individuated in non-individualistic ways. These methods of individuation are consonant with the aims of psychology and indeed those of many other special sciences.

15 *Intentional Properties and Causation*

In "A Modal Argument for Narrow Content"[a] Jerry Fodor tries to show that psychological properties typed by ordinary intentional propositional content (which he calls 'broad content') cannot be associated with distinctive causal powers for purposes of psychological taxonomizing. Causal powers are relevantly distinctive insofar as they are distinguished from twin-earth psychological properties. Thus Fodor attempts to show that ordinary intentional propositional content cannot be basic for taxonomizing causal powers in psychology. I think that he does not succeed.

Before discussing his argument, I want to remark on his methodology. Fodor calls his argument *"apriori"*. He seems to mean by this only that it is the sort of argument that could be given from an armchair (p. 12). Certainly, most of his claims (for example, the claim about H- and T-particles) do not seem to be apriori in any traditional sense. Something is a T-particle at time t if it is a physical particle and the coin in Fodor's hand at time t is tails up. Our knowledge that being a T-particle is not having any particular causal power is perfectly obvious apart from any particular investigation; but it clearly relies broadly on our empirical experience.

Fodor takes his proposal to be justified by its sorting examples, like the T-particle example, and by its respecting Humean intuitions about causation. It seems to me that he is simply attempting to generalize about causal explanation in the empirical sciences. This is certainly a philosophically valuable enterprise. But I think that it is treacherous when its conclusions appear to be in opposition to actual scientific practice.

Fodor's conclusion does appear to be in opposition to the actual practice of psychological explanation. Psychologists use ordinary content in many of their causal explanations. There is no wholesale movement in intentional psychology to make its explanations more "general", or more in accord with Fodor's conception of causally relevant kinds, by replacing ordinary content attributions with attributions of another sort of content (which he calls 'narrow content').

I am indebted to Ned Block for several very valuable criticisms.

[a] J. Fodor, "A Modal Argument for Narrow Content", *The Journal of Philosophy*, 88 (1991), 5–26. Subsequent page references to this article are given parenthetically in the text.

Narrow content seems to play no explicit role that would replace that of ordinary content. So I think that there is strong armchair reason to think that Fodor's argument will not establish its conclusion. I think that it is another in a long line of philosophical proposals to revise science. Such proposals have a poor track record; they have given philosophy a bad name. Fodor is advocating a change in the formulation of scientific generalizations rather than a flat-out denial of scientific claims. But I think that it is no more likely to be scientifically useful than its more notorious ancestors. Let us consider the argument itself.

Fodor begins by assuming that differences in intentional properties are the only relevant differences between the behavior of a person and a twin-earth twin (p. 7). I think that this is a mistake. Non-intentional descriptions of behavioral relations between an individual and specific kinds in his or her environment seem to be a significant part of what psychology is interested in.

Fodor dismisses non-intentionally and relationally described behavior (for example, getting water) by reference to his "cross-context" test. He maintains, 'you have to judge identity and difference of causal powers in a way that bears the counterfactuals in mind, namely, *across* contexts rather than *within* contexts' (p. 8). The idea is that a twin would get water if placed on Earth, and an earthling would get twater if placed on Twin Earth, given that they made the same requesting sounds in their respective languages. Fodor concludes that the behavior of the two protagonists, on Earth and Twin Earth, is the same as far as psychological taxonomy and causal power are concerned.

Fodor is certainly right that causal power is a counterfactual notion. But his test, at least in the way he applies it, is useless for individuating causal powers. The trouble is that deciding which contexts are relevant for determining and distinguishing causal powers is not independent of assumptions about how to individuate explanatory kinds.[1]

Imagine that a heart and an organ that pumps digestive waste (from a completely different evolutionary scheme) were physically indistinguishable up to their boundaries. Clearly they would be of two different biological kinds, with different causal powers, on any conception of causal power that would be relevant to biological taxonomy. Judging the heart's causal powers presupposes that it is connected to a particular type of bodily environment, with a particular sort of function in that environment. One cannot count being connected to such a body to pump blood as just one of many contexts that the heart might be in, if one wants to understand the range of its biologically relevant causal powers. It would show a serious misconception of biological kinds to argue that the causal powers and taxonomically relevant effects of the heart and its physical twin are the same because if one hooked up the waste pump to the heart's body, it would pump blood and cause the blood vessels to dilate; and that if one hooked the heart to the waste pump's body, it would move waste.

---

[1] I have made this point with essentially the example that follows in "Individuation and Causation in Psychology", *Pacific Philosophical Quarterly*, 70 (1989), 303–322 (Ch. 14 above).

But that is how Fodor argues regarding relational behavioral effects of psychological states. The argument ignores the fact that specific relations between an entity and its normal environment may be of interest to a special science, and fundamental to its causal taxonomy. Causal power is judged against background assumptions about what kind of thing is being evaluated. And kinds are sometimes what they are because of their relations to, and functions within, a specific environment. Fodor's treatment of any environment as being on a par with other "contexts" for testing causal powers is in effect an assimilation of the special sciences to physics. It certainly begs the question against my view.

The test gives no reason to think that psychology should not be, or is not, interested in explaining non-intentional behavioral relations between an individual and specific sorts of things in his or her environment. In fact, psychology is engaged in explaining many successes and failures that relate an individual's intentional states to kinds of things in the individual's environment: specific successes or failures in perception, in knowledge, in action. I see no good reason to think that psychology does or should gloss these explanations of success or adaptation in environmentally neutral ways (as Fodor attempts to do in his Appendix).

Fodor concentrates his discussion on intentionally described behavior. He does so because he thinks that such descriptions pass his cross-context test (p. 8). He therefore devises a further condition which is supposed to show that ordinary intentional psychological states are not distinctive causal powers with respect to intentionally described behavior.

Fodor offers a necessary condition for when a difference between having causal properties CP1 and CP2 is a difference in "causal powers" in virtue of the difference's being responsible for a certain difference between effect properties EP1 and EP2. (The difference in causal properties CP1 and CP2 is said to be responsible for the difference between the effect properties in the same sense that if CP2 had been instantiated instead of CP1, the effect would have had property EP2 instead of EP1; and if CP1 had been instantiated instead of CP2, the effect would have had EP1 instead of EP2; (p. 9).

Fodor never formulates his condition in final form. But his core answer is:

(C): Only when it is not a conceptual truth that causes that differ in that one has CP1 where the other has CP2 have effects that differ in that one has EP1 where the other has EP2. (p. 19)

The idea is that being a meteor can be a causal power in virtue of the fact that meteors are responsible for craters because the relation between the difference between meteors and rock-twins-of-meteors which are not meteors and their respective effects (the effects: making craters and whatever effects the rock-twins have) is 'non-conceptual' (p. 20). By contrast, Fodor says, "it is conceptually necessary that people who have water thoughts (rather than twater thoughts) produce water behavior (rather than twater behavior)" (p. 21). So being a water thought (a thought that involves the concept *water*) cannot be a distinctive causal power in virtue of the fact that water thoughts are responsible for water behavior. Fodor thinks that his condition is a necessary condition on causal properties' being 'psychological natural kinds' (p. 14).

Fodor stipulates that condition C is not to apply to causal properties that are individuated *as* causal powers with certain specific sorts of effects. He cites being a camshaft and being soluble in water as properties that are non-contingently causal powers of their characteristic effects. The problem Fodor anticipates is that characteristic camshaft effects (lifting valves of certain sorts) necessarily have the effect properties which the property of being a camshaft is conceptually associated with. And any such effects will be different, on conceptual grounds, from characteristic effects of physical-camshaft-twins that have different functions. Yet it would seem that being a camshaft is a distinctive causal power in good standing. So condition C should not apply to such causal properties, canonically described.

By contrast, Fodor assumes that being a meteor is only contingently a causal power with respect to such effects as making craters. And he explicitly says that being a water thought is contingently a distinctive causal power with respect to its effects on behavior characterized, intentionally, in terms of the concept *water*. More generally, he believes that specific propositional attitudes characterized in the usual way are only contingently causal powers with respect to intentionally described behavior characterized in terms that indicate intentional elements in the propositional attitudes (p. 19). So condition C is applicable to them.

Since Fodor believes that propositional attitudes characterized in the usual way fail condition C, he concludes that they are not causal powers in virtue of their characteristic intentionally described effect properties: they do not differ in their causal power from propositional attitudes of twin-earth counterparts. That is, it is a conceptual truth that 'broad content' propositional attitudes differ in their characteristic intentionally described effect properties from those of their "broad content" twins. So condition C is violated. So "broad content" propositional attitudes do not differ in causal power from their twins. I find the complexity of these formulations unappealing, and less than immediately intuitive. I characterize Fodor's position to have it on the table for discussion.

There's more complexity than I have so far mentioned. Fodor has to do some patching of his core answer (pp. 21–22). For by redescribing causal properties or effect properties, one can produce a non-conceptual relation between concepts of any given pair of properties. Fodor does not make fully clear what his patch is to be, but as Ned Block has pointed out, it appears that the line of response that he proposes cannot solve the problem. For in all the examples he gives (pp. 21–25) the properties he cites could still be redescribed to produce statements that are about the same properties but that are not conceptually necessary. The problem is that conceptual necessity is (if anything) a property of relations between concepts of properties, not of relations between properties.

In my view, however, this is not a fundamental problem for Fodor. I think that he can and should speak of canonical descriptions (or canonical conceptions) of properties—descriptions (or conceptions) that are candidates for use in explanatory theories. 'Being a meteor', 'being a water thought', 'being phlogiston', and so on are of this sort. 'Being Harry's favorite property' is not. At least I am willing to accept this emendation, despite its vagueness. I agree also not to cavil over the notion of conceptual necessity. Given that we assume that we are testing canonical descriptions (or conceptions) of the property of being a water thought, I think Fodor need not do any patching on his original proposal at all.

I want now to return to Fodor's assumption that having thoughts involving the concept *water* are not themselves necessarily distinctive causal powers with respect to behavioral effects intentionally described in terms of the concept *water*. To put it another way, Fodor assumes that it is contingent that 'having mental states that differ in their broad content is having mental states that differ in their causal powers' (pp. 16, 24–25).

As noted, he contrasts the property of having thoughts whose intentional content involves the concept of water with the property of being water-soluble. He observes that it is not contingent that having this latter property is having a distinctive causal power (pp. 17–18). And he thinks that it is 'reasonably untendentious' to assume that having intentional thoughts are different in this regard:

friends of broad content argue that it perfectly well *could turn out*—that there is no metaphysical reason why it should not turn out—that having mental states that differ in their broad content is having mental states that differ in their causal powers. (For example, it could turn out that there are causal laws that distinguish between twins.) But I do not remember hearing anyone argue that having mental states that differ in the way that the mental states of twins do *just is* having mental states that differ in their causal powers. On the contrary, according to the usual understanding, it is their causal *histories* that distinguish the mental states of twins. And the intuition about features of causal history is that some of them are causal powers (e.g. *having been dropped in transit*...) and some of them are not (e.g. ... *having been born on a Tuesday*) and it is contingent which are which. (p. 18)

I cannot speak for others. But this articulation of Fodor's assumption contains several misunderstandings of the point of view that has motivated my anti-individualism. I will discuss some of them as a preliminary to discussing the assumption.

What distinguishes the twins is not confined to their causal histories. Their propositional attitudes themselves differ. Their intentionally described behavior differs. Their interactions with their environments, including their effects on their environments, differ. I believe that intentional ascriptions of psychological states and specific relational behavioral descriptions are taxonomically primitive: they characterize psychological kinds. Some of the other properties of a person not shared with the person's twin are *not* psychological kinds. In particular, I think it highly unlikely that the historical individuating conditions of specific psychological states will be psychological kinds.

It is for psychology and other scientific enterprises an empirical question whether and to what extent they will make use of ordinary propositional attitude ascriptions in their explanations. I believe that the question whether they will use ordinary propositional attitude ascriptions is already settled for psychology and a wide range of other explanatory endeavors. But perhaps in some cases it could, in principle, 'turn out' otherwise.

An analogous epistemological point applies to the property of being water-soluble. Water solubility is in itself a causal notion. Let us suppose that it serves some explanatory enterprises (though it may in fact be explicable in more general terms). It could have 'turned out' that there was no such property or that it had no distinctive explanatory role.

We can also say about water solubility that it is necessarily a causal notion, and that it is individuated partly in terms of its effects. So its canonical description implies necessary or conceptual relations between the causal property and appropriately described effects. On the supposition that it is an explanatorily useful property, anything that has it is taxonomically or explanatorily distinct from anything that lacks it.

I think that in these respects intentional psychological properties are similar. They necessarily have causal implications as such. They are scientifically and causally relevant kinds.[2] And many of them bear a conceptual relation to standard conceptions of the properties that are causally effected by them. (I shall return to the sense in which this is so.) Given, as I think, that ordinary intentional properties are causally relevant kinds, they are necessarily distinct from other causally relevant properties, including twin-earth analogs.

Fodor is right that much of the focus of the discussion of anti-individualism has been on the role of causal-historical antecedents in concept individuation. One reason for this focus is that the arguments for anti-individualism grew out of previous work on reference in the philosophy of language.[3] Another reason, at least for me, is that in view of the failure of behaviorism and the programmatic, almost empty, character of all the sorts of functionalist reductionism that I know of, it is difficult to state in an illuminating, even sketchy, way what causal relations most psychological states bear to behavior (intentionally characterized or otherwise). It is approximately as difficult as psychology is.

Nevertheless, I think that it is probably a fault of some expositions within this tradition (a fault I myself am guilty of) that there has been so much more emphasis, in the account of attitude individuation, on historical chains leading up to employment of a concept, than on the individual's activity in interacting with an environment. Still, even causal-historical antecedents have consistently been said to involve *interaction* between individuals and their environments. Interaction is not passive reception of input.

[2] Cf. my "Mind–Body Causation and Explanatory Practice", in J. Heil and A. Mele (eds.), *Mental Causation* (Oxford: Oxford University Press 1993) (Ch. 16 below).
[3] Cf. my "Philosophy of Language and Mind, 1950–1990", *The Philosophical Review*, 100 (1992), esp. pp. 45 ff. (Ch. 20 below).

In any case, it seems to me clearly true that specific actions by individuals on their environment are part of what is involved in individuating ordinary intentional contents. This is what underlies the conceptual relation between certain sorts of behavior and intentional psychological states. For example, what an individual perceives is not independent of what the individual or conspecifics can discriminate.[4]

The theory of perception takes for granted that among the things that in a patterned way cause perceptual representations, the kinds of things that are represented can, in most cases, only be those that the creature's perceptual apparatus can function, under appropriate conditions, to discriminate. Discrimination here is a behavioral as well as teleological notion. But it is a notion whose application is circumscribed by the possibilities for discrimination in the individual's normal environment. Necessarily, things perceived, in optimum or normal conditions, function in some way not only in a species' or individual's causal history but in the species' members' actions on the world. The individuation of various beliefs about macro-objects and properties also depend on looser but still significant relations to the individual's acting on the relevant objects or properties.

Despite the relative concentration on historical antecedents in parts of the anti-individualist tradition, it is strange that Fodor regards his assumption as untendentious. Fodor would be begging the question to assume that ordinary intentional psychological properties, standardly conceived, are not distinctive causal and explanatory kinds. But it is obvious that if they have causal implications, some ordinary intentional properties, under their standard conceptions, bear conceptual relations to some of the properties that are causally effected by them, standardly conceived. These effect properties include both intentionally described behavior and behavior described in terms of relations to specific kinds of things in the environment. That ordinary intentional properties are necessarily distinct from twin analogs in their causal implications follows from the anti-individualist view that they are taxonomically relevant kinds. It is not an independent question.

Fodor's attribution of the view that it could 'turn out' that there are ordinary intentional causal laws (or causal law-like generalizations) is at best misleading. He purports to be talking about necessity. But 'could turn out' talk is epistemic, not modal in the ordinary senses. Epistemic contingency is irrelevant to the application of condition C. It may well be that Fodor has confused an epistemic view with a metaphysical or causal-taxonomical view.

---

[4] B. O'Shaughnessy, *The Will* (Cambridge: Cambridge University Press, 1980), ii. ch. 8; M. Davies, "Individualism and Perceptual Content", *Mind*, 100 (1991), 461–484; *idem*, "Perceptual Content and Local Supervenience", *Proceedings of the Aristotelian Society*, 92 (1992), 21–45. I think that by concentrating on the role of behavior in perceptual-state individuation, one can produce a simpler, stronger argument for anti-individualism than the general philosophical one I give in 'Individualism and Psychology' (Ch. 9 above).

Fodor's main argument rests on the assumption that ordinary intentional psychological states are unlike being a camshaft and water solubility in that they are not necessarily causal powers and are not necessarily distinct in their causal implications from twin-earth analogs. Since this assumption is mistaken, the argument is inapplicable.

In a brief note, Fodor anticipates this response late in his paper (n. 22). He claims that if ordinary intentional states are like water solubility in being both conceptually and causally connected to their behavioral effects—and in a way that distinguishes them from their twin analogs—then there is even less reason to think them causally and taxonomically significant:

> the broad content psychological generalizations that distinguish twins (like, 'if you have water wants [rather than twater wants] then you drill for water [rather than twater]') themselves all come out conceptually necessary ... The moral would then be: no causal laws about broad intentional states as such ... It is true that being soluble is a causal power even though it is conceptually connected to dissolving. But the price for thus evading condition C is the 'quasi-logical' status of 'if soluble then dissolves'. (n. 22)[5]

But this point contains a simple fallacy. The fact that there is some conceptual connection between explanans and explanandum (or antecedent and consequent) does not mean that the psychological generalizations come out to be conceptually necessary. It does not preclude their being interesting causal law-like statements. The conceptual link between antecedent and consequent may be merely that 'water' occurs in both (intensionally in the former, either intensionally or extensionally in the latter), and that being a thought about water has some causal implications or other, with respect to water.[6] It does not follow that the consequent follows conceptually from the antecedent.

---

[5] I am sure that Fodor knows that nothing about twater would occur in a psychological generalization about water. His point must be that 'water' really occurs primitively in the generalization. I must also point out that Fodor's idea that 'wants water' means something like 'thirsty and born here' (p. 17) is wildly inaccurate. As I have shown, 'water' contains no indexical element. Cf. my "Other Bodies", in A. Woodfield (ed.), *Thought and Object* (Oxford: Oxford University Press, 1982) (Ch. 4 above). At best he is proposing some replacement for the ordinary use of 'water' in psychological discourse.

[6] It is important not to oversimplify here. Having water thoughts does not necessitate the existence of water. One can imagine a chemist who has theorized about the existence of H_2O and has imagined and visualized the macro-properties of H_2O. Such a being could have water thoughts but lack any causal relations to water. So having water thoughts cannot necessitate having causal relations to water, except relative to fairly strong parameters stating optimal conditions. In cases where a thinker has water thoughts but there is no water, the water thoughts will necessitate causal relations to instances of other physical kinds in the thinker's environment. And there will be necessary causal relations to acts or actions intentionally characterized in terms of the concept *water*. But the causal relations to actual entities in the thinker's environment that are necessitated by having the concept *water* are quite complicated and merely bring in relations to and concepts of *some* kinds in the thinker's actual environment. (I made this point years ago in "Other Bodies".) None of this constitutes the slightest concession to the idea that beings on Twin Earth, in the relevant thought experiments, have the concept *water*.

In fact, psychological law-like generalizations do sometimes have such conceptual links between statements about psychological antecedents and statements about behavior. And if they amounted to no more than 'if something is a water-type thought, it tends under optimal circumstances to cause water-related or water-conceived behavior', they would yield no real insight into causal relations.[7] But such generalizations in intentional psychology presuppose or contain existence assumptions that are contingent. For example, some generalizations presuppose or entail that water thoughts exist. They also contain detailed specifications of conditions in their antecedents and consequents. The detail makes the generalizations scientifically interesting, as well as contingent.[8]

One can see this by thinking about the heart case again. One could plausibly claim that it is a conceptual truth that hearts differ from twin waste-pumps in that they pump blood. One could plausibly claim that it is conceptually necessary that if something is a heart, then when functioning normally, it pumps blood. Although these are true statements, they do not provide deep insight into causal relations. If physiology contented itself with such statements, it would certainly be remiss. But these points do nothing to show that hearts are not taxonomically significant kinds.

The interest for physiology lies first in the existence of hearts and blood. This is both contingent and empirically known. Interest lies second and more richly in the account of how much blood a given type of heart pumps, in what particular ways it pumps it, in what ways pumping action causes blood vessels to dilate, and so on. Answers to these questions are non-trivial, contingent causal truths, even though 'heart' and 'blood' are conceptually connected.

Psychology is broadly like that. Many of its intentional notions are individuated partly in terms of very broadly described cause–effect relations. This form of individuation insures some conceptual relations between taxonomically relevant descriptions of causes and taxonomically relevant descriptions of effects. This is one of the grains of truth in functionalism. But these conceptual

---

[7] Fodor describes the relevant necessary statements in rather puzzling ways. 'If soluble then dissolves' and 'Having water thoughts is identical to having (*inter alia*) the power to drill for water' and 'if you have water wants … then you drill for water' are obviously not necessary. I have done the best I can on Fodor's behalf in formulating rough necessities of the sort he seems to be gesturing toward. I think that when one fills out what the necessities really are—involving as they do terms like 'normally', 'in appropriate circumstances'—they come to seem familiar and harmless. Filling them out by determining relevant circumstances both produces contingent statements and illustrates how hard and complex causal generalizations in intentional psychology are.

[8] Fodor's mistake here seems to me to infect his main condition on being a causal power, even if one waives the point that Fodor's mistaken presupposition about intentional psychological properties makes the condition irrelevant. The idea of the condition (pp. 19–20) seems to be that if a conceptual connection between properties of a cause and properties of its effect is not based on individuating the cause as a causal power, then the conceptual connection prevents a causal relation between those properties from being of any taxonomical interest. But this seems to me to be a more subtle form of the same fallacy I have just criticized. The conceptual connection between the properties need not be so full that it allows no room for a taxonomically interesting connection.

relations provide only a broad frame for psychological theorizing. They do not make intentional psychology anything like trivial.

Fodor's main argument does not succeed because it fails to apply to the cases at issue. His subsidiary argument that typical statements about causal properties that are individuated partly in terms of effect properties are "quasi-logical" and useless for science is based on a fallacy.

The difficulty with Fodor's attempt to apply Humean and Rylean intuitions about causation is that the conceptual relations between descriptions of causes and effects occur at a very high level of abstraction. The relevant propositional attitude concepts have causal implications. But the implications are very general. They are at the level: something is not a perception unless it functions in a system for causing discriminative behavior; one cannot attribute perception of rough texturedness to an organism unless its perceptual system functions to cause it to respond to or otherwise discriminate rough texturedness under environmentally normal circumstances; water thoughts enter in some way, under some appropriate conditions, into causing behavior having to do with water, or at least behavior whose intentional description involves the concept of water. Some intentional psychological properties have even looser causal implications than these. Psychological law-like generalizations, by contrast, are much more specific. They involve statements of specific, contingent conditions that must be satisfied for the causal relations to occur.

Arguments against the scientific relevance of intentional notions that invoke Humean principles or Rylean intuitions are likely to gloss over (as Fodor's does) the enormous difficulty and complexity of stating a true, interesting law-like generalization in psychology. In my view, such arguments tend to carry on bad habits of behaviorism and physics-worship. The habits can remain even in those who are to be admired for what they have done to undermine behaviorism and over-simple pictures of the special sciences.

16 *Mind–Body Causation and Explanatory Practice*

In recent years a number of philosophers have worried about whether we can reasonably believe that mental properties are causally efficacious. They are concerned whether the intentional 'aspects' or qualitative 'aspects' of mental events are epiphenomenal—that is, lacking in causal power and irrelevant to causal transactions. They typically assume that mental events themselves are causes. But this is supposed to be ensured by the prior assumption that mental events are physical events. Individual mental events are assumed to be instantiations or tokens of physical event-kinds. The doubt is whether the mental 'aspects' of these states and events play any significant role in causal processes.

I think that these worries can be met within the materialist metaphysical framework in which they arise. I will say a little about what I think is wrong with some of the more prominent sorts of argument that lead to epiphenomenalism. But what interests me more is the very existence of the worries. I think that they are symptomatic of a mistaken set of philosophical priorities. Materialist metaphysics has been given more weight than it deserves. Reflection on explanatory practice has been given too little. The metaphysical grounds that support the worries are vastly less strong than the more ordinary grounds we already have for rejecting them.

I shall first outline the worries about epiphenomenalism, and identify some of the weak spots in the arguments for them. Then I shall explain why I think that the starting point for the worries is itself dubious. Finally I shall generalize a little about the misguided priorities (as I see them) that engender these worries.

1

The picture that leads to the worries about epiphenomenalism begins with a plausible idea. It is that certain non-intentionally described states or events that 'underlie' mental states and events participate in causal processes that are instances of physical laws that do not mention mentality. I want to leave open

I am grateful to Ned Block for several suggestions.

what 'underlie' is to mean here. I will assume, however, at least that mental states and events would not occur if some 'underlying' physical states and events did not occur. There are no gaps in these physical chains of events. So, for example, there are underlying, gapless neural processes that are instances of laws of neurophysiology; and the mental events would not occur if some such processes did not occur. I have no serious doubts about this view.

These physical states and events are usually thought to 'underlie' the mental states and events in a more specific sense. They are held to be token-identical with them. I do not accept this materialist claim. But it is widely accepted, largely because of its supposed virtues in clarifying mental causation. From the time of Descartes it has often been thought that there is some mystery in how mental and physical events can interact. This and other materialist views purport to dispel the mystery by holding that there is only one sort of causation—a relation between physical events. In this section, I will accept this ontology, though only for the sake of argument.

The worry about epiphenomenalism arises by considering that some properties of events (or states) are relevant to their causal relations, while others are not. The property of being the third large explosion in a given country during the last ten years may be irrelevant to that explosion's causing certain damage, whereas the heat of the explosion would be relevant. The question is whether mentalistic properties are causally efficacious, or whether mentalistic descriptions of properties are relevant to understanding causation. Many philosophers have developed more confidence in the causal efficacy of the underlying neural properties than in that of the 'intentional aspects' of mental events. If those neural processes are going on, the body's movements, and hence what we count as behavior, will depend on the properties of those processes. The intentional or phenomenal 'aspects' of the mental events might, they think, be irrelevant or at best quite derivative and indirect—epiphenomenal on the real underlying causal processes.

A comparison of mental properties to properties like phenotypes in biology is typical. There are regular, even—assuming richly filled-in background conditions—loosely nomological, relations between the phenotypes of parents and phenotypes of their immediate offspring. But the phenotypes of the parents are causally inefficacious in producing those of their offspring. The real causal efficacy derives from the parental genotypes. Some philosophers appear to be seriously concerned that intentional kinds are, like phenotypes, part of a nomologically describable system, but not causally efficacious in their own right.

What motivates these worries? Broadly and crudely speaking, it is the picture that the underlying processes are occurring anyway and that the mental events really derive their causal efficacy from the physical properties which are the real agents of causation. This picture leads to the idea that the mental properties are superfluous. Even if the mental properties were not separable from the physical properties (because they necessarily supervened on them), they would be in a sense along for the ride, since the primary mechanisms of causation are located in the underlying physical properties.

Let us cast this sort of motivation into an argument. One could assume: (*A*) that mental event-tokens are identical with physical event-tokens; (*B*) that the causal powers of a physical event are determined only by its physical properties; and (*C*) that mental properties are not reducible to physical properties. From these assumptions, it may seem to follow that a mental event's mental properties play no role in determining its causal powers.

Here is another argument for the picture: Assume (a) that the world of physical events and properties is a complete and closed system, in the sense that physical events can be caused only by virtue of physical properties of other physical events; (b) that mental properties are not reducible to physical properties. It may again seem to follow that no physical events can be caused by virtue of mental properties, even if these mental properties are properties of physical events. The argument does leave open the possibility that mental properties of mental events are causally efficacious with respect to other mental properties of mental events. But if mental causation has no outlet among physical events, it is surely a peculiarly limited sorted of causation.[1]

Let us begin with the first argument. As is common in arguments for epiphenomenalism, the key phrases leave much clarity to be desired. 'Is determined by' is a case in point. It could mean 'supervenes on', 'is explained by', or 'is individuated by'. For reasons that will emerge, I need not choose among these readings. (*B*) is problematic on all of them.

It is also not clear what is to be included in the notion of a physical property. In particular, it is unclear whether various relations to the environment count among the physical 'properties'. If they do not, the premiss is difficult to defend. I will assume that a very broad notion of physical property is intended—one that encompasses relations to the environment which are described in non-mentalistic, non-intentional terms.

The fundamental unclarity lies in the notion of causal power.[2] The causal powers of a kind of event are to be understood in terms of the patterns of causation that events of that kind enter into. Such patterns are identified as explanatory in causal explanations. And the properties that 'determine' the causal powers of an event are those that enter into causal explanations. The second premise is plausible only insofar as one considers the causal powers of a physical event to be got only through patterns of properties described in the physical sciences, or in other commonsense explanations in physical terms. The sense in which only physical properties determine the causal powers of a physical event is just that within the patterns of causation described in the physical sciences and commonsense physicalistic discourse, physical properties suffice to provide a basis for the

---

[1] For a discussion of such arguments with which I have some sympathy, see Robert Van Gulick, "Who's in Charge Here? And Who's Doing All the Work?", in J. Heil and A. Mele (eds.), *Mental Causation* (Oxford: Oxford University Press, 1993), ch. 13. My criticisms of these arguments differ from his, but are for the most part compatible.

[2] Cf. my "Individualism and Causation in Psychology", *Pacific Philosophical Quarterly*, 70 (1989), 303–322, (Ch. 14 above) for a detailed account of my understanding of causal power.

existence and understanding of the causal powers of physical events; and no other properties enter in. Both the chains of causation and the patterns of explanation are in no need of supplementation from outside the realm of physical properties or physicalistic discourse. This is a tempting and plausible interpretation of the second premise. But on this interpretation the conclusion will not follow.

If physical events have mental properties, one is not entitled to the view that only physical properties (properties specified in the physical sciences or in ordinary physicalistic discourse) determine all the causal powers of a physical event (as opposed to merely all the causal powers associated with physicalistic explanations of the physical event), unless one can show that mentalistic explanation is either non-causal or fails to describe patterns of causal properties. For the causal powers of a physical event that is mental might include possible effects that are specified in mentalistic explanation. No one has shown that mentalistic explanation is either non-causal or non-descriptive. Nor is either view plausible.

Normally we consider an entity's causal powers relative to the kind in terms of which the entity is specified. For example, in asking for the causal powers of the heart, we implicitly expect physiological patterns of properties to be cited. We do not expect citation of powers that would be studied by physics. Pumping blood is usually considered relevant; squashing a bug if dropped from a ladder is not. If we were to specify the heart as a physical object of such and such physical dimensions, the latter property would seem relevant. The second premise (B) of the argument attracts an interpretation that is plausible but insufficient for the argument because the mental events are specified as physical. Then mental properties seem irrelevant to its causal powers. But if it is specified as mental ('What are the causal powers of a thought that it is raining?'), the idea that only properties specified in the physical sciences are relevant to determining the causal powers seems outlandish. Thus one cannot just take the second assumption of the argument as a generalized self-evident metaphysical principle.[3] Interpreted in a way that leaves the argument valid, the premise is either false or question-begging.

---

[3] Sometimes the second premise is stated, 'The causal powers of a physical event are *completely* determined by its physical properties.' This premise has substantially the same difficulties as the one I discuss. This premise is, however, weaker in that it allows the possibility that although the physical properties completely determine the causal powers of a physical event, mental properties may also play a role in determining those powers. To complete the argument, one needs a premise excluding 'overdetermination'. Issues about 'overdetermination' are fairly similar to those that I am discussing. I might say, however, that I find the term extremely misleading inasmuch as it assimilates different levels or ranges of causal interaction to ordinary cases in which (say) physical causes occur simultaneously and each is sufficient unto itself for their common effect. There are deep differences in the two cases.

I might add here that in all these arguments, a materialist must have some explanation for regarding mental properties as material in character. Their existence must not be seen as incompatible with the materialism. I think that this is not an easy problem, but there are various solutions that seem to satisfy many materialists. And since I am accepting materialism in this section for the sake of argument, I shall not pursue the matter.

Let us turn to the second argument. Problems with the second argument lie in the first premise, (a). The claim that physical events can be caused only by virtue of physical properties of other physical events has problems entirely analogous to those that beset the first argument. The existence of a closed system reflects a pattern of causal relations and of causal explanation that needs no supplementation from the outside. There are no gaps. It does not follow from this that such a system excludes or overrides causal relations or causal explanation in terms of properties from outside the system. Indeed, if it did follow, as has often been pointed out, there would be no room for causal efficacy in the special sciences, even in natural sciences like chemistry and physiology. For there is no gap (other than perhaps quantum gaps) in the causal relations explained in terms of the properties of physics. But few are tempted by the idea that physical events cannot be caused in virtue of physiological properties of physical events.

Is the causal efficacy of properties cited in chemistry and physiology dependent on the reducibility of the properties cited in these fields to those cited in physics? That seems almost equally outlandish. It is a wide-open empirical question whether properties of these special sciences are reducible to those cited in physics. In fact, it seems very unlikely that general reduction is possible. The causal relevance of the properties of these special sciences seems independent of questions of reducibility.

Weaknesses in the foregoing arguments are widely known. But there remains a sense of unease. Many seem disturbed by the picture of mental properties supervening on physical properties and just going along for the ride. Thus there have been various attempts to state what kind of supervenience relations would 'allow' mental properties to be causally efficacious even though they supervene on physical properties.[a]

These projects can be interesting. But in my view, the worries about epiphenomenalism have an air of make-believe. It is much surer that epiphenomenalism is false than that the various assumptions (even including the materialist assumptions) that have been thought to lead to it are true. It is also much surer that epiphenomenalism is false than that the various attempts to show it false or avoidable by appeal to counterfactuals, accounts of laws, or supervenience, are true. Epiphenomenalism is often taken as a serious metaphysical option. But it is better seen as at best a source of pressure for clarifying our common conceptions. It is rather like one of the less plausible scepticisms, which can be used as an instrument for philosophical clarification, but which has little real persuasive force. I think that a different, less metaphysical attitude in thinking about the problem would be more realistic and fruitful.

The irony is that by trying to clarify mentalistic causation, many materialists have come to believe that there is a serious metaphysical issue whether

---

[a] Jaegwon Kim, "Epiphenomenal and Supervenient Causation", *Midwest Studies in Philosophy*, 9 (1984), 257–270; Ernest Sosa, "Mind–Body Interaction and Supervenient Causation", *Midwest Studies in Philosophy*, 9 (1984), 271–281.

mentalistic characterizations have any causal relevance at all. I think that this is tantamount to admitting that materialism has failed to illumine mental causation. But such illumination has been advertised as materialism's chief selling-point. Although materialism is not forced to accept epiphenomenalism, the very fact that the view is taken so seriously as a metaphysical option suggests that something has gone wrong in the search for clarification.

One cannot understand mentalistic causation (causation involving mentalistic or intentional properties) and mental causal powers by concentrating on properties characterized in the physical sciences. Our understanding of mental causation derives primarily from our understanding of mentalistic explanation, independently of our knowledge—or better, despite our ignorance—of the underlying processes. Materialist accounts have allowed too wide a gap between their metaphysics of mental causation and what we actually know about the nature and existence of mentalistic causation, which derives almost entirely from mentalistic explanations and observations.

2

So far I have not questioned the materialist metaphysics that helps ground the worries about epiphenomenalism. In this section I want to advance reasons for doubting the most common form of materialism and its centrality in understanding mental causation.

There is certainly reason to believe that underlying our mental states and processes are physical, chemical, biological, and neural processes that proceed according to their own laws. Some such physical processes are probably necessary if intentional (or phenomenal) mental events are to be causes of behavior. They seem necessary even for the mental events to exist. But, in my view, the nature of the relation between mental events and these physical processes is thoroughly unclear. The most widely accepted account of the relation is the materialist token-identity theory.

Some years ago I gave an argument against a significant version of the materialist token-identity theory.[b] The version I had in mind holds that each mental-state instance and event-token is identical with a physical-state instance or event-token that instantiates a physical natural kind specified in some actual natural science, or specifiable in some reasonable extension of the natural sciences as we now know them. Different mental event-tokens of the same mental event type may be tokens of different physical natural kinds.

The requirement that the physical event-token instantiate a physical kind specifiable in a natural science (physics, chemistry, biology, neurophysiology, and so on) is meant to ensure that the materialist utilize a non-question-begging

[b] Burge, "Individualism and the Mental" *Midwest Studies in Philosophy*, 4 (1979), 73–121 (Ch. 5 above).

identification that is not only uncontroversially physical, but plays some role in explanation of physical causation. I think that there are materialist views that are less committal than this one. My argument does not defeat these views. I shall remark on some of them later.

The argument against this sort of token-identity theory is partly based on twin earth thought experiments that I shall presume are familiar.[4] According to these thought experiments, it is possible for a person's body, considered in isolation from its relations to the environment, to be physiologically and molecularly the same even if the person were to think thoughts that have different intentional content. The difference in content depends on differences in the individual's historical relations to his or her environment. For example, it is possible for a person who has borne some historical relation (perhaps through vision or interlocution) to aluminum or arthritis to think that aluminum is a light metal or that arthritis is a painful disease, even though the person has no dispositions that would enable him to discriminate aluminum or arthritis from all other actual or possible metals or diseases—except by thinking of it as aluminum or arthritis. Counterfactual environments are possible in which one of these other 'look-alike' metals or diseases plays the same role in the acquisition and production of thoughts that aluminum and arthritis actually do. In such counterfactual environments the person might, for all intents and purposes, have a body that is a chemical and physiological duplicate of the actual person's body. Yet the person would be thinking thoughts with different content. The person would not be thinking that aluminum is a light metal or that arthritis is a painful disease.

I shall take it for granted that these thought experiments are sound, as so far described. The first premise of the argument against the token-identity theory is strongly suggested (though not entailed) by the thought experiments:

(1) It is possible for a person to think thoughts with different contents even though all event-tokens that occur in the individual's body, that are plausible candidates for identification with mental events, and that are specifiable by physical sciences such as physics, chemistry, and neurophysiology, are the same.

The second premise is less specifically related to the thought experiments:

(2) No occurrence of a thought could have a different intentional content and be the very same token-event or event-particular.

---

[4] Ibid.; Burge, "Other Bodies", in A. Woodfield (ed.), *Thought and Object: Essays on Intentionality* (Oxford: Clarendon Press, 1982), 97–120; *idem*, "Cartesian Error and the Objectivity of Perception", in P. Pettit and J. McDavell (eds.), *Subject, Thought, and Context* (Oxford: Clarendon Press, 1986), 117–136; *idem*, "Intellectual Norms and the Foundations of Mind", *The Journal of Philosophy*, 83 (1986), 697–720; *idem*, "Wherein is Language Social?", in A. George (ed.), *Reflections on Chomsky* (Oxford: Blackwell, 1989), 175–191 (Chs. 4, 7, 10, 11 above). The thought experiments use the methodology set out in Hilary Putnam, "The Meaning of 'Meaning'", in *Philosophical Papers*, ii (Cambridge: Cambridge University Press, 1975), 215–271.

Now take any physical event-token *b* in the individual's body that is a plausible candidate for being identical with the individual's occurrent thought (mental event-token) *a* that aluminum is a light metal (or that arthritis is a painful disease). By (1), there are possible situations in which the same token *b* occurs, but in which there occur only thoughts (mental event-tokens) with different intentional content. By (2), none of these thought occurrences is the very same token event as *a*. So since *b* could occur without *a*'s occurring, *b* cannot be identical with *a*.

This argument has been criticized by Donald Davidson. Davidson accepts the second premise, calling its denial 'not merely implausible but absurd. If two mental events have different contents, they are surely different events.' He does not squarely confront the first premise. But he appears to reject it. He thinks that the relevant thought experiments show that 'people who are in all relevant respects similar ... can differ in what they mean or think. ... But of course there is *something* different about them, even in the physical world; their causal histories are different.'[5]

I find this response unconvincing. There certainly are physical differences between actual and counterfactual situations in the relevant thought experiments. The question is whether there are always physically different entities that are plausible candidates for being identical with the different mental events or state-instances. The different physical causal histories are not plausible candidates. These histories do not have the same causes or effects that the relevant mental events (states) do. Moreover, it is doubtful that relevantly described causal histories instantiate explanatory natural kinds in any of the physical sciences.

One might think that since, in the counterfactual situation, there are differences at least in the remote causal ancestry of every relevant physical event in the individual's body, every such event would be a different event-token from any event-token in the actual situation. Events are, on this view, different just by virtue of having some difference in their causal histories.[6] But this seems an extremely implausible view of event identity. It seems to me clearly possible to consider the same event-token in an individual's body in a counterfactual situation, without being committed to the view that every event in the causal ancestry of that event, however remote, remains token- (or type-) identical. Much counterfactual reasoning about events depends on not being so inflexible. We frequently talk about a particular event under counterfactual suppositions in

[5] The quotations are from D. Davidson, "Knowing one's own Mind", *Proceedings of the American Philosophical Association*, 60 (1987), 452. Davidson has helpfully confirmed his rejection of premise (1) in private communication.

[6] This may be a consequence of Davidson's criterion for individuating events; cf. D. Davidson, "The Individuation of Events", in N. Rescher (ed.), *Essays in Honor of Carl G. Hempel* (Dordrecht: Reidel, 1969), 216–234. But since the criterion is not formulated modally, it is not clear that Davidson intends to apply the criterion in all counterfactual situations. He does, however, consider at least one counterfactual situation in discussing it.

which it is not assumed that every prior event in the history of the world that is causally linked with it is the same.[7]

Suppose I get my thoughts about aluminum from reading books. In the counterfactual situation I see identical-looking print. The salient difference lies at the end of a long causal chain: the counterfactual chain goes back to some other metal; the actual one goes back to aluminum. On the view we are considering, every event in the two chains must be different, a different particular. So the physiologically characterized events in my brain caused by reading the print cannot be token-identical in the two cases. What is objectionable about this view is that it makes the individuation of brain events depend on matters that are irrelevant to the physiology of the brain. I know of nothing in our explanatory practices that would support such a metaphysical view.

As far as I can see, in numerous cases it is possible for all physical (token-) events that are candidates for identification with intentional mental events to remain the same in counterfactual situations while the relevant mental events, the thoughts, differ. I do not see the slightest plausibility in the idea that there are always physical events—identifiable with the mental events and specifiable in the natural sciences—whose identity will, under all possible counterfactual circumstances, vary exactly when the mental events vary. At any rate, objections of the sort Davidson raises need to show, in the light of the thought experiments, what differences in physical events might plausibly be token-identical with the different mental events.

There is another element in Davidson's resistance to my argument. He holds that an appreciation of the external factors that enter into our common ways of identifying mental states does not discredit a token-identity theory. He cites sunburn as an example of a state whose identification is environmentally dependent. Davidson thinks, plausibly, that a particular sunburn is token-identical with a

---

[7] Davidson, ('Knowing one's own Mind', 451–453) concedes that events in the individual's body can be type-identical in the relevant actual and counterfactual situations. But he gives no reason for thinking that events in the individual's body cannot be token-identical—the same individual events—between actual and counterfactual situations.

There is an unexplained suggestion, p. 453, that he thinks that 'essentialist' assumptions might be playing a role in my argument. I do not mind being committed to some types of essentialism. But my argument does not depend on essentialism. All modal claims (including the one in the second premise) can be interpreted as supported by the best available methods of individuation. In the first premise I have not made a claim about essence or necessity at all, only one about possibility. To counter this claim, Davidson would have to appeal to a certain impossibility. He would have to deny that it is possible that an event could be the same token event if, counterfactually, its causal ancestry differs in any of the ways needed to yield different thoughts. This denial would itself seem to me to suggest an extreme form of essentialism about individual events. It suggests that the entire causal ancestry of an event is always part of the essence of that event. The denial could be rephrased in terms of methods of individuation (cf. above), but it seems to me to have no support in our actual explanatory practices. Davidson does think that events are the same if and only if they have the same causes and effects (cf. note 8). But for the present purposes, he needs to hold that it is impossible for an event to have been the same if it had had any differences in causal history. As far as I know, he has not defended this modal thesis. I suspect that it is indefensible.

particular state of the skin. And he thinks that mental states and events are broadly analogous to sunburn.

I think the sunburn example irrelevant to my argument. My argument does not claim that no non-individualistically characterized states or events can be identified with states or events in the individual's body. It claims only that some mental states and events cannot be.[8] The state of being sunburned is, I agree, token-identical with a physiologically specifiable state (instance) of the skin. But the state of being sunburned is relevantly unlike a state of belief, or a thought-event. In the first place, we know how to identify sunburned states of the skin in systematic and explanatory ways that are completely independent of the fact that they are sunburns. That is part of what makes plausible the identification of a sunburn with a physiological state of the skin. We can see the effect of the sun on the skin, and give a chemical or physiological account of that effect. Significantly, this account need not make any assumptions about whether a celestial body caused that effect. We have no such ways of identifying states of the body that (putatively) are beliefs, independently of assumptions about the beliefs. I think that this difference reflects our ignorance of the relation between beliefs and states of the body. It is not incompatible with an identity theory, but it renders questionable the easy analogy to cases where identities are obvious.

In the second place, the analog of my argument would not work for sunburns in the way the argument works for thoughts. The analogue of the first premise seems true for sunburn. That is, the very same (instance-identical) state of the same skin, specifiable in physiological terms, could (metaphysically could) have been caused by something other than the rays of the sun. This seems true because there are uncontroversial and obvious ways of identifying sunburns with physiologically specifiable states (state-instances) of the skin. These specifications are deeply explanatory and seem to be individuatively relevant. Yet they do not presume anything about those states deriving from the sun's rays.[9]

---

[8] Ibid. 452 says I may make the mistake of thinking that the thought experiments by themselves are incompatible with the token-identity theory. His further discussion seems to suggest that I do make this mistake. I have never thought this, and I have never written anything that entails it. In a later paper, "The Myth of the Subjective", in M. Krausz (ed.), *Relativism: Interpretation and Confrontation* (Notre Dame, Ind.: University of Notre Dame Press, 1989), 159–172, Davidson says that the argument behind my denial of the token-identity theory 'assumes that if a state or event is identified (perhaps necessarily, if it is a mental state or event) by reference to things outside of the body, then the state or event itself must be outside the body, or at least not identical with any event in the body'. I do think that certain mental events that are necessarily individuated by reference to things outside the body are not identical with any event in the body describable via kind terms of the physical sciences. But I have never taken this view as an assumption. I have argued for it. Davidson's discussion does not go to the heart of our disagreement. What follows should make the point clearer.
[9] In my view, therefore, the sunburn example does not line up very well with Davidson's criticism of my argument—since he wishes to deny premise (1). Davidson very likely denies that the analog of (1) holds for sunburn. Cf. Davidson, "Knowing One's Own Mind", 451–455, where he concedes only that the state of the skin might remain type-identical. But he gives no reason for holding that an instance-identical state of the skin could not have been caused by anything other than the sun. Perhaps he thinks that states are analogous to events in (necessarily) being instance-identical only if

On the other hand, the analog of premise (2) seems to fail for sunburn. I think that we have no grounds to think that if a physiologically specifiable state (instance) of the skin had not been a sunburn, it would have been impossible for it to have been the same state (instance) as one that is. Again, our ability to identify states of the skin with sunburns and fit them into a systematic, individuatively relevant scheme of explanation that prescinds from anything about the sun supports this view. The kind *sunburn*, by contrast, fits into a much less systematic, informative, and important explanatory scheme—if it fits into any such scheme at all. Its claim to individuate state-instances across counterfactual situations is far less strong than the physiological scheme. Similarly, its claim to provide a fundamental form of individuation (as premise (2) claims for intentional contents) is substantially less strong than the claim of mental kinds. The failure of analogy, in these respects, between sunburn and thoughts makes the example incapable of undermining my argument.

Whereas Davidson doubts premise (1) of the argument, some token-identity theories have been taken as denying premise (2). It is common to hold that intentional states and events can be type-identified with functional states and that these states could be realized by a variety of physical states or events. The realizing physical states and events are supposed to be instance- or token-identical with the mental states or events. This view does not entail a denial of (2). But it is usually also assumed, at least implicitly, that the identity of the underlying physical states and events is independent of their exact functional role in a given system. If this is assumed, then this sort of theory would be committed to denying (2).

Such a theory seems very unpromising. There is little in our explanatory practice to encourage identification of intentional mental types with non-intentionally specified functional types.[10] The identification of intentional mental tokens with tokens specified in the natural sciences has, I think, even less clear support in explanatory practice. But what I want to centre on is the main reason for accepting (2).

The system of intentional content attribution is the fundamental means of identifying intentional mental states and events in psychological explanation and in our self-attributions. In fact, we have no other systematic way of identifying such states and events. Davidson holds that (2) is intuitively obvious and denials of it are absurd. I agree. But I think that it can also be justified by noting that it is our only way of individuating intentional mental events that provides systematic

they have the same causes (cf. note 6). But I see no metaphysical or even physiological impossibility in thinking of a given state-instance as having been arranged by light rays with exactly the same physical powers and vectors as the sun's which, however, did not emanate from the sun. Whether Davidson holds the analogue of premise (2) for sunburn is unclear to me. It appears, however, that he probably would hold that no state-instance of a sunburn could be caused by something other than the sun and be the very same state-instance. As noted below, I find this implausible.

[10] For a recent discussion of reasons for this charge, cf. Hilary Putnam, *Representation and Reality* (Cambridge, Mass.: MIT Press, 1988).

understanding, description, and explanation of mental events and intentional activity. Such cognitive practices are our most reliable way of knowing the nature of what exists.

I know of no plausible or even serious arguments against (2).[11] But failure to hold it firmly in mind is a major source of the misguided worries about epiphenomenalism. Insofar as one allows oneself to think that intentional contents are only contingently associated with a thought-event, one is in a position to imagine that one can hold constant a neural event supposedly identical with a mental event, while imagining the mental/physical event to have a different content. Supposing that the causal laws connecting the neural processes are sufficient for their effects, one is led to wonder wherein the intentional properties are causally relevant. This conceit can naturally be seen to lie behind the view that the intentional content of mental states and events is a mere epiphenomenal 'aspect' of those events—the view that I noted in the first paragraph of this paper.

But in fact, such content is the explanatory and identificatory centre of those events. We have little else to go on in talking about the causal powers and ontology of the mental. Systematic, informative, important explanatory schemes—like our mentalistic one—usually (there are special cases) make the strongest claim for providing individuating descriptions that indicate what is essential to the identities of individuals, particulars, or instances.[12] It seems to me that any metaphysical theory that seeks to illumine mental causation or the ontology of mental events that denies (2) is hopelessly misdirected.

As I have been noting, systematic, informative, important explanatory schemes of events and states are also our strongest indications of causal relevance. The idea that the causal relations described in psychology are really or most fundamentally causal only under some other description seems extremely tenuous and doubtful. I see no reason to think that there is anything in the idea, now common among philosophers, that in some sense the 'real' causal work is being done at a lower level. I also see no reason to think that we can understand mentalistic causation through some analysis of supervenience (although I think that understanding the sense in which mental events supervene on the physical is an important enterprise). Our understanding of mental causation derives not primarily from re-descriptions in physical terms.[13] It derives

---

[11] I have heard it suggested that although (2) is not true, it is true that there could not be two events that are mentally the same if they had different contents. (2) is still denied because the same physical event could allegedly be identical with a mental event that had one content, in the actual situation, or with a mental event that had another content, in the counterfactual situation. It is not the same thought content, but it is the same thought/neural event. This subtlety does not seem to me to count for much in defending opposition to (2). The remarks in the preceding paragraph still seem to apply.

[12] Again, one can reparse talk about essence into talk about the most fundamental method for identifying individuals and reidentifying them under counterfactual considerations; cf. note 7.

[13] Or worse yet, in syntactical terms. One might well grant that many psychological states and events involve operations on syntactic entities. One may also see such inner mental syntactic items

primarily from our understanding of mentalistic explanation. This understanding is largely independent of reference to the underlying processes.

Davidson's profoundly stimulating argument for a token-identity theory seems to me flawed by a subtle analog of the tendency to underrate the centrality of cognitive practice in understanding mental causation and ontology.[c] The argument partly relies on the premise that causal relations between events must be backed by (entail the existence of) laws of a complete, closed system of explanation, where the predicates of these laws are true of the events that are causally related. Davidson conjoins this premise with the assumption that there are causal relations between mental and physical events and the assumption (for which he argues) that mentalistic explanations cannot themselves be part of a complete, closed system of explanation. From these three premises he concludes that mental event-tokens must fall under predicates of physical laws that do form part of a complete, closed explanatory system. As far as I can see, these must be the laws of physics.

I think that we do not know, and cannot know apriori, that causal statements entail the existence of laws or explanatory systems that have such specific properties. We cannot know apriori this much about the form of the laws of nature, described by any science. Nor can we know apriori the relations among the ontologies and causal schemes of the various sciences. That is, we cannot know apriori that the laws, or nomological generalizations, of psychology describe events that have any very specific relation to events that fall under the laws of any other science. I think that there is no reason, much less any apriori reason, to accept Davidson's first premise. Thus we cannot know apriori that mental events that are causes fall under any other (non-mentalistic) sort of law.

Our best guide to the nature of mental causation and ontology lies in understanding our best means of explaining and describing mental events. Our actual cognitive practice lends little credence to the idea that intentional mental events fall under exceptionless physical laws, or instantiate physical descriptions of the most fundamental natural science.

Let us return to the argument against the form of token-identity theory that I described at the outset (a form that Davidson's argument was intended to support). Since premises (1) and (2) seem strongly plausible and free of serious counter-arguments, the argument seems to me forceful and sound. The most

---

as expressing intentional content. But the idea that the brain is sensitive only to syntactic shape, not to content, seems to me a misleading metaphor. The brain is sensitive to neural forms. One may think of there being causal relations among syntactic entities, but this is already to describe causation at a higher level of abstraction than that of brain physiology. If causation can be described at that level, it can also be described at the level of intentional content. I see little ground for seeing the syntactic properties as prior to intentional properties in the order of causal relevance. Syntax is attributed to serve explanations that are fundamentally intentional. In my view, there is no non-artificial sense in which syntax is ontologically or causally more secure.

[c] D. Davidson, "Mental Events", in L. Foster and J. Swauson (eds.), *Experience and Theory* (Amherst, Mass.: University of Massachusetts Press, 1970), 79–101; repr. in Davidson, *Essays on Actions and Events* (Oxford: Clarendon Press, 1980).

common metaphysical ground for worries about epiphenomenalism seems on weak ground.

There are less committal forms of materialism about mental events. All such forms must take mental event-tokens to be physical event-tokens that are not instances of kinds described by any of the natural sciences. Perhaps this is not an intrinsically implausible claim. Particular wars, avalanches, thunderstorms, meal-cookings may not fall under any natural event-kind describable in any natural science. I doubt that there is ever any one definite token event that instantiates kinds of a natural science, even physics, with which an event-token of these kinds can be identified. Yet they are clearly physical events. Maybe mental events are like that.

On the other hand, these analogies seem merely hopeful. The relevant descriptions are uncontroversially physical. The problem with identifying them with events described in physics lies merely in their complexity and in the fact that they fall into patterns that are salient for macro-descriptions, but not particularly useful for systematic explanation. By contrast, psychological states do fall into systematic patterns which explanation can make use of. But these patterns do not seem to involve ordinary physical properties (like mass, energy, composition, and so on) that physical explanations and descriptions make use of.[14] So the view that these are, in the ordinary sense, physical patterns seems doubtful.

In any case, such forms of materialism provide little new insight into mental causation, as long as the relevant physical events with which the mental events are supposedly token-identical remain unidentified in non-mentalistic terms. There is little in current cognitive practice to encourage the view that any such descriptions of central intentional state-instances or event-tokens are forthcoming. So even if such a liberalized version of materialism were true, it would offer little help in understanding mental causation.

3

The problem about mental causation that is usually raised as a means of motivating an appeal to materialism is that of explaining a mechanism that would make possible causal interaction between two such different things as a physical event (or substance) and a mental event (or substance). Materialists hold that the problem disappears if mental events are seen as physical. This problem was posed by Descartes; and he professed himself baffled by it. The problem was acute for Descartes because he viewed mental and physical entities as substances in

---

[14] The composition relation is probably the critical one. There are forms of materialism that maintain that all objects are decomposable into inorganic physical particles. Apart from the fact that these forms do not apply very well to properties or events (not to speak of objects like numbers, intentional contents, methods), they make a claim for the relevance of physical composition to our understanding of mental entities that seems to me (so far) quite unsupported by anything that we know.

the old-fashioned sense—entities that were not dependent on anything else for their nature or existence. But mental events and other mental entities like minds are not substances in the old-fashioned sense. So there is for us no antecedent problem of admitting various sorts of constitutive and existential dependency of the mental on the physical. It is not obvious, however, that this dependency need involve material constitution—the mental events being identical with or made up of physical events.

I have no satisfying response to the problem of explaining a mechanism. But I am sure that there is less reason to think it a decisive consideration in favor of materialism than is often thought. What is unclear is whether the question is an appropriate one in the first place. Demanding that there be an account of mechanism in mind–body causation is tantamount to demanding a physical model for understanding such causation. It is far from obvious that such a model is appropriate. It is not even obvious why any model is needed. The argument I have just cited presents no clearly formulated problem about mental causation that need force us to embrace materialism, including the computer model's version of materialism, as a solution. The demand for a mechanism is tantamount to an implicit demand for a materialist solution.

A better articulated argument for materialism along similar lines goes as follows. Physical effects are caused by prior physical states or events according to approximately deterministic physical laws. Mental causes bring about physical movements of our bodies. If such causation did not consist in physical processes, there would be departures from the approximately deterministic physical patterns described by physical laws. It would interfere with, alter, or otherwise 'make a difference' in the physical outcomes. But there is no reason to think that this happens. Physical antecedent states suffice for the physical effects. Appeal to mental causation that does not consist in physical causation appears, on this reasoning, to require us to doubt the adequacy of current forms of physical explanation, even within the physical domain. So such appeal should be rejected.

This reasoning seems to me to have some force. But I think that it is not as forceful as it may appear. Why should mental causes alter or interfere with the physical system if they do not materially consist in physical processes? Thinking that they must, surely depends on thinking of mental causes on a physical model—as providing an extra 'bump' on the effect. The idea seems to be that a cause must transfer a bit of energy or exert a force on the effect. On such a model, mental causes would deflect a physical effect off the course a physical cause alone would set it on. Cases where the mental cause and the physical cause yield the same physical outcome—cases of 'overdetermination'—will be seen, on such a model, as coincidences that must be abnormal. So appeals to overdetermination by mental causes and physical causes will seem unattractive as a gloss on the general failure of mental causes to interfere with or alter the physical outcomes expected on purely physical grounds.

But whether the physical model of mental causation is appropriate is, again, part of what is at issue. As we have seen, one can specify various ways in which mental causes 'make a difference' which do not conflict with physical explanations. The differences they make are specified by psychological causal explanations, and by counterfactuals associated with these explanations. Such 'differences' made by psychological causes do not require that gaps be left in physical chains of causation. They do not seem to depend on any specific assumptions at all about the physical events underlying the mental causes.

I think that we have reason, just from considering explanatory goals and practice—before ontology is even considered—to think that mentalistic and physicalistic accounts of causal processes will not interfere with one another. Part of the point of referring to mental states lies in explaining intentional activity that involves (or is identical with) physical movement. A man's running to the store is explained by his believing that his child would suffer without the needed medicine and by his decision not to wait on a doctor. We think that the man's running is caused by the formation of his belief and by his decision.

It would be perverse to think that such mental events must interfere with or alter, or fill some gap in, the chain of physiological events leading up to and including the movements of his muscles in running. It would be perverse to think that the mentalistic explanation excludes or interferes with non-intentional explanations of the physical movement. I think that these ideas seem perverse not because we know that the mental events are material. They seem perverse because we know that the two causal explanations are explaining the same physical effect as the outcome of two very different patterns of events. The explanations of these patterns answer two very different types of inquiry. Neither type of explanation makes essential, specific assumptions about the other. So the relation between the entities appealed to in the different explanations cannot be read off the causal implications of either or both types of explanation. The perversity of thinking that mental causes must fill gaps in physical chains of events probably has its source in traditional dualism, or in libertarian worries about free will. But the perversity remains regardless of its source.

The upshot of this reasoning is that we have no ground for assuming that the failure of mental causes to interfere in the physical chain of events must be explained in terms of mental causes' consisting in physical events. Interference would be surprising, given antecedent assumptions about mental and physical explanation. So non-interference is in no need of explanation in ontological terms.

There are surely some systematic, even necessary, relations between mental events and underlying physical processes. We have good reason to believe that mental processes depend on underlying physical processes. By probing or damaging parts of the brain we can bring about, affect, or ruin mental states and processes. But the relations of identity and physical composition are relations that have specific scientific uses. For example, we explain the behavior of a molecule in terms of the behavior of its component parts. It is far from clear that these compositional relations have a systematic scientific use in bridging psychology and neurophysiology (cf. note 15). They are guesses about what sorts of relation might obtain. But they seem to me just one set of possibilities for accounting for relations between entities referred to in these very different explanatory enterprises. What form an inter-level account might take seems to me to be an open question.

I find it plausible to believe in some sort of broad supervenience thesis: no changes in mental states without some sort of change in physical states. But the inference to materialism is, I think, a metaphysical speculation which has come, misleadingly, to seem a relatively obvious scientific or commonsensical bromide.

As long as mentalistic explanation yields knowledge and understanding, and as long as that explanation is (sometimes) causal, we can firmly believe that mind–body causation is a part of the world. The primary way of understanding such causation is by understanding mentalistic causal and explanatory statements in the ordinary, non-philosophical sense of 'understanding'. How much more illumination philosophy or neuro-psychology can offer remains to be seen. At any rate, mentalistic explanation and mental causation do not need validation from materialist metaphysics.

It seems to me that philosophers should be more relaxed about whether or not some form of materialism is true. I think it a thoroughly open—and not very momentous—question whether there is any point in insisting that mental events are, in any clear sense, physical. Maybe science will never make use of anything more than limited correlations with the lower, more automatic parts of the cognitive system. Maybe identities or part–whole relations will never have systematic use. Maybe the traditional idea of a category difference will maintain a presence in scientific practice. What matters is that our mentalistic explanations work and that they do not conflict with our physicalistic explanations. As philosophers, we want a well-founded understanding of how these explanations, and their subject matters, relate to one another. But it serves no purpose to over-dramatize the conflict between different ontological approaches or the merits of the materialist approach.

The flood of projects over the last two decades that attempt to fit mental causation or mental ontology into a 'naturalistic picture of the world' strikes me as having more in common with political or religious ideology than with a philosophy that maintains perspective on the difference between what is known and what is speculated. Materialism is not established, or even clearly supported, by science. Metaphysics should venture beyond science with an acute sense of its liabilities.

4

I have argued that epiphenomenalism need not be seen as a serious metaphysical option even if materialism is true. The probity of mentalistic causal explanation is deeper than the metaphysical considerations that call it into question. I have also argued that materialist metaphysics is not the most plausible starting point for reasoning about mind–body causation. Explanatory practice is.

I think it more natural and fruitful to begin by assuming, defeasibly perhaps but firmly, that attributions of intentional mental events are central to psychological explanation both in ordinary life and in various parts of psychology. We may also assume that intentional mental events are often causes and that psychological explanation is often a form of causal explanation. Given these assumptions, the 'worry' about epiphenomenalism seems very remote. For if intentional mental events are type-individuated in terms of their intentional 'aspects'—if those aspects are the fundamental explanatory aspects—and if such events enter into causal relations and are cited (in terms of those aspects) in explanations, then there seems to be every reason to conclude that those aspects are causally efficacious. None of the metaphysical considerations advanced in current discussion seem to me remotely strong enough to threaten this conclusion.[15]

I shall conclude by mentioning a further reason for thinking that intentional events are, as such, causally efficacious. Why is it that philosophers who discuss epiphenomenalism are worried about it? Why should one not take a more disinterested attitude?

Part of the answer lies in the fact that many philosophers instinctively feel that if epiphenomenalism were a consequence of their metaphysics, their metaphysics would be in trouble.[16] This is good philosophical sense. Outside our philosophical studies, we all know that epiphenomenalism is not true.

But there is a deeper reason why epiphenomenalism should seem intellectually unattractive. Much of the interest of psychological explanation, both in psychology and in ordinary discourse, lies in helping us understand ourselves as agents. Causal implications are built into our intentional concepts and intentional modes of explanation. We think that we make things happen because we make decisions or will to do things. We think that we make assertions, form theories, and create cultures, because we think certain thoughts and have certain goals—and we express and fulfill them. In this context, we identify ourselves primarily in terms of our intentional mental aspects—our wants, our thoughts, our values. Our agency consists in our wants', willings', thoughts', values' as such (under these 'aspects') having some sort of efficacy in the world. Our mental events' having the intentional characters that they have is, in individual instances, what we define our agency in terms of.

---

[15] The fact that intentional mental events are appealed to, as such, in explanations by itself differentiates them from phenotypes. Phenotypes are explananda in biology, but intentional mental events are part of causal explanations in psychology and everyday life—not simply the explananda for explanations. It is a mark of much of the discussion in this area that such simple differences in explanatory status are not so much as mentioned. The metaphysics of the situation is often discussed in virtual isolation from explanatory practice.

[16] Cf. N. Block, "Can the Mind Change the World?", in G. Boolos (ed.), *Meaning and Method: Essays in Honor of Hilary Putnam* (Cambridge: Cambridge University Press, 1990), 137–170, for a clear statement of this view.

Most of our intellectual and practical norms and evaluations presuppose that we are agents. If our willing or deciding made something happen, but that event's being a willing or deciding were not causally efficacious (so that the efficacy resided in some underlying neural property), then the agency would not be ours. If our theoretical deliberations were not ours to control, we could not see ourselves as being the authors of our theories; nor could we criticize ourselves as deliberators. Most normative evaluations of our intellectual and practical activities would be empty.

If intentional psychological explanation 'made sense' of what we did, 'rationalized' it, but did not provide insight into the nature of any causal efficacy, it would lose much of its point. It would provide no insight into the various forms of agency that give life its meaning and purpose, and psychology its special interest.

I am not here asserting that it is inconceivable that psychological explanation could break down—or at least be very much more limited than we conceive it as being. I think that the question of conceivability is quite subtle and complex. The point is that this form of psychological explanation has not in the least broken down. It works very well, within familiar limits, in ordinary life; it is used extensively in psychology and the social sciences; and it is needed in understanding physical science, indeed any sort of rational enterprise. We have reason to believe that it provides explanatory insights. But then, as I have noted, there is a deep connection between intentional psychological explanation and the view it provides of ourselves as agents, on one hand, and the attribution of some sort of causal efficacy to intentional mental states and events as such, on the other.

I think that these are not the only reasons for this form of attribution. But even if they were, it would leave the attribution so deeply entrenched that there is no real hope that epiphenomenalism could become a credible view. Epiphenomenalism is better seen as an instrument, like scepticism, for clarifying our most deeply held beliefs. It seems to me, however, that the traditional scepticisms about agency, will, and responsibility are more penetrating tools for this purpose.

Postscript to "Mind–Body Causation and Explanatory Practice"

"Mind-Body Causation and Explanatory Practice" is out of step with the philo-sophical temper of the times. I take a distant, sceptical attitude toward the prevailing physicalism, or materialism, in philosophy of mind. I also defend my old argument, first stated in "Individualism and the Mental" (Chapter 5 above), that one popular form of materialism, the token identity theory, is false.

I attempt no satisfying account of the mind–body problem. My primary interest lies in articulating dissatisfaction with the particular approach to the problem that has dominated discussions since the mid-twentieth century.

I believe that discussions of the mind–body problem often show poor per-spective on what we know and what we do not know. Metaphysical posi-tions—like materialism or physicalism—are held in common among many philosophers with a firmness and fervor that are out of proportion to the strength of the grounds for holding them. Such positions are not clearly supported by explanations in common sense or the sciences. Nor do they have strong intuitive support.

There is, of course, a long-standing, justified, general sense that the mind depends on the body. However, materialist views in philosophy make very particular claims about the relations between psychological events or proper-ties and physical events or properties. Such views require relations of iden-tity, constitution, realization, or the like. No one of these specific relations is clearly supported by actual scientific explanation. I think that all lack strong intuitive support—beyond the support for the generalized sense of dependence.

In the article, I held that the issues over mental causation that had begun to arise from within materialist points of view showed the metaphysical situation to be less clear-cut and more difficult than common philosophical opinion took it to be. I maintained that metaphysical positions in this area should be occu-pied and reflected upon with considerably more diffidence, and with a greater openness to reflecting on alternatives.

Similarly, the metaphysical view epiphenomenalism, which is flatly incom-patible with what we know from scientific and commonsense explanations, is widely taken as a genuine contender for the truth, although, unlike physical-ism, it is not widely held. The reason why the view is taken seriously is that it can appear to be implied by some of the metaphysical opinions that are them-selves too firmly held. Here again, I maintained that a great deal of philosophy had lost perspective on the distinction between what we know and understand,

I am indebted to Ned Block for helpful advice.

on one hand, and what we are in the position of groping to understand, on the other.[1]

I believe that these points remain valid. My repeating them here is witness to their having had rather little effect. I believe that part of the problem is that large shifts in philosophical attitude usually proceed only slowly. In some cases, however, misunderstanding has helped block adequate appreciation of the points that I made. I want to discuss a response that embodies both a fair amount of misunderstanding and a version of the syndrome that provoked my scepticism.

Writing as if my criticism of materialist metaphysics were a criticism of doing metaphysics at all, Jaegwon Kim responds to my paper by arguing that there is indeed a problem of mental causation and that a metaphysics that engages it is worth doing. Those points are true. Kim's spirited claims in this vein are irrelevant to what I wrote.

Kim quotes my statement,

Materialist metaphysics has been given more weight than it deserves. Reflection on explanatory practice has been given too little.

He associates this statement with the much stronger claim of Lynne Rudder Baker:

If we reverse the priority of explanation and causation that is favored by the metaphysician, the problem of mental causation just melts away.[2]

Kim asks:

Would the problem of mental causation take its leave if we did less metaphysics, as Burge and Baker urge, and instead focused our attention on psychological explanation?[3]

This take on my view is very much mistaken. I do not accept Baker's claim that the problem of mental causation would 'melt away' if one shifted perspective. I did not, and do not, think that any such problem can be made to 'take its leave' by focusing on psychological explanation, and doing less metaphysics. I do not advocate doing less metaphysics.[4] I have no objection to counting the problem of understanding mental causation as a *metaphysical*

---

[1] I applied these methodological points to particular issues regarding mind–body causation. I believe that parallel points apply even more strongly to certain other areas of metaphysics. For the most part, philosophy of mind has taken at least rough account of what (little) is known about the mind and its relation to the brain or body. In some other areas of metaphysics, the discussion has proceeded without any serious contact with what science has had to say on the relevant topic. I have in mind, for example, discussions of the nature of time, the relation between existence and time, the nature of physical bodies, implications for contact in body–body causation, and much of the discussion of causation itself.

[2] Lynne Rudder Baker, 'Metaphysics and Mental Causation', in J. Heil and A. Mele (eds.), *Mental Causation* (Oxford: Clarendon Press, 1993), 92–93.

[3] Jaegwon Kim, *Mind in a Physical World* (Cambridge, Mass.: MIT Press, 1999), 60–62.

[4] The scope of Kim's 'as Baker and Burge urge' is ambiguous. His assumption about what I urge is mistaken on either interpretation.

problem. I believe that very few philosophical problems are easily solved or deflated. I do not believe that problems regarding mental causation are among these few.

I recognize that there are difficulties in achieving a satisfactory understanding of mental causation, though I think that the ways these difficulties have usually been posed, from Descartes onward, have been unproductive. I think that the problem has usually been posed so as to suggest that there is some definite conflict or tension in the very notion of mind–body causation. I believe that this suggestion has never been made good. It was not made good by Descartes or by Princess Elisabeth of Bohemia (who raised the issue with Descartes). It has not been made good by modern materialists. Beginning one's inquiry by taking such a suggestion seriously, rather than beginning with a firm grip on what we know from good psychological and physical causal explanations, has tended to distort philosophical discussion. My paper was partly a complaint about such distortion. I believe that by reflecting more on explanation in science and common sense, one can gain a better starting point and perspective on the problem of mind–body causation.

As noted, I also maintained that a particular view, epiphenomenalism, has been taken more seriously, as a contender for the truth, than it deserves. I held that epiphenomenalism is a non-starter. I argued that epiphenomenalism can serve at best as a foil in trying to better understand mental causation. One can use any valid argument that leads to epiphenomenalism as a *reductio* of the argument's set of premises.

Kim writes that he agrees with my attitude toward epiphenomenalism. He maintains, 'the problem of mental causation is ... the problem of showing *how* mental causation is possible, not *whether* it is possible'. He continues:

The issue is *how to make our metaphysics consistent with mental causation*, and the choice that we need to make is between various *metaphysical alternatives*, not between some recondite metaphysical principle on the one hand and some cherished epistemological practice or principle on the other. This of course is not to say that metaphysics and epistemology are necessarily independent ...[5]

As we shall see, however, Kim does not disengage his own reasoning from talk of mental causation's being in 'jeopardy'—jeopardy engendered by what I believe to be insubstantial metaphysical considerations. In fact, I believe that because of specific aspects of Kim's eventual reductionism, his own position amounts to a form of epiphenomenalism.

Mental causation does need to be better understood, particularly in relation to physical causation. I conceive this problem in terms of better understanding rather than in terms of explaining the possibility of mental causation. I think its possibility is best explained by reflecting on its actuality rather than by appealing to putative metaphysical principles, as Kim does. Perhaps this difference

---

[5] Kim, *Mind in a Physical World*, 62.

is merely one of strategy. I do not deny that metaphysical exploration and speculation can be fruitful when it is done with a keen sense of its limitations.

I have more substantive differences with the last part of Kim's statement. Part of my point was that we cannot assume that we need to *make a choice* between various metaphysical alternatives if the available alternatives do not have a firm rational or evidential basis. Metaphysics should sometimes be carried on in a more exploratory and speculative spirit.

The issue is not between metaphysics and epistemology, two branches of philosophy. It is not a matter of making a choice between doing metaphysics and doing science, as the quoted paragraph seems to suggest my view to be. The issue is that certain forms of metaphysics do not keep in perspective what we know and what we do not know—including what we know from science. Such forms rely on metaphysical principles that are not rationally or empirically supported. Most of what we know (or are warranted in believing) about mental causation resides in causal explanations in science and common sense. In my view, metaphysics in this area has progressed very little beyond them.

Kim claims that our understanding of belief–desire explanation as causal derives from Davidson's argument that reasons are causes:

If, as Burge says, we 'may assume' that belief–desire explanation is a form of causal explanation, we owe this license substantially to Davidson. What carried the day for the causal view was Davidson's philosophical argument, not the pervasiveness of our explanatory practice of rationalizing actions in terms of belief and desire. There was no disagreement on the explanatory practice; the debate was about its nature and rationale.

Kim seems to think that explanatory practice in psychology and common sense was innocent of evident causal commitments until Davidson's philosophical (indeed Kim holds, metaphysical) arguments came along to indicate their causal character.[6]

I admire Davidson's defense of regarding psychological explanation as causal.[7] I think, however, that Kim's account takes too narrow a view of the dialectical situation in which Davidson's defense was mounted. Davidson resisted a set of aberrant philosophical views that systematically either ignored or were suspicious of scientific explanation in psychology and that offered what was in fact a revisionist view of commonsense explanation. Ordinary and scientific explanatory practice did not need Davidson to show it to be causal. Philosophy, during one of its less admirable periods, did.

Kim seems to think that actual scientific explanation in psychology is prima facie neutral as to whether psychological events or properties are causally efficacious, and that such explanation needs metaphysics to determine the issue. I

---

[6] Kim, *Mind in a Physical World*, 62–63. The quote is from p. 63.

[7] Donald Davidson, 'Actions, Reasons, and Causes', *The Journal of Philosophy*, 60 (1963); repr. in his *Essays on Actions and Events* (Oxford: Clarendon Press, 1980).

think that such a view is completely mistaken. We are entitled to assume that psychological explanation is causal unless powerful arguments arise to the contrary. We do not need metaphysics to license the assumption. Mental causation is solidly supported by science (not to speak of common sense). No metaphysics—at least, no metaphysics that has emerged so far—is in a position to put mental causation 'in jeopardy'.

I think that Kim's position is yet another example of greater confidence in a metaphysics about the mind–body problem than the relevant arguments warrant. I would like to develop this view in more detail.

Kim thinks that the principal problem for understanding mental causation is what he calls 'the exclusion problem'. The problem is: 'Given that every physical event that has a cause has a physical cause, how is a mental cause also possible?'[8]

As noted, I think that the first answer to this question lies in looking at actual mental causation—at the specifics of causal explanations in psychology and common sense. We need to recognize from the outset that the psychological properties appealed to in causal psychological explanations of physical events are among the causal factors. No ground to doubt the legitimacy of appeal to them as causes has so far been raised. Given that we know that there is neuro-physical causation of the same movement, we know that the psychological and the neuro-physical causation do not compete. I believe that we have no intuition that we need take seriously that they do compete. I think that intuitions that suggest such competition derive from questionable, poorly supported metaphysics or from dubious metaphors. Any such intuitions are in conflict with what we know from scientific and commonsense explanations.

Kim wants to press a puzzlement or a sense of 'tension' here that I think is not well motivated. He thinks that it is natural to regard the presence of the physical cause as a *threat to exclude* the presence of a mental cause. Thus, his name for the problem. Sometimes he writes that the physical cause can make the mental cause seem 'dispensable' or can put it in 'jeopardy'.[9]

I find this approach artificial. I think that given what we know from psychological causal explanation, we should assume from the beginning that any sense of tension is an illusion that must derive from some misunderstanding. Now in a way, Kim agrees that the sense of tension is an illusion. He wants to leverage the sense of tension into an acceptance of his reductionist view of psychological properties, and psychological explanation.[10] Where we differ is that I think that the sense of tension is not only an illusion, but is itself largely artificially induced.

---

[8] Ibid. 37–38.

[9] Ibid. 42, 45.

[10] Kim presents his view as a reductionist view, but the notion of reduction that he invokes seems to me not at all like reductions in science. In many respects, the view seems more eliminationist or epiphenomenalist, at least about representational states. I shall, however, continue to call it a reductionist view.

Kim states that the exclusion problem arises 'for anyone with the kind of broadly physicalist outlook that many philosophers, including myself, find compelling or, at least, plausible and attractive'.[11] This is to say that the exclusion problem arises from within physicalist metaphysics. Its force or intuitiveness is, I think, dubious independently of the metaphysics. It is very doubtful that it can be used to motivate or support physicalist metaphysics, or any particular version of such metaphysics.

Kim tries to build the sense of tension between mental and physical causes into a *reductio* argument that leads to epiphenomenalism. He wants to use the argument not to support epiphenomenalism, but to support his reduction of mental properties to physical properties. I think that there is more than one dubious or very speculative step in the argument. So I think that it cannot be used to target any one premise as the mistaken one in generating epiphenomenalism.

The argument begins with a sub-argument that mental properties *supervene* on physical properties in the sense that

> if something instantiates any mental property M at t, there is a physical base property P such that the thing has P at t, and necessarily anything with P at a time has M at that time.

Kim's argument for this principle seems to me very strange. He bases his argument on '*the principle of physical causal closure*':

If you pick any physical event and trace out its causal ancestry or posterity, that will never take you outside the physical domain. That is, no causal chain will ever cross the boundary between the physical and the nonphysical. ... If you reject this principle, you are ipso facto rejecting the in-principle completability of physics—that is, the possibility of a complete and comprehensive physical theory of all physical phenomena. For you would be saying that any complete explanatory theory of the physical domain must invoke non-physical causal agents.[12]

---

[11] Ibid. 30. Kim opens his book by announcing his commitment to a 'broadly physicalist outlook'. There is no detailed discussion of what such an outlook is. Kim says only that it is an outlook according to which 'the world' is 'fundamentally physical'. There are many questions to be raised about this idea and how it is supposed to apply to various cases (the mathematical 'world', the 'worlds' of value, right and wrong, beauty, rational justification, semantics, indeed mind). I find this sort of generalized rhetoric, which is certainly not peculiar to Kim, unilluminating. The rhetoric is very far from the expression of a definite, warranted belief.

[12] Ibid. 40. Kim cites Jerry Fodor as holding that the very intelligibility of mental causation depends on mind–body supervenience. He apparently regards the principle of physical causal closure as a way of articulating support for Fodor's blanket and apparently otherwise unsupported claim. Cf. Jerry Fodor, *Psychosemantics* (Cambridge, Mass.: MIT Press, 1987), 42. I think that Fodor's claim is wild, and that Kim's way of supporting it is implausible. I think that intelligibility lies in psychological causal explanation. Such explanation may invite philosophical supplement and interpretation. But its intelligibility hardly depends on some extremely general, abstract, and scientifically idle principle like the supervenience principle. I think that scientific explanation in psychology would go on attributing mental causation intelligibly and fruitfully regardless of the truth or falsity of supervenience, or indeed regardless of the truth or falsity of physicalism. From conversation, I believe that Fodor's present view is now closer to mine than it was when he made this statement.

Kim maintains that if mind–body supervenience fails, and if causation from the mental to the physical occurs, this principle would be false. I think that Kim's claim here is correct, almost regardless of how the physical causal closure principle is interpreted.

The formulation of the principle does, however, leave something to be desired. What is it to be taken 'outside the physical domain'? What is meant by 'agents'? It appears from the context that Kim intends to include as 'agents' any causal factors—properties, relations, events, and so on. Normally, we would say that a theory in purely physical terms, such as a physics or a biology, would leave out psychological causal factors, including psychological events and properties. Of course, if psychological properties were themselves physical, the principle would not be violated. Many—perhaps most—materialist philosophers, however, regard psychological properties as irreducible to (and not identical with) physical properties. So the principle as Kim appears to interpret it would not be accepted even by many materialists. Kim does not argue for the principle. He simply surrounds it with misleading rhetoric.

For example, Kim misleadingly claims that the principle is a necessary condition on taking a physical theory to give a complete theory of physical phenomena. This claim is certainly untrue, given what is *ordinarily* meant by the idea that one can given a complete physical theory of physical phenomena. What is ordinarily meant is that physical theory can explain physical phenomena by reference to causes specified in physical vocabulary, and by reference to laws expressed in physical vocabulary, where there are no gaps in the causal chains or causal explanations. This normal understanding of the completeability of the physical sciences does not prejudge any relation that those sciences bear to the human or psychological sciences, except that the latter sciences will not specify causes that intrude on the course of physical causation or on the lawfulness of the physical laws. (This understanding of the completeability of the physical sciences does not even entail supervenience.) Kim's principle makes unnecessary his complex argument for reduction of the psychological to the physical. Assuming that mind–body causation is not epiphenomenal, the principle already entails reduction or elimination of the psychological. I regard Kim's argument for supervenience as implausible because his premise is so strong.[13]

Should we accept supervenience? I find it plausible. Yet I know of no interesting argument for it. I do not think it irrational to suspend belief about it,

---

[13] In a subsequent book Kim states a closure principle that is similar to what I just (independently) wrote is the ordinary understanding of what is meant by the completeability of the physical sciences. Kim does not state that he has revised his understanding of closure. I think that he must have done so, however. For the new principle is not taken to support supervenience. In the later book Kim accepts supervenience as a separate basic principle, rather than something to be argued for from any closure principle. Cf. Jaegwon Kim, *Physicalism, Or Something Near Enough* (Princeton: Princeton University Press, 2005), 15–16, 21–22, 43–44. This procedure seems to me an improvement on the earlier work. The improvement does not affect anything except for my criticism of the earlier closure principle.

given the extreme generality of its modal claim, given that there is no strong argument for it, and given that it is neither evident in itself nor strongly supported by scientific evidence. I will accept it for the sake of argument. In what follows, let us remember that its epistemic credentials are not very strong.

Kim gives an argument that assumes supervenience and purports to lead to epiphenomenalism. Suppose that an instance of mental property M causes another mental property M^* to be instantiated. Given supervenience, M^* has a physical supervenience base P^*. At this point, Kim attempts to get the reader to share his sense that there is a tension between mental causation of M^* and the relation between the supervenience base P^* and M^*. (Note that this is a different 'tension' from that which Kim believes occurs between mental and physical causes of the same physical event. For it is not assumed that P^* causes M^*. We shall return to the supposed tension between mental and physical causes of the same physical event.) I regard this sense of tension between causation and supervenience as bogus. I would like to scrutinize how Kim explains it.

Kim asks, 'Where does the instance of M^* come from? How does M^* get instantiated on this occasion?' He regards the two answers

(a) because by hypothesis M caused M^* to be instantiated,

and

(b) because, by supervenience, P^*, the physical supervenience base of M^*, is instantiated on this occasion,

as in 'real tension'.

(a) and (b) are answers to different questions. One is a causal answer. The other simply cites M^*'s supervenience base. Although Kim is aware of the difference between causation and supervenient determination, his formulation of the two answers runs together the different notions, misleadingly expressed by 'because' in the remainder of his discussion. I believe that if one keeps the difference steadily in view, the supposed tension itself comes to seem illusory.

Let us look at his attempts to bring out the tension:

> I hope that you are like me in seeing a real tension between these two answers: Under the assumption of mind–body supervenience, M^* occurs because its supervenience base P^* occurs, and as long as P^* occurs, M^* must occur no matter what other events preceded this instance of M^*—in particular, regardless of whether or not an instance of M preceded it. This puts the claim of M to be a cause of M^* in jeopardy: P^* alone seems fully responsible for, and capable of accounting for, the occurrence of M^*. As long as P^*, or another base property of M^*, is present, that absolutely guarantees the presence of M^*, and unless such a base is there on this occasion, M^* can't be there either.[14]

Assuming supervenience, if P^* occurs, M^* must occur, no matter whether the physical cause (P) of P^* occurs or whether the mental cause (M) of M^*

---

[14] Kim, *Mind in a Physical World*, 42.

occurs. Unless the causal relation between an effect and its cause is metaphysically necessary, it is metaphysically possible that the effect, whether mental or physical, of a cause, whether mental or physical, could (metaphysically) have been instantiated, even though the cause were not. Most philosophers who think about these things believe that a given effect metaphysically could in many instances have had another cause. This point hardly puts 'in jeopardy' the claim that the given effect, whether mental or physical, has the cause, or causes, that it has. If the cause of a given effect *is* metaphysically necessary, then the point that the effect occurs regardless of whether the cause occurs is idle.[15]

To put the point another way: Kim writes that P^* alone 'seems fully responsible for, and capable of accounting for, the occurrence of M^*'. To be sure, on assumption of supervenience, and given that P^* occurs, M^* must occur. But P^* is not the cause of M^*.[16] Causes are not in general metaphysically sufficient for their effects. Moreover, unlike the cause of M^*, at least a portion of its supervenience base is simultaneous with M^*. Supervenience is a matter of how things hang together. Causation is a matter of how the things that hang together come about. Since P^* is not causally responsible for M^*, its role as supervenience base could hardly put the claim that M^* has a mental cause in jeopardy.

Kim's formulation may encourage another mistake. Not only does his use of his notion of 'responsibility' encourage the idea that causation and the base–supervenient relation are in some way in competition for 'responsibility' for M^*. His notion of *accounting* encourages conflating these two relations with explanation. P^* surely does not explain M^* causally. Citing a physical supervenience base of M^* hardly gives a satisfying 'account' of its occurrence. It certainly does not obviate the need for a psychological explanatory account of M^*. Kim's initial questions, which elicit answers (a) and (b), are unspecific in just the ways that invite the answers which tend to run together importantly different issues—causation, supervenience, explanation.

In a later book, Kim tries to bolster his claim that there is a 'tension' between base–supervenient determination and mental causation.[17] He counts this claim the 'fundamental idea' of his argument. Kim repeats his earlier point that as long as the supervenient base is in place, the mental occurrence must occur, no matter what happened before that occurrence. I think this point is ineffectual, for the reasons given two and three paragraphs back. Base–supervenient determination is not causation and cannot do its job.

---

[15] Note again that we are not yet discussing a supposed competition between physical and mental *causal* competitors. Here the supposed competition is between a mental cause of M^* and a physical supervenience base of M^*. My point here is that the supervenience base no more puts the mental cause of M^* in jeopardy than it puts its own physical cause, P, or a physical cause of M^*, in jeopardy.

[16] Kim makes this assumption also. Cf. ibid, 44.

[17] Kim, *Physicalism, Or Something Near Enough*, 36–38.

Kim appeals to the theologian Jonathan Edwards as the first philosopher who saw the alleged tension. Kim attributes to Edwards the view that there is a tension between what he calls vertical determination and horizontal causation. He attributes the further view that vertical determination excludes horizontal causation. He calls this pair of views 'Edwards's Dictum'. Kim gives no evidence that Edwards was committed to Edwards's Dictum.

Edwards held that there are no temporally persisting objects (hence, also no horizontal object-to-object causation) because he believed that

God is the sustaining cause of the created world at every instant of time. There are no persisting things because at every moment God creates, or recreates, the entire world *ex nihilo*—that is what it means to say that God is the sustaining cause of the world.[18]

Kim explains that on Edwards's view, God's being a sustaining cause renders causation between temporally successive events nugatory. For Edwards thinks that if God's sustaining causation were withdrawn, the whole world would vanish, regardless of what had happened before. So putative other, preceding causes do not causally influence anything that comes after them.

Kim holds that it is 'simple' to see how Edwards's Dictum, which Kim takes to have been illustrated in the theological doctrine, applies to the mind–body case, 'causing trouble for mental causation':

Mind–body supervenience, or the idea that the mental is physically 'realized'—in fact, any serious doctrine of mind–body dependence will do—plays the role of vertical determination, or dependence, and mental causation, or any 'higher-level' causation is the horizontal causation at issue. The tension between vertical determination and horizontal causation, or the former's threat to preempt and void the latter, has been, at least for me, at the heart of the worries about mental causation.[19]

Let us, for the sake of argument, take Edwards's view to have full intuitive force. The view is that God's causation preempts other putative causation. Edwards argues: if God's sustaining causation were withdrawn, the preceding horizontal events would have occurred and the successive events would not have occurred. This argument tends to support the view that the preceding horizontal events are not really causes. Everything hinges on God's sustaining causation. Nothing hinges on any putative causal power of the preceding horizontal events.

Kim takes two significant missteps in his use of Edwards's views to support his own view that base–supervenience determination is in tension with mental causation (the first half of what he calls, misleadingly I think, 'Edwards's Dictum'.)

One misstep lies in his gloss on Edwards. Kim runs Edwards's divine 'vertical' causation together with 'vertical' supervenience determination. Some of the intuitive force in Edwards's position derives from God's sustaining action's

---

[18] Kim, *Physicalism, Or Something Near Enough*, 37. The words are Kim's.
[19] Ibid. 38.

being *causal*. God's causation can seem to be in competition with ordinary causation. But base–supervenience determination is not causation. As I argued above, it cannot, even prima facie, take the place of causation in accounting for how things occur. In comparing Edwards's view about God's causation with his own view about supervenience determination, Kim has simply mixed apples with oranges—yet again.

Kim's second misstep is a failure to note the main source of Edwards's view that 'horizontal' causation between temporally successive events is illusory. Edwards's argument that God's causation preempts ordinary putative causation is based on a counterfactual claim that Kim nowhere replicates in his own account. If God's causation of the later event had been withdrawn, on Edwards's view, the antecedent event that is putatively the 'horizontal' cause would have existed, but would not have brought about any later event. No later event would have existed.

The supervenience case is disanalogous. Suppose that the physical supervenience base P^* of the mental effect M^* had not occurred. Then either M^* would have occurred with another supervenience base or it would not have occurred. If it did occur, there is no evident reason why M could not been its psychological cause. Suppose M^* did not occur. Then either M (with *its* supervenience base P) did or did not occur. If M did not occur, it cannot be charged with being causally ineffective. If M and P did occur, there is no evident reason why they would not have been causally effective. In any normal counterfactual world, they would remain causally effective. Since they did not cause M^* and P^* respectively, there would be different causal conditions or laws, and they would have had other effects. None of these cases parallels Edwards's.

Edwards's argument depends on assuming that God can sustain the world to any given point and then withdraw support, depriving earlier events of any successors (hence of any effects). These assumptions about God's power have no analogs in ordinary counterfactual reasoning about physical and mental conditions in a supervenience relation. Edwards's view does not parallel Kim's. So Kim's attempt to use Edwards's view to bolster (or even illustrate) his claim that there is a tension between base–supervenient determination and mental causation is ineffective. It rests on compound conflations.

The deeper source of Kim's claiming tension where there is none is his arguing from metaphysical intuitions that abstract from what we know from causal explanation in science and common sense. Here we come again to the main the point of my original article: Our confidence in citing mental causes resides, or should reside, in psychological causal explanations. Nothing that Kim cites in his metaphysical discussion bears on psychological explanation. So nothing that he cites puts the hypothesis that M^* has a mental cause M 'in jeopardy'.

Kim proposes to resolve the tension that he has purportedly identified by appealing to a new principle:

M caused M^* by causing P^*.

Kim thinks that it is justification enough of this claim that it helps resolve the alleged tension. He adds that 'there may be' a plausible principle that justifies this principle by entailing it:

To cause a supervenient property to be instantiated, you must cause its base property (or one of its [possible] base properties) to be instantiated.[20]

I see no reason to believe these principles. Causal explanations in psychology certainly attribute mind–body causation. They do so primarily where mental states or events cause bodily action-movement. We have no independent reason to think that all mental causes of mental effects cause physical effects that are supervenience bases of their mental effects. It is not independently evident—much less scientifically supported—that every mental event or property that causes a mental event, in every inference for example, causes some physical event or condition that is the supervenience base of its mental effect. Although one can construct a metaphysics that entails this claim, the claim is not supported by scientific explanation or intuitive reflection. I see no reason given so far to be any more favorable than agnostic about these principles.

If one reflects on what the supervenience bases of certain particular thoughts would be, supposing (as we are) that they have such bases, the principles seem wildly *implausible*. Take an occurrent thought that mercury occurs in Lake Baakal. Suppose that this thought is caused by prior thoughts and inferential steps. What is the supervenience base of this mental event?

I believe that I have given strong reasons to believe anti-individualism. I think that anti-individualism is in various ways supported or presupposed by relevant science. Some of the arguments for anti-individualism indicate that the supervenience bases of empirical thoughts are not local to the body of the individual. The supervenience base of a thought about mercury and Lake Baakal would involve a complex pattern of individual–environment relations, including causal-perceptual relations to objects in the environment. The supervenience base of such thoughts is a massively complex pattern that includes states in the thinker's body at the time of the thought, but extends over large stretches of space and time. Such a pattern is not local to the individual's body. The supervenience base of any belief or thought that might be a cause of the thought will also be complex, trans-temporal, and spread out in space.[21]

It would be to stretch matters to count such patterns as properties at all. They are surely not instances of any natural kinds. They are trans-temporal physical conditions, radically spread out in space as well as time. It is not plausible to

---

[20] Kim, *Physicalism, Or Something Near Enough*, 42, my insertion of the bracketed word. I do not understand how Kim understands the first principle if it is not already equivalent to the second. The first principle is evidently a generalization, not a claim about any particular mental or physical occurrences. And it is hard to see why Kim would think that it is merely contingent.

[21] Phenomenal properties may supervene on neural states. So this argument applies only to representational psychological states, but these are the states that are most prominent in causal psychological explanations.

think of them as causes of anything. The idea that the physical supervenience base of the thought is caused by the supervenience base of another mental state or event—or that a mental state or event causes such a supervenience base—has no intuitive or scientific plausibility.

I do not claim that it is incoherent to construct a metaphysics according to which there are physical–physical or mental–physical causal relations that take these sorts of supervenience bases as causal 'agents'. But I think that such a metaphysics has no claim on our belief. I see no explanatory potential in such a view. Both commonsense and scientific causal explanations take mental and physical causation to be spatially and temporally more local than any such metaphysics could allow. I believe that we have reason to dismiss such metaphysics. The relevant physical causation is to be understood in terms of causation among neural states. Neural states are not a supervenience base for at least many mental states.

Where does the argument go from this stage? Kim holds that any mental cause M of any mental effect M^* causes M^* by causing the physical supervenience base P^* of M^*. He also holds that P^* will have its own physical cause P. Then it seems that P^* has two causes—M and P. He then holds that we can 'see reasons for taking P as preempting the claim of M as a cause of P^*.'[22]

The reasons that Kim cites in this particular argument are stated rather cursorily. He rejects the idea that the mental and physical causes of a given physical effect are to be taken as jointly 'sufficient' but individually 'insufficient' for their effects. He regards this view as incompatible with our understanding of both mind–body and physical causation. Kim further rejects the idea that the mental cause is sufficient for the physical effect and the physical cause is sufficient for the same physical effect. He rejects this idea by appealing to the physical causal closure principle.[23]

From these rejections he moves quickly to the view that mental causation is epiphenomenal, and the physical cause is doing all the causal 'work'. Since he believes that this is an undesirable conclusion, he does not accept it. His favored solution is to reduce all mental causal factors to physical factors, thereby purportedly restoring causal efficacy to the mental causal factors. I will return to the notion of 'work'.

I believe that the argument that Kim offers has too many difficulties to support his favored solution. I have not rejected supervenience, but I believe that its epistemic credentials are not strong. In what follows, I will ignore the 'broadly physicalist outlook' which drives so much of what is supposed to seem plausible. I will ignore the under-explained but apparently question-begging and overly strong principle of physical causal closure. I will ignore the implausible idea that

---

[22] Ibid. 43.

[23] Ibid. 44–45. There are elements in Kim's argumentation in these pages, in particular his appeal to a closest possible world argument to criticize overdetermination, that I find obscure and unsound. I will not discuss these elements in his argument.

mental causes cause mental effects always (or necessarily) by causing physical supervenience bases of those effects. I will ignore the idea that mental causes always cause physical effects.

I believe that the basic philosophical issues regarding mental causation are independent of assumptions about supervenience. What is at issue is, on the surface, relatively simple.

Psychological causal explanation indicates that mental events and mental properties are causally relevant. Sometimes mental–physical causation occurs. In such causation some mental events or states cause some physical event or state, where the mental aspects of the causes are causally efficacious.[24] Any physical event has a physical cause, with physical properties that are causally efficacious. So any physical effect of a mental cause will have a physical cause. Both mental and physical causes have properties that are causally relevant or efficacious. What is the relationship between the mental and physical causes (and their properties) in such cases?

There is a natural impulse to deal with the question by holding that the causes and properties are 'the same'. This answer sounds good until one gets into the details of 'sameness'. Token-identity claims, type-identity claims, claims that the mental is 'made out of' the physical, claims that mental explanation or properties are reducible to physical explanation or properties, claims that mental properties are second-order functional properties of physical properties—all have specific difficulties. I argued against the first in my paper. I think that the others bear no close relation to what we know from the sciences. Some of them fall into epiphenomenalism.[25]

---

[24] I need not take a position on how often mind–body causation occurs. It is enough that it is adverted to in a good bit of psychological explanation, and that the idea of mental causation being entirely confined to causing mental effects is almost as unacceptable as epiphenomenalism.

[25] I have not discussed Kim's specific solution. This solution appeals to a reduction of psychological properties (at least those with intentionality) to functional properties, and then what he calls a further reduction of the latter properties, through reducing their realizations, to physical properties. I find his *notion* of reduction in this second stage very questionable. I also find the reduction of intentional psychological properties to functional properties a paradigmatically ungrounded philosophical claim. Analytic functionalism purports to give a conceptual analysis of psychological explanation into purely functional (causal role) terms. No plausible, or even specific, presentation of such an analysis has been given in a single case, for a specification of a single mental state-type, much less for all psychological discourse. The causal roles associated with specific psychological states like specific beliefs (beliefs like DNA contains a phosphate group or there is a red object on the distant hill) are too various to seem to admit such an analysis. So a specific account is needed. One cannot simply appeal to the general program. Moreover, the emptiness of specifications of causal roles makes the claim of conceptual equivalence incredible to disinterested reflection. To see this, reflect on even a schematic specification that uses only vocabulary that includes 'causes' and non-representational terms for stimuli and for behavioral response. No disinterested reflection will enable one to take seriously the idea that the specification has the same meaning or conceptual content as a mentalistic specification of a state.

Empirical functionalism takes the functional specification to yield not conceptual equivalence, but an account of the nature or constitution of representational psychological states. Empirical functionalism is, I think, no better off than analytic functionalism. Such a specification is far removed from any explanation that goes on in science. No science employs the functionalist theory envisioned by

I think a more exploratory, less committal metaphysical approach is more rational, and accords better with what we know. I think that our metaphysics is not yet very strong, epistemically, on these matters. What are strong are the claims that mind–body causation occurs, and that there are no gaps in the chains of body–body causation. Metaphysics should be pursued with a strong sense of its poor track record, and without writing as if metaphysical intuitions or principles are in a position to threaten mental causation, or put it in jeopardy.

I continue to advocate giving more attention to one largely unexplored line of inquiry. I doubt that there is any rational ground to think that a belief that a physical effect has both a mental cause and a physical cause forces a choice between maintaining that the causes are 'the same' and maintaining that they are 'in competition' or 'in tension'. I think that the credentials of any claim that such a choice is forced on us should be viewed much more critically. Alternative ways of understanding joint mental and physical causation invite more exploration.

In any case, I have so far found no ground to support the view that there is competition or tension between mental and physical causes. The explanation and motivation of the 'exclusion problem' from supervenience considerations are not persuasive. What other motivation might be marshaled?

Kim claims:

As long as each [the mental cause and the physical cause] claims to be a full cause of the event to be explained, a tension is created and we are entitled to ask, indeed compelled to ask, how the two purported causes are related to each other.[26]

We are certainly entitled to ask how the causes are related to one another. Let us also ask whether there is any antecedent reason to think that there is a tension, exclusion, or competition among physical and mental causes of the same physical event.[27]

---

functionalism, for example, a Ramsified functionalist theory. Any such theory would be devoid of any explanatory power. One cannot remove the theoretical terms (in this case, the mentalistic terms) from a scientific explanation and expect to have a comparable theoretical explanation. One cannot obtain equal, much less superior, power in giving causal psychological explanations by omitting the mentalist terms of the explanation in terms of blank descriptions of causal roles. Accounts of the nature of psychological states should illuminate the explanatory power of psychological explanation. (In fact, analytic functionalism should also illuminate the explanatory power of psychological explanation that it purports to analyze, but it fails to.) Again, not a single specific identification between mental properties and such functionalist properties has ever been carried through. The very idea that all of cognitive psychology can be reduced to some other theory that does not make any use of representational notions has no support in the way the relevant sciences are developing. Empirical functionalism is a tribute to the isolation of philosophy from scientific explanation. Both forms of functionalism seem to me to be waves of hands, without cognitive substance. As I indicated earlier, Kim's eventual position really leaves mental causation without any genuine causal role. For on his view, functional properties *per se* lack any genuine causal power. They free-ride on the underlying first-order physical causal powers. So Kim's eventual position falls into epiphenomenalism. See *Mind in a Physical World*, ch. 4.

[26] Ibid. 66.
[27] In this part of his discussion, Kim again misrepresents my views. In the first place, he argues again as if the issue were whether there is a place for metaphysical inquiry at all. As I have noted,

The quoted passage suggests that mental and physical causes 'claim' to be 'full' causes of the event to be explained. Causes do not make claims. Who makes this claim? Neither psychological nor physical explanation makes any claims about the other. The only sense in which we can reasonably say that the physical cause has a 'claim' to be the full cause is that it is causally sufficient. It is sufficient to make the physical effect occur. Citing it within a physical explanation is also sufficient to explain the physical effect in the terms of the physical explanation. Similarly, for the mental cause and the psychological explanation. The mental cause is causally sufficient to make the physical effect occur. Citing the mental cause within a psychological explanation is sufficient to explain the physical effect in the terms of the psychological explanation.

This situation leaves us with a question about how the causes are related, but it does not leave us with competition or tension. We can assume some sort of coordination or connection between the causes (insofar as they are distinct), since their causing the same effect is certainly not coincidental. There is no abstract compelling reason to think that this coordination or connection is just the causes being 'the same'.

We assume, and the psychology tends to assume, that there is a physical cause of the physical effect. This is to say that the claim of 'fullness' by psychology does not exclude the physical explanation. Similarly, the physical explanation is certainly open to there being a mental cause, as long as it does not interfere with the physical explanation. The only reasonably grounded notions of 'full cause' are compatible with there being, in the relevant cases, coordinated, non-competing sufficient causes, mental and physical.

Kim also claims that the 'exclusion problem' arises 'from the very notion of causal explanation and what strikes me as a perfectly intuitive and ordinary understanding of the causal relation'.[28] As I have just indicated, the different causal *explanations* do *not* seem to be mutually exclusive or in competition. No argument that Kim gives provides any non-question-begging ground to accept his view that there is competition among mental and physical *causes*.

There is, perhaps, an understanding of the causal relation from which intuitions like Kim's about exclusion naturally arise. This is the understanding of

this was never the issue for me. In the second place, he quotes the paragraph in Section 3 of my paper, in which I claimed that it is 'perverse' to think that mentalistic explanation excludes or interferes with non-intentional (non-mentalist) explanation of physical movement. However, he uses ellipses to omit a key sentence in the paragraph. This omission makes it appear that I give a direct argument for my view that it is perverse to believe in exclusion or interference between mental and physical causes. The argument is made to appear to proceed directly from the premise that neither type of explanation (mental or physical) makes essential, specific assumptions about the other. Kim criticizes this argument. I did not give quite this argument. In fact, I use this premise only to support the view that 'the relation between the entities appealed to in the different explanations cannot be read off the causal implications of either or both types of explanation'. This is just to say that sciences do not give us an account of a relation between mental and physical causes—hardly a controversial point. The perversity, in my view, derives from reflecting on the *particular* nature of the 'very different types of inquiry' embodied in psychological and physical explanation.

[28]   Ibid. 66–67.

causation as occurring among physical events. In the physical domain, cases of different causes of the same outcome commonly fall into one of three categories. Either they are unusual cases of coincidental overdetermination. Or they are cases in which one causal factor is constituted of or otherwise 'resolvable' into the other.[29] Or they are cases in which the different causes are partial and in need of each other's physical contributions for their effect. None of these cases seems to fit mental causation.

In later work, Kim distills these claims about the causal relation into what he calls the Principle of Causal Exclusion:

> If an event e has a sufficient cause c at t, no event at t distinct from c can be a cause of e (unless this is a genuine case of causal overdetermination).

Kim understands overdetermination to involve 'two or more separate and independent causal chains intersecting at a common effect'. The separate and independent clause suggests that causal overdetermination is a matter of a certain coincidence or accident. Kim and I would agree that overdetermination in this sense is unusual and that mental and physical causes of a physical effect are not cases of overdetermination in this sense.[30]

Kim takes the Causal Exclusion principle to be 'virtually an analytic truth with not much content'.[31] This strikes me as an amazing claim. It is surely a consequence of intuitions about causation guided by his metaphysical view. I think any notion of causation according to which the Principle of Causal Exclusion is virtually 'analytic' has lost touch with any notion of causation that is used in scientific or commonsense explanation.

Science certainly does not take mental and physical causation of a physical effect to exclude one another. Any such mental causation and physical causation are non-accidentally related. They are not independent. And hence they do not constitute a case of overdetermination, as Kim uses the term. There is certainly either a prima facie assumption that the mental and physical causes are distinct or at least an open question whether they are distinct. Nothing in commonsense or scientific usage supports the 'virtual analyticity' of the Principle of Causal Exclusion.

Kim holds that each science claims its cause to be 'sufficient' and not 'partial'.[32] He takes this claim to be evidence of competition. Our best understanding of sufficiency derives from the sufficiency of causal explanations within each

---

[29] Actually, the relations among different causes postulated in different physical sciences (say biology and physics, or geology and physics) are not understood in real depth. So this talk of constituency and resolvability is a wave of the hand. It is potentially misleading. I believe that the mind–body problem is much more difficult than the macro–micro physical problem. Even so, it would be a mistake to think that handling the latter problem is simple or straightforward.

[30] Kim, *Physicalism, Or Something Near Enough*, The principle is stated on p. 17. The construal of overdetermination is stated on p. 48. I think that the principle has serious difficulties in understanding even relations between instances of causation at different physical levels of explanation. Kim discusses this issue at some length on pp. 52–69. I find various aspects of this discussion unpersuasive, but I will not discuss these aspects here.

[31] Ibid. 51.

[32] Ibid. 53, 37–38.

science's domain. Neither physics nor psychology makes claims about the causes asserted by the other science. Insofar as a physical or mental event causes a physical event, it brings it about. In that sense, each cause is sufficient. I see no ground for either cause to be taken to exclude the other. We need to understand the relation while assuming that each cause has whatever sufficiency its causal power requires.

Kim asks, given that the physical cause is 'sufficient', what 'work' remains for the mental cause. It is not clear to me what makes this question seem forceful to him. I am inclined to think that the question trades on unclarified notions of sufficiency and work. The notion of work has homes both in physics and in talk of physical labor. The notion may elicit thinking of the psychological cause as like a further physical cause, offering an extra infusion of energy that is in fact not needed to supplement an already sufficient physical cause. Here mental causation would be implicitly regarded as a form of physical causation. In such a role it can easily seem to be an intrusive, competing, physical-like cause.

Alternatively, it may be that one can sustain a notion of work that is neutral as between mental and physical work. The idea of physical cause using up all the work so that there is no work left for the mental cause still seems to trade on a kind of hydraulic model. According to this model, so much energy is needed to get the job done. Given that enough energy is expended to get the job done by the physical cause, the mental cause is left without any need to expend its energy. This idea too seems to import a conception of the relation between physical and mental causation that is not sanctioned by ordinary explanations in the physical and human sciences. So it is reasonable to distrust the metaphor underlying the 'work' questions.

I believe that there is no strong, independent source of the idea that causation in psychology is in tension with causation in the natural sciences. The sense of tension is a product of assumptions of ungrounded metaphysics, or of metaphors which when held up against what we know, couched in literal terms, do not carry rational weight. The sense of tension is not an independently supported claim that a metaphysics is needed to explain.

If one asks, more neutrally, how the mental cause's causation is to be understood in relation to the physical cause's causation, we have, I think, a legitimate and unbiased question.

When we know from psychological explanation that mental events cause a physical event, where the mental properties are relevant to the causation, we also know from physiological explanation that there are physical events that cause the same physical event, where their physical properties are relevant to the causation. Each type of causal explanation is 'complete' (sufficient) on its own terms. But how are we to view the matter from a perspective that includes all the causal explanations and all the posited causal relations?

We assume that the mental cause could be effective only if there is a physical cause. Many are inclined to think that the physical cause would be effective regardless of whether there were a mental cause—sufficient to itself. This 'regardless' is problematic. It is true that the physical explanation does not need the psychological explanation to explain the caused physical event. However, the same is true of the psychological explanation. Psychological explanation need not appeal to an underlying physical story (which is largely unknown, in any detail, in actual cases) in order to give its causal explanation. We believe that the psychological causation could not occur without there being physical causation. It is hard to see how the particular physical causation could occur and there be no mental causation. There certainly remains an instinctive sense that the mental depends on the physical in a way that the physical does not depend on the mental. This sense is, I think, poorly understood.

The most common recent way to answer our question, 'How is the mental cause's causation is to be understood in relation to the physical cause's causation?', is to try to spell out in a satisfying way the idea that the causes are 'basically the same'. I think that this strategy has so far not yielded an account of 'basically the same' that provides a satisfying answer to the mind–body problem. And it is striking that among materialists there is no agreed-upon specific account of the 'sameness'. Another way to answer the question is to try to clarify the notion of mental causation in a way that accords with the idea that the mental and physical are not in competition and operate non-coincidentally and in concert. The two types of causation clearly operate together in some systematic way. What that way is remains to be understood. I believe that this second strategy has been under-explored.

The mind–body problem is the problem of understanding the relation between mental events and properties and physical events and properties. I think that there is no future in attempts to argue from an assumption about tension or exclusion to a conclusion about the mind–body relation. Our understanding of mental causation is no better than our understanding of the mind–body relation. The relation between mental and physical causation is not well understood, both because we have not solved the mind–body problem and because we do not have a satisfying understanding of mental causation, or indeed any causation. I include myself in this 'we'.

I think that an open attitude to exploring these matters is a better cognitive position than a metaphysics that assumes a vague generalized physicalism, and leans on visions of mind–body competition that are not grounded in anything that we know.

There is certainly reason to expect illumination from the progress of the sciences. At relatively primitive levels of the psychological, close connections have been established between psychological and neural causation. In understanding low-level vision, for example, the neural pathways and the functions of neural structures in visual processing are better understood than they were two decades ago. This knowledge should give us better tools for understanding mind–body relations. Even in these sorts of cases, a precise and satisfying characterization of the relations seems to me still to lie well ahead of us. Whether systematic, scientifically tractable correlations occur between neural pathways and higher levels of perception and cognition is more doubtful, and certainly an open question.

The mind–body problem is difficult partly because the notion of causation itself is not well understood in philosophy. It is difficult partly because of the variety of ways in which psychological events and properties relate to physical events and properties. The problem is certainly not confined to understanding consciousness. It remains puzzling even for the representational aspects of mind.

17 *Two Kinds of Consciousness*

I want to develop some ideas about consciousness that derive from reflection on a distinction between phenomenal consciousness and access consciousness drawn by Ned Block.[1] I accept a version of such a distinction, and I think that Block's drawing it is a significant contribution. But I believe that Block has not drawn it quite right. I will maintain three primary points. First, access consciousness—indeed, any sort of consciousness—in an individual presupposes the existence of phenomenal consciousness in that individual. Second, the relevant notion of access consciousness is not captured by the idea of a state's being poised for use in rational activity, even if it is assumed that the individual is phenomenally conscious. The relations between access consciousness and phenomenal consciousness need detailed exploration. But access conscious states, and even events, need not themselves be phenomenally conscious. Third, although phenomenal qualities are individuated in terms of what it is like to feel or be conscious of them, one may have phenomenal states or events with phenomenal qualities that one is unconscious of. Thus, phenomenal qualities themselves do not guarantee phenomenal consciousness. To be phenomenally conscious, phenomenal states, or their phenomenal qualities, must be sensed or felt by the individual subject.

Block explicates phenomenally conscious states and properties as experiential states and properties. He says that the totality of experiential properties of a state are 'what it is like' to have it. He notes that we have phenomenally conscious states when we exercise our senses or have pains. More generally, phenomenally conscious properties are said to be the 'experiential' properties of sensations, feelings, perceptions, thoughts, wants, and emotions.[2] I do not believe that 'experiential' coincides with 'phenomenally conscious,' but I will not press the point here. Ordinary pain and other sensations provide paradigms for phenomenally conscious states. And Block's use of the notions of sensed phenomenality or felt quality, and of 'what it is like' to have a state, elicits recognition of a type of consciousness that is broadly familiar.

---

[1] Ned Block, "On a Confusion about a Function of Consciousness," *Behavioral and Brain Sciences*, 18 (1995), 227–247.

[2] Ibid.

I will assume that phenomenal properties are distinct from intentional properties (in roughly Brentano's sense[a]) and from functional properties. Moreover, by virtue of being phenomenal, a property is not necessarily either intentional or functional. I assume that there not only can be but are phenomenal properties that are not intentional. At least they need not indicate anything beyond themselves. These assumptions are not universally accepted. I state them here to clarify my discussion.

Some intentional states and events—some thoughts, for example—seem to have phenomenal states or properties as an essential aspect of their content. Thus, associated with the intentional content of typical perceptual judgments is a phenomenal element that is part of, or at least necessary to, the content—inseparable from the way of thinking, or mode of presentation, of the perceived entities. A normal visual judgment about a visually presented red surface would have a different content—or would be a different visual judgment—if the phenomenal aspect associated with the judgment were relevantly different (though the different visual judgment might still represent a red surface). Since I think that phenomenal consciousness is essential to individuating phenomenal properties, phenomenal consciousness seems to play a role in type-individuating certain intentional contents—hence certain intentional states and events.

It is a multifaceted question whether phenomenal aspects of intentional content could have had, or could have been associated with, different intentional content. In many cases, the answer to this question is affirmative. One can imagine that the causal antecedents and cognitive use of given phenomenal aspects could have been different in such a way as to make for different intentional content. For example, it seems to me that the tactile feeling of cold—an essential element of the content of some tactile judgments about cold surfaces—could, in a different environment (perhaps with different neural wiring associating the sensations with different action, and with different conceptual training), have played a part in representing warmth in surfaces or any of various other physical properties. In such a case the phenomenal aspects of the tactile feeling would be the same, even though it is no longer a feeling of cold. This is one ground for distinguishing between phenomenal and intentional aspects of experience. At least in those perceptual judgments whose content involves phenomenal elements that make reference to entities in the environment of the thinker, there is always the possibility of some degree of referential flexibility for the phenomenal elements. In other cases, such flexibility is absent. Phenomenal elements surely have some sort of primacy in sensorily based thoughts about those very elements. Whether there are restrictions on the degree of representational flexibility in various other cases is an interesting question, which I leave open.

I believe that the notion of phenomenal consciousness is the core notion of consciousness. Any being that is not phenomenally conscious is not conscious

---

[a]   F. Brentano, *Psychology from an Empirical Standpoint* (original in German: Leipzig, 1874).

in any sense. There are no zombies that lack phenomenal consciousness but are conscious in some further way. I will return to this point.

Block distinguishes phenomenal consciousness from access consciousness. He writes that a state is access conscious 'if, in virtue of one's having the state, a representation of its content is ... poised to be used as a premise in reasoning, poised for *rational* control of action and poised for rational control of speech'. He adds that the last condition is not necessary for access consciousness, despite its centrality for practical purposes.

I will use the term 'rational-access consciousness' for the sort of consciousness that I think Block is on to but does not correctly characterize. I will begin with some points of agreement. Rational-access conscious states and events—paradigmatically thoughts—are necessarily intentional. Most such states refer or purport to refer to things beyond themselves. Phenomenally conscious states do not, as such, necessarily or essentially involve purported intentional relations to objects of reference beyond themselves. Rational-access consciousness is a consciousness of things through or by means of 'conscious' thoughts, perceptions, and concepts.

Rational-access consciousness is not the same as phenomenal consciousness. One can have rational-access consciousness with respect to intentional states or events that lack any phenomenological types as essential elements. Conscious mathematical beliefs or thoughts are examples. Rational-access consciousness is not simply phenomenal consciousness within content elements of certain intentional states or events. Further, rational-access consciousness of an intentional event need not have any essentially phenomenal aspects. As will emerge, I think that one can have rational-access consciousness with respect to an event but lack any phenomenal consciousness of that event.

Moreover, I think that one can have phenomenal consciousness of a given state but lack rational-access consciousness of it, as Block emphasizes. If one 'sees stars' in a drunken stupor but cannot reason with or about that state, the images might be phenomenally conscious, but thoughts with or about such a state might be unconscious in the sense that they are not rationally accessible.

I hold with Block that access to central rational powers and rational activity of an individual is a necessary condition for a kind of consciousness having to do with rational access. But I believe, contrary to Block, that poised accessibility to central rational activity is not a sufficient condition for any sort of consciousness. No matter how accessible and no matter how poised for use in reasoning, rational control of action, or rational control of speech a thought may be, it can still fail to be conscious in every way. As noted, I think that a phenomenal zombie, no matter how freely rational, is not conscious in any sense.

A being that lacks phenomenal consciousness altogether could not be conscious in any way. It would not, for example, have imageless conscious thought.

---

[3] Ibid.

Phenomenal consciousness need not be part of a thought or of its articulation in order for the thought to be rational-access conscious. But there must be some phenomenal consciousness—some sensed or imaged what-it-is-like quality—in the individual for a thought to count as conscious in any sense. The individual may close his or her eyes and think imageless thoughts with a surround of subliminal, phenomenally conscious blackness. Or the individual might have some sort of super blindsight but have some other sensations or a capacity to articulate thoughts through phenomenal verbalizations. But lacking some such frame of phenomenal consciousness, one's thinking could not be conscious in any way. A phenomenal zombie has no consciousness—no matter how efficiently rational its behavior, verbalizations, and reasoning. I do not know how to defend this view. I do not know why it is true. But despite a literature replete with assumptions to the contrary, I find it compelling. I think that the view is a reflection of the fact that phenomenal consciousness is the core notion.

Thus, potential use is not the same as consciousness. If there is a distinctive sort of consciousness having to do with rational access, as I think there is, being poised for use in rational activity is not a sufficient condition for it, only a necessary condition. It is an empirical question, not a matter of conceptual analysis, whether intentional states or events that are poised for rational use are always, or in individual cases, conscious in any way.

Perhaps in a phenomenally conscious individual, being poised for use in central rational activity, and being poised for being brought into rational-access occurrently conscious thought, suffice for standing states, such as beliefs, to have, in one sense, rational-access consciousness. They are conscious proleptically, through their accessibility to being made occurrently conscious. But accessibility to use in central rational activity—even in a phenomenally conscious individual—does not suffice for an intentional event to be rational-access conscious.

Some of the nonphenomenal mental events that enter into our highest practical and theoretical reasoning, and that are as poised as possible for free interaction with other rationally controlled mental states and events, are not occurrently conscious in any way. I may be imaging a rainy night in Salisbury while thinking about philosophy. I could bring the philosophical thoughts to consciousness at any moment, and they may be fully available to all other rational activity. But they could be unconscious—with my being unconscious in those moments of all the philosophical points my mind is working on—until I bring them to consciousness.

These are empirical suppositions. What seems clear is a more modest point: the supposition that thoughts might be freely accessible, even in a being that meets the general condition of being phenomenally conscious, but not be in the sort of actual occurrent relation that entails conscious thought is conceptually coherent. Accessibility is one thing; actual occurrent consciousness (of any kind) is another.

Thus, what makes rational-access conscious states and events conscious is not primarily their representational aspects nor their accessibility to rational activity. Similarly, I do not accept the view that rational-access consciousness is a functional notion. I am inclined to believe that no notion of consciousness is a fully functional notion. This is not so much a firmly held theoretical view as a conjectural inference from the intuitive failures of the various functionalist attempts to account for anything I mean by 'consciousness'.

I cannot pretend to have a clear reflective understanding of my notion of rational-access consciousness. But I will hazard some remarks that I hope will prove constructive. I will focus mainly on the rational-access consciousness of intentional events, such as thoughts or judgments. I have already indicated that I accept two necessary conditions. First, to be rational-access conscious, a state or event must be poised for use in the central rational operations of an individual (animal or person). Second, rational-access consciousness must maintain at least a general connection to phenomenal consciousness in the individual. I do not, however, believe that to be rational-access conscious, a state or event must be phenomenally conscious. The connection between the two kinds of consciousness is loose, though phenomenal consciousness often seems to be a factor in the consciousness of rational-access conscious events.

Because it seems to me that we phenomenally conscious beings might have unconscious thought that is fully rationally accessible (cf. the Salisbury example), I do not think that the two necessary conditions I have articulated are sufficient for rational-access consciousness. I do not have a full account. Instead of trying for one, I will canvass some examples of conscious thoughts. (I do not claim that any of these cases represents necessary conditions, though I assume they meet sufficient conditions, given that the two necessary conditions are satisfied.)

Thoughts type-individuated partly in terms of phenomenal elements, at least when these elements are phenomenally conscious, form one subclass of rational-access conscious thoughts. When such thoughts meet the condition of being accessible to the central rational activity of an individual, they are rational-access conscious. A visual judgment, or occurrent visual belief, that involves a sensation of a red surface will be rational-access conscious, assuming that the sensation is phenomenally conscious and that the rational-accessibility condition is met.

Verbally articulated thoughts also normally count as rational-access conscious, again assuming the necessary access condition is met. The relevant notion of articulation will often involve phenomenal consciousness again. Certainly when the symbols are verbalized through visual, auditory, or tactile symbol images that are phenomenally conscious, the thought expressed by the symbols is conscious. There are, of course, different theories about the relations between the symbols and the thought contents. On my view, the symbols are not usually identifiable with the content, nor are they normally essential elements of the content. They merely express something that is more abstract. In my view, in such cases, no essential element of the thoughts or thought contents need be phenomenally conscious for the thoughts to be rational-access conscious. Yet the fact that the symbols that express the content are tokened by phenomenally conscious states seems sufficient to make the thoughts expressed by the symbols conscious (assuming as always that the general rational-accessibility condition is met).

Sometimes we seem to use shorthand in silent thought, with some phenomenal representation of a symbol standing for a whole thought (where we could articulate the thought immediately if called upon). Such thoughts seem to be typically rational-access conscious.

To be rational-access conscious through verbalization, a thought need not be phenomenally articulated or abbreviated. Often we verbalize our thoughts unreflectively and immediately in a public manner, without any prior phenomenally conscious inner articulation. Lacking special obstructions, articulated thoughts of this sort seem, given rational accessibility, to count as rational-access conscious, even if they briefly precede the articulation in time.

I think there are rational-access conscious thoughts that are neither symbolically articulated nor involve phenomenally conscious states as content-essential elements. These may be what used to be called 'imageless thoughts.' They bear perhaps the loosest relation to phenomenal consciousness. As I have indicated, some of our imageless unarticulated thoughts seem rationally accessible but not conscious in any sense (cf. the Salisbury example). What would make such thoughts rational-access conscious?

When one is aware of the occurrence of thoughts as they occur, and the thoughts have immediate accessibility to rational operations, then imageless unarticulated thoughts seem to count as rational-access conscious. (One may lack a conscious thought of their content.) The notion of awareness of the occurrence of thoughts obviously calls for further comment. It is not merely the occurrence of a higher-order thought; such higher-order thoughts might still be unconscious. But the relevant awareness of the occurrence of one's thoughts seems not always to involve phenomenal consciousness. I think that there are nonphenomenal sorts of conscious awareness of one's mental activity. For example, when one gets a solution to a problem, one may be consciously aware of the event of one's getting it, yet lack any phenomenal marker for the thought or (so far) any articulation of the solution. One 'just knows' one has a conclusion.

I do not think that one must be aware of the occurrence of a thought in order for it to be rational-access conscious. One might be phenomenally conscious of some marker of the subject matter and then go on thinking, in an appropriately controlled, guiding way, without making further use of such individual elements of consciousness or event awareness. Or the nonphenomenal awareness may attach to the general process of thinking, involving some general guiding by the individual of the stages of the process, without awareness of particular occurrences within the process. I do not know how to provide a satisfying generalization. Clearly these matters are in need of further exploration and articulation.

Whether there are further major types of rational-access consciousness, whether I have correctly characterized conscious imageless thought (as far as that characterization goes), and what further necessary conditions apply to rational-access consciousness seem thoroughly open questions. What is clear is that rational-access consciousness cannot count as a type of consciousness unless there is more to it than being poised for rational operations, even if these occur within a frame of phenomenal consciousness. Often this 'something more' derives from some specific connection between the thought and some element of phenomenal consciousness. I have suggested that this is not always so.

Some of the interest of the notion of rational-access consciousness is that it is connected to the notions of rationality and agency. Availability to the central executive powers of a higher animal or person is surely connected to what it is to be an individual agent—and, with the right associated abilities, to what it is to be a person. It seems correct and insightful of Block to have separated this type of consciousness, associated with access to higher-order cognitive abilities, from the ontogenetically more basic type of consciousness associated with phenomenal field and feel.

Let me return now to phenomenal consciousness. Phenomenal consciousness seems to play a role in typing some kinds of mental states and events, whereas rational-access consciousness does not. A given belief, and perhaps a given token thought event, could go into and out of rational-access consciousness and remain the same state or event. Further, whether an intentional state or event bears an access relation to central rational powers does not seem essential to being what it is, at least in most cases. But phenomenal consciousness is fundamental to typing phenomenal properties, and phenomenal properties are fundamental to typing phenomenal mental states and events. The way a pain feels is essential or basic to what pain, and what a pain, is. The same is true with other sensations and feelings. I think nothing could be a pain, a token event of pain, and lack the what-it-is-likeness or characteristic feel or phenomenal properties that individuate pain. As I have noted, phenomenal properties also seem to be part of the type-individuation of certain thoughts, for example, certain perceptual judgments, whose content seems necessarily associated with phenomenal states.

It would be easy to infer from this point that phenomenal states and events must be phenomenally conscious at every moment of their existence, but I do not think that this is so. It seems to me that phenomenal states can be phenomenally unconscious. Pains that are not felt at all because of some distraction or other obstruction are sometimes examples. They may remain pains even though they are not felt, not conscious for the individual, at some times.

What it is like to feel pain, pain's phenomenal quality, is essential to the type and token individuation of pains. A pain essentially has phenomenal qualities at every moment. But pains and other sensations can be phenomenally unconscious—not actually felt by their possessor—at a given time. I distinguish what-it-is-likeness (phenomenality) from what it is occurrently like for the individual (phenomenal consciousness). Phenomenality is individuated, necessarily, in terms of how such a state actually feels to individuals. But states with phenomenal qualities need not be felt at all times by an individual who has them.

Of course, one must distinguish subliminal unattended-to conscious feeling from lack of all feeling, or unconsciousness. If a pain is not felt at all at some time by the individual who has it, it is not conscious for the individual at that time. And the idea of a pain that is conscious but not conscious for any individual seems incoherent. Some individual subject (however rudimentary the individual's cognitive or sensory capacities) must be associated with a conscious state.[4]

It would be a mistake to respond to these points by claiming that putative cases of unconscious phenomenal states are always cases of phenomenally conscious events that are rational-access unconscious. An unfelt pain is not the same as a felt pain that is not accessible to rational operations. I have endorsed the idea that a subject might sense sensations but be unable to access them for rational operations. These would be cases of phenomenal consciousness without rational-access consciousness. But it also seems possible that there are sensations that are temporarily not felt or sensed by the individual—sensations that have no phenomenal consciousness for the individual. This is not a lack of rational access, and it is not a lack of higher-order thought or belief. It is a lack of sensing or feeling or imaging by the individual. Such sensations might or might not be accessible (by means other than being phenomenally conscious with respect to them) to central rational operations. There seems no conceptual reason that a phenomenal event could not be unfelt (hence phenomenally unconscious), even while it remained fully accessible to rational operations, by some other means.

Unfelt sensations remain sensations (phenomenal states) because there is a way that it is like to feel them, and they are individuated in terms of their qualitative features; and because they meet empirical criteria of sensibility and sensation continuity. In most cases, the onset of a pain feels different from the bringing to consciousness of a pain that has been unconscious. And there are rough criteria for when a pain remains the same even when it comes into or goes out of consciousness. Some of these criteria are commonsensical; some may result from further empirical discovery.

For those who do not believe that phenomenal states necessarily have representational properties, there is a further reason for not assimilating unconscious phenomenal states to conscious phenomenal states that are rational-access unconscious. Sensations that are not representational are trivially noncandidates for

---

[4] I am tempted by the idea that phenomenal consciousness is at bottom a transitive relation between a subject and a state or event. Although the phenomenal quality of phenomenally conscious states does not as such represent anything, there may be some relation of sensing or feeling (not of higher-order thought or belief) between the individual and the phenomenal state or event that is intrinsic to phenomenal consciousness. Similarly, phenomenal states, when conscious, may in some sense indicate themselves reflexively. They are sensed by way of themselves. I am aware that this 'act-object picture' is objectionable to some philosophers. I am not committed to it except as a prima facie feature of surface grammar. But I think that surface grammar is often hard to rearrange convincingly for metaphysical purposes. As far as epistemology is concerned, I certainly do not maintain that sensations are the fundamental objects of perception, when, for example, we are perceiving physical objects by way of sensations.

being rational-access conscious. I think that those sensations too could be either (phenomenally) conscious or unconscious for certain periods of time. In those cases one cannot match the difference with a difference between the sensations' being phenomenally conscious and rational-access unconscious. Nor does it seem that putative cases of unconscious phenomenal states are always cases of unattended-to phenomenally conscious states. One could attend to phenomenally unconscious states (by other means than feeling them) and fail to attend to states that are still phenomenally though subliminally conscious.

Phenomenal states, with phenomenal qualities, may be unconscious through more than mere lack of attention (though distraction can be one source of their lack of consciousness). It seems to me empirically possible and certainly conceptually possible that the cases involving hypnosis for suppressing pain and those involving epileptics who have 'blanked out' but succeed in driving a car may turn out to be cases in which limited use is made of information that is phenomenally registered but unavailable to both phenomenal and rational-access consciousness. It may be that there is no feeling of a pain (a pain that is nevertheless present) for the hypnotic. There may be no way that it is actually and occurrently like for the epileptic to drive the car. Perhaps what enables the epileptic to operate is the phenomenally registered information (which has phenomenal what-it-is-like qualities that are simply not actually felt by the individual), operating through limited unconscious mental and sensory-motor procedures. But the phenomenal states and the information might be in no sense conscious. In these cases, it would not be mere distraction of attention, or lack of rational access, that accounts for the individual's failure to feel or be conscious with respect to the phenomenal states. Again, what is important for my purposes is not whether these empirical conjectures are correct but that the distinctions mark conceptual possibilities.

Unfelt pains or other sensations must be susceptible to phenomenal consciousness, if attentional or other obstructions to consciousness were removed. And what it is like for one to feel them, to be conscious with respect to them, is part of what individuates them as pains or other sensations. But to be a sensation or other state with phenomenal qualities does not entail that it is phenomenally conscious at every moment.

The mere fact that a token of a kind of state or event can go unconscious and remain the same token does not show that consciousness does not help to type-individuate that kind of thing. It is an interesting and difficult question to explain these issues of individuation in more depth and detail.

Distinguishing phenomenal consciousness and rational-access consciousness is important to understanding how different types or aspects of consciousness feature in the fundamental notions of mentality, agency, and personhood. Such understanding will be deepened when it is liberated from ideological and programmatic preoccupations with materialism and functionalism that have dominated the revival of philosophical interest in consciousness.

18 *Reflections on Two Kinds of Consciousness*

In recent years, something like Ned Block's distinction between phenomenal consciousness and access consciousness has continued to show itself to be valuable and durable. Phenomenal consciousness is the sort of consciousness that consists in there being some way that it is like for an individual to be in a mental state. Access consciousness is the sort of consciousness that consists in a mental state's being accessible to—indeed, I think accessed by—an individual through his or her rational, cognitive powers. There appears to be mounting evidence that a person can have phenomenal consciousness even though the person has no rational, cognitive access to it. That is, a person can have a rich phenomenal consciousness—for example, a full, consciously apprehended visual field with all its subject matter—yet at the same time the person cannot form a belief that makes use of the consciousness, much less represent the phenomenal aspects of the consciousness as such; and the person cannot form a propositional memory from it or of it.[1]

This result is in one way unsurprising. Phenomenal consciousness is a matter of phenomenal feeling or sensing. Access consciousness involves the occurrence of rational, cognitive attitudes–belief, propositional memory, reasoning. Feeling and sensing, on one hand, and rational cognition, on the other, are distinct psychological capacities. There are almost certainly animals that are phenomenally conscious but lack any rational, cognitive powers—propositional attitudes. Where there are distinct capacities that are phylogenetically separable, there is very likely the possibility of dissociation within an individual that has both. Block not only outlined such a distinction. He marshaled evidence that dissociation occurs. He has thereby enriched our sense of the borders between sensibility and rational cognition.

I have benefited from several conversations with Ned Block.

[1] Block first draws the distinction in 'On a Confusion about a Function of Consciousness', *The Behavioral and Brain Sciences*, 18 (1995), 227–247. The 'what it is like' formulation derives, of course, from Thomas Nagel, 'What is it Like to Be a Bat?', *The Philosophical Review*, 83 (1974), 435–450. For a more recent discussion of empirical evidence for the two types of consciousness, see Ned Block, 'Two Neural Correlates of Consciousness', *Trends in Cognitive Sciences*, 9 (2005), 46–52. Block discusses further evidence in 'The Methodological Puzzle of the Neural Basis of Phenomenal Consciousness' (forthcoming). The present paper develops some reflections in my 'Two Kinds of Consciousness', in *The Nature of Consciousness*, N. Block, O. Flanagan, and G. Güzeldere (eds.) (Cambridge, Mass.: MIT Press, 1997) (Ch. 17 above).

While this separation of types of consciousness seems to me to be of great importance, there remain questions about how to characterize both types of consciousness. I stand by the view that phenomenal consciousness is the basic sort, and that one cannot have any other sort without having that one. A zombie that lacks phenomenal consciousness lacks consciousness in any sense. The exact nature of the dependence between access consciousness and phenomenal consciousness remains, I think, elusive and puzzling.

I

I raised a problem for understanding the notion of access consciousness in 'Two Kinds of Consciousness'(Ch. 17 above). The problem is that access consciousness, or what I called 'rational-access consciousness', like any sort of consciousness, is an occurrent condition. Block's original characterization of access consciousness was dispositional. A state was supposed to be access conscious if it is 'poised' for use in rational activity. But no matter how poised for use, realization, or occurrence a state may be, it can still be unconscious in a natural and straightforward sense. What turns disposition into occurrence?

There are, of course, beliefs that are not occurrently activated but that are easily accessible to consciousness. We may count such beliefs 'conscious beliefs' proleptically. There is definitely a sense in which they are not conscious, and perhaps a derivative sense in which they are conscious. They are accessible to consciousness, but they are not part of consciousness. Since the consciousness attributed to such beliefs is understood in terms of accessibility to occurrent consciousness, we need to understand what this occurrent rational or cognitive consciousness is. We have an intuitive understanding. I would like a better reflective understanding.

For Block's immediate purposes of showing that phenomenal consciousness can occur without access consciousness, intuitive understanding is enough. We have sufficient intuitive grip on a notion of conscious belief to enable us to judge most cases of absence and presence. Beliefs lodged in the Freudian unconscious, no matter how occurrently active, are not access conscious. Beliefs that are intentionally asserted by a wide-awake person are. Block wants to show that phenomenal consciousness—a robust sensory array with qualitative, phenomenal, 'what it is like' character—can occur without conscious belief, or even any accessibility to conscious belief. This point can be made without providing a general characterization of rational access consciousness.

In 'Two Kinds of Consciousness' I tried to better understand rational-access consciousness by considering cases in which this sort of consciousness bears various relations to phenomenal consciousness. For example, a thought that uses phenomenally conscious imagery in its representational content is a rational-access conscious thought. The thought is accessed by the individual through the phenomenal elements in it. The phenomenally conscious imagery itself is rational-access conscious as well. It is occurrently phenomenally conscious and occurrently accessed by the individual's rational capacity.

Such a case provides a rather direct relation between rational-access consciousness and phenomenal consciousness. Among other sorts of relations that I cited, I would like to concentrate on one, as a second example. An individual who is phenomenally conscious and who thinks an imageless thought that is under direct rational control is thinking consciously. The individual is phenomenally conscious, but no particular elements in the phenomenal consciousness are made use of in the thought. Yet the individual initiates, guides, directs, directly controls the thought. Such thinking is a type of rational-access consciousness.

The relation between the rational, propositional aspect and the conscious access aspect of the thought is very different in the two cases. In the former case the conscious access aspect is provided by the phenomenal consciousness in, or used by, the thought itself. In the latter case, the thought content does not contain or make use of any particular phenomenally conscious element. How does its being in the same mind with phenomenal consciousness and being directed under the individual's direct control make it conscious?

What is the relation between occurrent, directed, direct control and rational-access consciousness? One can control some of one's states without their being conscious. One can learn actively to control goose bumps on one's skin, or one's heart rate, or perhaps one's unconscious anger or unconscious thoughts. In such cases, the control seems indirect. Occurrently exercised, direct control of thoughts, at least by an individual who is phenomenally conscious while doing so, seems to imply that the thoughts are conscious (though I think not necessarily that the individual is conscious of the control of them). I would like better reflective understanding of what the connection is here.

Occurrently exercised, direct control is certainly not a necessary condition on rational-access consciousness. Some rational-access conscious thoughts simply come upon one. These seem to be thoughts more closely connected to some sort of phenomenal consciousness. They operate on or make use of particular, qualitative, conscious elements. They make use of conscious perception, imagery, verbalization, or the like.

In some cases, however, occurrently exercised direct control seems sufficient for rational-access consciousness, given that the individual is phenomenally conscious. The thought itself can be rational-access conscious even though it does not operate on or make use of particular phenomenally conscious elements, *if* it is under the direct control of the individual. This is the example of the attentively guided imageless thinking, or only intermittently imaged or verbalized thinking, that is under direct control. I want to connect this point with some issues about what it is to be a conscious individual, and about psychological agency.

Both phenomenal consciousness and rational-access consciousness are necessarily occurrent states of the *whole individual*. In fact, both phenomenal consciousness and rational-access consciousness seem to be closely associated with conceptions of what is the individual's *own* in a proprietary sense of 'own'.

Modular mental processes and other unconscious mental processes are, in different senses, sub-individual. They occur within the individual's psychology, but they are primarily attributable to psychological subsystems. They are attributable to the individual psychological subject only derivatively. For an individual with rational powers, both phenomenal consciousness and rational-access consciousness seem in some way to be the constitutive core or base of the individual's psychology or mind. They are fundamental to what counts as non-derivatively the individual's own. They play a constitutive role in determining what it is to be an individual subject, even though the vast bulk of psychological processing in an individual mind is unconscious in both ways.

I call conscious individuals *individual subjects*. Being an individual subject requires phenomenal consciousness. Phenomenal consciousness is the base of conscious mental life. Being an individual subject that exercises autonomous rational cognitive powers requires rational-access consciousness as well. That part of such an individual's rational, cognitive psychology that is occurrently rational-access conscious or that can be brought to occurrent rational-access consciousness is attributable to the *individual* as distinguished from just the individual's subsystems. Both types of consciousness are constitutive of what is an individual's own.

The idea that those mental states or events that are occurrently conscious, or can be brought to occurrent consciousness, are the individual's *own* goes back at least to Kant.[2] The dispositional power to bring a state to occurrent consciousness is obviously constitutively explained in terms of occurrent consciousness itself.[3] Kant was interested in the proprietary ownership that resides in a capacity for rational *self-consciousness*—the capacity to attach I think to one's representations. I think that Kant's higher-level notion of being a *self-conscious* psychological subject with powers of thought and intentional action is constitutively posterior to a more primitive notion. The more primitive notion centers on individuals that are capable of propositional attitudes—thought and intentional action—but are not necessarily capable of self-consciousness. I think that rational agency—occurrently exercised direct control of thought and action—is developmentally and phylogenetically, as well as conceptually, prior to self-conscious rational agency. In both cases, what it is to be an individual rational subject is constitutively determined by capacities constitutively explained in terms of rational-access consciousness.[4]

---

[2] Immanuel Kant, *Critique of Pure Reason*, trans. P. Guyer and A. W. Wood (Cambridge: Cambridge University Press, 1998), B131–135.

[3] Constitutive explanation is not always one-way. Here I think, as Kant also thought, that the dispositional power to bring a state to consciousness is part of the explanation of what it is to be a self; but a self is constitutively involved in what it is to be such a dispositional power (it is constitutively a power of a self). As I shall indicate, a similar reciprocity connects the notion of self with the notion of rational access consciousness.

[4] There may be a yet more primitive notion of ownership along this general line. Phenomenally conscious sensory states are certainly an animal's *own*, phylogenetically prior to propositional attitudes. Perhaps the relevant animals are able to bring to phenomenal consciousness states of sensory

Four paragraphs back, I conjectured that occurrently exercised direct control of occurrent rational processes plays some constitutive role in rational-access consciousness. What is the connection between individual subjecthood and ownership, just discussed, and occurrently exercised direct control?

Rational agency—occurrently exercised direct control of rational processes—is necessarily a power of the whole individual. With respect to active aspects of rational, propositional occurrences, I think that the notion of occurrently exercised *direct* control by the *individual* entails occurrent conscious access to what is under direct control. When propositional representational contents are directly *used* by the individual (not just useable or passively received), they are conscious. *Being used, or being under occurrently exercised direct control, by the individual* entails being rational-access conscious.[5] I think that this point may illumine individual mental agency and rational-access consciousness, as well as what it is to be a rational individual subject.

I conjecture that where rational-access conscious thoughts *are not* under exercised direct control, they are fully the individual's *only* inasmuch as they operate on or make use of particular elements of phenomenal consciousness. They count as rational-access conscious only insofar as these rational cognitive powers operate on or make use of the passive, sensory aspects of the individual's proprietary psychological core—phenomenal consciousness.

In such cases, I think that the thoughts are both phenomenally conscious and rational-access conscious. They are phenomenally conscious because they operate on or make use of qualitative elements that are phenomenally conscious. They are rational-access conscious because the phenomenally conscious elements that they make use of yield access to the thoughts that use them. Explicit verbalizations of thoughts or incorporations of phenomenal elements into the representational contents of thoughts make the thoughts accessible by clothing them in sensory garb. The access is occurrent proprietary ownership of the propositional thought through the thought's being informed by elements from the individual's sensory core. So the thought and the phenomenal sensory elements are both rational-access conscious.

Where thoughts *are* under exercised direct control, they are rational-access conscious by virtue of being the individual's rational acts. The access is occurrent proprietary ownership of the thought through its being the direct expression of the individual's core rational agency. Access can be overdetermined. If the thought is under the exercised direct control of the individual and makes use of phenomenal elements, it is accessible in both ways. It is also both rational-access conscious and phenomenally conscious. If the thought is imageless, is not

---

memory or sensory imagination. Any non-occurrent states over which an animal had such power would also count as the animal's own. On the other hand, if the relevant animals lack such power, then ownership would be restricted to occurrent phenomenally conscious states.

[5] I am always assuming a background of phenomenal consciousness, although the thought need not make use of particular aspects of the phenomenal consciousness.

spelled out through some sort of verbalization, and is not associated with any other phenomenal element particular to the thought, then it is not phenomenally conscious. But it can remain rational-access conscious if it is a direct exercise of the individual's agency.

It was part of Block's original characterization of access consciousness that it be 'poised for direct control of thought and action'. I criticized this view for treating consciousness as dispositional ('poised'), whereas consciousness is occurrent. I think that what it is for a propositional attitude to be the individual's own *is* a partly dispositional notion. Psychological ownership of propositional attitudes is to be explicated in terms of occurrent consciousness or a capacity to bring such attitudes to consciousness. Reciprocally, this dispositional power is explicated in terms of rational-access consciousness. And rational-access consciousness is constitutively intertwined with occurrently exercised direct control.

Intertwined with, not reducible to. As I noted, some occurrent thoughts that are rational-access conscious are not the products of occurrently exercised direct control. They simply occur to one. These thoughts are rational-access conscious, I have conjectured, because elements in them make use of particular elements of phenomenal consciousness. Even these thoughts tend to come under control, once they occur. They can be used in further thought and action that is directly controlled. That is, they can be co-opted for direct control, at least in normal non-pathological circumstances. One can begin to reason in an active way from a daydream. Of course, control of propositional attitudes should not be understood in terms of some meta-monitoring process operating upon them. The idea is simply that the attitudes are directly attributable to the individual as exercises of psychological agency.

The circle of constitutive dependence here is narrow. Rational-access consciousness and individual, occurrently exercised, direct control of propositional thoughts are different notions. There are mutual entailment relations between them, however. Direct control of propositional attitudes by the individual entails that the attitudes (and any phenomenal states that they operate on or make use of) are rational-access conscious for the individual. Being a rational-access conscious thought entails either being directly and occurrently controlled or being associated with making use of particular phenomenally conscious elements. In both cases, the rational-access conscious state is *accessed* by the individual through engagement of his or her rational powers. And of course, phenomenally conscious sensory states that are made use of by thoughts are also rational-access conscious.

The primitive core of being an individual subject is having a base of phenomenal consciousness. Where the individual subject has powers for thought and intentional action, the individual subject has rational-access consciousness as well. Much thought and action is generated by psychological processes that are unconscious. Our basic notion of an individual subject with powers for thought and action, however, takes these unconscious processes as functioning to serve the whole individual. In all individual subjects, whether capable of thought and intentional action or not, the basic kind of consciousness, phenomenal consciousness, plays some constitutive role in an individual's having a mind or a psychology. For individual subjects with powers of thought and intentional action, occurrent access to the individual of propositional events (and phenomenally conscious states that the propositional events make use of) is constitutive of being a *rational* individual subject. Being such a subject entails complex but constitutive relations not only to consciousness but also to rational agency.[6]

II

I turn now from rational-access consciousness to the basic sort of consciousness—phenomenal consciousness. Examples of phenomenally conscious states are felt pains, felt tickles, felt hunger pangs; qualitative elements in conscious vision, hearing, smell, or taste; feelings of tiredness or strain from effort; the feels associated with touch; phenomenal blur, phenomenal static; and so on. Most of these examples derive from aspects of sensory capacities. Some might be parts of feedback loops in primitive action systems.

Understanding phenomenal consciousness depends on distinguishing it from other things. One is better placed to understand what it is if one is clear about what it is not.

---

[6] Thus, for example, having propositional attitudes requires being able to use their propositional structure in inference, which is a psychological act. So, even though not all rational-access thoughts are active, some must be. I think that there can be active elements in elementary phenomenal consciousness as well. A frog probably lacks propositional attitudes, but it may be phenomenally conscious. I suppose that it may be capable of feeling pain. Perhaps it has a rudimentary phenomenally conscious visual field. There is empirical reason to think that selective attention, or orientation to certain primed areas, occurs with respect to one or another aspect of a sensory array even in frogs. Cf. D. J. Ingle, 'Selective Visual Attention in Frogs', *Science*, 188 (1975), 1033–1035. Thus selective attention is not necessarily associated with systems of propositional attitudes. As the notion of attention is here employed in psychology, attention is not necessarily associated with any kind of consciousness either. There is some evidence that sub-propositional, selective orientation within a stimulus array occurs with human blind-sight patients. Cf. A. David Milner and Melvyn A. Goodale, *The Visual Brain in Action* (Oxford: Oxford University Press, 1995), 180–183. I conjecture that where selective attention, or selective orientation, occurs in sub-propositional, non-rational aspects of a psychology, it is a psychological *act* by an individual only if it operates within phenomenal consciousness.

The examples from frogs and blindsight concern consciousness and agency in sub-propositional perceptual systems. But conscious agency may be even more primitive. Some animals that lack sense-perceptual systems, let alone propositional attitudes, might well be phenomenally conscious. A mark of a sense-perceptual system is a capacity for representational objectification and perceptual constancies. Aspects of our own sensory capacities, which can be phenomenally conscious, are not sense-perceptual. Cf. my 'Perception', *International Journal of Psychoanalysis*, 84 (2003), 157–167; 'Perceptual Entitlement', *Philosophy and Phenomenological Research*, 67 (2003), 503–548. Such pre-perceptual animals would be capable of feeling pain, simple tingles, and so on. Whether they might also be capable of directing attention to one or another aspect of phenomenal consciousness is, as far as I know, an open question. Answering such questions lies at the heart of understanding the most primitive cases of psychological agency.

Phenomenal consciousness is not attention. The states that I have listed can be phenomenally conscious whether or not they are attended to, and whether or not things sensed through them are attended to. When they are not the objects of attention, and when attention does not operate through them, however, the consciousness is commonly less intense or robust.

Phenomenal consciousness is not thought or conception.[7] Phenomenally conscious qualities are aspects of our sensory systems, or other relatively primitive systems, which are distinct from systems of propositional attitudes. Certain animals—perhaps lower mammals, almost surely many birds and many fish—cannot think, but are phenomenally conscious. (Cf. note 27.) There are also the experiments cited by Block (note 1) that indicate that in humans phenomenally conscious states can be inaccessible to capacities for thought. The idea that consciousness is thought, whether first-order or second-order, is in my view empirically unacceptable. When thought is phenomenally conscious, its being phenomenally conscious derives from its making use of phenomenal qualities that derive from more primitive psychological systems.

Phenomenal consciousness is not perception or perceptual representation. Perception, as I understand it, is a sensory capacity for objectification. It is commonly marked by perceptual constancies—capacities that enable an individual to treat objective, environmental properties systematically as the same under a wide variety of proximal stimulations and perspectives.

Underlying the perceptual constancies are sensory subsystems that systematically filter proximal stimulation that is not relevant to distal stimulation. Phenomenal or qualitative aspects of perceptual systems are used as vehicles of perceptual representation. Many perceptions are thereby phenomenally conscious. But the qualitative aspects of sensation are not correctly explained in terms of any such notion of objectification.[8]

Is phenomenal consciousness representation? The term 'representation' is troublesome in discussions of consciousness. Many standard issues in the area turn on what is meant by the term. Most discussions, even many that claim that consciousness is to be understood in terms of representation, never bother to explicate the term. The term has many uses in philosophy. I will not be able to provide an extensive explication or defense of my use, but I will say a few things.

Some authors take a type of state or condition *A* to 'represent' a state or condition *B* if the former is a regular or nomological or causal consequence of

---

[7] I take thought to be propositional. I take concepts to be certain components in propositional, representational thought contents. Concepts mark aspects of propositional abilities.

[8] Since phenomenal aspects of perceptual systems are used as vehicles in many perceptual systems, they become part of perceptual modes of presentation, part of perceptual representational content. I think that these representational roles are never reductively constitutive. Most philosophical views that try to reduce phenomenality to representation help themselves to very broad—I would say debased—notions of representation, or representational content, that have no independent explanatory value. For reasons given below, I think that even debased notions of representation fail to capture some types of phenomenal consciousness.

the latter. On this type of view, smoke could be taken to represent fire. I do not use the term that way. Some philosophers add to the preceding type of condition a further one: that the regular or nomological or causal relation has a biological function for an organism. On this type of view a plant's growing in a certain direction or an amoeba's state of being caused to move in a certain direction could represent light or some chemical compound. I do not use the term 'representation' in this way either. I call this latter sort of usage 'information registration'.[9] I distinguish between representation and information registration.

One reason why I draw this distinction is that information registration can easily be dispensed with in favor of causal (or correlational, or nomological) notions and notions of biological function. I take 'representation' to be a term with some prima facie independent explanatory bite. Genuine *perceptual* representation cannot be dispensed with in some psychological explanation. At least, no one knows how to dispense with it. We do not need a further notion, beyond causal (correlational, nomological) and functional notions, to explain a plant's or an amoeba's sensitivities. I reserve 'perception' and 'representation' for cases where psychological explanation needs them.

Since 'representation' is, prima facie, a primitive theoretical term, I do not have a definition for it. One sign of the presence of genuine representation, however, is an explanatory paradigm in psychology in which the explanation is geared to explaining individuals' going into veridical or non-veridical states—getting things right or wrong. Such explanation is not a rewarding enterprise in the case of plants and amoebae. It is not a rewarding enterprise even in scientific work on many sensory systems in many more complex animal organisms. Insofar as one can count these various organisms as getting something right or wrong, the explanation reduces to the organism's being in a sensory state that serves, or fails to serve, its survival or reproduction. These explanations do not need to appeal to conditions of veridicality. Nor is it particularly intuitive to do so. In the case of visual perception, by contrast, a complex, challenging type of explanation has centered on this very problem.[10] Representational states are fundamentally states of the sort that can be veridical or non-veridical. A genuinely distinctive notion of representation can, I think, be developed by taking such explanations as cue. The most primitive type of representation in this sense is, I conjecture, perceptual representation, in the sense of 'perception' explained earlier. Further types of representation include belief, thought, intention, assertion, certain types of memory, and so on. The theoretical term 'representation' must find its place through use, combining example and theory.

---

[9] There is, of course, a thinner, purely statistical notion of information carrying that does not imply anything about function. I think the richer notion that I am employing is more useful in understanding the physiology of sensory systems.

[10] I explain the form of this sort of explanation in some detail in 'Disjunctivism and Perceptual Psychology', forthcoming in *Philosophical Topics*.

Given this understanding of 'representation', I believe that phenomenal consciousness is not in itself, and in general, representation. It is certainly not in itself, and in general, perceptual representation, which I believe to be the most primitive sort of representation. Pain is a paradigm of phenomenal consciousness. Pain is not perceived, and it is not perception of bodily damage. It lacks the marks of true sensory perceptual representation, or, I think, any other genuine representation. There are no objectifying elements in the sensing of pain. There is no distinction in the sensation of pain between mere proximal stimulation and stimulation that comes from a distal source. Similarly, there is no capacity, in the mechanisms for pain's registering information about bodily damage, to distinguish between proximal and distal information. There are no perceptual constancies in this information-registration system. There is no *evident* rewarding type of explanation that centers on either getting the pain right or getting the bodily damage right. Most pain registers information about, and so is functionally related to, damage in certain locations in the body. Pain registers information about bodily damage and bodily location without *perceptually representing* either. (Cf. note 15 below.)

Pain's registering information without perceptually representing anything can be usefully compared to other non-perceptual sensory systems, like that of a bacterium's sensing the location of oxygen or light, or a worm's geotactic sensing of up or down. Pain is phenomenally conscious. Presumably the bacterium's sensory events and probably the worm's geotactic sense (like many of our own sensory capacities for balance) are not phenomenally conscious. The difference between all of these non-perceptual information-registering systems and genuine perceptual systems is huge, and of great importance for understanding mind. The notion of registering information requires no systematic powers of objectification. There are no internal mechanisms to distill the distal from the proximal. There is no evident need for perceptual representational kinds in explaining the sensory function of the painfulness of pain.[11]

Phenomenal consciousness is not in itself, in general, registering of information. Phenomenally conscious states usually do register information about other things. That is, usually there is a systematic law-like relation between phenomenally conscious states and further properties that functions to relate the individual to those properties in order to further survival for reproduction. I think, however, that it is not part of the nature of *some* phenomenal qualities to represent or

---

[11] I shall elaborate the distinction between sensory registration of information and perceptual representation in further work. Cf. my 'Perception'. The objectification that is the mark of perceptual representation is pre-intellectual. It can reside in capacities of an automatically operating perceptual system that systematically filters out noise and irrelevant aspects of the proximal stimulus array to form representations of relevant distal conditions. Such capacities are absent in mere sensory systems that respond simply to proximal stimulation. The proximal stimulation may be reliably connected to some distal situation that is relevant to biological function. But nothing in the sensory system is geared to making the distinction systematically. In such cases, the sensory system may *register information about* or *register* the distal situation; but it does not perceptually represent it.

register any particular information, in this sense, about anything further.[12] Some qualitative aspects of phenomenally conscious states depend purely on underlying transactions in the brain, not on causal or functional relations to anything further about which they register information. These qualitative aspects do not *constitutively* function to register any specific information—although many do in fact register information. I believe that this point applies to the most primitive sorts of phenomenal qualities.

Take the hurtful or painful quality of pain, for example. This quality in fact registers information about bodily damage. A pain can be produced by stimulating the central nervous system, even as normal neural pathways to the areas of bodily damage that the pain normally registers information about are blocked or severed. Further, it has been conjectured by neuro-scientists as empirically plausible, given what we know about the neural structure of the brain, that the pain centers of the brain would continue to cause the hurtful quality of pain even if they had been wired to connect to peripheral sensors for touch.[13] Then the lightest touch of the skin would have produced painful feelings. If the wiring had been naturally in place from the beginning of a creature's or species' life, then pain would never have had the biological function of conveying information about bodily damage; but it would have retained its hurtful or painful feeling. It follows from this conjecture that the hurtful quality of pain is not constitutively associated with registering information about bodily damage. It could have registered entirely different information, about touch.[14] I think that this conjecture is both extremely plausible and empirically testable. If it is correct, as it seems to be, then we have empirical ground for rejecting the identification—or even the constitutive connection—of the relevant phenomenal quality (hurtfulness) with any particular information-registering properties. I believe that similar points apply for other primitive qualities—the feel of cold, heat, hunger, stress. All of these might have signaled different bodily conditions than they in fact do.[15]

---

[12] Cf. Ned Block, 'Mental Paint', in M. Hahn and B. Ramberg (eds.), *Reflections and Replies: Essays on the Philosophy of Tyler Burge* (Cambridge, Mass.: MIT Press, 2003); and my 'Qualia and Intentional Content: Reply to Block', ibid.

[13] V. S. Ramachandran, 'Behavioral and Magnetoencephalographic Correlates of Plasticity in the Adult Human Brain', *Proceedings of the National Academy of Sciences USA*, 90 (1993), 10,413–10,420, esp. p. 10418.

[14] It is no argument to claim that such a species could not have evolved. In the first place, this is not obviously true. In some environments the slightest touch might be sufficiently dangerous to register strong alarm signals. In the second place, the issue is not over what is evolutionarily plausible, but over what is constitutive of painfulness. With respect to this issue, mere physical or metaphysical possibility suffices to separate properties. The physical connections could be established non-evolutionarily.

[15] I believe that these points apply better to the hurtful quality of the pain than to its locational feel. I take it that the pain's being-in-the-foot feeling may well have a *constitutive* informational element. This topographic aspect of phenomenal feel seems to me plausibly associated with the well-known way in which phenomenal topography, like neural topography in the central nervous system, functionally mimics the topography of peripheral areas of the body which normally cause their activation. Of course, it does not follow from this point that even the being-in-the-foot aspect of

The hurtful quality of pain does not represent anything perceptually. It is not perception of, or as of, anything. It does register information. But it does not constitutively register the information that it in fact registers. I think that the hurtful quality of pain does not *constitutively* register any information at all. Thus I think pain could have been the result of only relatively random stimulations, or of psychological noise. I will not argue this particular point. There are other phenomenal qualities—phenomenal aspects of phenomenally conscious states—that not only represent nothing. They have no function, and do not register sensory information at all.

Psychological theories must always allow for psychological noise. Psychological noise does not have a function and thus does not register information. It is not systematically correlated with anything that the animal or its sensory system makes use of. In some cases, the animal could not even learn to make use of it. It is an interference with or degradation of function. Some psychological noise is phenomenal. Visual blur is an instance of phenomenal psychological noise. Visual blur has no function and does not naturally register information for the individual. Phenomenal psychological noise cannot be assimilated to the (functional) registration of information.

What can we say in a more positive vein about phenomenal consciousness? A phenomenally conscious state is always a state of an individual psychological subject. The state is conscious for the individual. This 'for' needs scrutiny. The conscious phenomenal aspects of a conscious state are present for, presented to, the individual. In this respect, phenomenal consciousness involves access.[16]

---

a pain's feeling is *purely* informational. This aspect of the phenomenal quality may be constitutively informational without its being identical with, or fully explained by, its informational aspect. At a minimum, the way in which the pain feels to be in the foot involves the hurtful way of feeling the pain. This aspect of the feeling does not seem to convey constitutively any particular information at all, as I have suggested in the text. For stimulating facts relevant to these points, see Ramachandran, "Behavioral and Magnetoencephalographic Correlates".

Although the locational aspects of pain may be constitutively information registering, I think that they are not perceptual. We can certainly regard a feeling of pain in the foot as mistaken if there is no foot or if the pain is 'referred pain'. But the error does not rest on the failure of an objectifying capacity. There is no such capacity. The error seems more one of a failure of function. In such cases, the pain does not fulfill its function of guiding the individual to a location. There is no explanatory need to type-identify the pain in terms of an *objectifying* sensory capacity for distilling the distal from the proximal and with representational content that sets veridicality conditions. The contrast with genuine perceptual psychology—centered in representational theories of vision, hearing, and active touch—is stark. The notion of representation is tied to veridicality conditions. Perhaps it could be separated from the objectification of perception.

Whether there is an empirically autonomous type of representation—with a genuinely explanatory appeal to veridicality conditions—that is weaker than perceptual representation, but stronger than information registration—and that fits the locational feel of pain—seems to me worthy of further reflection. I am provisionally doubtful. I see no *evident* need for a systematic explanation that takes representational success and failure as one of the central explananda, and representational states as an explanatory kind, in accounting for the mechanism of pain formation for signaling bodily location.

[16] Partly for this reason, I prefer 'rational-access consciousness' to Block's 'access consciousness'. Since phenomenal consciousness also involves access for the individual, one needs to specify

We need to remember, firmly, what this access is not. It is not attention, conception, thought, perception, or information registration. An individual need not be conscious of the qualitative or sensory elements in a conscious state *as* sensory elements. They need not be conceptualized. They need not be categorized perceptually. The access is phenomenal, sensory—in the way that conscious sensations are, trivially, sensed.

There is a relation in this sensory access. We have intransitive uses of 'is conscious', analogous to 'is awake'. But if an individual is conscious in this intransitive sense, then necessarily there are instantiated qualitative aspects of the consciousness which are *conscious for* the individual.[17] Some phenomenal aspects are presented to, present to, present for, or conscious for, the individual in consciousness. I think that understanding this relation is fundamental to understanding phenomenal consciousness and what it is to be an individual subject.

A certain philosophical tradition inveighs against construing phenomenal consciousness as involving an 'act–object' relation.[18] There is something to this tradition. Sensing and phenomenal consciousness are not themselves acts. The aspects of phenomenal states that are phenomenally conscious for an individual are not objects, in most commonsense uses of the term. They are not objects of perception. They are not objects of reference, at least not by virtue of being phenomenally conscious. And they are not individuals. They are aspects, aspect instances, of psychological states. Psychological states are states of individuals. On the other hand, they are real; they have causal powers; and they can enter into relations. Pains, the phenomenal quality of blur, hunger pangs, and so on are events or properties that are conscious for individuals. They are presented to, present for, individuals. Their being conscious for an individual is a relation.

what sort of access is at issue. For rational-access consciousness, the relevant kind of access involves the employment of propositional attitudes, which I take to imply a capacity for rational inference.

[17] I would also say that the individual is 'conscious of' these aspects. But this phrase, together with 'aware of', easily misleads. The 'of' suggests attention, representation, reference. For example, consider phenomenally conscious vision. It may help to think of such vision in a rat rather than a human, since the human case brings in more intuitive distractions. If we say that the rat is conscious of the cheese, we are less inclined to say that the rat is conscious of the visual sensations in its visual field. Saying that will suggest, at least to many, that the rat *attends to* its visual sensations, or *perceives* them, or perceives them *as* visual sensations, or perhaps even *thinks* about them. (The point about attention shows in the fact that we are more willing to say that the individual is conscious of the pain or of a tickle. The individual's attention is likely to be directed to the pain or tickle rather than to its cause.) None of these suggestions is acceptable. Many will withhold 'conscious of' from its applications to such cases because of the suggestions. For this reason, 'conscious for' and 'presented to' seem to me better, less committal-seeming locutions for relations of phenomenal consciousness between individuals and sensations or the qualitative aspects of psychological states. I will, however, use all these locutions, since I think that the implicatures that accompany the 'conscious of' locution can be cancelled.

[18] Sydney Shoemaker, "Self-Knowledge and 'Inner Sense' ", *Philosophy and Phenomenological Research*, 54 (1994), 249–314; repr. in *The First-Person Perspective and Other Essays* (Cambridge: Cambridge University Press, 1996).

Some philosophers have maintained that the putative relation should be collapsed into a one-place property. For example, the sensation sensed is sometimes treated in an adverbial manner, as a feature or way of being conscious: individual ____ is conscious painfully, individual ____ is conscious in the visual-blur way. Of course, conscious sensations are aspects of psychological states, which are, in turn, states of individuals. So, ontologically, there is something to these locutions. Adverbs do connote properties of properties. But sensed sensations, occurrent qualitative aspects of consciousness, are also timeable states or events. They are instantiated aspects of consciousness. They have causal powers. Since they themselves can have a number of properties and relations, I think it impossibly stultifying to avoid referring to them—to avoid quantifying over them and making singular reference to them. Psychological explanation makes reference to these entities. I take the relational locutions to be unexceptionable. The visual blur is conscious for the individual. The individual is conscious of the pain. The individual feels the hunger pang. The tickle is present to, and presented to, the individual's consciousness.

For a qualitative aspect of a psychological state to be conscious for an individual is for that aspect (aspect instance) to be an element or aspect of the consciousness.[19] The relation between individual and qualitative aspects of psychological states that are conscious for the individual is not epistemically robust. The relation is not representational. It expresses no sort of perception or knowledge. Still, I think that it is worth taking very seriously.

The relation is not that of just any property to its bearer. The aspects of consciousness in phenomenally conscious states are present for the individual, whether or not they are attended to or represented. They are accessible to—indeed, accessed by—the individual. Although they are not necessarily accessible to whatever rational powers the individual has, phenomenal consciousness in itself involves phenomenal qualities' being conscious for, present for, the individual. They are presented to the individual's consciousness. This presentational relation is fundamental to phenomenal consciousness. I think that this relation can be recognized apriori, by reflection on what it is to be phenomenally conscious. Phenomenal consciousness is consciousness for an individual. Conscious phenomenal qualities are present for, and presented to, an individual.

The individual may or may not have rational powers. The individual may or may not be a self. The individual may or may not have perception in the full-blown objectifying sense in which I understand 'perception'. But consciousness is necessarily and constitutively presentational. The presentation is to an individual subject.

---

[19] Prima facie, any psychological state that has conscious qualitative aspects may also have other properties that are not conscious for the individual. This may be disputed. It is a serious issue in some forms of the mind–body problem.

The key to avoiding mistakes here is, I think, to allow the relational and presentational elements some scope in one's thinking, without misinterpreting phenomenal consciousness to be a form of perception or representation. This misinterpretation is, I believe, one of the root mistakes of the sense-data tradition and of Russell's 'knowledge by acquaintance'. Phenomenally conscious aspects of psychological states are not objects of perception, or data (evidence) to which one normally adverts in representing something else. They may be vehicular elements in perception or in information registration. They can have those roles. For example, phenomenally conscious sensations can figure in visual perception—say, conscious perception as of a moving object. Many phenomenally conscious sensations commonly register non-perceptual information.

Although phenomenally conscious states can figure in perception and in information registration and thus serve perceptual-representational and informational functions, the relational and presentational features constitutive of phenomenal consciousness itself are not in general constitutively functional. As I have indicated, some phenomenally conscious elements of conscious states do not have a function at all. At least, many of those that do have a function could have lacked the one they have. When phenomenally conscious sensations do figure in perception or information registration, there remains the presentational relation of these sensations to the individual. They are conscious for the individual, presented to the individual, no matter how unattended to, unperceived, unreferred to, unrepresented, and uninformative they may be.

The presentational, 'consciousness-for', aspect of the relation between phenomenally conscious states and the individual does have some things in common with representation. Phenomenally conscious qualities are present for the individual. They are presented to the individual in consciousness. Of course, an individual with capacities for propositional attitudes can have beliefs about phenomenal qualities. These are, I think, fallible. One can believe that one is in pain when one is not; and one can believe that one is not in pain when one is. But phenomenal consciousness itself is phylogenetically prior to propositional attitudes. It is fundamentally a sensory capacity.

There is a natural temptation to take an individual's feeling pain as a special case of the sort of sensory perception involved in, for example, the individual's seeing a red glow on the horizon. There is a natural temptation to take visual blur's being a phenomenally conscious element of a visual state for the individual as a special case of the sort of perception involved in the individual's seeing a highlight on an illuminated surface. The temptation is to count the cases special in that they cannot fail. If the pain or visual blur is presented to one in phenomenal consciousness, there can be no failure of 'perception' of these phenomenal elements. Phenomenal consciousness has been regarded as an infallible intentionality or representation.

These temptations should be firmly resisted. Phenomenal consciousness is indeed a presentation to the individual that cannot fail. It cannot fail, not because it is an infallible representation, but because it is not a representation with veridicality conditions at all. It can neither fail nor succeed.[20] Either phenomenal aspects of psychological states are present for, presented to, the individual in consciousness, or they are not. There is no question of right or wrong. It is a matter of presence or absence.

The presence is not spatial. The presence is to or for the individual's consciousness. Conscious phenomenal aspects of conscious states are presented to the individual, to the individual's consciousness.

This point encourages the question, How are conscious sensations presented? How are they present for the individual? How are phenomenal qualities like pain, visual blur, or the cold visceral sensation associated with objectless depression, phenomenally conscious for the individual?

These questions bring out part of why it has been perennially tempting to assimilate consciousness, phenomenal consciousness, to a kind of reference or representation. For entities are also presented to the individual through perception, thought, and other types of representation. The questions asked in the preceding paragraph have analogs for representational states: How is the individual conscious of the table? How is the table presented to the individual in perception? How is the individual thinking of this point in the triangle? What is the mode of presentation by which the point is present to the individual's thought?

The answers to these latter questions cite a representational content: perhaps a perceptual attributive or an applied concept. These are components of

---

[20] A recently popular view of pain is to regard it as perception of bodily damage, or of some property associated with bodily damage. For reasons mentioned earlier, I think that this view conflates information registration with perception. Some versions of the view also conflate the feeling of pain with the information that the feeling of pain registers about something further (bodily damage or even bodily location). The view has invoked some strange collateral positions. It has been maintained that in phantom limb cases, individuals hallucinate pain: they have no pain. This claim seems to me to be absurdly off the rails. No supplementary patter about how theoretical considerations can force revision of intuition should distract one from the weakness of such a view. A more subtle position, which I think has also gone wrong because of thinking of pain sensation too much on an analogy with perception, is that of Sydney Shoemaker, 'Introspection and Phenomenal Character', in David J. Chalmers (ed.), *Philosophy of Mind* (Oxford: Oxford University Press, 2002), 464. Shoemaker maintains that the somatic experience of pain perceptually represents a phenomenal property. The phenomenal property is supposed to be a relational property: roughly, the disposition of the bodily damage to cause the somatic experience. The somatic experience is not to be identified with either the bodily damage or the dispositional phenomenal appearance property of the damage. Shoemaker claims that somatic experiences are what we are averse to, and that they are better candidates for being pains than the phenomenal properties. But he does not regard them as good candidates, as will emerge. Since the phenomenal properties are dispositional properties of the damage, we *can*, according to the view, presumably hallucinate them. To his credit Shoemaker avoids claiming that we hallucinate pain, where the somatic experience is not caused by damage. But of the somatic experiences, he claims that they are not felt, 'just as visual experiences are not seen'. So if pains were the somatic experiences, they would not be felt. According to the theory, what we do feel is not something we are averse to; and nothing that we feel is pain. Without calling attention to these results, Shoemaker blames the awkwardness of mapping his theory onto intuition on 'our ordinary talk of pains'. He concludes that nothing is an ideal candidate for being pain as we ordinarily talk about it. It seems to me that these results reveal a theory gone awry.

the representational content of perception or thought. In the case of phenomenal consciousness of pain, visual blur, or hunger pang, one can seem to need analogous answers. It can seem that the consciousness of the pain, or the presentation of the pain to the individual's consciousness, is just a special type of sensory reference or representation.

As I have been maintaining, such a view would be mistaken. The situation is, rather, the reverse. Phenomenally conscious perception and phenomenally conscious thought are special cases of presentation to the individual.[21] Thus phenomenally conscious representation is a special case of presentation to the individual. So is non-representational information registration that involves phenomenal consciousness. Presentation of aspects of phenomenal states to the individual's phenomenal consciousness is not in itself a case of representation, or (at least not in general) information registration.

Asked with caution, the question 'How are phenomenally conscious aspects of psychological states present for the individual, or presented to the individual?' is not a bad one. There are certainly wrong answers to it! The phenomenally conscious aspects of psychological states are not presented through some representational content. We are not phenomenally conscious of our pain—we do not feel the pain—through some further mode of presentation. As is often noted, the pain is not separate from a mode of presentation as the rigid body is separate from the perceptual representation (or the perceptual content, or perception) that represents it. The pain is, however, present to and presented to the mind. How? It is presented to the individual through itself. The pain is its own mode of presentation. In this weak sense, there is a reflexive element in phenomenal consciousness.

Again, this reflexiveness should not be conceived as self-reference. It is not reference. It is not representation. The difference between self-reference in thought or language and the reflexive element in phenomenal consciousness of pain or visual blur is far more impressive than any similarity. Still, phenomenal consciousness involves a kind of access. Not rational access. It is access for the individual to the sensation, or to qualitative aspects of psychological states. The access is by way of phenomenal consciousness—by way of the person's feeling or sensing those aspects, having them in phenomenal consciousness. The sensation is sensed by the individual, or is conscious for the individual, *through* the sensation and through nothing further. The sensation's being presented to the individual in phenomenal consciousness does not entail that it is used to represent or refer to anything, even itself.

As I just indicated, there is reflexiveness in self-referential thoughts. Some of these are rational-access conscious. So the difference between phenomenal consciousness and rational-access consciousness is not that in the case of

---

[21] Rational-access consciousness may be a special case of a yet broader generic notion of presentation to the individual. I will confine my discussion here to phenomenal consciousness.

thought, the mode of presentation is always distinct from what it represents. Self-referential reflexiveness in thought has a logical form, which falls under norms for logical transformation. No such norms govern phenomenal consciousness *per se*. Reflexiveness in phenomenal consciousness is not representation. It is presentational consciousness in the absence of representation.

Rational-access consciousness is reflexive only in special cases. Reflexiveness is not a constitutive aspect of rational-access consciousness. Only few conscious thoughts are self-referential. Moreover, unconscious thoughts can surely be self-referential.

Reflexiveness is important to understanding *thought* primarily at the level of self-consciousness. Self-consciousness is rational-access consciousness that involves attribution of psychological states to oneself as such. A certain *type* of self-consciousness always involves a self-referential element. This reflexiveness is not the kind involved in phenomenal consciousness.

So phenomenal consciousness is not self-consciousness. But phenomenal consciousness is, I think, *always* reflexive. I conjecture that reflexiveness is a constitutive feature of phenomenal consciousness.

I have been emphasizing the negative. Reflexiveness is a feature of the presentational relation in phenomenal consciousness through the absence of a further mode of presentation. Given that reflexiveness gets its putative purchase only through absence, one can reasonably ask whether it is an idle wheel. What is the point of the extra place in the relation of consciousness between an individual and a sensational aspect of a psychological state, if the place does not add anything? Could we not do equally well with the relation

(sensation) _____ is presented in phenomenal consciousness to (individual) _____

or

(pain) _____ is phenomenally conscious for (individual) _____

or

individual _____ is phenomenally conscious of (visual blur) _____ ?

I think that the answer to this question hinges on whether a third argument place, which putatively engenders reflexiveness, really *is* idle.

The locutions just highlighted can certainly be understood as indicating simple two-place relations. Perhaps they all indicate the same relation. If we were to confine our consideration to phenomenal consciousness *per se*, with no consideration of the way in which phenomenal consciousness figures in other psychological states, then the third argument place would be idle. I think, however, that there is much to be said for considering phenomenally conscious presentation as pivotal in a wider range of mental phenomena.

---

[21] On the third locution, see note 17.

Consider these relation instances:

(i) (sensation) ____ is presented in phenomenal consciousness to (individual) ____ through (sensation) ____

(pain) ____ is phenomenally conscious for (individual) ____ through (pain) ____

individual ____ is phenomenally conscious of (visual blur) ____ through (visual blur) ____

(ii) (rigid body) ____ is presented in phenomenal consciousness to (individual) ____ through (perception) ____

(rigid body) ____ is phenomenally conscious for (individual) ____ through (perception) ____

(individual) ____ is phenomenally conscious of (rigid body) ____ through (perception) ____

(iii) (wound) ____ is presented in phenomenal consciousness to (individual) ____ through (pain) ____

(wound) ____ is phenomenally conscious for (individual) ____ through (pain) ____

(individual) ____ is phenomenally conscious of (wound) ____ through (pain) ____

(iv) (table) ____ is presented in phenomenal consciousness to (individual) ____ through (concept) ____

(table) ____ is phenomenally conscious for (individual) ____ through (concept) ____

(individual) ____ is phenomenally conscious of (table) ____ through (concept) ____ [22]

If it is reasonable to regard the relation or relations in each group as being the same relations as in the other groups, then the third argument place is not idle. If presentation or consciousness-for is the same relation in phenomenally conscious sensing sensation, phenomenally conscious perception, phenomenally conscious information registration, and phenomenally conscious thought, then the reflexiveness exhibited in the first group is not idle. I think that it *is* reasonable to regard phenomenal consciousness as present in phenomenally conscious perception, information registration, and thought. Presentation to an individual, phenomenal consciousness for an individual, can occur in all these cases.

Consider groups (ii) and (iii). The rigid body is presented to the individual through a perceptual representation. The individual is conscious of the wound

---

[22] I am assuming that at least the first relation in groups (i), (ii), (iii), and (iv) is the same relation. Similarly, for the second relation in the four groups, and the third and fourth. So the role of the locutions in the parentheses is not to indicate part of the relation. It is to indicate relevant *relata* that can enter into the relevant relation. Group (i) concerns feeling sensations, or being phenomenally conscious in the most primitive way. Group (ii) concerns phenomenal consciousness in perception. Group (iii) concerns phenomenal consciousness in information registration. Group (iv) concerns phenomenal consciousness in thought.

through the pain. In these cases what is presented to, or conscious for, the individual, and what the individual is conscious of, is something other than a qualitative aspect of a phenomenal state. The mode of presentation is different from what is presented. So in groups (ii) and (iii), there is no reflexiveness.

In group (ii) the mode of presentation is a perceptual state or perceptual content. What is presented is different (for example, a rigid body or a shape or color). So there is no reflexiveness. I doubt that reflexiveness is even possible for genuine perception. In group (iii) the mode of presentation is an information-registering state or sensation. If the information-registering state is non-perceptual but phenomenally conscious, the mode of presentation must be a qualitative state, a conscious sensation (type or token). What is informationally presented is different from the mode of presentation. What the conscious sensation registers information about (for example, bodily damage, or heat) is different from itself. So again, there is no reflexiveness.[23]

The same point applies with respect to group (iv). The phenomenally conscious thought that represents the table is certainly not reflexive. The subject matter of most thoughts is not presented, or represented, reflexively. Even phenomenally conscious thoughts as of qualitative states are not reflexive. In cases of *thought* about a sensation or quality, the phenomenally conscious thought (which I think is also rational-access conscious) may employ or make use of sensory, phenomenal elements in the conceptual mode by which the sensation or quality is presented. That is, the phenomenal quality may be presented in thought through the application of a phenomenal concept. The concept may incorporate the very phenomenal quality, as an iconic archetype, into its mode of presentation. The quality that is employed by the conceptual ability can be a sensation or sensation-memory. Or it can be an element in a representational image or perception. In any case, the concept is not identical with the quality. The concept is essentially representational, constitutively has a logical form, and has essential relations to truth. The quality is not essentially representational, constitutively lacks in itself a logical form, and lacks essential relations to truth. So, even though the quality is a part of the concept's mode of presentation, it is not the same as the conceptual mode of presentation.[24] So, again the presentation to the individual in thought is not reflexive. Clearly, reflexiveness is not a constitutive feature of thought in general. There is, as I indicated, self-referential thought. Its reflexiveness is representational, indeed conceptual. A mode of representation represents itself. The reflexiveness of phenomenal consciousness is the

---

[23] It is probably a constitutive, necessary truth about perception that a perceived object is never identical with its perceptual mode of presentation. I am inclined to think that an analogous point applies to information registration. I can think of no cases in which a conscious qualitative sensation registers information only about itself, in the sense of 'information registration' discussed earlier. Even if there are such cases, they are not constitutive of information registration. So reflexiveness is not constitutive of information registration *per se*, as it is of phenomenal consciousness *per se*.

[24] The demonstrative-like application of the concept is also not identical to any occurrence of the quality, which in itself is not a representational application of anything.

reflexiveness of absence of representation. So it is certainly to be distinguished from the reflexiveness of self-reference in thought.

If what is phenomenally presented to, or phenomenally conscious for, the individual is the qualitative aspect of a phenomenal state—of a sensation—(group (i)), *and* if the phenomenal consciousness is considered in itself and not as an element in a more complex psychological phenomenon, then the mode of presentation—what goes in the third place of the relation—is the same as what is presented. The sensation is presented to the individual through itself.[25] This is reflexiveness in the phenomenal consciousness relation or relations.

Whenever presentations to the individual through perception, information registration, or thought are phenomenally conscious, there is a phenomenally conscious qualitative state that is the vehicle of, or an aspect of, the perceptual state, or that is an aspect of the information-registering state, or that is an expression of, element in, or aspect of a propositional attitude. In other words, whenever a relation in group (ii), or group (iii), or group (iv) holds, a relation in group (i) holds, as a sub-element of the phenomenal consciousness in perception, information registration, or thought. In such group (i) cases, the qualitative state or aspect of a state is presented to the individual in phenomenal consciousness as well. It is its own mode of presentation. It is not perceived in group (ii) cases, and it need not be attended to. It is not the functionally relevant information in group (iii) cases. It may be thought about in group (iv) cases, but in such cases the conceptual mode of presentation is not identical with the qualitative element that is presented. Still, in these cases, there remains the basic relation that is constitutive of phenomenal consciousness. In this relation the qualitative element is presented to the individual and conscious for the individual through itself. (Cf. note 16.) Phenomenal consciousness, in and of itself, is reflexive. The reflexiveness of the phenomenal-consciousness relation distinguishes it from other sorts of presentations to the individual's mind, which may also be phenomenally conscious.

---

[25] Since phenomenal qualities are constitutive aspects of the core individual subject, there is an approximation to ego-presentation in phenomenal consciousness. But nothing presents the ego as a whole, or as such. There is no phenomenal quality that is the 'presentational to me' quality. Beyond the hurt, there is no further 'to me-ish' quality in sensing pain. There is a *de se* aspect of primitive *perceptual* states; this aspect is *representational*. We human sophisticates can represent, in thought, anything, including pain, as presented *to us*. Such ego representations overlay phenomenal consciousness. They are not present in phenomenal consciousness *per se*, or in non-perceptual, non-representational systems of phenomenal consciousness. The ego-connection in such systems is not representational. It resides in the presentation to an individual that is constitutive of phenomenal consciousness itself. And it resides in the functional connection between having sensations and individuals' being disposed to react so as to benefit themselves. A claim that there is a 'me-ish' *phenomenal quality* at any stage of phylogenetic complexity would be mistaken. Hume and Kant rightly denied such a claim. Cf. David Hume, *Treatise of Human Nature*, ed. L. A. Selby Bigge (Oxford: Oxford University Press, 1965; first pub. 1899), 252; Kant, *Critique of Pure Reason*, B132, B157, B275–277. One is not phenomenally presented with a self, or proto-self. One is presented with phenomenal qualities.

In fact, reflexive phenomenal consciousness is what makes perceptual representation, non-perceptual information-registering phenomenal states, and thought phenomenally conscious. Relations in group (i) underlie relations in groups (ii), (iii), and (iv). The former relations make the latter relations phenomenally conscious. The former relations lie at the base of phenomenal consciousness. The connection to this base in the latter three groups makes non-reflexive cases and reflexive ones instances of phenomenal consciousness. The connection also unifies phenomenal consciousness.

Thus, given that phenomenal presentation to the individual, or phenomenal consciousness for the individual, is present in all these cases, the question of mode of presentation is not idle. Non-representational reflexiveness in presentation to an individual is a constitutively necessary condition on phenomenal consciousness. Such reflexiveness is present in, and constitutively necessary of, any phenomenal consciousness in perception, information registration, and thought. Presentations that are distinctive of perception, information registration, and most thought are not reflexive. Where a thought is reflexive by way of its representational content, this reflexiveness differs from the reflexiveness of phenomenal consciousness *per se* precisely in being representational. Of course, by employing phenomenal elements in its representational content, a self-referential thought can be phenomenally conscious. Phenomenal elements can figure in the self-reference. But what makes the thought phenomenally conscious is a non-representational reflexive presentation to the individual. What makes it self-referential is a representational reflexive presentation.

Reflexiveness is a constitutively necessary condition on phenomenal consciousness. It can be present in perception and information registration, when they are phenomenally conscious; but reflexiveness is not constitutive of perception or information registration. What they present to the individual in consciousness is not presented reflexively. Reflexive presentation is what makes these types of psychological processes conscious, but it is not what makes them cases of information registration or perception. Indeed, being phenomenally conscious is probably neither necessary nor sufficient for a state to be either an information-registering state or a perceptual state.

There are simple animals like bees that are known to have visual perception, with an array of objectifying representations and perceptual constancies, but about which we do not know whether they are conscious.[26] There is certainly no apriori connection between perceiving and being conscious. We appear to have an adequate empirical grip on the nature of bees' visual perception without

---

[26] Even though bees exhibit many visual constancies, the neural circuitry underlying their visual systems is relatively simple. It is much simpler than the corresponding circuitry underlying the visual systems of birds and fish. This is why I think it more plausible to conjecture that birds and fish are visually phenomenally conscious than that bees are. Of course, visual phenomenal consciousness is a relatively complex type. The phenomenal consciousness of pain, or of other sensations that do not serve perceptual systems, probably has a simpler neural basis and a phylogenetically earlier origin than phenomenal consciousness in vision.

assuming that they are conscious. Further, many sensory states deriving from the human dorsal visual stream are unconscious. Yet they exhibit the objectification, the sort of filtering mechanisms, and the perceptual constancies that mark perception. That is, they discriminate distal conditions under a wide variety of stimulus conditions and do so by standard perceptual means.[27] So there is empirical reason to believe that phenomenal consciousness is not constitutively necessary for perception.

Phenomenal consciousness is not constitutively sufficient for perception. Pain and visual blur are phenomenally conscious, but are not perceptions.

Visual blur shows that phenomenal consciousness is not sufficient for information registration. The numerous non-conscious information-registering states—sensitivity to light in amoeba, for example—show that phenomenal consciousness is not necessary for information registration. Amoebae are surely not conscious.

Other things besides qualitative sensations can be *sensorily* presented in phenomenal consciousness, insofar as the sensations do participate in perceptual or other sensory information-registering enterprises. When other things besides qualitative sensations are presented in purely sensory phenomenal consciousness, the presentation is through modes of presentation that differ from the things presented. (Cf. note 24.) So these presentations are not reflexive. But the concomitant presence of a non-representational reflexive presentation is what makes these presentations phenomenally conscious.

III

There may be a further point about the form of consciousness in (group (i)) phenomenal consciousness *per se*. To explain this point, I must return to an idea

---

[27] Cf. Milner and Goodale, *The Visual Brain in Action*; Yves Rossetti and Laude Pastille, 'Several "Vision for Action" Systems: A Guide to Dissociating and Integrating Dorsal and Ventral Functions (Tutorial)', in Wolfgang Prinz and Bernhard Hamill (eds.), *Common Mechanisms in Perception and Action* (Oxford: Oxford University Press, 2002). Some of this literature follows Milner and Goodale in using the term 'perception' in what I regard as a misleading and non-standard way. Often the term is applied only to transactions in the ventral system. But there is no scientific basis, especially in the larger context of perceptual psychology, for this usage. The basic mechanisms postulated to account for representational success and failure are common to dorsal and ventral systems, and to conscious and unconscious visual representation. Both conscious and unconscious representational contents can be veridical or non-veridical. Both exhibit perceptual constancies and other fundamental perceptual representational capacities. Both involve complex filtering mechanisms. Both share some of the same basic routes for yielding representational successes (e.g. depth perception). In fact, there is evidence that many unattended-to states in the ventral system that are counted perceptual (in the narrow sense of Milner and Goodale) are unconscious. So this narrow usage of the term 'perception' does not clearly correspond to a conscious–unconscious distinction. In my view, the term 'perception' should be applied to objectifying aspects of sensory systems, regardless of whether these are conscious. This is the more nearly standard usage in visual psychology. I think that perception is fundamentally to be understood in terms of a way of realizing representational function, not in phenomenological terms.

in 'Two Kinds of Consciousness'. This is the idea that one might distinguish between phenomenal consciousness and instantiated phenomenal qualities, or between *phenomenally conscious* sensation and phenomenal qualitative states, or sensations, that may or may not be phenomenally conscious.

According to such a distinction, an individual could have a pain while not consciously feeling it at all times. I want to explain the distinction before discussing whether it is of any empirical use, whether it actually applies to any real cases. In entertaining such a distinction, I am not merely supposing that the individual does not attend to the pain. I mean that the individual does not feel it. It is not phenomenally conscious for the individual. Yet the individual still has it. The pain is individuated partly in terms of how it consciously feels. It is, constitutively, an instance of a way of feeling. An enduring, occurrent, phenomenal, psychological condition that feels that way could go in and out of consciousness—could be felt or not—if distraction or some other interference intervened.

Roughly speaking, the continuity of the sensation, the pain, would depend on at least three facts. It would depend on the fact that it would be felt in roughly the same way if it were to come back into consciousness. It would depend on the fact that its basic cause and its causal powers are the same. And it would depend on the fact that phenomenal consciousness of it—its presentation to the individual—is masked by some interference. As I noted in 'Two Kinds of Consciousness', regaining consciousness of a sensation seems phenomenally different from being conscious of the initial onset of a sensation.

The conceptual distinction is this. On the view that I am exploring, an occurrent phenomenal quality is *constitutively* individuated in terms of how it *would be* felt if it were to become conscious. Its nature is constitutively, not just causally or dispositionally, related to occurrently conscious ways of feeling. This constitutive point is what makes the quality *phenomenal* even when it is not actually conscious. On this view, the unfelt pain is still a pain—not just a neural state or a dispositional state that happens to be capable of producing pain under the right conditions—even though it is not occurrently felt and is not conscious for the individual.

The alternative view does not recognize or make use of the distinction. On the alternative view, a phenomenal quality could not be phenomenal unless it is occurrently conscious at all times at which it occurs. On this view, phenomenal qualities are constitutively *occurrently* conscious. On this view, whenever some people say that one has phenomenal qualities that are unfelt, one should say instead that one is in a state, perhaps a neural state, that sometimes causes occurrently felt phenomenal qualities but bears no constitutive relation to them. On the view I am exploring, phenomenal qualities are *constitutively capable* of being occurrently conscious. The view might add that such qualities are occurrently conscious unless certain masking or interfering conditions occur. This constitutive capability—this association in the *nature* of the state with occurrent phenomenal consciousness—is what makes the unconscious state a phenomenal state.[28]

I have just defended the conceptual coherence of the distinction between phenomenal qualities of a psychological state and phenomenal consciousness of them. It is a further question whether the distinction has a definite empirical application. If it does not have such application, then I assume that there are no unconscious phenomenal qualities—no unfelt pains. Then (further), as far as I can see, all occurrently instantiated phenomenal qualities could be required constitutively to be always conscious.

I am not strongly committed one way or the other on this empirical issue. I simply want to keep it open. I am interested in exploring the empirical possibility of the more liberal form of individuation, which makes use of a distinction between being a phenomenal quality and being an occurrently conscious phenomenal quality.

There are obvious anecdotal cases where there is some temptation to apply the distinction. It is common to say that the soldier lost consciousness of the (persisting) pain from his or her wound until the battle was over. Of course, it is easy to redescribe such cases so as not to assume that a pain persists when it is not felt. There also appears to be some place for the distinction in some uses of the way many of us ordinarily think about sensations. The locution of being conscious of one's pain suggests cases where distraction might make one not conscious of one's pain—not (phenomenally) conscious of a pain that one has. Again, it is easy to see how to explain these locutions away so as to deprive them of literal empirical application.

Whether there are solid empirical applications of the distinction may depend on whether there is a place in more rigorous psychological explanation for constitutively phenomenal psychological states with causal powers even during times when they are not consciously felt. Take a case in which one is tempted to regard a pain as persisting even though it is unconscious. Is there a place in a systematic psychological theory for attributing occurrent causal relations where the cause or effect is distinctively phenomenal—constitutively individuated in phenomenal terms? If so, then there is empirical application for the distinction between felt and unfelt pains. If, on the contrary, in all such cases causal explanation of occurrent causal relations can dispense with psychological explanations that appeal to phenomenal states, then perhaps there will be no empirical application for the conceptual distinction.

I think that science should try to maximize the scope of its explanatory notions. I think that the notion of a psychological state individuated in terms of

---

[28] Such a distinction would in no way interfere with finding underlying neural mechanisms. One would expect to find one level or array of neural activity that corresponds to unconscious phenomenal states, and another level or array that corresponds to conscious phenomenal states. The key issue about whether this conceptual distinction has actual application to a difference in the real world centers on the character of psychological explanation, as I shall argue below—not on the relation between the psychological explanation and underlying neural explanations.

what it is like to feel or be conscious is explanatory. Such states have causal powers and vulnerabilities. So I think that one should be alive to the possibility that causal explanation in phenomenal terms does not lapse at every moment when an individual is not occurrently conscious in the relevant way. I conjecture, for the sake of exploration, that there is a causal-explanatory role for such phenomenal continuants at times when they go out of consciousness.

As I have indicated, this view of the relation between phenomenal qualities and their being phenomenally conscious is not fundamental to my thinking about phenomenal consciousness. If it is correct, however, it would further highlight the *presentational* nature of phenomenal consciousness. The point can be brought out in two ways.

First, if feeling a phenomenal quality like pain is to be distinguished from merely occurrently having the phenomenal quality (the pain), reflexiveness is *not* a feature of the phenomenal state itself. The pain is not reflexive on its own, as a self-referential thought content might be. For if a pain is unfelt by, or not conscious for, the individual that has it, there is no *way* that the pain is, at that time, presented to the individual. Unconscious pain would become conscious in being presented to the individual through itself. Reflexiveness is, unmomentously but constitutively, how a phenomenal quality or sensation is presented to, or conscious for, the individual. It is presented to, conscious for, the individual through itself. Reflexiveness is a feature of the relation of phenomenal consciousness between the individual and the phenomenal state. In a weak sense, it is part of the form of the consciousness when the qualitative aspects of a psychological state are conscious for the individual. Reflexiveness is relevant entirely to the presentational aspect of phenomenally conscious states. It is relevant entirely to presentation to the individual. Phenomenal consciousness consists in such presentation.

Second, consider the following reasoning. A pain is correctly individuated partly in terms of a way of feeling. But a *way* of feeling is an abstraction that can be instantiated in different individuals and at different times in the same individual. The same can be said for *what it is like* to feel pain. That is an abstraction too. A phenomenally conscious pain is, of course, not an abstraction. It is an occurrent, instantiated condition. Suppose that an individual can have a pain without feeling it—without its being conscious for the individual, without its being presented to the individual. Then the pain's being instantiated is not sufficient for its being phenomenally conscious. On this supposition, a state's being individuated by a characteristic way of feeling (or way of being presented, or what it is like to feel it) *and* being instantiated do not suffice for the state's being phenomenally conscious. Being occurrently phenomenally conscious (at all times) is not a necessary feature of the pain itself. For the pain to be phenomenally conscious, it must be in the right relation to the individual. It must be conscious for, or presented to, the individual.

These two points are really at most supplementary. The idea that there is a place for a distinction between having a pain and being phenomenally conscious of the pain is just exploratory. If it is correct, it throws the basic point into sharper relief. But the basic point that I have made about phenomenal consciousness is independent. The basic point is that phenomenal consciousness is constitutively a non-representational, reflexive presentation relation between an occurrent qualitative state and an individual.

The presentation relation between an occurrent qualitative state and an individual is evident in our common understanding of the notions *way of feeling* and *what it is like*: way of feeling *for the individual*, what it is like *for the individual*. The relation can be recognized through apriori reflection. No qualitative conscious state can fail to be conscious for an individual. The state is accessible to, present for, conscious for, presented to, the individual. All of the key notions for phenomenal consciousness mandate presentation to or for an individual. One can, of course, specify qualitative states that are essentially conscious—*conscious* pain, for example. Any such states must, however, at least implicitly entail this presentational relation to the individual.

This point about the role of a non-representational relation in phenomenal consciousness could be regarded as adding a new dimension, over and above the qualitative aspects of consciousness, to what is hard or difficult about understanding consciousness.[29] I do not see things quite that way. I think that this relation is an apriori and necessary aspect of what it is to be a phenomenally conscious quality or qualitative condition. What it is like has always been what it is like for an individual. Such phenomenal qualities are by nature either occurrently, or capable of being, presented to, present to, conscious for an individual.[30]

Constitutive reciprocity reigns here, as it does with respect to rational-access consciousness. There is a constitutive role for an individual subject in what it is to be a phenomenal quality. Being conscious for an individual is part of what it is to be a qualitative phenomenal state. Reciprocally, what it is to be

---

[29] Although I cannot go into the matter here, I do not accept the usual framework in which the 'hard problem' of understanding consciousness is raised or answered. This framework invites a reduction of phenomenal consciousness, or substitute for it, as a condition of understanding. Then the discussion either maintains that some reduction is correct, or that because it is incorrect, we do not understand consciousness. Then philosophers who hold the latter position divide as to whether we will ever understand consciousness. 'Is it an ultimate mystery?', they ask. All this makes good magazine copy. But it is not the way scientific understanding tends to go. I see no scientific or commonsensical reason why understanding consciousness must take any such reductive form. It would be enough to integrate consciousness into a systematic empirical theory, connecting it in some systematic way to other psychological capacities and to underlying neural conditions. We are coming to understand representation in that way—not by reducing it to functional, neural, or other matters. Such reductions do not succeed for representation any more than they do for consciousness. But the integration of representation into empirical theory is dissolving the sense that representation needs reduction or 'naturalization'. Naturalization is best taken to be empirical systematization and integration. It is not best taken as reduction to some privileged set of terms (in the physical sciences or elsewhere). It is also not best taken as purification of subjective elements for a universal 'objective' point of view. Our main difficulty with consciousness is that we do not yet know how to integrate it into empirical theory. I see no reason to doubt that that day will come.

[30] Even if occurrent phenomenal qualities can fail to be phenomenally conscious, their phenomenality is still to be explained in terms of a would-be way of being occurrently presented.

a certain sort of individual, a conscious individual, is constitutively associated with an occurrent, presentational relation to such qualitative states. Phenomenal consciousness is relevant to demarcating certain sorts of individuals, individual subjects—individuals with a conscious mental life. Such individuals include selves or persons. But they are not confined to selves or persons. There are surely conscious individuals that are neither. For all individual subjects, the constitutive core—though not necessarily the bulk—of their psychological lives is phenomenal consciousness, a presentational relation to certain sensory aspects of their psychological lives. This core constitutes a primitive type of subjectivity—non-representational phenomenal subjectivity.

Any substantive value in these reflections lies in their uncovering a unified form for phenomenally conscious mental life—presentation to the individual in phenomenal consciousness. Central aspects of phenomenally conscious mental life vary in the formal structure of the presentation. In particular, the variations center on what is presented and how. But non-representational reflexiveness in presentation underlies, and is constitutive of, the phenomenal consciousness in all these variations.

These reflections on the role of non-representational reflexiveness in phenomenal consciousness are at best pointers to differences between phenomenally conscious sensing and conscious *representation*, whether in perception or in thought. The pointing may be too 'formal' to constitute rich insight into the content of the difference. We should not, however, belittle whatever insight we can gain into these difficult matters. One day we will gain more.

19 *Descartes on Anti-individualism*

In 'Cartesian Error and the Objectivity of Perception'[1], I made what I now regard as an important mistake in the interpretation of Descartes. I construed him as an individualist about thoughts. In this paper I would like to explain why this construal is at best doubtful. I would also like to use the occasion to explore Descartes's views of mental substances and mental attributes, and about reference to the physical world.

Individualism is the view that the individuation of all an individual's mental states and events does not depend in any way on relations the individual bears to a wider environment. As noted, I interpreted Descartes to be an individualist. I interpreted him as holding that the individuation of all mental states and events—or at least, all thoughts—was independent of any relations to a wider environment, prototypically, the physical environment. I realized this mistake shortly after making it, and signaled my awareness of it in a subsequent paper.[2] But I did not explain in any detail why I had changed my mind. I would like to do better here.

I took Descartes to be an individualist on the basis of two considerations. One was his elaboration of the Demon thought experiment in *Meditation* I. That thought experiment presumes that one might have the thoughts that one has even if there were no physical world at all. So it presumes that one's thoughts are what they are independently of any relations to the physical world. The second consideration derived from Descartes's substance dualism. It seemed to me that insofar as he thought that minds are substances whose existence and nature are

---

This paper is largely a lightly edited excerpt from a longer, previously published essay that took the form of a reply to an article by my colleague Calvin Normore. My reply, 'Descartes, Bare Concepts, and Anti-Individualism', was published, together with Normore's article in M. Hahn and B. Ramberg (eds.), *Reflections and Replies: Essays on the Philosophy of Tyler Burge* (Cambridge, Mass.: MIT Press, 2003). The present article contains a few additions, not present in my essay as previously published

[1] Cf. 'Cartesian Error and the Objectivity of Perception', in P. Pettit and J. McDowell (eds.), *Subject, Thought, and Context* (New York: Oxford University Press, 1986) (Ch. 7 above).

[2] Cf. 'Individualism and Self-Knowledge', *The Journal of Philosophy*, 85 (1988), 649–663, note 4.

independent of any physical reality, he had to think that thoughts were also thus independent.

The first consideration is relatively easy to undermine, at least as it stands. What is individualistic in Descartes is the presentation of the demon thought experiment in *Meditation* I. What I said in 'Cartesian Error and the Objectivity of Perception' about individualistic intuitions that might be drawn from that thought experiment—my criticism of moving without argument from knowledge of one's actual thoughts to knowledge of what one's thoughts would be in counterfactual situations—still seems to me right and to the point. This invalid transition is easy to fall for. It has seduced others. Descartes himself blurs the distinction between self-knowledge and metaphysical knowledge, in such a way as to encourage the transition.

Nevertheless, my attribution of individualism to Descartes was badly grounded. Descartes holds that the thought experiment of *Meditation* I is not ultimately coherent. God is invoked as a necessary principle for making our intentional mental contents (ideas) conform to basic natures in the objective world. This is to give God a role prima facie analogous to the role of causal history and evolutionary design in determining contents. The general caste of Descartes' account appears in many ways congenial to anti-individualism.

Whether Descartes is an anti-individualist, however, is complex and not completely clear. Descartes does not say much about the individuation of mental states. For that matter, he says little about the individuation of minds or of physical objects. I want to explain why the issue is interpretatively complex.

I

Individualism is consistent with Descartes's claim that God insures that our clear and distinct ideas apply to objective natures. If one held that there are no individuation conditions on what it is to have a given idea of an objective nature that make reference to anything outside the mind, one could regard God's role as simply to insure that the ideas that we have always correspond to objective natures. For example, one could hold that what it is to have an idea requires that no further explanatory conditions be met. God's necessarily making a match between the world and ideas so conceived would *not* entail that there are anti-individualist conditions on the individuation of thoughts. It would entail only that there is a necessary match between our ideas and their objects. Necessity is one thing. Individuation is a further thing. The appeal to God's veracity is congenial to anti-individualism, but does not entail it.

Descartes also has a causal principle: There must be as much reality, 'formally', in the cause as there is in the effect. The principle requires that the *objective reality* (roughly the representational content) of an idea be caused by something whose *formal reality* (roughly, intrinsic reality of the object or referent) is as much or greater than the reality purportedly represented by the idea.[3] Descartes may understand degrees of reality in terms of explanatory priority.[4] The principle would require that the representational nature of an idea of a rock be explained in terms of a cause which has an ontological status at least equal to that of a rock. Thus a rock would do.

In its focus on explanation, this principle is closer to bearing on individuation conditions than the invocation of God's veracity. But the principle is too weak to entail anti-individualism. The finite thinker will have an ontological status sufficient to explain the objective reality of all the thinker's ideas except for the idea of God (for which God must be invoked, according to Descartes's ontological argument). It is consistent with the principle, stated in the abstract, that the mind can be the explanatory basis for all its own ideas. So the principle is again consistent with individualistic individuation conditions for objectively and empirically referring ideas.[5]

It appears to me, however, that the main drift of Descartes's reasoning is to explain the representational nature of one's ideas in terms of the objects that those ideas represent. The appeal to God's veracity seems to function as a guarantee that this natural direction of explanation, especially for reference to objects in the physical world, can be relied upon, as long as we as thinkers avoid invoking materially false or confused ideas.[6]

For example, consider this passage from *Meditation* III:

And although the reality which I am considering in my ideas is merely objective reality, I must not on that account suppose that the same reality need not exist formally in the causes of my ideas, but that it is enough for it to be present in them objectively. For just as the objective mode of being belongs to ideas by their very nature, so the formal mode of being belongs to the causes of ideas—or at least the first and most important ones—by *their* very nature. And although one idea may perhaps originate from another, there cannot be an infinite regress here; eventually

---

[3] René Descartes, *Meditations*, III, in *The Philosophical Writings of Descartes*, II, trans. J. Cottingham, R. Stoothoff, and D. Murdoch (Cambridge: Cambridge University Press, 1984), 28, and in *Œuvres de Descartes*, ed. Ch. Adam and P. Tannery (Paris: CNRS, 1964–76), henceforth AT, VII, 40–41.

[4] Cf. Calvin Normore, 'Meaning and Objective Being: Descartes and His Sources', in Amélie Rorty (ed.), *Essays on Descartes' Meditations* (Berkeley: University of California Press, 1986).

[5] I have one caveat about Normore's presentation of Descartes on these matters. Normore reads Descartes as an externalist 'in the sense that the content of our ideas depends on their causes—but on the cause of the objective reality of the idea not the cause of its formal reality'. It is not sufficient to be an anti-individualist (or externalist) that one hold that the content of our ideas depends on their causes. One needs the further points that the causes are external to the individual and that the dependence is individuative, not merely causal.

[6] I read *Meditations* III and VI as illustrating this drift. I think that this issue in interpreting Descartes is worth further investigation. I have benefited from several conversations with Normore in my remarks about Descartes. Normore recommends further reflection on God's creation of real possible natures. God's idea and the natures are created in the same act. Nevertheless, Normore sees Descartes, here as elsewhere, as tending to take the nature that the idea refers to as explanatorily prior to the idea.

one must reach a primary idea, the cause of which will be like an archetype which contains formally all the reality which is present only objectively in the idea.[7]

The phrase 'same reality' and the causal account of the objective reality (or intentional content) of ideas seem distinctly anti-individualist in spirit. Our ideas of objective physical space, for example, seem to be explained in terms of our being causally related to spatial shapes.[8]

When Descartes discusses the material truth or falsity of ideas, he may appear to individuate ideas independently of objects with formal reality that are independent of the mind. He claims that the idea of a chimera is no more a false idea than the idea of a goat. He notes that it is just as true that he imagines the one as the other. To be a false idea is to be an idea that represents a non-thing as a thing. Thus it appears that Descartes believes that the idea of a chimera does not in itself represent something as real that is not real. In any case, Descartes believes that 'there can be no ideas which are not as it were of things'. This 'as it were' is not easy to interpret. But I think that Descartes means that all ideas are representational, they have representational content, even though not all ideas represent (refer to a real referent)—and even though not all ideas that do not refer to a real referent represent something as real. I take it that he means that chimera and illusory dagger do not purport to represent something real, even though they are representational.[9]

Anti-individualism does not require that all ideas that are individuated in terms of a wider environment in fact refer to anything in the wider environment. Many ideas obtain their representational content by being related (by theory, construction, amalgamation, or other means) to other ideas that do refer to elements in the environment. Both types of ideas derive their content partly through causal or other non-representational relations to the environment. Descartes's development of the early stages of scepticism in *Meditation* I shows that he has a masterful sense of the variety of ways in which an idea can be dependent for its representational meaning or content on a wider environment, without succeeding in referring to anything (real) in the environment. The failure of some ideas to

---

[7] Descartes, *Meditations*, III, in *Philosophical Writings of Descartes*, II, 29; AT, VII, 41–42. I am indebted to Calvin Normore for discussion of this passage and other passages in Descartes's interchange with Arnauld in the fourth set of Objections and Replies. The essay as a whole has benefited from several conversations with him and with Deborah Brown.

[8] A similar line of thought occurs in his discussion of the perception of color. In *Principles*, I, 70, Descartes writes:

It is clear, then, that when we say that we perceive colours in objects, this is really just the same as saying that we perceive something in the objects whose nature we do not know, but which produces in us a certain very clear and vivid sensation which we call the sensation of colour.

Descartes insists that it would be an error to judge that color had a particular *nature* on the basis of its being perceived as color. His account, however, does not question that the sensation is of color, or that its being a sensation of color depends on its having a cause external to the individual.

[9] *Meditations*, III; AT VII, 37, 43–44.

refer does not show that all ideas, or even that those non-referring ideas, do not owe their representational meaning or content to some ideas that refer to things in the wider environment—things that tend to cause those ideas. Descartes's rejection of the Demon hypothesis as being impossible or incoherent is, I think, associated with his view that all ideas, including non-referring ones, owe their representational content to things beyond them—things that cause at least some ideas which are successfully referential.

Since Descartes does not explicitly discuss individuation conditions of ideas, my anti-individualist reading requires some judgment. Still, I take the spirit of Descartes's work to be broadly anti-individualist.

In my formulation of individualism in 'Cartesian Error and the Objectivity of Perception', I indicated some awareness of these issues. I explicitly excluded appeals to God as means of preventing one from being an individualist.[10] I do think that there are serious difficulties with Descartes's invocation of theology to guarantee clear and distinct ideas in his account of veridicality and content determination. The appeal is not only epistemically tenuous. I think that it, together with his extreme reductionist conception of physical reality, may have led him to underrate how large a role mundane, empirical, macro-objects and properties play in content determination.

On the other hand, no historically sensitive account of early modern rationalist views can afford to bracket the role of God. I believe that my indulging in such bracketing led to under-rating anti-individualist elements in Descartes. I have come to think that there were fewer individualists prior to the twentieth century than I had formerly supposed. Despite the new science criticism of Aristotelian metaphysics and of commonsense epistemology by nearly all the great early modern figures, the enormous influence of the anti-individualism of Aristotle carries deeply into the early modern period.

II

The second consideration that led me to my misinterpretation of Descartes concerns his dualism. Issues surrounding this consideration seem to me very complex. What needs to be explored is how individuation of mental states in terms of relations to objects outside the individual's mind is to be squared with Descartes's strong form of dualism. Anti-individualism limits the metaphysical independence of mental states and events from the non-mental. But Descartes's view of mind, as a substance whose principal essential attribute is thought,

---

[10] I wrote, 'Individualism is the view that an individual person or animal's mental state or event kinds ... can in principle be individuated in complete independence of the natures of empirical objects, properties, or relations (excepting those in the individual's own body ...)—and similarly do not depend essentially on the natures of the minds or activities of other (*non-divine*) individuals' (my retrospective emphasis). Cf. 'Cartesian Error and the Objectivity of Perception', 193 above.

is prima facie incompatible with ontological dependence of mind on the non-mental. For finite substances are independent for their existence and nature of anything else except God.

Insofar as Descartes is not an individualist, he must have reconciled these views by holding that mental states and events that are about body are not *essential* to any given mind, or to being a mind.[11] Mental events about body are for him *modes* of mind (contingent properties). Such mental events are not *attributes* (necessary ones). (A *principal attribute* is an attribute that is constitutive of the entity's nature or essence and explains other attributes.) Anti-individualism does not itself maintain that to have a mind, one must have thoughts about body. It claims that, as a matter of individuation, to have certain thoughts, including specific ideas of body, one must be in causal relations to a wider environment. It is open to Descartes to agree that particular thoughts about body and even having innate ideas like that of extension, are metaphysically dependent on their non-mental objects, without conceding that mind itself is thus dependent. So although this sort of reconciliation involves, to be sure, other difficulties, it does make Cartesian dualism prima facie compatible with anti-individualism.

Of course, conceding to anti-individualism that thoughts of body are dependent for their natures not only on mind but on body opens a view of Cartesian dualism that is different from the common construal of it. On such a position, some particular thoughts, which Descartes would count as modes of a mind, are necessarily dependent on physical properties. So not just aspects of sensation and imagination, but even aspects of some acts of intellection are, on this position, explanatorily dependent on body. Aside from God, only mental substances (particular minds) and mental attributes derivative from the principal mental attribute (the attribute, thinking) seem to be completely independent of physical substances.

It is important to see how far the exclusion of ideas of body from essential attributes of mind might extend in the Cartesian scheme, if it is to be anti-individualistic. For Descartes, the basic idea of body is the idea of extension. Extension, considered in abstraction from actual matter, is supposed to be the fundamental idea in geometry. Geometry is not, according to Descartes, about corporeal extension. It does not depend epistemically on perception of the physical world. It is not committed to the existence of corporeal substance.

---

[11] God's mental events are special and may not be subject to anti-individualist considerations. The objects of God's mind depend on his creating them through his thinking them. See, however, note 4. Moreover, I will assume that Descartes's holding that a human mind's idea of God depends on the existence of God is not incompatible with his substance dualism, since no finite substance is completely independent of God. Similarly, I assume that the fact that Descartes holds that God could bring about anything, including the falsity of eternal truths, does not show that Descartes was an individualist. Even though he thinks that relations between having ideas about body and being in relation to the physical environment is, in this sense, contingent, I take the issue to remain alive. If anti-individualist principles were, like mathematical truths, necessary except for the qualification about God's power, then I would regard Descartes as an anti-individualist. I owe this point to Carl G. Anderson.

Descartes seems, however, to think that the shapes studied in geometry are not ontologically independent of possible or actual shapes that can be instantiated in corporeal substance. Descartes's view, like most early modern views about why geometry applies to actual physical space, depends on the claim that such shapes are essentially *possible* modes of matter, studied independently of whether they are actually instantiated. This dependence on possible modes of matter is, I think, an ontological dependence. Ontology in the early modern period was probably more centrally concerned with possibility than with actuality. So the objects of geometry are not ontologically independent of corporeal substance, in Descartes's view. An anti-individualist account of ideas and thoughts about geometric shapes would be committed to some dependency relation between the abstract shapes (the objects of geometrical reasoning) and having those ideas. If such objects of geometrical reasoning, the shapes, are not ontologically independent of (corporeal) extension, then thoughts and ideas about them are not ontologically independent either. If this line of reasoning is correct, Descartes should hold that having geometrical ideas is inessential to being a thinking mind.

What of arithmetical ideas, ideas of number? These, unlike geometrical ideas, Descartes does not associate essentially with physical substances or properties. He classes them with substance, duration, and order as 'items that extend to all classes of things'.[12] Ideas of number are independent of what they are applied to in counting (*Principles of Philosophy*, I, 55, 58.) It follows that they are independent of geometrical ideas. They would also not depend on some relation to space or physical reality to be what they are, inasmuch as they have a universal application.

I find this interesting. Despite his discovery of analytic geometry and his sophisticated use of algebra, Descartes joined the tradition, dominant since the Greek mathematicians, that held that geometry is more basic than arithmetic or algebra. Geometry was supposed to be the foundation of mathematics. (I shall return to this point in Section III.) But the exact sense in which it is foundational is important for our purposes. Descartes regarded proofs in geometry as necessary epistemic bases for some beliefs about number—for example, belief in the real numbers. But it is unclear to me how far this epistemic dependence was supposed to extend. It seems clear, however, that Descartes did not hold, as many mathematicians in his day did, that number is ontologically grounded in geometric proportions. As Frege noted, number, unlike geometrical lines and shapes, is applicable to all things (through sortals)—so to thoughts as well as bodies. Descartes seems to have anticipated this insight, although he would not have joined Frege in regarding numbers as among the commitments of logic or

---

[12] Cf. *Principles of Philosophy*, I, 48. Descartes also mentions common notions that apply cross-categorially in *Rules for the Direction of the Mind*, AT X, 419; in *The Philosophical Writings of Descartes*, I, trans. J. Cottingham, R. Stoothoff, and D. Murdoch (Cambridge: Cambridge University Press, 1984), 45. In the *Rules* passage, Descartes mentions existence, unity, duration as, common notions that are attributed 'indifferently, now to corporeal things, now to spirits'.

as being abstract, mind-independent objects. In any case, I think that Descartes, as anti-individualist, was free to regard the idea of number as essential to mind.

If ideas of both body and geometrical shape are inessential to mind, what remains? One could imagine a view that *no* particular thought- or idea-*types* are necessary for mind, as long as the mind has some thoughts and ideas. On this view, all specific intentional (or in Descartes's terminology, 'objective') content is contingent with respect to mind and minds.

Two versions of the position can be distinguished here. One is that the representational content (for Descartes, objective reality) of particular thoughts could be different while those thoughts as events (their 'formal reality')—and by extension the mind—remained the same. I think that, as a substantive view, this position is incoherent. Our only individuative grip on the identity of particular thoughts involves their intentional or representational content—primarily the concepts with which the thoughts represent referents.

The other version of the position is as follows. Although particular thoughts would be different if their contents were different, the mind is metaphysically independent for its identity not only from the identity of any particular thought events, but also from having any particular thought contents or idea-types. That is, there are *no* particular idea-types that a mind must have in order to be a mind. I will come back to the question of what the identity of mind would then consist in. But it would have to consist in something (perhaps a field of consciousness and some type of thinking or other) that is what it is independently of the content of any particular mental activity or process. For all particular thoughts, and all particular types of intentional content, would be contingent modes of a mind.

This second version holds that thinking is necessary to being a mind. It holds that it is not necessary that any particular kinds of thoughts be thought. And it holds that it is not necessary that a mind have any particular idea-types or concepts. This view simply denies that there are any thoughts, ideas, or concepts that are constitutively necessary and universal to all thinking minds. This is an interesting view, not obviously false, I think. Aristotle and Kant represent a tradition of maintaining that there are fundamental, universal categories of all thought. Their lists, which include a number of traditional metaphysical notions, have not persuaded many. There remains for some an inclination to think that having a few simple logical notions associated with negation, conjunction, and implication, perhaps simple arithmetical ideas, is necessary to being a thinking mind. I share such an inclination. Justifying it, however, is a difficult matter. Such a view must confront the variety of different 'non-standard' logics and the apparent possibility of taking different connectives as fundamental even within classical logic. As regards arithmetical notions, one must explain why thinking cannot proceed without sortals and counting, and getting by with mass concepts and notions of more and less.

I doubt that either of the positions just outlined is Descartes's. I believe it likely that Descartes held instead that having available to reflection the innate ideas <u>thought</u> and <u>God</u> is essential to being a mind. I think that Descartes believed that from the idea of <u>thought</u> (or <u>mind</u>) or of <u>God</u>, other ideas, such as those of objective reality and <u>cause</u> (and perhaps <u>substance</u>, <u>number</u>, <u>order</u>, <u>duration</u>) can be derived by reflection. I conjecture that knowledge associated with the *cogito* and the ontological argument are thought by Descartes to be necessarily available to any thinking mind. If he is an anti-individualist as well as a substance dualist, however, I think that he must hold that thoughts about the material world and about geometrical shapes are, though central to our actual mental histories, not essential to being a mind.

The view that thoughts and knowledge of mind and of God are more basic—in the sense of necessarily more fundamental to the essence of any thinking mind—than thoughts and knowledge of body and mathematics is, of course, deeply un-Kantian. As an account of all thinking minds, I find such a view unacceptable. Thoughts about thought, let alone thoughts about God, seem absent from some minds—the minds of animals and young children—that nevertheless think about body and can engage in simple counting.

On the other hand, I think that the closely related question whether thoughts of mind are *conceptually independent* of thoughts of body—and the question whether knowledge of mind is conceptually independent of knowledge of body—are more complicated than most neo-Kantian, post-Strawsonian discussion has suggested.

I have been discussing Descartes's dualist view of *mind* in the context of anti-individualism. I want to consider now his dualist view of *particular minds* in the same context. Descartes claims that one cannot conceive of mental substance without its principal attribute, thinking. As we have seen, this principal attribute must be regarded as independent of any particular thought events. What are particular minds for Descartes? And what more can be said about the principal attribute of minds?

If one regards the principal attribute, thinking, as a generic essence common to all minds, one must ask what individuates particular minds. I think that there is no evidence that Descartes thought of mental substances as immaterial 'soul stuff'. Understanding immaterial substances on such a model is in effect to treat them as material and immaterial at the same time. Such a view misses what is special about mind, and part of what is interesting about Descartes's dualism. Descartes's mental substances are not, I think, best construed as distinguished by a special kind of constitution or stuff.

There is reason to believe that Descartes saw the principal attribute of a mental substance as not (or not merely) generic and common to all mental substances, but as particular and concrete. Thus in a late letter to Arnauld, he writes:

I tried to remove the ambiguity of the word 'thought' in articles 63 and 64 of the first part of the *Principles*. Just as extension, which constitutes the nature of body, differs greatly from the various shapes or modes of extension which it may assume, so thought, or a thinking nature, which I think contributes the essence of human mind, is far different from any particular act of thinking. It depends on the mind itself whether it produces this or that particular act of thinking, but not that it is a thinking thing; just as it depends on a flame, as an efficient cause, whether it turns to this side or that, but not that it is an extended substance. So by 'thought' I do not mean some universal which includes all modes of thinking, but a particular nature, which takes on those modes, just as extension is a nature that takes on all shapes.[13]

I will discuss two issues raised by this passage.

First, the last sentence of the passage suggests that thinking is a nature that is particularized in the individual mind. Yet, in its particularity, it is seen as independent of any particular act of thinking. What could thinking be, so understood? It seems clear that thinking can be understood generically, as common to all particular acts of thinking. But what would thinking be, understood as both particular (or concrete) and independent of particular acts of thinking?

I reject as grotesque the idea that there is actual thinking independent of particular intentional or representational content. I see no reason to think Descartes was committed to such an idea. Perhaps, though, Descartes thought that something like a reflexive self-attribution, expressible as *I think*, implicitly attaches to every thought. All instances of such an attachment, somehow regarded as a continuous generative activity, might be seen to constitute the principal attribute of the mind, as a 'particular nature'. I think that this is the most promising starting point for understanding Descartes's notion. (Cf. *Principles of Philosophy*, I, 7–9.)

Compatibly, one might also take thinking, the 'particular nature', to be a reflexive *consciousness* or awareness. Such a view is at least loosely suggested in *Principles of Philosophy*, I, 9. This view would allow the field of consciousness to take on particular images and ideas as forms, on a loose analogy to matter taking on particular shapes. Perhaps the active element in Descartes's chosen description of the relevant particular nature—'thinking'—could be seen as necessarily conscious. So the relevant type of consciousness might be understood in terms of the reflexive self-consciousness, expressible as I think, mentioned above. The reflexive self-consciousness involved in the continuing I think is filled out by particular thoughts, which are themselves contingent modes of mind.

I would regard such a view as hyper-intellectualized if it were applied to all thinking minds. Animals and children think, but lack a concept of thinking. They do not think about thinking. I think that Descartes's own view is probably hyper-intellectualized. He would certainly not allow that animals think. He makes some concession in my direction by holding that the relevant consciousness or awareness is to be regarded as present in sensing as well as thinking (*Principles of Philosophy*, I, 9). But I do think it nearly certain that he thought that the idea thinking substance has to be available to every mind. I think this view

[13] Descartes to Arnauld, 29, July 1648, in Descartes, *Philosophical Letters*, trans. Anthony Kenny (Minneapolis: University of Minnesota Press, 1981). I am indebted to Deborah Brown for calling my attention to this passage.

mistaken. I also regard as mistaken Descartes's apparent view that minds must always, at all times, be both conscious and thinking or sensing, if they are to continue to exist.

Still, I think that Descartes's remarks about consciousness as an aspect of the nature of mind are worth reflecting upon if one considers consciousness at different levels of mind. In particular, I think that there are interesting issues about the relation between intellectual reflexive self-consciousness and ordinary phenomenal consciousness.[14] There are also interesting issues about the relation between reflexive consciousness in the activity of thinking (through implicit attachment of *I think* to thoughts) and consciousness of oneself as intellectual agent.

This brings me to the second issue from the quoted passage that I wish to discuss. There is an obscurity in Descartes over the relation between the mental agent and its agency—between the mind and its thinking. There is no obscurity about Descartes's view of the relation between mental substance and its particular contingent thoughts. Descartes is emphatic that the mind and its modes, its thinking events (whether active or passive), are to be distinguished.[15] But the matter is more problematic regarding the relation between mental substance and its principal attribute, thinking—especially inasmuch as thinking is considered a 'particular nature' in the individual thinker.

Neither a field of consciousness, nor reflexive consciousness in the form *I think*, nor whatever else thinking itself might be—*is* the mental agent. The agent is a being that engages in such reflexive acts, that has the relevant self-consciousness. To identify the agent with any of these would be to make a category mistake. An ontological view of mental substance that takes the agent simply to be entirely exhausted by its principal attribute, thinking, seems to me incoherent. Thinking must be the activity of a categorially distinct agent of thinking.

It is clear that Descartes is not committed to mental substances as bare particulars, or as having some further constitution, or stuff, beyond their thinking natures. Thinking is the principal essential attribute of the mind. No other essential property is, on his view, needed for the mind to be a substance. Neither the substance nor the attribute could exist or be understood without the other, and substance is known only through its principal attribute.

But Descartes speaks of the mind as 'producing' thoughts. He often seems to respect the distinction that I am emphasizing, by writing of the mind as a thinking thing. Moreover, as I have noted, he is very firm that particular thoughts, modes (contingent properties), are not the same as the thinking thing, the thinker or mind that does the thinking in particular cases. On the other hand, there are

---

[14] See my 'Reflections on Two Kinds of Consciousness' (Ch. 18 above).

[15] Cf. Descartes's reply to Hobbes's worry that Descartes had reduced the thinking agent to thinking—the second objection in the Third Set of Replies, in *Philosophical Writings of Descartes*, II, 122–124.

passages where he seems to identify thinking, as a principal attribute (essential property) and particular nature, with substance. (Cf. *Principles of Philosophy*, I, 63.) Some scholars have interpreted these passages in a way that risks attributing to Descartes the category mistake that I have warned about.[16]

In the passage quoted above, Descartes draws an analogy between thinking and a flame, which might be taken to suggest that thinking, considered as principal attribute, is a process that does not inhere in some further thing, a thinker. The other analogy, in the passage quoted, between thinking, as a principal attribute of the mind which can take on particular thoughts as modes, and material extension, which as a 'particular nature' can take on different shapes, raises similar worries. This analogy seems to leave no room for a further distinction between thinking, the attribute, and the mind, as agent—the thing that thinks. For in the case of the corporeal substance, the principal attribute, material extension, takes on further shapes as contingent modes; but there is no need to distinguish between this attribute and a further underlying substance. In my view, although reflexive consciousness, as principal attribute of the mind, might take on particular thoughts as contingent modes, reflexive consciousness (*I think*) must be the consciousness of an agent that has such consciousness.

Descartes's official account of the distinction between a substance and its principal attribute in the *Principles of Philosophy*, I, 60, 62, is not much help. In those passages, he discusses three relevant distinctions. First, he cites a *real distinction*, which holds between substances, which God could separate. Second, there is a distinction *regarding mode*, which holds between substances and their contingent properties or modes. Third, he mentions a *conceptual distinction* (or distinction in reason), which holds between a substance and an attribute of that substance without which the substance is unintelligible. Descartes says that the latter distinction is recognized in our inability to perceive clearly the idea of the substance if we exclude from it the attribute in question. This latter distinction holds between the thinking thing and thinking, its principal attribute construed presumably as a particular nature in the sense of the letter quoted above. Mental substance and its principle attribute are merely conceptually distinct, or distinct in reason, in this technical sense.

One might read 'merely conceptually distinct' (or 'distinct in reason') in a way that would require that thinking substance and its principal attribute are exactly the same at the ontological level, only thought about in different ways. This view seems, at least at first blush, to fall into attributing the mistake of identifying agent and act, when it is applied to thinking substance.

The view that the thinking agent can be understood essentially and purely in terms of its thinking seems to me interesting and characteristically Cartesian.

---

[16] There is a body of scholarly opinion that takes Descartes to hold that mental substance 'consists' in its principal attribute. As far as I know, however, the problem that I have been raising has not been addressed. For a brief discussion of this construal of Descartes, see Marleen Rozemond, *Descartes's Dualism* (Cambridge, Mass.: Harvard University Press, 1998), 8–12.

Such a view might resist the move of insisting on conceptual grounds that the agent have a further constitution, one more basic than its thinking.[17] But there remains the need to explicate some distinction between thinking agent and the activity of thinking. If there is no distinction between substance and principal attribute, indeed some ontological distinction, then Descartes is committed to a category mistake. The problem of making room for a distinction between an act and its agent (hence, in Descartes's scheme, between mental substance and its principal attribute, thinking) has no analog in the relation between bodily substance and its principal attribute, material extension.

I think that Descartes is in a position to solve this problem, *even if he identifies substance and attribute in some ontological sense.* The difference between the two principal attributes, material extension and thinking, itself seems to provide a basis for drawing the categorial distinction that I am after. If the principal attribute of a thinker, as a particular nature, is continuous reflexive self-consciousness, then the attribute itself, as expressed in I think, requires a distinction between thinker (what is indicated by *I*) and attribute (what is indicated by think). If this conjecture is right, then Descartes's account of thinking as a particular essential nature yields the desired asymmetry between the principal attributes of material and thinking substances.

Before leaving this point, I want to say a bit more about Descartes's conceptual distinction, or *distinction in reason,* mentioned above. This is a distinction that holds between any substance and its principal attribute. In a letter of about 1645, commenting on the distinction, Descartes states that conceptual distinctions, or distinctions in reason, must have a 'foundation in reality'.[18] Descartes contrasts conceptual distinctions, or distinctions in reason, with a distinction made purely by the mind—a *rationis ratiocinantes.* Descartes says that he does not recognize a *rationis ratiocinantes.* Traditionally, a purported example of this latter sort of distinction would be a distinction between *definiens* and *definiendum* in a real definition—between man and rational animal, for example. Descartes apparently would say that reason (as opposed to the language) draws no distinction in this case. Descartes denies that the distinction between substance and principal attribute is a distinction made purely by reason, and claims that the distinction has a foundation in reality.

Descartes seems to associate distinctions in reason with the distinction between essence and existence. In any given case, the essence of a corporeal body and the existence of the same body are for Descartes the same. Although the thought of Peter is different from the thought of humanity, 'in Peter himself,

---

[17] This is a move that Sellars pressed. I am not convinced by Sellars's view. I shall discuss the matter elsewhere. Cf. Wilfrid Sellars, 'This I or he or it (the thing) that thinks' (Presidential Address, *Proceedings of the American Philosophical Association,* 1970).

[18] Cf. Descartes, Letter to ***, 1645 or 1646, in Descartes, *Philosophical Letters,* 187. I owe this reference and useful discussion of this issue to Lilli Alanen. For discussion of the distinction, see her 'On Descartes' Argument for Dualism and the Distinction between Different Kinds of Beings', in S. Knuuttila and J. Hintikka (eds.), *The Logic of Being* (Dordrecht: Reidel, 1986).

being a man is nothing other than being Peter'. Similarly, in a corporeal substance, being an instance of material extension is nothing other than being the
corporeal substance. The essence can, however, be thought about independently
of the existence. And this difference in thought has a foundation in 'objective
reality' inasmuch as the difference in thought contents is not created by reason
(it is not a *rationis ratiocinantes*), but is grounded in objective ways of thinking.

Descartes's nominalism about natures prevents him from regarding this difference in 'objective reality' as being grounded in an ontology of universal
natures. I am not sure that with his thin nominalistic resources he can give a
satisfactory account of the objectivity (or 'foundation in reality') of the distinction between substance and attribute—an account of why the distinction in
thought is objective. In any case, I think that anti-individualism will require
him to say more than he does. But as far as I can see, he has the resources
to avoid the particular incoherence of identifying agent and agency that I have
been worrying about.

There remains, of course, the notorious question—pressed by Kant in the
Paralogisms section of *Critique of Pure Reason*—as to how, in the context of
his substance dualism, Descartes individuates *individual minds*. Suppose that
we do allow that there is an agent of thought, and (for the sake of argument)
that this is the fundamental mind substance. What is it about this agent that
individualizes it? Not the particular thoughts it thinks. They could be different
while the agent remains the same. Not the general attribute of thought. That
is common to different thinking agents. There is no evidence that Descartes
appeals to 'mental stuff'. As noted, such an appeal would lose the insight that
mind is deeply different from body. It would miss the role of intentionality and
point of view in making thinking agents what they are. There is the neo-Kantian
route of demanding a body as a necessary condition for individuating a mind.
The arguments for that view are tantalizing, but I do not think them decisive. At
any rate, given his dualism, Descartes cannot appeal to the brain or to 'external'
physical objects to help individuate particular mental substances.

Is there any way to think coherently about the individuation problem purely
from the point of view of Descartes's version of dualism? Perhaps one should
take seriously Descartes's apparent tack of simply regarding individuation of
particular minds as primitive: We individuate a mind by conceiving it as an agent
of particular mental acts. The same mind could have produced other thoughts
instead. We count a mind the same by reference to some type of continuity of
a changing point of view. (I would insist that the agent has not only conscious
active thinking, but powers, faculties, concepts, and other mental dispositions
that are present even when mental activity is not.) I believe that Descartes may
be on to something important in regarding thinkers as consisting not in some
special sort of stuff, but in particular instances of the special type of agency,
power, consciousness, and point of view involved in thinking.

What is interesting and challenging here is to explain why immaterial *constitution* and bodily *constitution* are not basic—and why the aforesaid mentalistic

features are the basic properties of minds or thinkers. A central challenge for a serious dualism should be to explain why the *fundamental* sortals can be activity sortals rather than constitution sortals. Another Kantian challenge is to show that a continuous thinker can be made sense of, using only mentalistic concepts. Whether or not these challenges can be met, I believe that reflection on these issues has so far not exhausted all possibility of progress. Descartes's dualism seems to me more interesting than traditional caricatures of it allow.

I have no interest in reviving a substance dualism, where 'substance' is taken in the old-fashioned sense—requiring complete ontological independence from anything else in the same ontologically basic category. I am not sure that *anything* is a substance in the old-fashioned sense. It is not obvious to me, however, that it is mistaken to suppose that mental agents and their mental powers, acts, and states are in no literal sense physical.

For the present, I am impressed with anti-individualistic elements in Descartes's account of mind. I think that anti-individualism is prima facie compatible with some form of dualism. These are profound historical and substantive issues that need more development.

III

I mentioned earlier that Descartes's appeal to God and his austere conception of physical reality may have played a role in his having so little to say about the detailed ways in which our thoughts depend for their individuation on particular relations to aspects of the physical environment. There is much to discuss here that I will not have space to go into. But I want to make a few remarks about Descartes's conception of physical reality, and of our ways of referring to it. In my view, Descartes's conception of physical reality and of our reference to it is much more different from ours than his conception of mental reality and of our ways of referring to *it*.

Descartes's conception of the ways we might fall into error is a perpetual challenge to attempts to answer scepticism.[19] He is sensitive to the fact that some of our representations are composites of other representations (griffins, satyrs). He challenges us to distinguish the representations that apply to genuine realities from implicitly composite ones that do not. Moreover, he is aware that some of our sensory systems are geared not to detect objects and properties as they really are, but rather to signal contrasts and changes that are potentially

---

[19] Normore speculates that I would say that in the 'Ur Demon world' all our thoughts are about the demon or about ourselves. He holds that Descartes would say that we have no general thoughts at all because there are no natures. What I would say depends on a more detailed account of the relation between the demon and us and of how the demon purportedly thinks. I am not committed to disagreeing with Descartes on this matter.

relevant to our survival or other practical needs.[20] Again he challenges us to distinguish veridical perception from practically useful but epistemically unreliable perception, and objective detection from practically useful sensory signals that do not function to detect objective properties at all. These points go very deep. They enrich the sceptic's arsenal in ways that are often not adequately appreciated today. Scepticism is not our primary topic, but some remarks on Descartes's view of reference to physical reality will enrich our discussion of his relation to anti-individualism.

Descartes's view of reference is, as far as I understand it, simpler than mine. I think it too simple. He tends to see unsuccessful reference with kind concepts as the result of our making, perhaps unconsciously, a fictitious combination out of basic ideas for simple natures or out of parts of simple natures. The idea of a satyr is a prime example.[21] There are, however, other ways of making referential errors with kind concepts—ways that Descartes does not seem to recognize. The concept phlogiston does not seem to be a composite built out of representations for simple natures. It is the product of an explanatory theory that is constitutively dependent not on combination from simpler elements, but on an inference from observational beliefs.

Descartes might, of course, extend the notion of combination to this case. He might insist that although we may not think that the concept of phlogiston is composite, it nevertheless is. But the notion of composition or combination would then seem to be so flexible as not to be very informative. I see no evidence that Descartes made use of what we now think of as scientific theoretical explanatory inference in his account of concept formation.

My colleague Calvin Normore holds that Descartes thinks that reference succeeds only when the explanatory cause of the mental event is the same as the explanatory cause of the content of the mental event (its objective reality). In such a case, the cause is identified with the referent. Whether or not it is Descartes's view, this view, too, appears to incorporate too simple a causal picture. A Martian scientist could refer to H_2O even though he or she bore no causal relation to H_2O and did not bear causal relations to all the factors postulated in the theory. Suppose that the scientist has causal relations to oxygen and hydrogen and, despite lacking any experimental causal relation to the particular sort of bonding connection between them, guesses or hypothesizes—near enough—the correct bonding relation. Then the object of the idea, H_2O, is not the explanatory cause of either the representational content or the mental event.

---

[20] For a recent discussion of empirical aspects of this point, see Kathleen Akins, 'Of Sensory Systems and the "Aboutness" of Mental States', *The Journal of Philosophy*, 93 (1996), 337–372.

[21] I take it that Normore is right that simple natures, for Descartes, do not include human or goat bodies. Although the ontological status of ordinary bodies is obscure, it seems to me that Descartes's satyr example in *Meditation* I is meant to exemplify a primary sort of error. Satyr representations are made up of parts that veridically apply to the simpler natures. The simpler elements one most immediately thinks of (human heads and torsos, goat legs) are not genuinely natures, but can be regarded as such for the sake of illustration. Ultimately the real simple natures are parts of extension.

Moreover, there is no straightforward sense in which the cause of the mental event is the same as the explanatory cause of its representational content. I do not see that explanations of psychological events and explanations of representational content are likely to track one another—in the simple way that Descartes seems to expect—in the case of complex theorizing.[22]

Nothing depends here on the referent's being a compound. It could be an element or even a type of elementary particle. A scientist could correctly postulate and refer to such kinds, without having a causal relation to their instances. Descartes might not have counted particles, elements, or compounds as genuine elements of the world—as simple natures. The paradigm for him is geometrically shaped matter. But I do not see that he has the resources to form a plausible account of how we come into a referential relation to actual physical kinds that we now recognize as kinds and to which we bear no causal or perceptual relations. The tools of perceptual, or quasi-perceptual, reference and combination seem inadequate to the task. Descartes may have thought that our only genuine referential relation to simple natures was quasi-perceptual.

One might maintain that given Descartes's austere and simple view of elementary natures and of the ways they relate to one another to form complexes (basically part–whole ways), he can afford to rely on his simple account of reference. Everyone has had causal relations to chunks of matter and to part–whole relations. Assuming that all geometrically possible combinations are innately available to our mathematical intuition, perhaps Descartes can hold that it is safe to assume that we bear causal relations to all the genuine constituents and have access to all the genuine relations needed to form all kinds that we in fact have ideas of. Then my objection would be to his ontology, which I shall discuss shortly.

I think that Descartes's over-simple account of reference is associated with his seeing all representation as a sort of perception, or a combination of perceptions. This picture underlies the tendency to see reference to an object or kind as dependent on causal relations to *that* object, or else 'combinations' of representations each of which bears causal relations to an object. I see Descartes as relying too little on discursive elements in concept formation (and hence conceptual reference)—elements that Kant and Frege emphasized.

It may seem surprising that Descartes was guided by such a picture, given his focus on the mathematicization of nature. The picture was encouraged by a venerable but now dated conception of mathematics. Although Descartes's unification of geometry and algebra began the process that eventually freed mathematics for a more abstract view of its subject matter, Descartes joined a dominant tradition, which ran even into Newton's early mathematical practice and motivated Kant's philosophy of mathematics, of seeing geometry as epistemically basic in mathematics. Geometry was supposed to be an abstraction from

---

[22] I cite such a case in my 'Other Bodies', in A. Woodfield (ed.), *Thought and Object* (Oxford: Oxford University Press, 1982) (Ch. 4. above).

our perceptual experience of objects in space. Thus Descartes seems to have seen the methods of mathematics as quasi-perceptual at their basics, with an attendant abstraction from empirical assumptions of actual existence.[23] Descartes saw geometry as studying the shapes of the physical world, with no presumption that they were actually materially instantiated.[24]

Both mathematics and the use of mathematics in physics have become increasingly independent of their geometrical origins. The progressively more abstract conceptions of mathematics and of physical explanation have forced a more complex picture of the representation of physical reality. The recognition that representation and mathematicization of physical reality can be tied to perception in only very loose and complex ways, involving theoretical explanatory inference, has been forced on us by these developments in the physical and mathematical sciences.[25]

Descartes's difficulty with theoretical reference to physical kinds that one bears no causal relation to was hidden by two elements of his philosophy. One is his extremely austere physical ontology, which admits only geometrical forms of matter as simple physical natures. Such an ontology seems to disallow not only nearly all commonsense macro-objects but even most of the natural kinds of present-day science. The other element is his tendency to blur the distinction between mathematical and physical kinds. Given the austere ontology, he did not need to worry about the sorts of theoretical kinds that I have mentioned. Given his view of physical kinds as being instances of geometrical kinds, he could believe that all the relevant basic kinds are available to perception informed by geometrical structures. More complicated kinds are constructible by geometrical reasoning from the simpler ones. But Descartes regards even the results of construction ultimately in quasi-perceptual terms rather than in terms of proof or formal construction.[26]

It must be said that an analog of the problem that I have raised for Descartes regarding reference to theoretical physical kinds faces us today. Once a modern distinction between mathematics and physics is in place, one needs to account for reference to mathematical objects (or functions) that are not in any straightforward sense physical properties. We have no causal relations to the objects. I think that we cannot plausibly help ourselves to the idea of a theoretical explanatory

---

[23] John A. Shuster, 'Descartes' *Mathesis Universalis*, 1619–28', in Stephen Gaukroger (ed.), *Descartes: Philosophy, Mathematics, and Physics* (Brignton: Harvester, 1980); Stephen Gaukroger, 'Descartes' Project for a Mathematical Physics', ibid. To Descartes's credit, he came to place less and less emphasis on the role of images in mathematical thinking.

[24] Descartes, *Conversations with Burman*, AT X, 160; *Descartes' Conversations with Burman*, ed. John Cottingham (Oxford: Clarendon Press, 1976), 23. Cf. *Meditations*, VI, AT VIII, 79–80.

[25] I believe that representation of most mathematical reality is in principle independent of perception, not only for its justification but also for individuation of its content. This is a complex issue that I will not pursue here.

[26] Cf. Ian Hacking, 'Leibniz and Descartes: Proof and Eternal Truths', *Proceedings of the British Academy*, 59 (1973), 4–16.

inference from perceptual references that are grounded causally. Cartesian mathematical perception of geometrical properties does not seem viable either, as a full account of reference to mathematical objects. Geometry is not a foundation for all mathematics. Moreover, pure geometry itself can no longer be seen to concern physical space directly. I think that accounting for mathematical knowledge and mathematical reference requires notions that Descartes did not employ. It requires notions of objective formal structures that inform thought and reason, and rational commitment to entities associated with these formal structures—a commitment that is implicit in the very practice of mathematical reasoning. This is a complex matter whose exploration is not in place here.

My difference with Descartes about reference is, as I have mentioned, associated with a difference with his conception of physical reality. As I have noted, Descartes has an extremely austere conception of physical reality. For him, physical reality is made up of extension and parts of extension. This is an impoverished conception even of the world of physics. The subsequent history of physics, beginning with Newton's recognition of forces as fundamental and continuing with the addition of dynamical and field relations to mechanical ones in the nineteenth and early twentieth centuries, has made Descartes's conception seem even more impoverished than it did to his contemporaries. Moreover, I do not accept Descartes's apparent reduction of physical reality to physics. There are chemical and biological kinds that are fundamental natural kinds.

Equally important, there are ordinary physical kinds that do not fit neatly into the sciences; and there are perceptible, artifactual, and social kinds that Descartes tends to treat as modes, or perhaps even constructs, acceptable in everyday practical life but unacceptable as basic in a serious account of reality. I take clouds, rainbows, brisket, rocks, the North Sea, arthritis, redness, shadows, cracks, rough-texturedness, sounds, cold, sofas, clothes, symphonies, the United States—as well as human bodies—to be kinds or individual entities that need not be reduced to parts of extension or of matter or to sequences of collections of particles. And they are not mere projections of our minds. Yet all of these are kinds or properties of *physical entities*, with the possible exception of symphonies and the United States.

My colleague Calvin Normore goes so far as to suggest that Descartes believes that we make such kinds in the sense that we 'project' 'principles of unity' for them. (I am not convinced by this reading of Descartes, incidentally. But there is no question that Descartes thought that such objects have *some* kind of ontologically secondary status.) Here again, I think that it is a mistake to think that such objects or kinds are 'ideal' or merely practical. I do not agree that they are in any sense constructed by us. Of course, most *artifacts* are dependent on our intentionally making them, causing them to come into existence more or less according to some plan. Once made, the artifacts are what they are, regardless of how we regard them. An amplifier is not a kind of thing only by courtesy of our 'projecting' a principle of unity whose reality lies entirely in our projection.

We fix on and represent kinds, features, and relations in the world. Often our representations reflect interests and needs special to us. One should not, however, conclude that since we represent a pattern only because it corresponds to some need or interest of ours that the pattern is a product or projection from our needs or representational abilities. The world is made up of individuals that instantiate a rich, hierarchical, cross-quilt of patterns made up of properties, relations, kinds. Science deals with those that submit to explanatory systematization that is relatively deep. A pattern, however, is, not less real for being local, or for being perceptible only by certain sensory modalities, or for being constitutively dependent on causal processes that do not fall under the systematic principles of some science. It seems to me that it is a mistake to regard reality fundamentally in terms of law. The unities and similarities that we make use of are for the most part quite independent of us, even where they are of special interest to us, and might be of no interest to some other species.

Even if Descartes does not hold the sort of conventionalism that Normore attributes to him (as I suspect he does not), his reductionistic picture of physical kinds is, I think, unacceptable. I believe that Descartes's view of physical reality can be seen, in retrospect, to be one of the more flamboyant, though in a certain way admirable, products of intellectual hubris. It is no longer a rationally warranted view of the physical world. Accepting the variety of types of concept formation and reference, and the variety of types of physical kinds in the world, calls for a more complex account of the individuation of mental kinds than Descartes gives. I am inclined to think that Descartes was an anti-individualist, but that because of his simple view of reference and of physical reality, he did not see it as a challenge worthy of his considerable powers to elaborate the doctrine of anti-individualism. I think that this is one reason why it is so hard to find clear and determinate statements of anti-individualism in his work. It remains a matter of judgment, rather than textual proof, that Descartes was an anti-individualist.

20 *Philosophy of Mind: 1950–2000*

I want to outline some of the main developments in the philosophy of mind in the last half of the twentieth century.[1]

Behaviorism dominated psychology during approximately the same period that logical positivism dominated philosophy. The principles of behaviorism are less easily stated than those of logical positivism. It is perhaps better seen as a method that eschewed use of mentalistic vocabulary in favor of terms that made reference to dispositions to behavior. Both movements aimed at banishing nonscientific speculation, and forcing theory to hew as closely as possible to methods of confirmation. Both methodological doctrines came to be seen as restrictive, even on the practice of science.

Behaviorism had a run of influence within philosophy. It was a favored view of some of the later positivists. They made use of the verificationist principle to attempt to dissolve the mind–body problem and the problem of other minds, declaring these problems meaningless. And they appealed to behavioral analyses of mentalistic terms as a way of maintaining strict experimental control on mentalistic language. The simplistic picture of confirmation associated with the verificationist principle, a picture that ignored the role of auxiliary hypotheses, paralleled and abetted the behaviorist blindness to the role of background assumptions in mentalistic attributions. As we shall see, this blindness led to the collapse of behaviorism.

In postwar, postpositivistic philosophy, the early logical constructionists thought that behavioristic language was the most suitable way to 'reconstruct' mentalistic language in scientific terms. Ordinary-language philosophers purported to find behavioristic underpinnings for ordinary language. Behaviorism influenced positivistic construals of psychology, Quine's theory of the indeterminacy

[1] This article consists mostly of the second half of my article 'Philosophy of Language and Mind, 1950–1990', *The Philosophical Review*, 101 (1992), 3–51. I have added further material that concentrates on the last decade of the century. I present a historical overview pitched to nonspecialists. The scope of the article has, of course, led to omission of many important topics—for example, personal identity, action theory, the innateness of mental structures, knowledge of language, the nature of psychological explanation, the nature of concepts, many strands in the mind–body problem, and the legacy of Wittgenstein. I am grateful to Ned Block, Susan Carey, and the editors of *The Philosophical Review* for good advice.

of translation, Ryle's work on the concept of mind, and Malcolm's explications of discourse about dreaming and sensations.[2] These philosophers shared a tendency to think that theorizing in psychology or philosophy of mind should dispense with mentalistic vocabulary, or interpret it in nonmentalistic terms, as far as possible. They thought that such vocabulary should be largely replaced with talk about stimulations and about dispositions to behavior. Some philosophers thought that ordinary mentalistic terms could be defined or adequately explicated (for any cognitively respectable purpose) in these latter terms. Others thought that ordinary mentalistic terms were hopelessly unscientific or philosophically misleading, so no real explication was possible.

The demise of behaviorism in philosophy is less easily attributed to a few decisive events than is the fall of logical positivism. There were a series of influential criticisms of behaviorism beginning in the late 1950s and extending on for a decade.[3] The main cause of the shift seemed, however, to be a gradually developed sense that behaviorist methods were unduly restrictive and theoretically unfruitful. A similar development was unfolding within psychology, linguistics, and computer science, with an array of nonbehaviorist articles in the late 1950s and early 1960s.[4]

The attempts to provide behavioristic *explications* of mentalistic terms fell prey to various instances of a single problem. The behavioristic explications succeeded only on the implicit assumption that the individual had certain background beliefs or wants. As a crude illustration, consider an explication of belief as a disposition to assert. Even ignoring the fact that 'assert' is not a behavioral notion, but presupposes assumptions about mind and meaning, the analysis could work only with the proviso that the subject wants to express his beliefs and knows what they are. Eliminating these mentalistic background assumptions proved an impossible task, given behaviorist methodological strictures.

---

[2] Gilbert Ryle, *The Concept of Mind* (London: Hutchison, 1949); Norman Malcolm, *Dreaming* (London: Routledge & Kegan Paul, 1959); W. V. Quine, *Word and Object* (Cambridge, Mass.: MIT Press, 1960).

[3] Roderick Chisholm, *Perceiving* (Ithaca, NY: Cornell University Press, 1957), ch. 11; Peter Geach, *Mental Acts* (London: Routledge, 1957), ch. 1; Noam Chomsky, review of *Verbal Behavior*, by B. F. Skinner, *Language*, 35 (1959), 26–58, repr. in J. A. Fodor and J. Katz (eds.), *The Structure of Language* (Englewood Cliffs, NJ: Prentice-Hall, 1964) Hilary Putnam, 'Brains and Behavior' (1963), in *Philosophical Papers*, ii (Cambridge: Cambridge University Press, 1975); Jerry Fodor, *Psychological Explanation* (New York: Random House, 1968).

[4] In psychology: George Miller, 'The Magic Number 7 Plus or Minus Two: Some Limits on Our Capacity for Processing Information', *Psychological Review*, 63 (1956), 81–97; J. Bruner, J. Goodnow, and G. Austin, *A Study of Thinking* (New York: John Wiley, 1956); G. Miller, E. Galanter, and K. Pribram, *Plans and the Structure of Behavior* (New York: Holt, Rinehart & Winston, 1960); G. Sperling, 'The Information Available in Brief Visual Presentations', *Psychological Monographs*, 24 (1960); Ulrich Neisser, 'The Multiplicity of Thought', *British Journal of Psychology*, 54 (1963), 1–14; M. I. Posner, 'Immediate Memory in Sequential Tasks', *Psychology Bulletin*, 60 (1963), 333–349; S. Sternberg, 'High-Speed Scanning in Human Memory', *Science*, 153 (1966), 652–654. In linguistics: Noam Chomsky, *Syntactic Structures* (The Hague: Mouton, 1957). In computer science: A. Newell, J. C. Shaw, and H. A. Simon, 'Elements of a Theory of Human Problem Solving', *Psychological Review*, 65 (1958), 151–166.

The problem, stated less methodologically, is that mental causes typically have their behavioral effects only because of their interactions with one another.

As behaviorism slipped from prominence in philosophy in the 1950s and early 1960s, it left two heirs, which gradually formed an uneasy alliance. One of these heirs was naturalism. The other was functionalism.

A doctrine I will call 'naturalism' (and sometimes called 'physicalism') emerged first as a distinctive point of view in the philosophy of mind in the early 1950s. This view maintains two tenets. One is that there are no mental states, properties, events, objects, sensations over and above ordinary physical entities, entities identifiable in the physical sciences or entities that common sense would regard as physical. The formulation's vague expression 'over and above' matches the doctrine's vagueness: the doctrine does not entail an identity theory in ontology. It does require some sort of materialism about the mind. Naturalism coupled this ontological position with an ideological or methodological demand. It demanded that mentalistic discourse be reduced, explained, or eliminated in favor of discourse that is 'acceptable', or on some views already found, in the natural or physical sciences. Thus, we find repeated calls for 'explaining' rationality or intentionality. In its materialism, naturalism emphasized ontology in a way that behaviorism did not. Its ideological program, however, continued the behaviorist attempt to make psychology and philosophy of mind more scientific by limiting the supposed excesses of mentalism.

Many of the later logical positivists were naturalists. But issues about mind tended to be submerged in the general positivist program. The mind–body problem began to receive direct attention from a naturalistic point of view in articles by Quine, Place, and Smart, in the 1950s.[5] Place and Smart tried to identify mental states and events—primarily sensations and after images—with physical states and events. Smart thought that one could identify types of sensations in a 'topic-neutral' way that would leave it open whether they were physical; he then predicted that each type of sensation would turn out to be a neural state of some kind. For example, he paraphrased 'I am having an afterimage of an orange' as 'I am in a state like the one I am in when I am seeing an orange'. He thought that this translation would overcome any conceptual obstacles to identifying mental states with physical states. It would sidestep, for example, issues about the qualitative properties of afterimages. Science was supposed to settle the mind–body problem empirically—in favor of what came to be known as *type–type identity theory*, or *central state materialism*.

During the mid to late 1960s materialism became one of the few orthodoxies in American philosophy. It is difficult to say why this happened. No single

[5] W. V. Quine, 'On Mental Entities' (1952), in *The Ways of Paradox* (New York: Random House, 1966); U. T. Place, 'Is Consciousness a Brain Process?', *British Journal of Psychology*, 47 (1956), 44–50; J. J. C. Smart, 'Sensations and Brain Processes', *The Philosophical Review*, 68 (1959), 141–156.

argument obtained widespread acceptance. Perhaps the success in biochemistry during the 1950s in providing some sense of the chemical underpinnings of biological facts encouraged the expectation that eventually mental facts would receive a similar explication in neural terms. Moreover, there were some spectacular advances in animal neurophysiology during the period.[6] Perhaps the attempts of the positivists and behaviorists to make philosophy scientific had as a natural outgrowth the view that philosophical problems would eventually be solved by progress in the natural sciences—with the help of analytical clarification by philosophers. In any case, several philosophers in the 1960s defended either some form of the type–type identity theory or some form of eliminationism (the view that mentalistic talk and mental entities would eventually lose their place in our attempts to describe and explain the world).[7]

The most influential paper of this period was written several years before: Sellars's 'Empiricism and the Philosophy of Mind' (1956). The article is a grand attempt to portray mental episodes as explanatory posits that hold a place in our conceptual scheme by virtue of their explanatory usefulness.[8] Sellars tried to undermine the view that knowledge of one's own mental events is intrinsically poses an obstacle to the empirical discovery that mental events are neural events. Although in my view the argumentation in this paper is not satisfyingly clear or convincing, the picture it paints of the status of mentalistic discourse is profoundly conceived.

Whereas materialism became widely accepted during the 1960s, issues surrounding naturalism's ideological demand remained intensely controversial. Putnam raised a serious objection to type-type identity theories of the sort that Smart had made popular. He suggested that it is implausible that a sensation like pain is identical with a single neural state in all the many organisms that feel pain, in view of their enormously varied physiologies. He also pointed out that it is even more implausible to think that any given type of thought—for example, a thought that thrice 3 is 9 or a thought that one's present situation is dangerous—is realized by the same physical state in every being that thinks it. Not only the probable existence of extraterrestrials, the variety of higher

[6] J. Y. Lettvin *et al.*, 'What the Frog's Eye Tells the Frog's Brain', *Proceedings of the Institute of Radio Engineers*, 47 (1959), 1940–1951; D. H. Hubel and T. N. Wiesel, 'Receptive Fields of Single Neurones in the Cat's Striate Cortex', *Journal of Physiology*, 148 (1959), 574–591; Hubel and Wiesel, 'Receptive Fields, Binocular Interaction, and Functional Architecture in the Cat's Visual Cortex', *Journal of Physiology* (London), 160 (1962), 106–154.

[7] The central state identity theory is defended in D. M. Armstrong, *A Materialist Theory of the Mind* (London: Routledge & Kegan Paul, 1968); David Lewis, 'An Argument for the Identity Theory', *The Journal of Philosophy*, 63 (1966), 17–25. Eliminative materialism, which derives from Quine, is defended in Paul Feyerabend, 'Materialism and the Mind–Body Problem', *The Review of Metaphysics*, 17 (1963), 49–66; Richard Rorty, 'Mind–Body Identity, Privacy, and Categories', *The Review of Metaphysics*, 19 (1965), 24–54; and Daniel Dennett, *Content and Consciousness* (New York: Routledge & Kegan Paul, 1969). Many of these works, and several other significant ones, are collected in O'Connor (ed.), *Modern Materialism: Readings on Mind–Body Identity* (New York: Harcourt, Brace, and World, 1969).

[8] In Wilfrid Sellars, *Science, Perception, and Reality* (London: Routledge & Kegan Paul, 1963).

animals, and the possibility of thinking robots (a possibility most materialists were eager to defend), but the plasticity of the brain seemed to make the type–type identity theory untenable.[9] Mental states seemed 'multirealizable'. Materialism maintained its dominance, but needed a new form. Putnam observation seemed to show that if mentalistic discourse was to be explicated in 'scientifically acceptable' terms, the terms would have to be more abstract than neural terms.

Responses to Putnam's observation led to a more specific materialist orthodoxy. The response proceeded on two fronts: ontological and ideological. Most materialists gave up the type–type identity theory in favor of an ontology that came to be known as the token identity theory. Although a mental state- or event-kind was not identified with any one physical (neural) kind, each instance of a mental state and each particular mental event token was held to be identical with some instance of a physical state or with some physical event token. This claim allowed that the occurrence of a thought that thrice 3 is 9 could be identical with the occurrence of one sort of physical event in one person, whereas a different occurrence of the same kind of thought could be identical with the occurrence of a different sort of physical event in another person.

Although this ontological position is still widely maintained, no one argument for it has gained wide acceptance. The commonest consideration adduced in its favor is its supposed virtue in simplifying our understanding of mind–body causation. Davidson gave a profound but controversial apriori argument along these lines.[10] He held, first, that there are causal relations between mental and physical events; second, that causal relations between events must be backed by laws of a complete, closed system of explanation ('backed' in the sense that the predicates of the laws must be true of the events that are causally related); third, that there are no psycho-physical or purely mentalistic laws that form a complete, closed system of explanation. He concluded that since there can be no psycho-physical or mentalistic laws that would provide the relevant backing for the causal relations between mental and physical events, there must be purely physical laws that back such relations. This is to say that physical predicates apply to mental events—that mental events are physical.

Davidson has not been ideally clear or constant in formulating and arguing for the third premise. But given the conception of 'complete, closed system' that he usually adverts to, this premise seems plausible. The second premise is more doubtful. I do not think it apriori true, or even clearly a heuristic principle of science or reason, that causal relations must be backed by any particular kind

[9] Hilary Putnam, 'The Nature of Mental States' (1967), in *Philosophical Papers*, ii; Ned Block and Jerry Fodor 'What Psychological States Are Not', *The Philosophical Review*, 81 (1972), 159–181.

[10] Donald Davidson, 'Mental Events' (1970), in *Essays on Actions and Events* (Oxford: Clarendon Press, 1980).

of law. I think that we learn the nature and scope of laws (and the variety of sorts of 'laws') that back causal relations through empirical investigation. It is not clear that psycho-physical counterfactual generalizations—or nonstrict 'laws'—cannot alone 'back' psychophysical causal relations.

Most philosophers accepted the token identity theory as the simplest account that both reconciled materialism with multirealizability and raised no metaphysical issues about mind–body causation. Insofar as the view rests on the hope of finding empirical correlations between types that would inductively support token identities, however, it seems highly speculative. Some philosophers adopted an even more liberal materialism. They held, roughly, that although an instance of a mental event kind may not be an instance of a physical natural kind, they are always *constituted* of events that are instances of physical natural kinds.[11]

In any case, materialism in one form or another has widespread support among North American philosophers, largely on grounds of its supposed virtues in interpreting causation between mental and physical events. There is a vague sense abroad that alternatives amount to superstition. One common idea is that there is some intrinsic mystery in seeing mental events, imagined as nonphysical, as interacting with physical events. Descartes thought this too; and perhaps there was some plausibility to it, given his conceptions of mental and physical substance. But Cartesian conceptions of substance are not at issue nowadays, and the exact nature of the problem in its modern form needs clearer articulation than it is usually given.

A better-reasoned argument along these lines goes as follows. Macrophysical effects depend on prior macrophysical states or events according to approximately deterministic patterns described by physical laws. Mental causes often give rise to physical movements of human bodies. If such causation did not consist in physical processes, it would yield departures from the approximately deterministic patterns described by physical laws. It would interfere with, disrupt, alter, or otherwise 'make a difference' in the physical outcomes. But there is no reason to think that this occurs. Physical antecedent states seem to suffice for the physical effects. Appeal to mentalistic causation that does not consist in physical causation appears, on this reasoning, to invoke physically ungrounded causation that requires us to doubt the adequacy of current forms of physical explanation, even within the physical realm. Not surprisingly, such invocation is widely thought to be unattractive.

---

[11] Geoffrey Hellman and Frank Wilson Thompson, 'Physicalist Materialism', *Noûs*, 11 (1977), 309–345; Richard Boyd, 'Materialism without Reductionism: What Physicalism Does Not Entail', in Ned Block (ed.), *Readings in Philosophy of Psychology*, i (Cambridge, Mass.: Harvard University Press, 1980). Another source of reformulations of materialism has been the discussion of supervenience principles. Cf. Jaegwon Kim, 'Causality, Identity, and Supervenience in the Mind–Body Problem', *Midwest Studies in Philosophy*, 4 (1979), 31–50. It is worth noting, however, that supervenience of the mental on the physical does not entail materialism.

This reasoning—and other parallel arguments focusing on the effect of physical processes on mental states—has some force, perhaps enough to nourish materialism indefinitely. But I think that materialism merits more scepticism than it has received in North American philosophy during the last two decades. At any rate, the argument just outlined is not as forceful as it may appear.

Why should mental causes of physical effects interfere with the physical system if they do not *consist in* physical processes? Thinking that they must surely depends heavily on thinking of mental causes on a physical model—as providing an extra 'bump' or transfer of energy on the physical effect. In such a context, instances of 'overdetermination'—two causes having the same effect—must seem to be aberrations. But whether the physical model of mental causation is appropriate is part of what is at issue. Moreover, the sense in which mental causes must 'make a difference' if they do not consist in physical processes is in need of substantial clarification. There are many ways of specifying differences they do make that do not conflict with physical explanations.

It seems to me that we have substantial reason, just from considering mentalistic and physicalistic explanatory goals and practice—before ontology is even considered—to think that mentalistic and physicalistic accounts of causal processes will not interfere with one another. They appeal to common causes (in explaining the physiology and psychology of cognitive processes, for example) and common or at least constitutively related effects (in physiological and psychological explanations of an instance of a man's running to a store, for example). It seems to me perverse, independently of ontological considerations, to assume that these explanations might interfere with one another. They make too few assumptions about one another to allow such an assumption.

There are surely *some* systematic, even necessary, relations between mental events and underlying physical processes. It seems overwhelmingly plausible that mental events depend on physical events in some way or other. But constitution, identity, and physical composition are relations that have specific scientific uses in explaining relations between entities invoked in physical chemistry and biochemistry. These relations so far have no systematic use in nonmetaphysical, scientific theories bridging psychology and neurophysiology. They seem to me to be just one set of possibilities for accounting for relations between entities referred to in these very different explanatory enterprises. Where science does not make clear use of such relations, philosophy should postulate them with some diffidence.

The apparent fact that there are no gaps in physical chains of causation and that mental causes do not disrupt the physical system is perhaps ground for some sort of broad supervenience thesis—no changes in mental states without some sort of change in physical states. But the inference to materialism is, I think, a metaphysical speculation that has come, misleadingly, to seem a relatively obvious scientific-commonsensical bromide.

The issue of mind–body causation is extremely complex and subtle. In recent years, this issue has become an object of intense interest. Much of the discussion concerns 'epiphenomenalism'.[12] The causal picture that motivates materialism is so firmly entrenched that many philosophers have come to worry that mental 'aspects' of events really do not 'make a difference': Maybe mental 'aspects' or properties are causally inert and just go along for a ride on physical properties of physical events, in something like the way that relations between phenotypal properties of parents and their offspring ride inertly and parasitically on underlying causal relations characterized by the genetic properties of parents and offspring. I think that these worries can be answered, even within a materialist framework. But I think that the very existence of the worries is the main point of philosophical interest. The worry about epiphenomenalism is, in my view, a sign that materialist theories have done a poor job of accounting for the relation between mind–body causal interaction and mentalistic explanation. They have done little to account for the fact that virtually all our knowledge and understanding of the nature and existence of mental causation derives from mentalistic explanations, not from nonintentional functionalist or neurological accounts.[13]

We determine the nature of the causation, and the sort of laws or law-like generalizations that accompany it, by scrutinizing actual explanations in psychology and ordinary discourse. If there turned out to be no clear sense in which mental events fell under predicates that are uncontroversially physical, then it would seem reasonable to count the mental events nonphysical. As far as I can see, there is no reason to be anything but relaxed in the face of this possibility. I see no powerful, clearly articulated reason for worrying about the existence of mind–body causation, or the gaplessness of chains of physical events, if this possibility were realized. What counts in supporting our belief in mind–body causation is the probity of mentalistic explanations. As long as they are informative and fruitful, we can assume that they are relating genuine events, whatever their metaphysical status.

Otherwise put: The theme in naturalism that deserves the status of orthodoxy is not its materialism and not its demand that mentalistic discourse be given some ideologically acceptable underpinning. It is its implicit insistence that one not countenance any form of explanation that will not stand the scrutiny of scientific and other well-established, pragmatically fruitful methods of communal check and testing. (More crudely, it is the opposition to miracles and to postulation of unverified interruptions in chains of causation among physical events.) But the relevant methods are to be drawn from reflection on what works in actual

---

[12] Cf., e.g., Jaegwon Kim, 'Epiphenomenal and Supervenient Causation', *Midwest Studies in Philosophy*, 9 (1984), 257–270; Ernest Sosa, 'Mind–Body Interaction and Supervenient Causation', ibid. 271–281; Ned Block, 'Can the Mind Change the World?', in G. Boolos (ed.), *Meaning and Method: Essays in Honor of Hilary Putnam* (Cambridge: Cambridge University Press, 1990).

[13] The lack of attention to our source of knowledge of mental causation is one reason why there has recently been a small outpouring of worries among materialists that a form of epiphenomenalism—the view that mentalistic properties or descriptions are causally irrelevant—must be taken seriously.

explanatory practice, not from metaphysical or ideological restrictions on these practices. These points are subject to various interpretations. But I think that taking them seriously motivates less confidence in materialist metaphysics than is common in North American philosophy.

I have been discussing ontological responses to Putnam's observation that various kinds of physical states could be, and are, associated with mental states of a given type. The ideological response to Putnam's observation was the development of a new paradigm for indicating how mental states could be given identifications in nonmentalistic terms. Philosophers looked not to neurophysiology but to computer programming as a source of inspiration. Identifying a mental state with some sort of abstract state of a computer appeared to avoid the problems of identifying mental kinds with neural kinds. And unlike the nonreductive forms of token-identity materialism, it promised means of explaining mentalistic notions in other terms, or at least of supplementing and illuminating mentalistic explanation. Most philosophers found the terms of this supplementation compatible with materialism. This new account came to be known as *functionalism*.[14]

The guiding intuition of functionalism was that what entirely determines what kind of state or event a mental state or event is, is its place in a causal or functional network in the mental life of the individual. The original stimulus to this view was a proposed analogy between the mind and a computer program. To specify such a program, one needed to specify possible inputs into the system, the operations that would pass the machine from one state to another, the states that the machine would pass through, and the output of the machine, given each possible input and given the states it was already in. The machine might be either deterministic or probabilistic. On most versions of functionalism, the internal states were to be specified purely in terms of their 'place' in the system of input and output—in terms of the possible dependency relations they bore to other states and ultimately to input and output. Input and output were to be specified in nonintentional, nonmentalistic terms. Types of mental states and events were supposed to be determined entirely by the relations of functional dependency within the whole system of input and output.

The notion of determination is subject to three main interpretations. One, the least ambitious and least reductive, claims only that each mental kind supervenes on a place in the functional system, in the sense that the individual would be in a different kind of mental state if and only if he were not in the

---

[14] Cf. A. M. Turing, 'Computing Machinery and Intelligence', *Mind*, 59 (1950), 433–460. Turing's article provided an impetus and a vivid illustration of the computer paradigm, but it was itself an expression of behaviorism about the mind. The papers that inspired machine functionalism were Hilary Putnam's 'Minds and Machines' (1960), 'Robots: Machines or Artificially Created Life?' (1964), and 'The Mental Life of Some Machines' (1967), in *Philosophical Papers*, ii. Putnam states an explicitly functionalist view in 'The Nature of Mental States' (1967), but the idea is not far from the surface of his earlier papers. A type of functionalism less tied to computers was proposed in Lewis, 'An Argument for the Identity Theory' (1966), and Armstrong, *A Materialist Theory of the Mind*.

functional state corresponding to that kind. The other two purport to say what mental kinds 'consist in'. One version ('analytic functionalism') claims that a functionalist specification of such relations explicates the meaning of mentalistic terms. Another ('scientific functionalism') makes the lesser claim that such a specification gives the true essence of mental kinds, in something like the way that molecular constitution gives the true essence of a natural kind like *water*. Both of these latter two versions claim that functionalist discourse provides the 'real explanatory power' latent in mentalistic explanation.[15].

Analytic and scientific functionalism are clearly liberalized heirs to behaviorism. They share with behaviorism the insistence on nonintentional specifications of input (stimulus) and output (response), and the belief that mentalistic explanation is somehow deficient and needs a nonmentalistic underpinning. They also expand on the behaviorist idea that mental states are individuated partly in terms of their relations. Whereas behaviorists focused largely on relations to behavior, functionalists included relations to other mental states, and relations to stimulating input into the system. This is an insight already present in Frege, who claimed that sense is inseparable from a network of inferential capacities.

It has been common to combine functionalism with token-identity materialism. Functionalism was supposed to provide insight into the nature of mental kinds, whereas token-identity materialism provided insight into the nature of mental particulars—into the instantiation of the mental kinds in particular individuals. The computer analogy seemed compelling to many: mentalistic discourse was a sort of gloss on an underlying network functional flow chart, which was ultimately realized in different physical ways in different machines or organisms. Thus neural descriptions were seen as lying at the bottom of a three-level hierarchy of descriptions of the same human subject.

The functionalist position—in its least reductionist garb—was given distinctive form by Fodor. Fodor maintained that the intentional content of propositional attitudes is irreducible via functionalist specifications. But he held that such content is expressed by inner mental representations that have syntactic properties, inner words and sentences that were presumed to be instantiated somehow in the brain. Fodor further claimed that mental representations have their causal roles in virtue of their formal or syntactic properties, and that the input and output of functionalist specifications should be seen as symbols.[16] This picture

---

[15] The nonreductive version is the least common. It is expressed in the introduction of Jerry Fodor's *RePresentations* (Cambridge, Mass.: MIT Press, 1981), but he maintains it neither very long before nor very long after. The analytic version may be found in Armstrong, *A Materialist Theory of Mind*; David Lewis, 'Psychophysical and Theoretical Identification', *Australasian Journal of Philosophy*, 50 (1972), 249–258; Sydney Shoemaker, 'Functionalism and Qualia' (1975), in his *Identity, Cause and Mind* (Cambridge: Cambridge University Press, 1984). Putnam proposed the scientific version in 'The Nature of Mental States'. A view more instrumentalist than functionalist but which bears broad comparison appears in Daniel Dennett, 'Intentional Systems', *The Journal of Philosophy*, 68 (1971), 87–106.

[16] Jerry A. Fodor, *The Language of Thought* (New York: Cravell, 1975) and *RePresentations*. Cf. also Hartry Field, 'Mental Representation', *Erkenntnis*, 13 (1978), 9–61.

brought the functionalist tradition into line with a fairly literal interpretation of the computer analogy: psychological explanation was modeled on *proofs* or other types of symbol manipulation by a digital computer. The causal aspects of psychological explanation were to be understood in terms of the physical relations among the particular neural states or events that instantiated the symbolic representations.

Something like this picture had been proposed by Sellars.[17] But Fodor presented his view as an interpretation of work in psycholinguistics and cognitive psychology. To many it gained plausibility because of its appeal to specific scientific practices. The picture and its relation to psychological theory are still very much in dispute.[18] Fodor's work drew attention from linguists, psychologists, and computer scientists. It also benefited from and helped further a significant shift in the degree to which the details of scientific practice were seen to be relevant to philosophical problems about mind.

Until the mid to late 1970s most philosophy in this area was carried on in a relatively apriori analytic spirit. Even those philosophers, such as type–type identity theorists or sceptics about mental states, who purported to take science as a model for philosophy of mind had little to say about the theories of any science. They saw themselves as freeing philosophy from obstacles to scientific progress (whose direction was often predicted with considerable confidence). This was true not only of the philosophy of mind, but of much of the rest of philosophy—even much of the philosophy of natural science, with the exception of historical work in the tradition of Thomas Kuhn.[19] It is an interesting question why such a shift occurred. A similar shift occurred in the philosophies of science and mathematics. Both disciplines undertook much more concentrated discussions of a wider variety of the details of scientific practice, beginning about fifteen years ago.[20] Philosophizing about biology, a science that had not

[17] Wilfrid Sellars, 'Some Reflections on Language Games' (1954), in *Science, Perception and Reality*. Cf. also Gilbert Harman, *Thought* (Princeton: Princeton University Press, 1973).

[18] For opposition from different angles to the computer analogy or to other aspects of the language-of-thought hypothesis, see Paul M. Churchland, *Scientific Realism and the Plasticity of Mind* (Cambridge: Cambridge University Press, 1979); Christopher Peacocke, *Sense and Content* (Oxford: Clarendon Press, 1983); Stephen Stich, *From Folk Psychology to Cognitive Science* (Cambridge, Mass.: MIT Press, 1983); Robert Stalnaker, *Inquiry* (Cambridge, Mass.: MIT Press, 1984); Daniel Dennett, *The Intentional Stance* (Cambridge, Mass.: MIT Press, 1987); Paul Smolensky, 'On the Proper Treatment of Connectionism', *The Journal of Behavioral and Brain Sciences*, 11 (1988), 1–74.

[19] T. S. Kuhn, *The Structure of Scientific Revolutions* (Chicago: University of Chicago Press, 1962).

[20] The change in the philosophy of physics was foreshadowed by early articles of Hilary Putnam's—e.g. 'An Examination of Grünbaum's Philosophy of Geometry' (1963), 'A Philosopher Looks at Quantum Mechanics' (1965), both in *Philosophical Papers*, i (Cambridge: Cambridge University Press, 1975). But it caught on and received new impetus with the articles of John Earman—e.g. 'Who's Afraid of Absolute Space?', *Australasian Journal of Philosophy*, 48 (1970), 287–319. For an overview of broadly analogous changes in the philosophy of mathematics, see Thomas Tymoczko (ed.), *New Directions in the Philosophy of Mathematics* (Boston: Birkhauser, 1985).

conformed to positivist conceptions of law and explanation, came to prominence in this period.

Perhaps it took two decades for the criticisms of positivism to be digested sufficiently for a more open-minded consideration of the actual practice of the sciences to develop. In any case, interest in the details of psychology should be seen in the context of intellectual movements outside the scope of this essay.

The demise of behaviorism might similarly be viewed as requiring a period of assimilation before psychology could be considered a worthwhile object of philosophical reflection. Of course, there was a more positive side to the reconsideration of the practice of psychology. The computer paradigm was a natural object of interest. The continuing success of Chomsky's program in linguistics, coupled as it was with claims that it was a part of a psychology of the mind, made philosophers increasingly interested in mentalistic psychology. And an intellectually substantial cognitive and developmental psychology, and psycholinguistics, offered new forms to questions relevant to traditional philosophical issues: the role of intentional content in explanation, the mind–body problem, differences between the natural and the human sciences, the relation between language and thought, the innateness and universality of various conceptual and linguistic structures, the scope and limits of human rationality.

How much the reflection on psychology will enrich and advance philosophical inquiry remains an open question. Quite a lot of the work in this area seems to me very unreflective. It is at best rare that scientific practice answers philosophical questions in a straightforward way. But philosophy has traditionally given and received aid in the rise of new sciences or new scientific paradigms.

Let us return to functionalism. Although functionalism has enjoyed substantial support—at least among specialists in the philosophy of mind—it has not lacked detractors. The analytic and scientific versions of functionalism have always been afflicted with a programmatic, unspecific character that has seemed to many to render them unilluminating as *accounts* of particular mental kinds.

There are more specific criticisms. Many philosophers find the application of any form of functionalism to sensations like pain or color sensations implausible. For them, the causal relations of the sensations seem less fundamental to their character than their qualitative aspects.[21]

Searle mounted a controversial argument, similar to some of those directed against the applicability of functionalism to qualitative aspects of sensations,

---

[21] Criticism of this aspect of functionalism may be found in Ned Block, 'Troubles with Functionalism', in C. W. Savage (ed.), *Minnesota Studies in the Philosophy of Science*, ix (Minneapolis: University of Minnesota Press, 1978), and 'Are Absent Qualia Impossible?' *The Philosophical Review*, 89 (1980), 257–274. An influential article with a different, but related, point is Thomas Nagel, 'What Is It Like to Be a Bat?', *The Philosophical Review*, 83 (1974), 435–450. Cf. also Frank Jackson, 'Epiphenomenal Qualia', *Philosophical Quarterly*, 32 (1982), 127–136. The numerous defenses of functionalism on this score include Sydney Shoemaker, 'Functionalism and Qualia' and 'Absent Qualia are Impossible—A Reply to Block', in *Identity, Cause and Mind*; and David Lewis, 'Mad Pain and Martian Pain' (1980), in his *Philosophical Papers*, i (New York: Oxford University Press, 1983).

to show that functionalism could not account for any propositional attitudes. He postulated a room in which stations are manned by a person who does not understand Chinese, but who memorizes the Chinese words of given instructions. These stations are postulated to correspond to the stages of processing a language. The person is able to produce appropriate Chinese sentences as output, given any Chinese sentence as input. Searle claimed that although the system could be set up to meet the functionalist requirements for understanding Chinese, there is no understanding of Chinese in the room. Most opponents claim that the whole system can be credited with understanding Chinese. Searle finds this reply unconvincing.[22]

A more complex issue concerns the specific formulation of a functionalist account. Clearly, people can share meanings and many beliefs even though they maintain very different theories about the world. Maintaining different theories entails making different inferences, which correspond to different causal relations among the different sets of mental states associated with the theories. So not just any network of causal relations among mental states and events can be relevant to a functional account, on pain of counting no one as sharing any beliefs or meanings. One needs to find a network that is common to all the possible inference networks and theories in which any given belief (or meaning) might be embedded. But it is very difficult to imagine there being such common causal networks for each given belief (or meaning).[23]

Another approach to understanding intentional content and mental kinds developed out of the work on reference. That work showed that proper names and natural kind expressions could succeed in referring even though the speaker's knowledge of the referent was incomplete or defective. Reference depends not just on background descriptions that the speaker associates with the relevant words, but on contextual, not purely cognitive relations that the speaker bears to entities that a term applies to.

The work on reference is relevant to the meaning of terms and to the identity of concepts. For the meaning of a wide range of nonindexical terms and the nature of a wide range of concepts are dependent on the referent or range of application in the sense that if the referent were different, the meaning of the term, and the associated concept, would be different. (Here let us simply take concepts to be elements in the intentional contents of propositional attitudes, elements that have referential aspects.) For example, different meanings or concepts would be expressed by the wordforms 'chair' and 'arthritis' if the word forms did not apply exactly to chairs and to instances of arthritis.

---

[22] John Searle, 'Minds, Brains, and Programs', *The Behavioral and Brain Sciences*, 3 (1980), 417–424. Searle's argument is anticipated in Ned Block, 'Troubles with Functionalism'.

[23] These problems have long been recognized. But as with some of the fundamental difficulties with positivism, such recognition does not always convince proponents of a program to give it up. For a summary of some of these problems, see Hilary Putnam, *Representation and Reality* (Cambridge, Mass.: MIT Press, 1988).

The points about reference can be extended to many such terms and concepts. An individual can think of a range of entities via such terms and concepts even though the thinker's knowledge of the entities is not complete enough to pick out that range of entities except through the employment of those terms and concepts. What the individual knows about the range of entities—and hence about those many meanings or concepts whose identities are not independent of their referential range of applications—need not provide a definition that distinguishes them from all other (possible) meanings or concepts. So the meanings of many terms—and the identities of many concepts—are what they are even though what the individual knows about the meaning or concept may be insufficient to determine it uniquely. Their identities are fixed by environmental factors that are not entirely captured in the explicatory or even discriminatory abilities of the individual, unless those discriminatory abilities include application of the concept itself. Since most propositional attitudes, like specific beliefs, are the kinds of mental kinds that they are because of the meanings, concepts, or intentional contents that are used to specify them, the identities of many mental kinds depend on environmental factors that are not entirely captured in the (nonintentionally specified) discriminatory abilities of the individual. I have just developed one motivation for what is called '*anti-individualism*'.

Anti-individualism is the view that not all of an individual's mental states and events can be type-individuated independently of the nature of the entities in the individual's environment. There is, on this view, a deep individuative relation between the individual's being in mental states of certain kinds and the nature of the individual's physical or social environments.

Anti-individualism was supported not only through abstract considerations from the theory of reference, but also through specific thought experiments. For example, one can imagine two individuals who are, for all relevant purposes, identical in the intrinsic physical nature and history of their bodies (described in isolation of their environments). But the two individuals can be imagined to have interacted with different metals (one aluminum, one an aluminum look-alike) in their respective environments. The metals need resemble one another only to the level of detail that the two individuals have noticed. The individuals know about as much about the metals as most ordinary people do, but neither could tell the difference if given the other metal. In such a case, it seems that one individual has thoughts like *aluminum is a light metal*, whereas the other individual (lacking any access to aluminum, even through interlocutors) has analogous thoughts about the other metal. Similar thought experiments appear to show that a person's thoughts can be dependent on relations to a social environment as well as a purely physical one. Some environmental dependence or other can be shown for nearly all empirically applicable terms or concepts.[24]

---

[24] Tyler Burge, 'Individualism and the Mental', *Midwest Studies in Philosophy*, 4 (1979), 73–121; 'Other Bodies', in A. Woodfield (ed.), *Thought and Object* (Oxford: Oxford University Press, 1982); 'Intellectual Norms and Foundations of Mind', *The Journal of Philosophy*, 83 (1986),

454   *Philosophy of Mind: 1950–2000*

The thought experiments made trouble for the standard forms of functionalism, which limited specifications of input and output to the surfaces of the individual. The thought experiments suggested that all an individual's internal functional transactions could remain constant, while his mental states (counterfactually) varied. Some philosophers proposed extending the functional network into the physical or social environments. Such a proposal reduces the reliance on the computer paradigm and requires a vastly more complex account. The main problems for it are those of accounting for (or specifying an illuminating supervenience base for) the notions of meaning, reference, and social dependence, in nonintentional terms. These are tasks commonly underestimated, in my view, because of the programmatic nature of the functionalist proposals.

Most philosophers seem to have accepted the thought experiments. But there remains disagreement about how they bear on mentalistic explanation, especially in psychology. Some have held that no notion of intentional content that is as dependent for its individuation on matters external to the individual could serve in explaining the individual's behavior. Many of these philosophers have tried to fashion surrogate notions of content or of 'mental' states to serve explanatory purposes. Others have maintained that such positions are based on mistakes and that the ordinary notions of intentional content and mental state can and do play a role in ordinary explanation and explanation in psychology. The debate concerns the interpretation of actual psychological practice and the relation between psychological explanation and explanation in other sciences.[25]

In my view, however, the main interest of the thought experiments lies in their giving new forms to many old issues. The arguments for anti-individualism are new. But the broad outline of the conclusion that they support is not. It is

697–720; 'Cartesian Error and the Objectivity of Perception', in R. Grimm and D. Merrill (eds.), *Contents of Thought* (Tucson: University of Arizona Press, 1988); 'Wherein is Language Social?', in A. George (ed.), *Reflections on Chomsky* (Oxford: Basil Blackwell, 1989) (Chs. 5, 4, 10, 7, 11 above). The thought experiments use the methodology set out in Hilary Putnam, 'The Meaning of "Meaning" ' (1975), in *Philosophical Papers*, ii. Putnam's argument, however, was not applied to intentional elements in mind or meaning. In fact, it contained remarks that are incompatible with anti-individualism about mental states. Much in subsequent papers is, however, anti-individualistic. Cf. 'Computational Psychology and Interpretation Theory', in *Philosophical Papers*, iii (Cambridge: Cambridge University Press, 1983); *Representation and Reality*, ch. 5. But ambivalences remain. Cf. ibid, 19–22.

[25] For versions of the former approach, see Stephen White, 'Partial Character and the Language of Thought', *Pacific Philosophical Quarterly*, 63 (1982), 347–365; Stephen Stich, 'On the Ascription of Content', in *Thought and Object*; Jerry Fodor, *Psychosemantics* (Cambridge, Mass.: MIT Press, 1987); Brian Loar, 'Social Content and Psychological Content', in Grimm and Merrill (eds.), *Contents of Thought*. For defenses of anti-individualistic conceptions of psychology, see Fred Dretske, *Knowledge and the Flow of Information* (Cambridge, Mass.: MIT Press, 1981); Tyler Burge, 'Individualism and Psychology', *The Philosophical Review*, 95 (1986), 3–45 (Ch. 9 above), and 'Individuation and Causation in Psychology', *Pacific Philosophical Quarterly*, 70 (1989), 303–22 (Ch. 14 above); Lynne Rudder Baker, *Saving Belief* (Princeton: Princeton University Press, 1987); and Robert Stalnaker, 'On What's in the Head', *Philosophical Perspectives*, 8 (1989), 287–316.

clearly maintained by Aristotle, Hegel, and Wittgenstein, and arguably present in Descartes and Kant.[26] Emergence of an old doctrine in a new form is a source of vitality in philosophy. Issues about self-knowledge, skepticism, apriori knowledge, personhood, the nature of meaning, the mind-body problem, are all deeply affected by considerations about necessary, individuative relations between an individual's mind and his environment. The line of development from the anti-descriptivist theories of reference to anti-individualist accounts of mind promises, I think, to enrich traditional philosophy.

In the last decade of the twentieth century, the relation between anti-individualism and other issues in philosophy came under intense scrutiny. I will discuss two areas that fall under this general heading. One is perception and perceptual thought. The other is self-knowledge. The decade was also marked by the emergence of widespread reflection on qualitative aspects of the mental, and on the nature of consciousness.

I begin with the two issues associated with anti-individualism. The first concerns issues about singular *de re* aspects of representation. I touch on two issues within this sub-area, both having to do with the nature of perceptual representation.

In *Languages of Art*, Nelson Goodman developed an account of the 'syntax' of pictorial representation that distinguishes it from propositional representation. Many have thought that Goodman's work points toward an account of nonpropositional form for perceptual representation. Roughly, Goodman counted nonpropositional representations—particularly drawings—as analog representations. Analog representations are analog if (for relevant purposes) dense. Representations are dense if between any two types there is a third. An associated idea is that in analog representations, every discernible difference in the representational medium makes a representational difference. There is much that is not right about Goodman's account, even for pictures. Still, many have thought that Goodman was on to an important distinction between perceptual and conceptual (propositional) representation, particularly regarding the second idea. Others pursued a similar path independently.[27]

---

[26] Descartes's Demon hypothesis is paradigmatically individualistic. But Descartes thought that the hypothesis was incoherent. His causal argument for the existence of the physical world (in *Meditation* VI) and his principle that the reality of ideas cannot exceed the reality of their objects are anti-individualistic in spirit. The question of whether Descartes was an individualist is very complex and entangled with his views about God. As regards Kant, the Refutation of Idealism (*Critique of Pure Reason*, B 274 ff.) contains a fundamentally anti-individualistic strategy. But the overall question of how to interpret Kant with regard to anti-individualism is, again, very complex, since it is bound up with the interpretation of his transcendental idealism.

[27] Nelson Goodman, *Languages of Art* (Indianapolis: Bobbs-Merrill, 1968); John Haugeland, 'Analog and Analog', *Philosophical Topics*, 12 (1981), 213–226; Fred Dretske, *Knowledge and the Flow of Information* (Oxford: Blackwell, 1981); Gareth Evans, *The Varieties of Reference* (Oxford: Oxford University Press, 1982); Christopher Peacocke, 'Perceptual Content', in J. Almog, J. Perry, and H. Wettstein (eds.), *Themes from Kaplan* (Oxford: Oxford University Press, 1989); *idem, A Study of Concepts* (Cambridge, Mass.: MIT Press, 1992).

Making the distinction in a clear and psychologically relevant way resists simple stories. There is the following baseline point that functions as a challenge: seemingly any representational content can be mimicked by or converted into propositional form. What distinguishes (some particular form of) nonpropositional, nonconceptual representational content? Since perception seems both to indicate particulars and to categorize them in certain ways, one has a prima facie analog of subject–predicate form implicit in perception.

Some have claimed that one cannot make sense of representation that plays a role in epistemology unless one takes the representation to be propositional and thus capable of yielding reasons.[28]

I believe that the position that distinguishes perceptual from conceptual representational form is correct. I believe this largely on empirical grounds. There is no need to appeal to propositionally marked states to explain the representational capacities, principally perceptual capacities, of numerous animals. But perception and action in these animals *is* best explained in terms of representational states. The representational organization of vision, hearing, and touch does not seem to be propositional. In most empirical work on these senses, no systematic attribution of propositional representations is made. Similarly, the representational organization of grasping or of eating does not seem to be propositional. No reasonable, full account can carry out the inquiry independently of empirical work in psychology. But the need for conceptual clarification in understanding the distinction seems to me to be deep and complex.

A related issue about perceptual representation concerns its semantics rather than its form. The issue centers on the nature of the relation between the singular element in perceptual belief and the particulars that the perceptual belief is about. Developing the view in anti-individualism that representational states are (commonly) individuated in terms of their relations to the environment, some, following Evans, maintained that a perceptual state and a perceptual belief could not be the same type of state or belief if it were a perception or belief about a different particular. Similarly, a given type of perceptual state or belief that is about a given particular could not have been the same if there had been an illusion of a particular instead of a genuine perceptual object in the environment.[29] On the other hand, there is both commonsense and scientific ground for thinking that the types of states that perceivers are in are the same as between veridical perceptions, perceptions of indiscernible duplicates, and

[28] John McDowell, *Mind and World* (Cambridge, Mass.: Harvard University Press, 1994). Cf. also the exchange between Peacocke and McDowell, *Philosophy and Phenomenological Research*, 57 (1998), 381–388, 414–419.

[29] Cf. Evans, *The Varieties of Reference*; John McDowell, 'Singular Thought and the Boundaries of Inner Space', in J. McDowell and P. Pettit (eds.), *Subject, Thought, and Context* (Oxford: Oxford University Press, 1986); Peacocke, *A Study of Concepts*; McDowell, *Mind and World*.

referential perceptual illusions.[30] This issue raises important questions about the nature of perceptual states and perceptual beliefs and about the nature of illusion.

A second large sub-area in the development of issues associated with anti-individualism bears on the nature of self-knowledge. Discussion centered on the question of whether anti-individualism is compatible with some sort of authoritative or privileged warrant for certain types of self-knowledge. Inevitably, this question forced reflection on the nature of self-knowledge and its role in various human pursuits. The issue was first raised in independent papers by Davidson and me. Each defended a type of compatibilism about the relation between anti-individualist individuation of certain mental states and a capacity to know nonempirically what those states are.[31] This claim was resisted or qualified by a number of philosophers.[32]

The bulk of the discussion came to center on the nature of self-knowledge—or rather, the nature of various types of self-knowledge. Some philosophers maintained that all self-knowledge is at least implicitly empirical. Some maintained that apparent cases of privileged or authoritative self-knowledge are to be understood in an expressivist or otherwise deflationary way. Others attempted to understand the apparently special character of some knowledge of what one is thinking or what one believes—without explaining that character away. What I regard as the most interesting developments of this approach appealed to some constitutive role of self-knowledge in having beliefs, in having a concept of belief, in being rational, or in being a deliberative person. These matters are complex, and deserve, I think, further development.[33]

I want to highlight one further area of intense discussion in the philosophy of mind in the 1990s. This one is largely independent of issues about anti-individualism. The area concerns the nature of qualitative experience, including

[30] John Searle, *Intentionality* (Cambridge: Cambridge University Press, 1983); Tyler Burge, 'Vision and Intentional Content', in E. Lepore and R. Van Gulick (eds.), *John Searle and his Critics* (Oxford: Blackwell, 1991).

[31] Donald Davidson, 'Knowing One's Own Mind', *Proceedings and Addresses of the American Philosophical Association*, 60 (1987), 441–458; Tyler Burge, 'Individualism and Self-Knowledge', *The Journal of Philosophy*, 85 (1988), 649–663.

[32] Paul Boghossian, 'Content and Self-Knowledge', *Philosophical Topics*, 17 (1989), 5–26; André Gallois, *The World Without, the Mind Within* (Cambridge: Cambridge University Press, 1996). For a collection of articles developing both sides of this issue, see P. Ludlow and N. Martin (eds.), *Externalism and Self-Knowledge* (Stanford, Calif.: CSLI Publications, 1998).

[33] Donald Davidson, 'First Person Authority', *Dialectica*, 38 (1984), 101–110, repr. in *Subjective, Intersubjective, Objective* (Oxford: Oxford University Press, 2001); Sydney Shoemaker, 'Self-Knowledge and "Inner Sense" ', *Philosophy and Phenomenological Research*, 54 (1994), 249–314, repr. in *The First-Person Perspective and Other Essays* (Cambridge: Cambridge University Press, 1996); Richard Moran, 'Interpretation Theory and the First-Person', *Philosophical Quarterly*, 44 (1994), 154–173; Tyler Burge, 'Our Entitlement to Self-Knowledge', *Proceedings of the Aristotelian Society*, 96 (1995), 1–26; Bernard Kobes, 'Mental Content and Hot Self-Knowledge', *Philosophical Topics*, 24 (1996), 71–99. A collection of articles that provides some indication of the range of this discussion is C. Wright, B. C. Smith, and C. Macdonald (eds.), *Knowing Our Own Minds* (Oxford: Oxford University Press, 1998).

the nature of consciousness. Consciousness and representationality, or aboutness, have long been regarded as the two major marks of mind. An important question is whether one mark can be reduced to the other; and if not, what relative places the two marks have in our understanding of mind.

The discussion of these matters at the end of the twentieth century must be seen against the background of four important papers. I have already mentioned two of these: Block's 'Troubles with Functionalism'[34] and Searle's 'Minds, Brains, and Programs'.[35] Each paper offers a forceful example that suggests that functionalist accounts of the representational aspects of mind fail to come to grips with qualitative aspects of experience. A third paper, Nagel's 'What is it Like to Be a Bat?',[36] offers a compelling way of thinking about qualitative aspects of experience, summarized in his phrase 'what it is like'. Finally, Jackson's 'Epiphenomenal Qualia',[37] gives an argument against materialism that features the difficulty of accounting for phenomenal qualities in material terms. These papers set many cross-currents going. I will not be able to survey nearly all of them. I will concentrate on one strand of development—the relation between qualitative and representational aspects of mind.

Many of the original responses to these papers focused on defending either functionalism or materialism—the original targets of the papers. As interest in strict forms of functionalism waned, the debate over functionalism was largely replaced by a closely related, but slightly different debate. Some functionalists took the tack of *assuming* that some form of functionalism is true of representational states, and then arguing that qualitative phenomena are essentially and solely representational. Others argued to the same conclusion with no antecedent commitment to functionalism.

Harman's 'The Intrinsic Quality of Experience'[38] claimed that qualitative aspects of experience are simply certain types of representational aspects of experience. Qualitative aspects of experience are the aspects that have to do with what it is like to have an experience, feeling, or sensation. Harman argued that putatively intrinsic aspects of experiences—for example, the felt quality of pain—had been conflated with intrinsic aspects of the 'intentional object' of an experience. Against the Jackson thought experiment he maintained that a person blind from birth fails to know what it is like to see something red because he or she does not have the full concept of red and so does not fully understand what it is for something to be red. Finally, Harman argued against invoking the inverted spectrum to show that representational constancy is compatible with qualitative difference. Harman's paper defended what came to be known

---

[34] In C. W. Savage (ed.), *Minnesota Studies in the Philosophy of Science*, ix (Minneapolis: University of Minnesota Press, 1978).

[35] *The Behavioral and Brain Sciences*, 3 (1980), 417–424.

[36] *The Philosophical Review*, 83 (1974), 435–450.

[37] *Philosophical Quarterly*, 37 (1982), 127–136.

[38] In J. Tomberlin (ed.), *Philosophical Perspectives*, iv (Atascadero, Calif.: Ridgeview Publishing Co., 1990).

as 'representationalism'—the view that qualitative aspects of experience are nothing other than representational aspects.

This paper was followed by—and in many cases it engendered—several further papers defending representationalist construals of qualitative mental phenomena.[39] The position was opposed by other philosophers, who maintained that phenomenal qualities, or phenomenal qualitative aspects of experience, commonly have representational content and representational functions but are not to be reduced to them.[40]

Most papers in this area, on both sides, pay what seems to me too little attention to what is to be meant by 'representation'. Harman admitted that his notion of intentional object is crude. I think it vulnerable. I think that the notion will not convincingly support the first of Harman's three arguments. There is, however, a clearer conception of representation that provides a basis for much of the representationalist discussion. According to this conception 'x represents y' should be understood roughly as: appropriate types of which x is an instance are dependent in a lawful or law-like way on appropriate types of which y is an instance, and this connection between x and y has functional value for the life of the organism that contains x.[41]

It is certainly plausible that on this conception of representation, qualitative color registrations are representational, if not constitutively, at least as a matter of fact. The view also suggests that pains and orgasms are representational. For example, a state of feeling pain is in a law-like relation to instances of bodily damage or disorder, and this relation surely has a functional value in the life of the organism. So the state of feeling pain 'represents' the bodily damage or disorder. This result has been embraced and defended by some representationalists.[42]

I believe that this notion of representation is too broad. It deems the states of very simple creatures to be 'representational states'. For example, it counts as representational states the sensory states underlying thermotactic responses of protozoa. One can coherently talk this way. Some psychologists and physiologists do talk this way. This notion of representation is, however, not needed to

---

[39] Fred Dretske, *Naturalizing the Mind* (Cambridge, Mass.: MIT Press, 1995); *idem.*, 'Phenomenal Externalism, or If Meanings Ain't in the Head, Where are Qualia?', in E. Villanueva (ed.), *Philosophical Issues, vii: Perception* (Atascadero, Calif.: Ridgeview, 1993); Michael Tye, *Ten Problems of Consciousness* (Cambridge, Mass.: MIT Press, 1995); Georges Rey, 'Sensational Sentences', in M. Davies and G. Humphreys (eds.), *Consciousness: Psychological and Philosophical Essays* (Oxford: Blackwell, 1992).

[40] Ned Block, 'Inverted Earth', *Philosophical Perspectives*, 4 (1990), 51–79; *idem.* 'Mental Paint and Mental Latex', in Villanueva (ed.), *Philosophical Issues, vii: Perception;*, Brian Loar, 'Phenomenal States', in N. Block, O. Flanagan, and G. Güzeldere (eds.), *The Nature of Consciousness* (Cambridge, Mass.: MIT Press, 1997; revision of original 1990 version); Colin McGinn, *The Problem of Consciousness* (Oxford: Blackwell, 1991).

[41] Dretske, *Naturalizing the Mind*, ch. 1. A similar but somewhat different view can be found in Ruth Millikan, *Language, Thought, and Other Biological Categories* (Cambridge, Mass.: MIT Press, 1984; and idem., 'Biosemantics', *The Journal of Philosophy*, 86 (1989), 281–297.

[42] Michael Tye, 'A Representational Theory of Pains and their Phenomenal Character', in J. Tomberlin (ed.), *Philosophical Perspectives*, ix (Atascadero, Calif.: Ridgeview, 1990).

explain such simple phenomena. It is a mere gloss on points that can be made in physiological, ecological, and functional terms. By contrast, a more intuitive, restrictive notion of representation does have prima facie explanatory force in the ethology of the perceptual and cognitive systems of less primitive animals and in the psychology of human beings. Dretske and others hope to reduce the more ordinary notion(s) of representation to the very broad one. I think that there is no ground for optimism about this project.[43]

Moreover, it is doubtful that the simple notion is one that opponents of representationalism have been concerned with when they doubt that qualitative aspects of experience are 'representational'. I believe that a less inclusive, or more specific, notion is needed to sort out issues between representationalists and their opponents.

Laying this issue aside, there remain difficulties for the representationalist position, even formulated with the broad notion of representation. One is that it produces unattractive results in cases like the feeling of pain. For example, one representationalist position holds that if an individual has a phantom limb, there is no pain—since there is no bodily damage that is functionally connected to the state of feeling pain; there is only a representation of pain that hallucinates the pain. This view has actually been embraced by some proponents of representationalism. It seems to me clearly unacceptable.

A second difficulty is that despite the inclusiveness of the cited conception of representation, there still appear to be qualitative states that do not 'represent' in this inclusive sense. There appear to be qualitative aspects of experience that have no function in the life of the organism. They constitute dysfunction or noise. Blurriness in a visual experience is an example. These cases have been treated as misrepresentations or as representations of blurriness, but it is hard to see that they have any representational function at all. They make no contribution to reproductive fitness, and they seem to get in the way of proper functions. This result is incompatible with the representationalist program.

Harman's second argument seems to me to beg the question. It does, however, highlight interesting and difficult issues about the relation between qualitative aspects of perception and representational aspects. In the case of (say) visual perception it is certainly hard to separate out qualitative aspects from representational aspects. We identify most qualitative aspects of perception with terms that indicate what is normally represented when one's consciousness is marked by those aspects. For example, although few philosophers still think that experience (by a normal-sighted person) of red is itself in any way red, we currently have no better, easily accessible, public way to characterize the qualitative aspect of the experience than in terms of its relation to red surfaces. This fact makes it

---

[43] Dretske relies partly on a view that in Mental representation, there is learning. In the relevant sense of learning, all animals and all unicellular organisms, including amoebae, learn. No animal is confined to fixed hard-wired, purely reflexive behavior. So Dretske's line seems to me not to do anything to solve the problem.

hard to see how to describe, much less explain, the qualitative aspect of experience in a way that abstracts from its representational role. And this difficulty encourages representationalism.

Opponents of representationalism typically maintain that the qualitative aspects of perception play a role in determining the mode of presentation or the representational content of the perception, and are not to be explained in terms of this role. The idea is that at least some aspects of qualitative states are dependent on the nature of the neural substrate and not on the sorts of correlations with objects of representation that determine representational content. This view seems to me correct. But it will provide little explanatory illumination until the relation between qualitative feels and neural underpinnings are better and more specifically understood.

Harman's third argument centers on the inverted spectrum. How to describe and evaluate this type of thought experiment remains difficult and disputed. I think that the case can be elaborated in various ways that make representationalism implausible. But the issues are very delicate and complex, and I will not try to review them here. There has been considerable, nuanced discussion of issues surrounding inverted spectra.[44]

One reason why the issue of representationalism has been of such interest is that it bears on the nature of consciousness. Qualitative or phenomenal states, as ordinarily felt, provide the most obvious instances of consciousness. Feelings involved in sensations like pains and tickles, phenomenal aspects of the experience of color or sound, the experience of warmth or of being touched, seem to be the paradigmatic center of consciousness. There are then issues about the relation between consciousness and representation that parallel those about the relation between qualitative aspects of experience and representation. In fact, positions on consciousness run the gamut from arguments that there is no such thing as qualitative aspects of experience, to functionalist reductionism, to simple representationalist views, to higher-order thought views, to claims that consciousness is irreducible, to claims that consciousness is both irreducible and a ground for dualist theories of mind.[45]

---

[44] Sydney Shoemaker, 'The Inverted Spectrum', *The Journal of Philosophy*, 74 (1982), 357–381; 'Intrasubjective/Intersubjective', in *The First-Person Perspective and Other Essays* (Cambridge: Cambridge University Press, 1996); Block, 'Inverted Earth'.

[45] Works representing these various positions, and intermediate ones, are as follows: Daniel Dennett, 'Quining Qualia', in A. Marcel and E. Bisiach (eds.), *Consciousness in Contemporary Science*, (Oxford: Oxford University Press, 1988); idem, *Consciousness Explained* (Boston: Little, Brown, 1991); Fred Dretske, 'Conscious Experience', *Mind*, 102 (1993), 263–283; idem, *Naturalizing the Mind*; David Rosenthal, 'Two Concepts of Consciousness', *Philosophical Studies*, 49 (1986), 329–359; John Searle, *The Rediscovery of Mind* (Cambridge, Mass.: MIT Press, 1992); Joseph Levine, 'On Leaving Out What It's Like', in M. Davies and G. Humphreys (eds.), *Consciousness*, (Oxford: Blackwell, 1993); Martin Davies, 'Externalism and Experience', in A. Clark, J. Ezquerro, and J. M. Larrazabal (eds.), *Philosophy and Cognitive Science: Categories, Consciousness, and Reasoning*, (Dordrecht: Kluwer, 1996); Charles Siewart, *The Significance of Consciousness* (Princeton: Princeton University Press, 1998); David Chalmers, *The Conscious Mind: In Search of a Fundamental Theory* (Oxford: Oxford University Press, 1996). For further discussion that hinges

The variety of theories about consciousness, and the depth of disagreement among theorists, suggests that there may be differences at the intuitive level—differences about the explanandum. Block suggested fruitfully that there are at least two notions of consciousness. One has to do with phenomenal, felt, qualitative aspects of experience. Another has to do with accessibility to rational deliberation, or at least to reflection and use in verbal and other rational enterprises.[46] Whether or not this view is correct, it seems to me to have engendered greater awareness of the complexity and elusiveness of the phenomena that have been discussed in philosophizing about consciousness.

Discussions of consciousness have opened up what had been a neglected, almost taboo subject in philosophy. This has been a good thing. On the other hand, it seems to me that progress toward genuine understanding has been at best mixed. The difficulty of the subject has provoked not only a number of wildly implausible theories. It has also encouraged what seems to me to be some backsliding in methodology and clarity of discussion in many presentations in this area. Metaphors, appeals to disputed and sketchily described introspection, unexplained terms, hastily and poorly explained technicalia, and grandiose programs have been more prominent than is good for a subject. These are early days. A certain amount of floundering is inevitable in initial work on a difficult topic. It may well be that a deeper scientific grip on relevant areas of neural, sensory, and cognitive psychology will be necessary before impressive progress emerges. It is well also to remember that many of the most fundamental aspects of our experience of the world—aspects that throw up some of the most basic and long-standing philosophical problems—have a way of remaining puzzling, despite progress in associated sciences. Consciousness may remain a case in point.

I want to close by summarizing some of the main changes in *both* philosophy of mind and philosophy of language in the second half of the twentieth century. Three major, possibly durable contributions in these areas during the period are the criticism of the positivist theory of meaning; the development of a vastly more sophisticated sense of logical form, as applied to natural language; and the fashioning of the nondescriptivist account of reference, with the extension of the line of thought associated with this account into the philosophy of mind. Different philosophers would, of course, provide different lists of achievements, given their own sense of what is true and important.

The dominant currents during the period are more easily agreed upon. The central event is the downfall of positivism and the reopening for discussion of

---

on more technical and methodological issues, see Ned Block and Robert Stalnaker, 'Conceptual Analysis, Dualism, and the Explanatory Gap', *The Philosophical Review*, 108 (1999), 1–46; David Chalmers and Frank Jackson, 'Conceptual Analysis and Reductive Explanation', *The Philosophical Review*, 110 (2001), 315–361. A good anthology is Block *et al.* (eds.), *The Nature of Consciousness*.

[46] Ned Block, 'On a Confusion about a Function of Consciousness', *The Behavioral and Brain Sciences*, 18 (1995), 227–247. Cf. Tyler Burge, 'Two Kinds of Consciousness' in Block *et al.* (eds.), *Nature of Consciousness* (Ch. 17 above).

virtually all the traditional problems in philosophy. This event was accompanied by the rediscovery of Frege, the application of logical theory to language, and the rise of the philosophy of language both as a preliminary to reflection on other subjects, and as a more nearly autonomous discipline. The computer paradigm and complex outgrowths of the philosophy of language have brought the philosophy of mind to dominance in the last decade.

Positivism left behind a strong orientation toward the methods of science. This orientation has fueled the acceptance of materialism in the philosophy of mind and, somewhat belatedly, the development of areas of philosophy (philosophy of physics, mathematics, biology, psychology, linguistics, social science) that take the specifics of scientific theories and practices into account.

For all this, the main direction of philosophy during the period has been toward a broader-based, more eclectic, less ideological approach to philosophical problems—and a greater receptivity to interplay between modern philosophy and the history of philosophy. Philosophy of mind emerged as an area of intense ferment not simply as a product of interaction between philosophy and such disciplines as psychology and linguistics. That ferment also represents a greater interest in traditional questions, questions about what is morally and intellectually distinctive about being human. It is hard to overemphasize the degree to which leading North American philosophers have since the 1950s broadened their sympathies toward traditional questions that still help frame what it is to lead a reflective life.

This broadening seems not to have seriously undermined the standards of rigor, clarity, and openness to communal check bequeathed by such figures as Frege, Russell, Carnap, Hempel, Gödel, Church, and Quine. Partly because of its close connection with the development of mathematical logic in this century, the standards of argument in philosophy have certainly been raised.

A corollary of this change, and of the personal example of the positivists in carrying on open, dispassionate discussion, has been the emergence of philosophical community. One of the glories of English-speaking philosophy in the last half-century has been the fruitful participation of many philosophers in the same discussions. Unlike much traditional philosophy and much philosophy in other parts of the world, English-speaking philosophy has been an open, public forum. The journals of the field, including notably *The Philosophical Review*, bear witness to a sharing of philosophical concerns, vocabularies, and methods of dispute. We now take this sharing for granted. But in historical perspective, it is remarkable. Although I think that philosophy is not and never will be a science, it has taken on this much of the spirit of science. That is, to my mind, the more important achievement.

This overview has provided at best a blurred glimpse of the enormous complexity and variety of discussion in philosophy mind during the last half-century. It is deficient as a picture not only in its oversimplifications and limited scope, but also in its failure to convey the life and nature of the animal. Philosophy is not primarily a body of doctrine, a series of conclusions or systems or movements. Philosophy, both as product and as activity, lies in the detailed posing of questions, the clarification of meaning, the development and criticism of argument, the working out of ideas and points of view. It resides in the angles, nuances, styles, struggles, and revisions of individual authors. In an overview of this sort, almost all the real philosophy must be omitted. For those not initiated into these issues, the foregoing is an invitation. For those who are initiated, it is a reminder—a reminder of the grandeur, richness, and intellectual substance of our subject.

Bibliography

WORKS BY BURGE

"Reference and Proper Names", *The Journal of Philosophy*, 70 (1973), 425–439.
"Demonstrative Constructions, Reference, and Truth", *The Journal of Philosophy*, 71 (1974), 205–223.
"On Knowledge and Convention", *The Philosophical Review*, 84 (1975), 249–255; Ch. 1 this volume.
"Belief *De Re*", *The Journal of Philosophy*, 74 (1977), 338–362; Ch. 3 this volume.
"Kaplan, Quine, and Suspended Belief", *Philosophical Studies*, 31 (1977), 197–203; Ch. 2 this volume.
"Self-Reference and Translation", in F. Guenthner and M. Guenthner (eds.), *Translation and Meaning* (London: Duckworth, 1977).
"Belief and Synonymy", *The Journal of Philosophy*, 75 (1978), 119–138.
"Frege and the Hierarchy", *Synthese*, 40 (1979), 265–289; repr. as ch. 4 in *Truth, Thought, Reason.*
"Individualism and the Mental", *Midwest Studies in Philosophy*, 4 (1979), 73–121; Ch. 5 this volume.
"Sinning against Frege", *The Philosophical Review*, 88 (1979), 398–432; repr. as ch. 5 in *Truth, Thought, Reason.*
"Other Bodies", in A. Woodfield (ed.), *Thought and Object* (Oxford: Oxford University Press, 1982), 97–120; Ch. 4 this volume.
"Two Thought Experiments Reviewed", *Notre Dame Journal of Formal Logic*, 23 (1982), 284–293; Ch. 6 this volume.
"Russell's Problem and Intentional Identity", in J. Tomberlin (ed.), *Agent, Language, and Structure of the World* (Indianapolis: Hackett Publishing Company, 1983).
"Frege on Extensions and Concepts, from 1884 to 1903", *The Philosophical Review*, 93 (1984), 3–34; repr. as ch. 7 in *Truth, Thought, Reason.*
"Cartesian Error and the Objectivity of Perception", in P. Pettit and J. McDowell (eds.), *Subject, Thought, and Context* (Oxford: Oxford University Press, 1986); repr. in R. Grimm and D. Merrill (eds.), *Contents of Thought* (Tucson: University of Arizona Press, 1988); Ch. 7 this volume.
"Frege on Truth", in L. Haaparanta and J. Hintikka (eds.), *Frege Synthesized* (Dordrecht: Reidel, 1986); repr. as ch. 3 in *Truth, Thought, Reason.*
"Individualism and Psychology", *The Philosophical Review*, 95 (1986), 3–45; Ch. 9 this volume.
"Intellectual Norms and Foundations of Mind", *The Journal of Philosophy*, 83 (1986), 697–720; Ch. 10 this volume.

"Authoritative Self-Knowledge and Perceptual Individualism", in R. Grimm and D. Merrill (eds.), *The Contents of Thought* (Tucson: University of Arizona Press, 1988); Ch. 8 this volume.

"Individualism and Self-Knowledge", *The Journal of Philosophy*, 85 (1988), 649–663.

"Individuation and Causation in Psychology", *Pacific Philosophical Quarterly*, 70 (1989), 303–322; Ch. 14 this volume.

"Wherein is Language Social?", in A. George (ed.), *Reflections on Chomsky* (Oxford: Blackwell, 1989); Ch. 11 this volume.

"Frege on Sense and Linguistic Meaning", in D. Bell and N. Cooper (eds.), *The Analytic Tradition* (Oxford: Blackwell, 1990); repr. as ch. 6 in *Truth, Thought, Reason.*

"Vision and Intentional Content", in E. Lepore and R. Van Gulick (eds.), *John Searle and his Critics* (Oxford and Cambridge, Mass.: Blackwell, 1991).

"Philosophy of Language and Mind, 1995–2003", *The Philosophical Review*, 101 (1992), 3–51; Ch. 20 this volume.

"Concepts, Definitions, and Meaning", *Metaphilosophy*, 24 (1993), 309–325; Ch. 12 this volume.

"Content Preservation", *The Philosophical Review*, 102 (1993), 457–488.

"Mind–Body Causation and Explanatory Practice", in J. Heil and A. Mele (eds.), *Mental Causation* (Oxford: Oxford University Press, 1993); Ch. 16 this volume.

"Intentional Properties and Causation", in C. MacDonald and G. MacDonald (eds.), *Philosophy and Psychology* (Oxford: Blackwell, 1995); Ch. 15 this volume.

"Two Kinds of Consciousness" (1995), in N. Block, O. Flanagan, and G. Guzeldere (eds.), *The Nature of Consciousness* (Cambridge, Mass.: MIT Press, 1997); originally published as "Zwei Arten von Bewusstsein", in T. Metzinger (ed.), *Bewusstsein* (Paderborn: Schoningh, 1995); Ch. 17 this volume.

"Our Entitlement to Self-Knowledge", *Proceedings of the Aristotelian Society*, 96 (1996), 91–116.

"Interlocution, Perception, and Memory", *Philosophical Studies*, 86 (1997), 21–47.

"Computer Proof, Apriori Knowledge, and Other Minds", *Philosophical Perspectives*, 12 (1998), 1–37.

"Frege on Knowing the Foundation", *Mind*, 107 (1998), 305–347; repr. as ch. 9 in *Truth, Thought, Reason.*

"Reason and the First-Person", in C. Wright, B. C. Smith, and C. Macdonald (eds.), *Knowing Our Own Minds* (Oxford: Clarendon Press, 1998).

"Comprehension and Interpretation", in L. Hahn (ed.), *The Philosophy of Donald Davidson* (Chicago: Open Court Publishers, 1999).

"Frege on Apriority", in P. Boghossian and C. Peacocke (eds.), *New Essays on the Apriori* (Oxford: Oxford University Press, 2000); repr. as ch. 10 in *Truth, Thought, Reason.*

"Concepts, Conceptions, Reflective Understanding: Reply to Peacocke", in M. Hahn and B. Ramberg (eds.), *Reflections and Replies: Essays on the Philosophy of Tyler Burge* (Cambridge, Mass.: MIT Press, 2003).

"Davidson and Forms of Anti-Individualism: Reply to Hahn", in M. Hahn and B. Ramberg (eds.), *Reflections and Replies: Essays on the Philosophy of Tyler Burge* (Cambridge, Mass.: MIT Press, 2003).

"Descartes, Bare Concepts, and Anti-Individualism: Reply to Normore", in M. Hahn and B. Ramberg (eds.), *Reflections and Replies: Essays on the Philosophy of Tyler Burge* (Cambridge, Mass.: MIT Press, 2003).

"Epiphenomenalism: Reply to Dretske", in M. Hahn and B. Ramberg (eds.), *Reflections and Replies: Essays on the Philosophy of Tyler Burge* (Cambridge, Mass.: MIT Press, 2003).

"The Indexical Strategy: Reply to Owens", in M. Hahn and B. Ramberg (eds.), *Reflections and Replies: Essays on the Philosophy of Tyler Burge* (Cambridge, Mass.: MIT Press, 2003).

"Logic and Analyticity", *Grazer Philosophische Studien*, 66 (2003), 199–249.

"Perception", *International Journal of Psychoanalysis*, 84 (2003), 157–167.

"Perceptual Entitlement", *Philosophy and Phenomenological Research*, 67 (2003), 503–548.

"Phenomenality and Reference: Reply to Loar", in M. Hahn and B. Ramberg (eds.), *Reflections and Replies: Essays on the Philosophy of Tyler Burge* (Cambridge, Mass.: MIT Press, 2003).

"Psychology and the Environment: Reply to Chomsky", in M. Hahn and B. Ramberg (eds.), *Reflections and Replies: Essays on the Philosophy of Tyler Burge* (Cambridge, Mass.: MIT Press, 2003).

"Qualia and Intentional Content: Reply to Block", in M. Hahn and B. Ramberg (eds.), *Reflections and Replies: Essays on the Philosophy of Tyler Burge* (Cambridge, Mass.: MIT Press, 2003).

"Social Anti-individualism, Objective Reference", *Philosophy and Phenomenological Research*, 67 (2003), 682–690; Ch. 13 this volume.

"Some Reflections on Scepticism: Reply to Stroud", in M. Hahn and B. Ramberg (eds.), *Reflections and Replies: Essays on the Philosophy of Tyler Burge* (Cambridge, Mass.: MIT Press, 2003).

"The Thought Experiments: Reply to Donnellan", in M. Hahn and B. Ramberg (eds.), *Reflections and Replies: Essays on the Philosophy of Tyler Burge* (Cambridge, Mass.: MIT Press, 2003).

Truth, Thought, Reason: Essays on Frege (Oxford: Clarendon Press, 2005).

"Disjunctivism and Perceptual Psychology", *Philosophical Topics* (forthcoming).

"Five Theses on *De Re* States and Attitudes", in P. Leonardi (ed.), [title unknown] (Oxford: Oxford University Press, forthcoming).

WORKS BY OTHER AUTHORS

Akins, Kathleen, "Of Sensory Systems and the 'Aboutness' of Mental States", *The Journal of Philosophy*, 93 (1996), 337–372.

Alanen, Lilli, "On Descartes' Argument for Dualism and the Distinction between Different Kinds of Beings", in S. Knuuttila and J. Hintikka (eds.), *The Logic of Being* (Dordrecht: Reidel, 1986).

Aristotle, *De Anima*, trans. David Ross (Oxford: Clarendon Press, 1961).

——*De Generatione et Corruptione*, trans. C. J. F. Williams (Oxford: Clarendon Press, 1982).

——*De Interpretatione*, in *Aristotle's Categories and De Interpretatione*, trans. J. L. Ackrill (Oxford: Clarendon Press, 1961).

Aristotle, *Posterior Analytics*, trans. J. Barnes (Oxford: Clarendon Press, 1975).

____ *Prior Analytics*, in *The Complete Works of Aristotle*, i, ed. J. Barnes (Princeton: Princeton University Press, 1984).

____ *Sophisticis Elenchis*, in *The Complete Works of Aristotle*, i, ed. J. Barnes (Princeton: Princeton University Press, 1984).

____ *Topics*, trans. Robin Smith (Oxford: Clarendon Press, 1997).

Armstrong, D. W., *A Materialist Theory of Mind* (London and New York: Routledge & Kegan Paul, 1968).

Baker, Lynne Rudder, *Saving Belief* (Princeton: Princeton University Press, 1987).

____ "Metaphysics and Mental Causation", in J. Heil and A. Mele (eds.), *Mental Causation* (Oxford: Clarendon Press, 1993).

Ballard, D. H., Hinton, G. E., and Sejnowski, T. J., "Parallel Vision Computation", *Nature*, 306 (1983), 21–26.

Bennett, Jonathan, *Kant's Analytic* (New York: Cambridge University Press, 1966).

____ "The Meaning-Nominalist Strategy", *Foundations of Language*, 10 (1974), 141–168.

Block, Ned, "Troubles with Functionalism", in C. W. Savage (ed.), *Minnesota Studies in the Philosophy of Science*, ix (Minneapolis: University of Minnesota Press, 1978).

____ "Are Absent Qualia Impossible?", *The Philosophical Review*, 89 (1980), 257–274.

____ "Advertisement for a Semantics for Psychology", in P. French *et al*. (eds.), *Midwest Studies in Philosophy*, 10 (Minneapolis: University of Minnesota Press, 1986).

____ "Can the Mind Change the World?", in G. Boolos (ed.), *Meaning and Method: Essays in Honor of Hilary Putnam* (Cambridge: Cambridge University Press, 1990).

____ "Inverted Earth", *Philosophical Perspectives*, 4 (1990), 51–79.

____ "On a Confusion about a Function of Consciousness", *The Behavioral and Brain Sciences*, 18 (1995), 227–247.

____ "Mental Paint and Mental Latex", in E. Villanueva (ed.), *Philosophical Issues*, vii: *Perception* (Atascadero, Calif.: Ridgeview Publishing Co., 1996).

____ "Mental Paint", in M. Hahn and B. Ramberg (eds.), *Reflections and Replies: Essays on the Philosophy of Tyler Burge* (Cambridge, Mass.: MIT Press, 2003).

____ "Two Neural Correlates of Consciousness", *Trends in Cognitive Sciences*, 9 (2005), 46–52.

____ "The Methodological Puzzle of the Neural Basis of Phenomenal Consciousness" (forthcoming).

____ and Fodor, Jerry, "What Psychological States are Not', *The Philosophical Review*, 81 (1972), 159–181.

____ and Stalnaker, Robert, "Conceptual Analysis, Dualism, and the Explanatory Gap", *Philosophical Review*, 108 (1999), 1–46.

____ Flanagan, O., and Guzeldere, G. (eds.), *The Nature of Consciousness* (Cambridge, Mass.: MIT Press, 1997).

Boghossian, Paul, "Content and Self-Knowledge", *Philosophical Topics*, 17 (1989), 5–26.

Boyd, Richard, "Materialism without Reductionism: What Physicalism Does Not

Entail", in N. Block (ed.), *Readings in the Philosophy of Psychology*, i (Cambridge, Mass.: Harvard University Press, 1980).

Brentano, F., *Psychology from an Empirical Standpoint*, orig. in German (Leipzig, 1874).

Brown, Roger, *A First Language: The Early Stages* (Cambridge, Mass.: Harvard University Press, 1973).

Bruner, J., Goodnow, J., and Austin, G., *A Study of Thinking* (New York: John Wiley, 1956).

Castaneda, Hector-Neri, "Indicators and Quasi-indicators", *American Philosophical Quarterly*, 4, 2 (Apr. 1967), 85–100.

Chalmers, David, *The Conscious Mind: In Search of a Fundamental Theory* (Oxford: Oxford University Press, 1996).

——and Jackson, Frank, "Conceptual Analysis and Reductive Explanation", *The Philosophical Review*, 110 (2001), 315–361.

Chisholm, Roderick, *Perceiving* (Ithaca, NY: Cornell University Press, 1957).

Chomsky, Noam, *Syntactic Structures* (The Hague: Mouton, 1957).

——Review of *Verbal Behavior* by B. F. Skinner, *Language*, 35 (1959), 26–58; repr. in J. A. Fodor and J. Katz (eds.), *The Structure of Language* (Englewood Cliffs, NJ: Prentice-Hall, 1964).

——*Aspects of the Theory of Syntax* (Cambridge, Mass.: MIT Press, 1965).

——*Rules and Representation* (Oxford: Blackwell, 1980).

——*Lectures on Government and Binding* (Dordrecht: Foris, 1982).

——*Knowledge of Language: Its Nature, Origin, and Use* (New York: Praeger, 1986).

Churchland, Paul M., *Scientific Realism and the Plasticity of Mind* (Cambridge: Cambridge University Press, 1979).

Davidson, Donald, "Actions, Reasons, and Causes", *The Journal of Philosophy*, 60 (1963), 685–700; repr. in *Essays on Actions and Events* (Oxford: Clarendon Press, 1980).

——"The Individuation of Events", in N. Rescher (ed.), *Essays in Honor of Carl G. Hempel* (Dordrecht: Reidel, 1969).

——"Mental Events", in L. Foster and J. Swanson (eds.), *Experience and Theory* (Amherst, Mass.: University of Massachusetts Press, 1970); repr. in *Essays on Actions and Events* (Oxford: Oxford University Press, 1980).

——"On the Very Idea of a Conceptual Scheme", *Proceedings and Addresses of the American Philosophical Association*, 47 (1973/4); repr. in *Inquiries into Truth and Interpretation* (Oxford: Clarendon Press, 1984).

——*Inquiries into Truth and Interpretation* (Oxford: Clarendon Press, 1984).

——"First Person Authority", *Dialectica*, 38 (1984), 101–110; repr. in *Subjective, Intersubjective, Objective* (Oxford: Oxford University Press, 2001).

——"Knowing One's Own Mind", *Proceedings and Addresses of the American Philosophical Association*, 60 (1987), 441–458; repr. in *Subjective, Intersubjective, Objective* (Oxford: Oxford University Press, 2001).

——"The Myth of the Subjective", in M. Krausz (ed.), *Relativism: Interpretation and Confrontation* (Notre Dame, Ind.: University of Notre Dame Press, 1989).

——"Epistemology Externalized", *Dialectica*, 45 (1991). 191–202; repr. in *Subjective, Intersubjective, Objective* (Oxford: Oxford University Press, 2001).

Davies, M., "Individualism and Perceptual Content", *Mind*, 100 (1991), 461–484.

_____ "Perceptual Content and Local Supervenience", *Proceedings of the Aristotelian Society*, 92 (1992), 21–45.

_____ "Externalism and Experience", in A. Clark, J. Ezquerro, and J. M. Larrazabal (eds.), *Philosophy and Cognitive Science: Categories, Consciousness, and Reasoning* (Dordrecht: Kluwer, 1996).

Dehaene, Stephen, *The Number Sense* (New York: Oxford University Press, 1997).

_____ "Precis of *The Number Sense*", *Mind and Language*, 16 (2001), 16–36.

Dennett, Daniel, *Content and Consciousness* (London: Routledge & Kegan Paul, 1969).

_____ "Intentional Systems", *The Journal of Philosophy*, 68 (1971), 87–106.

_____ *The Intentional Stance* (Cambridge, Mass.: MIT Press, 1987).

_____ "Quining Qualia", in A. Marcel and E. Bisiach (eds.), *Consciousness in Contemporary Science* (Oxford: Oxford University Press, 1988).

_____ *Consciousness Explained* (Boston: Little, Brown, 1991).

Descartes, Rene, *Philosophical Works*, ed. E. Haldane and G. R. T. Ross, 2 vols. (New York: Dover, 1955).

_____ *Rules for the Direction of the Mind*, in *Philosophical Works*, ed. E. Haldane and G. R. T. Ross (New York: Dover, 1955).

_____ *Principles of Philosophy*, in *Philosophical Works*, ed. E. Haldane and G. R. T. Ross (New York: Dover, 1955).

_____ *Replies*, in *Philosophical Works*, ed. E. Haldane and G. R. T. Ross (New York: Dover, 1955).

_____ *Oeuvres de Descartes*, ed. Ch. Adam and P. Tannery (Paris: CNRS, 1964–76).

_____ *The Philosophical Writings of Descartes*, trans. J. Cottingham, R. Stoothoff, and D. Murdoch (Cambridge: Cambridge University Press, 1984).

_____ *Descartes' Conversations with Burman*, ed. J. Cottingham (Oxford: Clarendon Press, 1976).

_____ *Philosophical Letters*, trans. A. Kenny (Minneapolis: University of Minnesota Press, 1981).

Devitt, Michael, "Suspension of Judgment: A Response to Heidelberger on Kaplan", *Journal of Philosophical Logic*, 5 (1976), 17–24.

Donnellan, Keith, "Reference and Definite Descriptions", *The Philosophical Review*, 75 (1966), 281–304.

_____ "Proper Names and Identifying Descriptions", *Synthese*, 21 (1970), 335–358; repr. in D. Davidson and G. Harman (eds.), *Semantics for Natural Language* (Dordrecht: Reidel, 1972).

_____ "Speaking of Nothing", *The Philosophical Review*, 83, 1 (1974), 3–31.

_____ "Burge Thought Experiments", in M. Hahn and B. Ramberg (eds.), *Reflections and Replies: Essays of the Philosophy of Tyler Burge* (Cambridge, Mass.: MIT Press, 2003).

Dretske, Fred, *Knowledge and the Flow of Information* (Oxford: Blackwell; Cambridge, Mass.: MIT Press, 1981).

_____ "Conscious Experience", *Mind*, 102 (1993), 263–283.

_____ "Phenomenal Externalism, or If Meanings Ain't in the Head, Where are Qualia?", in E. Villanueva (ed.), *Philosophical Issues*, vii (Atascadero, Calif.: Ridgeview Publishing Co., 1993).

____*Naturalizing the Mind* (Cambridge, Mass.: MIT Press, 1995).

Earman, John, "Who's Afraid of Absolute Space?", *Australasian Journal of Philosophy*, 48 (1970), 287–319.

Evans, Gareth, *The Varieties of Reference* (Oxford: Oxford University Press, 1982).

Feldman, Fred, "Kripke on the Identity Theory", *The Journal of Philosophy*, 71 (1974), 665–676.

Feyerabend, Paul, "Materialism and the Mind-Body Problem", *The Review of Metaphysics*, 17 (1963), 49–66.

Field, Hartry, "Mental Representation", *Erkenntnis*, 13 (1978), 9–61.

Fodor, Jerry, *Psychological Explanation* (New York: Random House, 1968).

____*The Language of Thought* (1975) (Cambridge, Mass.: Harvard University Press, 1979).

____"Methodological Solipsism Considered as a Research Strategy in Cognitive Psychology", *Behavioral and Brain Sciences*, 3 (1980), 63–73; repr. in *RePresentations* (Cambridge, Mass.: MIT Press, 1981).

____*RePresentations* (Cambridge, Mass.: MIT Press, 1981).

____*Psychosemantics* (Cambridge, Mass.: MIT Press, 1987).

____"A Modal Argument for Narrow Content", *The Journal of Philosophy*, 88 (1991), 5–26.

Frappoli, Maria J., and Romero, Esther (eds.), *Meaning, Basic Self-Knowledge, and Mind: Essays on Tyler Burge* (Stanford, Calif.: CSLI Publications, 2003).

Frege, Gottlob, "On Sense and Reference", in P. T. Geach and M. Black (eds.), *Translations of the Philosophical Writings of Gottlob Frege* (Oxford: Blackwell, 1966).

____*The Foundations of Arithmetic*, ed. J. L. Austin (Evanston, Ill.: Northwestern University Press, 1968).

____"The Thought", in E. D. Klemke (ed.), *Essays on Frege* (Urbana, Ill.: University of Illinois Press, 1968).

Gallois, Andre, *The World Without, the Mind Within* (Cambridge: Cambridge University Press, 1996).

Gaukroger, Stephen, "Descartes' Project for a Mathematical Physics", in Gaukroger (ed.), *Descartes: Philosophy, Mathematics, and Physics* (Brighton: Harvester, 1980).

Geach, Peter, *Mental Acts* (London: Routledge, 1957).

Gelman, S. A., and Markham, E. M., "Young Children's Inductions from Natural Kinds: The Role of Categories and Appearances", *Child Development*, 58 (1987), 1532–1541.

Geroch, Robert, *General Relativity, from A to B* (Chicago: University of Chicago Press, 1978).

Godfrey-Smith, Peter, *Complexity and the Function of Mind in Nature* (Cambridge: Cambridge University Press, 1996).

Goodman, Nelson, *Languages of Art* (Indianapolis: Bobbs-Merrill, 1968).

Grice, H. P., "Meaning", *Philosophical Review*, 66 (1957), 377–388.

____"Utterer's Meaning, Sentence-Meaning, and Word-Meaning", *Foundations of Language*, 4 (1968), 225–242.

Hacking, Ian, "Leibniz and Descartes: Proof and Eternal Truths", *Proceedings of the British Academy*, 59 (1973), 4–16.

Hahn, Martin, and Ramberg, Bjorn (eds.), *Reflections and Replies: Essays on the Philosophy of Tyler Burge* (Cambridge, Mass.: MIT Press, 2003).

Harman, Gilbert, "Three Levels of Meaning", *The Journal of Philosophy*, 65 (1968), 155–65.

—— "An Introduction to 'Translation and Meaning'", in D. Davidson and J. Hintikka (eds.), *Words and Objections* (Dordrecht: Reidel, 1969).

—— *Thought* (Princeton: Princeton University Press, 1973).

—— "The Intrinsic Quality of Experience" in J. Tomberlin (ed.), *Philosophical Perspectives*, iv (Atascadero, Calif.: Ridgeview Publishing Co., 1990).

Haugeland, John, "Analog and Analog", *Philosophical Topics*, 12 (1981), 213–226.

Heidelberger, Herbert, "Kaplan on Quine and Suspension of Judgment", *Journal of Philosophical Logic*, 3 (1974), 441–443.

Hellman, Geoffrey, and Thompson, Frank Wilson, "Physicalist Materialism", *Nous*, 11 (1977), 309–345.

Hubel, D. H., and Wiesel, T. N., "Receptive Fields of Single Neurones in the Cat's Striate Cortex", *Journal of Physiology*, 148 (1959), 574–591.

—— —— "Receptive Fields, Binocular Interaction, and Functional Architecture in the Cat's Visual Cortex", *Journal of Physiology* (London), 160 (1962), 106–154.

Hume, David, *A Treatise of Human Nature*, ed. L. A. Selby-Bigge (Oxford: Clarendon Press, 1965; first pub. 1899).

Ingle, D. J., "Selective Visual Attention in Frogs", *Science*, 188 (1975), 1033–1035.

Jackson, Frank, "Epiphenomenal Qualia", *Philosophical Quarterly*, 32 (1982), 127–136.

Kant, Immanuel, *Critique of Pure Reason* (1781, 1787), trans. N. K. Smith (New York: St Martin's Press, 1965); trans. P. Guyer and A. W. Wood (Cambridge: Cambridge University Press, 1998).

Kaplan, David, "Quantifying In", in D. Davidson and J. Hintikka (eds.), *Words and Objections: Essays on the Work of W. V. Quine* (Dordrecht: Reidel, 1969); repr. in L. Linsky (ed.), *Reference and Modality* (Oxford: Oxford University Press, 1971).

—— "Dthat", in P. Cole (ed.), *Syntax and Semantics*, ix (New York: Academic Press, 1978).

Kim, Jaegwon, "Causality, Identity, and Supervenience in the Mind–Body Problem", *Midwest Studies in Philosophy*, 4 (1979), 31–50.

—— "Epiphenomenal and Supervenient Causation", *Midwest Studies in Philosophy*, 9 (1984), 257–270.

—— *Mind in a Physical World* (Cambridge, Mass.: MIT Press, 1999).

—— *Physicalism, Or Something Near Enough* (Princeton: Princeton University Press, 2005).

Kneale, W., "Modality De Dicto and De Re", in E. Nagel, P. Suppes, and A. Tarski (eds.), *Logic, Methodology, and the Philosophy of Science* (Stanford, Calif.: Stanford University Press, 1962).

Kobes, Bernard, "Individualism and the Cognitive Sciences" (unpub. diss. UCLA, 1986).

—— "Mental Content and Hot Self-Knowledge", *Philosophical Topics*, 24 (1996), 71–99.

Kripke, Saul, *Naming and Necessity* (Cambridge, Mass.: Harvard University Press, 1972).

____ "Naming and Necessity", in D. Davidson and G. Harman (eds.), *Semantics for Natural Language* (Dordrecht: Reidel, 1972).

____ *Wittgenstein on Rules and Private Language* (Cambridge, Mass.: Harvard University Press, 1982).

Kuhn, T. S., *The Structure of Scientific Revolutions* (Chicago: University of Chicago Press, 1962).

Leibniz, G. W., *Philosophical Papers and Letters*, trans. and ed. L. Loemker (Chicago: University of Chicago Press, 1956).

Lettvin, Y., *et al.*, "What the Frog's Eye Tells the Frog's Brain", *Proceedings of the Institute of Radio Engineers*, 47 (1959), 1940–1951.

Levine, Joseph, "On Leaving Out What It's Like", in M. Davies and G. Humphreys (eds.), *Consciousness* (Oxford: Blackwell, 1993).

Lewis, David, "An Argument for the Identity Theory", *The Journal of Philosophy*, 63 (1966), 17–25.

____ *Convention: A Philosophical Study* (Cambridge, Mass.: Harvard University Press, 1969).

____ "Psychophysical and Theoretical Identifications", *Australasian Journal of Philosophy*, 50 (1972), 249–258.

____ "Language and Languages", in K. Gunderson (ed.), *Minnesota Studies in the Philosophy of Science*, vii (Minneapolis: University of Minnesota Press, 1975).

____ "Radical Interpretation", *Synthese*, 23 (1974), 331–344.

____ "Mad Pain and Martian Pain" (1980), in *Philosophical Papers*, i (New York: Oxford University Press, 1983).

Loar, Brian, "Reference and Propositional Attitudes", *The Philosophical Review*, 80 (1972), 43–62.

____ "Social Content and Psychological Content", in Robert Grimm and Daniel Merrill (eds.), *Contents of Thought* (Tucson: University of Arizona Press, 1988).

____ "Phenomenal States", in N. Block, O. Flanagan, and G. Guzeldere (eds.), *The Nature of Consciousness* (Cambridge, Mass.: MIT Press, 1998; 1st pub. 1997).

Ludlow, P., and Martin, N. (eds.), *Externalism and Self-Knowledge* (Stanford, Calif.: CSLI Publications, 1998).

Lycan, William G., "Kripke and the Materialists", *The Journal of Philosophy*, 71 (1974), 677–689.

Lyons, John, *Introduction to Theoretical Linguistics* (Cambridge: Cambridge University Press, 1968).

McDowell, John, "Singular Thought and the Boundaries of Inner Space", in P. Pettit and J. McDowell (eds.), *Subject, Thought and Context* (Oxford: Oxford University Press, 1986).

____ *Mind and World* (Cambridge, Mass.: Harvard University Press, 1994).

____ "Reply to Commentators", *Philosophy and Phenomenological Research* 57 (1998), 403–431.

McGinn, Colin, "Anomalous Monism and Kripke's Cartesian Intuitions", *Analysis*, 37 (1977), 78–80.

____ "Charity, Interpretation and Belief", *The Journal of Philosophy*, 74 (1977), 521–535.

____ "The Structure of Content", in A. Woodfield (ed.), *Thought and Object* (Oxford: Oxford University Press, 1982).

McGinn, Colin, *The Problem of Consciousness* (Oxford: Blackwell, 1991).

Malcolm, Norman, *Dreaming* (London: Routledge & Kegan Paul, 1959).

Marr, David, *Vision* (San Francisco: W. H. Freeman, 1982).

_____ and Hildreth, E., "Theory of Edge Detection", *Proceedings of the Royal Society of London*, B207 (1980), 187–217.

_____ and Poggio, T., "A Computational Theory of Human Stereo Vision", *Proceedings of the Royal Society of London*, B204 (1979), 301–328.

Mates, Benson, "Synonymity", in L. Linsky (ed.), *Semantics and the Philosophy of Language* (Urbana, Ill.: University of Illinois Press, 1952).

Matthews, Robert J., "Comments", in R. Grimm and D. Merrill (eds.), *The Contents of Thought* (Tucson: University of Arizona Press, 1985).

Mill, John Stuart, *A System of Logic* (1843) (London: Longmans, Green and Co., 1865; New York: Harper & Brothers, 1893).

Miller, George, "The Magic Number 7 Plus or Minus Two: Some Limits on Our Capacity for Processing Information", *Psychological Review*, 63 (1956), 81–97.

_____ Galanter, E., and Pribram, K., *Plans and the Structure of Behavior* (New York: Holt, Rinehart & Winston, 1960).

Millikan, Ruth, *Language, Thought, and Other Biological Categories* (Cambridge, Mass.: MIT Press, 1984).

_____ "Biosemantics", *The Journal of Philosophy*, 86 (1989), 281–297.

Milner, A. David, and Goodale, Melvyn A., *The Visual Brain in Action* (Oxford: Oxford University Press, 1995).

Moore, G. E., *Principia Ethica* (1903) (Cambridge: Cambridge University Press, 1966).

Moran, Richard, "Interpretation Theory and the First-Person", *Philosophical Quarterly*, 44 (1994), 154–173.

Nagel, Thomas, "What is it Like to Be a Bat?", *The Philosophical Review*, 83 (1974), 435–450.

Neisser, Ulrich, "The Multiplicity of Thought", *British Journal of Psychology*, 54 (1963), 1–14.

Newell, E., Shaw, J. C., and Simon, H. A., "Elements of a Theory of Human Problem Solving", *Psychological Review*, 65 (1958), 151–166.

Newton, Sir Isaac, *The Mathematical Works of Isaac Newton*, ed. D. T. Whiteside, 2 vols. (New York: Johnson Reprint Corporation, 1964).

Normore, Calvin, "Meaning and Objective Being: Descartes and His Sources", in A. Rorty (ed.), *Essays on Descartes' Meditations* (Berkeley: University of California Press, 1986).

_____ ,"Burge, Descartes, and US", in M. Hahn and B. Ramberg (eds.), *Reflections and Replies: Essays on The Philosophy of Tyler Burge* (Cambridge, Mass.: MIT Press, 2003).

O'Connor, John (ed.), *Modern Materialism: Readings on Mind–Body Identity* (New York: Harcourt, Brace, and World, 1969).

O'Shaughnessy, Brian, *The Will* (Cambridge: Cambridge University Press, 1980).

Parsons, Charles, "The Transcendental Aesthetic", in P. Guyer (ed.), *The Cambridge Companion to Kant* (Cambridge: Cambridge University Press, 1992).

Peacocke, Christopher, *Sense and Content* (Oxford: Clarendon Press, 1983).

—— "Perceptual Content", in J. Almog, J. Perry, and H. Wettstein (eds.), *Themes from Kaplan* (Oxford: Oxford University Press, 1989).

—— *A Study of Concepts* (Cambridge, Mass.: MIT Press, 1992).

—— "Nonconceptual Content Defended" *Philosophy and Phenomenological Research* 57 (1998), 381–388.

—— "Implicit Conceptions, Understanding, and Rationality", in M. Hahn and B. Ramberg (eds.), *Reflections and Replies: Essays on the Philosophy of Tyler Burger* (Cambridge, Mass.: MIT Press, 2003).

Pessin, Andrew, and Goldberg, Sanford (eds.), *The Twin Earth Chronicles* (London: M. E. Sharpe, 1996).

Pitcher, George, *A Theory of Perception* (Princeton: Princeton University Press, 1971).

Place, U. T., "Is Consciousness a Brain Process?", *British Journal of Psychology*, 47 (1956), 44–50.

Plantinga, Alvin, "De Dicto and De Re", *Nous*, 3 (1969), 235–258.

Plato, *Phaedo*, in *The Collected Dialogues of Plato*, trans. E. Hamilton and H. Cairns (New York: Pantheon Books, 1961).

—— *Phaedrus*, in *The Collected Dialogues of Plato*, trans. E. Hamilton and H. Cairns (New York: Pantheon Books, 1961).

Posner, M. I., "Immediate Memory in Sequential Tasks", *Psychological Bulletin*, 60 (1963), 333–349.

Povanelli, Daniel, *Folk Physics for Chimps* (Oxford: Oxford University Press, 2000).

Putnam, Hilary, "Minds and Machines" (1960), in *Philosophical Papers*, ii (Cambridge: Cambridge University Press, 1975).

—— "The Analytic and the Synthetic" (1962), repr. in *Philosophical Papers*, ii (Cambridge: Cambridge University Press, 1975).

—— "Brains and Behavior" (1963), in *Philosophical Papers*, ii (Cambridge: Cambridge University Press, 1975).

—— "An Examination of Grünbaum's Philosophy of Geometry" (1963), in *Philosophical Papers*, i (Cambridge: Cambridge University Press, 1975).

—— "A Memo on Conventionalism" (1959), in *Philosophical Papers*, i (Cambridge: Cambridge University Press, 1975).

—— "Robots: Machines or Artificially Created Life" (1964), in *Philosophical Papers*, ii (Cambridge: Cambridge University Press, 1975).

—— "A Philosopher Looks at Quantum Mechanics" (1965), in *Philosophical Papers*, i (Cambridge: Cambridge University Press, 1975).

—— "The Mental Life of Some Machines" (1967), in *Philosophical Papers*, ii (Cambridge: Cambridge University Press, 1975).

—— "The Nature of Mental States" (1967), in *Philosophical Papers*, ii (Cambridge: Cambridge University Press, 1975).

—— "Is Semantics Possible?" (1970), in *Philosophical Papers*, ii (Cambridge: Cambridge University Press, 1975).

—— "Explanation and Reference" (1973), in *Philosophical Papers*, ii (Cambridge: Cambridge University Press, 1975).

—— "Comment on Wilfrid Sellars", *Synthese*, 27 (1974), 445–455.

—— "Language and Reality" (1975), in *Philosophical Papers*, ii (Cambridge: Cambridge University Press, 1975).

Putnam, Hilary, "The Meaning of 'Meaning'" (1975), in *Philosophical Papers*, ii (Cambridge: Cambridge University Press, 1975).

――――"Computational Psychology and Interpretation Theory" (1983), in *Philosophical Papers*, iii (Cambridge: Cambridge University Press, 1983).

――――*Representation and Reality* (Cambridge, Mass.: MIT Press, 1988).

Quine, W. V., "Truth by Convention" (1935), in *The Ways of Paradox* (New York: Random House, 1966).

――――"On Mental Entities" (1952), repr. in *The Ways of Paradox* (New York: Random House, 1966).

Quine, W. V., "Two Dogmas of Empiricism" (1953), in *From a Logical Point of View* (New York: Harper & Row, 1963).

――――"Carnap and Logical Truth" (1954), in *The Ways of Paradox* (New York: Random House, 1966).

――――"Quantifiers and Propositional Attitudes", *The Journal of Philosophy*, 53 (1956), 177–187; repr. in his *The Ways of Paradox* (New York: Random House, 1966).

――――"Truth by Convention", (1936) in *The Ways of Paradox* (New York: Random House, 1966).

――――*Word and Object* (Cambridge, Mass.: MIT Press, 1960).

――――*Theories and Things* (Cambridge, Mass.: Harvard University Press, 1981).

Ramachandran, V. S., "Behavioral and Magnetoencephalographic Correlates of Plasticity in the Adult Human Brain", *Proceedings of the National Academy of Sciences USA*, 90 (1993), 10,413–10,420.

Rey, Georges, "Concepts and Stereotypes", *Cognition*, 15 (1983), 237–262.

――――"Concepts and Conceptions: A Reply to Smith, Medin and Rips", *Cognition*, 19 (1985), 297–303.

――――"Sensational Sentences", in M. Davies and G. Humphreys (eds.), *Consciousness: Psychological and Philosophical Essays* (Oxford: Blackwell, 1992).

Robins, R. H., *A Short History of Linguistics* (London: Longman, 1967).

Rorty, Richard, "Mind–Body Identity, Privacy, and Categories", *Review of Metaphysics*, 19 (1965), 24–54.

Rosch, Eleanor, and Lloyd, Barbara, *Cognition and Categorization* (Hillsdale, NJ: Erlbaum, 1978).

――――Mervis, C. B., Gray, W., Johnson, D., and Boyes-Graem, P., "Basic Objects in Natural Categories", *Cognitive Psychology*, 8 (1976), 382–439.

Rosenthal, David, "Two Concepts of Consciousness", *Philosophical Studies*, 49 (1986), 329–359.

Rossetti, Yves, and Pastille, Laude, "Several 'Vision for Action' Systems: A Guide to Dissociating and Integrating Dorsal and Ventral Functions (Tutorial)", in W. Prinz and B. Hamill (eds.), *Common Mechanisms in Perception and Action* (Oxford: Oxford University Press, 2002).

Rozemond, Marleen, *Descartes's Dualism* (Cambridge, Mass.: Harvard University Press, 1998).

Russell, Bertrand, *The Problems of Philosophy* (1912) (London: Oxford University Press, 1982).

――――"Knowledge by Acquaintance and Knowledge by Description" (1912), in *The Problems of Philosophy*.

――――*Our Knowledge of the External World* (1914) (London: Allen & Unwin, 1952).

Russell, Bertrand, "The Philosophy of Logical Atomism" (1918), in R. C. Marsh (ed.), *Logic and Knowledge: Essays 1901–1950* (London: Unwin Hyman, 1956).

—— *The Analysis of Matter* (New York: Dover, 1954).

—— *Mysticism and Logic* (London: Allen & Unwin, 1959).

Ryle, Gilbert, *The Concept of Mind* (London: Hutchinson, 1949).

Schiffer, Stephen, *Meaning* (Oxford: Oxford University Press, 1972).

Searle, John, "Minds, Brains, and Programs", *The Behavioral and Brain Sciences*, 3 (1980), 417–424.

—— *Intentionality* (Cambridge: Cambridge University Press, 1983).

—— *The Rediscovery of Mind* (Cambridge, Mass.: MIT Press, 1992).

Sellars, Wilfrid, "Some Reflections on Language Games" (1954), repr. in *Science, Perception, and Reality* (London: Routledge & Kegan Paul, 1963).

—— *Science, Perception, and Reality* (London: Routledge & Kegan Paul, 1963).

—— "... this I or he or it (the thing) which thinks ... ", Presidential Address, *Proceedings and Addresses of the American Philosophical Association*, 44 (1971), 5–31.

Shoemaker, Sidney, "Functionalism and Qualia", *Philosophical Studies*, 27 (1975), 291–315; repr. in *Identity, Cause and Mind* (Cambridge: Cambridge University Press, 1984).

—— "The Inverted Spectrum", *The Journal of Philosophy*, 74 (1982), 357–381.

—— "Absent Qualia are Impossible—A Reply to Block", in *Identity, Cause and Mind* (Cambridge: Cambridge University Press, 1984).

—— "Self-Knowledge and 'Inner Sense'", *Philosophy and Phenomenological Research*, 54 (1994), 249–314; repr. in *The First-Person Perspective and Other Essays* (Cambridge: Cambridge University Press, 1996).

—— "Intrasubjective/Intersubjective", in *The First-Person Perspective and Other Essays* (Cambridge: Cambridge University Press, 1996).

—— "Introspection and Phenomenal Character", in D. J. Chalmers (ed.), *Philosophy of Mind* (Oxford: Oxford University Press, 2002).

Shuster, John A., "Descartes' *Mathesis Universalis*, 1619–28", in S. Gaukroger (ed.), *Descartes: Philosophy, Mathematics, and Physics* (Brighton: Harvester, 1980).

Siewart, Charles, *The Significance of Consciousness* (Princeton: Princeton University Press, 1998).

Smart, J. J. C., "Sensations and Brain Processes", *The Philosophical Review*, 68 (1959), 141–156.

—— "Further Thoughts on the Identity Theory", *The Monist*, 56 (1972), 149–162.

Smith, Edward, and Medin, Douglas, *Categories and Concepts* (Cambridge, Mass.: Harvard University Press, 1981).

Smolensky, Paul, "On the Proper Treatment of Connectionism", *The Journal of Behavioral and Brain Sciences*, 11 (1988), 1–74.

Sosa, Ernest, "Mind–Body Interaction and Supervenient Causation", *Midwest Studies in Philosophy*, 9 (1984), 271–281.

Sperling, G., "The Information Available in Brief Visual Presentations", *Psychological Monographs*, 24 (1960).

Stalnaker, Robert, *Inquiry* (Cambridge, Mass.: MIT Press, 1984).

—— "On What's in the Head", in J. Tomberlin (ed.), *Philosophical Perspectives*, iii. 287–316 (Atascadero, Calif.: Ridgeview Publishing Co., 1989); repr. in A. Pessin and S. Goldberg (eds.), *The Twin Earth Chronicles* (London: M. E. Sharpe, 1996).

Sternberg, S., "High-Speed Scanning in Human Memory", *Science*, 153 (1966), 652–664.

Stich, Stephen, "On the Ascription of Content", in A. Woodfield (ed.), *Thought and Object* (Oxford: Oxford University Press, 1982).

_____ *From Folk Psychology to Cognitive Science* (Cambridge, Mass.: MIT Press, 1983).

Stillings, Neil, "Modularity and Naturalism in Theories of Vision", in J. L. Garfield (ed.), *Modularity in Knowledge Representation and Natural-Language Understanding* (Cambridge, Mass.: MIT Press, 1987).

Strawson, P. F., "Singular Terms, Ontology and Identity", *Mind*, 65 (1956), 433–454.

Strawson, P. F., *Individuals* (1959) (Garden City, NY: Anchor, 1963).

Temin, Marc, "The Relational Sense of Indirect Discourse", *The Journal of Philosophy*, 72 (1975), 287–306.

Tomasello, Michael, and Call, Josep, *Primate Cognition* (Oxford: Oxford University Press, 1997).

Turing, A. M., "Computing Machinery and Intelligence", *Mind*, 59 (1950), 433–60.

Tversky, Amos, "Features of Similarity", *Psychological Review*, 84 (1977), 327–352.

Tye, Michael, "A Representational Theory of Pains and their Phenomenal Character", in J. Tomberlin (ed.), *Philosophical Perspectives*, ix (Atascadero, Calif.: Ridgeview Publishing Co., 1990).

_____ *Ten Problems of Consciousness* (Cambridge, Mass.: MIT Press, 1995).

Tymoczko, Thomas (ed.), *New Directions in the Philosophy of Mathematics* (Boston: Birkhauser, 1985).

Ullman, Shimon, *The Interpretation of Visual Motion* (Cambridge, Mass.: MIT Press, 1979).

Van Gulick, Robert, "Metaphysical Arguments for Internalism and Why They Don't Work", in S. Silvers (ed.), *ReRepresentation*, Synthese Philosophy Series (Dordrecht: Kluwer, 1988).

_____ "Who's in Charge Here? And Who's Doing All the Work?", in J. Heil and A. Mele (eds.), *Mental Causation* (Oxford: Oxford University Press, 1993).

Wallace, John, "Belief and Satisfaction", *Nous*, 6 (1972), 85–95.

Westfall, Richard S., *Never at Rest: A Biography of Isaac Newton* (Cambridge: Cambridge University Press, 1980).

White, Stephen, "Partial Character and the Language of Thought", *Pacific Philosophical Quarterly*, 63 (1982), 347–365.

Whiteside, D. T., *The Mathematical Principles Underlying Newton's* Principia (Glasgow: University of Glasgow Press, 1970).

William of Sherwood, *Introduction to Logic*, trans. and ed. Norman Kretzmann (Minneapolis: University of Minnesota Press, 1966).

Wright, C., Smith, B. C., and Macdonald, C. (eds.), *Knowing Our Own Minds* (Oxford: Oxford University Press, 1998).

Author Index

Subject Index

The main objective of this index is not to provide a quick look-up or a tool for browsers. The index is constructed to aid study. In many of the longer entries or in the entries for technical terms, however, the reader who wants to find basic or elementary passages will find them through *italicized* numerals.

486 *Subject Index*